THE LONGMAN READER SIXTH EDITION

BRIEF EDITION

Judith Nadell

John Langan
Atlantic Cape Community College

Eliza A. Comodromos
Rutgers, The State University of New Jersey

Longman

New York   San Francisco   Boston
London   Toronto   Sydney   Tokyo   Singapore   Madrid
Mexico City   Munich   Paris   Cape Town   Hong Kong   Montreal

Editor-in-Chief: Joseph Opiela
Vice President: Eben W. Ludlow
Executive Marketing Manager: Ann Stypuloski
Supplements Editor: Donna Campion
Media Supplements Editor: Nancy Garcia
Production Manager: Douglas Bell
Project Coordination, Text Design, and Electronic Page Makeup: Elm Street
    Publishing Services, Inc.
Cover Designer/Manager: John Callahan
Cover Photo: Annapurna south face at dawn, courtesy FPG International
Senior Manufacturing Buyer: Dennis J. Para
Printer and Binder: R.R. Donnelley & Sons, Harrisonburg
Cover Printer: Coral Graphic Services

For permission to use copyrighted material, grateful acknowledgment is made to the
copyright holders on pp. 550–552, which are hereby made part of this copyright page.

Library of Congress Cataloging-in-Publication Data
Nadell, Judith.
    The Longman reader: Brief edition / Judith Nadell, John Langan, Eliza A.
    Comodromos—6th ed./Brief ed.
        p. cm.
    This is a truncated version of the 6th ed. (full version), containing a wide variety
    of reading selections. These selections are aimed at helping students become more
    active readers, thinkers, and writers—Publisher's info.
    Includes bibliographical references and index.
    ISBN 0-321-11295-4
    1. College readers. 2. English language—Rhetoric—Problems, exercises, etc.
    3. Report writing—Problems, exercises, etc. I. Langan, John, 1942– II.
    Comodromos, Eliza A. III. Title.

PE1417.N33 2003
808'.042—dc21   2002066055

Please visit our website at http://www.ablongman.com/nadell

ISBN 0-321-11295-4

1 2 3 4 5 6 7 8 9 10—DOH—05 04 03 02

ABOUT THE AUTHORS

Judith Nadell was until several years ago Associate Professor of Communications at Rowan University (New Jersey). During her eighteen years at Rowan, she coordinated the introductory course in the Freshman Writing Sequence and served as Director of the Writing Lab. In the past several years, she has developed a special interest in grassroots literacy. Besides designing an adult-literacy project, a children's reading-enrichment program, and a family-literacy initiative, she has worked as a volunteer tutor and a tutor trainer in the programs. A Phi Beta Kappa graduate of Tufts University, she received a doctorate from Columbia University. She is author of *Becoming a Read-Aloud Coach* (Townsend Press) and coauthor of *Doing Well in College* (McGraw-Hill), *Vocabulary Basics* (Townsend Press), and *The Longman Writer*. The recipient of a New Jersey award for excellence in the teaching of writing, Judith Nadell lives with her coauthor husband, John Langan, near Philadelphia.

John Langan has taught reading and writing courses at Atlantic Cape Community College near the New Jersey shore for more than twenty years. He earned an advanced degree in reading at Glassboro State College and another in writing at Rutgers University. Active in a mentoring program, he designed a reading-enrichment program for inner-city high school students and recently wrote a motivational and learning skills guidebook, *Ten Skills You Really Need to Succeed in College*. Coauthor of *The Longman Writer* and author of a series of college textbooks on both reading and writing, he has published widely with McGraw-Hill Book Company, Townsend Press, and Longman. His books include *English Skills, Reading and Study Skills,* and *College Writing Skills*.

Eliza A. Comodromos has taught composition and developmental writing in the English departments of both Rutgers University and John Jay College of Criminal Justice. After graduating with a bachelor's degree in English and French from La Salle University, she did graduate work at the City University of New York Graduate School and went on to earn an advanced degree at Rutgers University, New Brunswick. A freelance editor and textbook consultant, Eliza Comodromos has delivered numerous papers at language and literature conferences around the country. Currently,   she teaches composition at Rutgers University and lives near Philadelphia.

CONTENTS

THEMATIC CONTENTS   xiii

PREFACE   xviii

1 THE READING PROCESS   1

Stage 1: Get an Overview of the Selection   2
Stage 2: Deepen Your Sense of the Selection   3
Stage 3: Evaluate the Selection   4

Ellen Goodman FAMILY COUNTERCULTURE   6
Parents are told to switch the dial if they don't want their kids
watching something on TV. But what should parents do if the
entire culture warrants being switched off?

2 THE WRITING PROCESS   13

Stage 1: Prewrite   14
Stage 2: Identify the Thesis   31
Stage 3: Support the Thesis With Evidence   36
Stage 4: Organize the Evidence   45
Stage 5: Write the First Draft   53
Stage 6: Revise the Essay   68

Student Essay   74
Commentary   76

3 DESCRIPTION   81

What Is Description?   81
How Description Fits Your Purpose and Audience   82
Suggestions for Using Description in an Essay   84
Student Essay   88
Commentary   90
Activities: Description   94

Gordon Parks   FLAVIO'S HOME   96
Having battled poverty and prejudice himself, writer-
photographer Gordon Parks visits a Brazilian slum and
finds, among the wretched thousands forgotten by the
outside world, a dying yet smiling boy.

Maya Angelou   SISTER FLOWERS   106
Hidden deep within herself after the trauma of a rape, a young
girl is escorted back into life by the grand lady of a small town.

E. B. White   ONCE MORE TO THE LAKE   115
Past, present, and future merge when White returns to a
beloved boyhood spot.

Additional Writing Topics   124

4 NARRATION   127

What Is Narration?   127
How Narration Fits Your Purpose and Audience   128
Suggestions for Using Narration in an Essay   128
Student Essay   135
Commentary   137
Activities: Narration   140

Annie Dillard   THE CHASE   142
On a lazy winter morning, several children throw perfectly
rounded snowballs at passing cars. Suddenly, one driver leaps
from his car and gives chase.

Langston Hughes   SALVATION   148
In the course of being "saved" during a revival meeting, a
young boy's life is changed forever.

Sophronia Liu SO TSI-FAI   153
The tragedy of a classmate's brief, hopeless life continues, more than twenty years later, to haunt the author.

Additional Writing Topics   159

5 EXEMPLIFICATION   161

What Is Exemplification?   161
How Exemplification Fits Your Purpose
    and Audience   162
Suggestions for Using Exemplification
    in an Essay   165
Student Essay   170
Commentary   172
Activities: Exemplification   176

Charles Sykes THE "VALUES" WASTELAND   178
In the quest to teach kids to be broad-minded and non-judgmental, have we compromised their ability to distinguish between right and wrong? A respected journalist thinks we have.

Beth Johnson BOMBS BURSTING IN AIR   189
Forced to share grim news with her children, the author reflects on life's fragility—and its beauty.

Barbara Ehrenreich WHAT I'VE LEARNED
    FROM MEN   196
Do men simper, smile, and chatter aimlessly in an effort to be "nice"? No, says the author, and neither should women.

Additional Writing Topics   203

6 DIVISION-CLASSIFICATION   205

What Is Division-Classification?   205
How Division-Classification Fits Your Purpose and
    Audience   207
Suggestions for Using Division-Classification
    in an Essay   209
Student Essay   214
Commentary   218
Activities: Division-Classification   221

William Lutz   DOUBLESPEAK   224
What do you call language that is specifically designed not to
communicate? William Lutz has a name for it—doublespeak.

Ann McClintock   PROPAGANDA TECHNIQUES IN
TODAY'S ADVERTISING   232
Propaganda is not just a tool of totalitarian states. American
advertisers also use propaganda to get us to buy their products.

Deborah Tannen   BUT WHAT DO YOU MEAN?   241
Could the way women communicate on the job ever work to
their disadvantage? Absolutely, says this professor of linguistics.

Additional Writing Topics   251

7 PROCESS ANALYSIS   253

What Is Process Analysis?   253
How Process Analysis Fits Your Purpose
and Audience   254
Suggestions for Using Process Analysis
in an Essay   256
Student Essay   262
Commentary   265
Activities: Process Analysis   268

Bill Bryson   YOUR NEW COMPUTER   271
Anyone who has ever read a computer manual, trying to figure
out whether to insert the red wire into the blue slot or the blue
wire into the red slot, will sympathize with Bryson's humorous
exasperation.

Nikki Giovanni   CAMPUS RACISM 101   278
The advice that Giovanni gives Black students for succeeding
at predominantly White institutions has relevance for nonmi-
norities, too.

Caroline Rego   THE FINE ART OF COMPLAINING   285
Shoddy service and malfunctioning products afflict us all, but
some of us complain more effectively than others.

Additional Writing Topics   292

8 COMPARISON-CONTRAST   295

What Is Comparison-Contrast?   295

How Comparison-Contrast Fits Your Purpose
and Audience   296
Suggestions for Using Comparison-Contrast
in an Essay   297
Student Essay   303
Commentary   305
Activities: Comparison-Contrast   309

Rachel Carson   A FABLE FOR TOMORROW   311
Ecologist Rachel Carson warns us that what seems like a nightmare will become all too real if we fail to protect the earth.

Richard Rodriguez   WORKERS   315
A summer job teaches a college student some important things about himself and the world of work.

Dave Barry   THE UGLY TRUTH ABOUT BEAUTY   323
Why do men tend to be unconcerned about their appearance while women seem obsessed with how they look? Humorist Dave Barry advances an interesting theory.

Additional Writing Topics   328

9 CAUSE-EFFECT   331

What Is Cause-Effect?   331
How Cause-Effect Fits Your Purpose
and Audience   332
Suggestions for Using Cause-Effect
in an Essay   333
Student Essay   340
Commentary   343
Activities: Cause-Effect   347

Stephen King   WHY WE CRAVE HORROR MOVIES   349
Who should know more about our appetite for horror than Stephen King? This maestro of the macabre shares his thoughts on why moviegoers eagerly pay to be terrified.

Lewis Thomas   THE LIE DETECTOR   354
Buried deep within us, Thomas believes, is something that hates a lie.

Jonathan Coleman   IS TECHNOLOGY MAKING
US INTIMATE STRANGERS?   359
Cell phones and beepers, e-mail and fax machines. We're electronically connected, every day, all day. So why, wonders Coleman, do we seem so isolated from others—and from ourselves?

Additional Writing Topics   364

10 DEFINITION   367

What Is Definition?   367
How Definition Fits Your Purpose and Audience   368
Suggestions for Using Definition in an Essay   369
Student Essay   373
Commentary   376
Activities: Definition   379

K. C. Cole   ENTROPY   381
A noted science writer observes that disorder is the natural order of things—in her life and in the universe at large.

James Gleick   LIFE AS TYPE A   387
Since they were first identified in a 1959 study, "Type A" people—those hurried, hassled, heart-attack-prone folks—have become part of our cultural landscape. But, says Gleick, there's a problem: The study was worthless.

William Raspberry   THE HANDICAP OF DEFINITION   394
Raspberry looks at the expectations that many of his fellow African-Americans have for themselves—and sees a serious problem.

Additional Writing Topics   399

11 ARGUMENTATION-PERSUASION   401

What Is Argumentation-Persuasion?   401
How Argumentation-Persuasion Fits Your Purpose and
    Audience   402
Suggestions for Using Argumentation-Persuasion in an
    Essay   407
Student Essay   426
Commentary   433
Activities: Argumentation-Persuasion   437

Mary Sherry   IN PRAISE OF THE "F" WORD   440
The fear of receiving a failing grade can go a long way toward
getting the attention of non-achieving students.

Yuh Ji-Yeon   LET'S TELL THE STORY OF
ALL AMERICA'S CULTURES   445
In school, the author's history books taught about the settling
of the West but not about the massacre of the native peoples
living there; about the American belief in equality, but not
about Americans denied citizenship because of their race.

Examining an Issue: Date Rape

Camille Paglia   RAPE: A BIGGER DANGER
THAN FEMINISTS KNOW   451
The widespread prevalence of date rape, says the author, is evi-
dence that feminism has failed young women.

Susan Jacoby   COMMON DECENCY   458
According to Jacoby, a man who forces himself on a woman is
neither misled nor confused; he's simply a rapist.

Examining an Issue: Affirmative Action

Roger Wilkins   RACISM HAS ITS PRIVILEGES   464
A longtime civil rights activist argues that the call to eliminate
affirmative-action programs is rooted in wrongheaded thinking,
willful ignorance, even outright lies.

Shelby Steele   AFFIRMATIVE ACTION: THE
PRICE OF PREFERENCE   475
Black writer and scholar Shelby Steele describes the discomfort
he experiences at the prospect of his own children being
offered preferential treatment because of their color.

Additional Writing Topics   483

12 COMBINING THE PATTERNS   485

The Patterns in Action: During the
Writing Process   485
The Patterns in Action: In an Essay   486

Virginia Woolf   THE DEATH OF THE MOTH   488
Watching the death throes of a moth leads Woolf to wonder at
the mystery of life and at the force that opposes it.

Martin Luther King, Jr.   WHERE DO WE GO
FROM HERE: COMMUNITY
OR CHAOS?   495
America's most influential civil rights leader pleads eloquently
for a drastic change in the way that governments pursue world
peace.

Joan Didion   THE SANTA ANA   500
Living within reach of the Santa Ana—a fierce, hot, unpre-
dictable wind—teaches us how tenuous our hold on life can be.

APPENDIX: A CONCISE GUIDE TO FINDING AND DOCUMENTING SOURCES   505

Using the Library to Find Books
on Your Subject   505
Using the Library to Find Reference
Works on Your Subject   508
Using the Library to Find Articles on
Your Subject   509
Using the Internet to Research Your Subject   513
Documenting Sources   519
What to Document   520
How to Document   520
List of Works Cited   525

GLOSSARY   533

ACKNOWLEDGMENTS   550

INDEX   553

THEMATIC
CONTENTS

COMMUNICATION AND LANGUAGE

Maya Angelou, Sister Flowers   106
Barbara Ehrenreich, What I've Learned From Men   196
William Lutz, Doublespeak   224
Ann McClintock, Propaganda Techniques in Today's Advertising   232
Deborah Tannen, But What Do You Mean?   241
Bill Bryson, Your New Computer   271
Caroline Rego, The Fine Art of Complaining   285
Dave Barry, The Ugly Truth About Beauty   323
Jonathan Coleman, Is Technology Making Us Intimate Strangers?   359
William Raspberry, The Handicap of Definition   394
Mary Sherry, In Praise of the "F" Word   440
Camille Paglia, Rape: A Bigger Danger Than Feminists Know   451
Susan Jacoby, Common Decency   458

EDUCATION AND WORK

Maya Angelou, Sister Flowers   106
Sophronia Liu, So Tsi-Fai   153
Charles Sykes, The "Values" Wasteland   178

Barbara Ehrenreich, What I've Learned From Men   196
Nikki Giovanni, Campus Racism 101   278
Caroline Rego, The Fine Art of Complaining   285
Richard Rodriguez, Workers   315
William Raspberry, The Handicap of Definition   394
Mary Sherry, In Praise of the "F" Word   440
Yuh Ji-Yeon, Let's Tell the Story of All America's Cultures   445
Roger Wilkins, Racism Has Its Privileges   464
Shelby Steele, Affirmative Action: The Price of Preference   475

ETHICS AND MORALITY

Ellen Goodman, Family Counterculture   6
Gordon Parks, Flavio's Home   96
Annie Dillard, The Chase   142
Langston Hughes, Salvation   148
Sophronia Liu, So Tsi-Fai   153
Charles Sykes, The "Values" Wasteland   178
William Lutz, Doublespeak   224
Ann McClintock, Propaganda Techniques in Today's Advertising   232
Stephen King, Why We Crave Horror Movies   349
Lewis Thomas, The Lie Detector   354
Jonathan Coleman, Is Technology Making Us Intimate Strangers?   359
Camille Paglia, Rape: A Bigger Danger Than Feminists Know   451
Susan Jacoby, Common Decency   458
Roger Wilkins, Racism Has Its Privileges   464
Shelby Steele, Affirmative Action: The Price of Preference   475
Martin Luther King, Jr., Where Do We Go From Here:
    Community or Chaos?   495

FAMILY AND CHILDREN

Ellen Goodman, Family Counterculture   6
Gordon Parks, Flavio's Home   96
Maya Angelou, Sister Flowers   106
E. B. White, Once More to the Lake   115
Annie Dillard, The Chase   142
Sophronia Liu, So Tsi-Fai   153
Charles Sykes, The "Values" Wasteland   178
Beth Johnson, Bombs Bursting in Air   189
Stephen King, Why We Crave Horror Movies   349
Jonathan Coleman, Is Technology Making Us Intimate Strangers?   359
William Raspberry, The Handicap of Definition   394
Mary Sherry, In Praise of the "F" Word   440

GOVERNMENT AND LAW

William Lutz, Doublespeak   224
Roger Wilkins, Racism Has Its Privileges   464
Shelby Steele, Affirmative Action: The Price of Preference   475
Martin Luther King, Jr., Where Do We Go From Here:
    Community or Chaos?   495

HUMAN GROUPS AND SOCIETY

Ellen Goodman, Family Counterculture   6
Gordon Parks, Flavio's Home   96
Maya Angelou, Sister Flowers   106
Annie Dillard, The Chase   142
Langston Hughes, Salvation   148
Sophronia Liu, So Tsi-Fai   153
Charles Sykes, The "Values" Wasteland   178
Barbara Ehrenreich, What I've Learned From Men   196
Deborah Tannen, But What Do You Mean?   241
Nikki Giovanni, Campus Racism 101   278
Richard Rodriguez, Workers   315
Dave Barry, The Ugly Truth About Beauty   323
Stephen King, Why We Crave Horror Movies   349
Jonathan Coleman, Is Technology Making Us Intimate Strangers?   359
James Gleick, Life As Type A   387
William Raspberry, The Handicap of Definition   394
Mary Sherry, In Praise of the "F" Word   440
Yuh Ji-Yeon, Let's Tell the Story of All America's Cultures   445
Camille Paglia, Rape: A Bigger Danger Than Feminists Know   451
Susan Jacoby, Common Decency   458
Roger Wilkins, Racism Has Its Privileges   464
Shelby Steele, Affirmative Action: The Price of Preference   475
Martin Luther King, Jr., Where Do We Go From Here:
    Community or Chaos?   495
Joan Didion, The Santa Ana   500

HUMOR AND SATIRE

Annie Dillard, The Chase   142
Barbara Ehrenreich, What I've Learned From Men   196
Bill Bryson, Your New Computer   271
Caroline Rego, The Fine Art of Complaining   285
Dave Barry, The Ugly Truth About Beauty   323

MEANING IN LIFE

Gordon Parks, Flavio's Home   96
Maya Angelou, Sister Flowers   106
Annie Dillard, The Chase   142
Langston Hughes, Salvation   148
Sophronia Liu, So Tsi-Fai   153
Charles Sykes, The "Values" Wasteland   178
Beth Johnson, Bombs Bursting in Air   189
Nikki Giovanni, Campus Racism 101   278
Rachel Carson, A Fable for Tomorrow   311
Richard Rodriguez, Workers   315
Lewis Thomas, The Lie Detector   354
Jonathan Coleman, Is Technology Making Us Intimate Strangers?   359
William Raspberry, The Handicap of Definition   394
Mary Sherry, In Praise of the "F" Word   440
Yuh Ji-Yeon, Let's Tell the Story of All America's Cultures   445
Virginia Woolf, The Death of the Moth   488
Joan Didion, The Santa Ana   500

MEMORIES AND AUTOBIOGRAPHY

Maya Angelou, Sister Flowers   106
E. B. White, Once More to the Lake   115
Annie Dillard, The Chase   142
Langston Hughes, Salvation   148
Sophronia Liu, So Tsi-Fai   153
Beth Johnson, Bombs Bursting in Air   189
Richard Rodriguez, Workers   315
Yuh Ji-Yeon, Let's Tell the Story of All America's Cultures   445

MEN AND WOMEN

Barbara Ehrenreich, What I've Learned From Men   196
Deborah Tannen, But What Do You Mean?   241
Dave Barry, The Ugly Truth About Beauty   323
Camille Paglia, Rape: A Bigger Danger Than Feminists Know   451
Susan Jacoby, Common Decency   458

NATURE, SCIENCE, AND HEALTH

Gordon Parks, Flavio's Home   96
E. B. White, Once More to the Lake   115

Rachel Carson, A Fable for Tomorrow   311
Lewis Thomas, The Lie Detector   354
K. C. Cole, Entropy   381
James Gleick, Life As Type A   387
Virginia Woolf, The Death of the Moth   488
Joan Didion, The Santa Ana   500

MEDIA AND TECHNOLOGY

Ellen Goodman, Family Counterculture   6
Ann McClintock, Propaganda Techniques in Today's Advertising   232
Bill Bryson, Your New Computer   271
Dave Barry, The Ugly Truth About Beauty   323
Stephen King, Why We Crave Horror Movies   349
Lewis Thomas, The Lie Detector   354
Jonathan Coleman, Is Technology Making Us Intimate Strangers?   359
James Gleick, Life As Type A   387

PREFACE

Our bookshelves, and perhaps yours, sag under the weight of all the readers published over the years. Semester after semester, we used to switch texts because we wanted more than was offered. For one thing, we found that many of the readers contained an all-too-predictable blend of selections, with the same pieces cropping up from one book to the next. We also discovered that the books provided students with little guidance on ways to read, think, and write about the selections. And so, when we first began working on the original long version of *The Longman Reader*, we aimed for a different kind of text—one that would offer fresh examples of professional prose, one that would take a more active role in helping students become stronger readers, thinkers, and writers.

As in the long version, our primary goal in this brief edition has been to enliven the mix of selections commonly appearing in readers. Although *The Longman Reader: Brief Edition* includes widely read and classic essays, a number of our selections have not yet appeared in other anthologies. Among these are Beth Johnson's "Bombs Bursting in Air," Gordon Parks's "Flavio's Home," Caroline Rego's "The Fine Art of Complaining," and Charles

Sykes's "The 'Values' Wasteland." We've been careful to choose selections that range widely in subject matter and approach, from the humorous to the informative, from personal meditation to polemic. We've also made sure that each selection captures students' interest and clearly illustrates a specific pattern of development or combination of patterns.

Our second concern has remained the quality of instruction in the book. As before, our objective has been to help students bridge the gap between the product and process approaches to reading and writing. Throughout, we describe possible sequences and structures but emphasize that such steps and formats are not meant to be viewed as rigid prescriptions; rather, they are strategies for helping students discover what works best in a particular situation. Such an approach, we've been told, does indeed help students read more critically, think more logically, and write more skillfully.

Gratified by the enthusiasm for the many editions of *The Longman Reader* in its original long version, we decided not to tinker with the book's essential structure in creating this *Brief Edition*. The main changes we've made are that (1) a small handful of activities in Chapter 2, "The Writing Process," have been streamlined and (2) the number of reading selections has been reduced from five to three in each of the rhetorical chapters, and from six to three in Chapter 12, "Combining the Patterns," yielding a total of 34 (as opposed to 58) highly engaging readings. Apart from these changes, the *Brief Edition* is otherwise exactly the same as the long version. The book's format remains as follows:

- **Chapter 1, "The Reading Process,"** is designed to reflect current theories about the interaction of reading, thinking, and writing. The chapter provides guided practice in a three-part process for reading with close attention and a high level of interpretive skill. This step-by-step process sharpens students' understanding of the book's selections and promotes the rigorous thinking needed to write effective essays. An activity at the end of the chapter gives students a chance to use the three-step process. First, they read an essay by journalist Ellen Goodman. The essay has been annotated both to show students the reading process in action and to illustrate how close critical reading can pave the way to promising writing topics. Then they respond to sample questions and writing assignments, all similar to those accompanying each of the book's selections. The chapter thus does more than just tell students how to sharpen their reading abilities; it guides them through a clearly sequenced plan for developing critical reading skills.

- **Chapter 2, "The Writing Process,"** introduces students to essay writing. To make the composing process easier for students to grasp, we provide a separate section for each of the following stages: prewriting, identifying a thesis, supporting the thesis with evidence, organizing the evidence, writing the first draft, and revising. From the start, we point out that the stages are fluid. Indeed, the case history of an evolving student paper illustrates just how recursive and individualized the writing process can be. Guided activities at the end of each section give students practice taking their essays through successive stages in the composing process.

  To illustrate the link between reading and writing, the writing chapter presents the progressive stages of a student paper written in response to Ellen Goodman's "Family Counterculture," the selection presented in Chapter 1. An easy-to-spot symbol in the margin (✎) makes it possible to locate—at a glance—this evolving student essay. Commentary following the student paper highlights the essay's strengths and points out spots that could use additional work. In short, by the end of the second chapter, the entire reading-writing process has been illustrated, from reading a selection to writing about it.

- **Chapters 3–11** of *The Longman Reader: Brief Edition* contain selections grouped according to **nine patterns of development:** description, narration, exemplification, division-classification, process analysis, comparison-contrast, cause-effect, definition, and argumentation-persuasion. The sequence progresses from the more personal and expressive patterns to the more public and analytic. However, because each chapter is self-contained, the patterns may be covered in any order. Instructors preferring a thematic approach will find the Thematic Contents helpful.

  The Longman Reader: Brief Edition treats the patterns separately because such an approach helps students grasp the distinctive characteristics of each pattern. At the same time, the book continually shows the way writers usually combine patterns in their work. We also encourage students to view the patterns as strategies for generating and organizing ideas. Writers, we explain, rarely set out to compose an essay in a specific pattern. Rather, they choose a pattern or combination of patterns because it suits their purpose, audience, and subject.

Each of the nine pattern-of-development chapters follows this format:

1. **A detailed explanation of the pattern** begins the chapter. The explanation includes (a) a definition of the pattern, (b) a description of the way the pattern helps a writer accommodate his or her purpose and audience, and (c) step-by-step guidelines for using the pattern.

2. Next, we present **an annotated student essay** using the pattern. Written in response to one of the professional selections in the chapter, each essay illustrates the characteristic features of the pattern discussed in the chapter.

3. **Commentary** after each student essay points out the blend of patterns in the piece, identifies the paper's strengths, and locates areas needing improvement. "First draft" and "revised" versions of one section of the essay reveal how the student writer went about revising, thus illustrating the relationship between the final draft and the steps taken to produce it.

4. The **professional selections** in the pattern-of-development chapters are accompanied by these items:
   - *A biographical note and "Pre-Reading Journal Entry"* give students a perspective on the author and create interest in the piece.
   - *Questions for Close Reading* help students dig into and interpret the selection. The first question asks them to identify the selection's thesis; the last provides work on vocabulary development.
   - *Questions About the Writer's Craft* deal with such matters as purpose, audience, tone, organization, sentence structure, diction, and figures of speech. The first question in the series (labeled "The Pattern") focuses on the distinctive features of the pattern used in the selection. And usually there's another question (labeled

"Other Patterns") that asks students to analyze the writer's use of additional patterns in the piece.

- *Writing Assignments,* five in all, follow each selection. Packed with suggestions on how to proceed, the assignments use the selection as a springboard. The first two assignments ask students to write an essay using the same pattern as the one used in the selection; the next two assignments encourage students to discover for themselves which combination of patterns would be most appropriate for an essay; the last assignment helps students turn the raw material in their journals into fully considered essays. Frequently, the assignments are preceded by the symbol ∞, indicating a cross-reference to at least one other selection in the book. By encouraging students to make connections among readings, such assignments broaden students' perspective and give them additional material to draw on when they write. These "paired assignments" will be especially welcome to instructors stressing recurring ideas and themes.

5. **Prewriting and revising activities,** placed in shaded boxes at the end of each chapter, help students understand the unique demands posed by the pattern being studied.

6. At the end of each pattern-of-development chapter are two sets of **Additional Writing Assignments:** "General Assignments" and "Assignments With a Specific Purpose and Audience." The first set provides open-ended topics that prompt students to discover the best way to use a specific pattern; the second set develops their sensitivity to rhetorical context by asking them to apply the pattern in a real-world situation.

- **Chapter 12, "Combining the Patterns,"** offers one essay by each of three very different prose stylists. Annotations on one of the selections show how writers often blend patterns of development in their work. The chapter also provides guidelines to help students analyze this fusing of patterns.

- An **Appendix, "A Concise Guide to Finding and Documenting Sources,"** provides guidelines for conducting library and Internet research and for citing print and electronic sources.

The Longman Reader: Brief Edition also includes a glossary that lists all the key terms presented in the text. In addition, a comprehensive *Instructor's Manual* contains the following: in-depth answers to the "Questions for Close Reading" and "Questions About the Writer's Craft"; suggested activities; pointers about using the book; a detailed syllabus; and an analysis of the blend of patterns in the selections in the "Combining the Patterns" chapter.

WHAT'S NEW IN THE SIXTH EDITION

In preparing this brief edition, we looked closely at scores of questionnaires completed by instructors using the long version. Their comments helped us identify new directions the book might take. Here are some of the new features of this brief edition of *The Longman Reader:*

- Most importantly, *every selection in the book* (both new and retained) *is framed by a new set of assignments: a "Pre-Reading Journal Entry" assignment before the piece and a "Writing Assignment Using a Journal Entry as a Starting Point" after the piece. Taken together, these two "bookend" assignments illustrate not only the connection between reading and writing but also the process involved in shaping a piece of writing.* The journal assignment "primes" students for the selection by encouraging them to explore—in a loose, unpressured way—their thoughts about an issue that will be raised in the selection. The journal entry thus motivates students to read the piece with extra care, attention, and personal investment. The journal assignment also paves the way to the "Writing Assignment Using a Journal Entry as a Starting Point." The latter assignment helps students translate the raw material in their journals into a full-length essay. By the time students reach this final assignment, the rough ideas in their journal entry will have been enriched by a careful reading of the selection, setting the stage for a more rigorously conceived essay.
- *Nearly one quarter of the selections are new.* Many of these readings were suggested by instructors across the country; others were chosen after a lengthy search through magazines, nonfiction collections, newspapers, autobiographies, and the

like. Whether written by a well-known figure such as Joan Didion ("The Santa Ana") or a relative newcomer such as Beth Johnson ("Bombs Bursting in Air"), the new selections are bound to stimulate strong writing on a variety of topics—gender, family life, education, race, mass culture, and morality, to name a few. When selecting new readings, we took special care to include humorous pieces (for example, Bill Bryson's "Your New Computer") as well as those written from the third-person point of view (for example, James Gleick's "Life As Type A"). Honoring the requests of many instructors, we also made an effort to find compelling pieces on the way technology affects our everyday lives. Jonathan Coleman's "Is Technology Making Us Intimate Strangers?" is one of several such pieces.

- *A provocative new selection in the reading-process chapter,* Ellen Goodman's "Family Counterculture," *provides the foundation for the student paper presented in the writing-process chapter.* Seeing such a direct connection between a selection and the writing it inspires helps students appreciate the *interdependence of the reading and writing process.*

- *Additional attention is given to the concept of peer review.* An expanded discussion provides students with guidelines for reacting to other students' work and for responding to the feedback they themselves receive. This emphasis on peer review encourages students to work together and learn from one another; it also helps students evaluate their own writing more incisively. For quick, easy reference, the inside front cover now features a checklist that can be used for peer review. And the book's companion website offers a peer-review checklist for each pattern of development.

- *Many assignments* (signaled by 🖥) *suggest that students might want to conduct research in the library and/or on the Internet as part of their preparation for an essay.* Most of these assignments are worded in such a way that the essay can be written without visiting the library or going online, but the research option is there for instructors and students who think an essay would benefit from the citation of outside sources. The companion website provides links to Internet sites that students will find helpful if they supplement an essay with research.

- *The value of collaborative learning is underscored more than ever.* Many assignments encourage students to investigate various sides of an issue by brainstorming with classmates, questioning friends, speaking with family members, or interviewing "experts." Such assignments help students formulate sound, well-reasoned opinions and steer them away from reflexive, off-the-cuff positions.

- *A greater number of linked assignments* (indicated by ∞) *help students make connections between selections,* thus broadening their perspectives and giving them additional material to draw upon when they write.

- The *research paper* has been *updated* to reflect the *most recent MLA guidelines regarding the use of electronic sources.*

- *A new section, "A Concise Guide to Finding and Documenting Sources," has been added.* This Appendix now includes *up-to-date information on both library and Internet research.* The Internet section discusses the advantages and pitfalls of conducting research online, presents suggestions for using online time efficiently, and offers guidelines for evaluating online materials. The Appendix also shows how to document print and electronic sources.

- *A Companion Website, www.ablongman.com/nadell,* offers a number of helpful features, including additional activities and assignments, the address of relevant websites for assignments calling for Internet research, and a variety of supplementary activities.

The Longman Reader: Brief Edition has one more important new feature: Eliza A. Comodromos joins the book's original team of authors. A freelance editor and textbook consultant, Eliza has taught a variety of college writing courses; her special interest is in freshman composition. Eliza's considerable talents have helped shape this new edition of the book. Her presence is indeed welcome.

ACKNOWLEDGMENTS

At Longman, our thanks go to Eben Ludlow for his perceptive editorial guidance and continued enthusiasm for the long and brief editions of *The Longman Reader.* We're also indebted to Amber Allen, Zak Semens, and Irene Sotiroff of Elm Street Publishing Services,

Inc., and Valerie Zaborski, Doug Bell, and Bill Russo of Longman for their skillful handling of the never-ending complexities of the production process.

For help in preparing the sixth edition of *The Longman Reader: Brief Edition,* we owe thanks to the insightful comments of these reviewers: Joseph A. Alvarez, Central Piedmont Community College; George Cox, Johnston Community College; Laurie Culbreth, Chipola Junior College; Nancy N. Frazer, Fairmont State College; Casey Gilson, Broward Community College; Roberta Grantham, Chipola Junior College; Harrabeth A. Haidusek, Lamar University; Mary L. Hurst, Cuyahoga Community College; Eleanor James, Montgomery County Community College; David Kelly, Dyersburg State Community College; Teri Maddox, Jackson State Community College; Grace C. Ocasio, Central Piedmont Community College; Richard Pepp, Massasoit Community College; Lillian Polak, Nassau Community College; Patricia M. Price, Virginia Western Community College; Taryn Rice, Johnston Community College; Rhonda Lemke Sanford, Fairmont State College; Rita J. Self, Lamar University; Charles Swannell, Burlington County College; Victor Uszerowicz, Miami-Dade Community College; Patricia M. Wheeler, Central Piedmont Community College; and Donnie Yeilding, Central Texas College.

Our work on this edition was influenced too by the many students who took advantage of the questionnaire at the back of the fifth edition to tell us which selections they preferred.

Several individuals from our at-home office deserve special thanks. During the preparation of the sixth edition, Karen Beardslee and Frank Smigiel provided valuable assistance with the apparatus. And we're especially grateful to Janet M. Goldstein for the insight she provided when it came time to refine the journal-to-essay writing assignments. Finally, as always, we're thankful to our students. Their reactions to various drafts of material sharpened our thinking and helped focus our work. And we are especially indebted to the ten students whose essays are included in the book. Their thoughtful, carefully revised papers dramatize the potential of student writing and the power of the composing process.

Judith Nadell
John Langan
Eliza A. Comodromos

1

THE READING
PROCESS

More than two hundred years ago, essayist Joseph Addison commented, "Of all the diversions of life, there is none so proper to fill up its empty spaces as the reading of useful and entertaining authors." Addison might have added that reading also challenges our beliefs, deepens our awareness, and stimulates our imagination.

Why, then, don't more people delight in reading? After all, most children feel great pleasure and pride when they first learn to read. As children grow older, though, the initially magical world of books is increasingly associated with homework, tests, and grades. Reading turns into an anxiety-producing chore. Also, as demands on a person's time accumulate throughout adolescence and adulthood, reading often gets pushed aside in favor of something that takes less effort. It's easier simply to switch on the television and passively view the ready-made images that flash across the screen. In contrast, it's almost impossible to remain passive while reading. Even a slick best-seller requires that the reader decode, visualize, and interpret what's on the page. The more challenging the material, the more actively involved the reader must be.

The essays we selected for this book call for active reading. Representing a broad mix of styles and subjects, the essays range from the classic to the contemporary. They contain language that will move you, images that will enlarge your understanding of other people, ideas that will transform your views on complex issues.

The selections serve other purposes as well. For one thing, they'll help you develop a repertoire of reading skills—abilities that will benefit you throughout life. Second, as you become a better reader, your own writing style will become more insightful and polished. Increasingly, you'll be able to draw on the ideas presented in the selections and employ the techniques that professional writers use to express such ideas. As novelist Saul Bellow has observed, "A writer is a reader moved to emulation."

In the pages ahead, we outline a three-stage approach for getting the most out of this book's selections. Our suggestions will enhance your understanding of the book's essays, as well as help you read other material with greater ease and assurance.

STAGE 1: GET AN OVERVIEW OF THE SELECTION

Ideally, you should get settled in a quiet place that encourages concentration. If you can focus your attention while sprawled on a bed or curled up in a chair, that's fine. But if you find that being very comfortable is more conducive to daydreaming and dozing off than it is to studying, avoid getting too relaxed.

Once you're settled, it's time to read the selection. To ensure a good first reading, try the following hints:

- Start by reading the biographical note that precedes the selection. By providing background information about the author, the biographical note helps you evaluate the writer's credibility as well as his or her slant on the subject. For example, if you know that Deborah Tannen is a linguistics professor at Georgetown University, you can better assess whether she is a credible source for the analysis she presents in her essay "But What Do You Mean?" (page 241).
- Do the *Pre-Reading Journal Entry* assignment, which precedes the selection. This assignment "primes" you for the piece by helping you to explore—in an easy, unpressured way—your thoughts about a key point raised in the selection. By preparing the journal entry, you're inspired to read the selection with

special care, attention, and personal investment. (For more on pre-reading journal entries, see pages 16–18 and 542.)

- Consider the selection's title. A good title often expresses the essay's main idea, giving you insight into the selection even before you read it. For example, the title of Ann McClintock's essay, "Propaganda Techniques in Today's Advertising" (page 232), suggests that the piece will examine the dark side of the advertising world. A title may also hint at a selection's tone. The title of Robert Barry's piece, "Becoming a Videoholic" (the student essay on page 262), points to an essay that's light in spirit, whereas Nikki Giovanni's "Campus Racism 101" (page 278) suggests a piece with a serious mood.

- Read the selection straight through purely for pleasure. Allow yourself to be drawn into the world the author has created. Just as you first see a painting from the doorway of a room and form an overall impression without perceiving the details, you can have a preliminary, subjective feeling about a reading selection. Moreover, because you bring your own experiences and viewpoints to the piece, your reading will be unique. As Ralph Waldo Emerson said, "Take the book, my friend, and read your eyes out; you will never find there what I find."

- After this initial reading of the selection, focus your first impressions by asking yourself whether you like the selection. In your own words, briefly describe the piece and your reaction to it.

STAGE 2: DEEPEN YOUR SENSE OF THE SELECTION

At this point, you're ready to move further into the selection. A second reading will help you identify the specific features that triggered your initial reaction. Here are some suggestions on how to proceed:

- Mark off the selection's main idea, or thesis, often found near the beginning or end. If the thesis isn't stated explicitly, write down your own version of the selection's main idea.
- Locate the main supporting evidence used to develop the thesis. You may even want to number in the margin each key supporting point.

- Take a minute to write "Yes" or "No" beside points with which you strongly agree or disagree. Your reaction to these points often explains your feelings about the aptness of the selection's ideas.
- Return to any unclear passages you encountered during the first reading. The feeling you now have for the piece as a whole will probably help you make sense of initially confusing spots. However, this second reading may also reveal that, in places, the writer's thinking isn't as clear as it could be.
- Use your dictionary to check the meanings of any unfamiliar words.
- Ask yourself if your initial impression of the selection has changed in any way as a result of this second reading. If your feelings *have* changed, try to determine why you reacted differently on this reading.

STAGE 3: EVALUATE THE SELECTION

Now that you have a good grasp of the selection, you may want to read it a third time, especially if the piece is long or complex. This time, your goal is to make judgments about the essay's effectiveness. Keep in mind, though, that you shouldn't evaluate the selection until after you have a strong hold on it. A negative, even a positive reaction is valid only if it's based on an accurate reading.

At first, you may feel uncomfortable about evaluating the work of a professional writer. But remember: Written material set in type only *seems* perfect; all writing can be fine-tuned. By identifying what does and doesn't work in others' writing, you're taking an important first step toward developing your own power as a writer. You might find it helpful at this point to get together with other students to discuss the selection. Comparing viewpoints often opens up a piece, enabling you to gain a clearer perspective on the selection and the author's approach.

To evaluate the essay, ask yourself the following questions:

1. *Where does support for the selection's thesis seem logical and sufficient? Where does support seem weak?* Which of the author's supporting facts, arguments, and examples seem pertinent and convincing? Which don't?

2. *Is the selection unified? If not, why not?* Where does something in the selection not seem relevant? Where are there any unnecessary digressions or detours?

3. *How does the writer make the selection move smoothly from beginning to end?* How does the writer create an easy flow between ideas? Are any parts of the essay abrupt and jarring? Which ones?

4. *Which stylistic devices are used to good effect in the selection?* Which pattern of development or combination of patterns does the writer use to develop the piece? Why do you think those patterns were selected? How do paragraph development, sentence structure, and word choice contribute to the piece's overall effect? What tone does the writer adopt? Where does the writer use figures of speech effectively? (The next chapter and the glossary explain these terms.)

5. *How does the selection encourage further thought?* What new perspective on an issue does the writer provide? What ideas has the selection prompted you to explore in an essay of your own?

It takes some work to follow the three-step approach just described, but the selections in *The Longman Reader: Brief Edition* are worth the effort. Bear in mind that none of the selections sprang full-blown from the pen of its author. Rather, each essay is the result of hours of work—hours of thinking, writing, rethinking, and revising. As a reader, you should show the same willingness to work with the selections, to read them carefully and thoughtfully. Henry David Thoreau, an avid reader and prolific writer, emphasized the importance of this kind of attentive reading when he advised that "books must be read as deliberately and unreservedly as they were written."

To illustrate the multi-stage reading process just described, we've annotated the professional essay that follows: "Family Counterculture" by Ellen Goodman. Note that annotations are provided in the margin of the essay as well as at the end of the essay. As you read Goodman's essay, try applying the three-stage sequence. You can measure your ability to dig into the selection by making your own annotations on Goodman's essay and then comparing them to ours. You can also see how well you evaluated the piece by answering the preceding five questions and then comparing your responses to ours on pages 9–11.

Ellen Goodman

The recipient of a Pulitzer Prize, Ellen Goodman (1941–) worked for *Newsweek* and the *Detroit Free Press* before joining the staff of the *Boston Globe* in the mid-1970s. A resident of the Boston area, Goodman writes a popular syndicated column that provides insightful commentary on life in the United States. Her pieces have appeared in a number of national publications, including *The Village Voice* and *McCalls*. Collections of her columns have been published in *Close to Home* (1979), *Turning Points* (1979), *At Large* (1981), *Keeping in Touch* (1985), *Making Sense* (1989), and *Value Judgments* (1993). Most recently, she coauthored *I Know Just What You Mean* (1999), a book that examines the complex nature of women's friendships. The following selection is from *Value Judgments*.

Pre-Reading Journal Entry

Television is often blamed for having a harmful effect on children. Do you think this criticism is merited? In what ways does TV exert a negative influence on children? In what ways does TV exert a positive influence on youngsters? Take a few minutes to respond to these questions in your journal.

Marginal Annotations

Family Counterculture

Interesting take on the term "counter-culture"

Time frame established

1   Sooner or later, most Americans become card-carrying members of the counterculture. This is not an underground holdout of hippies. No beads are required. All you need to join is a child.

Light humor. Easy, casual tone

Time frame picked up

Thesis, developed overall by cause-effect pattern

2   At some point between Lamaze and the PTA, it becomes clear that one of your main jobs as a parent is to counter the culture. What the media delivers to children by the masses, you are expected to rebut one at a time.

First research-based example to support thesis

3   The latest evidence of this frustrating piece of the parenting job description came from pediatricians. This summer, the American Academy of Pediatrics called for a ban on television food ads. Their plea was hard on the heels of a study

showing that one Saturday morning of TV cartoons contained 202 junk-food ads.

The kids see, want, and nag. That is, after all, the theory behind advertising to children, since few six-year-olds have their own trust funds. The end result, said the pediatricians, is obesity and high cholesterol.

Their call for a ban was predictably attacked by the grocers' association. But it was also attacked by people assembled under the umbrella marked "parental responsibility." We don't need bans, said these "PR" people, we need parents who know how to say "no."

Well, I bow to no one in my capacity for naysaying. I agree that it's a well-honed skill of child raising. By the time my daughter was seven, she qualified as a media critic.

But it occurs to me now that the call for "parental responsibility" is increasing in direct proportion to the irresponsibility of the marketplace. Parents are expected to protect their children from an increasingly hostile environment.

Are the kids being sold junk food? Just say no. Is TV bad? Turn it off. Are there messages about sex, drugs, violence all around? Counter the culture.

Mothers and fathers are expected to screen virtually every aspect of their children's lives. To check the ratings on the movies, to read the labels on the CDs, to find out if there's MTV in the house next door. All the while keeping in touch with school and, in their free time, earning a living.

In real life, most parents do a great deal of this monitoring and just-say-no-ing. Any trip to the supermarket produces at least one scene of a child grabbing for something only to have it returned to the shelf by a frazzled parent. An extraordinary number of the family arguments are over the goodies—sneakers, clothes, games— that the young know only because of ads.

Marginal annotations:

Relevant paragraph? Identifies Goodman as a parent, but interrupts flow

Transition doesn't work but would if ¶6 were cut.

Series of questions and brief answers consistent with overall casual tone.

Brief real-life examples support thesis.

Fragments

More examples

Paragraph numbers: 4, 5, 6, 7, 8, 9, 10

Another weak transition—no contrast

Restatement of thesis

Second research-based example to support thesis

Citing an expert reinforces thesis.

Restatement of thesis

Comparison-contrast pattern—signaled by "once," "Today," "Once," and "Now"

Restatement of thesis

Conveys the challenges that parents face

But at times it seems that the media have 11
become the mainstream culture in children's lives. Parents have become the alternative.

Barbara Dafoe Whitehead, a research associ- 12
ate at the Institute for American Values, found this out in interviews with middle-class parents. "A common complaint I heard from parents was their sense of being overwhelmed by the culture. They felt their voice was a lot weaker. And they felt relatively more helpless than their parents.

"Parents," she notes, "see themselves in a 13
struggle for the hearts and minds of their own children." It isn't that they can't say no. It's that there's so much more to say no to.

Without wallowing in false nostalgia, there 14
has been a fundamental shift. Americans once expected parents to raise their children in accordance with the dominant cultural messages. Today they are expected to raise their children in opposition.

Once the chorus of cultural values was full 15
of ministers, teachers, neighbors, leaders. They demanded more conformity, but offered more support. Now the messengers are Ninja Turtles, Madonna, rap groups, and celebrities pushing sneakers. Parents are considered "responsible" only if they are successful in their resistance.

It's what makes child raising harder. It's why 16
parents feel more isolated. It's not just that American families have less time with their kids. It's that we have to spend more of this time doing battle with our own culture.

It's rather like trying to get your kids to eat 17
their green beans after they've been told all day about the wonders of Milky Way. Come to think of it, it's exactly like that.

Annotations at End of Selection

Thesis: First stated in paragraph 2 (". . . it becomes clear that one of your main jobs as a parent is to counter the culture. What the media delivers to children by the masses, you are expected to rebut one at a time.") and then restated in paragraphs 11 ("the media have become the mainstream culture in children's lives. Parents have become the alternative."); 13 (Parents are frustrated, not because ". . . they can't say no. It's that there's so much more to say no to."); and 16 ("It's not just that American families have less time with their kids. It's that we have to spend more of this time doing battle with our own culture.").

First reading: A quick take on a serious subject. Informal tone and to-the-point style gets to the heart of the media vs. parenting problem. Easy to relate to.

Second and third readings:
1. Uses the findings of the American Academy of Pediatrics, a statement made by Barbara Dafoe Whitehead, and a number of brief examples to illustrate the relentless work parents must do to counter the culture.
2. Uses cause-effect overall to support thesis and comparison/contrast to show how parenting nowadays is more difficult than it used to be.
3. Not everything works (reference to her daughter as a media critic, repetitive and often inappropriate use of "but" as a transition), but overall the essay succeeds.
4. At first, the ending seems weak. But it feels just right after an additional reading. Shows how parents' attempts to counter the culture are as commonplace as their attempts to get kids to eat vegetables. It's an ongoing and constant battle that makes parenting more difficult than it has to be and less enjoyable than it should be.
5. Possible essay topics: A humorous paper about the strategies kids use to get around their parents' saying "no" or a serious paper on the negative effects on kids of another aspect of television culture (cable television, MTV, tabloid-style talk shows, and so on).

The following answers to the questions on pages 4–5 will help crystallize your reaction to Goodman's essay.

1. *Where does support for the selection's thesis seem logical and sufficient? Where does support seem weak?*

   Goodman begins to provide evidence for her thesis when she cites the American Academy of Pediatrics's call for a "ban on television food ads" (paragraphs 3–5). The ban followed a study showing that kids are exposed to 202 junk-food ads during a single Saturday morning of television cartoons. Goodman further buoys her thesis with a list of brief "countering the culture" examples (8–10) and a slightly more detailed example (10) describing the parent-child conflicts that occur on a typical trip to the supermarket. By citing Barbara Dafoe Whitehead's findings later on (12–13), Goodman further reinforces her point that the need for constant rebuttal makes parenting especially frustrating: Because parents have to say "no" to virtually everything, more and more family time ends up being spent "doing battle" with the culture (16).

2. *Is the selection unified? If not, why not?*

In the first two paragraphs, Goodman identifies the problem and then provides solid evidence of its existence (3–4, 8–10). But Goodman's comments in paragraph 6 about her daughter's skill as a media critic seem distracting. Even so, paragraph 6 serves a purpose because it establishes Goodman's credibility by showing that she, too, is a parent and has been compelled to be a constant naysayer with her child. From paragraph 7 on, the piece stays on course by focusing on the way parents have to compete with the media for control of their children. The concluding paragraphs (16–17) reinforce Goodman's thesis by suggesting that parents' struggle to counteract the media is as common—and as exasperating—as trying to get children to eat their vegetables when all the kids want is to gorge on candy.

3. *How does the writer make the selection move smoothly from beginning to end?*

The first two paragraphs of Goodman's essay are clearly connected: The phrase "sooner or later" at the beginning of the first paragraph establishes a time frame that is then picked up at the beginning of the second paragraph with the phrase "at some point between Lamaze and the PTA." And Goodman's use in paragraph 3 of the word *this* ("The latest evidence of *this* frustrating piece of the parenting job description . . .") provides a link to the preceding paragraph. Other connecting strategies can be found in the piece. For example, the words *once, Today, Once,* and *Now* in paragraphs 14–15 provide an easy-to-follow contrast between parenting in earlier times and parenting in this era. However, because paragraph 6 contains a distracting aside, the contrast implied by the word *But* at the beginning of paragraph 7 doesn't work. Nor does Goodman's use of the word *But* at the beginning of paragraph 11 work; the point there emphasizes rather than contrasts with the one made in paragraph 10. From this point on, though, the essay is tightly written and moves smoothly along to its conclusion.

4. *Which stylistic devices are used to good effect in the selection?*

Goodman uses several patterns of development in her essay. The selection as a whole shows the *effect* of the mass media on kids and their parents. In paragraphs 3 and 12, Goodman provides *examples in the form of research data* to support her thesis, while paragraphs 8–10 provide a series of *brief real-life examples.* Paragraphs 12–15 use *contrast,* and paragraph 17 makes a *comparison* to punctuate Goodman's concluding point. Throughout, Goodman's *informal, conversational tone* draws readers in, and her *no-holds-barred style* drives her point home forcefully. In paragraph 8, she uses a *question and answer format* ("Are the kids being sold junk food? Just say no.") and *short sentences* ("Turn it off" and "Counter the culture") to illustrate how pervasive the situation is. And in paragraph 9, she uses *fragments* ("To check the ratings . . ." and "All the while keeping in touch with school . . .") to focus attention on the problem. These varied stylistic devices help make the essay a quick, enjoyable read. Finally, although Goodman is concerned about the corrosive effects of the media, she leavens her essay with dashes of *humor*. For example, the image of parents as counter-culturists (1) and the comments about green beans and Milky Ways (17) probably elicit smiles or gentle laughter from most readers.

5. *How does the selection encourage further thought?*

Goodman's essay touches on a problem most parents face at some time or another—having to counter the culture in order to protect their children. Her main concern is how difficult it is for parents to say "no" to virtually every aspect of the culture. Although Goodman offers no immediate solutions, her presentation of the issue urges us to decide for ourselves which aspects of the culture should be countered and which should not.

If, for each essay you read in this book, you consider the preceding questions, you'll be able to respond thoughtfully to the *Questions for Close Reading* and *Questions About the Writer's Craft* presented after each selection. Your responses will, in turn, prepare you for the writing assignments that follow the questions. Interesting and varied, the assignments invite you to examine issues raised by the selections and encourage you to experiment with various writing styles and organizational patterns.

Following are some sample questions and writing assignments based on the Goodman essay; all are similar to the sort that appear later in this book. Note that the final writing assignment paves the way for a student essay, the stages of which are illustrated in Chapter 2.

Questions for Close Reading

1. According to Goodman, what does it mean to "counter the culture"? Why is it harder now than ever before?
2. Which two groups, according to Goodman, protested the American Academy of Pediatrics's ban on television food ads? Which of these two groups does she take more seriously? Why?

Questions About the Writer's Craft

1. What audience do you think Goodman had in mind when she wrote this piece? How do you know? Where does she address this audience directly?
2. What word appears four times in paragraph 16? Why do you think Goodman repeats this word so often? What is the effect of this repetition?

Writing Assignments

1. Goodman believes that parents are forced to say "no" to almost everything the media offer. Write an essay illustrating the idea that not everything the media present is bad for children.
2. Goodman implies that, in some ways, today's world is hostile to children. Do you agree? Drawing upon but not limiting yourself to the material in your pre-reading journal, write an essay in which you support or reject this viewpoint.

The benefits of active reading are many. Books in general and the selections in *The Longman Reader: Brief Edition* in particular will bring you face to face with issues that concern all of us. If you study the selections and the questions that follow them, you'll be on the way to discovering ideas for your own papers. Chapter 2, "The Writing Process," offers practical suggestions for turning those ideas into well-organized, thoughtful essays.

2

THE WRITING PROCESS

Not many people retire at age thirty-eight. But Michel Montaigne, a sixteenth-century French attorney, did exactly that. Montaigne retired at a young age because he wanted to read, think, and write about all the subjects that interested him. After spending years getting his ideas down on paper, Montaigne finally published his short prose pieces. He called them *essays*—French for "trials" or "attempts."

In fact, all writing is an attempt to transform ideas into words, thus giving order and meaning to life. By using the term *essais,* Montaigne acknowledged that a written piece is never really finished. Of course, writers have to stop at some point, especially if they have deadlines to meet. But, as all experienced writers know, even after they dot the final *i,* cross the final *t,* and say "That's it," there's always something that could have been explored further or expressed a little better.

Because writing is a process, shaky starts and changes in direction aren't uncommon. Although there's no way to eliminate the work needed to write effectively, certain approaches can make the process more manageable and rewarding. This chapter describes a sequence of steps for writing essays. Familiarity with a specific sequence develops your awareness of strategies and choices, making you feel more confident when it comes time to write. You're less likely to look at a blank piece of paper and think, "Help! Now what do I do?" During the sequence, you do the following:

1. Prewrite
2. Identify the thesis
3. Support the thesis with evidence
4. Organize the evidence
5. Write the first draft
6. Revise the essay

We present the sequence as a series of stages, but we urge you not to view it as a rigid formula that must be followed step by unchanging step. Most people develop personalized approaches to the writing process. Some writers mull over a topic in their heads, then move quickly into a promising first draft; others outline their essays in detail before beginning to write. Between these two extremes are any number of effective approaches. The sequence here can be streamlined, juggled around, or otherwise altered to fit individual writing styles as well as the requirements of specific assignments.

STAGE 1: PREWRITE

Prewriting refers to strategies you can use to generate ideas *before* starting the first draft of a paper. Prewriting techniques are like the warm-ups you do before going out to jog—they loosen you up, get you moving, and help you to develop a sense of well-being and confidence. Since prewriting techniques encourage imaginative exploration, they also help you discover what interests you most about your subject. Having such a focus early in the writing process keeps you from plunging into your initial draft without first giving some thought to what you want to say.

Prewriting can help in other ways, too. When we write, we often sabotage our ability to generate material because we continually critique what we put down on paper. During prewriting, you deliberately ignore your internal critic. Your purpose is simply to get ideas down on paper *without evaluating* their effectiveness. Writing without immediately judging what you produce can be liberating. Once you feel less pressure, you'll probably find that you can generate a good deal of material. And that can make your confidence soar.

Keep a Journal

Of all the prewriting techniques, keeping a journal (daily or almost daily) is the one most likely to make writing a part of your life. Some journal entries focus on a single theme; others wander from topic to topic. Your starting point may be a dream, a snippet of overheard conversation, a video on MTV, a political cartoon, an issue raised in class or in your reading—anything that surprises, interests, angers, depresses, confuses, or amuses you. You may also use a journal to experiment with your writing style—say, to vary your sentence structure if you tend to use predictable patterns.

Here is a fairly focused excerpt from a student's journal:

Today I had to show Paul around school. He and Mom got here by 9. I didn't let on that this was the earliest I've gotten up all semester! He got out of the car looking kind of nervous. Maybe he thought his big brother would be different after a couple of months of college. I walked him around part of the campus and then he went with me to Am. Civ. and then to lunch. He met Greg and some other guys. Everyone seemed to like him. He's got a nice, quiet sense of humor. When I went to Bio., I told him that he could walk around on his own since he wasn't crazy about sitting in on a science class. But he said "I'd rather stick with you." Was he flattering me or was he just scared? Anyway it made me feel good. Later when he was leaving, he told me he's definitely going to apply. I guess that'd be kind of nice, having him here. Mom thinks it's great and she's pushing it. I don't know. I feel kind of like it would invade my privacy. I found this school and have made a life for myself here. Let him find his own school! But it could be great having my kid brother here. I guess this is a classic case of what my psych teacher calls ambivalence. Part of me wants him to come, and part of me doesn't! (November 10)

Although some instructors collect students' journals, you needn't be overly concerned with spelling, grammar, sentence structure, or organization. While journal writing is typically more structured than freewriting (see page 25), you don't have to strive for entries that read like mini-essays. In fact, sometimes you may find it helpful

to use a simple list (see the journal entry on page 24) when recording your thoughts about a subject. The important thing is to let
your journal writing prompt reflection and new insights, providing
you with material to draw upon in your writing. It is, then, a good
idea to reread each week's entries to identify recurring themes and
concerns. Keep a list of these issues at the back of your journal,
under a heading like "Possible Essay Subjects." Here, for instance,
are a few topics suggested by the preceding journal entry: deciding
which college to attend, leaving home, sibling rivalry. Each of these
topics could be developed in a full-length essay.

The Pre-Reading Journal.   To reinforce the value of journal writing, we've included a journal assignment before every selection in
the book. This assignment, called *Pre-Reading Journal Entry,*
"primes" you for the piece by encouraging you to explore—in a tentative fashion—your thoughts about an issue that will be raised in
the selection. Here, once again, is the *Pre-Reading Journal Entry*
assignment that precedes Ellen Goodman's "Family Counterculture" (page 6):

> Television is often blamed for having a harmful effect on
> children. Do you think this criticism is merited? In what
> ways does TV exert a negative influence on children? In
> what ways does TV exert a positive influence on young-
> sters? Take a few minutes to respond to these questions in
> your journal.

The following journal entry shows how one student, Harriet
Davids, responded to the journal assignment. A thirty-eight-year-
old college student and mother of two young teenagers, Harriet was
understandably intrigued by the assignment. As you'll see, Harriet
used a listing strategy to prepare her journal entry. She found that
lists were perfect for dealing with the essentially "for or against"
nature of the journal assignment.

TV's Negative Influence on Kids	TV's Positive Influence on Kids
Teaches negative behaviors (violence, sex, swearing, drugs, alcohol, etc.)	Teaches important educational concepts (<u>Sesame Street</u>, shows on The Learning Channel, etc.)
Cuts down on imagination and creativity	Exposes kids to new images and worlds (<u>Reading Rainbow</u>, <u>Mister Rogers' Neighborhood</u>)
Cuts down on time spent with parents (talking, reading, playing games together)	Can inspire important discussions (about morals, sexuality, drugs, etc.) between kids and parents
Encourages parents' lack of involvement with kids	Gives parents a needed break from kids
Encourages isolation (watching screen rather than interacting with other kids)	Creates common ground among kids, basis of conversations and games
De-emphasizes reading and creates need for constant stimulation	Encourages kids to slow down and read books based on a TV series or show (the <u>Arthur</u> and the <u>Clifford, the Big Red Dog</u> series, <u>The Bookworm Bunch</u>, etc.)
Promotes materialism (commercials)	Can be used by parents to teach kids that they can't have everything they see

The journal assignment and subsequent journal entry do more than prepare you to read a selection with extra care and attention; they also pave the way to a full-length essay. Here's how. The final assignment following each selection is called *Writing Assignment Using a Journal Entry as a Starting Point*. This assignment helps you to translate the raw material in your journal entry into a thoughtful, well-considered essay. By the time you get to the assignment, the rough ideas in your journal entry will have been enriched by your reading of the selection. (For an example of a writing assignment that draws upon material in a pre-reading journal entry, turn to page 105.)

As you've just seen, journal writing can stimulate thinking in a loose, unstructured way; journal writing can also prompt the focused thinking required by a specific writing assignment. When you have a specific piece to write, you should approach prewriting in a purposeful, focused manner. You need to:

- Understand the boundaries of the assignment.
- Determine your purpose, audience, and tone.
- Discover your essay's limited subject.
- Generate raw material about your limited subject.
- Organize the raw material.

We'll discuss each of these steps in turn. But first, here's a practical tip: If you don't use a word processor during the prewriting stage, try using a pencil and scrap paper. They're less intimidating than pen, typewriter, and "official" paper; they also reinforce the notion that prewriting is tentative and exploratory.

Understand the Boundaries of the Assignment

You shouldn't start writing a paper until you know what's expected. First, clarify the *kind of paper* the instructor has in mind. Assume the instructor asks you to discuss the key ideas in an assigned reading. What does the instructor want you to do? Should you include a brief summary of the selection? Should you compare the author's ideas with your own view of the subject? Should you determine if the author's view is supported by valid evidence?

If you're not sure about an assignment, ask your instructor—not the student next to you, who may be as confused as you—to make the requirements clear. Most instructors are more than willing to provide an explanation. They would rather take a few minutes of class time to explain the assignment than spend hours reading dozens of student essays that miss the mark.

Second, find out *how long* the paper is expected to be. Many instructors will indicate the approximate length of the papers they assign. If no length requirements are provided, discuss with the instructor what you plan to cover and indicate how long you think your paper will be. The instructor will either give you the go-ahead or help you refine the direction and scope of your work.

Determine Your Purpose, Audience, and Tone

Once you understand the requirements for a writing assignment, you're ready to begin thinking about the essay. What is its *purpose?* For what *audience* will it be written? What *tone* will you use? Later on, you may modify your decisions about these issues. That's fine. But you need to understand the way these considerations influence your work in the early phases of the writing process.

Purpose.   The papers you write in college are usually meant to *inform* or *explain,* to *convince* or *persuade,* and sometimes to *entertain.* In practice, writing often combines purposes. You might, for example, write an essay trying to *convince* people to support a new trash recycling program in your community. But before you win readers over, you most likely would have to *explain* something about current waste disposal technology.

When purposes blend this way, the predominant one determines the essay's content, organization, emphasis, and choice of words. Assume you're writing about a political campaign. If your primary goal is to *entertain,* to take a gentle poke at two candidates, you might start with several accounts of one candidate's "foot-in-mouth" disease and then describe the attempts of the other candidate, a multimillionaire, to portray himself as an average Joe. Your language, full of exaggeration, would reflect your objective. But if your primary purpose is to *persuade* readers that the candidates are incompetent and shouldn't be elected, you might adopt a serious, straightforward style. Rather than poke fun at one candidate's gaffes, you would use them to illustrate her insensitivity to important issues. Similarly, the other candidate's posturing would be presented, not as a foolish pretension, but as evidence of his lack of judgment.

Audience.   To write effectively, you need to identify who your readers are and to take their expectations and needs into account. An essay about the artificial preservatives in the food served by the campus cafeteria would take one form if submitted to your chemistry professor and a very different one if written for the college newspaper. The chemistry paper would probably be formal and technical, complete with chemical formulations and scientific data: "Distillation revealed sodium benzoate particles suspended in a gelatinous medium." But such technical material would be inappropriate in a newspaper column intended for general readers. In this case, you might provide specific examples of cafeteria foods containing additives—"Those deliciously smoky cold cuts are loaded with nitrates and nitrites, both known to cause cancer in laboratory animals"—and suggest ways to eat more healthily—"Pass by the deli counter and fill up instead on vegetarian pizza and fruit juices."

Ask yourself the following questions when analyzing your audience:

- What are my readers' age, sex, and educational level?
- What are their political, religious, and other beliefs?
- What interests and needs motivate my audience?
- How much do my readers already know about my subject?
- Do they have any misconceptions?
- What biases do they have about me, my subject, my opinion?
- How do my readers expect me to relate to them?
- What values do I share with my readers that will help me communicate with them?

Tone.   Just as your voice may project a range of feelings, your writing can convey one or more *tones*, or emotional states: enthusiasm, anger, resignation, and so on. Tone is integral to meaning; it permeates writing and reflects your attitude toward yourself, your purpose, your subject, and your readers. How do you project tone? You pay close attention to sentence structure and word choice.

Sentence structure refers to the way sentences are shaped. Although the two paragraphs that follow deal with exactly the same subject, note how differences in sentence structure create sharply dissimilar tones:

> During the 1960s, many inner-city minorities considered the police an occupying force and an oppressive agent of control. As a result, violence against police grew in poorer neighborhoods, as did the number of residents killed by police.

An occupying force. An agent of control. An oppressor. That's how many inner-city minorities in the '60s viewed the police. Violence against police soared. Police killings of residents mounted.

Informative in its approach, the first paragraph projects a neutral, almost dispassionate tone. The sentences are fairly long, and clear transitions ("During the 1960s"; "As a result") mark the progression of thought. But the second paragraph, with its dramatic, almost alarmist tone, seems intended to elicit a strong emotional response; its short sentences, fragments, and abrupt transitions reflect the turbulence of earlier times.

Word choice also plays a role in establishing the tone of an essay. Words have *denotations,* neutral dictionary meanings, as well as *connotations,* emotional associations that go beyond the literal meaning. The word *beach,* for instance, is defined in the dictionary as "a nearly level stretch of pebbles and sand beside a body of water." This definition, however, doesn't capture individual responses to the word. For some, *beach* suggests warmth and relaxation; for others, it calls up images of hospital waste and sewage washed up on a once-clean stretch of shoreline.

Since tone and meaning are tightly bound, you must be sensitive to the emotional nuances of words. In a respectful essay about police officers, you wouldn't refer to *cops, narcs,* or *flatfoots;* such terms convey a contempt inconsistent with the tone intended. Your words must also convey tone clearly. Suppose you're writing a satirical piece criticizing a local beauty pageant. Dubbing the participants "livestock on view" leaves no question about your tone. But if you simply referred to the participants as "attractive young women," readers might be unsure of your attitude. Remember, readers can't read your mind, only your paper.

Discover Your Essay's Limited Subject

Once you have a firm grasp of the assignment's boundaries and have determined your purpose, audience, and tone, you're ready to focus on a limited aspect of the general assignment. Because too broad a subject can result in a diffuse, rambling essay, be sure to restrict your general subject before starting to write.

The following examples show the difference between general subjects that are too broad for an essay and limited subjects that are appropriate and workable. The examples, of course, represent only a few among many possibilities.

General Subject	Less General	Limited
Education	Computers in education	Computers in elementary school arithmetic classes
	High school education	High school electives
Transportation	Low-cost travel	Hitchhiking
	Getting around a metropolitan area	The transit system in a nearby city
Work	Planning for a career	College internships
	Women in the work force	Women's success as managers

How do you move from a general to a narrow subject. Imagine that you're asked to prepare a straightforward, informative essay for your writing class. The writing assignment (#2 on page 12), prompted by Ellen Goodman's essay "Family Counterculture," is an extension of the journal-writing assignment on page 6.

> Goodman implies that, in some ways, today's world is hostile to children. Do you agree? Drawing upon but not limiting yourself to the material in your pre-reading journal, write an essay in which you support or reject this viewpoint.

You might feel unsure about how to proceed. But two techniques can help you limit such a general assignment. Keeping your purpose, audience, and tone in mind, you may *question* or *brainstorm* the general subject. These two techniques have a paradoxical effect. Although they encourage you to roam freely over a subject, they also help restrict the discussion by revealing which aspects of the subject interest you most.

1. Question the general subject.   One way to narrow a subject is to ask a series of *who, how, why, where, when,* and *what* questions.

The following example shows how Harriet Davids, the mother of
two young teenagers, used this technique to limit the Goodman
assignment.

You may recall that, before reading Goodman's essay, Harriet
had used her journal to explore TV's effect on children (see page
17). After reading "Family Counterculture," Harriet concluded that
she essentially agreed with Goodman; like Goodman, she felt that
parents nowadays are indeed forced to raise their kids in an "increasingly hostile environment." She was pleased that the writing assignment gave her an opportunity to expand preliminary ideas she had
jotted down in her journal.

Harriet soon realized that she had to narrow the Goodman
assignment. She started by asking a number of pointed questions
about the general topic. As she proceeded, she was aware that the
same questions could have led to different limited subjects—just as
other questions would have.

General Subject: We live in a world that is difficult, even hostile to
children.

Question	Limited Subject
Where do kids go to escape?	Television, which makes the world seem even more dangerous (violence, sex, etc.). Also malls and the Internet
Who is to blame for the difficult conditions under which children grow up?	Parents' casual attitude toward child-rearing
How have schools contributed to the problems children face?	Not enough counseling programs for kids in distress
Why do children feel frightened?	Divorce
When are children most vulnerable?	The special problems of adolescents
What dangers or fears should parents discuss with their children?	AIDS, drugs, alcohol, war, terrorism

2. Brainstorm the general subject.   Another way to focus on a limited subject is to list quickly everything about the general topic that pops into your mind. Working vertically down the page, jot down brief words, phrases, and abbreviations to capture your free-floating thoughts. Writing in complete sentences will slow you down. Don't try to organize or censor your ideas. Even the most fleeting, random, or seemingly outrageous thoughts can be productive.

Here's an example of the brainstorming that Harriet Davids generated in an effort to gather even more material on the Goodman assignment:

General Subject: We live in a world that is difficult, even hostile to children.

- TV--shows corrupt politicians, casual sex, drugs, alcohol, foul language, violence
- Kids babysat by TV
- Not enough guidance from parents
- Kids raise themselves
- Too many divorces
- Parents squabbling over material goods in settlements
- Money too important
- Kids feel unimportant
- Families move a lot
- I moved in fourth grade--hated it
- Rootless feeling
- Nobody graduates from high school in the same district they went to kindergarten in
- Drug abuse all over, in little kids' schools
- Pop music glorifies drugs
- Kids not innocent--know too much
- Single-parent homes
- Day care problems
- Abuse of little kids in day care
- TV coverage of day care abuse frightens kids
- Perfect families on TV make kids feel inadequate

As you can see, questioning and brainstorming suggest many possible limited subjects. To identify especially promising ones, reread your material. What arouses your interest, anger, or curiosity? What themes seem to dominate and cut to the heart of the matter? Star or circle ideas with potential.

After marking the material, write several phrases or sentences summarizing the most promising limited subjects. These, for example, are just a few that emerged from Harriet Davids's questioning and brainstorming for the Goodman assignment:

- TV partly to blame for children having such a hard time
- Relocation stressful to children
- Schools also at fault
- The special problems that parents face raising children today

Harriet decided to write on the last of these limited subjects—the special problems that parents face raising children today. This topic, in turn, is the focus of our discussion in the pages ahead.

Generate Raw Material About Your Limited Subject

When a limited subject strikes you as having possibilities, your next step is to see if you have enough interesting and insightful things to say about the subject to write an effective essay. To find out if you do, you may use any or all of the following techniques:

1. Freewrite on your limited subject. *Freewriting* means jotting down in rough sentences or phrases everything that comes to mind. To capture this continuous stream of thought, write nonstop for ten minutes or more. Don't censor anything; put down whatever pops into your head. Don't reread, edit, or pay attention to organization, spelling, or grammar. If your mind goes blank, repeat words until another thought emerges.

Here is part of the freewriting that Harriet Davids generated about her limited subject, "The special problems that parents face raising children today":

Parents today have tough problems to face. Lots of dangers. Drugs and alcohol for one thing. Also crimes of violence against kids. Parents also have to keep up with cost of living, everything costs more, kids want and expect more. Television? The Internet? Another thing is Playboy, Penthouse. Internet sites featuring sex. Sexy ads on TV, movies deal with sex. Kids grow up too fast, too fast. Drugs. Little kids can't handle knowing too much at an early age. Both parents at work much of the day. Finding good day care a real problem. Lots of latchkey kids. Another problem is getting kids to do homework, lots of other things to do. Especially playing on the computer and going to the mall! When I was young, we did homework after dinner, no excuses accepted by my parents.

2. Brainstorm your limited subject.   Let your mind wander freely, as you did when using brainstorming to narrow your subject. This time, though, list every idea, fact, and example that occurs to you about your limited subject. Use brief words and phrases so you don't get bogged down writing full sentences. For now, don't worry whether ideas fit together or whether the points listed make sense.

To gather additional material on her limited subject for the Goodman assignment ("The special problems that parents face raising children today"), Harriet Davids brainstormed the following list:

- Trying to raise kids when both parents work
- Prices of everything outrageous, even when both parents work
- Commercials make kids want more of everything
- Clothes so important
- Day care not always the answer--cases of abuse
- Day care very expensive
- Sex everywhere--TV, movies, magazines
- Sexy clothes on little kids. Absurd!
- Sexual abuse of kids
- Violence against kids when parents abuse drugs
- Acid, "Ecstasy," heroin, AIDS
- Schools have to teach kids about these things
- Schools doing too much--not as good as they used to be
- Not enough homework assigned--kids unprepared
- Distractions from homework--malls, TV, phones, stereos, MTV, Internet, computer games

3. Use group brainstorming.   Brainstorming can also be conducted as a group activity. Thrashing out ideas with other people stretches the imagination, revealing possibilities you may not have considered on your own. Group brainstorming doesn't have to be conducted in a formal classroom situation. You can bounce ideas around with friends and family anywhere—over lunch, at the student center, and so on.

4. Map out the limited subject.   If you're the kind of person who doodles while thinking, you may want to try *mapping*, sometimes called *diagramming* or *clustering.* Like other prewriting techniques, mapping proceeds rapidly and encourages the free flow of ideas. Begin by expressing your limited subject in a crisp phrase and placing it in the center of a blank sheet of paper. As ideas come to you, put them along lines or in boxes or circles around the limited subject. Draw arrows and lines to show the relationships among ideas. Don't stop there, however. Focus on each idea; as subpoints and details come to you, connect them to their source idea, again using boxes, lines, circles, or arrows to clarify how everything relates.

5. Use the patterns of development.   Throughout this book, we show how writers use various patterns of development (narration, process analysis, definition, and so on), singly or in combination, to develop and organize their ideas. Because each pattern has its own distinctive logic, the patterns encourage you, when you prewrite, to think about a subject in different ways, causing insights to surface that might otherwise remain submerged.

The various patterns of development are discussed in detail in Chapters 3–11. At this point, though, you should find the following chart helpful. It not only summarizes the broad purpose of each pattern but also shows the way each pattern can generate different raw material for the limited subject of Harriet Davids's essay:

Limited Subject: The special problems that parents face raising children today.

Pattern	Purpose	Raw Material
Description	To detail what a person, place, or object is like	Detail the sights and sounds of a glitzy mall that attracts kids
Narration	To relate an event	Recount what happened when neighbors tried to forbid their kids from going to a rock concert
Exemplification	To provide specific instances or examples	Offer examples of family arguments. Can a friend known to use drugs visit? Can a child go to a party where alcohol will be served? Can parents outlaw MTV?

Pattern	Purpose	Raw Material
Division-classification	To divide something into parts or to group related things in categories	Identify components of a TV commercial that distorts kids' values
		Classify the kinds of commercials that make it difficult to teach kids values
Process analysis	To explain how something happens or how something is done	Explain step by step how family life can disintegrate when parents have to work all the time to make ends meet
Comparison-contrast	To point out similarities and/or dissimilarities	Contrast families today with those of a generation ago
Cause-effect	To analyze reasons and consequences	Explain why parents are not around to be with their kids: Industry's failure to provide day care and inflexibility about granting time off for parents with sick kids
		Explain the consequences of absentee parents: Kids feel unloved; they're undisciplined; they take on adult responsibility too early
Definition	To explain the meaning of a term or concept	What is meant by "tough love"?
Argumentation-persuasion	To win people over to a point of view	Convince parents to work with schools to develop programs that make kids feel safer and more secure

(For more on ways to use the patterns of development in different phases of the writing process, see pages 37–38, 45–46, and 485–487.)

6. Conduct research.   Depending on your topic, you may find it helpful to visit the library and/or to go online to identify books and articles about your limited subject. (See pages 505–519 for hints on conducting research.) At this point, you don't need to read closely the material you find. Just skim and perhaps take a few brief notes on ideas and points that could be useful.

If researching the Goodman assignment, for instance, Harriet Davids could look under such headings and subheadings as the following:

> Day care
> Drug abuse
> Family
> Parent-child relationship
>   Child abuse
>   Children of divorced parents
>   Children of working mothers
> School and home

Organize the Raw Material

Once you generate the raw material for your limited subject, you're ready to shape your rough, preliminary ideas. Preparing a *scratch outline* or *scratch list* is an effective strategy. On pages 48–52, we talk about the more formal outline you may need later on in the writing process. Here we show how a rough outline or scratch list can impose order on the tentative ideas generated during prewriting.

Reread your exploratory thoughts about the limited subject. Cross out anything not appropriate for your purpose, audience, and tone; add points that didn't originally occur to you. Star or circle compelling items that warrant further development. Then draw arrows between related items, your goal being to group such material under a common heading. Finally, determine what seems to be the best order for those headings.

By giving you a sense of the way your free-form material might fit together, a scratch outline makes the writing process more manageable. You're less likely to feel overwhelmed once you actually start writing because you'll already have some idea about how to shape your material into a meaningful statement. Remember, though, the scratch outline can, and most likely will, be modified along the way.

The following scratch outline shows how Harriet Davids began to shape her brainstorming (page 24) into a more organized format. Note the way she eliminated some items (for example, the point about outrageous prices), added others (for example, the point about video arcades), and grouped the brainstormed items under four main headings, with the appropriate details listed underneath. (If you'd like to see Harriet's more formal outline and her first draft, turn to pages 50–51 and 66–67.)

Limited Subject: The special problems that parents face raising children today.

1. Day care for two-career families
   - Expensive
   - Before-school problems
   - After-school problems

2. Distractions from homework
   - Stereos, televisions, and computers in room at home
   - Places to go--malls, video arcades, fast-food restaurants, rock concerts

3. Sexually explicit materials
   - Magazines and books
   - Television shows
   - Internet
   - MTV
   - Movies
   - Rock posters

4. Life-threatening dangers
   - AIDS
   - Drugs
   - Drinking
   - Violence against children (by sitters, in day care, etc.)

The prewriting strategies just described provide a solid foundation for the next stages of your work. But invention and imaginative exploration don't end when prewriting is completed. As you'll see, remaining open to new ideas is crucial during all phases of the writing process.

Activities: Prewrite

1. Number the items in each set from 1 (*broadest subject*) to 5 (*most limited subject*):

Set A	Set B
Abortion	Business Majors

Controversial social issue	Students' majors
Cutting state abortion funds	College students
Federal funding of abortions	Kinds of students on campus
Social issues	Why many students major in business

2. Which of the following topics are too broad for an essay of two to five typewritten pages: soap operas' appeal to college students; day care; trying to "kick" the junk-food habit; male and female relationships; international terrorism?

3. Use the techniques indicated in parentheses to limit each general topic listed below. Then, identify a specific purpose, audience, and tone for the one limited subject you consider most interesting. Next, with the help of the patterns of development, generate raw material about that limited subject. (You may find it helpful to work with others when developing this material.) Finally, shape your raw material into a scratch outline—crossing out, combining, and adding ideas as needed. (Save your scratch outline so you can work with it further after reading about the next stage in the writing process.)

Friendship (*journal writing*)
Malls (*mapping*)
Leisure (*freewriting*)
Television (*brainstorming*)
Required courses (*group brainstorming*)
Manners (*questioning*)

STAGE 2: IDENTIFY THE THESIS

The process of prewriting—discovering a limited subject and generating ideas about it—prepares you for the next stage in writing an essay: identifying the paper's *thesis,* or controlling idea. Presenting your opinion on a subject, the thesis should focus on an interesting and significant issue, one that engages your energies and merits your consideration. You may think of the thesis as the essay's hub—the central point around which all the other material revolves. Your thesis determines what does and does not belong in the essay. The thesis, especially when it occurs early in an essay, also helps focus the reader on the piece's central point.

Sometimes the thesis emerges early in the prewriting stage, particularly if a special angle on your limited topic sparks your interest or becomes readily apparent. Often, though, you'll need to do some work to determine your thesis. For some topics, you may need to do some library research. For others, the best way to identify a promising thesis is to look through your prewriting and ask yourself questions such as these: "What statement does all this prewriting support? What aspect of the limited subject is covered in most detail? What is the focus of the most provocative material?"

For a look at the process of finding the thesis within prewriting material, glance back at the scratch outline (page 30) that Harriet Davids prepared for the limited subject "The special problems that parents face raising children today." Harriet devised the following thesis to capture the focus of this prewriting: "Being a parent today is much more difficult than it was a generation ago." (The full outline for Harriet's paper appears on pages 50–51; the first draft on pages 66–67; the final draft on pages 74–76.)

Writing an Effective Thesis

What makes a thesis effective? Generally expressed in one or two sentences, a thesis statement often has two parts. One part presents your paper's *limited subject;* the other presents your *point of view,* or *attitude,* about that subject. Here are some examples of the way you might move from general subject to limited subject to thesis statement. In each thesis statement, the limited subject is underlined once and the attitude twice.

General Subject	Limited Subject	Thesis
Education	Computers in elementary school arithmetic classes	Computer programs in arithmetic can individualize instruction more effectively than the average elementary schoolteacher can.
Transportation	A metropolitan transit system	Although the city's transit system still has problems, it has become safer and more efficient in the last two years.

General Subject	Limited Subject	Thesis
Work	College internships	College internships provide valuable opportunities to students uncertain about what to do after graduation.
Our anti-child world	Special problems that parents face raising children today	Being a parent today is much more difficult than it was a generation ago.

(*Reminder:* The last of these thesis statements is the one that Harriet Davids devised for the essay she planned to write in response to the assignment on page 12. Harriet's prewriting appears on pages 24 and 30. You can find her first draft on pages 66–67.)

Because identifying your thesis statement is an important step in writing a sharply focused essay, you need to avoid three common problems that lead to an ineffective thesis.

Don't make an announcement.   Some writers use the thesis statement merely to announce the limited subject of their paper and forget to indicate their attitude toward the subject. Such statements are announcements of intent, not thesis statements.

Compare the following three announcements with the thesis statements beside them.

Announcements	Thesis Statements
My essay will discuss whether a student pub should exist on campus.	This college should not allow a student pub on campus.
Handgun legislation is the subject of this paper.	Banning handguns is the first step toward controlling crime in the United States.
I want to discuss cable television.	Cable television has not delivered on its promise to provide an alternative to network programming.

Don't make a factual statement.   Your thesis and thus your essay should focus on an issue capable of being developed. If a fact is used as a thesis, you have no place to go; a fact generally doesn't invite much discussion.

Notice the difference between these factual statements and thesis statements:

Factual Statements	Thesis Statements
Many businesses pollute the environment.	Tax penalties should be levied against businesses that pollute the environment.
Nowadays, many movies are violent.	Movie violence provides a healthy outlet for aggression.
The population of the United States is growing older.	The aging of the U.S. population will eventually create a crisis in the delivery of health-care services.

Don't make a broad statement.   Avoid stating your thesis in vague, general, or sweeping terms. Broad statements make it difficult for readers to grasp your essay's point. Moreover, if you start with a broad thesis, you're saddled with the impossible task of trying to develop a book-length idea in an essay that runs only several pages.

The following examples contrast statements that are too broad with thesis statements that are focused effectively

Broad Statements	Thesis Statements
Nowadays, high school education is often meaningless.	High school diplomas have been devalued by grade inflation.
Newspapers cater to the taste of the American public.	The success of *USA Today* indicates that people want newspapers that are easy to read and entertaining.
The computer revolution is not all that we have been led to believe it is.	Home computers are still an impractical purchase for many people.

You have considerable freedom regarding the placement of the thesis in an essay. The thesis is often stated near the beginning, but it may be delayed, especially if you need to provide background information before it can be understood. Sometimes the thesis is reiterated—using fresh words—in the essay's conclusion or elsewhere.

You may even leave the thesis unstated, relying on strong evidence to convey the essay's central idea.

One final point: Once you start writing your first draft, some feelings, thoughts, and examples may emerge that qualify, even contradict, your initial thesis. Don't resist these new ideas; they frequently move you toward a clearer statement of your main point. Remember, though, your essay must have a thesis. Without this central concept, you have no reason for writing.

Activities: Identify the Thesis

1. For the following limited subject, four possible thesis statements are given. Indicate whether each is an announcement (*A*), a factual statement (*FS*), too broad a statement (*TB*), or an effective thesis (*OK*). Then, for the effective thesis, identify a possible purpose, audience, and tone.

   Limited Subject: The ethics of treating severely handicapped infants

   Some babies born with severe handicaps have been allowed to die.
   There are many serious issues involved in the treatment of handicapped newborns.
   The government should pass legislation requiring medical treatment for handicapped newborns.
   This essay will analyze the controversy surrounding the treatment of severely handicapped babies who would die without medical care.

2. Below you'll find listed the key points in an essay. Based on the information provided, prepare a possible thesis for the essay.

   • We do not know how engineering new forms of life might affect the earth's delicate ecological balance.
   • Another danger of genetic research is its potential for unleashing new forms of disease.
   • Even beneficial attempts to eliminate genetic defects could contribute to the dangerous idea that only perfect individuals are entitled to live.

3. Following are four pairs of general and limited subjects. Generate an appropriate thesis statement for each pair. Select one thesis, and determine which pattern of development would support it most

effectively. Use that pattern to draft a paragraph developing the thesis. (Save the paragraph so you can work with it further after reading about the next stage in the writing process.)

General Subject	Limited Subject
Psychology	The power struggles in a classroom
Health	Doctors' attitudes toward patients
U.S. politics	Television's coverage of presidential campaigns
Work	Minimum-wage jobs for young people

4. Return to the scratch outline you prepared for activity 3 on page 31. After examining the outline, identify a thesis that conveys the central idea behind most of the raw material. Then, ask others to evaluate your thesis in light of the material in the outline. Finally, keeping the thesis—as well as your purpose, audience, and tone—in mind, refine the scratch outline by deleting inappropriate items, adding relevant ones, and indicating where more material is needed. (Save your refined scratch outline and thesis so you can work with them further after reading about the next stage in the writing process.)

STAGE 3: SUPPORT THE THESIS WITH EVIDENCE

After identifying a preliminary thesis, you should develop the evidence needed to support the central idea. Such supporting material grounds your essay, showing readers you have good reason for feeling as you do about your subject. Your evidence also adds interest and color to your writing. In college essays of five hundred to fifteen hundred words, you usually need at least three major points of evidence to develop your thesis. These major points—each focusing on related but separate aspects of the thesis—eventually become the supporting paragraphs in the body of the essay.

What Is Evidence?

By *evidence,* we mean a number of different kinds of support. *Examples* are just one option. To develop your thesis, you might also include *reasons, facts, details, statistics, anecdotes,* and *quotations from experts.* Imagine you're writing an essay with the thesis, "People normally unconcerned about the environment can be galvanized to constructive action if they feel personally affected by an environmental problem." You could support this thesis with any combination of the following types of evidence:

- *Examples* of successful recycling efforts in several neighborhoods.
- *Reasons* why people got involved in a neighborhood recycling effort.
- *Facts* about other residents' efforts to preserve the quality of their well water.
- *Details* about the steps that people can take to get involved in environmental issues.
- *Statistics* showing the number of Americans concerned about the environment.
- An *anecdote* about your involvement in environmental efforts.
- A *quotation* from a well-known scientist about the impact that citizens can have on environmental legislation.

Where Do You Find Evidence?

Where do you find the examples, anecdotes, details, and other types of evidence needed to support your thesis? As you saw when you followed Harriet Davids's strategies for gathering material for an essay (pages 23–29), a good deal of evidence is generated during the prewriting stage. In this phase of the writing process, you tap into your personal experiences, draw upon other people's observations, perhaps interview a person with special knowledge about your subject. The library, with its abundant material, is another rich source of supporting evidence. In addition, the various patterns of development are a valuable source of evidence.

How the Patterns of Development Help Generate Evidence

On pages 27–28, we discussed the way patterns of development help generate material about a limited subject. The same patterns also help develop support for a thesis. The following chart shows how they generate evidence for this thesis: "To those who haven't done it, babysitting looks easy. In practice, though, babysitting can be difficult, frightening, even dangerous."

Pattern	Evidence Generated
Description	Details about a child who, while being babysat, was badly hurt.
Narration	Story about the time a friend babysat an ill child whose condition was worsened by the babysitter's actions.
Exemplification	Examples of potential babysitting problems: an infant rolls off a changing table; a toddler sticks objects in an electric outlet; a school-age child is bitten by a neighborhood dog.
Division-classification	A typical babysitting evening divided into stages: playing with the kids; putting them to bed; dealing with their nighttime fears once they're in bed.
	Classify kids' nighttime fears: of monsters under their beds; of bad dreams; of being abandoned by their parents.
Process analysis	Step-by-step account of what a babysitter should do if a child becomes ill or injured.
Comparison-contrast	Contrast between two babysitters: one well-prepared, the other unprepared.
Cause-effect	Why children have temper tantrums; the effect of such tantrums on an unskilled babysitter.
Definition	What is meant by a *skilled* babysitter?
Argumentation-persuasion	A proposal for a babysitting training program.

(For more on ways to use the patterns of development in different phases of the writing process, see pages 27–28, 45–46, and 485–487.)

Characteristics of Evidence

No matter how it is generated, all types of supporting evidence share the characteristics described in the following sections. You should keep these characteristics in mind as you review your thesis and scratch outline. That way, you can make the changes needed to strengthen the evidence gathered earlier. As you'll see shortly,

Harriet Davids focused on many of these issues as she worked with the evidence she collected during the prewriting phase.

The evidence is relevant and unified.   All the evidence in an essay must clearly support the thesis. It makes no difference how riveting material might be; if it doesn't *relate directly* to the essay's central point, the evidence should be eliminated. Irrelevant material can weaken your position by implying that no relevant support exists. It also distracts readers from your controlling idea, thus disrupting the paper's overall unity.

The following paragraph, taken from an essay illustrating recent changes in Americans' television-viewing habits, demonstrates the importance of unified evidence. The paragraph focuses on people's reasons for switching from network to cable television. As you'll see, the paragraph lacks unity because it contains points (underlined) unrelated to its main idea. Specifically, the comments about cable's foul language should be deleted. Although these observations bring up interesting points, they shift the paragraph's focus. If the writer wants to present a balanced view of the pros and cons of cable and network television, these points *should* be covered, but in *another paragraph*.

Nonunified Support

Many people consider cable TV an improvement over network television. For one thing, viewers usually prefer the movies on cable. Unlike network films, cable movies are often only months old, they have not been edited by censors, and they are not interrupted by commercials. Growing numbers of people also feel that cable specials are superior to the ones the networks grind out. Cable viewers may enjoy such pop stars as Billy Joel, Mariah Carey, or Chris Rock in concert, whereas the networks continue to broadcast tired Bob Hope variety shows and boring awards ceremonies. There is, however, one problem with cable comedians. The foul language many of them use makes it hard to watch these cable specials with children. The networks, in contrast, generally present "clean" shows that parents and children can watch together. Then, too, cable TV offers viewers more flexibility since it schedules shows at various times over the month. People working night shifts or attending evening classes can see movies in the afternoon, and viewers missing the first twenty minutes of a show can always catch them later. It's not surprising that cable viewership is growing while network ratings have taken a plunge.

Early in the writing process, Harriet Davids was aware of the importance of relevant evidence. Take a moment to compare Harriet's brainstorming (pages 24 and 26) and her scratch outline (page 30). Even though Harriet hadn't identified her thesis when she prepared the scratch outline, she realized she should delete a number of items on the reshaped version of her brainstorming—for example, the second item and third-to-last item ("prices of everything outrageous" and "schools doing too much"). Harriet eliminated these points because they weren't consistent with the focus of her limited subject.

The evidence is specific.   When evidence is vague and general, readers lose interest in what you're saying, become skeptical of your ideas' validity, and feel puzzled about your meaning. In contrast, *specific, concrete evidence* provides sharp *word pictures* that engage your readers, persuade them that your thinking is sound, and clarify meaning.

Consider, for example, the differences between the following two sentences: "The young man had trouble lifting the box out of an old car" and "Joe, only twenty years old but more than fifty pounds overweight, struggled to lift the heavy wooden crate out of the rusty, dented Chevrolet." The first sentence, filled with generalities, is fuzzy and imprecise while the second sentence, filled with specifics, is crisp and clear.

As the preceding sentences illustrate, three strategies can be used, singly or in combination, to make writing specific. First, you can provide answers to *who, which, what,* and similar *questions.* (The question "How does the car look?" prompts a change in which "an old car" becomes "a rusty, dented Chevrolet.") Second, you can use *vigorous verbs* ("had trouble lifting" becomes "struggled to lift"). Finally, you can replace *vague, abstract* nouns with *vivid, concrete* nouns or phrases ("the young man" becomes "Joe, only twenty years old but more than fifty pounds overweight").

Following are two versions of a paragraph from an essay about trends in the business community. Although both paragraphs focus on one such trend—flexible working hours—note how the first version's bland language fails to engage the reader and how its vague generalities leave the meaning unclear. What, for example, is meant by the term "flex-time scheduling"? The second paragraph answers this question (as well as several others) with clear specifics; it also uses strong, energetic language. As a result, the second paragraph is more informative and more interesting than the first.

Nonspecific Support

More and more companies have begun to realize that flex-time scheduling offers advantages. Several companies outside Boston have tried flex-time scheduling and are pleased with the way the system reduces the difficulties their employees face getting to work. Studies show that flex-time scheduling also increases productivity, reduces on-the-job conflict, and minimizes work-related accidents.

Specific Support

More and more companies have begun to realize that flex-time scheduling offers advantages over a rigid 9-to-5 routine. Along suburban Boston's Route 128, such companies as Compugraphics and Consolidated Paper now permit employees to schedule their arrival any time between 6 A.M. and 11 A.M. The corporations report that the number of rush-hour jams and accidents has fallen dramatically. As a result, employees no longer arrive at work weighed down by tension induced by choking clouds of exhaust fumes and the blaring horns of gridlocked drivers. Studies sponsored by the journal Business Quarterly show that this more mellow state of mind benefits corporations. Traffic-stressed employees begin their workday anxious and exasperated, still grinding their teeth at their fellow commuters, their frustration often spilling over into their performance at work. By contrast, stress-free employees work more productively and take fewer days off. They are more tolerant of coworkers and customers, and less likely to balloon minor irritations into major confrontations. Perhaps most importantly, employees arriving at work relatively free of stress can focus their attention on working safely. They rack up significantly fewer on-the-job accidents, such as falls and injuries resulting from careless handling of dangerous equipment. Flex-time improves employee well-being, and as well-being rises, so do company profits.

 At this point, it will be helpful to compare once again Harriet Davids's brainstorming (page 24 and 26) and her scratch outline (page 30). Note the way she added new details to make her brainstorming more specific. For example, to the item "Distractions from homework," she added the new examples "video arcades," "fast-food restaurants," and "rock concerts." And, as you'll see when you read Harriet's first and final drafts (pages 66–67 and 74–76), she added many more vigorous specifics during later stages of the writing process.

The evidence is adequate.   Readers won't automatically accept your thesis; you need to provide *enough specific evidence* to support your viewpoint. On occasion, a single extended example will suffice. Generally, though, you'll need a variety of evidence: facts, examples, reasons, personal observations, expert opinion, and so on.

Following are two versions of a paragraph from a paper showing how difficult it is to get personal, attentive service nowadays at gas stations, supermarkets, and department stores. Both paragraphs focus on the problem at gas stations, but one paragraph is much more effective. As you'll see, the first paragraph starts with good specific support, yet fails to provide enough of it. The second paragraph offers additional examples, descriptive details, and dialogue—all of which make the writing stronger and more convincing.

Inadequate Support

Gas stations are a good example of this impersonal attitude. At many stations, attendants have even stopped pumping gas. Motorists pull up to a combination convenience store and gas island where an attendant is enclosed in a glass booth with a tray for taking money. The driver must get out of the car, pump the gas, and walk over to the booth to pay. That's a real inconvenience, especially when compared with the way service stations used to be run.

Adequate Support

Gas stations are a good example of this impersonal attitude. At many stations, attendants have even stopped pumping gas. Motorists pull up to a combination convenience store and gas island where an attendant is enclosed in a glass booth with a tray for taking money. The driver must get out of the car, pump the gas, and walk over to the booth to pay. Even at stations that still have "pump jockeys," employees seldom ask, "Check your oil?" or wash windshields, although they may grudgingly point out the location of the bucket and squeegee. And customers with a balky engine or a nonfunctioning heater are usually out of luck. Why? Many gas stations have eliminated on-duty mechanics. The skillful mechanic who could replace a belt or fix a tire in a few minutes has been replaced by a teenager in a jumpsuit who doesn't know a carburetor from a charge card and couldn't care less.

Now take a final look at Harriet Davids's scratch outline (page 30). You'll see that Harriet realized she needed more than one block of supporting material to develop her limited subject; that's why she identified four separate blocks of evidence (day care, homework distractions, sexual material, and dangers). When Harriet prepared her first and final drafts (pages 66–67 and 74–76), she decided to eliminate the material about day care. But she added so many more specific and dramatic details that her evidence was more than sufficient.

The evidence is accurate.   When you have a strong belief and want readers to see things your way, you may be tempted to overstate or downplay facts, disregard information, misquote, or make up details. Suppose you plan to write an essay making the point that dormitory security is lax. You begin supporting your thesis by narrating the time you were nearly mugged in your dorm hallway. Realizing the essay would be more persuasive if you also mentioned other episodes, you decide to invent some material. Perhaps you describe several supposed burglaries on your dorm floor or exaggerate the amount of time it took campus security to respond to an emergency call from a residence hall. Yes, you've supported your point—but at the expense of truth.

The evidence is representative.   Using representative evidence means that you rely on the typical, the usual, to show that your point is valid. Contrary to the maxim, exceptions don't prove the rule. Perhaps you plan to write an essay contending that the value of seat belts has been exaggerated. To support your position, you mention a friend who survived a head-on collision without wearing a seat belt. Such an example isn't representative because the facts and figures on accidents suggest your friend's survival was a fluke.

Borrowed evidence is documented.   If you include evidence from outside sources (books, articles, interviews), you need to acknowledge where that information comes from. If you don't, readers may consider your evidence nothing more than your point of view, or they may regard as dishonest your failure to cite your indebtedness to others for ideas that obviously aren't your own.

For help in documenting sources in brief, informal papers, turn to page 410. For information on acknowledging sources in longer, more formal papers, refer to the Appendix (pages 519–532).

Strong supporting evidence is at the heart of effective writing. Without it, essays lack energy and fail to convey the writer's perspective. Such lifeless writing is more apt to put readers to sleep than to engage their interest and convince them that the points being made are valid. Taking the time to accumulate solid supporting material is, then, a critical step in the writing process.

Activities: Support the Thesis with Evidence

1. Below you'll find listed a thesis statement and four points of support. Identify the one point that is off target.

   Thesis: The United States is becoming a homogenized country.
   Regional accents vanishing
   Chain stores blanket country
   Americans proud of their ethnic identities
   Metropolitan areas almost indistinguishable from one another

2. For each of the following thesis statements, develop three points of relevant support. Then use the patterns of development to generate evidence for each point of support.

   Thesis: The trend toward disposable, throwaway products has gone too far.
   Thesis: The local (or college) library fails to meet the needs of those it is supposed to serve.
   Thesis: Television portrays men as incompetent creatures.

3. Choose one of the following thesis statements. Then identify an appropriate purpose, audience, and tone for an essay with this thesis. Using freewriting, mapping, or the questioning technique, generate at least three supporting points for the thesis. Last, using the appropriate pattern of development, write a paragraph about one of the points, making sure your evidence reflects the characteristics discussed in these pages. Alternatively, you may go ahead and prepare the first draft of an essay having the selected thesis. (If you choose the second option, you may want to turn to page 65 to see a diagram showing how to organize a first draft.) Save whatever you prepare so you can work with it further after reading about the next stage in the writing process.

   - Teenagers should (or should not) be able to obtain birth-control devices without their parents' permission.
   - All of us can take steps to reduce the country's trash crisis.
   - Drug education programs in public schools are (or are not) effective.

4. Retrieve the paragraph you wrote in response to activity 3 on pages 35–36. Keeping in mind the characteristics of effective evidence discussed in pages 38–43, make whatever changes are needed to strengthen the paragraph. (Save the paragraph so you can work with it further after reading about the next stage in the writing process.)

5. Look at the thesis and refined scratch outline you prepared in response to activity 4 on page 36. Where do you see gaps in the support for your thesis? By brainstorming with others, generate material to fill these gaps. If some of the new points generated suggest that you should modify your thesis, make the appropriate changes now. (Save this material so you can work with it further after reading about the next stage in the writing process.)

STAGE 4: ORGANIZE THE EVIDENCE

After you've generated supporting evidence, you're ready to *organize* that material. Even highly compelling evidence won't illustrate the validity of your thesis or achieve your purpose if readers have to plow through a maze of chaotic evidence. Some writers can move quickly from generating support to writing a clearly structured first draft. (They usually say they have sequenced their ideas in their heads.) Most, however, need to spend some time sorting out their thoughts on paper before starting the first draft; otherwise, they tend to lose their way in a tangle of ideas.

When moving to the organizing stage, you should have in front of you your scratch outline (see pages 29–30) and thesis plus any supporting material you've accumulated since you did your prewriting. To find a logical framework for all this material, you'll need to (1) determine which pattern of development is implied in your evidence, (2) select one of four basic approaches for organizing your evidence, and (3) outline your evidence. These issues are discussed in the pages ahead.

Use the Patterns of Development

As you saw on pages 27–28 and 37–38, the patterns of development (definition, narration, process analysis, and others) can help you develop prewriting material and generate evidence for a thesis. In the organizing stage, the patterns provide frameworks for presenting evidence in an orderly, accessible way. Here's how.

Each pattern of development has its own internal logic that makes it appropriate for some writing purposes but not for others. (You may find it helpful at this point to turn to pages 27–28 so you can review the broad purpose of each pattern.) Once you see which pattern (or combination of patterns) is implied by your purpose, you can block out your paper's general structure. Imagine that you're writing an essay *explaining why* some students drop out of college during the first semester. You might organize the essay around a three-part discussion of the key *causes* contributing to the difficulty that students have adjusting to college: (1) they miss friends and family, (2) they take inappropriate courses, and (3) they experience conflicts with roommates. As you can see, your choice of pattern of development significantly influences your essay's content and organization.

Some essays follow a single pattern, but most blend them, with a predominant pattern providing the piece's organizational framework. In our example essay, you might include a brief *description* of an overwhelmed first-year college student; you might *define* the psychological term "separation anxiety"; you might end the paper by briefly explaining a *process* for making students' adjustment to college easier. Still, the essay's overall organizational pattern would be *cause-effect* since the paper's primary purpose is to explain why students drop out of college. (For more information on the way patterns often blend in writing, see Chapter 12, "Combining the Patterns.")

Although writers often combine the patterns of development, your composition instructor may ask you to write an essay organized according to a single pattern. Such an assignment helps you understand a particular pattern's unique demands. Keep in mind, though, that most writing begins not with a specific pattern but with a specific *purpose*. The pattern or combination of patterns used to develop and organize an essay evolves out of that purpose.

Select an Organizational Approach

No matter which pattern(s) of development you select, you need to know four general approaches for organizing supporting evidence. These are explained below.

Chronological approach.   When an essay is organized *chronologically,* supporting material is arranged in a clear time sequence, usually starting with what happened first and ending with what happened last. Occasionally, chronological sequences can be rearranged to create flashback or flashforward effects, two techniques discussed in Chapter 4 on narration. Essays using narration (for example, an experience with prejudice) or process analysis (for instance, how to deliver an effective speech) are most likely to be organized chronologically. The paper on public speaking might use a time sequence to present its points: how to prepare a few days before the presentation is due; what to do right before the speech; what to concentrate on during the speech itself. (For examples of chronologically arranged student essays, turn to pages 136 and 262.)

Spatial approach.   When you arrange supporting evidence *spatially*, you discuss details as they occur in space, or from certain locations. This strategy is particularly appropriate for description. Imagine that you plan to write an essay describing the joyous times you spent as a child playing by a towering old oak tree in the neighborhood park. Using spatial organization, you start by describing the rich animal life (the plump earthworms, swarming anthills, and numerous animal tracks) you observed while hunkered down *at the base* of the tree. Next, you re-create the contented feeling you experienced sitting on a branch *in the middle* of the tree. Finally, you end by describing the glorious view of the world you had *from the top* of the tree.

Although spatial arrangement is flexible (you could, for instance, start with a description from the top of the tree), you should always proceed systematically. And once you select a particular spatial order, you should usually maintain that sequence throughout the essay; otherwise, readers may get lost along the way. (A spatially arranged student essay appears on page 88.)

Emphatic approach.   In *emphatic* order, the most compelling evidence is saved for last. This arrangement is based on the psychological principle that people remember best what they experience last. Emphatic order has built-in momentum because it starts with the least important point and builds to the most significant. This method is especially effective in argumentation-persuasion essays, in papers developed through examples, and in pieces involving comparison-contrast, division-classification, or causal analysis.

Consider an essay analyzing the negative effect that workaholic parents can have on their children. The paper might start with a brief discussion of relatively minor effects such as the family's eating mostly frozen or takeout foods. Paragraphs on more serious effects might follow: children get no parental help with homework; they try to resolve personal problems without parental advice. Finally, the essay might close with a detailed discussion of the most significant effect—children's lack of self-esteem because they feel unimportant in their parents' lives. (The student essays on pages 170, 303, and 374 all use an emphatic arrangement.)

Simple-to-complex approach.   A final way to organize an essay is to proceed from relatively *simple* concepts to more *complex* ones. By starting with easy-to-grasp, generally accepted evidence, you establish rapport with your readers and assure them that the essay is firmly grounded in shared experience. In contrast, if you open with difficult or highly technical material, you risk confusing and alienating your audience.

Assume you plan to write a paper arguing that your college has endangered students' health by not making an all-out effort to remove asbestos from dormitories and classroom buildings. It probably wouldn't be a good idea to begin with a medically sophisticated explanation of precisely how asbestos damages lung tissue. Instead, you might start with an observation that is likely to be familiar to your readers—one that is part of their everyday experience. You could, for example, open with a description of asbestos—as readers might see it—wrapped around air ducts and furnaces or used as electrical insulation and fireproofing material. Having provided a basic, easy-to-visualize description, you could then go on to explain the complicated process by which asbestos can cause chronic lung inflammation. (See page 341 for an example of a student essay using the simple-to-complex arrangement.)

Depending on your purpose, any one of these four organizational approaches might be appropriate. For example, assume that you planned to write an essay developing Harriet Davids's thesis: "Being a parent today is much more difficult than it was a generation ago." To emphasize that the various stages in children's lives present parents with different difficulties, you'd probably select a *chronological* sequence. To show that the challenges that parents face vary depending on whether children are at home, at school, or in the world at large, you'd probably choose a *spatial* sequence. To stress the range of problems that parents face (from less to more serious), you'd probably use an *emphatic* sequence. To illustrate today's confusing array of theories for raising children, you might take a *simple-to-complex* approach, moving from the basic to the most sophisticated theories.

Prepare an Outline

Do you, if asked to submit an outline, prepare it *after* you've written the essay? If you do, we hope to convince you that having an outline—a skeletal version of your paper—*before* you begin the first draft makes the writing process much more manageable. The outline helps you organize your thoughts beforehand, and it guides your writing as you work on the draft. Even though ideas continue to evolve during the draft, an outline clarifies how ideas fit together, which points are major, which should come first, and so on. An outline may also reveal places where evidence is weak, underscoring the need, perhaps, for more prewriting.

Like previous stages in the writing process, outlining is individualized. Some people prepare highly structured outlines; others make only a few informal jottings. Sometimes outlining will go quickly, with points falling easily into place; at other times you'll have to work hard to figure out how points are related. If that happens, be glad you caught the problem while outlining rather than while writing the first draft.

To prepare an effective outline, you should reread and evaluate your scratch outline and thesis as well as any other evidence you've generated since the prewriting stage. Then decide which pattern of development (description, cause-effect, and so on) seems to be suggested by your evidence. Also determine whether your evidence lends itself to a chronological, a spatial, an emphatic, or a simple-to-complex order. Having done all that, you're ready to identify and sequence your main and supporting points.

The amount of detail in an outline will vary according to the paper's length and the instructor's requirements. A scratch outline (like the one on page 30) is often sufficient, but for longer papers, you'll probably need a more detailed and formal outline. In such cases, the suggestions in the accompanying checklist will help you develop a sound plan. Feel free to modify these guidelines to suit your needs.

Outlining Checklist

- Write your purpose, audience, tone, and thesis at the top of the outlining page.
- Below the thesis, enter the pattern of development that seems to be implied by the evidence you've accumulated.
- Also record which of the four organizational approaches would be most effective in sequencing your evidence.
- Reevaluate your supporting material. Delete anything that doesn't develop the thesis or that isn't appropriate for your purpose, audience, and tone.
- Add any new points or material. Group related items together. Give each group a heading that represents a main topic in support of your thesis.

- Label these main topics with Roman numerals (I, II, III, and so on). Let the order of the numerals indicate the best sequence.
- Identify subtopics and group them under the appropriate main topics. Indent and label these subtopics with capital letters (A, B, C, and so on). Let the order of the letters indicate the best sequence.
- Identify supporting points (often, reasons and examples) and group them under the appropriate subtopics. Indent and label these supporting points with Arabic numbers (1, 2, 3, and so on). Let the numbers indicate the best sequence.
- Identify specific details (secondary examples, facts, statistics, expert opinions, quotations) and group them under the appropriate supporting points. Indent and label these specific details with lowercase letters (a, b, c, and so on). Let the letters indicate the best sequence.
- Examine your outline, looking for places where evidence is weak. Where appropriate, add new evidence.
- Double-check that all main topics, subtopics, supporting points, and specific details develop some aspect of the thesis. Also confirm that all items are arranged in the most logical order.

The sample outline that follows develops the thesis "Being a parent today is much more difficult than it was a generation ago." You may remember that this is the thesis that Harriet Davids devised for the essay she planned to write in response to the assignment on page 12. Harriet's scratch list appears on page 26. When you compare Harriet's scratch list and outline, you'll find some differences. On the whole, the outline contains more specifics, but it doesn't include all the material in the scratch list. For example, after reconsidering her purpose, audience, tone, and thesis, Harriet decided to omit from her outline the section on day care and the points about rock concerts, MTV, rock posters, and AIDS.

The plan shown below is called a *topic outline* because it uses phrases, or topics, for each entry. For a lengthier or more complex paper, a *sentence outline* would be more appropriate.

Purpose: To inform

Audience: Instructor as well as class members, most of whom are 18-20 years old

Tone: Serious and straightforward

Thesis: Being a parent today is much more difficult than it was a generation ago.

Pattern of development: Exemplification

Organizational approach: Emphatic order

  I. Distractions from homework
    A. At home
      1. Stereos, radios, tapes
      2. Television--esp. on MTV
      3. Computers
    B. Outside home
      1. Malls
      2. Video arcades
      3. Fast-food restaurants

 II. Sexually explicit materials
    A. In print
      1. Sex magazines
        a. <u>Playboy</u>
        b. <u>Penthouse</u>
      2. Pornographic books
    B. In movies
      1. Seduction scenes
      2. Casual sex
    C. On television
      1. Soap operas
      2. R-rated comedians
      3. R-rated movies on cable
    D. Internet
      1. Easy-to-access adult chat rooms
      2. Easy-to-access pornographic websites

III. Increased dangers
    A. Drugs--peer pressure
    B. Alcohol--peer pressure
    C. Violent crimes against children

(If you'd like to see the first draft that resulted from Harriet's outline, turn to pages 66–67. Hints for moving from an outline to a first draft appear on pages 53–55.)

Before starting to write your first draft, show your outline to several people (your instructor, friends, classmates). Their reactions will indicate whether your proposed organization is appropriate for your thesis, purpose, audience, and tone. Their comments can also highlight areas needing additional work. After making whatever changes are needed, you're in a good position to go ahead and write the first draft of your essay.

Activities: Organize the Evidence

1. The thesis statement below is followed by a scrambled list of supporting points. Prepare an outline for a potential essay, making sure to distinguish between major and secondary points.

   Thesis: Our schools, now in crisis, could be improved in several ways.

   Certification requirements for teachers
   Schedules
   Teachers
   Longer school year
   Merit pay for outstanding teachers
   Curriculum
   Better textbooks for classroom use
   Longer school days
   More challenging content in courses

2. Assume you plan to write an essay based on the following brief outline, which consists of a thesis and several points of support. Determine which pattern of development (pages 45–46) you would probably use for the essay's overall framework. Also identify which organizational approach (pages 46–48) you would most likely adopt to sequence the points of support listed. Then, use one or more patterns of development to generate material to support those points. Having done that, review the material generated, deleting, adding, combining, and arranging ideas in logical order. Finally, make an outline for the body of the essay. (Save your outline so you can work with it further after reading about the next stage in the writing process.)

   Thesis: Friends of the opposite sex fall into one of several categories: the pal, the confidant, or the pest.

   • Frequently, an opposite-sex friend is simply a "pal."
   • Sometimes, though, a pal turns, step by step, into a confidant.
   • If a confidant begins to have romantic thoughts, he or she may become a pest, thus disrupting the friendship.

3. Retrieve the writing you prepared in response to activity 3 or 4 on page 44. As needed, reshape that material, applying the organizational principles discussed in these pages. Be sure, for example, that you select the approach (chronological, spatial, emphatic, or simple-to-complex) that would be most appropriate, given your main idea, purpose, audience, and tone. (Save whatever you prepare so you can work with it further after reading about the next stage in the writing process.)

4. Look again at the thesis and scratch outline you refined and elaborated in response to activity 5 on page 45. Reevaluate this material by deleting, adding, combining, and rearranging ideas as needed. Also, keeping your purpose, audience, and tone in mind, consider whether a chronological, a spatial, an emphatic, or a simple-to-complex approach will be most appropriate. Now prepare an outline of your ideas. Finally, ask at least one person to evaluate your organizational plan. (Save your outline. After reading about the next stage in the writing process, you can use it to write the essay's first draft.)

STAGE 5: WRITE THE FIRST DRAFT

After prewriting, deciding on a thesis, and developing and organizing evidence, you're ready to write a *first draft*—a rough, provisional version of your essay. Because of your work in the preceding stages, the first draft may flow quite smoothly. But don't be discouraged if it doesn't. You may find that your thesis has to be reshaped, that a point no longer fits, that you need to return to a prewriting activity to generate additional material. Such stopping and starting is to be expected. Writing the first draft is a process of discovery, involving the continual clarification and refining of ideas.

How to Proceed

There's no single right way to prepare a first draft. Some writers rely heavily on their scratch lists or outlines; others glance at them only occasionally. Some people write the first draft in longhand; others use a typewriter or a computer.

However you choose to proceed, consider the following suggestions when moving from an outline or scratch list to a first draft:

- Make the outline's *main topics* (I, II, III) the *topic sentences* of the essay's supporting paragraphs. (Topic sentences are discussed later on pages 55–56.)
- Make the outline's *subtopics* (A, B, C) the *subpoints* in each paragraph.
- Make the outline's *supporting points* (1, 2, 3) the key *examples* and *reasons* in each paragraph.
- Make the outline's *specific details* (a, b, c) the *secondary examples, facts, statistics, expert opinions,* and *quotations* in each paragraph.

(To see how one student, Harriet Davids, moved from outline to first draft, turn to pages 65–67.)

Although outlines and lists are valuable for guiding your work, don't be so dependent on them that you shy away from new ideas that surface during your writing of the first draft. If promising new thoughts pop up, jot them down in the margin. Then, at the appropriate point, go back and evaluate them: Do they support your thesis? Are they appropriate for your essay's purpose, audience, and tone? If so, go ahead and include the material in your draft.

It's easy to get bogged down while preparing the first draft if you try to edit as you write. Remember: A draft isn't intended to be perfect. For the time being, adopt a relaxed, noncritical attitude. Working as quickly as you can, don't stop to check spelling, correct grammar, or refine sentence structure. Save these tasks for later. One good way to help remind you that the first draft is tentative is to use scrap paper and pencil. Writing on alternate lines also underscores your intention to revise later on, when the extra space will make it easier to add and delete material. Similarly, writing on only one side of the paper can prove helpful if, during revision, you decide to move a section to another part of the paper.

What should you do if you get stuck while writing your first draft? Stay calm and try to write something—no matter how awkward or imprecise it may seem. Just jot a reminder to yourself in the margin ("Fix this," "Redo," or "Ugh!") to fine-tune the section later. Or leave a blank space to hold a spot for the right words when they finally break loose. It may also help to reread—out loud is best—what you've already written. Regaining a sense of the larger context is often enough to get you moving again. You might also try talking your way through a troublesome section. By speaking aloud, you tap your natural oral fluency and put it to work in your writing.

If a section of the essay strikes you as particularly difficult, don't spend time struggling with it. Move on to an easier section, write that, and then return to the challenging part. If you're still getting nowhere, take a break. Watch television, listen to music, talk with friends. While you're relaxing, your thoughts may loosen up and untangle the knotty section.

Because you read essays from beginning to end, you may assume that writers work the same way, starting with the introduction and going straight through to the conclusion. Often, however, this isn't the case. In fact, since an introduction depends so heavily on everything that follows, it's usually best to write the introduction *after* the essay's body.

When preparing your first draft, you may find it helpful to follow this sequence:

1. Write the supporting paragraphs.
2. Connect ideas in the supporting paragraphs.
3. Write the introduction.
4. Write the conclusion.
5. Write the title.

Write the Supporting Paragraphs

Drawn from the main sections in your outline or scratch list, each *supporting paragraph* should develop an aspect of your essay's thesis. Besides containing relevant, concrete, and sufficient evidence (see pages 36–43), a strong supporting paragraph is (1) often focused by a topic sentence and (2) organized around one or more patterns of development. We'll focus on both features in the pages ahead. As you read our discussion, though, keep in mind that you shouldn't expect your draft paragraphs to be perfect; you'll have a chance to revise them later on.

Use topic sentences.   Frequently, each supporting paragraph in an essay is focused by a *topic sentence* that functions as a kind of mini-thesis for the paragraph. Generally one or two sentences in length, the topic sentence usually appears at or near the beginning of the paragraph. However, it may also appear at the end, in the middle, or—with varied wording—several times within the paragraph.

Regardless of its length or location, the topic sentence states the paragraph's main idea. The other sentences in the paragraph provide support for this central point in the form of examples, facts, expert opinion, and so on. Like a thesis statement, the topic sentence *signals the paragraph's subject* and frequently *indicates the writer's attitude* toward that subject. In the topic sentences that follow, the subject of the paragraph is underlined once and the attitude toward that subject is underlined twice:

> Some students select a particular field of study for the wrong reasons.
>
> The ocean dumping of radioactive waste is a ticking time bomb.
>
> Several contemporary rock groups show unexpected sensitivity to social issues.
>
> Political candidates are sold like slickly packaged products.

As you work on the first draft, you may find yourself writing paragraphs without paying too much attention to topic sentences. That's fine, as long as you evaluate the paragraphs later on. When revising, you can provide a topic sentence for a paragraph that needs a sharper focus, recast a topic sentence for a paragraph that ended up taking an unexpected turn, even eliminate a topic sentence altogether if a paragraph's content is sufficiently unified to imply its point.

Use the patterns of development.   As you saw on pages 45–46, an entire essay can be organized around one or more patterns of development (narration, process analysis, definition, and so forth). These patterns can also provide the organizational framework for an essay's supporting paragraphs. Assume you're writing an article for your town newspaper with the thesis "Year-round residents of an ocean community must take an active role in safeguarding the seashore environment." Your supporting paragraphs could develop this thesis through a variety of patterns, with each paragraph's topic sentence suggesting a specific pattern or combination of patterns. For example, one paragraph might start with the topic sentence "In a nearby ocean community, signs of environmental danger are everywhere" and go on to *describe* a seaside town with polluted waters, blighted trees, and diseased marine life. The next paragraph might have the topic sentence "Fortunately, not all seaside towns are plagued by such environmental problems" and continue by *contrasting* the troubled community with another, more ecologically sound shore town. A later paragraph, focused by the topic sentence "Residents can get involved in a variety of pro-environment activities," might use *division-classification* to elaborate on activities at the neighborhood, town, and municipal levels.

Connect Ideas in the Supporting Paragraphs

While writing the supporting paragraphs, you can try to smooth out the progression of ideas within and between paragraphs. In a *coherent* essay, the relationship between points is clear; readers can easily follow the development of your thoughts. (Sometimes, working on coherence causes a first draft to get bogged down; if this happens, move on, and wait until the revision stage to focus on such matters.)

The following paragraph lacks coherence for two main reasons. First, it sequences ideas improperly. (The idea about the toll attendants' being cut off from coworkers is introduced, dropped, then picked up again. References to motorists are similarly scattered throughout the paragraph.) Second, it doesn't indicate how individual ideas are related. (What, for example, is the connection between drivers who pass by without saying anything and attendants who have to work at night?)

Incoherent Support

Collecting tolls on the turnpike must be one of the loneliest jobs in the world. Each toll attendant sits in his or her booth, cut off from other attendants. Many drivers pass by each booth. None stays long enough for a brief "hello." Most don't acknowledge the attendant at all. Many toll attendants work at night, pushing them "out of synch" with the rest of the world. And sometimes the attendants have to deal with rude drivers who treat them like non-people, swearing at them for the long lines at the tollgate. Attendants also dislike how cut off they feel from their coworkers. Except for infrequent breaks, they have little chance to chat with each other and swap horror stories--small pleasures that would make their otherwise routine jobs bearable.

Coherent Support

Collecting tolls on the turnpike must be one of the loneliest jobs in the world. First of all, although many drivers pass by the attendants, none stays long enough for more than a brief "hello." Most drivers, in fact, don't acknowledge the toll collectors at all, with the exception of those rude drivers who treat the attendants like non-people, swearing at them for the long lines at the tollgate. Then, too, many toll attendants work at night, pushing them further "out of synch" with the rest of the world. Worst of all, attendants say, is how isolated they feel from their coworkers. Each attendant sits in his or her booth, cut off from other attendants. Except for infrequent breaks, they have little chance to chat with each other and swap horror stories--small pleasures that would make their otherwise routine jobs bearable.

To avoid the kinds of problems found in the incoherent paragraph, use—as the revised version does—two key strategies: (1) a clearly *chronological, spatial, emphatic* (*"Worst of all,* attendants say . . ."), or *simple-to-complex* approach and (2) *signal devices* (*"First of all,* although many drivers pass by . . .") to show how ideas are connected. For a discussion of the four organizational approaches, see pages 46–48. The following paragraphs describe signal devices.

Once you determine a logical approach for presenting your points, you need to make sure readers can follow the progression of those points. Signal devices provide readers with cues, reminding them where they have been and indicating where they are going.

Aim to include some signals—however awkward or temporary—in your first draft. If you find you *can't,* that's probably a warning that your ideas may not be arranged logically. A light touch should be your goal with such signals. Too many call attention to themselves, making the essay mechanical and plodding. In any case, here are some signaling devices to consider:

1. Transitions.   Words and phrases that ease readers from one idea to another are called *transitions.* Among such signals are the following:

Time	Space	Addition	Examples
first	above	moreover	for instance
next	below	also	for example
now	next to	furthermore	to illustrate
finally	behind	in addition	specifically

Contrast	Comparison	Summary
but	similarly	therefore
however	also	thus
otherwise	likewise	in short
on the one/other hand	too	in conclusion

Here's an earlier paragraph from this chapter. Note how the itali-cized transitions show readers how ideas fit together.

> *After* you've generated supporting evidence, you're ready to organize that material. Even highly compelling evidence won't illustrate the validity of your thesis or achieve your purpose if the readers have to plow through a maze of chaotic evidence. Some writers can move quickly from gen-erating support to writing a clearly structured first draft. (They usually say they have sequenced their ideas in their heads.) Most, *however,* need to spend some time sorting out their thoughts on paper before starting the first draft; *oth-erwise,* they tend to lose their way in a tangle of ideas.

2. Bridging sentences.   Although bridging sentences may be used within a paragraph, they are more often used to move readers from one paragraph to the next. Look again at the first sentence in the preceding paragraph. Note that the sentence consists of two parts: The first part reminds readers that the previous discussion focused on techniques for generating evidence; the second part tells readers that the focus will now be the organization of such evidence.

3. Repeated words, synonyms, and pronouns.   The repetition of important words maintains continuity, reassures readers that they are on the right track, and highlights key ideas. Synonyms—words sim-ilar in meaning to key words or phrases—also provide coherence, while making it possible to avoid unimaginative and tedious repeti-tions. Finally, pronouns (*he, she, it, they, this, that*) enhance coherence by causing readers to think back to the original word the pronoun replaces (antecedent). When using pronouns, however, be sure there is no ambiguity about antecedents.

Reprinted here is another paragraph from this chapter. Repeated words have been underlined once, synonyms underlined twice, and pronouns printed in italic type to illustrate how these techniques were used to integrate the paragraph's ideas.

> The process of prewriting—discovering a limited subject and generating ideas about *it*—prepares you for the next stage in writing an essay: identifying the paper's thesis or controlling idea. Presenting your opinion on a subject, the

<u>thesis</u> should focus on an interesting and significant issue, *one* that engages your energies and merits your consideration. You may think of the <u>thesis</u> as the essay's <u>hub</u>—the <u>central point</u> around which all the other material revolves. Your <u>thesis</u> determines what does and does not belong in the essay. The <u>thesis</u>, especially when *it* occurs early in an essay, also helps focus the reader on the piece's central point.

Write the Introduction

Many writers don't prepare an introduction until they have started to revise; others feel more comfortable if their first draft includes in basic form all parts of the final essay. If that's how you feel, you'll probably write the introduction as you complete your first draft. No matter when you prepare it, keep in mind how crucial the introduction is to your essay's success. Specifically, the introduction serves three distinct functions: It arouses readers' interest, introduces your subject, and presents your thesis.

The length of your introduction will vary according to your paper's scope and purpose. Most essays you write, however, will be served best by a one- or two-paragraph beginning. To write an effective introduction, use any of the following methods, singly or in combination. The thesis statement in each sample introduction is underlined.

Broad Statement Narrowing to a Limited Subject

For generations, morality has been molded primarily by parents, religion, and schools. Children traditionally acquired their ideas about what is right and wrong, which goals are important in life, and how other people should be treated from these three sources collectively. But in the past few decades, a single force--television--has undermined the beneficial influence that parents, religion, and school have on children's moral development. Indeed, <u>television often implants in children negative values about sex, work, and family life.</u>

Brief Anecdote

At a local high school recently, students in a psychology course were given a hint of what it is like to be the parents of a newborn. Each "parent" had to carry a raw egg around at all times to symbolize the responsibilities of parenthood. The egg could not be left alone; it limited the "parents'" activities; it placed a full-time emotional burden on

"Mom" and "Dad." This class exercise illustrates a common problem facing the majority of new mothers and fathers. Most people receive little preparation for the job of being parents.

Idea That Is the Opposite of the One Developed

We hear a great deal about divorce's disastrous impact on children. We are deluged with advice on ways to make divorce as painless as possible for youngsters; we listen to heartbreaking stories about the confused, grieving children of divorced parents. Little attention has been paid, however, to a different kind of effect that divorce may have on children. Children from divorced families may become skilled manipulators, playing off one parent against the other, worsening an already painful situation.

Series of Short Questions

What happens if a child is caught vandalizing school property? What happens if a child goes for a joyride in a stolen car and accidentally hits a pedestrian? Should parents be liable for their children's mistakes? Should parents have to pay what might be hundreds of thousands of dollars in damages? Adults have begun to think seriously about such questions because the laws concerning the limits of parental responsibility are changing rapidly. With unfortunate frequency, courts have begun to hold parents legally and financially accountable for their children's misdeeds.

Quotation

Educator Neil Postman believes that television has blurred the line between childhood and adulthood. According to Postman, "All the secrets that a print culture kept from children . . . are revealed all at once by media that do not, and cannot, exclude any audience." This media barrage of information, once intended only for adults, has changed childhood for the worse.

Refutation of a Common Belief

Adolescents care only about material things; their lives revolve around brand-name sneakers, designer jeans, the latest fad in stereo equipment. They resist education, don't read, barely know who is president, mainline rock 'n' roll, experiment with drugs, and exist on a steady diet of Ring-Dings, nachos, and beer. This is what many adults, including parents, seem to believe about the young. The reality is, however, that young people today show more maturity and common sense than most adults give them credit for.

Dramatic Fact or Statistic

Seventy percent of the respondents in a poll conducted by columnist Ann Landers stated that if they could live their lives over, they would choose not to have children. This startling statistic makes one wonder what these people believed parenthood would be like. <u>Most parents, it seems, have unrealistic expectations about their children.</u> Parents want their children to accept their values, follow their paths, and succeed where they failed.

Introductory paragraphs sometimes end with a *plan of development:* a quick preview of the essay's major points in the order in which those points will be discussed. The plan of development may be part of the thesis (as in the first sample introduction) or it may immediately follow the thesis (as in the last sample introduction). Because the plan of development outlines the essay's organizational structure, it helps prepare the reader for the essay's progression of ideas. In a brief essay, readers can often keep track of the ideas without this extra help. In a longer paper, though, a plan of development can be an effective unifying device since it highlights the main ideas the essay will develop.

Write the Conclusion

You may have come across essays that ended with jarring abruptness because they had no conclusions at all. Other papers may have had conclusions, but they sputtered to a weak close, a sure sign that the writers had run out of steam and wanted to finish as quickly as possible. Just as satisfying closes are an important part of everyday life (we feel cheated if dinner doesn't end with dessert or if a friend leaves without saying goodbye), a strong conclusion is an important part of an effective essay. Generally one or two paragraphs in length, the conclusion should give the reader a feeling of completeness and finality. One way to achieve this sense of "rounding off" is to return to an image, idea, or anecdote from the introduction. Because people tend to remember most clearly the points they read last, the conclusion is also a good place to remind readers of your thesis. You may also use the conclusion to make a final point about your subject. Be careful, though, not to open an entirely new line of thought at the essay's close.

Illustrated briefly here are several strategies for writing sound conclusions. These techniques may be used singly or in combination. The first strategy, the summary conclusion, can be especially helpful in long, complex essays since readers may appreciate a review of your points. Tacked onto a short essay, though, a summary conclusion often seems boring and mechanical.

Summary

Contrary to what many adults think, most adolescents are not only aware of the important issues of the times but also deeply concerned about them. They are sensitive to the plight of the homeless, the destruction of the environment, and the pitfalls of rampant materialism. Indeed, today's young people are not less mature and sensible than their parents were. If anything, they are more so.

Prediction

The growing tendency on the part of the judicial system to hold parents responsible for the actions of their wayward children can have a disturbing impact on all of us. Parents will feel bitter toward their own children and cynical about a system that holds them accountable for the actions of minors. Children, continuing to escape the consequences of their actions, will become even more lawless and destructive. Society cannot afford two such possibilities.

Quotation

The comic W. C. Fields is reputed to have said, "Anyone who hates children and dogs can't be all bad." Most people do not share Fields's cynicism. Viewing childhood as a time of purity, they are alarmed at the way television exposes children to the seamy side of life, stripping youngsters of their innocence and giving them a glib sophistication that is a poor substitute for wisdom.

Statistic

Granted, divorce may, in some cases, be the best thing for families torn apart by parents who battle one another. However, in longitudinal studies of children from divorced families, psychologist Judith Wallerstein found that only 10 percent of the youngsters felt relief at their parents' divorce; the remaining 90 percent felt devastated. Such statistics surely call into question parents' claims that they are divorcing for their children's sake.

Recommendation or Call for Action

It is a mistake to leave parenting to instinct. Instead, we should make parenting skills a required course in schools. In addition, a nationwide hotline should be established to help parents deal with crises. Such training and continuing support would help adults deal more effectively with many of the problems they face as parents.

Write the Title

Some writers say that they began a certain piece with only a title in mind. But for most people, writing a title is a finishing touch. Although creating a title for your paper is usually one of the last steps in writing an essay, it shouldn't be done haphazardly. It may take time to write an effective title—one that hints at the essay's thesis and snares the reader's interest.

Good titles may make use of the following techniques: repetition of sounds ("Affirmative Action: The Price of Preference"); questions ("Is Technology Making Us Intimate Strangers?"); and humor ("Becoming a Videoholic"). More often, though, titles are straightforward phrases derived from the essay's subject or thesis: "The Chase" and "Why Computers Don't Belong in the Classroom," for example.

Pull It All Together

Now that you know how to prepare a first draft, you might find it helpful to examine the accompanying illustration to see how the different parts of a draft can fit together. Keep in mind that not every essay you write will take this shape. As your purpose, audience, and tone change, so will your essay's structure. An introduction or conclusion, for instance, may be developed in more than one paragraph; the thesis statement may be implied or delayed until the essay's middle or end; not all paragraphs may have topic sentences; and several supporting paragraphs may be needed to develop a single topic sentence. Even so, the basic format presented here offers a strategy for organizing a variety of writing assignments—from term papers to lab reports. Once you feel comfortable with the structure, you have a foundation on which to base your variations. (This book's student and professional essays illustrate some possibilities.) Even when using a specific format, you always have room to give your spirit and imagination free play. The language you use, the details you select, the perspective you offer are uniquely yours. They are what make your essay different from everyone else's.

Introductory Paragraph(s)	Opening comments Thesis statement Plan of development (optional)
Supporting Paragraphs	Topic sentence 1 Specific details
	Topic sentence 2 Specific details
	Topic sentence 3 Specific details
Concluding Paragraph(s)	Closing comments

Sample First Draft

Here is the first draft of Harriet Davids's essay. (The assignment and prewriting for the essay appear on pages 22, 23–26, and 30.) Harriet wrote the draft in one sitting. Working at a computer, she started by typing her thesis at the top of the first page. Then, following the guidelines on page 54, she moved the material in her outline (page 51) to her draft. Harriet worked rapidly; she started with the first body paragraph and wrote straight through to the last supporting paragraph.

By moving quickly, Harriet got down her essay's basic text rather easily. Once she felt she had captured in rough form what she wanted to say, she reread her draft to get a sense of how she might open and close the essay. Then she drafted her introduction and conclusion; both appear here, together with the body of the essay. The commentary following the draft will give you a clearer sense of how Harriet proceeded.

Challenges for Today's Parents
by Harriet Davids

Thesis: Being a parent today is much more difficult than it was a generation ago.

Raising children used to be much simpler in the '50s and '60s. I remember TV images from that era showing that parenting involved simply teaching kids to clean their rooms, do their homework, and _____(ADD SPECIFICS). But being a parent today is much more difficult because nowadays parents have to shield/protect kids from lots of things, like distractions from schoolwork, from sexual material, from dangerous situations.

Parents have to control all the new distractions/temptations that turn kids away from schoolwork. These days many kids have stereos, computers, and televisions in their rooms. Certainly, my girls can't resist the urge to listen to MTV and go online, especially if it's time to do homework. Unfortunately, though, kids aren't assigned much homework and what is assigned too often is busywork. And there are even more distractions outside the home. Teens no longer hang out/congregate on the corner where Dad and Mom can yell to them to come home and do homework. Instead they hang out at the mall, in video arcades, and fast-food restaurants. Obviously, parents and school can't compete with all this.

Also (WEAK TRANS.) parents have to help kids develop responsible sexual values even though sex is everywhere. Kids see sex magazines and dirty paperbacks in the corner store where they used to get candy and comic books. And instead of the artsy nude shots of the past, kids see ronchey (SP?), explicit shots in Playboy and Penthouse. And movies have sexy stuff in them today. Teachers seduce students and people treat sex casually/as a sport. Not exactly traditional values. TV is no better. Kids see soap-opera characters in bed and cable shows full of nudity by just flipping the dial (FIX). Even worse is what's on the Internet. Too easy for kids to access chat rooms and websites dealing with adult, sometimes pornographic material. The situation has gotten so out of hand that maybe the government should establish guidelines on what's permissible.

Worst of all are the life-threatening dangers that parents must help children fend off over the years. With older kids, drugs fall into place as a main concern (AWK). Peer pressure to try drugs is bigger (WRONG WORD) to kids than their parents' warnings. Other kinds of warnings are common when children are small. Then parents fear violence since news shows constantly report stories of little children being abused (ADD SPECIFICS). And when kids aren't much older, they have to resist the pressure to drink. Alcohol has always attracted kids, but nowadays they are drinking more and this can be deadly, especially when drinking is combined with driving (REDO).

Most adults love their children and want to be good parents. But it's difficult because the world seems stacked against young people. Even Holden Caufield (SP?) had trouble dealing with society's confusing pressures. Parents must give their children some freedom but not so much that the kids lose sight of what's important.

Commentary

As you can see, Harriet's draft is rough. Because she knew she would revise later on (page 68), she "zapped out" the draft in an informal, colloquial style. For example, she occasionally expressed her thoughts in fragments ("Not exactly traditional values"), relied heavily on "and" as a transition, and used slangy expressions such as "kids," "dirty paperbacks," and "lots of things." Similarly, rather than fine-tuning, Harriet simply used capital letters to type parenthetic notes to herself: "REDO" or "FIX" to signal awkward sentences; "ADD SPECIFICS" to mark overly general statements; "WRONG WORD" after an imprecise word; "SP?" to remind herself to check spelling in the dictionary; "WEAK TRANS." to indicate where a stronger signaling device was needed. Note, too, that she used slashes between alternative word choices and left a blank space when wording just wouldn't come. (Harriet's final draft appears on pages 74–76.)

Writing a first draft may seem like quite a challenge, but the tips offered in these pages should help you proceed with confidence. Indeed, as you work on the draft, you may be surprised how much you enjoy writing. After all, this is your chance to get down on paper something you want to say.

Activities: Write the First Draft

1. Retrieve the writing you prepared in response to activity 3 on page 53. Applying the principles just presented, rework that material. If you wrote a single paragraph earlier, expand the material into a full essay draft. If you prepared an essay, strengthen what you wrote. In both cases, remember to consider your purpose, audience, and tone as you write the body of the essay as well as its introduction and conclusion. (Save your draft so you can rework it even further after reading about the next stage in the writing process.)

2. Referring to the outline you prepared in response to activity 2 or activity 4 on pages 52 and 53, draft the body of your essay, making your evidence as strong as possible. As you work, keep your purpose, audience, and tone in mind. After reading what you've prepared, go ahead and draft a rough introduction, conclusion, and title. Finally, ask at least one other person to react to your draft by listing its strengths and weaknesses. (Save the draft so you can work with it further after reading about the next stage in the writing process.)

STAGE 6: REVISE THE ESSAY

By now, you've probably abandoned any preconceptions you might have had about good writers sitting down and creating a finished product in one easy step. Alexander Pope's comment that "true ease in writing comes from art, not chance" is as true today as it was more than two hundred years ago. Writing that seems effortlessly clear is often the result of sustained work, not of good luck or even inborn talent. And much of this work takes place during the final stage of the writing process when ideas, paragraphs, sentences, and words are refined and reshaped.

Professional writers—novelists, journalists, textbook authors— seldom submit a piece of writing that hasn't been revised. They recognize that rough, unpolished work doesn't do them justice. What's more, they often look forward to revising. Columnist Ellen Goodman puts it this way: "What makes me happy is rewriting. . . . It's like cleaning house, getting rid of all the junk, getting things in the right order, tightening up."

In a sense, revision occurs throughout the writing process: At some earlier stage, you may have dropped an idea, overhauled your thesis, or shifted paragraph order. What, then, is different about the rewriting that occurs in the revision stage? The answer has to do with the literal meaning of the word *revision*—to resee, or to see again. Genuine revision involves casting clear eyes on your work, viewing it as though you're a reader rather than the writer. Revision means that you go through your paper looking for trouble, ready to pick a fight with your own writing. And then you must be willing to sit down and make the changes needed for your writing to be as effective as possible.

Revision is not, as some believe, simply touch-up work—changing a sentence here or a word there, eliminating spelling errors, typing a neat final copy. Revision means cutting deadwood, rearranging paragraphs, substituting new words for old ones, recasting sentences, improving coherence, even generating new material when appropriate. Because such work is challenging, you may resist revision or feel shaky about how to proceed.

Strategies to Make Revision Easier

The following pointers should help get you going if you balk at or feel overwhelmed by revising.

- *Set your draft aside for a while* before revising. When you pick up your paper again, you'll have a fresh, more objective point of view.
- *Work from typed material* whenever possible. Having your essay in neutral typed letters instead of in your own familiar writing helps you see the paper impartially, as if someone else had written it. Each time you make major changes, try to retype that section so that you can see it anew.
- *Read your draft aloud* as often as you can. Hearing how your writing sounds helps you pick up problems that you passed by before: places where sentences are awkward, meaning is ambiguous, words are imprecise. Even better, have another person read aloud to you what you have written. If the reader slows to a crawl over a murky paragraph or trips over a convoluted sentence, you know where you have to do some rewriting.
- *Participate in peer review.* Many instructors include in-class or at-home peer review as a regular part of a composition

course. Peer review—the critical reading of another person's writing with the intention of suggesting changes—accomplishes several important goals. First, peer review helps you gain a more objective perspective on your work. When you write something, you're often too close to what you've prepared to evaluate it fairly; you may have trouble seeing where the writing is strong and where it needs to be strengthened. Peer review supplies the fresh, neutral perspective you need. Second, reviewing your classmates' work broadens your own composing options. You may be inspired to experiment with a technique you admired in a classmate's writing but wouldn't have thought of on your own. Finally, peer review trains you to be a better reader and critic of your *own* writing. When you get into the habit of critically reading other students' writing, you become more adept at critiquing your own.

An important note: Preparing a helpful peer review is a skill that takes time to develop. At first, you, like many students, may be too easy or too critical. Effective peer review calls for rigor and care; you should give classmates the conscientious feedback that you hope for in return. Peer review also requires tact and kindness; feedback should always be constructive and include observations about what works well in a piece of writing. People have difficulty mustering the energy to revise if they feel there's nothing worth revising.

If your instructor doesn't require peer review, you can set up peer review sessions on your own, adapting the suggestions here to fit your needs. Start by selecting readers who are objective (not a love-struck admirer or doting grandparent) and skilled enough to provide useful commentary. To ensure that you leave peer review sessions with specific observations about what does and doesn't work in your writing, give your readers a clear sense of what you want from them. If you simply ask, "How's this?" you may receive a vague comment like "It's not very effective." What you want are concrete observations and suggestions: "I'm confused because what you say in the fifth sentence contradicts what you say in the second."

To promote such specific responses, ask your readers targeted (preferably written) questions like "I'm having trouble moving from my second to my third point. How can I make the transition smoother?" Such questions require more than "yes" or "no" responses; they encourage readers to dig into your writing where you sense it needs work. You may develop your own questions, or you may adapt the checklist on pages 72–74 and at the front of the book. (If it's feasible, encourage readers to *write* their responses to your questions.)

If you're most concerned about your draft's overall meaning (pages 72–73), readers don't necessarily need a copy of your essay. The draft can be read aloud so everyone can hear it. However, if you want feedback on individual paragraphs (page 73) or on specific sentences and words (page 73), you should supply readers with copies of your draft.

- *Evaluate and respond to peer review.* Accepting criticism isn't easy (even if you asked for it), and not all peer reviewers will be diplomatic. Even so, try to listen with an open mind to those giving you feedback. Take notes on their oral observations and/or have them fill out the checklist described above. Later, when you're ready to revise your paper, reread your notes. Which reviewer remarks seem valid? Which don't? Rank the problems and solutions that your reviewers identified, designating the most critical as number 1. Based on the peer feedback, enter your own notes for revising in the margins of a clean copy of your draft. This way, you'll know exactly what changes need to be made in your draft as you proceed. Then, keeping the problems and remedies in mind, start revising. If you've been working on a computer, type in your changes, or handwrite changes directly on the draft above the appropriate line. (Rework extensive sections on a separate piece of paper.) When revising, always keep in mind that you may not agree with every reviewer suggestion. That's fine. It's *your* paper, and it's *your* decision to implement or reject the suggestions made by your peers.
- *Evaluate and respond to instructor feedback.* Most likely, your peers won't be the only ones giving you feedback. Your instructor will also react to your early or final draft. Like many students, you may be tempted to look only briefly at your instructor's comments. Perhaps you've "had it" with the essay and don't want to think about revising it to reflect the instructor's remarks. And if there's a grade on the essay,

you may think that's the only thing that counts. But remember: Although grades are important, comments are even more so. They can help you *improve* your writing—if not in this paper, then in the next one. If you don't understand or agree with the instructor's observations, don't hesitate to request a conference. Getting together gives both you and the instructor a chance to clarify your respective points of view.

- *View revision as a series of steps.* Don't try to tackle all of a draft's problems at once; instead, proceed step by step. (The feedback chart and annotation system described above will help you do just that.) Whenever possible, read your draft several times, each time focusing on different issues and asking yourself different questions. Move from a broad view of the draft to an up close look at its mechanics.

The following checklist describes a number of questions you and your readers can ask when moving through the various steps in the revising process. (To see how one student, Harriet Davids, used the checklist when revising, turn to pages 78–79.) Keep in mind, though, that there are no hard-and-fast rules about the revision steps outlined here. Everyone approaches revision differently. There are bound to be occasions when you have time for only one quick pass over a draft. And with experience, you'll learn how to streamline the process so you can focus on the most critical issues for a particular piece of writing. Feel free, then, to adapt our suggestions to your individual needs.

Peer Review/Revision Checklist

First Step: Revise Overall Meaning and Structure

- Considering the essay's purpose, audience, and tone (pages 19–21), in what ways does or doesn't the paper accomplish what was intended?
- What is the essay's thesis (pages 32–35)? Is it stated explicitly, or is it implied? If the perceived thesis isn't what was intended, what changes need to be made?
- What are the essay's main points of support (pages 36–37)? If any of these stray from or contradict the thesis (pages 38–39), what changes need to be made?
- Are the main points arranged in a chronological, spatial, emphatic, or simple-to-complex sequence (pages 46–48)? How does this organizational format reinforce the thesis?

- Which patterns of development (pages 45–46) provide the essay's organizational framework? How do these patterns reinforce the thesis?

Second Step: Revise Paragraph Development

- Where in each paragraph does support seem irrelevant, vague, insufficient, inaccurate, or nonrepresentative (pages 38–43)? What could be done to remedy these problems?
- By what organizational principles (pages 46–48) are the ideas in each paragraph arranged? Why is this the most effective arrangement?
- What signal devices (pages 58–60) are used to connect ideas within and between paragraphs? Where are there too few signals or too many?
- What strategies are used to open (pages 60–62) and close (pages 62–64) the essay? How could the introduction and conclusion be made more effective?

Third Step: Revise Sentences and Words

- Which sentences seem inconsistent with the essay's intended tone (pages 20–21)? How could the problem be corrected?
- Where does sentence structure become monotonous and predictable (pages 88 and 134)? How could a different sentence pattern add variety?
- Which words are vague and overly general (pages 86–88 and 132–134)? How could the language be made more vigorous and concrete?
- Where does gender-biased language (pages 540–541) appear? How could the problem be eliminated?

Fourth Step: Proofread for Grammar, Punctuation, and Typing Errors

- A note about proofreading: Although proofing seems to involve relatively minor matters, an accumulation of small errors—misspellings, typos, misplaced commas—can distract readers and sabotage an otherwise strong essay. So before handing in the final draft of your essay, proofread it closely, keeping a dictionary and English handbook nearby. When proofing, people tend to see what they think is on the page rather than what really is there. Reading the essay out loud and backwards, starting with the last word first, can highlight errors that otherwise might slip by.

STUDENT ESSAY

In this chapter, we've taken you through the various stages in the writing process. You've seen how Harriet Davids used prewriting (pages 23–26 and 30) and outlining (page 51) to arrive at her first draft (pages 66–67). In the following pages, you'll look at Harriet's final draft—the paper she submitted to her instructor.

Harriet, a thirty-eight-year-old college student and mother of two teenagers, wanted to write an informative paper with a straightforward, serious tone. While preparing her essay, she kept in mind that her audience would include her course instructor as well as her classmates, many of them considerably younger than she. This is the assignment that prompted Harriet's essay:

> Goodman implies that, in some ways, today's world is hostile to children. Do you agree? Drawing upon but not limiting yourself to the material in your pre-reading journal, write an essay in which you support or reject this viewpoint.

Harriet's essay is annotated so that you can see how it illustrates the essay format described on page 65. As you read her essay, try to determine how well it reflects the principles of effective writing. The commentary following the paper will help you look at the essay more closely and give you some sense of the way Harriet went about revising her first draft.

Challenges for Today's Parents
by Harriet Davids

Introduction   Reruns of situation comedies from the 1950s and   1
early 1960s dramatize the kinds of problems that parents used to have with their children. The Cleavers scold Beaver for not washing his hands before dinner; the Andersons ground Bud for not doing his homework; the Nelsons dock little Ricky's allowance because he keeps forgetting to clean his room. But

Thesis ————— times have changed dramatically. Being a parent today is much more difficult than it was a generation

Plan of development	ago. Parents nowadays must protect their children from a growing number of distractions, from sexually explicit material, and from life-threatening situations.
First supporting paragraph **Topic sentence**	Today's parents must try, first of all, to control all 2 the new distractions that tempt children away from schoolwork. At home, a child may have a room furnished with a stereo, television, and computer. Not many young people can resist the urge to listen to CDs, go online, play computer games, or watch MTV--especially if it is time to do schoolwork. Outside the home, the distractions are even more alluring. Children no longer "hang out" on a neighborhood corner within earshot of Mom or Dad's reminder to come in and do homework. Instead, they congregate in vast shopping malls, buzzing video arcades, and gleaming fast-food restaurants. Parents and school assignments have obvious difficulty competing with such enticing alternatives.
Second supporting paragraph **Topic sentence with link to previous paragraph**	Besides dealing with these distractions, parents 3 have to shield their children from a flood of sexually explicit materials. Today, children can find sex magazines and pornographic paperbacks in the same corner store that once offered only comics and candy. Children will not see the fuzzily photographed nudes that a previous generation did but will encounter the hard-core raunchiness of Playboy or Penthouse. Moreover, the movies young people attend often focus on highly sexual situations. It is difficult to teach children traditional values when films show teachers seducing students and young people treating sex as a casual sport. Unfortunately, television, with its often heavily sexual content, is no better. With just a flick of the dial, children can see soap-opera stars cavorting in bed or watch cable programs where nudity is common. But the sexually graphic content of TV shows is nothing compared to the seamy material on the Internet. Many parents report that their children, sometimes without intending to, access pornographic chat rooms and websites that haunt the youngsters for months afterward.
Third supporting paragraph **Topic sentence with emphasis signal**	Most disturbing to parents today, however, is 4 the increase in life-threatening dangers that face young people. When children are small, parents fear that their youngsters may be victims of violence.

Every news program seems to carry a report about a mass murderer who preys on young girls, a deviant who has buried six boys in his cellar, or an organized child pornography ring that molests preschoolers. When children are older, parents begin to worry about their kids' use of drugs. Peer pressure to experiment with drugs is often stronger than parents' warnings. This pressure to experiment can be fatal. Finally, even if young people escape the hazards associated with drugs, they must still resist the pressure to drink. Although alcohol has always held an attraction for teenagers, reports indicate that they are drinking more than ever before. As many parents know, the consequences of this attraction can be deadly--especially when drinking is combined with driving.

Conclusion

References to TV shows recall introduction

Within one generation, the world as a place to   5
raise children has changed dramatically. One wonders how yesterday's parents would have dealt with today's problems. Could the Andersons have kept Bud away from MTV? Could the Nelsons have shielded little Ricky from sexually explicit material on the Internet? Could the Cleavers have protected Beaver from drugs and alcohol? Parents must be aware of all these distractions and dangers yet be willing to give their children the freedom they need to become responsible adults. It is not an easy task.

COMMENTARY

Introduction and thesis.   The opening paragraph attracts readers' interest by recalling several vintage television shows that have almost become part of our cultural heritage. Harriet begins with these examples from the past because they offer such a sharp contrast to the present, thus underscoring the idea expressed in her *thesis:* "Being a parent today is much more difficult than it was a generation ago." Opening in this way, with material that serves as a striking contrast to what follows, is a common and effective strategy. Note, too, that Harriet's thesis states the paper's subject (being a parent) as well as her attitude toward the subject (the job is more demanding than it was years ago).

Plan of development.   Harriet follows her thesis with a *plan of development* that anticipates the three major points to be covered in the essay's supporting paragraphs. Unfortunately, this particular plan of development is somewhat mechanical, with the major points being trotted past the reader in one long, awkward sentence. To deal with the problem, Harriet could have rewritten the sentence or eliminated the plan of development altogether, ending the introduction with her thesis.

Patterns of development.   Although Harriet develops her thesis primarily through *examples,* she also draws on two other patterns of development. The whole paper implies a *contrast* between the way life is now and the way it used to be. The essay also contains an element of *causal analysis* since all the factors that Harriet cites affect children and the way they are raised.

Purpose, audience, and tone.   Given the essay's *purpose* and *audience,* Harriet adopts a serious *tone,* providing no-nonsense evidence to support her thesis. But assume she had been asked by her daughters' school newspaper to write a humorous column about the trials and tribulations that parents face raising children. Aiming for a different tone, purpose, and audience, Harriet would have taken another approach. Drawing on her experience as a mother of two teenage daughters, she might have confessed how she survives MTV's flash and dazzle, as well as the din of stereos blasting rock music at all hours: she stuffs her ears with cotton, hides her daughters' CDs, and cuts off the electricity. This material—with its personalized perspective, exaggeration, and light tone—would be appropriate.

Organization.   Structuring the essay around a series of *relevant* and *specific examples,* Harriet uses *emphatic order* to sequence the paper's three main points: that a growing number of distractions, sexually explicit materials, and life-threatening situations make parenting difficult nowadays. The third supporting paragraph begins with the words "Most disturbing to parents today . . . ," signaling that Harriet feels particular concern about the physical dangers children face. Moreover, she uses basic organizational strategies to sequence the supporting examples within each paragraph. The details in the first supporting paragraph are organized *spatially,* starting with distractions at home and moving to those outside the home. The second supporting paragraph arranges examples *emphatically*. Harriet starts with sexually explicit publications and ends with the "seamy material on the Internet," which is even more disturbing than TV's "heavily sexual content." The third and final supporting paragraph is organized *chronologically;* it begins by discussing dangers to small children and concludes by talking about teenagers.

The essay also displays Harriet's familiarity with other kinds of organizational strategies. Each supporting paragraph opens with a *topic sentence*. Further, *signal devices* are used throughout the paper to show how ideas are related to one another: *transitions* ("Instead, they congregate in vast shopping malls"; "Moreover, the movies young people attend often focus on highly sexual situations"); *repetition* ("sexual situations" and "sexual content"); *synonyms* ("distractions . . . enticing alternatives" and "life-threatening . . . fatal"); *pronouns* ("young people . . . they"); and *bridging sentences* ("Besides dealing with these distractions, parents have to shield their children from a flood of sexually explicit material").

Two minor problems.   Harriet's efforts to write a well-organized essay result in a somewhat predictable structure. It might have been better had she rewritten one of the paragraphs, perhaps embedding the topic sentence in the middle of the paragraph or saving it for the end. Similarly, Harriet's signal devices are a little heavy-handed. Even so, an essay with a sharp focus and clear signals is preferable to one with a confusing or inaccessible structure. As she gains more experience, Harriet can work on making the structure of her essays more subtle.

Conclusion.   Harriet brings the essay to a satisfying *close* by reminding readers of the paper's central idea and three main points. The final paragraph also extends the essay's scope by introducing a new but related issue: that parents have to strike a balance between their need to provide limitations and their children's need for freedom.

Revising the first draft.   With the help of several classmates, Harriet reworked her essay a number of times. Using the checklist on pages 72–74 to focus their feedback, Harriet's revising team offered various suggestions to strengthen the paper. To get a sense of Harriet's revising process, compare the final version of her conclusion (page 76) with the original version reprinted here.

Original Version of Conclusion

Most adults love their children and want to be good parents. But it's difficult because the world seems stacked against young people. Even Holden Caulfield had trouble dealing with society's pressures. Parents must give their children some freedom but not so much that kids lose sight of what's important.

As soon as Harriet heard her paper read aloud during a group session, she realized the conclusion didn't work at all, but she wisely waited to rework the conclusion until after she had fine-tuned the rest of the essay. At that point, she made marginal annotations summarizing the problems that she and her editing group detected in the conclusion. Together, they identified three problems, numbered in order of importance. First, the conclusion seemed tacked on, rather like a tired afterthought. Second, the allusion to *The Catcher in the Rye* misrepresented the essay's focus since Harriet discusses children of all ages, not just teens. Third, the first sentence in the conclusion was bland and boring.

Keeping these points in mind, Harriet decided to scrap her original conclusion. Working at a word processor, she prepared a much stronger concluding paragraph. Besides eliminating the distracting reference to Holden Caulfield, she replaced the shopworn opening sentence ("Most adults love their children . . . ") with three interesting and rhythmical questions ("Could the Andersons . . . ? Could the Nelsons . . . ? Could the Cleavers . . . ?"). Because these questions recall the essay's main points and echo the introduction's reference to vintage television shows, they help unify Harriet's paper and bring it to a satisfying close.

These are just a few of the changes Harriet made when reworking her essay. Realizing that writing is a process, she left herself enough time to revise. She was gratified by her classmates' responses to what she had written and pleased by the lively discussion her essay provoked. Early in her composition course, Harriet learned that attention to the various stages in the writing process yields satisfying results, for writer and reader alike.

Activity: Revise the Essay

Return to the draft you wrote in response to either activity 1 or activity 2 on page 68. Also look at any written feedback you received on the draft. To identify any further problems in the draft, get together with several people (classmates, friends, or family members) and request that one of them read the draft aloud to you. Then ask your audience focused questions about the areas you sense need work, or use the checklist on pages 72–74 to focus the feedback. In either case, summarize and rank the comments on a feedback chart or in marginal annotations. Then, using the comments as a guide, go ahead and revise the draft. Either type a new version or do your revising by hand, perhaps on a photocopy of the draft. Don't forget to proofread closely before submitting the paper to your instructor.

3

DESCRIPTION

WHAT IS DESCRIPTION?

All of us respond in a strong way to sensory stimulation. The sweet perfume of a candy shop takes us back to childhood; the blank white walls of the campus infirmary remind us of long vigils at a hospital where a grandmother lay dying; the screech of a subway car sets our nerves on edge.

Without any sensory stimulation, we sink into a less-than-human state. Neglected babies, left alone with no human touch, no colors, no lullabies, become withdrawn and unresponsive. And prisoners dread solitary confinement, knowing that the sensory deprivation can be unbearable, even to the point of madness.

Because sensory impressions are so potent, descriptive writing has a unique power and appeal. *Description* can be defined as the expression, in vivid language, of what the five senses experience. A richly rendered description freezes a subject in time, evoking sights, smells, sounds, textures, and tastes in such a way that readers become one with the writer's world.

HOW DESCRIPTION FITS YOUR PURPOSE AND AUDIENCE

Description can be a supportive technique that develops part of an essay, or it can be the dominant technique used throughout an essay. Here are some examples of the way description can help you meet the objective of an essay developed chiefly through another pattern of development:

- In a *causal analysis* showing the *consequences* of pet overpopulation, you might describe the desperate appearance of a pack of starving stray dogs.
- In an *argumentation-persuasion* essay urging more rigorous handgun control, you might start with a description of a violent family confrontation that ended in murder.
- In a *process analysis* explaining the pleasure of making ice cream at home, you might describe the beauty of an old-fashioned, hand-cranked ice-cream maker.
- In a *narrative essay* recounting a day in the life of a street musician, you might describe the musician's energy and the joyous appreciation of passersby.

In each case, the essay's overall purpose would affect the amount of description needed.

Your readers also influence how much description to include. As you write, ask yourself, "What do my particular readers need to know to understand and experience keenly what I'm describing? What descriptive details will they enjoy most?" Your answers to these and similar questions will help you tailor your description to specific readers. Consider an article intended for professional horticulturists; its purpose is to explain a new technique for controlling spider mites. Because of readers' expertise, there would be little need for a lengthy description of the insects. Written for a college newspaper, however, the article would probably provide a detailed description of the mites so student gardeners could distinguish between the pesky parasites and flecks of dust.

While your purpose and audience define *how much* to describe, you have great freedom deciding *what* to describe. Description is especially suited to objects (your car or desk, for example), but you can also describe a person, an animal, a place, a time, and a phenomenon or concept. You might write an effective description about a friend who runs marathons (person), a pair of ducks who return each year to a neighbor's pond (animals), the kitchen of a fast-food restaurant (place), a period when you were unemployed (time), the "fight or flight" response to danger (phenomenon or concept).

Description can be divided into two types: *objective* and *subjective*. In an objective description, you describe the subject in a straightforward and literal way, without revealing your attitude or feelings. Reporters, as well as technical and scientific writers, specialize in objective description; their jobs depend on their ability to detail experiences without emotional bias. For example, a reporter may write an unemotional account of a township meeting that ended in a fistfight. Or a marine biologist may write a factual report describing the way sea mammals are killed by the plastic refuse (sandwich wrappings, straws, fishing lines) that humans throw into the ocean.

In contrast, when writing a subjective description, you convey a highly personal view of your subject and seek to elicit a strong emotional response from your readers. Such subjective descriptions often take the form of reflective pieces or character studies. For example, in an essay describing the rich plant life in an inner-city garden, you might reflect on people's longing to connect with the soil and express admiration for the gardeners' hard work—an admiration you'd like readers to share. Or, in a character study of your grandfather, you might describe his stern appearance and gentle behavior, hoping that the contradiction will move readers as much as it moves you.

The *tone* of a subjective description is determined by your purpose, your attitude toward the subject, and the reader response you wish to evoke. Consider an essay about a dynamic woman who runs a center for disturbed children. If your goal is to make readers admire the woman, your tone will be serious and appreciative. But if you want to criticize the woman's high-pressure tactics and create distaste for her management style, your tone will be disapproving and severe.

The language of a descriptive piece also depends, to a great extent, on whether your purpose is primarily objective or subjective. If the description is objective, the language is straightforward, precise, and factual. Such *denotative* language consists of neutral dictionary meanings. If you want to describe as dispassionately as possible fans' violent behavior at a football game, you might write about the "large crowd" and its "mass movement onto the field." But if you are shocked by the fans' behavior and want to write a subjective piece that inspires similar outrage in readers, then you might write about the "swelling mob" and its "rowdy stampede onto the field." In the latter case, the language used would be *connotative* and emotionally charged so that readers would share your feelings.

Subjective and objective descriptions often overlap. Sometimes a single sentence contains both objective and subjective elements: "Although his hands were large and misshapen by arthritis, they were gentle to the touch, inspiring confidence and trust." Other times, part of an essay may provide a factual description (the physical appearance of a summer cabin your family rented), while another part of the essay may be highly subjective (how you felt in the cabin, sitting in front of a fire on a rainy day).

SUGGESTIONS FOR USING DESCRIPTION IN AN ESSAY

The following suggestions will be helpful whether you use description as a dominant or a supportive pattern of development.

1. Focus a descriptive essay around a dominant impression. Like other kinds of writing, a descriptive essay must have a thesis, or main point. In a descriptive essay with a subjective slant, the thesis usually centers on the *dominant impression* you have about your subject. Suppose you decide to write an essay on your ninth-grade history teacher, Ms. Hazzard. You want the paper to convey how unconventional and flamboyant she was. The essay could, of course, focus on a different dominant impression—how insensitive she could be to students, for example. What's important is that you establish—early in the paper—the dominant impression you intend to convey. Although descriptive essays often imply, rather than explicitly state, the dominant impression, that impression should be unmistakable.

2. Select the details to include. The power of description hinges on your ability to select from all possible details only those that support the dominant impression. All others, no matter how vivid or interesting, must be left out. If you're describing how flamboyant Ms. Hazzard could be, the details in the following paragraph would be appropriate.

A large-boned woman, Ms. Hazzard wore her bright red hair piled on top of her head, where it perched precariously. By the end of class, wayward strands of hair tumbled down and fell into eyes fringed by spiky false eyelashes. Ms. Hazzard's nails, filed into crisp points, were painted either bloody burgundy or neon pink. Plastic bangle bracelets, also either burgundy or pink, clattered up and down her ample arms as she scrawled on the board the historical dates that had, she claimed, "changed the world."

Such details—the heavy eye makeup, stiletto nails, gaudy bracelets—contribute to the impression of a flamboyant, unusual person. Even if you remembered times that Ms. Hazzard seemed perfectly conventional and understated, most likely you wouldn't describe those times since they contradict the dominant impression.

You must also be selective in the *number of details* you include. Having a dominant impression helps you eliminate many details gathered during prewriting, but there still will be choices to make. For example, it would be inappropriate to describe in exhaustive detail everything in a messy room:

The brown desk, made of a grained plastic laminate, is directly under a small window covered by a torn yellow-and-gold plaid curtain. In the left corner of the desk are four crumbled balls of blue-lined yellow paper, three red markers, two fine-point blue pens, an ink eraser, and four letters, two bearing special wildlife stamps. A green down-filled vest and a red cable-knit sweater are thrown over the back of the bright blue metal bridge chair pushed under the desk. Under the chair is an oval braided rug, its once brilliant blues and greens spotted by old coffee stains.

Readers will be reluctant to wade through such undifferentiated specifics. Even more important, such excessive detailing dilutes the focus of the essay. You end up with a seemingly endless list of specifics rather than with a carefully crafted picture in words. In this regard, sculptors and writers are similar—what they take away is as important as what they leave in.

Perhaps you're wondering how to generate the details that support your dominant impression. As you can imagine, you have to develop heightened powers of observation and recall. To sharpen these key faculties, it can be helpful to make up a chart with separate columns for each of the five senses. If you can observe your subject directly, enter in the appropriate columns what you see, hear, taste, and so on. If you're attempting to remember something from the past, try to recollect details under each of these sense headings. Ask yourself questions ("How did it smell? What did I hear?") and list each memory recaptured. You'll be surprised how this simple technique can tune you in to your experiences and help uncover the specific details needed to develop your dominant impression.

3. Organize the descriptive details. Select the organizational pattern (or combination of patterns) that best supports your dominant impression. The paragraphs in a descriptive essay are usually sequenced *spatially* (from top to bottom, interior to exterior, near to far) or *chronologically* (as the subject is experienced in time). But the paragraphs can also be ordered *emphatically* (ending with your subject's most striking elements) or by *sensory impression* (first smell, then taste, then touch, and so on).

You might, for instance, use a *spatial* pattern to organize a description of a large city as you viewed it from the air, a taxi, and a subway car. A description of your first day on a new job might move *chronologically,* starting with how you felt the first hour on the job and proceeding through the rest of the day. In a paper describing a bout with the flu, you might arrange details *emphatically,* beginning with a description of your low-level aches and pains and concluding with an account of your raging fever. An essay about a neighborhood garbage dump, euphemistically called an "ecology landfill" by its owners, could be organized by *sensory impressions:* the sights of the dump, its smells, its sounds. Regardless of the organizational pattern you use, provide enough *signal devices* (for example, *about, next, worst of all*) so that readers can follow the description easily.

Finally, although descriptive essays don't always have conventional topic sentences, each descriptive paragraph should have a clear focus. Often this focus is indicated by a sentence early in the paragraph that names the scene, object, or individual to be described. Such a sentence functions as a kind of *informal topic sentence;* the paragraph's descriptive details then develop that topic sentence.

4. Use vivid sensory language and varied sentence structure. The connotative language typical of subjective description should be richly evocative. The words you select must etch in readers' minds the same picture that you have in yours. For this reason, rather than relying on vague generalities, you must use language that involves readers' senses. Consider the difference between the following paired descriptions:

Vague	Vivid
The food was unappetizing.	The stew congealed into an oval pool of milky-brown fat.
The toothpaste was refreshing.	The toothpaste, tasting minty sweet, felt good against slippery teeth, free finally from braces.
Filled with passengers and baggage, the car moved slowly down the road.	Burdened with its load of clamoring children and well-worn suitcases, the car labored down the interstate on bald tires and worn shocks, emitting puffs of blue exhaust and an occasional backfire.

Unlike the *concrete, sensory-packed* sentences on the right, the sentences on the left fail to create vivid word pictures that engage readers. While all good writing blends abstract and concrete language, descriptive writing demands an abundance of specific sensory language.

Keep in mind, too, that *verbs pack more of a wallop* than adverbs. The following sentence has to rely on adverbs (italicized) because its verbs are so weak: "She walked *casually* into the room and *deliberately* tried not to pay much attention to their stares." Rewritten, so that verbs (italicized), not adverbs, do the bulk of the work, the sentence becomes more powerful: "She *strolled* into the room and *ignored* their stares."

Figures of speech—nonliteral, imaginative comparisons between two basically dissimilar things—are another way to enliven descriptive writing. *Similes* use the words *like* or *as* when comparing; *metaphors* state or imply that two things being compared are alike; and *personification* attributes human characteristics to inanimate things.

The examples that follow show how effective figurative language can be in descriptive writing.

Moving as jerkily as a marionette on strings, the old man picked himself up off the sidewalk and staggered down the street. (*simile*)

Stalking their prey, the hall monitors remained hidden in the corridors, motionless and ready to spring on any unsuspecting student who dared to sneak into class late. (*metaphor*)

The scoop of vanilla ice cream, plain and unadorned, cried out for hot-fudge sauce and a sprinkling of sliced pecans. (*personification*)

Finally, when writing descriptive passages, you need to *vary sentence structure*. Don't use the same subject-verb pattern in all sentences. The second example above, for instance, could have been written as follows: "The hall monitors stalked their prey. They hid in the corridors. They remained motionless and ready to spring on any unsuspecting student who tried to sneak into class late." But the sentence is richer and more interesting when the descriptive elements are embedded, eliminating what would otherwise have been a clipped and predictable subject-verb pattern.

STUDENT ESSAY

The following student essay was written by Marie Martinez in response to this assignment:

The essay "Once More to the Lake" is an evocative piece about a spot that had special meaning in E. B. White's life. Write an essay about a place that holds rich significance for you, centering the description on a dominant impression.

While reading Marie's paper, try to determine how well it applies the principles of description. The annotations on Marie's paper and the commentary following it will help you look at the essay more closely.

Salt Marsh
by Marie Martinez

Introduction   In one of his journals, Thoreau told of the difficul-   1
ty he had escaping the obligations and cares of soci-
ety: "It sometimes happens that I cannot easily shake
off the village. The thought of some work will run in

my head and I am not where my body is--I am out of my senses. In my walks I . . . return to my senses." All of us feel out of our senses at times. Overwhelmed by problems or everyday annoyances, we lose touch with sensory pleasures as we spend our days in noisy cities and stuffy classrooms. Just as Thoreau walked in the woods to return to his senses, I have a special place where I return to mine: the salt marsh behind my grandparents' house.

My grandparents live on the East Coast, a mile or so inland from the sea. Between the ocean and the mainland is a wide fringe of salt marsh. A salt marsh is not a swamp, but an expanse of dark, spongy soil threaded with saltwater creeks and clothed in a kind of grass called salt meadow hay. All the water in the marsh rises and falls daily with the ocean tides, an endless cycle that changes the look of the marsh-- partly flooded or mostly dry--as the day progresses.

Heading out to the marsh from my grandparents' house, I follow a short path through the woods. As I walk along, a sharp smell of salt mixed with the rich aroma of peaty soil fills my nostrils. I am always amazed by the way the path changes with the sea- sons. Sometimes I walk in the brilliant green of spring, sometimes in the tawny gold of autumn, sometimes in the grayish tan of winter. No matter the season, the grass flanking the trail is often flattened into swirls, like thick Van Gogh brush strokes that curve and recurve in circular patterns. No people come here. The peacefulness heals me like a sooth- ing drug.

After a few minutes, the trail suddenly opens up to a view that calms me no matter how upset or dis- couraged I might be: a line of tall waving reeds bor- dering and nearly hiding the salt marsh creek. To get to the creek, I part the reeds.

The creek is a narrow body of water no more than fifteen feet wide, and it ebbs and flows as the ocean currents sweep toward the land or rush back toward the sea. The creek winds in a sinuous pattern so that I cannot see its beginning or end, the places where it trickles into the marsh or spills into the open ocean. Little brown birds dip in and out of the reeds on the far shore of the creek, making a special

Margin annotations:

Dominant impression (thesis)

Informal topic sentence: Definition paragraph

2

Informal topic sentence: First paragraph in a four-part spatial sequence

3

Simile

Informal topic sentence: Second paragraph in the spatial sequence

4

Informal topic sentence: Third paragraph in the spatial sequence

5

"tweep-tweep" sound peculiar to the marsh. When I stand at low tide on the shore of the creek, I am on a miniature cliff, for the bank of the creek falls abruptly and steeply into the water. Below me, green grasses wave and shimmer under the water while tiny minnows flash their silvery sides as they dart through the underwater tangles.

Informal topic sentence: Last paragraph in the spatial sequence → The creek water is often much warmer than the ocean, so I can swim there in three seasons. Sitting on the edge of the creek, I scoop some water into my hand, rub my face and neck, then ease into the water. Where the creek is shallow, my feet sink into a foot of *Simile* muck that feels like mashed potatoes mixed with motor oil. But once I become accustomed to it, I enjoy squishing the slimy mud through my toes. Sometimes I feel brushing past my legs the blue crabs that live in the creek. Other times, I hear the splash of a turtle or an otter as it slips from the shore into the water. Otherwise, it is silent. The salty water is buoyant and lifts my spirits as I stroke through it to reach the middle of the creek. There in the center, I float weightlessly, surrounded by tall reeds that reduce the world to water and sky. I am at peace.   6

Conclusion The salt marsh is not the kind of dramatic landscape found on picture postcards. There are no soaring mountains, sandy beaches, or lush valleys. The marsh is a flat world that some consider dull and uninviting. I am glad most people do not respond to the marsh's subtle beauty because that means I can be alone there. *Echo of idea in introduction* Just as the rising tide sweeps over the marsh, floating debris out to the ocean, the marsh washes away my concerns and restores me to my senses.   7

COMMENTARY

The dominant impression.   Marie responded to the assignment by writing a moving tribute to a place having special meaning for her—the salt marsh near her grandparents' home. Like most descriptive pieces, Marie's essay is organized around a *dominant impression:* the marsh's peaceful solitude and gentle, natural beauty. The essay's introduction provides a context for the dominant impression by comparing the pleasure Marie experiences in the marsh to the happiness Thoreau felt in his walks around Walden Pond.

Other patterns of development.   Before developing the essay's dominant impression, Marie uses the second paragraph to *define* a salt marsh. An *objective description,* the definition clarifies that a salt marsh—with its spongy soil, haylike grass, and ebbing tides—is not to be confused with a swamp. Because Marie offers such a factual definition, readers have the background needed to enjoy the personalized view that follows.

Besides the definition paragraph and the comparison in the opening paragraph, the essay contains a strong element of *causal analysis:* Throughout, Marie describes the marsh's effect on her.

Sensory language.   At times, Marie develops the essay's dominant impression explicitly, as when she writes "No people come here" (paragraph 3) and "I am at peace" (6). But Marie generally uses the more subtle techniques characteristic of *subjective description* to convey the dominant impression. First of all, she fills the essay with strong *connotative language,* rich with *sensory images.* The third paragraph describes what she smells (the "sharp smell of salt mixed with the rich aroma of peaty soil") and what she sees ("brilliant green," "tawny gold," and "grayish tan"). In the fifth paragraph, she tells us that she hears the chirping sounds of small birds. And the sixth paragraph includes vigorous descriptions of how the marsh feels to Marie's touch. She splashes water on her face and neck; she digs her toes into the mud at the bottom of the creek; she delights in the delicate brushing of crabs against her legs.

Figurative language, vigorous verbs, and varied sentence structure.   You might also have noted that *figurative language, energetic verbs,* and *varied sentence patterns* contribute to the essay's descriptive power. Marie develops a *simile* in the third paragraph when she compares the flattened swirls of swamp grass to the brush strokes in a painting by Van Gogh. Later she uses another simile when she writes that the creek's thick mud feels "like mashed potatoes mixed with motor oil." Moreover, throughout the essay, she uses lively verbs ("shimmer," "flash") to capture the marsh's magical quality. Similarly, Marie enhances descriptive passages by varying the length of her sentences. Long, fairly elaborate sentences are interspersed with short, dramatic statements. In the third paragraph, for example, the long sentence describing the circular swirls of swamp grass is followed by the brief statement "No people come here." And the sixth paragraph uses two short sentences ("Otherwise, it is silent" and "I am at peace") to punctuate the paragraph's longer sentences.

Organization.   We can follow Marie's journey through the marsh because she uses an easy-to-follow combination of *spatial, chronological,* and *emphatic* patterns to sequence her experience. The essay relies primarily on a spatial arrangement since the four body paragraphs focus on the different spots that Marie reaches: first, the path behind her grandparents' house (paragraph 3); then the area bordering the creek (4); next, her view of the creek (5); last, the creek itself (6). Each stage of her walk is signaled by an *informal topic sentence* near the start of each paragraph. Furthermore, *signal devices* (marked by italics here) indicate not only her location but also the chronological passage of time: "*As* I walk along, a sharp smell . . . fills my nostrils" (3); "*After* a few minutes, the trail suddenly opens up . . ." (4); "*Below* me, green grasses wave . . ." (5). And to call attention to the creek's serene beauty, Marie saves for last the description of the peace she feels while floating in the creek.

An inappropriate figure of speech.   Although the four body paragraphs focus on the distinctive qualities of each location, Marie runs into a minor problem in the third paragraph. Take a moment to reread that paragraph's last sentence. Comparing the peace of the marsh to the effect of a "soothing drug" is jarring. The effectiveness of Marie's essay hinges on her ability to create a picture of a pure, natural world. A reference to drugs is inappropriate. Now, reread the paragraph aloud, stopping after "No people come here." Note how much more in keeping with the essay's dominant impression the paragraph is when the reference to drugs is omitted.

Conclusion.   The concluding paragraph brings the essay to a graceful close. The powerful *simile* found in the last sentence contains an implied reference to Thoreau and to Marie's earlier statement about the joy to be found in special places having restorative powers. Such an allusion echoes, with good effect, the paper's opening comments.

Revising the first draft.   When Marie met with some classmates during a group feedback session, the students agreed that Marie's first draft was strong and moving. But they also said that they had difficulty following her route through the marsh; they found her third paragraph especially confusing. Marie kept track of her classmates' comments on a separate piece of paper and then entered them, numbered in order of importance, in the margin of her first draft. Reprinted here is the original version of Marie's third paragraph.

Original Version of the Third Paragraph

As I head out to the marsh from the house, I follow a short trail through the woods. A smell of salt mixed with the aroma of soil fills my nostrils. The end of the trail suddenly opens up to a view that calms me no matter how upset or discouraged I might be: a line of tall waving reeds bordering the salt marsh creek. Civilization seems far away as I walk the path of flattened grass and finally reach my goal, the salt marsh creek hidden behind the tall waving reeds. The path changes with the seasons; sometimes I walk in the brilliant green of spring, sometimes in the tawny gold of autumn, sometimes in the quiet grayish tan of winter. In some areas, the grass is flattened into swirls that make the marsh resemble one of those paintings by Van Gogh. No people come here. The peacefulness heals me like a soothing drug. The path stops at the line of tall waving reeds, standing upright at the border of the creek. I part the reeds to get to the creek.

When Marie looked more carefully at the paragraph, she agreed it was confusing. For one thing, the paragraph's third and fourth sentences indicated that she had come to the path's end and had reached the reeds bordering the creek. In the following sentences, however, she was on the path again. Then, at the end, she was back at the creek, as if she had just arrived there. Marie resolved this confusion by breaking the single paragraph into two separate ones—the first describing the walk along the path, the second describing her arrival at the creek. This restructuring, especially when combined with clearer transitions, eliminated the confusion.

While revising her essay, Marie also intensified the sensory images in her original paragraph. She changed the "smell of salt and soil" to the "sharp smell of salt mixed with the rich aroma of peaty soil." And when she added the phrase "thick Van Gogh brush strokes that curve and recurve in circular patterns," she made the comparison between the marsh grass and a Van Gogh painting more vivid.

These are just some of the changes Marie made while rewriting her paper. Her skillful revisions provided the polish needed to make an already strong essay even more evocative.

ACTIVITIES: DESCRIPTION

Prewriting Activities

1. Imagine you're writing two essays: One explains the *process* by which students get "burned out"; the other *argues* that being a spendthrift is better (or worse) than being frugal. Jot down ways you might use description in each essay.

2. Go to a place on campus where students congregate. In preparation for an *objective* description of this place, make notes of various sights, sounds, smells, and textures, as well as the overall "feel" of the place. Then, in preparation for a *subjective* description, observe and take notes on another sheet of paper. Compare the two sets of material. What differences do you see in word choice and selection of details?

Revising Activities

3. Revise each of the following sentence sets twice. The first time, create an unmistakable mood; the second time, create a sharply contrasting mood. To convey atmosphere, vary sentence structure, use vigorous verbs, provide rich sensory details, and pay special attention to words' connotations.
   a. The card players sat around the table. The table was old. The players were, too.
   b. A long line formed outside the movie theater. People didn't want to miss the show. The movie had received a lot of attention recently.
   c. A girl walked down the street in her first pair of high heels. This was a new experience for her.

4. The following descriptive paragraph is from the first draft of an essay showing that personal growth may result when romanticized notions and reality collide. How effective is the paragraph in illustrating the essay's thesis? Which details are powerful? Which could be more concrete? Which should be deleted? Where should sentence structure be more varied? How could the description be made more coherent? Revise the paragraph, correcting any problems you

discover and adding whatever sensory details are needed to enliven the description. Feel free to break the paragraph into two or more separate ones.

As a child, I was intrigued by stories about the farm in Harrison County, Maine, where my father spent his teens. Being raised on a farm seemed more interesting than growing up in the suburbs. So about a year ago, I decided to see for myself what the farm was like. I got there by driving on Route 334, a surprisingly easy-to-drive, four-lane highway that had recently been built with matching state and federal funds. I turned into the dirt road leading to the farm and got out of my car. It had been washed and waxed for the occasion. Then I headed for a dirt-colored barn. Its roof was full of huge, rotted holes. As I rounded the bushes, I saw the house. It too was dirt-colored. Its paint must have worn off decades ago. A couple of dead-looking old cars were sprawled in front of the barn. They were dented and windowless. Also by the barn was an ancient refrigerator, crushed like a discarded accordion. The porch steps to the house were slanted and wobbly. Through the open windows came a stale smell and the sound of television. Looking in the front door screen, I could see two chickens jumping around inside. Everything looked dirty both inside and out. Secretly grateful that no one answered my knock, I bolted down the stairs, got into my clean, shiny car, and drove away.

Gordon Parks

The son of deeply religious tenant farmers, Gordon Parks (1912–) grew up in Kansas knowing both the comforts of familial love and the torments of poverty and racism. Sent as a teenager to live with his sister in Minnesota after his mother's death, Parks was thrown out on his own in a frigid winter by his brother-in-law. To support himself, Parks worked as a janitor in a flophouse and as a piano player in a bordello. These and other odd jobs gave Parks the means to buy his first camera. Fascinated by photographic images, Parks studied the masters and eventually developed his own powers as a photographer. So evocative were his photographic studies that both *Life* and *Vogue* brought him on staff, the first Black photographer to be hired by the two magazines. Parks's prodigious creativity has found expression in filmmaking (*Shaft* in 1971), musical composition (both classical and jazz), fiction, nonfiction, and poetry (titles include *The Learning Tree, A Choice of Weapons, To Smile in Autumn, Arias in Silence,* and *Glimpses Toward Infinity,* published, respectively, in 1986, 1987, 1988, 1994, and 1996). But it is Parks's photographic essays, covering five decades of American life, that have brought him the most acclaim. In the following essay, taken from his 1990 autobiography, *Voices in the Mirror,* Parks tells the story behind one of his most memorable photographic works—that of a twelve-year-old boy and his family, living in the slums of Rio de Janeiro.

Pre-Reading Journal Entry

The problem of poverty has provoked a wide array of proposed solutions. One controversial proposal argues that the government should pay poor women financial incentives to use birth control. What do you think of this proposal? Why is such a policy controversial? Use your journal to explore your thinking on this issue.

Flavio's Home

I've never lost my fierce grudge against poverty. It is the most   1
savage of all human afflictions, claiming victims who can't mobilize their efforts against it, who often lack strength to digest what little food they scrounge up to survive. It keeps growing, multiplying, spreading like a cancer. In my wanderings I attack it wherever I can—in barrios, slums and favelas.

Catacumba was the name of the favela[1] where I found Flavio da   2
Silva. It was wickedly hot. The noon sun baked the mud-rot of the
wet mountainside. Garbage and human excrement clogged the
open sewers snaking down the slopes. José Gallo, a *Life* reporter,
and I rested in the shade of a jacaranda tree halfway up Rio de
Janeiro's most infamous deathtrap. Below and above us were a maze
of shacks, but in the distance alongside the beach stood the gleam-
ing white homes of the rich.

Breathing hard, balancing a tin of water on his head, a small boy   3
climbed toward us. He was miserably thin, naked but for filthy
denim shorts. His legs resembled sticks covered with skin and
screwed into his feet. Death was all over him, in his sunken eyes,
cheeks and jaundiced coloring. He stopped for breath, coughing,
his chest heaving as water slopped over his bony shoulders. Then
jerking sideways like a mechanical toy, he smiled a smile I will never
forget. Turning, he went on up the mountainside.

The detailed *Life* assignment in my back pocket was to find an   4
impoverished father with a family, to examine his earnings, political
leanings, religion, friends, dreams and frustrations. I had been sent
to do an essay on poverty. This frail boy bent under his load said
more to me about poverty than a dozen poor fathers. I touched
Gallo, and we got up and followed the boy to where he entered a
shack near the top of the mountainside. It was a leaning crumpled
place of old plankings with a rusted tin roof. From inside we heard
the babblings of several children. José knocked. The door opened
and the boy stood smiling with a bawling naked baby in his arms.

Still smiling, he whacked the baby's rump, invited us in and   5
offered us a box to sit on. The only other recognizable furniture was
a sagging bed and a broken baby's crib. Flavio was twelve, and with
Gallo acting as interpreter, he introduced his younger brothers and
sisters: "Mario, the bad one; Baptista, the good one; Albia, Isabel
and the baby Zacarias." Two other girls burst into the shack,
screaming and pounding on one another. Flavio jumped in and part-
ed them. "Shut up, you two." He pointed at the older girl. "That's
Maria, the nasty one." She spit in his face. He smacked her and
pointed to the smaller sister. "That's Luzia. She thinks she's pretty."

Having finished the introductions, he went to build a fire under   6
the stove—a rusted, bent top of an old gas range resting on several

---

[1]Slums on the outskirts of Rio de Janeiro, Brazil, inhabited by seven hundred thousand people (editors' note).

bricks. Beneath it was a piece of tin that caught the hot coals. The shack was about six by ten feet. Its grimy walls were a patchwork of misshapen boards with large gaps between them, revealing other shacks below stilted against the slopes. The floor, rotting under layers of grease and dirt, caught shafts of light slanting down through spaces in the roof. A large hole in the far corner served as a toilet. Beneath that hole was the sloping mountainside. Pockets of poverty in New York's Harlem, on Chicago's south side, in Puerto Rico's infamous El Fungito seemed pale by comparison. None of them had prepared me for this one in the favela of Catacumba.

Flavio washed rice in a large dishpan, then washed Zacarias's   7
feet in the same water. But even that dirty water wasn't to be wasted. He tossed in a chunk of lye soap and ordered each child to wash up. When they were finished he splashed the water over the dirty floor, and, dropping to his knees, he scrubbed the planks until the black suds sank in. Just before sundown he put beans on the stove to warm, then left, saying he would be back shortly. "Don't let them burn," he cautioned Maria. "If they do and Poppa beats me, you'll get it later." Maria, happy to get at the licking spoon, switched over and began to stir the beans. Then slyly she dipped out a spoonful and swallowed them. Luzia eyed her. "I see you. I'm going to tell on you for stealing our supper."

Maria's eyes flashed anger. "You do and I'll beat you, you little   8
bitch." Luzia threw a stick at Maria and fled out the door. Zacarias dropped off to sleep. Mario, the bad one, slouched in a corner and sucked his thumb. Isabel and Albia sat on the floor clinging to each other with a strange tenderness. Isabel held onto Albia's hair and Albia clutched at Isabel's neck. They appeared frozen in an act of quiet violence.

Flavio returned with wood, dumped it beside the stove and sat   9
down to rest for a few minutes, then went down the mountain for more water. It was dark when he finally came back, his body sagging from exhaustion. No longer smiling, he suddenly had the look of an old man and by now we could see that he kept the family going. In the closed torment of that pitiful shack, he was waging a hopeless battle against starvation. The da Silva children were living in a coffin.

When at last the parents came in, Gallo and I seemed to be part   10
of the family. Flavio had already told them we were there. "Gordunn Americano!" Luzia said, pointing at me. José, the father, viewed us

with skepticism. Nair, his pregnant wife, seemed tired beyond speaking. Hardly acknowledging our presence, she picked up Zacarias, placed him on her shoulder and gently patted his behind. Flavio scurried about like a frightened rat, his silence plainly expressing the fear he held of his father. Impatiently, José da Silva waited for Flavio to serve dinner. He sat in the center of the bed with his legs crossed beneath him, frowning, waiting. There were only three tin plates. Flavio filled them with black beans and rice, then placed them before his father. José da Silva tasted them, chewed for several moments, then nodded his approval for the others to start. Only he and Nair had spoons; the children ate with their fingers. Flavio ate off the top of a coffee can. Afraid to offer us food, he edged his rice and beans toward us, gesturing for us to take some. We refused. He smiled, knowing we understood.

Later, when we got down to the difficult business of obtaining 11 permission from José da Silva to photograph his family, he hemmed and hawed, wallowing in the pleasant authority of the decision maker. He finally gave in, but his manner told us that he expected something in return. As we were saying good night Flavio began to cough violently. For a few moments his lungs seemed to be tearing apart. I wanted to get away as quickly as possible. It was cowardly of me, but the bluish cast of his skin beneath the sweat, the choking and spitting were suddenly unbearable.

Gallo and I moved cautiously down through the darkness try- 12 ing not to appear as strangers. The Catacumba was no place for strangers after sundown. Desperate criminals hid out there. To hunt them out, the police came in packs, but only in daylight. Gallo cautioned me. "If you get caught up here after dark it's best to stay at the da Silvas' until morning." As we drove toward the city the large white buildings of the rich loomed up. The world behind us seemed like a bad dream. I had already decided to get the boy Flavio to a doctor, and as quickly as possible.

The plush lobby of my hotel on the Copacabana waterfront was 13 crammed with people in formal attire. With the stink of the favela in my clothes, I hurried to the elevator hoping no passengers would be aboard. But as the door was closing a beautiful girl in a white lace gown stepped in. I moved as far away as possible. Her escort entered behind her, swept her into his arms and they indulged in a kiss that lasted until they exited on the next floor. Neither of them seemed to realize that I was there. The room I returned to seemed to be

oversized; the da Silva shack would have fitted into one corner of it.
The steak dinner I had would have fed the da Silvas for three days.

Billowing clouds blanketed Mount Corcovado as we approached   14
the favela the following morning. Suddenly the sun burst through,
silhouetting Cristo Redentor, the towering sculpture of Christ with
arms extended, its back turned against the slopes of Catacumba. The
square at the entrance to the favela bustled with hundreds of favelados. Long lines waited at the sole water spigot. Others waited at the
only toilet on the entire mountainside. Women, unable to pay for
soap, beat dirt from their wash at laundry tubs. Men, burdened with
lumber, picks and shovels and tools important to their existence
threaded their way through the noisy throngs. Dogs snarled, barked
and fought. Woodsmoke mixed with the stench of rotting things. In
the mist curling over the higher paths, columns of favelados climbed
like ants with wood and water cans on their heads.

We came upon Nair bent over her tub of wash. She wiped away   15
sweat with her apron and managed a smile. We asked for her husband and she pointed to a tiny shack off to her right. This was José's
store, where he sold kerosene and bleach. He was sitting on a box,
dozing. Sensing our presence, he awoke and commenced complaining about his back. "It kills me. The doctors don't help because I
have no money. Always talk and a little pink pill that does no good.
Ah, what is to become of me?" A woman came to buy bleach. He
filled her bottle. She dropped a few coins and as she walked away his
eyes stayed on her backside until she was out of sight. Then he was
complaining about his back again.

"How much do you earn a day?" Gallo asked.   16
"Seventy-five cents. On a good day maybe a dollar."   17
"Why aren't the kids in school?"   18
"I don't have money for the clothes they need to go to school."   19
"Has Flavio seen a doctor?"   20
He pointed to a one-story wooden building. "That's the clinic   21
right there. They're mad because I built my store in front of their
place. I won't tear it down so they won't help my kids. Talk, talk,
talk and pink pills." We bid him good-bye and started climbing, following mud trails, jutting rock, slime-filled holes and shack after
shack propped against the slopes on shaky pilings. We sidestepped a
dead cat covered with maggots. I held my breath for an instant, only
to inhale the stench of human excrement and garbage. Bare feet and

legs with open sores climbed above us—evils of the terrible soil they trod every day, and there were seven hundred thousand or more afflicted people in favelas around Rio alone. Touching me, Gallo pointed to Flavio climbing ahead of us carrying firewood. He stopped to glance at a man descending with a small coffin on his shoulder. A woman and a small child followed him. When I lifted my camera, grumbling erupted from a group of men sharing beer beneath a tree.

"They're threatening," Gallo said. "Keep moving. They fear 22 cameras. Think they're evil eyes bringing bad luck." Turning to watch the funeral procession, Flavio caught sight of us and waited. When we took the wood from him he protested, saying he was used to carrying it. He gave in when I hung my camera around his neck. Then, beaming, he climbed on ahead of us.

The fog had lifted and in the crisp morning light the shack 23 looked more squalid. Inside the kids seemed even noisier. Flavio smiled and spoke above their racket. "Someday I want to live in a real house on a real street with good pots and pans and a bed with sheets." He lit the fire to warm leftovers from the night before. Stale rice and beans—for breakfast and supper. No lunch; midday eating was out of the question. Smoke rose and curled up through the ceiling's cracks. An air current forced it back, filling the place and Flavio's lungs with fumes. A coughing spasm doubled him up, turned his skin blue under viscous sweat. I handed him a cup of water, but he waved it away. His stomach tightened as he dropped to his knees. His veins throbbed as if they would burst. Frustrated, we could only watch; there was nothing we could do to help. Strangely, none of his brothers or sisters appeared to notice. None of them stopped doing whatever they were doing. Perhaps they had seen it too often. After five interminable minutes it was over, and he got to his feet, smiling as though it had all been a joke. "Maria, it's time for Zacarias to be washed!"

"But there's rice in the pan!" 24

"Dump it in another pan—and don't spill water!" 25

Maria picked up Zacarias, who screamed, not wanting to be 26 washed. Irritated, Maria gave him a solid smack on his bare bottom. Flavio stepped over and gave her the same, then a free-for-all started with Flavio, Maria and Mario slinging fists at one another. Mario got one in the eye and fled the shack calling Flavio a dirty son-of-a-bitch. Zacarias wound up on the floor sucking his thumb and escaping his washing. The black bean and rice breakfast helped to get things back to normal. Now it was time to get Flavio to the doctor.

The clinic was crowded with patients—mothers and children   27
covered with open sores, a paralytic teenager, a man with an ear in a state of decay, an aged blind couple holding hands in doubled darkness. Throughout the place came wailings of hunger and hurt. Flavio sat nervously between Gallo and me. "What will the doctor do to me?" he kept asking.

"We'll see. We'll wait and see."   28

In all, there were over fifty people. Finally, after two hours, it   29
was Flavio's turn and he broke out in a sweat, though he smiled at the nurse as he passed through the door to the doctor's office. The nurse ignored it; in this place of misery, smiles were unexpected.

The doctor, a large, beady-eyed man with a crew cut, had an air   30
of impatience. Hardly acknowledging our presence, he began to examine the frightened Flavio. "Open your mouth. Say 'Ah.' Jump up and down. Breathe out. Take off those pants. Bend over. Stand up. Cough. Cough louder. Louder." He did it all with such cold efficiency. Then he spoke to us in English so Flavio wouldn't under-stand. "This little chap has just about had it." My heart sank. Flavio was smiling, happy to be over with the examination. He was hand-ed a bottle of cough medicine and a small box of pink pills, then asked to step outside and wait.

"This the da Silva kid?"   31

"Yes."   32

"What's your interest in him?"   33

"We want to help in some way."   34

"I'm afraid you're too late. He's wasted with bronchial asthma,   35
malnutrition and, I suspect, tuberculosis. His heart, lungs and teeth are all bad." He paused and wearily rubbed his forehead. "All that at the ripe old age of twelve. And these hills are packed with other kids just as bad off. Last year ten thousand died from dysentery alone. But what can we do? You saw what's waiting outside. It's like this every day. There's hardly enough money to buy aspirin. A few wealthy people who care help keep us going." He was quiet for a moment. "Maybe the right climate, the right diet, and constant medical care might . . ." He stopped and shook his head. "Naw. That poor lad's finished. He might last another year—maybe not." We thanked him and left.

"What did he say?" Flavio asked as we scaled the hill.   36

"Everything's going to be all right, Flav. There's nothing to 37
worry about."

It had clouded over again by the time we reached the top. The 38
rain swept in, clearing the mountain of Corcovado. The huge Christ
figure loomed up again with clouds swirling around it. And to it I
said a quick prayer for the boy walking beside us. He smiled as if he
had read my thoughts. "Papa says 'El Cristo' has turned his back on
the *favela*."

"You're going to be all right, Flavio." 39

"I'm not scared of death. It's my brothers and sisters I worry 40
about. What would they do?"

"You'll be all right, Flavio."[2] 41

---

[2]Parks's photo-essay on Flavio generated an unprecedented response from *Life* readers. Indeed, they sent so much money to the da Silvas that the family was able to leave
the *favela* for better living conditions. Parks brought Flavio to the United States for
medical treatment, and the boy's health was restored. However, Flavio's story didn't
have an unqualifiedly happy ending. Although he overcame his illness and later married and had a family, Flavio continuously fantasized about returning to the United
States, convinced that only by returning to America could he improve his life. His
obsession eventually eroded the promise of his life in Brazil (editors' note).

Questions for Close Reading

1. What is the selection's thesis (or dominant impression)? Locate the sen-
   tence(s) in which Parks states his main idea. If he doesn't state the thesis explicitly, express it in your own words.
2. What is Flavio's family like? Why does Flavio have so much responsibility in the household?
3. What are some of the distinctive characteristics of Flavio's neighborhood
   and home?
4. What seems to be the basis of Flavio's fear of giving food to Parks and
   Gallo? What did Parks and Gallo understand that led them to refuse?
5. Refer to your dictionary as needed to define the following words used in
   the selection: *barrios* (paragraph 1), *jacaranda* (2), *jaundiced* (3), and
   spigot (14).

Questions About the Writer's Craft

1. **The pattern.** Without stating it explicitly, Parks conveys a dominant
   impression about Flavio. What is that impression? What details create it?

2. **Other patterns.** When relating how Flavio performs numerous household tasks, Parks describes several processes. How do these step-by-step explanations reinforce Parks's dominant impression of Flavio?

3. Parks provides numerous sensory specifics to depict Flavio's home. Look closely, for example, at the description in paragraph 6. Which words and phrases convey strong sensory images? How does Parks use transitions to help the reader move from one sensory image to another?

4. Paragraph 13 includes a scene that occurs in Parks's hotel. What's the effect of this scene? What does it contribute to the essay that the most detailed description of the *favela* could not?

Writing Assignments Using Description as a Pattern of Development

1. Parks paints a wrenching portrait of a person who remains vibrant and hopeful even though he is suffering greatly—from physical illness, poverty, overwork, and worry. Write a description about someone you know who has shown courage or other positive qualities during a time of personal trouble. Include, as Parks does, plentiful details about the person's appearance and behavior so that you don't have to state directly what you admire about the person. Maya Angelou's "Sister Flowers" (page 106) shows how one writer conveys the special quality of an admirable individual.

2. Parks presents an unforgettable description of the *favela* and the living conditions there. Write an essay about a region, city, neighborhood, or building that also projects an overwhelming negative feeling. Include only those details that convey your dominant impression, and provide— as Parks does— vivid sensory language to convey your attitude toward your subject.

Writing Assignments Using Other Patterns of Development

3. The doctor reports that a few wealthy people contribute to the clinic, but the reader can tell from the scene in Parks's hotel that most people are insensitive to those less fortunate. Write an essay describing a specific situation that you feel reflects people's tendency to ignore the difficulties of others. Analyze why people distance themselves from the problem; then present specific steps that could be taken to sensitize them to the situation. Sophronia Liu's "So Tsi-Fai" (page 153) will provide some perspective on the way people harden themselves to the pain of others.

4. Although Parks celebrates Flavio's generosity of spirit, the writer also illustrates the brutalizing effect of an impoverished environment. Prepare an essay in which you also show that setting, architecture, even

furnishings can influence mood and behavior. You may, as Parks does, focus on the corrosive effect of a negative environment, or you may write about the nurturing effect of a positive environment. Possible subjects include a park in the middle of a city, a bus terminal, and a college library.

Writing Assignments Using a Journal Entry as a Starting Point

5. Write an essay explaining why you think impoverished women should—or should not—be paid financial incentives to practice birth control. To help define your position, review your pre-reading journal entry, and interview classmates, friends, and family members to get their opinions. Consider supplementing this informal research with material gathered in the library and/or on the Internet. Weigh all the evidence carefully before formulating your position.

Maya Angelou

Born Marguerite Johnson in 1928, Maya Angelou spent her childhood in Stamps, Arkansas, with her brother, Bailey, and her grandmother, "Momma." Although her youth was difficult—she was raped at age eight and a mother at sixteen—Angelou somehow managed to thrive. Multi-talented, she later worked as a professional dancer, starred in an off-Broadway play, appeared in the television miniseries *Roots,* served as a coordinator for the Southern Christian Leadership Conference, and wrote several well-received volumes of poetry—among them *Oh Pray My Wings Are Gonna Fit Me Well* (1975) and *And Still I Rise* (1996). She has also written children's books, including *My Painted House, My Friendly Chicken, and Me* (1994) and *Kofi and His Magic* (1996) and, most recently, wrote a collection of essays called *Even the Stars Look Lonesome* (1997). A professor at Wake Forest University since 1991, Angelou delivered at the 1993 presidential inauguration a stirring poem written for the occasion. The recipient of numerous honorary doctorates, Angelou is best known for her series of five autobiographical books, starting with *I Know Why the Caged Bird Sings* (1970) and concluding with *All God's Children Need Traveling Shoes* (1986). The following essay is taken from *I Know Why the Caged Bird Sings.*

Pre-Reading Journal Entry

Growing up isn't easy. In your journal, list several challenges you've had to face in your life. In each case, was there someone who served as a "lifeline," providing you with crucial guidance and support? Who was that individual? How did this person steer you through the difficulty?

Sister Flowers

For nearly a year [after I was raped], I sopped around the house, 1
the Store, the school and the church, like an old biscuit, dirty and inedible. Then I met, or rather got to know, the lady who threw me my first life line.

Mrs. Bertha Flowers was the aristocrat of Black Stamps. She had 2
the grace of control to appear warm in the coldest weather, and on the Arkansas summer days it seemed she had a private breeze which swirled around, cooling her. She was thin without the taut look of wiry people, and her printed voile dresses and flowered hats were as

right for her as denim overalls for a farmer. She was our side's answer
to the richest white woman in town.

Her skin was a rich black that would have peeled like a plum if   3
snagged, but then no one would have thought of getting close
enough to Mrs. Flowers to ruffle her dress, let alone snag her skin.
She didn't encourage familiarity. She wore gloves too.

I don't think I ever saw Mrs. Flowers laugh, but she smiled   4
often. A slow widening of her thin black lips to show even, small
white teeth, then the slow effortless closing. When she chose to
smile on me, I always wanted to thank her. The action was so graceful and inclusively benign.

She was one of the few gentlewomen I have ever known, and   5
has remained throughout my life the measure of what a human
being can be.

Momma had a strange relationship with her. Most often when   6
she passed on the road in front of the Store, she spoke to Momma
in that soft yet carrying voice, "Good day, Mrs. Henderson."
Momma responded with "How you, Sister Flowers?"

Mrs. Flowers didn't belong to our church, nor was she   7
Momma's familiar. Why on earth did she insist on calling her Sister
Flowers? Shame made me want to hide my face. Mrs. Flowers
deserved better than to be called Sister. Then, Momma left out the
verb. Why not ask, "How *are* you, *Mrs.* Flowers?" With the unbal-
anced passion of the young, I hated her for showing her ignorance
to Mrs. Flowers. It didn't occur to me for many years that they were
as alike as sisters, separated only by formal education.

Although I was upset, neither of the women was in the least   8
shaken by what I thought an unceremonious greeting. Mrs. Flowers
would continue her easy gait up the hill to her little bungalow, and
Momma kept on shelling peas or doing whatever had brought her
to the front porch.

Occasionally, though, Mrs. Flowers would drift off the road and   9
down to the Store and Momma would say to me, "Sister, you go on
and play." As she left I would hear the beginning of an intimate conversation. Momma persistently using the wrong verb, or none at all.

"Brother and Sister Wilcox is sho'ly the meanest—" "Is,"   10
Momma? "Is"? Oh, please, not "is," Momma, for two or more. But
they talked, and from the side of the building where I waited for the
ground to open up and swallow me, I heard the soft-voiced Mrs.
Flowers and the textured voice of my grandmother merging and
melting. They were interrupted from time to time by giggles that

must have come from Mrs. Flowers (Momma never giggled in her life). Then she was gone.

She appealed to me because she was like people I had never met 11
personally. Like women in English novels who walked the moors (whatever they were) with their loyal dogs racing at a respectful distance. Like the women who sat in front of roaring fireplaces, drinking tea incessantly from silver trays full of scones and crumpets. Women who walked over the "heath" and read morocco-bound books and had two last names divided by a hyphen. It would be safe to say that she made me proud to be Negro, just by being herself.

She acted just as refined as whitefolks in the movies and books 12
and she was more beautiful, for none of them could have come near that warm color without looking gray by comparison.

It was fortunate that I never saw her in the company of 13
powhitefolks. For since they tend to think of their whiteness as an evenizer, I'm certain that I would have had to hear her spoken to commonly as Bertha, and my image of her would have been shattered like the unmendable Humpty-Dumpty.

One summer afternoon, sweet-milk fresh in my memory, she 14
stopped at the Store to buy provisions. Another Negro woman of her health and age would have been expected to carry the paper sacks home in one hand, but Momma said, "Sister Flowers, I'll send Bailey up to your house with these things."

She smiled that slow dragging smile, "Thank you, Mrs. 15
Henderson. I'd prefer Marguerite, though." My name was beautiful when she said it. "I've been meaning to talk to her, anyway." They gave each other age-group looks.

Momma said, "Well, that's all right then. Sister, go and change 16
your dress. You going to Sister Flowers's."

The chifforobe was a maze. What on earth did one put on to go 17
to Mrs. Flowers's house? I knew I shouldn't put on a Sunday dress. It might be sacrilegious. Certainly not a house dress, since I was already wearing a fresh one. I chose a school dress, naturally. It was formal without suggesting that going to Mrs. Flowers's house was equivalent to attending church.

I trusted myself back into the Store. 18

"Now, don't you look nice." I had chosen the right thing, for 19
once. . . .

There was a little path beside the rocky road, and Mrs. Flowers 20
walked in front swinging her arms and picking her way over the stones.

She said, without turning her head, to me, "I hear you're doing   21
very good school work, Marguerite, but that it's all written. The
teachers report that they have trouble getting you to talk in class."
We passed the triangular farm on our left and the path widened to
allow us to walk together. I hung back in the separate unasked and
unanswerable questions.

"Come and walk along with me, Marguerite." I couldn't have   22
refused even if I wanted to. She pronounced my name so nicely. Or
more correctly, she spoke each word with such clarity that I was certain a foreigner who didn't understand English could have understood her.

"Now no one is going to make you talk—possibly no one can.   23
But bear in mind, language is man's way of communicating with his
fellow man and it is language alone which separates him from the
lower animals." That was a totally new idea to me, and I would need
time to think about it.

"Your grandmother says you read a lot. Every chance you get.   24
That's good, but not good enough. Words mean more than what is
set down on paper. It takes the human voice to infuse them with the
shades of deeper meaning."

I memorized the part about the human voice infusing words. It   25
seemed so valid and poetic.

She said she was going to give me some books and that I not   26
only must read them, I must read them aloud. She suggested that I
try to make a sentence sound in as many different ways as possible.

"I'll accept no excuse if you return a book to me that has been   27
badly handled." My imagination boggled at the punishment I
would deserve if in fact I did abuse a book of Mrs. Flowers's. Death
would be too kind and brief.

The odors in the house surprised me. Somehow I had never   28
connected Mrs. Flowers with food or eating or any other common
experience of common people. There must have been an outhouse,
too, but my mind never recorded it.

The sweet scent of vanilla had met us as she opened the door.   29

"I made tea cookies this morning. You see, I had planned to   30
invite you for cookies and lemonade so we could have this little chat.
The lemonade is in the icebox."

It followed that Mrs. Flowers would have ice on an ordinary   31
day, when most families in our town bought ice late on Saturdays
only a few times during the summer to be used in the wooden ice-
cream freezers.

She took the bags from me and disappeared through the   32
kitchen door. I looked around the room that I had never in my
wildest fantasies imagined I would see. Browned photographs leered
or threatened from the walls and the white, freshly done curtains
pushed against themselves and against the wind. I wanted to gobble
up the room entire and take it to Bailey, who would help me analyze and enjoy it.

"Have a seat, Marguerite. Over there by the table." She carried   33
a platter covered with a tea towel. Although she warned that she
hadn't tried her hand at baking sweets for some time, I was certain
that like everything else about her the cookies would be perfect.

They were flat round wafers, slightly browned on the edges and   34
butter-yellow in the center. With the cold lemonade they were sufficient for childhood's lifelong diet. Remembering my manners, I
took nice little lady-like bites off the edges. She said she had made
them expressly for me and that she had a few in the kitchen that I
could take home to my brother. So I jammed one whole cake in my
mouth and the rough crumbs scratched the insides of my jaws, and
if I hadn't had to swallow, it would have been a dream come true.

As I ate she began the first of what we later called "my lessons   35
in living." She said that I must always be intolerant of ignorance but
understanding of illiteracy. That some people, unable to go to
school, were more educated and even more intelligent than college
professors. She encouraged me to listen carefully to what country
people called mother wit. That in those homely sayings was couched
the collective wisdom of generations.

When I finished the cookies she brushed off the table and   36
brought a thick, small book from the bookcase. I had read *A Tale
of Two Cities* and found it up to my standards as a romantic novel.
She opened the first page and I heard poetry for the first time in
my life.

"It was the best of times and the worst of times . . ." Her voice   37
slid in and curved down through and over the words. She was nearly singing. I wanted to look at the pages. Were they the same that I
had read? Or were there notes, music, lined on the pages, as in a
hymn book? Her sounds began cascading gently. I knew from listening to a thousand preachers that she was nearing the end of her
reading, and I hadn't really heard, heard to understand, a single
word.

"How do you like that?"   38

It occurred to me that she expected a response. The sweet vanil- 39
la flavor was still on my tongue and her reading was a wonder in my
ears. I had to speak.

I said, "Yes, ma'am." It was the least I could do, but it was the 40
most also.

"There's one more thing. Take this book of poems and memo- 41
rize one for me. Next time you pay me a visit, I want you to recite."

I have tried often to search behind the sophistication of years for 42
the enchantment I so easily found in those gifts. The essence escapes
but its aura remains. To be allowed, no, invited, into the private lives
of strangers, and to share their joys and fears, was a chance to
exchange the Southern bitter wormwood for a cup of mead with
Beowulf[1] or a hot cup of tea and milk with Oliver Twist.[2] When I
said aloud, "It is a far, far better thing that I do, than I have ever
done . . ."[3] tears of love filled my eyes at my selflessness.

On that first day, I ran down the hill and into the road (few cars 43
ever came along it) and had the good sense to stop running before
I reached the Store.

I was liked, and what a difference it made. I was respected not 44
as Mrs. Henderson's grandchild or Bailey's sister but for just being
Marguerite Johnson.

Childhood's logic never asks to be proved (all conclusions are 45
absolute). I didn't question why Mrs. Flowers had singled me out
for attention, nor did it occur to me that Momma might have asked
her to give me a little talking to. All I cared about was that she had
made tea cookies for *me* and read to *me* from her favorite book. It
was enough to prove that she liked me.

---

[1]The hero of an Old English epic poem dating from the eighth century (editors'
note).
[2]The main character in Charles Dickens's novel *Oliver Twist* (1837) (editors' note).
[3]The last words of Sydney Carton, the selfless hero of Charles Dickens's novel *A
Tale of Two Cities* (1859) (editors' note).

Questions for Close Reading

1. What is the selection's thesis (or dominant impression)? Locate the sen-
   tence(s) in which Angelou states her main idea. If she doesn't state the
   thesis explicitly, express it in your own words.

2. Angelou states that Mrs. Flowers "has remained throughout my life the measure of what a human being can be" (paragraph 5). What does Angelou admire about Mrs. Flowers?

3. Why is young Angelou so ashamed of Momma when Mrs. Flowers is around? How do Momma and Mrs. Flowers behave with each other?

4. What are the "lessons in living" that Angelou receives from Mrs. Flowers during their first visit? How do you think these lessons might have subsequently influenced Angelou?

5. Refer to your dictionary as needed to define the following words used in the selection: *taut* (paragraph 2), *voile* (2), *benign* (4), *unceremonious* (8), *gait* (8), *moors* (11), *incessantly* (11), *scones* (11), *crumpets* (11), *heath* (11), *chifforobe* (17), *sacrilegious* (17), *infuse* (24), *couched* (35), and *aura* (42).

Questions About the Writer's Craft

1. **The pattern.** Reread the essay, focusing on the descriptive passages first of Mrs. Flowers and then of Angelou's visit to Mrs. Flowers's house. To what senses does Angelou appeal in these passages? What method of organization (see pages 46–48) does she use to order these sensory details?

2. To enrich the description of her eventful encounter with Mrs. Flowers, Angelou draws upon figures of speech (see pages 87–88). Consider, for example, the similes in paragraphs 1 and 11. How do these figures of speech contribute to the essay's dominant impression?

3. **Other patterns.** Because Angelou's description has a strong narrative component, it isn't surprising that there's a considerable amount of dialogue in the selection. For example, in paragraphs 7 and 10, Angelou quotes Momma's incorrect grammar. She then provides an imagined conversation in which the young Angelou scolds Momma and corrects her speech. What do these imagined scoldings of Momma reveal about young Angelou? How do they relate to Mrs. Flowers's subsequent "lessons in life"?

4. Although it's not the focus of this selection, the issue of race remains in the background of Angelou's portrait of Mrs. Flowers. Where in the selection does Angelou imply that race was a fact of life in her town? How does this specter of racism help Angelou underscore the significance of her encounter with Mrs. Flowers?

Writing Assignments Using Description as a Pattern of Development

1. At one time or another, just about all of us have met someone who taught us to see ourselves more clearly and helped us understand what we wanted from life. Write an essay describing such a person. Focus on the individual's personal qualities, as a way of depicting the role he or she

played in your life. Be sure not to limit yourself to an objective description. Subjective description, filled with lively language and figures of speech, will serve you well as you provide a portrait of this special person.

∞ **2.** Thrilled by the spectacle of Mrs. Flowers's interesting home, Angelou says she wanted to "gobble up the room entire" and share it with her brother. Write an essay describing in detail a place that vividly survives in your memory. You may describe a setting that you visited only once or a familiar setting that holds a special place in your heart. Before you write, list the qualities and sensory impressions you associate with this special place; then refine the list so that all details support your dominant impression. You may want to read E. B. White's "Once More to the Lake" (page 115) to see how a professional writer evokes the qualities of a special place in his life.

Writing Assignments Using Other Patterns of Development

∞ **3.** When the young Angelou discovers, thanks to Mrs. Flowers, the thrill of acceptance, she experiences a kind of *epiphany*—a moment of enlightenment. Write an essay about an event in your life that represented a kind of epiphany. You might write about a positive discovery, such as when you realized you had a special talent for something, or about a negative discovery, such as when you realized that a beloved family member had a serious flaw. To make the point that the moment was a turning point in your life, start by describing what kind of person you were before the discovery. Then narrate the actual incident, using vivid details and dialogue to make the event come alive. End by discussing the importance of this epiphany in your life. For additional accounts of personal epiphanies, you might read Langston Hughes's "Salvation" (page 148) and Beth Johnson's "Bombs Bursting in Air" (page 189).

4. Think of an activity that engages you completely, one that provides—as reading does for Angelou—an opportunity for growth and expansion. Possibilities include reading, writing, playing an instrument, doing crafts, dancing, hiking, playing a sport, cooking, or traveling. Write an essay in which you argue the merits of your chosen pastime. Assume that some of your readers are highly skeptical. To win them over, you'll need to provide convincing examples that demonstrate the pleasure and benefits you have discovered in the activity.

Writing Assignments Using a Journal Entry as a Starting Point

5. Write an essay about a time when someone threw you a much-needed "lifeline" at a challenging time. Review your pre-reading journal entry, selecting *one* time when a person's encouragement and support made a

great difference in your life. Be sure to describe the challenge you faced
before recounting the specific details of the person's help. Dialogue and
descriptive details will help you re-create the power of the experience.

E. B. White

Elwyn Brooks White (1899–1985) is considered one of America's finest essayists. For many years, White was a member of the *New Yorker* magazine staff and wrote the magazine's popular column "The Talk of the Town." He also wrote children's books, including the classic *Charlotte's Web* (1952), and was the coauthor with William Strunk, Jr., of the renowned guide for writers, *The Elements of Style* (1959). But most memorable are the essays White produced during his life—gems of clarity, wit, and heartfelt expression. White's contribution to literature earned him many awards, including the Presidential Medal of Freedom and the National Medal for Literature. The classic essay reprinted here is taken from *The Essays of E. B. White* (1977).

Pre-Reading Journal Entry

In your journal, list at least two occasions—either serious or humorous— that made you keenly aware that you were growing older. What was it about each situation that forced this realization upon you? How did the realization affect you? Did it please or distress you? Jot down as many details about each instance as you can.

Once More to the Lake

One summer, along about 1904, my father rented a camp on a 1 lake in Maine and took us all there for the month of August. We all got ringworm from some kittens and had to rub Pond's Extract on our arms and legs night and morning, and my father rolled over in a canoe with all his clothes on; but outside of that the vacation was a success and from then on none of us ever thought there was any place in the world like that lake in Maine. We returned summer after summer—always on August 1 for one month. I have since become a salt-water man, but sometimes in summer there are days when the restlessness of the tides and the fearful cold of the sea water and the incessant wind that blows across the afternoon and into the evening make me wish for the placidity of a lake in the woods. A few weeks ago this feeling got so strong I bought myself a couple of bass hooks and a spinner and returned to the lake where we used to go, for a week's fishing and to revisit old haunts.

I took along my son, who had never had any fresh water up his nose and who had seen lily pads only from train windows. On the journey over to the lake I began to wonder what it would be like. I wondered how time would have marred this unique, this holy spot—the coves and streams, the hills that the sun set behind, the camps and the paths behind the camps. I was sure that the tarred road would have found it out, and I wondered in what other ways it would be desolated. It is strange how much you can remember about places like that once you allow your mind to return into the grooves that lead back. You remember one thing, and that suddenly reminds you of another thing. I guess I remembered clearest of all the early mornings, when the lake was cool and motionless, remembered how the bedroom smelled of the lumber it was made of and of the wet woods whose scent entered through the screen. The partitions in the camp were thin and did not extend clear to the top of the rooms, and as I was always the first up I would dress softly so as not to wake the others, and sneak out into the sweet outdoors and start out in the canoe, keeping close along the shore in the long shadows of the pines. I remembered being very careful never to rub my paddle against the gunwale for fear of disturbing the stillness of the cathedral.

The lake had never been what you would call a wild lake. There were cottages sprinkled around the shores, and it was in farming country although the shores of the lake were quite heavily wooded. Some of the cottages were owned by nearby farmers, and you would live at the shore and eat your meals at the farmhouse. That's what our family did. But although it wasn't wild, it was a fairly large and undisturbed lake and there were places in it that, to a child at least, seemed infinitely remote and primeval.

I was right about the tar: it led to within half a mile of the shore. But when I got back there, with my boy, and we settled into a camp near a farmhouse and into the kind of summertime I had known, I could tell that it was going to be pretty much the same as it had been before—I knew it, lying in bed the first morning, smelling the bedroom and hearing the boy sneak quietly out and go off along the shore in a boat. I began to sustain the illusion that he was I, and therefore, by simple transposition, that I was my father. This sensation persisted, kept cropping up all the time we were there. It was not an entirely new feeling, but in this setting it grew much stronger. I seemed to be living a dual existence. I would be in the middle of some simple act, I would be picking up a bait box or laying down a table fork, or I would be saying something, and suddenly it would be not I but my father who was saying the words or making the gesture. It gave me a creepy sensation.

We went fishing the first morning. I felt the same damp moss   5
covering the worms in the bait can, and saw the dragonfly alight on the tip of my rod as it hovered a few inches from the surface of the water. It was the arrival of this fly that convinced me beyond any doubt that everything was as it always had been, that the years were a mirage and that there had been no years. The small waves were the same, chucking the rowboat under the chin as we fished at anchor, and the boat was the same boat, the same color green and the ribs broken in the same places, and under the floorboards the same fresh-water leavings and débris—the dead helgramite, the wisps of moss, the rusty discarded fishhook, the dried blood from yesterday's catch. We stared silently at the tips of our rods, at the dragonflies that came and went. I lowered the tip of mine into the water, tentatively, pensively dislodging the fly, which darted two feet away, poised, darted two feet back, and came to rest again a little farther up the rod. There had been no years between the ducking of this dragonfly and the other one—the one that was part of memory. I looked at the boy, who was silently watching his fly, and it was my hands that held his rod, my eyes watching. I felt dizzy and didn't know which rod I was at the end of.

We caught two bass, hauling them in briskly as though they   6
were mackerel, pulling them over the side of the boat in a businesslike manner without any landing net, and stunning them with a blow on the back of the head. When we got back for a swim before lunch, the lake was exactly where we had left it, the same number of inches from the dock, and there was only the merest suggestion of a breeze. This seemed an utterly enchanted sea, this lake you could leave to its own devices for a few hours and come back to, and find that it had not stirred, this constant and trustworthy body of water. In the shallows, the dark, water-soaked sticks and twigs, smooth and old, were undulating in clusters on the bottom against the clean ribbed sand, and the track of the mussel was plain. A school of minnows swam by, each minnow with its small individual shadow, doubling the attendance, so clear and sharp in the sunlight. Some of the

other campers were in swimming, along the shore, one of them with a cake of soap, and the water felt thin and clear and unsubstantial. Over the years there had been this person with the cake of soap, this cultist, and here he was. There had been no years.

Up to the farmhouse to dinner through the teeming, dusty   7 field, the road under our sneakers was only a two-track road. The middle track was missing, the one with the marks of the hooves and the splotches of dried, flaky manure. There had always been three tracks to choose from in choosing which track to walk in; now the choice was narrowed down to two. For a moment I missed terribly the middle alternative. But the way led past the tennis court, and something about the way it lay there in the sun reassured me; the tape had loosened along the backline, the alleys were green with plantains and other weeds, and the net (installed in June and removed in September) sagged in the dry noon, and the whole place steamed with midday heat and hunger and emptiness. There was a choice of pie for dessert, and one was blueberry and one was apple, and the waitresses were the same country girls, there having been no passage of time, only the illusion of it as in a dropped curtain—the waitresses were still fifteen; their hair had been washed, that was the only difference—they had been to the movies and seen the pretty girls with the clean hair.

Summertime, oh, summertime, pattern of life indelible, the   8 fade-proof lake, the woods unshatterable, the pasture with the sweetfern and the juniper forever and ever, summer without end; this was the background, and the life along the shore was the design, the cottagers with their innocent and tranquil design, their tiny docks with the flagpole and the American flag floating against the white clouds in the blue sky, the little paths over the roots of the trees leading from camp to camp and the paths leading back to the outhouses and the can of lime for sprinkling, and at the souvenir counters at the store the miniature birch-bark canoes and the post-cards that showed things looking a little better than they looked. This was the American family at play, escaping the city heat, won-dering whether the newcomers in the camp at the head of the cove were "common" or "nice," wondering whether it was true that the people who drove up for Sunday dinner at the farmhouse were turned away because there wasn't enough chicken.

It seemed to me, as I kept remembering all this, that those times   9 and those summers had been infinitely precious and worth saving.

There had been jollity and peace and goodness. The arriving (at the beginning of August) had been so big a business in itself, at the railway station the farm wagon drawn up, the first smell of the pine-laden air, the first glimpse of the smiling farmer, and the great importance of the trunks and your father's enormous authority in such matters, and the feel of the wagon under you for the long ten-mile haul, and at the top of the last long hill catching the first view of the lake after eleven months of not seeing this cherished body of water. The shouts and cries of the other campers when they saw you, and the trunks to be unpacked, to give up their rich burden. (Arriving was less exciting nowadays, when you sneaked up in your car and parked it under a tree near the camp and took out the bags and in five minutes it was all over, no fuss, no loud wonderful fuss about trunks.)

Peace and goodness and jollity. The only thing that was wrong   10
now, really, was the sound of the place, an unfamiliar nervous sound of the outboard motors. This was the note that jarred, the one thing that would sometimes break the illusion and set the years moving. In those other summertimes all motors were inboard; and when they were at a little distance, the noise they made was a sedative, an ingredient of summer sleep. They were one-cylinder and two-cylinder engines, and some were make-and-break and some were jump-spark, but they all made a sleepy sound across the lake. The one-lungers throbbed and fluttered, and the twin-cylinder ones purred and purred, and that was a quiet sound, too. But now the campers all had outboards. In the daytime, in the hot mornings, these motors made a petulant, irritable sound; at night, in the still evening when the afterglow lit the water, they whined about one's ears like mosquitoes. My boy loved our rented outboard, and his great desire was to achieve single-handed mastery over it, and authority, and he soon learned the trick of choking it a little (but not too much), and the adjustment of the needle valve. Watching him I would remember the things you could do with the old one-cylinder engine with the heavy flywheel, how you could have it eating out of your hand if you got really close to it spiritually. Motorboats in those days didn't have clutches, and you would make a landing by shutting off the motor at the proper time and coasting in with a dead rudder. But there was a way of reversing them, if you learned the trick, by cutting the switch and putting it on again exactly on the final dying revolution of the flywheel, so

that it would kick back against compression and begin reversing. Approaching a dock in a strong following breeze, it was difficult to slow up sufficiently by the ordinary coasting method, and if a boy felt he had complete mastery over his motor, he was tempted to keep it running beyond its time and then reverse it a few feet from the dock. It took a cool nerve, because if you threw the switch a twentieth of a second too soon you would catch the flywheel when it still had speed enough to go up past center, and the boat would leap ahead, charging bullfashion at the dock.

11   We had a good week at the camp. The bass were biting well and the sun shone endlessly, day after day. We would be tired at night and lie down in the accumulated heat of the little bedrooms after the long hot day and the breeze would stir almost imperceptibly outside and the smell of the swamp drift in through the rusty screens. Sleep would come easily and in the morning the red squirrel would be on the roof, tapping out his gay routine. I kept remembering everything, lying in bed in the mornings—the small steamboat that had a long rounded stern like the lip of a Ubangi, and how quietly she ran on the moonlight sails, when the older boys played their mandolins and the girls sang and we ate doughnuts dipped in sugar, and how sweet the music was on the water in the shining night, and what it had felt like to think about girls then. After breakfast we would go up to the store and the things were in the same place—the minnows in a bottle, the plugs and spinners disarranged and pawed over by the youngsters from the boys' camp, the Fig Newtons and the Beeman's gum. Outside, the road was tarred and cars stood in front of the store. Inside, all was just as it had always been, except there was more Coca-Cola and not so much Moxie and root beer and birch beer and sarsaparilla. We would walk out with the bottle of pop apiece and sometimes the pop would backfire up our noses and hurt. We explored the streams, quietly, where the turtles slid off the sunny logs and dug their way into the soft bottom; and we lay on the town wharf and fed worms to the tame bass. Everywhere we went I had trouble making out which was I, the one walking at my side, the one walking in my pants.

12   One afternoon while we were there at the lake a thunderstorm came up. It was like the revival of an old melodrama that I had seen long ago with childish awe. The second-act climax of the drama of the electrical disturbance over a lake in America had not changed in any important respect. This was the big scene, still the big scene. The whole thing was so familiar, the first feeling of oppression and

heat and a general air around camp of not wanting to go very far away. In midafternoon (it was all the same) a curious darkening of the sky, and a lull in everything that had made life tick; and then the way the boats suddenly swung the other way at their moorings with the coming of a breeze out of the new quarter, and premonitory rumble. Then the kettle drum, then the snare, then the bass drum and cymbals, then cackling light against the dark, and the gods grinning and licking their chops in the hills. Afterward the calm, the rain steadily rustling in the calm lake, the return of light and hope and spirits, and the campers running out in joy and relief to go swimming in the rain, their bright cries perpetuating the deathless joke about how they were getting simply drenched, and the children screaming with delight at the new sensation of bathing in the rain, and the joke about getting drenched linking the generations in a strong indestructible chain. And the comedian who waded in carrying an umbrella.

When the others went swimming, my son said he was going in, too. He pulled his dripping trunks from the line where they had hung all through the shower and wrung them out. Languidly, and with no thought of going in, I watched him, his hard little body, skinny and bare, saw him wince slightly as he pulled up around his vitals the small, soggy, icy garment. As he buckled the swollen belt, suddenly my groin felt the chill of death.   13

Questions for Close Reading

1. What is the selection's thesis (or dominant impression)? Locate the sentence(s) in which White states his main idea. If he doesn't state the thesis explicitly, express it in your own words.
2. Why does White return to the lake in Maine he had visited as a child? Why do you think he has waited to revisit it until he has a young son to bring along?
3. Several times in the essay, White notes that he felt as if he were his own father—and that his son became his childhood self. What event first prompts this sensation? What actions and thoughts cause it to recur?
4. How is the latest visit to the lake similar to White's childhood summers? What differences does White notice? What effects do the differences have on him?
5. Refer to your dictionary as needed to define the following words used in the selection: *incessant* (paragraph 1), *placidity* (1), *primeval* (3), *transposition* (4), *undulating* (6), *indelible* (8), *petulant* (10), and *languidly* (13).

Questions About the Writer's Craft

1. **The pattern.** Through vivid language, descriptive writing evokes sensory experiences. In "Once More to the Lake," White overlays two sets of sensory details: those of the present-day lake and those of the lake as it was in his boyhood. Which set of details is more objective? Which seems sharper and more powerful? Why?

2. To describe the lake, White chooses many words and phrases with religious connotations. Give some examples. What might have been his purpose in using such language?

3. **Other patterns.** In paragraph 12, White uses a metaphor to describe a thunderstorm. To what does he compare a thunderstorm? Why does he make this comparison?

4. White refers to "the chill of death" in the final paragraph. What brings on this feeling? Why does he feel it "in his groin"? Where has this idea been hinted at previously in the essay?

Writing Assignments Using Description as a Pattern of Development

1. Write an essay describing a special place in your life. The place need not be a natural setting like White's lake; it could be a city or building that has meant a great deal to you. Use sensory details and figurative language, as White does, to enliven your description and convey the place's significance for you. Before writing, read Maya Angelou's "Sister Flowers" (page 106) to see how a professional writer conveys the special qualities of a memorable childhood place.

2. White was fortunate that his lake had remained virtually unchanged. But many other special spots have been destroyed or are threatened with destruction. Write an essay describing a place (a park, a school, an old-fashioned ice-cream parlor) that is "infinitely precious and worth saving." For your dominant theme, show which aspects of your subject make it worthy of being preserved for future generations. Before writing your essay, you might want to read Rachel Carson's "A Fable for Tomorrow" (page 311), an essay that laments the loss of a special place.

Writing Assignments Using Other Patterns of Development

3. Sometimes, we, like White, are suddenly reminded of the nearness of death: a crushed animal lies in the road, a politician is assassinated, a classmate is killed in a car crash. Write an essay about a time you were forced to think about mortality. Explain what happened and describe your thoughts and feelings afterwards.

4. Have your older relatives attempted to share with you some special experiences of their younger years? Have you done the same thing with your own children, nephews, or nieces? You may have taken loved ones to a special place, as White did, or listened to stories or looked at photographs. Write an essay recounting such an experience. Explain the motivations of the older generation and the effects on the younger one.

Writing Assignments Using a Journal Entry as a Starting Point

5. Write an essay narrating an incident that reminded you that you weren't as young as you used to be. Review your pre-reading journal entry, selecting the *one* occasion you would most enjoy writing about. Draw upon the specifics in your journal, providing additional details about both external circumstances and your internal state of mind. End your essay by discussing how your realization affected your subsequent thoughts and actions.

Additional Writing Topics

DESCRIPTION

General Assignments

Write an essay using description to develop any of the following topics. Remember that an effective description focuses on a dominant impression and arranges details in a way that best supports that impression. Your details—vivid and appealing to the senses—should be carefully chosen so that the essay isn't overburdened with material of secondary importance. When writing, keep in mind that varied sentence structure and imaginative figures of speech are ways to make a descriptive piece compelling.

1. A favorite item of clothing
2. A school as a young child might see it
3. A hospital room you visited or stayed in
4. An individualist's appearance
5. A coffee shop, a bus shelter, a newsstand, or some other small place
6. A parade or victory celebration
7. A banana, a squash, or another fruit or vegetable
8. A particular drawer in a desk or bureau
9. A houseplant
10. A "media event"
11. A dorm room
12. An elderly person
13. An attractive man or woman
14. A prosthetic device or wheelchair
15. A TV, film, or music celebrity
16. A student lounge
17. A once-in-a-lifetime event
18. The inside of something, such as a cave, boat, car, shed, or machine
19. A friend, a roommate, or another person you know well
20. An essential gadget or a useless gadget

Assignments With a Specific Purpose and Audience

1. For an audience of incoming first-year students, prepare a speech describing registration day at your college. Use specific details to help prepare students for the actual event. Choose an adjective that represents your dominant impression of the experience, and keep that word in mind as you write.

2. As a subscriber to a dating service, you've been asked to submit a description of the kind of person you'd like to meet. Describe your ideal date. Focus on specifics about physical appearance, personal habits, character traits, and interests.

3. Your college has decided to replace an old campus structure (for example, a dorm or dining hall) with a new version. Write a letter of protest to the administration, describing the place so vividly and appealingly that its value and need for preservation are unquestionable.

4. As a staff member of the campus newspaper, you have been asked to write a weekly column of social news and gossip. For your first column, you plan to describe a recent campus event—a dance, party, concert, or other social activity. With a straightforward or tongue-in-cheek tone, describe where the event was held, the appearance of the people who attended, and so on.

5. Students at your college have complained that the course catalog is inaccurate. Its course descriptions are often brief, misleading, or just plain incorrect. You're part of a student-faculty group responsible for revising the catalog. Write a full and accurate description of a course with which you're familiar. Tell exactly what the course is about, who teaches it, and how it is run.

6. As a resident of a particular town, you're angered by the appearance of a certain spot and by the activities that take place there. Write a letter to the town council, describing in detail the undesirable nature of this place (a video arcade, an adult bookstore, a bar, a bus station, a neglected park or beach). End with some suggestions about ways to improve the situation.

4

NARRATION

WHAT IS NARRATION?

Human beings are instinctively storytellers. In prehistoric times, our
ancestors huddled around campfires to hear tales of hunting and
magic. In ancient times, warriors gathered in halls to listen to bards
praise in song the exploits of epic heroes. Things are no different
today. Boisterous children invariably settle down to listen when their
parents read to them; millions of people tune in day after day to the
ongoing drama of their favorite soap operas; vacationers sit motionless on the beach, caught up in the latest best-sellers; and all of us
enjoy saying, "Just listen to what happened to me today." Our
hunger for storytelling is a basic part of us.

Narration means telling a single story or several related stories.
The story can be a means to an end, a way to support a main idea or
thesis. For instance, to demonstrate that television has become the
constant companion of many children, you might narrate a typical
child's day in front of the television—starting with frantic cartoons in
the morning and ending with dizzy situation comedies at night.
Or to support the point that the college registration process should
be reformed, you could tell the tale of a chaotic morning spent trying to enroll in classes.

Narration is powerful. Every public speaker, from politician to classroom teacher, knows that stories capture the attention of listeners as nothing else can. Narration speaks to us strongly because it is about us; we want to know what happened to others, not simply because we're curious, but because their experiences shed light on the nature of our own lives. Narration lends force to opinions, triggers the flow of memory, and evokes places and times in ways that are compelling and affecting.

HOW NARRATION FITS YOUR PURPOSE AND AUDIENCE

Because narratives tell a story, you may think they are found only in novels or short stories. But narration can also appear in essays, sometimes as a supplemental pattern of development. For example, if your purpose in a paper is to *persuade* apathetic readers that airport security regulations must be followed strictly, you might lead off with a brief account of an armed terrorist who easily boarded a plane. In a paper *defining* good teaching, you might keep readers engaged by including satirical anecdotes about one hapless instructor, the antithesis of an effective teacher. An essay on the *effects* of an overburdened judicial system might provide—in an attempt to involve readers—a dramatic account of the way one clearly guilty murderer plea-bargained his way to freedom.

In addition to providing effective support in one section of your paper, narration can also serve as an essay's dominant pattern of development. In fact, most of this chapter shows you how to use a single extended narrative to convey a central point and share with readers your view of what happened. You might choose to narrate the events of a day spent with your three-year-old nephew as a way of revealing how you rediscovered the importance of family life. Or you might relate the story of your roommate's mugging, evoking the powerlessness and terror of being a victim. Any story can form the basis for a narrative essay as long as you convey the essence of the experience and evoke its meaning.

SUGGESTIONS FOR USING NARRATION IN AN ESSAY

The following suggestions will be helpful whether you use narration as a dominant or a supportive pattern of development.

1. Identify the conflict in the event. The power of many narratives is rooted in a special kind of tension that "hooks" readers and makes them want to follow the story to its end. This narrative tension is often a by-product of some form of *conflict* within the story. Many narratives revolve around an internal dilemma experienced by a key person in the story. Or the conflict may be between people in the story or between a pivotal character and some social institution or natural phenomenon.

2. Identify the point of the narrative. In *The Adventures of Huckleberry Finn,* Mark Twain warned: "Persons attempting to find a motive in this narrative will be prosecuted; persons attempting to find a moral in it will be banished; persons attempting to find a plot in it will be shot." Twain was, of course, being ironic; his novel's richness lies in its "motives" and "morals." Similarly, when you recount a narrative, it's your responsibility to convey the event's *significance* or *meaning.* In other words, be sure readers are clear about your *narrative point,* or thesis.

Suppose you decide to write about the time you got locked in a mall late at night. Your narrative might focus on the way the mall looked after hours and the way you struggled with mounting terror. But you would also use the narrative to make a point. Perhaps you want to emphasize that fear can be instructive. Or your point might be that malls have a disturbing, surreal underside. You could state this thesis explicitly. ("After hours, the mall shed its cheerful daytime demeanor and took on a more sinister quality.") Or you could refrain from stating the thesis directly, relying on your details and language to convey the point of the narrative: "The mannequins stared at me with glazed eyes and frozen smiles" and "The steel grates pulled over each store's entrance glinted in the cold light, making each shop look like a prison cell."

3. Develop only those details that advance the narrative point. You know from experience that nothing is more boring than a storyteller who gets sidetracked and drags out a story with nonessential details. If a friend started to tell about the time his car broke down in the middle of an expressway—but interrupted his story to complain at length about the slipshod work done by his auto repair shop—you might clench your teeth in annoyance, wishing your friend would hurry up and get back to the interesting part of the story.

Brainstorming ("What happened? When? Where? Who was involved? Why did it happen?") can be valuable for helping you amass narrative details. Then, after generating the specifics, you cull out the nonessential and devote your energies to the key specifics needed to advance your narrative point. When telling a story, you maintain an effective narrative pace by focusing on that point and eliminating details that don't support it. A good narrative depends not only on what is included, but also on what has been left out.

But how do you determine which specifics to omit, which to treat briefly, and which to emphasize? Having a clear sense of your narrative point and knowing your audience are crucial. Assume you're writing a narrative about a disastrous get-acquainted dance sponsored by your college the first week of the academic year. In addition to telling what happened, you want to make a point; perhaps you want to emphasize that, despite the college's good intentions, such official events actually make it difficult to meet people. With this purpose in mind, you might write about how stiff and unnatural students seemed, all dressed up in their best clothes; you might narrate snatches of strained conversation you overheard; you might describe the way males gathered on one side of the room, females on the other—reverting to behaviors supposedly abandoned in fifth grade. All these details would support your narrative point.

Because you don't want to get waylaid by detours that lead away from that point, you would leave out details about the top-notch band and the appetizing refreshments at the dance. The music and food may have been surprisingly good, but since these details don't advance the point you want to make, they should be omitted.

You also need to keep your audience in mind when selecting narrative details. If the audience consists of your instructor and other students—all of them familiar with the new student center where the dance was held—specific details about the center probably wouldn't have to be provided. But imagine that the essay is going to appear in the quarterly magazine published by the college's community relations office. Many of the magazine's readers are former graduates who haven't been on campus for several years. They may need some additional specifics about the student center: its location, how many people it holds, how it is furnished.

As you write, keep asking yourself, "Is this detail or character or snippet of conversation essential? Does my audience need this detail to understand the conflict in the situation? Does this detail advance or intensify the narrative action?" Summarize details that have some importance but do not deserve lengthy treatment ("Two hours went by . . ."). And try to limit *narrative commentary*—statements that tell rather than show what happened—since such remarks interrupt the narrative flow. Focus instead on the specifics that propel action forward in a vigorous way.

Sometimes, especially if the narrative re-creates an event from the past, you won't be able to remember what happened detail for detail. In such a case, you should take advantage of what is called *dramatic license*. Using as a guide your powers of recall as well as the perspective you now have of that particular time, feel free to reshape events to suit your narrative point.

4. Organize the narrative sequence. All of us know the traditional beginning of fairy tales: "Once upon a time. . . ." Every narrative begins somewhere, presents a span of time, and ends at a certain point. Frequently, you'll want to use a straightforward time order, following the event *chronologically* from beginning to end: first this happened, next this happened, finally this happened.

But sometimes a strict chronological recounting may not be effective—especially if the high point of the narrative gets lost somewhere in the middle of the time sequence. To avoid that possibility, you may want to disrupt chronology, plunge the reader into the middle of the story, and then return in a *flashback* to the beginning of the tale. You're probably familiar with the way flashback is used on television and in film. You see someone appealing to the main character for financial help, then return to an earlier time when both were students in the same class, before learning how the rest of the story unfolds. Narratives can also use *flashforward*. You give readers a glimpse of the future (the main character being jailed) before the story continues in the present (the events leading to the arrest). These techniques shift the story onto several planes and keep it from becoming a step-by-step, predictable account. Reserve flashforwards and flashbacks, however, for crucial incidents only, since breaking out of chronological order acts as emphasis. Here are examples of how flashback and flashforward can be used in narrative writing:

Flashback

Standing behind the wooden counter, Greg wielded his knife expertly as he shucked clams--one every ten seconds--with practiced ease. The scene contrasted sharply with his first day on the job, when his hands broke out in blisters and when splitting each shell was like prying open a safe.

Flashforward

Rushing to move my car from the no-parking zone, I waved a quick goodbye to Karen as she climbed the steps to the bus. I didn't know then that by the time I picked her up at the bus station later that day, she had made a decision that would affect both our lives.

Whether or not you choose to include flashbacks or flashforwards in an essay, remember to limit the time span covered by the narrative. Otherwise, you will have trouble generating the details needed to give the story depth and meaning. Also, regardless of the time sequence you select, organize the tale so that it drives toward a strong finish. Be careful that your story doesn't trail off into minor, anticlimactic details.

5. Make the narrative easy to follow.   Describing each distinct action in a separate paragraph helps readers grasp the flow of events. Although narrative essays don't always have conventional topic sentences, each narrative paragraph should have a clear focus. Often this focus is indicated by a sentence early in the paragraph that directs attention to the action taking place. Such a sentence functions as a kind of *informal topic sentence;* the rest of the paragraph then develops that topic sentence. You should also be sure to use time signals when narrating a story. Words like *now, then, next, after,* and *later* ensure that your reader won't get lost as the story progresses.

6. Make the narrative vigorous and immediate.   A compelling narrative provides an abundance of specific details, making readers feel as if they're experiencing the story being told. Readers must be able to see, hear, touch, smell, and taste the event you're narrating. *Vivid sensory description* is, therefore, an essential part of an effective narrative. Not only do specific sensory details make writing a pleasure to read—we all enjoy learning the particulars about people, places, and things—but they also give the narrative the stamp of reality. The specifics convince the reader that the event being described actually did, or could, occur.

Compare the following excerpts from a narrative essay. The first version is lifeless and dull; the revised version, packed with sensory images, grabs readers with its sense of foreboding:

That eventful day started out like every other summer day. My sister Tricia and I made several elaborate mud pies, which we decorated with care. A little later on, as we were spraying each other with the garden hose, we heard my father walk up the path.

That sad summer day started out uneventfully enough. My sister Tricia and I spent a few hours mixing and decorating mud pies. Our hands caked with dry mud, we sprinkled each lopsided pie with alternating rows of dandelion and clover petals. Later when the sun got hotter, we tossed our white T-shirts over the red picket fence--forgetting my grandmother's frequent warnings to be more ladylike. Our sweaty backs bared to the sun, we doused each other with icy sprays from the garden hose. Caught up in the primitive pleasure of it all, we barely heard my father as he walked up the garden path, the gravel crunching under his heavy work boots.

A caution: Sensory language enlivens narration, but it also slows the pace. Be sure that the slower pace suits your purpose. For example, a lengthy description fits an account of a leisurely summer vacation but is inappropriate in a tale about a frantic search for a misplaced wallet.

Another way to create an aura of narrative immediacy is to use *dialogue* while telling a story. Our sense of other people comes, in part, from what they say and from the way they sound. Conversational exchanges allow the reader to experience characters directly. Compare the following fragments of a narrative, one with dialogue and one without, noting how much more energetic the second version is.

When I finally found my way back to the campsite, the trail guide commented on my disheveled appearance.

When I finally found my way back to the campsite, the trail guide took one look at me and drawled, "What on earth happened to you, Daniel Boone? You look as though you've been dragged through a haystack backwards."

"I'd look a lot worse if I hadn't run back here. When a bullet whizzes by me, I don't stick around to see who's doing the shooting."

Note that, when using dialogue, you generally begin a new paragraph to indicate a shift from one person's speech to another's (as in the second example above).

Using *varied sentence structure* is another strategy for making narratives lively and vigorous. Sentences that plod along predictably (subject-verb, subject-verb) put readers to sleep. Experiment with your sentences by juggling length and sentence type; mix long and short sentences, simple and complex. Compare the following original and revised versions to get an idea of how effective varied sentence rhythm can be in narrative writing.

Original

The store manager went to the walk-in refrigerator every day. The heavy metal door clanged shut behind her. I had visions of her freezing to death among the hanging carcasses. The shiny door finally swung open. She waddled out.

Revised

Each time the store manager went to the walk-in refrigerator, the heavy metal door clanged shut behind her. Visions of her freezing to death among the hanging carcasses crept into my mind until the shiny door finally swung open and she waddled out.

Original

The yellow-and-blue-striped fish struggled on the line. Its scales shimmered in the sunlight. Its tail waved frantically. I saw its desire to live. I decided to let it go.

Revised

Scales shimmering in the sunlight, tail waving frantically, the yellow-and-blue-striped fish struggled on the line. Seeing its desire to live, I let it go.

Finally, *vigorous verbs* lend energy to narratives. Use active verb forms ("The boss *yelled at* him") rather than passive ones ("He *was yelled at* by the boss"), and try to replace anemic *to be* verbs ("She *was* a good basketball player") with more dynamic constructions ("She *played* basketball well").

7. Keep your point of view and verb tense consistent. All stories have a *narrator,* the person who tells the story. If you, as narrator, tell a story as you experienced it, the story is written in the *first-person point of view* ("*I* saw the dog pull loose"). But if you observed the event (or heard about it from others) and want to tell how someone else experienced the incident, you would use the *third-person point of view* ("*Anne* saw the dog pull loose"). Each point of view has advantages and limitations. First person allows you to express ordinarily private thoughts and to re-create an event as you actually experienced it. This point of view is limited, though, in its ability to depict the inner thoughts of other people involved in the event. By way of contrast, third person makes it easier to provide insight into the thoughts of all the participants. However, its objective, broad perspective may undercut some of the subjective immediacy typical of the "I was there" point of view. No matter which point of view you select, stay with that vantage point throughout the entire narrative.

Knowing whether to use the *past* or *present tense* ("I *strolled* into the room" as opposed to "I *stroll* into the room") is important. In most narrations, the past tense predominates, enabling the writer to span a considerable period of time. Although more rarely used, the present tense can be powerful for events of short duration—a wrestling match or a medical emergency, for instance. A narrative in the present tense prolongs each moment, intensifying the reader's sense of participation. Be careful, though; unless the event is intense and fast-paced, the present tense can seem contrived. Whichever tense you choose, avoid shifting midstream—starting, let's say, in the past tense ("she skated") and switching to present ("she runs").

STUDENT ESSAY

The following student essay was written by Paul Monahan in response to this assignment.

> In "Salvation," Langston Hughes tells about an incident in which he felt pressured to act in a manner that ran counter to his better instincts. Write a narrative about a time when you faced a disturbing conflict and ended up doing something you later regretted.

While reading Paul's paper, try to determine how well it applies the principles of narration. The annotations on Paul's paper and the commentary following it will help you look at the essay more closely.

If Only
by Paul Monahan

<table>
<tr>
<td>Introduction</td>
<td>

Having worked at a 7-Eleven store for two years, I thought I had become successful at what our manager calls "customer relations." I firmly believed that a friendly smile and an automatic "sir," "ma'am," and "thank you" would see me through any situation that might arise, from soothing impatient or unpleasant people to apologizing for giving out the wrong change. But the other night an old woman shattered my belief that a glib response could smooth over the rough spots of dealing with other human beings.</td>
<td>1</td>
</tr>
</table>

Narrative Point (thesis)

Informal topic sentence → The moment she entered, the woman presented a sharp contrast to our shiny store with its bright lighting and neatly arranged shelves. Walking as if each step were painful, she slowly pushed open the glass door and hobbled down the nearest aisle. She coughed dryly, wheezing with each breath. On a forty-degree night, she was wearing only a faded print dress, a thin, light beige sweater too small to button, and black vinyl slippers with the backs cut out to expose calloused heels. There were no stockings or socks on her splotchy, blue-veined legs.

Sensory details

2

After strolling around the store for several minutes, the old woman stopped in front of the rows of canned vegetables. She picked up some corn niblets and stared with a strange intensity at the label. At that point, I decided to be a good, courteous employee and asked her if she needed help. As I stood close to her, my smile became harder to maintain; her red-rimmed eyes were partially closed by yellowish crusts; her hands were covered with layer upon layer of grime, and the stale smell of sweat rose in a thick vaporous cloud from her clothes.

Informal topic sentence

Sensory details

3

Start of dialogue → "I need some food," she muttered in reply to my bright "Can I help you?"

4

"Are you looking for corn, ma'am?"

5

"I need some food," she repeated. "Any kind."

6

"Well, the corn is ninety-five cents," I said in my most helpful voice. "Or, if you like, we have a special on bologna today."

7

"I can't pay," she said.   8

Conflict ———————▶ For a second, I was tempted to say, "Take the   9
established   corn." But the employee rules flooded into my mind:
                   Remain polite, but do not let customers get the best
                   of you. Let them know that you are in control. For a
                   moment, I even entertained the idea that this was
                   some sort of test, and that this woman was someone
                   from the head office, testing my loyalty. I responded
                   dutifully, "I'm sorry, ma'am, but I can't give away
                   anything free."

Informal topic ——▶ The old woman's face collapsed a bit more, if   10
sentence   that were possible, and her hands trembled as she
                   put the can back on the shelf. She shuffled past me
                   toward the door, her torn and dirty clothing barely
                   covering her bent back.

Conclusion   Moments after she left, I rushed out the door   11
                   with the can of corn, but she was nowhere in sight.
                   For the rest of my shift, the image of the woman
                   haunted me. I had been young, healthy, and smug.
Echoing of   She had been old, sick, and desperate. Wishing with
narrative point   all my heart that I had acted like a human being
in the   rather than a robot, I was saddened to realize how
introduction   fragile a hold we have on our better instincts.

COMMENTARY

Point of view, tense, and conflict.   Paul chose to write "If Only"
from the *first-person point of view*, a logical choice because he
appears as a main character in his own story. Using the *past tense*,
Paul recounts an incident filled with *conflicts*—between him and the
woman and between his fear of breaking the rules and his human
instinct to help someone in need.

Narrative point.   It isn't always necessary to state the *narrative
point* of an essay; it can be implied. But Paul decided to express the
controlling idea of his narrative in two places—in the introduction
("But the other night an old woman shattered my belief that a glib
response could smooth over the rough spots of dealing with other
human beings") and again in the conclusion, where he expands his
idea about rote responses overriding impulses of independent judgment and compassion. All of the essay's *narrative details* contribute

to the point of the piece; Paul does not include any extraneous information that would detract from the central idea he wants to convey.

Organization and other patterns of development.   The narrative is *organized chronologically,* from the moment the woman enters the store to Paul's reaction after she leaves. Paul limits the narrative's time span. The entire incident probably occurs in under ten minutes, yet the introduction serves as a kind of *flashback* by providing some necessary background about Paul's past experiences. To help the reader follow the course of the narrative, Paul uses *time signals: "The moment* she entered, the woman presented a sharp contrast" (paragraph 2); "*At that point,* I decided to be a good, courteous employee" (3); "*For the rest of my shift,* the image of the woman haunted me" (11).

The paragraphs (except for those consisting solely of dialogue) also contain *informal topic sentences* that direct attention to the specific stage of action being narrated. Indeed, each paragraph focuses on a distinct event: the elderly woman's actions when she first enters the store, the encounter between Paul and the woman, Paul's resulting inner conflict, the woman's subsequent response, and Paul's delayed reaction.

This chain of events, with one action leading to another, illustrates that the *cause-effect* pattern underlies the essay's basic structure. And another pattern—*description*—gives dramatic immediacy to the events being recounted. Throughout, rich sensory details engage the reader's interest. For instance, the sentence "her red-rimmed eyes were partially closed by yellowish crusts" (3) vividly recreates the woman's appearance while also suggesting Paul's inner reaction to the woman.

Dialogue and sentence structure.   Paul uses other techniques to add energy and interest to his narrative. For one thing, he dramatizes his conflict with the woman through *dialogue* that crackles with tension. And he achieves a vigorous narrative pace by *varying the length and structure of his sentences.* In the second paragraph, a short sentence ("There were no stockings or socks on her splotchy, blue-veined legs") alternates with a longer one ("On a forty-degree night, she was wearing only a faded print dress, a thin, light beige sweater too small to button, and black vinyl slippers with the backs cut out to expose calloused heels"). Some sentences in the essay open with a subject and verb ("She coughed dryly"), while others start with dependent clauses or participial phrases ("As I stood close to her, my smile became harder to maintain"; "Walking as if each step were painful, she slowly pushed open the glass door") or with a prepositional phrase ("For a second, I was tempted").

Revising the first draft. Comparing the final version of the essay's third paragraph, shown above, with the preliminary version reprinted below reveals some of the changes Paul made while revising the essay.

Original Version of the Third Paragraph

After sneezing and hacking her way around the store, the old woman stopped in front of the vegetable shelves. She picked up a can of corn and stared at the label. She stayed like this for several minutes. Then I walked over to her and asked if I could be of help.

After putting the original draft aside for a while, Paul reread his paper aloud and realized the third paragraph especially lacked power. So he decided to add compelling descriptive details about the woman ("the stale smell of sweat," for example). When revising, he also worked to reduce the paragraph's choppiness. By expanding and combining sentences, he gave the paragraph an easier, more graceful rhythm. Much of the time, revision involves paring down excess material. In this case, though, Paul made the right decision to elaborate his sentences. Furthermore, he added the following comment to the third paragraph: "I decided to be a good, courteous employee." These few words introduce an appropriate note of irony and serve to echo the essay's controlling idea.

Finally, Paul decided to omit the words "sneezing and hacking" because he realized they were too comic or light for his subject. Still, the first sentence in the revised paragraph is somewhat jarring. The word *strolling* isn't quite appropriate since it implies a leisurely grace inconsistent with the impression he wants to convey. Replacing *strolling* with, say, *shuffling* would bring the image more into line with the essay's overall mood.

Despite this slight problem, Paul's revisions are right on the mark. The changes he made strengthened his essay, turning it into a more evocative, more polished piece of narrative writing.

ACTIVITIES: NARRATION

Prewriting Activities

1. Imagine you're writing two essays: One analyzes the *effect* of insensitive teachers on young children; the other *argues* the importance of family traditions. With the help of your journal or freewriting, identify different narratives you could use to open each essay.

2. For each of the situations below, identify two different conflicts that would make a story worth relating. Then prepare six to ten lines of natural-sounding dialogue for each potential conflict in *one* of the situations.
   a. Going to the supermarket with a friend
   b. Telling your parents which college you've decided to attend
   c. Participating in a demonstration
   d. Preparing for an exam in a difficult course

Revising Activities

3. Revise each of the following narrative sentence groups twice: once with words that carry negative connotations, and again with words that carry positive connotations. Use varied sentence structure, sensory details, and vigorous verbs to convey mood.
   a. The bell rang. It rang loudly. Students knew the last day of class was over.
   b. Last weekend, our neighbors burned leaves in their yard. We went over to speak with them.
   c. The sun shone in through my bedroom window. It made me sit up in bed. Daylight was finally here, I told myself.

4. The following paragraph is the introduction from the first draft of an essay proposing harsher penalties for drunk drivers. Revise this narrative paragraph to make it more effective. How can you make sentence structure less predictable? Which details should you delete? As you revise, provide language that conveys the event's sights, smells, and sounds. Also, clarify the chronological sequence.

   As I drove down the street in my bright blue sports car, I saw a car coming rapidly around the curve. The car didn't slow down as it headed toward the traffic light. The light turned yellow and then red. A young couple, dressed like models, started crossing the street. When the woman saw the car, she called out to her husband.

He jumped onto the shoulder. The man wasn't hurt but, seconds later, it was clear the woman was. I ran to a nearby emergency phone and called the police. The ambulance arrived, but the woman was already dead. The driver, who looked terrible, failed the sobriety test, and the police found out that he had two previous offenses. It's apparent that better ways have to be found for getting drunk drivers off the road.

Annie Dillard

Pilgrim at Tinker Creek (1974) is probably Annie Dillard's best-known work. A collection of lyrical observations and reflections about the natural world, *Pilgrim* was awarded a Pulitzer Prize for general nonfiction. Born in 1945, Dillard is currently Adjunct Professor at Wesleyan University in Connecticut and a contributing editor at *Harper's*. Over the years, she has published a variety of books: *Tickets for a Prayer Wheel* (1974), a book of poetry; *Holy the Firm* (1978), *Teaching a Stone to Talk* (1982), *The Annie Dillard Reader* (1994), and *Mornings Like This* (1995), collections of essays; *Living by Fiction* (1982), literary criticism; *Encounters With Chinese Writers* (1984) and *For the Time Being* (1999), narrative nonfiction; *An American Childhood* (1987), an autobiography; and *The Writing Life* (1989), miscellaneous reflections on writing. Her first novel, *The Living*, was published to critical acclaim in 1992. The following selection is from *An American Childhood*.

Pre-Reading Journal Entry

Use your journal to reminisce about several of your memorable childhood and/or adolescent adventures that involved a confrontation with an adult. Some events may be amusing, while others may be serious. What happened? Who was involved? What was the outcome? Writing quickly, immerse yourself in your memories, recapturing as best you can your thoughts and feelings at the time of the incident.

The Chase

Some boys taught me to play football. This was fine sport. You thought up a new strategy for every play and whispered it to the others. You went out for a pass, fooling everyone. Best, you got to throw yourself mightily at someone's running legs. Either you brought him down or you hit the ground flat out on your chin, with your arms empty before you. It was all or nothing. If you hesitated in fear, you would miss and get hurt: you would take a hard fall while the kid got away, or you would get kicked in the face while the kid got away. But if you flung yourself wholeheartedly at the back of his knees—if you gathered and joined body and soul and pointed them diving fearlessly—then you likely wouldn't get hurt, and you'd stop the ball. Your fate, and your team's score, depended on your concentration and courage. Nothing girls did could compare with it.

Boys welcomed me at baseball, too, for I had, through enthusiastic practice, what was weirdly known as a boy's arm. In winter, in the snow, there was neither baseball or football, so the boys and I threw snowballs at passing cars. I got in trouble throwing snowballs, and have seldom been happier since. 2

On one weekday morning after Christmas, six inches of new snow had just fallen. We were standing up to our boot tops in snow on a front yard on trafficked Reynolds Street, waiting for cars. The cars traveled Reynolds Street slowly and evenly; they were targets all but wrapped in red ribbons, cream puffs. We couldn't miss. 3

I was seven; the boys were eight, nine, and ten. The oldest two Fahey boys were there—Mikey and Peter—polite blond boys who lived near me on Lloyd Street, and who already had four brothers and sisters. My parents approved Mikey and Peter Fahey. Chickie McBride was there, a tough kid, and Billy Paul and Mackie Kean too, from across Reynolds, where the boys grew up dark and furious, grew up skinny, knowing, and skilled. We had all drifted from our houses that morning looking for action, and had found it here on Reynolds Street. 4

It was cloudy but cold. The cars' tires laid behind them on the snowy street a complex trail of beige chunks like crenellated castle walls. I had stepped on some earlier; they squeaked. We could have wished for more traffic. When a car came, we all popped it one. In the intervals between cars we reverted to the natural solitude of children. 5

I started making an iceball—a perfect iceball, from perfectly white snow, perfectly spherical, and squeezed perfectly translucent so no snow remained all the way through. (The Fahey boys and I considered it unfair actually to throw an iceball at somebody, but it had been known to happen.) 6

I had just embarked on the iceball project when we heard tire chains come clanking from afar. A black Buick was moving toward us down the street. We all spread out, banged together some regular snowballs, took aim, and, when the Buick drew nigh, fired. 7

A soft snowball hit the driver's windshield right before the driver's face. It made a smashed star with a hump in the middle. 8

Often, of course, we hit our target, but this time, the only time in all of life, the car pulled over and stopped. Its wide black 9 door opened; a man got out of it, running. He didn't even close the car door.

He ran after us, and we ran away from him, up the snowy   10
Reynolds sidewalk. At the corner, I looked back; incredibly, he was still after us. He was in city clothes: a suit and tie, street shoes. Any normal adult would have quit, having sprung us into flight and made his point. This man was gaining on us. He was a thin man, all action. All of a sudden, we were running for our lives.

Wordless, we split up. We were on our turf; we could lose our-   11
selves in the neighborhood backyards, everyone for himself. I paused and considered. Everyone had vanished except Mikey Fahey, who was just rounding the corner of a yellow brick house. Poor Mikey, I trailed him. The driver of the Buick sensibly picked the two of us to follow. The man apparently had all day.

He chased Mikey and me around the yellow house and up a   12
backyard path we knew by heart: under a low tree, up a bank, through a hedge, down some snowy steps, and across the grocery store's delivery driveway. We smashed through a gap in another hedge, entered a scruffy backyard and ran around its back porch and tight between houses to Edgerton Avenue; we ran across Edgerton to an alley and up our own sliding woodpile to the Halls' front yard; he kept coming. We ran up Lloyd Street and wound through mazy backyards toward the steep hilltop at Willard and Lang.

He chased us silently, block after block. He chased us silently   13
over picket fences, through thorny hedges, between houses, around garbage cans, and across streets. Every time I glanced back, choking for breath, I expected he would have quit. He must have been as breathless as we were. His jacket strained over his body. It was an immense discovery, pounding into my hot head with every sliding, joyous step, that this ordinary adult evidently knew what I thought only children who trained at football knew: that you have to fling yourself at what you're doing, you have to point yourself, forget yourself, aim, dive.

Mikey and I had nowhere to go, in our own neighborhood or   14
out of it, but away from this man who was chasing us. He impelled us forward; we compelled him to follow our route. The air was cold; every breath tore my throat. We kept running, block after block; we kept improvising, backyard after backyard, running a frantic course and choosing it simultaneously, failing always to find small places or hard places to slow him down, and discovering always, exhilarated,

dismayed, that only bare speed could save us—for he would never give up, this man—and we were losing speed.

He chased us through the backyard labyrinths of ten blocks before he caught us by our jackets. He caught us and we all stopped.   15

We three stood staggering, half blinded, coughing, in an   16
obscure hilltop backyard: a man in his twenties, a boy, a girl. He had released our jackets, our pursuer, our captor, our hero: he knew we weren't going anywhere. We all played by the rules. Mikey and I unzipped our jackets. I pulled off my sopping mittens. Our tracks multiplied in the backyard's new snow. We had been breaking new snow all morning. We didn't look at each other. I was cherishing my excitement. The man's lower pants legs were wet; his cuffs were full of snow, and there was a prow of snow beneath them on his shoes and socks. Some trees bordered the little flat backyard, some messy winter trees. There was no one around: a clearing in a grove, and we the only players.

It was a long time before he could speak. I had some difficulty   17
at first, recalling why we were there. My lips felt swollen; I couldn't see out of the sides of my eyes; I kept coughing.

"You stupid kids," he began perfunctorily.   18

We listened perfunctorily indeed, if we listened at all, for the   19
chewing out was redundant, a mere formality, and beside the point. The point was that he had chased us passionately without giving up, and so he had caught us. Now he came down to earth. I wanted the glory to last forever.

But how could the glory have lasted forever? We could have run   20
through every backyard in North America until we got to Panama. But when he trapped us at the lip of the Panama Canal, what precisely could he have done to prolong the drama of the chase and cap its glory? I brooded about this for the next few years. He could only have fried Mikey Fahey and me in boiling oil, say, or dismembered us piecemeal, or staked us to anthills. None of which I really wanted, and none of which any adult was likely to do, even in the spirit of fun. He could only chew us out there in the Panamanian jungle, after months or years of exalting pursuit. He could only begin, "You stupid kids," and continue in his ordinary Pittsburgh accent with his normal righteous anger and the usual common sense.

If in that snowy backyard the driver of the black Buick had cut   21
off our heads, Mikey's and mine, I would have died happy, for nothing has required so much of me since as being chased all over

Pittsburgh in the middle of winter—running terrified, exhausted—by this sainted, skinny, furious redheaded man who wished to have a word with us. I don't know how he found his way back to his car.

Questions for Close Reading

1. What is the selection's thesis (or narrative point)? Locate the sentence(s) in which Dillard states her main idea. If Dillard doesn't state the thesis explicitly, express it in your own words.
2. In the first paragraph, Dillard describes football as a "fine sport." Which aspects of the sport does she refer to when illustrating her point? Which aspect is most important? Why?
3. Why was the driver's decision to follow Dillard and Mikey "sensible"?
4. Dillard dubs her pursuer "our hero" (paragraph 16) and says he was "sainted" (21). What is it about the man that merits these words of praise?
5. Refer to your dictionary as needed to define the following words used in the selection: *crenellated* (paragraph 5), *spherical* (6), *translucent* (6), *embarked* (7), *simultaneously* (14), *dismayed* (14), *labyrinths* (15), *prow* (16), *perfunctorily* (18), and *redundant* (19).

Questions About the Writer's Craft

1. **The pattern.** Dillard draws upon sensory details, play-by-play action, varied sentence length, and repetition to create a narrative filled with drama and suspense. Locate examples of each of these techniques and explain how the strategy keeps readers on the edge of their seats.
2. What key word does Dillard repeat in paragraph 6? Why do you suppose she repeats this word? What is the effect?
3. **Other patterns.** In paragraphs 12 and 13, Dillard provides a number of spatial signals to help readers track the path she and Mikey followed. Identify the signals and comment on their effectiveness.
4. There is only one place in the essay where someone actually speaks. Locate this instance of dialogue. Why do you think Dillard chose to include only this one piece of dialogue?

Writing Assignments Using Narration as a Pattern of Development

1. The chase tested Dillard—and she rose to the challenge. In a narrative of your own, write about a challenge that you responded to in a way that made you feel proud. Perhaps you triumphed over a serious illness, succeeded in a difficult sporting event, or worked hard not to lash out verbally at someone who had hurt you. Like Dillard, use vivid narrative

details to convey how you reacted and why you felt good about your reaction.

2. Like Dillard, most of us—at some point in our lives—have done something that crossed traditional gender lines. If you're female, you might have built some bookshelves. If you're male, you might have prepared a special dinner for friends. Write an essay about a time you engaged in what might be considered a "gender-bending" activity. Where appropriate, use sensory details and dialogue to convey how you and others felt about what you did. Before writing, you may want to read one or more of the following essays exploring gender-based behaviors: Barbara Ehrenreich's "What I've Learned From Men" (page 196), Deborah Tannen's "But What Do You Mean?" (page 241), and Dave Barry's "The Ugly Truth About Beauty" (page 323).

Writing Assignments Using Other Patterns of Development

3. Dillard believes that there are times we should "fling" ourselves at an experience and "dive" in with abandon. In an essay, argue the opposing point of view. Defend the position that there are times in life when a measured, thoughtful response is called for even though the common tendency is to act impulsively. Select convincing examples to support your position, showing how a more spontaneous approach could be harmful or counterproductive.

4. At one time or another, all children do things they shouldn't. Focus on *one* negative thing that children do in the classroom, at home, or in a public place, and write an essay showing that adults' typical response to the behavior is far from effective. Contrast adults' usual response with what you think adults should do to handle the problem behavior more effectively. Before writing, you might consider investigating your topic in the library and/or on the Internet.

Writing Assignments Using a Journal Entry as a Starting Point

5. Reread your pre-reading journal entry, and choose the *one* memory that conveys most dramatically a collision between the world of children (or adolescents) and the world of adults. Write an essay about this event. Make the conflict real and immediate by providing rich sensory details about the place and people involved. Reveal, either implicitly or explicitly, your current perspective on the event. Before you begin writing, read Langston Hughes's "Salvation" (page 148) for inspiration in depicting this clash between child and adult worlds.

Langston Hughes

One of the foremost members of the 1920s literary movement known as the Harlem Renaissance, Langston Hughes (1902–67) committed himself to portraying the richness of Black life in the United States. A poet and a writer of short stories, Hughes was greatly influenced by the rhythms of blues and jazz. In his later years, he published two autobiographical works, *The Big Sea* (1940) and *I Wonder as I Wander* (1956), and he wrote a history of the National Association for the Advancement of Colored People (NAACP). The following selection is from *The Big Sea*.

Pre-Reading Journal Entry

Young people often feel pressured by family and community to adopt certain values, beliefs, or traditions. In your journal, reflect on some of the pressures that you've experienced. What was your response to these pressures? What have been the consequences of your response? Do you think your experience with these family or community pressures was unique or fairly common?

Salvation

I was saved from sin when I was going on thirteen. But not really saved. It happened like this. There was a big revival at my Auntie Reed's church. Every night for weeks there had been much preaching, singing, praying, and shouting, and some very hardened sinners had been brought to Christ, and the membership of the church had grown by leaps and bounds. Then just before the revival ended, they held a special meeting for children, "to bring the young lambs to the fold." My aunt spoke of it for days ahead. That night I was escorted to the front row and placed on the mourners' bench with all the other young sinners, who had not yet been brought to Jesus.

My aunt told me that when you were saved you saw a light, and something happened to you inside! And Jesus came into your life! And God was with you from then on! She said you could see and hear and feel Jesus in your soul. I believed her. I had heard a great many old people say the same thing and it seemed to me they ought

1

2

to know. So I sat there calmly in the hot, crowded church, waiting
for Jesus to come to me.

The preacher preached a wonderful rhythmical sermon, all   3
moans and shouts and lonely cries and dire pictures of hell, and then
he sang a song about the ninety and nine safe in the fold, but one
little lamb was left out in the cold. Then he said: "Won't you come?
Won't you come to Jesus? Young lambs, won't you come?" And he
held out his arms to all us young sinners there on the mourners'
bench. And the little girls cried. And some of them jumped up and
went to Jesus right away. But most of us just sat there.

A great many older people came and knelt around us and   4
prayed, old women with jet-black faces and braided hair, old men
with work-gnarled hands. And the church sang a song about the
lower lights are burning, some poor sinners to be saved. And the
whole building rocked with prayer and song.

Still I kept waiting to *see* Jesus.   5

Finally all the young people had gone to the altar and were   6
saved, but one boy and me. He was a rounder's son named Westley.
Westley and I were surrounded by sisters and deacons praying. It
was very hot in the church, and getting late now. Finally Westley
said to me in a whisper: "God damn! I'm tired o' sitting here. Let's
get up and be saved." So he got up and was saved.

Then I was left all alone on the mourners' bench. My aunt came   7
and knelt at my knees and cried, while prayers and songs swirled all
around me in the little church. The whole congregation prayed for
me alone, in a mighty wail of moans and voices. And I kept waiting
serenely for Jesus, waiting, waiting—but he didn't come. I wanted
to see him, but nothing happened to me. Nothing! I wanted something to happen to me, but nothing happened.

I heard the songs and the minister saying: "Why don't you   8
come? My dear child, why don't you come to Jesus? Jesus is waiting
for you. He wants you. Why don't you come? Sister Reed, what is
this child's name?"

"Langston," my aunt sobbed.   9

"Langston, why don't you come? Why don't you come and be   10
saved? Oh, Lamb of God! Why don't you come?"

Now it was really getting late. I began to be ashamed of myself,   11
holding everything up so long. I began to wonder what God thought
about Westley, who certainly hadn't seen Jesus either, but who was
now sitting proudly on the platform, swinging his knickerbockered

legs and grinning down at me, surrounded by deacons and old women on their knees praying. God had not struck Westley dead for taking his name in vain or for lying in the temple. So I decided that maybe to save further trouble, I'd better lie, too, and say that Jesus had come, and get up and be saved.

So I got up.   12

Suddenly the whole room broke into a sea of shouting, as they   13
saw me rise. Waves of rejoicing swept the place. Women leaped in the air. My aunt threw her arms around me. The minister took me by the hand and led me to the platform.

When things quieted down, in a hushed silence, punctuated by   14
a few ecstatic "Amens," all the new young lambs were blessed in the name of God. Then joyous singing filled the room.

That night, for the last time in my life but one—for I was a big   15
boy twelve years old—I cried. I cried, in bed alone, and couldn't stop. I buried my head under the quilts, but my aunt heard me. She woke up and told my uncle I was crying because the Holy Ghost had come into my life, and because I had seen Jesus. But I was really crying because I couldn't bear to tell her that I had lied, that I had deceived everybody in the church, and I hadn't seen Jesus, and that now I didn't believe there was a Jesus any more, since he didn't come to help me.

Questions for Close Reading

1. What is the selection's thesis (or narrative point)? Locate the sentence(s) in which Hughes states his main idea. If Hughes doesn't state the thesis explicitly, express it in your own words.
2. During the revival meeting, what pressures are put on the young Langston to get up and be saved?
3. How does Westley's attitude differ from Hughes's?
4. Does the narrator's Auntie Reed really understand him? Why can't he tell her the truth about his experience in the church?
5. Refer to your dictionary as needed to define the following words used in the selection: *revival* (paragraph 1), *knickerbockered* (11), *punctuated* (14), and *ecstatic* (14).

Questions About the Writer's Craft

1. **The pattern.** A narrative's power can often be traced to a conflict within the event being recounted. What conflict does the narrator of "Salvation" experience? How does Hughes create tension about this conflict?

2. What key role does Westley serve in the resolution of the narrator's dilemma? How does Hughes's inclusion of Westley in the story help us to understand the narrator better?

3. **Other Patterns.** The thirteenth paragraph presents a metaphor of the church as an ocean. What images develop this metaphor? What does the metaphor tell us about Hughes's feelings and those of the church people?

4. The singing of hymns is a major part of this religious service. Why do you think Hughes has the narrator reveal the subjects and even the lyrics of some of the hymns?

Writing Assignments Using Narration as a Pattern of Development

1. Like Hughes, we sometimes believe that deception is our best alternative. Write a narrative about a time you felt deception was the best way either to protect those you care about or to maintain the respect of those important to you.

2. Write a narrative essay about a chain of events that caused you to become disillusioned about a person or institution you had previously regarded highly. Begin as Hughes does by presenting your initial beliefs. Relate the sequence of events that changed your evaluation of the person or organization. In the conclusion, explain the short- and long-term effects of the incident. For more accounts of childhood disillusionment, read Sophronia Liu's "So Tsi-Fai" (page 153) and Beth Johnson's "Bombs Bursting in Air" (page 189).

Writing Assignments Using Other Patterns of Development

3. Hughes writes, "My aunt told me that when you were saved, you saw a light, and something happened to you inside! And Jesus came into your life!" What causes people to change their beliefs? Do such changes come from waiting calmly, as Hughes tried to do in church, or must they come from a more active process? Write an essay explaining your viewpoint. You may use process analysis, causal analysis, or some other organizational pattern to develop your thesis. Be sure to include specific examples to support your understanding of the way beliefs change.

4. Write a persuasive essay arguing either that lying is sometimes right or that lying is always wrong. Apply your thesis to particular situations and show how lying is or is not the right course of action. Remember to acknowledge the opposing viewpoint. William Lutz's "Doublespeak" (page 224) and Lewis Thomas's "The Lie Detector" (page 354) may help you define your position. You might even mention these authors' perspectives in your essay.

Writing Assignments Using a Journal Entry as a Starting Point

5. Review your pre-reading journal entry, and select *one* family or community pressure with which you've had to contend. Then write an essay examining the effect that this pressure has had on you. Refer to your journal as you prepare to explain the values, beliefs, or traditions that you were expected to adopt. Discuss your response to this pressure and how your reaction has affected you.

Sophronia Liu

In 1973, at the age of twenty, Sophronia Liu came to the United States from her native Hong Kong. She earned a bachelor's degree in English and French and a master's degree in English from the University of South Dakota. She now makes her home in the Minneapolis-St. Paul area, where she is active as an organizer and educational consultant within the Asian-American community. An actress as well as a writer, Liu is a founding member of The Asian American Renaissance, a grassroots organization dedicated to building the Asian-American community through the arts. For her community work, she received a Governor's Award from the State of Minnesota. Liu's writing has appeared in *Colors Magazine, Making More Waves, Asian American Renaissance Journal,* and other publications. Currently, she is completing a memoir and her first full-length play, based on her family's stories. Initially written in response to a class assignment, the selection below was published in the feminist journal *Hurricane Alice* in 1986.

Pre-Reading Journal Entry

Think of at least two times in your childhood or adolescence when you witnessed—as an observer, participant, or victim—someone being bullied. In each case, reflect, in your journal, on these questions: What do you think made the person a target for bullying? Who were the offenders? What do you think provoked the bullying? What impact did this incident have on the people involved?

So Tsi-Fai

Voices, images, scenes from the past—twenty-three years ago,   1
when I was in sixth grade:

"Let us bow our heads in silent prayer for the soul of So Tsi-fai.   2
Let us pray for God's forgiveness for this boy's rash taking of his
own life . . ." Sister Marie (Mung Gu-liang). My sixth-grade English
teacher. Missionary nun from Paris. Principal of The Little Flower's
School. Disciplinarian, perfectionist, authority figure: awesome and
awful in my ten-year-old eyes.

"I don't need any supper. I have drunk enough insecticide." So   3
Tsi-fai. My fourteen-year-old classmate. Daredevil; good-for-noth-
ing lazybones (according to Mung Gu-liang). Bright black eyes,
disheveled hair, defiant sneer, creased and greasy uniform, dirty
hands, careless walk, shuffling feet. Standing in the corner for being
late, for forgetting his homework, for talking in class, for using foul
language. ("Shame on you! Go wash your mouth with soap!" Mung
Gu-liang's sharp command. He did, and came back with a grin.) So
Tsi-fai: Sticking his tongue out behind Mung Gu-liang's back, passing secret notes to his friends, kept behind after school, sent to the
Principal's office for repeated offenses. So Tsi-fai: incorrigible, hopeless, and without hope.

It was a Monday in late November when we heard of his death,   4
returning to school after the weekend with our parents' signatures
on our midterm reports. So Tsi-fai also showed his report to his
father, we were told later. He flunked three out of the fourteen subjects: English Grammar, Arithmetic, and Chinese Dictation. He
missed each one by one to three marks. That wasn't so bad. But he
was a hopeless case. Overaged, stubborn, and uncooperative; a
repeated offender of school rules, scourge of all teachers; who was
going to give him a lenient passing grade? Besides, being a few
months over the maximum age—fourteen—for sixth graders, he
wasn't even allowed to sit for the Secondary School Entrance Exam.

All sixth graders in Hong Kong had to pass the SSE before they   5
could obtain a seat in secondary school. In 1964 when I took the
exam, there were more than twenty thousand candidates. About
seven thousand of us passed: four thousand were sent to government and subsidized schools, the other three thousand to private
and grant-in-aid schools. I came in around no. 2000; I was lucky.
Without the public exam, there would be no secondary school for
So Tsi-fai. His future was sealed.

Looking at the report card with three red marks on it, his father   6
was furious. So Tsi-fai was the oldest son. There were three younger
children. His father was a vegetable farmer with a few plots of land
in Wong Juk-hang, by the sea. His mother worked in a local factory. So Tsi-fai helped in the fields, cooked for the family, and washed
his own clothes. ("Filthy, dirty boy!" gasped Mung Gu-liang.
"Grime behind the ears, black rims on the fingernails, dirty collar,
crumpled shirt. Why doesn't your mother iron your shirt?") Both
his parents were illiterate. So Tsi-fai was their biggest hope: He
made it to the sixth grade.

Who woke him up for school every morning and had breakfast 7
waiting for him? Nobody. ("Time for school! Get up! Eat your
rice!" Ma nagged and screamed. The aroma of steamed rice and
Chinese sausages spread all over the house. "Drink your tea! Eat
your oranges! Wash your face! And remember to wash behind your
ears!") And who helped So Tsi-fai do his homework? Nobody. Did
he have older brothers like mine who knew all about the arithmetic
of rowing a boat against the currents or with the currents, how to
count the feet of chickens and rabbits in the same cage, the present
perfect continuous tense of "to live" and the future perfect tense of
"to succeed"? None. Nil. So Tsi-fai was a lost cause.

I came in first in both terms that year, the star pupil. So Tsi-fai was 8
one of the last in the class: He was lazy; he didn't care. Or did he?

When his father scolded him, So Tsi-fai left the house. When he 9
showed up again, late for supper, he announced, "I don't need any
supper. I have drunk enough insecticide." Just like another one of his
practical jokes. The insecticide was stored in the field for his father's
vegetables. He was rushed to the hospital; dead upon arrival.

"He gulped for a last breath and was gone," an uncle told us at 10
the funeral. "But his eyes wouldn't shut. So I said in his ear, 'You go
now and rest in peace.' And I smoothed my hand over his eyelids.
His face was all purple."

His face was still purple when we saw him in his coffin. Eyes 11
shut tight, nostrils dilated and white as if fire and anger might shoot
out, any minute.

In class that Monday morning, Sister Marie led us in prayer. 12
"Let us pray that God will forgive him for his sins." We said the
Lord's Prayer and the Hail Mary. We bowed our heads. I sat in my
chair, frozen and dazed, thinking of the deadly chill in the morgue,
the smell of disinfectant, ether, and dead flesh.

"Bang!" went a gust of wind, forcing open a leaf of the double 13
door leading to the back balcony. "Flap, flap, flap." The door swung
in the wind. We could see the treetops by the hillside rustling to and
fro against a pale blue sky. An imperceptible presence had drifted in
with the wind. The same careless walk and shuffling feet, the same
daredevil air—except that the eyes were lusterless, dripping blood;
the tongue hanging out, gasping for air. As usual, he was late. But
he had come back to claim his place.

"I died a tragic death," his voice said. "I have as much right as 14
you to be here. This is my seat." We heard him; we knew he was back.

. . . So Tsi-fai: Standing in the corner for being late, for forget-   15
ting his homework, for talking in class, for using foul language. So
Tsi-fai: Palm outstretched, chest sticking out, holding his breath:
"Tat. Tat. Tat." Down came the teacher's wooden ruler, twenty
times on each hand. Never batting an eyelash: then back to facing the
wall in the corner by the door. So Tsi-fai: grimy shirt, disheveled hair,
defiant sneer. So Tsi-fai. Incorrigible, hopeless, and without hope.

The girls in front gasped and shrank back in their chairs. Mung   16
Gu-liang went to the door, held the doorknob in one hand, poked
her head out, and peered into the empty balcony. Then, with a
determined jerk, she pulled the door shut. Quickly crossing herself,
she returned to the teacher's desk. Her black cross swung upon the
front of her gray habit as she hurried across the room. "Don't be
silly!" she scolded the frightened girls in the front row.

What really happened? After all these years, my mind is still   17
haunted by this scene. What happened to So Tsi-fai? What happened
to me? What happened to all of us that year in sixth grade, when we
were green and young and ready to fling our arms out for the world?
All of a sudden, death claimed one of us and he was gone.

Who arbitrates between life and death? Who decides which life   18
is worth preserving and prospering, and which to nip in its bud?
How did it happen that I, at ten, turned out to be the star pupil, the
lucky one, while my friend, a peasant's son, was shoveled under the
heap and lost forever? How could it happen that this world would
close off a young boy's life at fourteen just because he was poor,
undisciplined, and lacked the training and support to pass his exams?
What really happened?

Today, twenty-three years later, So Tsi-fai's ghost still haunts   19
me. "I died a tragic death. I have as much right as you to be here.
This is my seat." The voice I heard twenty-three years ago in my
sixth-grade classroom follows me in my dreams. Is there anything I
can do to lay it to rest?

Questions for Close Reading

1. What is the selection's thesis (or narrative point)? Locate the sentence(s)
in which Liu states her main idea. If she doesn't state the narrative point
explicitly, express it in your own words.
2. What is the immediate cause of So Tsi-fai's suicide? What other factors
also come into play? Why might he have chosen the method to kill himself that he did?

3. How did Liu's home life compare to that of So Tsi-fai? What connections do you see between each one's family life and academic progress?
4. What does So Tsi-fai say when he returns as a ghost? What do his words indicate about his perception of the educational system—and of his place in it?
5. Refer to your dictionary as needed to define the following words used in the selection: *defiant* (paragraph 3), *incorrigible* (3), *scourge* (4), *subsidized* (5), *dilated* (11), *ether* (12), *imperceptible* (13), *lusterless* (13), and *arbitrates* (18).

Questions About the Writer's Craft

1. **The pattern.** Most narratives establish a conflict and then move to its resolution. In "So Tsi-Fai," however, the reader knows by paragraph 2 that the boy will commit suicide; flashbacks and flashforwards comprise the rest of the essay. Locate these flashbacks and flashforwards. How does Liu signal these time shifts?
2. Liu describes a number of relationships filled with conflict. Identify as many of these conflicted relationships as you can. How do they heighten the essay's narrative tension?
3. In paragraphs 3, 6, and 7, Liu calls attention to certain conversations by placing quotations in parentheses. How do these parenthetical quotations reinforce the contrast between the different ways the author and So Tsi-fai were treated?
4. Throughout the essay, Liu repeats significant material. For example, she repeats the boy's last words twice (3 and 9) as well as whole passages of description (3 and 15). What effect do you think Liu intended these repetitions to have? How do they support her narrative point?

Writing Assignments Using Narration as a Pattern of Development

1. The death of So Tsi-fai marks the end of the author's childhood, the end of the time when she was "green and young and ready to fling [her] arms out for the world." Write an essay about a time when you were forced to grow up suddenly or were faced with a sobering reality. Your moment of lost innocence might have occurred when you were a child; perhaps you had to cope with illness or divorce. Or your moment of loss may have come when you were an adult; maybe you learned about a relative's unsavory business practices or a respected boss's discriminatory hiring practices. Use vivid description and revealing dialogue to convey the tension and conflict you felt in the moment of discovery. Remember, though, to include only those details that reinforce your narrative point. Before writing, you may want to read Langston Hughes's "Salvation" (page 148) for a powerful depiction of lost innocence.

2. Liu depicts the unfairness of an educational system that penalizes children simply because they are disadvantaged. Brainstorm with others to identify injustices that exist in our educational system. You might, for example, decide that teachers single out males for discipline, that students with learning disabilities get a second-rate education, that student athletes receive preferential treatment at grading time. Focusing on a specific educational level, select *one* such type of unfairness, and write an essay recounting two or three dramatic incidents of this inequity. To depict each incident fully, you'll need to reconstruct conversations and provide vivid narrative details, always keeping in mind the narrative point you want to make.

Writing Assignments Using Other Patterns of Development

3. Liu writes, "After all these years, my mind is still haunted by this scene." All of us have witnessed dramatic events that continue to exert power over us even though they occurred in the past. Write an essay showing the effects of such an event on your life, behavior, attitudes, and values. Begin with a brief account of the event; then explain its consequences for you, making sure your discussion honors the inevitable complexity of cause-effect relationships.

4. Liu's teacher clearly has no concern for her students' self-esteem, a factor that many consider crucial to children's well-being and success. Brainstorm with others to identify as many strategies as possible that elementary school teachers could use to strengthen students' self-image. Select what you consider to be the most compelling strategies, and categorize them into types, such as "group work," "independent study," "leadership experiences," "teacher-student conferences," and so on. Then write an essay explaining the techniques and their value. Be sure to illustrate the strategies with specific examples drawn from your own and other people's experiences. Maya Angelou's "Sister Flowers" (page 106) and Mary Sherry's "In Praise of the 'F' Word" (page 440) will provide insight into the development of a healthy self-esteem.

Writing Assignments Using a Journal Entry as a Starting Point

5. Review your pre-reading journal entry, and select the most dramatic instance of bullying you witnessed as a child or adolescent. Then write an essay in which you analyze the causes and effects of the bullying incident. At the end of the essay, suggest ways that the bullying might have been prevented. To deepen your understanding of the bullying phenomenon, consider doing some research in the library and/or on the Internet.

Additional Writing Topics

NARRATION

General Assignments

Prepare an essay on any of the following topics, using narration as the paper's dominant method of development. Be sure to select details that advance the essay's narrative purpose; you may even want to experiment with flashback or flashforward. In any case, keep the sequence of events clear by using transitional cues. Within the limited time span covered, use vigorous details and varied sentence structure to enliven the narrative. Tell the story from a consistent point of view.

1. An emergency that brought out the best or worst in you
2. The hazards of taking children out to eat
3. An incident that made you believe in fate
4. Your best or worst day at school or work
5. A major decision
6. An encounter with a machine
7. An important learning experience
8. A narrow escape
9. Your first date, first day on the job, or first anything
10. A memorable childhood experience
11. A fairy tale the way you would like to hear it told
12. A painful moment
13. An incredible but true story
14. A significant family event
15. An experience in which a certain emotion (pride, anger, regret, or some other) was dominant

Assignments With a Specific Purpose and Audience

1. As the fund-raiser for a particular organization (for example, Red Cross, SPCA, Big Brothers/Big Sisters), you're sending a newsletter to contributors. Support your cause by telling the story of a time when your organization made all the difference—the blood donation that saved a life, the animal that was rescued from abuse, and so on.
2. A friend of yours has seen someone cheat on a test, shoplift, or violate an employer's trust. In a letter, convince this friend to inform the instructor, store owner, or employer by narrating an incident in which a witness did (or did not) speak up in such a situation. Tell what happened as a result.

3. You have had a disturbing encounter with one of the people who seem to have "fallen through the cracks" of society—a street person, an unwanted child, or anyone else who is alone and abandoned. Write a letter to the local newspaper describing this encounter. Your purpose is to arouse people's indignation and compassion and to get help for such unfortunates.

4. Write an article for your old high school newspaper. The article will be read primarily by seniors who are planning to go away to college next year. In the article, narrate a story that points to some truth about the "breaking away" stage of life.

5. A close friend has written a letter to you telling about a bad experience that he or she had with a teacher, employer, doctor, repairperson, or some other professional. On the basis of that single experience, your friend now negatively stereotypes the entire profession. Write a letter to your friend balancing his or her cynical picture by narrating a story that shows the "flip side" of this profession—someone who made every effort to help.

6. Your younger brother, sister, relative, or neighborhood friend can't wait to be your age. By narrating an appropriate story, show the young person that your age isn't as wonderful as he or she thinks. Be sure to select a story that the person can understand and appreciate.

5

EXEMPLIFICATION

WHAT IS EXEMPLIFICATION?

If someone asked you, "Have you been to any good restaurants lately?" you probably wouldn't answer "Yes" and then immediately change the subject. Most likely, you would go on to illustrate with *examples*. Perhaps you'd give the names of restaurants you've enjoyed and talk briefly about the specific things you liked: the attractive prices, the tasty main courses, the pleasant service, the tempting desserts. Such examples and details are needed to convince others that your opinion—in this or any matter—is valid. Similarly, when you talk about larger and more important issues, people won't pay much attention to your opinion if all you do is string together vague generalizations: "We have to do something about acid rain. It's had disastrous consequences for the environment. Its negative effects increase every year. Action must be taken to control the problem." To be taken seriously and to convince others that your point is well-founded, you must provide specific supporting examples: "The forests in the Adirondacks are dying"; "Yesterday's rainfall was fifty times more acidic than normal"; "Pine Lake, in the northern part of the state, was once a great fishing spot but now has no fish population."

Examples are equally important when you write an essay. It's not fuzzy generalities and highfalutin abstractions that make writing impressive. Just the opposite is true. Facts, anecdotes, statistics, details, opinions, and observations are at the heart of effective writing, giving your work substance and solidity.

HOW EXEMPLIFICATION FITS
YOUR PURPOSE AND AUDIENCE

The wording of assignments and essay exam questions may signal the need for specific examples:

> Soap operas, whether shown during the day or in the evening, are among the most popular television programs. Why do you think this is so? Provide specific examples to support your position.

> Some observers claim that college students are less interested in learning than in getting ahead in their careers. Cite evidence to support or refute this claim.

> A growing number of people feel that parents should not allow young children to participate in highly competitive team sports. Basing your conclusion on your own experiences and observations, indicate whether you think this point of view is reasonable.

Such phrases as "Provide specific examples," "Cite evidence," and "Basing your conclusion on your own experiences and observations" signal that each essay would be developed through examples.

Usually, though, you won't be told so explicitly to provide examples. Instead, as you think about the best way to achieve your essay's purpose, you'll see the need for illustrative details—no matter which patterns of development you use. For instance, to *persuade* skeptical readers that the country needs a national health system, you might mention specific cases to dramatize the inadequacy of our current health-care system: a family bankrupted by medical bills; an uninsured accident victim turned away by a hospital; a chronically ill person rapidly deteriorating because he didn't have enough money to visit a doctor. Or imagine a lightly satiric piece that pokes fun at cat lovers. Insisting that "cat people" are pretty strange creatures, you might make your point—and make readers chuckle—with a series of examples *contrasting* cat lovers and dog lovers: the qualities admired by each group (loyalty in dogs versus independence in cats) and the different expectations each group has for its pets (dog lovers want Fido to be obedient and lovable, whereas cat lovers are satisfied with Felix's occasional spurts of docility and affection). Similarly, you would supply examples in a *causal analysis* speculating on the likely impact of a proposed tuition hike at your college. To convince the college administration of the probable negative effects of such a hike, you might cite the following examples: articles reporting a nationwide upswing in student transfers to less expensive schools; statistics indicating a significant drop in grades among already employed students forced to work more hours to pay increased tuition costs; interviews with students too financially strapped to continue their college education.

Whether you use examples as the primary or a supplemental method of development, they serve a number of important purposes. For one thing, examples make writing *interesting*. Assume you're writing an essay showing that television commercials are biased against women. Your essay would be lifeless and boring if all it did was repeat, in a general way, that commercials present stereotyped views of women.

An anti-female bias is rampant in television commercials. It is very much alive, yet most viewers seem to take it all in stride. Few people protest the obviously sexist characters and statements in such commercials. Surely, these commercials misrepresent the way most of us live.

Without interesting particulars, readers may respond, "Who cares?" But if you provide specific examples, you'll attract your readers' attention:

Sexism is rampant in television commercials. Although millions of women hold responsible jobs outside the home, commercials continue to portray women as simple creatures who spend most of their time thinking about wax buildup, cottony-soft bathroom tissue, and static-free clothes. Men, apparently, have better things to do than fret over such mundane household matters. How many commercials can you recall that depict men proclaiming the virtues of squeaky-clean dishes or sparkling bathrooms? Not many.

Examples also make writing *persuasive*. Most writing conveys a point, but many readers are reluctant to accept someone else's point of view unless evidence demonstrates its validity. Imagine you're writing an essay showing that latchkey children are more self-sufficient and emotionally secure than children who return from school to a home where a parent awaits them. Your thesis is obviously controversial. Without specific examples—from your own experience, personal observations, or research studies—your readers would undoubtedly question your position's validity.

Further, examples *help explain* difficult, abstract, or unusual ideas. Suppose you're assigned an essay on a complex subject such as inflation, zero population growth, or radiation exposure. As a writer, you have a responsibility to your readers to make these difficult concepts concrete and understandable. If writing an essay on radiation exposure in everyday life, you might start by providing specific examples of home appliances that emit radiation—color televisions, computers, and microwave ovens—and tell exactly how much radiation we absorb in a typical day from such equipment. To illustrate further the extent of our radiation exposure, you could also provide specifics about unavoidable sources of natural radiation (the sun, for instance) and details about the widespread use of radiation in medicine (X rays, radiation therapy). These examples would ground your discussion, making it immediate and concrete, preventing it from flying off into the vague and theoretical.

Finally, examples *help prevent unintended ambiguity*. All of us have experienced the frustration of having someone misinterpret what we say. In face-to-face communication, we can provide on-the-spot clarification. In writing, however, instantaneous feedback isn't available, so it's crucial that meaning be as unambiguous as possible. Examples will help.

Assume you're writing an essay asserting that ineffective teaching is on the rise in today's high schools. To clarify what you mean by "ineffective," you provide examples: the instructor who spends so much time disciplining unruly students that he never gets around to teaching; the moonlighting teacher who is so tired in class that she regularly takes naps during tests; and the teacher who accepts obviously plagiarized reports because he's grateful that students hand in something. Without such concrete examples, your readers will supply their own ideas—and these may not be what you had in mind. Readers might imagine "ineffective" to mean harsh and punitive, whereas your concrete examples would show that you intend it to mean out of control and irresponsible. Such specifics help prevent misunderstanding.

SUGGESTIONS FOR USING EXEMPLIFICATION IN AN ESSAY

The following suggestions will be helpful whether you use examples as a dominant or a supportive pattern of development.

1. Generate examples. Where do you get the examples to develop your essay? The first batch of examples is generated during the prewriting stage. With your purpose and thesis in mind, you make a broad sweep for examples, using brainstorming, freewriting, the mapping technique—whichever prewriting technique you prefer. During this preliminary search for examples, you may also read through your journal for relevant specifics, interview other people, or conduct library research.

Examples can take several forms, including specific names (of people, places, products, and so on), anecdotes, personal observations, expert opinion, as well as facts, statistics, and case studies gathered through research. While prewriting, try to generate more examples than you think you'll need. Starting with abundance—and then picking out the strongest examples—will give you a firm base on which to build the essay. If you have a great deal of trouble finding examples to support your thesis, you may need to revise the thesis; you may be trying to support an idea that has little validity. On the other hand, while prewriting, you may unearth numerous examples but find that many of them contradict the point you started out to support. If that happens, don't hesitate to recast your central point, always remembering that your thesis and examples must fit.

2. Select the examples to include. Once you've used prewriting to generate as many examples as possible, you're ready to limit your examples to the strongest ones. Keeping your purpose, thesis, and audience in mind, ask yourself several key questions: "Which examples support my thesis? Which do not? Which are most convincing? Which are most likely to interest readers and clarify meaning?"

You may include several brief examples within a single sentence:

The French people's fascination with some American literary figures, such as Poe and Hawthorne, is understandable, but their great respect for "artists" like comedian Jerry Lewis is a mystery.

Or you may develop a paragraph with a number of "for instances":

> A uniquely American style of movie-acting reached its peak in the 1950s. Certain charismatic actors completely abandoned the stage techniques and tradition that had been the foundation of acting up to that time. Instead of articulating their lines clearly, the actors mumbled; instead of making firm eye contact with their colleagues, they hung their heads, shifted their eyes, even talked with their eyes closed. Marlon Brando, Montgomery Clift, and James Dean were three actors who exemplified this new trend.

As the preceding paragraph shows, *several examples* are usually needed to make a point. An essay with the thesis "Rock videos are dangerously violent" wouldn't be convincing if you gave only one example of a violent rock video. Several strong examples would be needed for readers to feel you had illustrated your point sufficiently.

As a general rule, you should strive for variety in the kinds of examples you include. For instance, you might choose a *personal-experience example* drawn from your own life or from the life of someone you know. Such examples pack the wallop of personal authority and lend drama to writing. Or you might include a *typical-case example,* an actual event or situation that did occur—but not to you or to anyone you know. (Perhaps you learned about the event through a magazine article, newspaper account, or television report.) The objective nature of such cases makes them especially convincing. You might also include a speculative or *hypothetical example* ("Imagine how difficult it must be for an elderly person to carry bags of groceries from the market to a bus stop several blocks away"). You'll find that hypothetical cases are effective for clarifying and dramatizing key points, but be sure to acknowledge that the example is indeed invented (*"Suppose* that . . ." or "Let's for a moment *assume* that . . ."). Make certain, too, that the invented situation is easily imagined and could conceivably happen. Finally, you might create a *generalized example*—one that is a composite of the typical or usual. Such generalized examples are often signaled by words that involve the reader (*"All of us,* at one time or another, have been driven to distraction by a trivial annoyance like the buzzing of a fly or the sting of a paper cut"), or they may refer to humanity in general ("When *most people* get a compliment, they perk up, preen, and think the praise-giver is blessed with astute powers of observation").

Occasionally, *one extended example,* fully developed with many details, can support an essay. It might be possible, for instance, to support the thesis "Federal legislation should raise the legal drinking age to twenty-one" with a single compelling, highly detailed example of the effects of one teenager's drunken-driving spree.

The examples you choose must also be *relevant;* that is, they must have direct bearing on the point you want to make. You would have a hard time convincing readers that Americans have callous attitudes toward the elderly if you described the wide range of new programs, all staffed by volunteers, at a well-financed center for senior citizens. Because these examples *contradict,* rather than support, your thesis, readers are apt to dismiss what you have to say.

Make certain, too, that your examples are *accurate.* Exercise special caution when using statistics. An old saying warns that there are lies, damned lies, and statistics—meaning that statistics can be misleading. A commercial may claim, "In a taste test, 80 percent of those questioned indicated that they preferred Fizzy Cola." Impressed? Don't be—at least, not until you find out how the test was conducted. Perhaps the subjects had to choose between Fizzy Cola and battery acid, or perhaps there were only five subjects, all Fizzy Cola vice presidents.

Finally, select *representative* examples. Picking the oddball, one-in-a-million example to support a point—and passing it off as typical—is dishonest. Consider an essay with the thesis "Part-time jobs contribute to academic success." Citing only one example of a student who works at a job twenty-five hours a week while earning straight A's isn't playing fair. Why not? You've made a *hasty generalization* based on only one case. To be convincing, you need to show how holding down a job affects *most* students' academic performance. (For more on hasty generalizations, see page 417.)

3. Develop your examples sufficiently.   To ensure that you get your ideas across, your examples must be *specific.* An essay on the types of heroes in American movies wouldn't succeed if you simply strung together a series of undeveloped examples in paragraphs like this one:

> Heroes in American movies usually fall into types. One kind of hero is the tight-lipped loner, men like Clint Eastwood and Humphrey Bogart. Another movie hero is the quiet, shy, or fumbling type who has appeared in movies since the beginning. The main characteristic of

this hero is lovableness, as seen in actors like Jimmy Stewart. Perhaps the most one-dimensional and predictable hero is the superman who battles tough odds. This kind of hero is best illustrated by Sylvester Stallone as Rocky and Rambo.

If you developed the essay in this way—if you moved from one undeveloped example to another—you would be doing little more than making a list. To be effective, key examples must be expanded in sufficient detail. The examples in the preceding paragraph could be developed in paragraphs of their own. You could, for instance, develop the first example this way:

Heroes can be tight-lipped loners who appear out of nowhere, form no permanent attachments, and walk, drive, or ride off into the sunset. In many of his Westerns, from the low-budget "spaghetti Westerns" of the 1960s to Unforgiven in 1992, Clint Eastwood personifies this kind of hero. He is remote, mysterious, and untalkative. Yet he guns down an evil sheriff, runs other villains out of town, and helps a handicapped girl--acts that cement his heroic status. The loner might also be Sam Spade as played by Humphrey Bogart. Spade solves the crime and sends the guilty off to jail, yet he holds his emotions in check and has no permanent ties beyond his faithful secretary and shabby office. One gets the feeling that he could walk away from these, too, if necessary. Even in The Right Stuff, an account of the United States's early astronauts, the scriptwriters mold Chuck Yeager, the man who broke the sound barrier, into a classic loner. Yeager, portrayed by the aloof Sam Shepard, has a wife, but he is nevertheless insular. Taking mute pride in his ability to distance himself from politicians, bureaucrats, even colleagues, he soars into space, dignified and detached.

(For hints on ways to make writing specific, see pages 40–41.)

4. Organize the examples. If, as is usually the case, several examples support your point, be sure that you present the examples in an *organized* manner. Often you'll find that other patterns of development (cause-effect, comparison-contrast, definition, and so on) suggest ways to sequence examples. Let's say you're writing an essay showing that stay-at-home vacations offer numerous opportunities to relax. You might begin the essay with examples that *contrast* stay-at-home and get-away vacations. Then you might move to a *process analysis* that illustrates different techniques for unwinding at home.

The essay might end with examples showing the *effect* of such leisurely at-home breaks.

Finally, you need to select an *organizational approach consistent* with your *purpose* and *thesis*. Imagine you're writing an essay about students' adjustment during the first months of college. The supporting examples could be arranged *chronologically*. You might start by illustrating the ambivalence many students feel the first day of college when their parents leave for home; you might then offer an anecdote or two about students' frequent calls to Mom and Dad during the opening weeks of the semester; the essay might close with an account of students' reluctance to leave campus at the midyear break.

Similarly, an essay demonstrating that a room often reflects the character of its occupant might be organized *spatially:* from the empty soda cans on the floor to the spitballs on the ceiling. In an essay illustrating the kinds of skills taught in a composition course, you might move from *simple* to *complex* examples: starting with relatively matter-of-fact skills such as spelling and punctuation and ending with more conceptually difficult skills such as formulating a thesis and organizing an essay. Last, the *emphatic sequence*—in which you lead from your first example to your final, most significant one—is another effective way to organize an essay with many examples. A paper about Americans' characteristic impatience might progress from minor examples (dependence on fast food, obsession with ever faster mail delivery) to more disturbing manifestations of impatience (using drugs as quick solutions to problems, advocating simple answers to complex international problems: "Bomb them!").

5. Choose a point of view. Many essays developed by illustration place the subject in the foreground and the writer in the background. Such an approach calls for the *third-person point of view*. For example, even if you draw examples from your own personal experience, you can present them without using the *first-person* "I." You might convert such personal material into generalized examples (see page 166), or you might describe the personal experience as if it happened to someone else. Of course, you may use the first person if the use of "I" will make the example more believable and dramatic. But remember: Just because an event happened to you personally doesn't mean you have to use the first-person point of view.

STUDENT ESSAY

The following student essay was written by Michael Pagano in response to this assignment:

> In "The 'Values' Wasteland," Charles Sykes contends that the American educational system fails to provide students with firm guidelines for making moral choices. In an essay of your own, critique another aspect of American society, using—as Sykes does—numerous compelling examples to support your viewpoint.

While reading Michael's paper, try to determine how effectively it applies the principles of exemplification. The annotations on Michael's paper and the commentary following it will help you look at the essay more closely.

Pursuit of Possessions
by Michael Pagano

Introduction   Anne Morrow Lindbergh, a well-known novel-   1
                      ist, essayist, and poet, once wrote that Americans
                      "who could choose simplicity, choose complica-
                      tion." Lindbergh herself was a prime example of this
                      phenomenon. Often in the spotlight as the wife of
                      the famed aviation pioneer Charles Lindbergh, she
                      also negotiated the demands of being a mother as
                      well as a writer. Not surprisingly, Lindbergh sought
                      to simplify her life. In one of her best-known essays,
                      "Channelled Whelk," she describes her escape to a
                      beach cottage, bare except for driftwood and
                      seashells. There she was happy. But few of us
                      Americans would be willing to simplify our lives as
Thesis ───────────   Lindbergh did. Instead, we choose to clutter our
                      lives with a stream of material possessions. And
                      what is the result of this mania for possessions?
Plan of ──────────▶ Much of our time goes to buying new things, deal-
development   ing with the complications they create, and work-
                      ing madly to buy more things or pay for the things
                      we already have.
Topic sentence ────▶ We devote a great deal of our lives to acquiring   2
                      the material goods we imagine are essential to our

The first of three paragraphs in a chronological sequence

well-being. Hours are spent planning and thinking about our future purchases. We window-shop for designer jogging shoes; we leaf through magazines looking at ads for elaborate stereo equipment; we research back issues of Consumer Reports to find out about recent developments in exercise equipment. Moreover, once we find what we are looking for, more time is taken up when we decide to actually buy the items. How do we find this time? That's easy. We turn evenings, weekends, and holidays--time that used to be set aside for family and friends--into shopping expeditions. No wonder family life is deteriorating and children spend so much time in front of television sets. Their parents are seldom around.

Topic sentence ——————►As soon as we take our new purchases home,   3

The second paragraph in the chronological sequence

A paragraph with many specific examples

they begin to complicate our lives. A sleek new sports car has to be washed, waxed, and vacuumed. A fashionable pair of skintight jeans can't be thrown in the washing machine but has to be taken to the dry cleaner. New stereo equipment has to be connected with a tangled network of cables to the TV, radio, and cassette deck. Eventually, of course, the inevitable happens. Our indispensable possessions break down and need to be repaired. The home computer starts to lose data, the microwave has to have its temperature controls adjusted, and the videotape recorder has to be serviced when a cassette becomes jammed in the machine.

Topic sentence ——————► After more time has gone by, we sometimes   4

The third paragraph in the chronological sequence

discover that our purchases don't suit us anymore, and so we decide to replace them. Before making our replacement purchases, though, we have to find ways to get rid of the old items. If we want to replace our black-and-white 19-inch television set with a 25-inch color set, we have to find time to put an ad in the classified section of the paper. Then we have to handle phone calls and set up times people can come to look at the TV. We could store the set in the basement--if we are lucky enough to find a spot that isn't already filled with other discarded

Topic sentence with emphasis signal

purchases.

——————► Worst of all, this mania for possessions often   5
influences our approach to work. It is not unusual for

people to take a second or even a third job to pay off the debt they fall into because they have over-bought. After paying for food, clothing, and shelter, many people see the rest of their paycheck go to Visa, MasterCard, department store charge accounts, and time payments. Panic sets in when they realize there simply is not enough money to cover all their expenses. Just to stay afloat, people may have to work overtime or take on additional jobs.

Conclusion
It is clear that many of us have allowed the pur-   6
suit of possessions to dominate our lives. We are so busy buying, maintaining, and paying for our world-ly goods that we do not have much time to think about what is really important. We should try to step back from our compulsive need for more of every-thing and get in touch with the basic values that are the real point of our lives.

COMMENTARY

Thesis, other patterns of development, and plan of development.   In "Pursuit of Possessions," Michael analyzes the American mania for acquiring material goods. He begins with a quotation from Anne Morrow Lindbergh and briefly explains Lindbergh's strategy for simplifying her life. The reference to Lindbergh gives Michael a chance to *contrast* the way she tried to lead her life with the acquisitive and frenzied way many Americans lead theirs. This contrast leads logically to the essay's *thesis:* "We choose to clutter our lives with a stream of material possessions."

Besides introducing the basic contrast at the heart of the essay, Michael's opening paragraph helps readers see that the essay contains an element of *causal analysis.* Michael asks, "What is the result of this mania for possessions?" and then answers that question in the next sentence. This sentence also serves as the essay's *plan of development* and reveals that Michael feels the pursuit of possessions negatively affects our lives in three key ways.

Essays of this length often don't need a plan of development. But since Michael's paper is filled with many *examples,* the plan of development helps readers see how all the details relate to the essay's central point.

Evidence.   Support for the thesis consists of numerous examples presented in the *first-person-plural point of view* ("*We* choose to clutter our lives . . . ," "*We* devote a great deal of our lives . . . ," and so on). Many of these examples seem drawn from Michael's, his friends', or his family's experiences; however, to emphasize the events' universality, Michael converts these essentially personal examples into generalized ones that "we" all experience.

These examples, in turn, are organized around the three major points signaled by the plan of development. Michael uses one paragraph to develop his first and third points and two paragraphs to develop his second point. Each of the four supporting paragraphs is focused by a *topic sentence* that appears at the start of the paragraph. The transitional phrase "Worst of all" (paragraph 5) signals that Michael has sequenced his major points *emphatically,* saving for last the issue he considers most significant: how the "mania for possessions . . . influences our approach to work."

Organizational strategies.   Emphatic order isn't Michael's only organizational technique. When reading the paper, you probably felt that there was an easy flow from one supporting paragraph to the next. How does Michael achieve such *coherence between paragraphs?* For one thing, he sequences paragraphs 2–4 *chronologically:* what happens before a purchase is made; what happens afterward. Secondly, topic sentences in paragraphs 3 and 4 include *signal devices* that indicate this passage of time. The topic sentences also strengthen coherence by *linking back* to the preceding paragraph: "*As soon as we take our new purchases home,* they . . . complicate our lives" and "*After more time has gone by,* we . . . discover that our purchases don't suit us anymore."

The same organizing strategies are used *within paragraphs* to make the essay coherent. Details in paragraphs 2 through 4 are sequenced chronologically, and to help readers follow the chronology, Michael uses *signal devices: "Moreover, once* we find what we are looking for, more time is taken up . . ." (2); "*Eventually,* of course, the inevitable happens" (3); "*Then* we have to handle phone calls . . ." (4).

Problems with paragraph development.   You probably recall that an essay developed primarily through exemplification must include examples that are *relevant, interesting, convincing, representative, accurate,* and *specific.* On the whole, Michael's examples meet these requirements. The third and fourth paragraphs, especially, include vigorous details that show how our mania for buying things can govern our lives. We may even laugh with self-recognition when reading about "skintight jeans [that] can't be thrown in the washing machine" or a basement "filled with other discarded purchases."

The fifth paragraph, however, is underdeveloped. We know that this paragraph presents what Michael considers his most significant point, but the paragraph's examples are rather *flat* and *unconvincing*. To make this final section more compelling, Michael could mention specific people who overspend, revealing how much they are in debt and how much they have to work to become solvent again. Or he could cite a television documentary or magazine article dealing with the issue of consumer debt. Such specifics would give the paragraph the solidity it now lacks.

Shift in tone.   The fifth paragraph has a second, more subtle problem; *a shift in tone*. Although Michael has, up to this point, been critical of our possession-mad culture, he has poked fun at our obsession and kept his tone conversational and gently satiric. In this paragraph, though, he adopts a serious tone and, in the next paragraph, his tone becomes even weightier, almost preachy. It is, of course, legitimate to have a serious message in a lightly satiric piece. In fact, most satiric writing has such an additional layer of meaning. But because Michael has trouble blending these two moods, there's a jarring shift in the essay.

Shift in focus.   The second paragraph shows another kind of shift—in *focus*. The paragraph's controlling idea is that too much time is spent acquiring possessions. However, starting with "No wonder family life is deteriorating," Michael includes two sentences that introduce a complex issue beyond the scope of the essay. Since these last two sentences disrupt the paragraph's unity, they should be deleted.

Revising the first draft.   Although the final version of the essay needs work in spots, it's much stronger than Michael's first draft. To see how Michael went about revising the draft, compare his paper's second and third supporting paragraphs with his draft version reprinted here.

Original Version of the Second Paragraph

Our lives are spent not only buying things but in dealing with the inevitable complications that are created by our newly acquired possessions. First, we have to find places to put all the objects we bring home. More clothes demand more closets; a second car demands more garage space; a home entertainment center requires elaborate shelving. We shouldn't be surprised that the average American family moves once every three years. A good many families move simply because they need more space to store all the things they buy. In addition, our possessions demand maintenance time. A person who gets a new car will spend hours washing it, waxing it, and vacuuming it. A new pair of jeans has to go to the dry cleaners. New stereo systems have to be connected to already existing equipment. Eventually, of course, the inevitable happens. Our new items need to be repaired. Or we get sick of them and decide to replace them. Before making our replacement purchases, though, we have to get rid of the old items. That can be a real inconvenience.

When Michael looked more closely at this paragraph, he realized it rambled and lacked energy. He started to revise the paragraph by tightening the first sentence, making it more focused and less awkward. Certainly, the revised sentence ("As soon as we take our new purchases home, they begin to complicate our lives") is crisper than the original. Next, he decided to omit the discussion about finding places to put new possessions; these sentences about inadequate closet, garage, and shelf space were so exaggerated that they undercut the valid point he wanted to make. He also chose to eliminate the sentences about the mobility of American families. This was, he felt, an interesting point, but it introduced an issue too complex to be included in the paragraph.

Michael strengthened the rest of the paragraph by making his examples more specific. A "new car" became a "sleek new sports car," and a "pair of jeans" became a "fashionable pair of skintight jeans." Michael also realized he had to do more than merely write, "Eventually, . . . our new items need to be repaired." This point had to be dramatized by sharp, convincing details. Therefore, Michael added lively examples to describe how high-tech possessions— microwaves, home computers, VCRs—break down. Similarly, Michael realized it wasn't enough simply to say, as he had in the original, that we run into problems when we try to replace out-of-favor purchases. Vigorous details were again needed to illustrate the point. Michael thus used a typical "replaceable" (an old black-and-white TV) as his key example and showed the annoyance involved in handling phone calls and setting up appointments so people could see the TV.

After adding these specifics, Michael realized he had enough material to devote a separate paragraph to the problems associated with replacing old purchases. By dividing his original paragraph, Michael ended up with two well-focused paragraphs, neither of which has the rambling quality found in the original.

In short, Michael strengthened his essay through substantial revision. Another round of rewriting would have made the essay stronger still. Even without this additional work, Michael's essay provides an interesting perspective on an American preoccupation.

ACTIVITIES: EXEMPLIFICATION

Prewriting Activities

1. Imagine you're writing two essays: One is a serious paper analyzing the factors that *cause* large numbers of public school teachers to leave the profession each year; the other is a light essay *defining* "preppie," "head banger," or some other slang term used to describe a kind of person. Jot down ways you might use examples in each essay.

2. Use mapping or another prewriting technique to gather examples illustrating the truth of *one* of the following familiar sayings. Then, using the same or a different prewriting technique, accumulate examples that counter the saying. Weigh both sets of examples to determine the saying's validity. After developing an appropriate thesis, decide which examples you would elaborate in an essay.

    a.   Haste makes waste.

    b.   There's no use crying over spilled milk.

    c.   A bird in the hand is worth two in the bush.

Revising Activities

3. The following paragraph is from the first draft of an essay about the decline of small-town shopping districts. The paragraph is meant to show what small towns can do to revitalize business. Revise the paragraph, strengthening it with specific and convincing examples.

A small town can compete with a large new mall for shoppers. But merchants must work together, modernizing the stores and making the town's main street pleasant, even fun to walk. They should also copy the malls' example by including attention-getting events as often as possible.

4. Reprinted here is a paragraph from the first draft of a light-spirited essay showing that Americans' pursuit of change for change's sake has drawbacks. The paragraph is meant to illustrate that infatuation with newness costs consumers money yet leads to no improvement in product quality. How effective is the paragraph? Which examples are specific and convincing? Which are not? Do any seem nonrepresentative, offensive, or sexist? How could the paragraph's organization be improved? Consider these questions as you rewrite the paragraph. Add specific examples where needed. Depending on the way you revise, you may want to break this one paragraph into several.

We end up paying for our passion for the new and improved. Trendy clothing styles convince us that last year's oufits are outdated, even though our old clothes are fine. Women are especially vulnerable in this regard. What, though, about items that have to be replaced periodically, like shampoo? Even slight changes lead to new formulations requiring retooling of the production process. That means increased manufacturing costs per item--all of which get passed on to us, the consumer. Then there are those items that tout new, trend-setting features that make earlier versions supposedly obsolete. Some manufacturers, for example, boast that their stereo or CD systems transmit an expanded-frequency range. The problem is that humans can't even hear such frequencies. But the high-tech feature dazzles men who are too naive to realize they're being hoodwinked.

Charles Sykes

A journalist whose work has appeared in the *New York Times,* the *Wall Street Journal,* and other leading newspapers, Charles Sykes (1954–) usually writes about education issues. His books include *ProfScam: Professors and the Demise of Higher Education* (1988), *The Hollow Men: Politics and Corruption in Higher Education* (1990), *A Nation of Victims: The Decay of the American Character* (1992), and *The End of Privacy* (1999). A senior fellow at the Wisconsin Policy Research Institute and host of a popular Milwaukee radio show, Sykes lectures widely on topics having to do with what he sees as the collapse of standards in American culture. The following excerpt is from Sykes's 1995 book, *Dumbing Down Our Kids: Why America's Children Feel Good About Themselves But Can't Read, Write, or Add.*

Pre-Reading Journal Entry

Recent studies reveal that sexual misbehavior, drug use, shoplifting, and cheating are on the rise among young people. In your journal, explore your thinking about young people's misconduct in two of these (or other) areas. Why do you think young people engage in such risky behavior?

The "Values" Wasteland

Eric Richardson was a seventeen-year-old member of the Spur 1
Posse, a group of boys accused of raping girls as young as ten years old. After their arrests, the posse members reportedly returned to school as heroes, applauded for their exploits by their fellow students. In talk show appearances and media interviews, the boys were unrepentant. "They pass out condoms, teach sex education and pregnancy this and pregnancy that," Eric said after polishing off a Nacho Supreme and necking with his girlfriend in a booth at the Taco Bell. "But they don't teach us any rules."[1] His response was too glib and too convenient; it wasn't our fault, he was saying, you taught us to be like this. No school, however misguided, can ever be

---

[1]Jane Gross, "Where 'Boys will be Boys,' And Adults Are Bewildered," *New York Times,* 29 March 1993.

blamed for a piece of work like Eric Richardson. Even so, the evidence suggests that his ethical compass is not an isolated aberration.

A 1988 study of more than 2,000 Rhode Island students in   2
grades six through nine found that two-thirds of the boys and half of the girls thought that "it was acceptable for a man to force sex on a woman" if they had been dating six months or more.[2] A write-in survey of 126,000 teenagers found that 25 to 40 percent of teens see nothing wrong with cheating on exams, stealing from employers, or keeping money that wasn't theirs. A seventeen-year-old high school senior explained: "A lot of it is a gray area. It's everybody doing their own thing."[3]

A 1992 survey by the Josephson Institute for Ethics of nearly   3
7,000 high school and college students, most of them from middle- and upper middle-class backgrounds, found the equivalent of a "hole in the moral ozone" among American youth.

- A third of high school students and 16 percent of college students said they have shoplifted in the last year. Nearly the same number (33 percent of high school students and 11 percent of college students) said they have stolen from their parents or relatives at least once.[4]
- One in eight college students admitted to committing an act of fraud, including borrowing money they did not intend to repay, and lying on financial aid or insurance forms.
- A third of high school and college students said they would lie to get a job. One in six said they have already done so at least once.
- More than 60 percent of high school students said they had cheated at least once on an exam.
- Forty percent of the high school students who participated in this survey admitted that they "were not completely honest" on at least one or two questions—meaning that they may have lied on a survey about lying.[5]

---

[2] J. Kikuchi, "Rhode Island Develops Successful Intervention Program for Adolescents," *National Coalition Against Sexual Assault Newsletter,* Fall 1988.
[3] *USA Weekend,* 21–22 August 1992.
[4] Gary Abrams, "Youth Gets Bad Marks in Morality," *Los Angeles Times,* 12 November 1992.
[5] Ibid.

"I think it's very easy to get through high school and college   4
these days and hardly ever hear, 'That's wrong,'" commented Patrick
McCarthy of Pasadena's Jefferson Center for Character Education.
Michael Josephson, the president of the Josephson Institute of
Ethics, describes a large and growing population as the "I-Deserve-
Its," or IDIs. "Their IDI-ology is exceptionally and dangerously self-
centered, preoccupied with personal needs, wants, don't-wants and
rights." In pursuit of success, or comfort, or self-gratification, the
IDIs are blithely willing to jettison traditional ethical restraints, and
as a result "IDIs are more likely to lie, cheat and engage in irresponsible behavior when it suits their purposes. IDIs act as if they need
whatever they want and deserve whatever they need. . . ."[6] American
youth's culture of entitlement cannot, of course, be laid solely at the
feet of the schools. If there has been an ethical meltdown among
young Americans we need to look first to their parents, communities,
the media, and even the churches for explanations. Society's shift
from a culture of self-control to one of self-gratification, self-actualization, and self-realization, and its changing norms regarding personal responsibility and character, was not restricted to the arena of
public education. Even so, the ethical state of America's young people may, at least in part, have something to do with the way our
schools teach them about right and wrong.

At one time, American students used to study historical role   5
models like Benjamin Franklin, Florence Nightingale, Thomas
Edison, Madame Curie, Abraham Lincoln, and George
Washington—whose stories were used to provide object lessons in
inventiveness, character, compassion, curiosity, and truthfulness.
Following Aristotle, ethicists recognized that humanity does not
become virtuous simply by precept, but by "nature, habit, rational principle." "We become just by the practice of just actions,"
Aristotle observed, "self-controlled by exercising self-control."
This process was most effectively begun by placing examples of
such virtues in front of young people for them to emulate. But
while Asian children continue to read about stories of perseverance, hard work, loyalty, duty, prudence, heroism, and honesty,
[educational researcher] Harold Stevenson finds that "For the
most part, such cultural models have been displaced in the United

---

[6]Michael Josephson, "Young America Is Looking Out for No. 1," *Los Angeles
Times,* 16 October 1990.

States today."[7] In its place, we provide children a jumbled smorgasbord of moral choices.

How Do You *Feel* About Cheating?

The course is officially about "citizenship," but the subject is values.[8] Specially prepared for students in the fourth to sixth grades, the class is designed to help students clarify and discover their own values on issues like lying and cheating. As a group or by secret ballot, the fourth, fifth, and sixth graders are asked: "How many of you . . . 6

Think children should have to work for their allowances?
Think most rules are dumb?
Think that there are times when cheating is ok?
Wish you didn't have grades in school?
Think prizes should be awarded for everything?"

The section on cheating asks students: "What are your attitudes toward cheating?" They are asked to complete the following statements:

Tests are _____
Grades are _____
The bad thing about cheating is _____
The good thing about cheating is _____
If there were no such things as grades, would your attitude toward cheating change?
Is school the only place cheating takes place? Where else does cheating take place?
Is it ever OK to cheat? When?

It is not clear whether there are ever any right and wrong 7 answers to these questions. The class takes a similar approach to lying. Students are asked, "Lying, What's Your View?". . . Children in the class are . . . presented with a series of ethical problems. They are not asked to define right and wrong or moral or immoral.

[7]Harold W. Stevenson and James W. Stigler, *The Learning Gap* (New York: Summit Books, 1992), pp. 85–86.
[8]"Citizenship: 4th–6th Grade," xeroxed worksheets, undated. Several copies were provided to me by parents whose children had been given the assignment during class.

Instead, they are asked to say which actions are "acceptable . . . and
. . . which are . . . unacceptable. Do any of the situations involve
lying?"

> A factory worker oversleeps and is late for work. He tells his
> supervisor that he was involved in a minor traffic accident.
> Janine just can't face a big history exam for which she hasn't
> studied. She convinces her mother that she has a terrible sore
> throat and must stay home.
> Bill runs into a friend he hasn't seen in months. The friend asks
> how he is. Bill smiles and answers "great!" even though his
> dog just died, he's flunking English, and he just broke up
> with his girlfriend. . . .

Such nonjudgmentalism is a feature of the approach known as   8
"values clarification," in which, as [journalist] William Kirk Kilpatrick writes, classroom discussions are turned into "'bull sessions'
where opinions go back and forth but conclusions are never
reached." . . . Many of these classes seem to be based on the rather
fantastic notion that since none of the civilizations anywhere in the
world throughout the entire sweep of human history has been able
to work out a moral code of conduct worthy of being passed on, we
should therefore leave it to fourth graders to work out questions of
right and wrong on their own.

The Values Clarifiers

The developers of Values Clarification and other nonjudgmen-   9
tal approaches to moral decision making often claimed to be value-
free, but their agenda was quite specific. Their bête noir was "moralizing" in any form. "Moralizing," the authors of *Values
Clarification: A Handbook of Practical Strategies for Teachers and
Students* wrote in 1978, "is the direct, although sometimes subtle
inculcation of the adults' values upon the young."9 For the authors
of the new curriculum, this was not merely authoritarian and stifling,
but also dangerous to the ethical health of children. By passing on a
set of moral values, they argued, parents were hampering the ability

---

9Sidney B. Simon, Leland W. Howe, and Howard Kirschenbaum, *Values
Clarification: A Handbook of Practical Strategies for Teachers and Students* (New
York: Hart Publishing, 1972), p. 15.

of children to come up with their own values. "Young people brought up by moralizing adults are not prepared to make their own responsible choices," they warned.[10] In any case, moralizing was no longer practical. Children were bombarded with so many different sets of values and parents were only some of the many voices they heard. In the end, they argue, every child had to make his own choices. That, of course, is true—making choices is the essence of free will. But where values clarification departed from older moral philosophies was in its contention that children do not need to be grounded in value systems or provided with moral road maps before they are asked to make such choices. Values clarifiers also did not care what values the child chose to follow. Specifically, values clarification did not concern itself with inculcating values such as self-control, honesty, responsibility, loyalty, prudence, duty, or justice. In its purest form, values clarification did not even argue that these virtues were superior or preferable to their opposites and had little to say about concepts of right and wrong. The goal of values clarification was not to create a virtuous young person, or young adult with character or probity; its goal was empowering youngsters to make their own decisions, *whatever those decisions were.* . . .

The assumption behind such programs was that children had   10 the capacity to develop character on their own; that students as young as third grade had the knowledge, insight, and cognitive abilities to wrestle through difficult dilemmas and thorny moral paradoxes without the benefit of a moral compass, either from parents or teachers. . . .

At the heart of the values clarification program was the effort to   11 have students develop an individual identity. One exercise was "Are You Someone Who . . ." followed by a long list of options, including: "is likely to marry someone of another religion?"; "is likely to grow a beard?"; "would consider joining the John Birch Society?"; "is apt to go out of your way to have a black (white) neighbor?"; "will subscribe to *Playboy* magazine?"; will change your religion?"; "will be likely to win a Nobel Peace Prize?"; "is apt to experiment with pot?"; "would get therapy on your own initiative?"; "will make a faithless husband? wife?"

The authors explain that such questions will cause students "to   12 consider more thoughtfully what they value, what they want out of

[10]Ibid., p. 16.

life and what type of persons they want to become."[11] But the questions send another message as well by treating the various options simply as different choices of apparently equal weight, like choices on a personality buffet line: Will you win the Nobel Prize or experiment with pot? Subscribe to *Playboy* or change your religion? There is no suggestion that growing a beard or cheating on your wife might be decisions that carry rather different moral weights.

13   Ultimately, the values clarification approach reduces moral choice to a matter of personal taste with no more basis in objective reality than a preference for a red car rather than a blue one. There is no right or wrong answer and no real ground to regard your own choice either as better or more valid than any other.

14   But is this really a process of working out moral values or is it simply a process of rationalization? Humans rationalize because it is convenient and it suits our interests. If we choose, we can shape morality to meet our inclinations and impulses, rather than try to shape our inclinations to accord with moral law. Moral reasoning, in contrast, involves asking whether an act is good, whether it is made with right intent, and examining the act's circumstances. To make such judgments requires an understanding of what the moral law might be, not simply how we feel about the act. But to take the subjective state of mind and make it the sole test of morality is to rationalize and call it moral reasoning. Checking one's inclinations is not the same as examining one's conscience, precisely because the conscience needs to be educated.

15   One would never get that idea from watching a values clarification "simulation" of a moral choice. In one popular exercise, students have to imagine that their class has been trapped in a cave-in. In the exercise, students are asked to imagine that they have to form a single line to work their way out of the cave. At any moment, another rock slide may close the way out. Those at the head of the line are therefore the most likely to survive. In the class exercise, each member of the class must give the reason he or she should be at the head of the line. The teacher tells them: "Your reasons can be of two kinds. You can tell us what you want to live for or what you have yet to get out of life that is important to you. Or you can talk about what you have to contribute to others in the world that would

[11]Ibid., p. 366.

justify your being near the front of the line." After hearing all of the pleas, the class then decides the order in which they will file out of the cave.[12]

Like other values clarification chestnuts, youngsters are asked to   16
make life-and-death decisions. But what are the practical implica-tions? Do students emerge from the class more empathetic? More willing to sacrifice for others? Are they likely to treat their peers with more respect? Show more self-restraint in the presence of their par-ents? Or are they likely to have a keener sense of their own egos? . . .

Other exercises ask students to choose who should be allowed   17
to stay in a fallout shelter (and who should be left to die) during a nuclear attack; to decide whether it is morally permissible for a poor man to steal a drug that his desperately ill wife needs; to work through the dilemma of trapped settlers who must decide whether to turn to cannibalism or starve to death; to put themselves in the place of a mother who must choose which of her two children she will save; and consider the ethical dilemma of a doctor who must decide to operate on an injured child despite the religious objections of the parents. "Like a roller-coaster ride," William Kilpatrick writes, "the dilemma approach can leave its passengers a bit breathless. That is one of its attractions. But like a roller-coaster ride, it may also leave them a bit disoriented—or more than a bit."[13] As entertaining as such problems may be, they are hardly a guide for developing a moral code; morality is more than solving a complex and perhaps even unsolvable puzzle. Take the case of the man whose wife is dying of an incurable illness and who needs a rare and expensive drug. Kilpatrick wonders whether youngsters who spend a diverting and lively class period debating whether stealing is right or wrong in this case would be less likely to steal themselves? Or lie? Or cheat? Or will they come to the conclusion that moral questions are inevitably so complicated, so fraught with doubt, that no one answer is necessarily ever any better than any other and that all moral questions come down in the end simply to a matter of opin-ion? Or will they get the idea that it is less important whether one steals or not than that one has developed a system of "valuing" with which one is comfortable?

---

[12]Ibid., p. 288.
[13]William Kirk Kilpatrick, *Why Johnny Can't Tell Right From Wrong* (New York: Simon & Schuster, 1992), p. 84.

One of the striking things about spending time with high school   18
students is the near universality of this notion that values are something they work out on their own. One frequent speaker on ethical
issues recounts his experience with high school students in which he
presents them with a typical values clarification dilemma. They must
imagine that they are on a lifeboat with another person and their
family dog; the students can save only one, so they must choose
either the human being, who is a complete stranger, or the beloved
and cherished family dog. Typically, some of the students choose to
save the dog and allow the man to die; most students choose to save
the human being. But then the speaker asks them what they thought
of their classmates who had opted for the dog over the man. Almost
never, says the speaker, do students say that those choices were
"wrong" or morally objectionable.14 Even for those who made the
correct moral choice, it was merely a matter of personal opinion, and
they refuse to be judgmental toward those who put the dog's life
ahead of the human being's. The concept that there might be universal and objective moral principles at stake is completely alien to
these youngsters.

Questions for Close Reading

1. What is the selection's thesis? Locate the sentence(s) in which Sykes
   states his main idea. If he doesn't state it directly, express it in your own
   words.
2. What, according to Sykes, is the difference between contemporary
   American education and American education in the past?
3. What group of people does Sykes blame for the erosion of morality in
   American education? What justification do these people provide for their
   approach?
4. Reread paragraphs 15 and 18. In each, Sykes describes a classroom exercise in "values clarification." What is the educational intent of the two
   exercises? How are they similar? How do they differ? What is Sykes's
   opinion of the two exercises?
5. Refer to your dictionary as needed to define the following words used in
   the selection: *unrepentant* (paragraph 1), *self-actualization* (4), *precept*
   (5), *emulate* (5), *perseverance* (5), *smorgasbord* (5), *bête noir* (9), *moralizing* (9), *cognitive* (10), *rationalization* (14), and *fraught* (17).

14Dennis Prager, conversation with author.

Questions About the Writer's Craft

1. **The pattern.** In the first three paragraphs of his essay, Sykes provides numerous examples to illustrate what he considers the moral looseness of young people. Why do you think he starts with the example of the seventeen-year-old rapist? In what ways is this example different from the examples he provides in paragraphs 2 and 3?
2. Why do you suppose Sykes entitles his essay "The 'Values' Wasteland"? Consider what each word means. Why do you think he puts quotation marks around the word "Values"?
3. In paragraphs 2 and 3, Sykes makes heavy use of statistics. Why do you suppose he cites statistics only in the beginning of the essay?
4. **Other patterns.** How would you characterize Sykes's tone? How does this tone reinforce his argument?

Writing Assignments Using Exemplification as a Pattern of Development

1. Sykes contends that modern education fails to teach morality. Do you agree? Write an essay illustrating the point that contemporary schooling blunts *or* enhances young people's moral sense. In either case, offer convincing examples from your own and other people's schooling to support your point of view. Consider opening your essay, as Sykes does, with a highly dramatic example.
2. Sykes believes that the moral fiber of young people has deteriorated. Interview classmates, friends, and family members of varying ages to see if they think that young people today are less moral than they were in earlier times. Ask each person to supply at least one example to illustrate his or her opinion. Review the examples, and decide whether you agree with or reject Sykes's position. Then write an essay in which you support your opinion, using the most compelling examples from your interviews as well as your own experiences and observations.

Writing Assignments Using Other Patterns of Development

3. Sykes believes that there are "universal and objective moral principles." Write an essay narrating a time when you faced a moral dilemma but knew deep down that there was only one moral way to act—even though such an action might have been to your personal disadvantage. Describe the situation, the conflict you experienced, and how you resolved the conflict. Before writing, read the following essays for insight into humans' moral impulse: Langston Hughes's "Salvation" (page 148) and Lewis Thomas's "The Lie Detector" (page 354).

4. Sykes writes that "we need to look first to . . . parents, communities, the media, and even the churches" to explain the "ethical meltdown" in young people. Focus on *one* of these forces, and write an essay analyzing the positive and negative effects it can have on young people's moral sense. To support your analysis, draw upon your own observations as well as those of friends, classmates, and family members.

Writing Assignments Using a Journal Entry as a Starting Point

5. Reread your pre-reading journal entry, and decide which *one* type of misconduct you think is most prevalent among young people nowadays. Then write an essay in which you illustrate the extent of the impropriety, using several persuasive examples to make your point. One section of the essay should explore causes of the misbehavior; another should discuss consequences. Brainstorming with others will help you identify examples, causes, and effects of the misbehavior. At the end of your essay, you might suggest steps that could be taken to set young people in the right direction. Also, consider supplementing your observations with information about your topic gathered in the library and/or on the Internet.

Beth Johnson

Beth Johnson (1956–) is a writer, occasional college teacher, and freelance editor. A graduate of Goshen College and Syracuse University, Johnson is the author of several college texts, including *Everyday Heroes* (1996) and the coauthor of *Voices and Values* (2002). Containing profiles of men and women who have triumphed over obstacles to achieve personal and academic success, *Everyday Heroes* has provided a motivational boost to college students nationwide. She lives with her husband and three children in Lederach, Pennsylvania. The following piece is one of several that Johnson has written about the complexities and wonders of life.

Pre-Reading Journal Entry

When you were young, did adults acknowledge the existence of life's tragedies, or did they deny such harsh truths? In your journal, list several difficult events that you observed or experienced firsthand as a child. How did the adults in your life explain these hardships? In each case, do you think the adults acted appropriately? If not, how should they have responded?

Bombs Bursting in Air

It's Friday night and we're at the Olympics, the Junior Olympics, that is. My son is on a relay-race team competing against fourth-graders from all over the school district. His little sister and I sit high in the stands, trying to pick Isaac out from the crowd of figures milling around on the field during these moments of pre-game confusion. The public address system sputters to life and summons our attention. "And now," the tinny voice rings out, "please join together in the singing of our national anthem."

"Oh saaay can you seeeeee," we begin. My arm rests around Maddie's shoulders. I am touching her a lot today, and she notices. "Mom, you're *squishing* me," she chides, wriggling from my grip. I content myself with stroking her hair. News that reached me today makes me need to feel her near. We pipe along, squeaking out the impossibly high note of "land of the freeeeeeeee." Maddie clowns, half-singing, half-shouting the lyrics, hitting the "b's" explosively on "bombs bursting in air."

1

2

Bombs indeed, I think, replaying the sound of my friend's voice   3
over the phone that afternoon: "Bumped her head sledding. Took
her in for an x-ray, just to make sure. There was something strange,
so they did more tests . . . a brain tumor . . . Children's Hospital in
Boston Tuesday . . . surgery, yes, right away. . . ." Maddie's playmate
Shannon, only five years old. We'd last seen her at Halloween,
dressed in her blue princess costume, and we'd talked of Furby and
Scooby-Doo and Tootsie Rolls. Now her parents were hurriedly
learning a new vocabulary—CAT scans, glioma, pediatric neurosurgery, and frontal lobe.[1] A bomb had exploded in their midst, and,
like troops under attack, they were rallying in response.

The games over, the children and I edge our way out of the   4
school parking lot, bumper to bumper with other parents ferrying
their families home. I tell the kids as casually as I can about
Shannon. "She'll have to have an operation. It's lucky, really, that
they found it by accident this way while it's small."

"I want to send her a present," Maddie announces. "That'd be   5
nice," I say, glad to keep the conversation on a positive note.

But my older son is with us now. Sam, who is thirteen, says,   6
"She'll be OK, though, right?" It's not a question, really; it's a statement that I must either agree with or contradict. I want to say yes.
I want to say of course she'll be all right. I want them to inhabit a
world where five-year-olds do not develop silent, mysterious
growths in their brains, where "malignancy" and "seizure" are
words for *New York Times* crossword puzzles, not for little girls.
They would accept my assurance; they would believe me and sleep
well tonight. But I can't; the bomb that exploded in Shannon's
home has sent splinters of shrapnel into ours as well, and they cannot be ignored or lied away. "We hope she'll be just fine," I finally
say. "She has very good doctors. She has wonderful parents who are
doing everything they can. The tumor is small. Shannon's strong
and healthy."

"*She'll* be OK," says Maddie matter-of-factly. "In school we   7
read about a little boy who had something wrong with his leg and
he had an operation and got better. Can we go to Dairy Queen?"

---

[1]A CAT scan is a computerized cross-sectional image of an internal body structure;
a glioma is a tumor in the brain or spinal cord; pediatric neurosurgery is surgery
performed on the nerves, brain, or spinal cord of a child; the frontal lobe is the
largest section of the brain (editors' note).

Bombs on the horizon don't faze Maddie. Not yet. I can just   8
barely remember from my own childhood the sense that still surrounds her, that feeling of being cocooned within reassuring walls
of security and order. Back then, Monday meant gym, Tuesday was
pizza in the cafeteria, Wednesday brought clarinet lessons. Teachers
stood in their familiar spots in the classrooms, telling us with reassuring simplicity that World War II happened because Hitler, a very
bad man, invaded Poland. Midterms and report cards, summer vacations and new notebooks in September gave a steady rhythm to the
world. It wasn't all necessarily happy—through the years there were
poor grades, grouchy teachers, exclusion from the desired social
group, dateless weekends when it seemed the rest of the world was
paired off—but it was familiar territory where we felt walled off
from the really bad things that happened to other people.

There were hints of them, though, even then. Looking back, I   9
recall the tiny shock waves, the tremors from far-off explosions that
occasionally rattled our shelter. There was the little girl who was
absent for a week and when she returned wasn't living with her
mother and stepfather anymore. There was a big girl who threw up
in the bathroom every morning and then disappeared from school.
A playful, friendly custodian was suddenly fired, and it had something to do with an angry parent. A teacher's husband had a heart
attack and died. These were interesting tidbits to report to our families over dinner, mostly out of morbid interest in seeing our parents
bite their lips and exchange glances.

As we got older, the bombs dropped closer. A friend's sister was   10
arrested for selling drugs; we saw her mother in tears at church that
Sunday. A boy I thought I knew, a school clown with a sweet
crooked grin, shot himself in the woods behind his house. A car full
of senior boys, going home from a dance where I'd been sent into
ecstasy when the cutest of them all greeted me by name, rounded a
curve too fast and crashed, killing them. We wept and hugged each
other in the halls. Our teachers listened to us grieve and tried to
comfort us, but their words came out impatient and almost angry. I
realize now that what sounded like anger was a helplessness to teach
us lessons we were still too young or too ignorant to learn. For
although our sorrow was real, we still had some sense of a protective curtain between us and the bombs. If only, we said. If only she
hadn't used drugs. If only he'd told someone how depressed he was.
If only they'd been more careful. *We* weren't like them; we were

careful. Like magical incantations, we recited the things that we would or wouldn't do in order to protect ourselves from such sad, unnecessary fates.

And then my best friend, a beautiful girl of sixteen, went to   11
sleep one January night and never woke up. I found myself shaken to the core of my being. My grief at the loss of my vibrant, laughing friend was great. But what really tilted my universe was the nakedness of my realization that there was no "if only." There were no drugs, no careless action, no crime, no accident, nothing I could focus on to explain away what had happened. She had simply died. Which could only mean that there was no magic barrier separating me and my loved ones from the bombs. We were as vulnerable as everyone else. For months the shock stayed with me. I sat in class watching my teachers draw diagrams of Saturn, talk about Watergate,[2] multiply fractions, and wondered at their apparent cheer and normalcy. Didn't they *know* we were all doomed? Didn't they know it was only a matter of time until one of us took a direct hit? What was the point of anything?

But time moved on, and I moved with it. College came and   12
went, graduate school, adulthood, middle age. My heightened sense of vulnerability began to subside, though I could never again slip fully into the soothing security of my younger days. I became more aware of the intertwining threads of joy, pain, and occasional tragedy that weave through all our lives. College was stimulating, exciting, full of friendship and challenge. I fell in love for the first time, reveled in its sweetness, then learned the painful lesson that love comes with no guarantee. A beloved professor lost two children to leukemia, but continued with skill and passion to introduce students to the riches of literature. My father grew ill, but the last day of his life, when I sat by his bed holding his hand, remains one of my sweetest memories. The marriage I'd entered into with optimism ended in bitter divorce, but produced three children whose existence is my daily delight. At every step along the way, I've seen that the most rewarding chapters of my life have contained parts that I not only would not have chosen, but would

[2]In June, 1972, supporters of Republican President Richard Nixon were caught breaking into the Democratic campaign headquarters in the Watergate office complex in Washington, D.C. The resulting investigation of the White House connection to the break-in led to President Nixon's eventual resignation in August, 1974 (editors' note).

have given much to avoid. But selecting just the good parts is not an option we are given.

The price of allowing ourselves to truly live, to love and be 13
loved, is (and it's the ultimate irony) the knowledge that the greater our investment in life, the larger the target we create. Of course, it is within our power to refuse friendship, shrink from love, live in isolation, and thus create for ourselves a nearly impenetrable bomb shelter. There are those among us who choose such an existence, the price of intimacy being too high. Looking about me, however, I see few such examples. Instead, I am moved by the courage with which most of us, ordinary folks, continue soldiering on. We fall in love, we bring our children into the world, we forge our friendships, we give our hearts, knowing with increasing certainty that we do so at our own risk. Still we move ahead with open arms, saying yes, yes to life.

Shannon's surgery is behind her; the prognosis is good. Her 14
mother reports that the family is returning to its normal routines, laughing again and talking of ordinary things, even while they step more gently, speak more quietly, are more aware of the precious fragility of life and of the blessing of every day that passes without explosion.

Bombs bursting in air. They can blind us, like fireworks at the 15
moment of explosion. If we close our eyes and turn away, all we see is their fiery image. But if we have the courage to keep our eyes open and welcoming, even bombs finally fade against the vastness of the starry sky.

Questions for Close Reading

1. What is the selection's thesis? Locate the sentence(s) in which Johnson states her main idea. If she doesn't state the thesis explicitly, express it in your own words.
2. In paragraph 2, Johnson describes her "need to feel her [daughter] near." What compels her to want to be physically close to her daughter? Why do you think Johnson responds this way?
3. In describing her family's responses to Shannon's illness, Johnson presents three reactions: Maddie's, Sam's, and her own. How do these responses differ? In what ways do Maddie's, Sam's, and Johnson's reactions typify the age groups to which they belong?
4. In paragraph 13, Johnson describes two basic ways people respond to life's inevitable "bombs." What are these ways? Which response does Johnson endorse?

5. Refer to your dictionary as needed to define the following words used in the selection: *ferrying* (paragraph 4), *shrapnel* (6), *faze* (8), *cocooned* (8), *tremors* (9), *incantations* (10), *vulnerable* (11), *intertwining* (12), *impenetrable* (13), *soldiering on* (13), *prognosis* (14), and *fragility* (14).

Questions About the Writer's Craft

1. **The pattern.** Although Johnson provides many examples of life's "bombs," she gives more weight to some examples than to others. Which examples does she emphasize? Which ones receive less attention? Why?

2. **Other patterns.** What important contrast does Johnson develop in paragraph 6? How does this contrast reinforce the essay's main idea?

3. Writers generally vary sentence structure in an effort to add interest to their work. But in paragraphs 9 and 10, Johnson employs a repetitive sentence structure. Where is the repetition in these two paragraphs? Why do you think she uses this technique?

4. Johnson develops her essay by means of an extended metaphor (see pages 87–88), using bombs as her central image. Identify all the places where Johnson draws upon language and imagery related to bombs and battles. What do you think Johnson hopes to achieve with this sustained metaphor?

Writing Assignments Using Exemplification as a Pattern of Development

1. In paragraphs 9 and 10, Johnson catalogues a number of events that made her increasingly aware of life's bombs. Write an essay of your own, illustrating how you came to recognize the inevitability of painful life events. Start by listing the difficult events you've encountered. Select the three most compelling occurrences, and do some freewriting to generate details about each. Before writing, decide whether you will order your examples chronologically or emphatically; use whichever illustrates more effectively your dawning realization of life's complexity. End with some conclusions about your ability to cope with difficult times.

2. Johnson describes her evolving understanding of life. In an essay of your own, show the way several events combined to change your understanding of a specific aspect of your life. Perhaps a number of incidents prompted you to reconsider career choices, end a relationship, or appreciate the importance of family. Cite only those events that illustrate your emerging understanding. Your decision to use either chronological or emphatic sequence depends on which illustrates more dramatically the change in your perception. To see how other writers describe their journeys of self-discovery, read Maya Angelou's "Sister Flowers" (page 106) and Richard Rodriguez's "Workers" (page 315).

Writing Assignments Using Other Patterns of Development

∞ 3. Johnson explores the lasting impact the death of her friend had on her life. Write an essay about the effect of a *single* bomb on your life. You might discuss getting left back in school, losing a loved one, seeing the dark side of someone you admired, and so on. Your causal analysis should make clear how the event affected your life. Perhaps the event had painful short-term consequences but positive long-term repercussions. Langston Hughes's "Salvation" (page 148) and Sophronia Liu's "So Tsi-Fai" (page 153) provide helpful models for examining the effects of a life-changing event.

💻 4. In an essay, offer readers a guide to surviving a specific life calamity. You might, for instance, explain how to survive a pet's death, a painful breakup, a financial hardship. Consider doing some library and/or Internet research on your subject. Combining your own insights with any material gathered through research, describe fully the steps readers should take to recover from the devastating events.

Writing Assignments Using a Journal Entry as a Starting Point

∞ 5. Johnson asserts that painful truths shouldn't "be ignored or lied away" by adults. Do you agree? Write an essay explaining why you think adults should protect children from harsh realities—or why they should present the whole truth, even when it's painful. Review your pre-reading journal entry, searching for strong examples to support your position. Discussing this topic with others will also help you shape your point of view, as will reading Yuh Ji-Yeon's "Let's Tell the Story of All America's Cultures" (page 445).

Barbara Ehrenreich

Barbara Ehrenreich (1941–) has been a college professor, investigative reporter, magazine editor, and social activist. A graduate of Reed College, Ehrenreich received her doctorate in biology from Rockefeller University. She has cowritten several books, including *For Her Own Good: 150 Years of the Experts' Advice to Women* (1978) and *Remaking Love: The Feminization of Sex* (1986). Her more recent books include *Fear of Falling: The Inner Life of the Middle Class* (1989), *The Worst Years of Our Lives* (1990), *Snarling Citizen: Essays* (1995), and the novel *Kipper's Game* (1993). A regular columnist for *Time, The Guardian,* and *The Nation,* Ehrenreich has published articles in many other magazines, such as *Esquire, Vogue,* and the *New Republic.* "What I've Learned From Men" first appeared in *Ms.* in 1985.

Pre-Reading Journal Entry

Drawing upon childhood experiences and recent observations, reflect in your journal about the way children's gender identity is formed. What traits do parents and society tend to encourage in boys? In girls? How do these gendered characteristics benefit and/or hinder boys and girls later in life?

What I've Learned From Men

For many years I believed that women had only one thing to 1
learn from men: how to get the attention of a waiter by some means short of kicking over the table and shrieking. Never in my life have I gotten the attention of a waiter, unless it was an off-duty waiter whose car I'd accidentally scraped in a parking lot somewhere. Men, however, can summon a maître d' just by thinking the word "coffee," and this is a power women would be well-advised to study. What else would we possibly want to learn from them? How to interrupt someone in mid-sentence as if you were performing an act of conversational euthanasia? How to drop a pair of socks three feet from an open hamper and keep right on walking? How to make those weird guttural gargling sounds in the bathroom?

But now, at mid-life, I am willing to admit that there are some 2
real and useful things to learn from men. Not from all men—in fact, we may have the most to learn from some of the men we like the

least. This realization does not mean that my feminist principles have gone soft with age: what I think women could learn from men is how to get *tough*. After more than a decade of consciousness-raising, assertiveness training, and hand-to-hand combat in the battle of the sexes, we're still too ladylike. Let me try that again—we're just too *damn* ladylike.

Here is an example from my own experience, a story that I 3
blush to recount. A few years ago, at an international conference held in an exotic and luxurious setting, a prestigious professor invited me to his room for what he said would be an intellectual discussion on matters of theoretical importance. So far, so good. I showed up promptly. But only minutes into the conversation—held in all-too-adjacent chairs—it emerged that he was interested in something more substantial than a meeting of minds. I was disgusted, but not enough to overcome 30-odd years of programming in ladylikeness. Every time his comments took a lecherous turn, I chattered distractingly; every time his hand found its way to my knee, I returned it as if it were something he had misplaced. This went on for an unconscionable period (as much as 20 minutes); then there was a minor scuffle, a dash for the door, and I was out—with nothing violated but my self-esteem. I, a full-grown feminist, conversant with such matters as rape crisis counseling and sexual harassment at the workplace, had behaved like a ninny—or, as I now understand it, like a lady.

The essence of ladylikeness is a persistent servility masked as 4
"niceness." For example, we (women) tend to assume that it is our responsibility to keep everything "nice" even when the person we are with is rude, aggressive, or emotionally AWOL. (In the above example, I was so busy taking responsibility for preserving the veneer of "niceness" that I almost forgot to take responsibility for myself.) In conversations with men, we do almost all the work: sociologists have observed that in male-female social interactions it's the woman who throws out leading questions and verbal encouragements ("So how did you *feel* about that?" and so on) while the man, typically, says "Hmmmm." Wherever we go, we're perpetually smiling—the on-cue smile, like the now-outmoded curtsy, being one of our culture's little rituals of submission. We're trained to feel embarrassed if we're praised, but if we see a criticism coming at us from miles down the road, we rush to acknowledge it. And when we're feeling aggressive or angry or resentful, we just tighten up our smiles

or turn them into rueful little moues. In short, we spend a great deal of time acting like wimps.

For contrast, think of the macho stars we love to watch. Think, 5 for example, of Mel Gibson facing down punk marauders in "The Road Warrior". . . John Travolta swaggering his way through the early scenes of "Saturday Night Fever". . . or Marlon Brando shrugging off the local law in "The Wild One." Would they simper their way through tight spots? Chatter aimlessly to keep the conversation going? Get all clutched up whenever they think they might—just might—have hurt someone's feelings? No, of course not, and therein, I think, lies their fascination for us.

The attraction of the "tough guy" is that he has—or at least 6 seems to have—what most of us lack, and that is an aura of power and control. In an article, feminist psychiatrist Jean Baker Miller writes that "a woman's using self-determined power for herself is equivalent to selfishness [and] destructiveness"—an equation that makes us want to avoid even the appearance of power. Miller cites cases of women who get depressed just when they're on the verge of success—and of women who do succeed and then bury their achievement in self-deprecation. As an example, she describes one company's periodic meetings to recognize outstanding salespeople: when a woman is asked to say a few words about her achievement, she tends to say something like, "Well, I really don't know how it happened. I guess I was just lucky this time." In contrast, the men will cheerfully own up to the hard work, intelligence, and so on, to which they owe their success. By putting herself down, a woman avoids feeling brazenly powerful and potentially "selfish"; she also does the traditional lady's work of trying to make everyone else feel better ("She's not really so smart, after all, just lucky").

So we might as well get a little tougher. And a good place to 7 start is by cutting back on the small acts of deference that we've been programmed to perform since girlhood. Like unnecessary smiling. For many women—waitresses, flight attendants, receptionists—smiling is an occupational requirement, but there's no reason for anyone to go around grinning when she's not being paid for it. I'd suggest that we save our off-duty smiles for when we truly feel like sharing them, and if you're not sure what to do with your face in the meantime, study Clint Eastwood's expressions—both of them.

Along the same lines, I think women should stop taking respon- 8 sibility for every human interaction we engage in. In a social encounter with a woman, the average man can go 25 minutes saying nothing more than "You don't say?" "Izzat so?" and, of course, "Hmmmm." Why should we do all the work? By taking so much responsibility for making conversations go well, we act as if we had much more at stake in the encounter than the other party—and that gives him (or her) the power advantage. Every now and then, we deserve to get more out of a conversation than we put into it: I'd suggest not offering information you'd rather not share ("I'm really terrified that my sales plan won't work") and not, out of sheer politeness, soliciting information you don't really want ("Wherever did you get that lovely tie?"). There will be pauses, but they don't have to be awkward for *you.*

It is true that some, perhaps most, men will interpret any   9
decrease in female deference as a deliberate act of hostility. Omit the free smiles and perky conversation-boosters and someone is bound to ask, "Well, what's come over *you* today?" For most of us, the first impulse is to stare at our feet and make vague references to a terminally ill aunt in Atlanta, but we should have as much right to be taciturn as the average (male) taxi driver. If you're taking a vacation from smiles and small talk and some fellow is moved to inquire about what's "bothering" you, just stare back levelly and say, the international debt crisis, the arms race, or the death of God.

There are all kinds of ways to toughen up—and potentially   10
move up—at work, and I leave the details to the purveyors of assertiveness training. But Jean Baker Miller's study underscores a fundamental principle that anyone can master on her own. We can stop acting less capable than we actually are. For example, in the matter of taking credit when credit is due, there's a key difference between saying "I was just lucky" and saying "I had a plan and it worked." If you take the credit you deserve, you're letting people know that you were confident you'd succeed all along, and that you fully intend to do so again.

Finally, we may be able to learn something from men about   11
what to do with anger. As a general rule, women get irritated: men get *mad.* We make tight little smiles of ladylike exasperation; they pound on desks and roar. I wouldn't recommend emulating the full basso profundo male tantrum, but women do need ways of expressing justified anger clearly, colorfully, and, when necessary, crudely. If you're not just irritated, but *pissed off,* it might help to say so.

I, for example, have rerun the scene with the prestigious pro-   12
fessor many times in my mind. And in my mind, I play it like Bogart. I start by moving my chair over to where I can look the professor

full in the face. I let him do the chattering, and when it becomes evident that he has nothing serious to say, I lean back and cross my arms, just to let him know that he's wasting my time. I do not smile, neither do I nod encouragement. Nor, of course, do I respond to his blandishments with apologetic shrugs and blushes. Then, at the first flicker of lechery, I stand up and announce coolly, "All right, I've had enough of this crap." Then I walk out—slowly, deliberately, confidently. Just like a man.

Or—now that I think of it—just like a woman.   13

Questions for Close Reading

1. What is the selection's thesis? Locate the sentence(s) in which Ehrenreich states her main idea. If she doesn't state the thesis explicitly, express it in your own words.

2. Why did Ehrenreich handle the lecherous professor as she did? In retrospect, how does she wish she had dealt with the situation? How does her current perspective of the way she should have behaved reinforce her thesis in the essay?

3. What does "behaving like a lady" mean, according to Ehrenreich? What is her opinion of "ladylike" behavior?

4. Why, in Ehrenreich's view, do we like "macho stars" (paragraph 5)? What can we learn from them?

5. Refer to your dictionary as needed to define the following words used in the selection: *euthanasia* (paragraph 1), *guttural* (1), *lecherous* (3), *distractingly* (3), *unconscionable* (3), *ninny* (3), *servility* (4), *veneer* (4), *moues* (4), *marauders* (5), *aura* (6), *brazenly* (6), *deference* (9), *taciturn* (9), *purveyors* (10), *emulating* (11), *basso profundo* (11), and *blandishments* (12).

Questions About the Writer's Craft

1. **The pattern.** In paragraphs 3 and 12, Ehrenreich uses her own personal experience as a key example. Why do you think she chooses to include this example? Why do you suppose she presents it so early in the essay and then returns to it at the end?

2. **Other patterns.** Locate places in the essay where Ehrenreich uses examples to contrast the different responses and behaviors of males and females. How do these contrasts help the writer develop her main idea?

3. Do you think that Ehrenreich is speaking primarily to a male or to a female audience? What in the essay makes you feel this way? Do you think that the author expects her audience to be positive, hostile, or neutral toward her ideas? What in the essay leads you to this conclusion?

4. In her attack on "ladylikeness," Ehrenreich deliberately avoids using a "ladylike" or "nice" tone. Which of her phrases or expressions seem to defy stereotypes about the way "ladies" should express themselves?

Writing Assignments Using Exemplification as a Pattern of Development

∞ **1.** If, as Ehrenreich suggests, women have much to learn from men, is it also true that men could learn from women? Write an essay illustrating your belief that men would indeed be better off if they acquired some attitudes and behaviors traditionally associated with women. Be sure to provide numerous examples from your own experience and observations. You may take a humorous or serious approach when showing that men should—in some respects—become more like women. Deborah Tannen's "But What Do You Mean?" (page 241) and Dave Barry's "The Ugly Truth About Beauty" (page 323) may spark some insight into characteristically male and female behavioral patterns.

∞ **2.** Ehrenreich points to the popularity of several "macho stars": Mel Gibson in *The Road Warrior,* John Travolta in *Saturday Night Fever,* Marlon Brando in *The Wild One,* and Clint Eastwood in anything. Choose several female characters from film or television who you feel provide positive role models for both males and females. Write an essay in which you use these characters as examples of the way that men and women should conduct their lives. Before writing, consider reading Maya Angelou's "Sister Flowers" (page 106), a loving portrait of a memorable female role model.

Writing Assignments Using Other Patterns of Development

∞ **3.** Ehrenreich suggests that some of the problems women experience in relationships and careers are of their own making—they smile too much, are too deferential, and fail to claim their own achievements. Pick one or two areas in which women tend to experience difficulty and write an essay arguing either that women sabotage themselves or that they are sabotaged by society's attitudes and expectations. Brainstorm with others to gather ideas for your paper. For other perspectives, you may want to read one or more of the following essays: Deborah Tannen's "But What Do You Mean?" (page 241), Dave Barry's "The Ugly Truth About Beauty" (page 323), Camille Paglia's "Rape: A Bigger Danger Than Feminists Know" (page 451), and Susan Jacoby's "Common Decency" (page 458).

∞ **4.** Like Ehrenreich, most of us have been subjected at one time or another to the inappropriate or unpleasant behavior of others: slurs on our abilities, interests, or appearance; derision about our sex or sexual preference; taunts about our race, religion, or ethnic background. Focus on *one* kind of insult, and brainstorm with others to identify ways for dealing with such an affront. Then write an essay describing different strategies for coping with the offensive behavior. Reach some conclusions about which approach is most effective. Deborah Tannen's "But What Do You Mean?" (page 241) and Caroline Rego's "The Fine Art of Complaining" (page 285) may spark some ideas worth exploring.

Writing Assignments Using a Journal Entry as a Starting Point

5. Drawing upon your pre-reading journal entry, write an essay in which you compare and/or contrast the qualities that parents and the culture at large nurture in boys with those they nurture in girls. Brainstorming with others will help you identify telling examples. Reach some conclusions about the long-term effects on children of these parental and societal influences. Consider supplementing your informal research with library and/or Internet information about the formation of children's gender identity.

Additional Writing Topics

EXEMPLIFICATION

General Assignments

Use examples to develop any one of the following topics into a well-organized essay. When writing the paper, choose enough relevant examples to support your thesis. Organize the material into a sequence that most effectively illustrates the thesis, keeping in mind that emphatic order is often the most compelling way to present specifics.

1. Many of today's drivers have dangerous habits.
2. Drug and alcohol abuse is (or is not) a serious problem among many young people.
3. One rule of restaurant dining is "Management often seems oblivious to problems that are perfectly obvious to customers."
4. Children today are not encouraged to use their imaginations.
5. The worst kind of hypocrite is a religious hypocrite.
6. The best things in life are definitely not free.
7. A part-time job is an important experience that every college student should have.
8. Many TV and magazine ads use sexual allusions to sell their products.
9. _____ (name someone you know well) is a _____ (use a quality: open-minded, dishonest, compulsive, reliable, gentle, and so on) person.
10. Television commercials stereotype the elderly (or another minority group).
11. Today, salespeople act as if they're doing you a favor by taking your money.
12. Most people behave decently in their daily interactions with each other.
13. Pettiness, jealousy, and selfishness abound in our daily interactions with each other.
14. You can tell a lot about people by observing what they wear and eat.
15. Too many Americans are overly concerned with being physically fit.
16. There are several study techniques that will help a student learn more efficiently.
17. Some teachers seem to enjoy turning tests into ordeals.
18. "How to avoid bad eating habits" is one course all college students should take.
19. More needs to be done to eliminate obstacles faced by the physically handicapped.
20. Some of the best presents are those that cost the least.

Assignments With a Specific Purpose and Audience

1. A friend of yours has taken a job in a big city or moved to a small town. To prepare your friend for this new environment, write a letter giving examples of what life in a big city or small town is like. You might focus on the benefits or dangers with which your friend is unlikely to be familiar.

2. Shopping for a new car, you become annoyed at how many safety features are available only as expensive options. Write a letter of complaint to the auto manufacturer, citing at least three examples of such options. Avoid sounding hostile.

3. Lately, many people at your college or workplace have been experiencing stress. As a member of the Campus (or Company) Committee on Morale, you've been asked to prepare a pamphlet illustrating different strategies for reducing stress. Decide what strategies you'll discuss and explain them with helpful examples.

4. Assume that you're an elementary school principal planning to give a speech in which you'll try to convince parents that television distorts children's perceptions of reality. Write the speech, illustrating your point with vivid examples.

5. A pet food company is having an annual contest to choose a new animal to feature in its advertising. To win the contest, you must convince the company that your pet is personable, playful, unique. Write an essay giving examples of your pet's special qualities.

6. For your college humor magazine, write an article on what you consider to be the "three best consumer products of the past twenty-five years." Support your opinion with lively, engaging specifics that are consistent with the magazine's offbeat and slightly ironic tone.

6

DIVISION-
CLASSIFICATION

WHAT IS DIVISION-CLASSIFICATION?

Imagine what life would be like if this is how an average day unfolded:

> You plan to stop at the supermarket for only five items, but your marketing takes over an hour because all the items in the store are jumbled together. Clerks put new shipments anywhere they please; the milk might be with the vegetables on Monday but with laundry detergent on Thursday. Next, you go to the drugstore to pick up some photos you left to be developed. You don't have time, though, to wait while the cashier roots through the large carton into which all the pickup envelopes have been thrown. You return to your car and decide to stop at the town hall to pay a parking ticket. But the town hall baffles you. The offices are unmarked, and there's not even a directory to tell you on which floor the Violations Bureau can be found. Annoyed,

you get back into your car and, minutes later, end up colliding with another car, which is driving toward you in your lane. When you wake up in the hospital, you find there are three other patients in your room: a middle-aged man with a heart problem, a young boy ready to have his tonsils removed, and a woman about to go into labor.

Such a muddled world, lacking the most basic forms of organization, would make daily life chaotic. All of us instinctively look for ways to order our environment. Without systems, categories, or sorting mechanisms, we'd be overwhelmed by life's complexity. An organization such as a college or university, for example, is made manageable by being divided into various schools (Liberal Arts, Performing Arts, Engineering, and so on). The schools are then separated into departments (English, History, Political Science), and each department's offerings are grouped into distinct categories— English, for instance, into Literature and Composition—before being further divided into specific courses.

The kind of ordering system we've been discussing is called *division-classification,* a logical way of thinking that allows us to make sense of a complex world. Division and classification, though separate processes, are often used together as complementary techniques. *Division* involves taking a single unit or concept, breaking the unit down into its parts, and then analyzing the connections among the parts and between the parts and the whole. For instance, if we wanted to organize the chaotic hospital described at the start of the chapter, we might think about how the single concept "a hospital" could be broken down into its components. We might come up with the following breakdown: pediatric wing, cardiac wing, maternity wing, and so on.

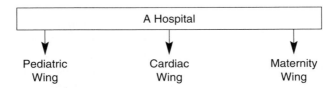

What we have just done involves division: We've taken a single entity (a hospital) and divided it into some of its component parts (wings), each with its own facilities and patients.

In contrast, *classification* brings two or more related items together and categorizes them according to type or kind. If the disorganized supermarket described earlier were to be restructured, the clerks would have to classify the separate items arriving at the loading dock. Cartons of lettuce, tomatoes, cucumbers, butter, yogurt, milk, shampoo, conditioner, and setting lotion would be assigned to the appropriate categories:

Lettuce	Butter	Shampoo
Tomatoes	Yogurt	Conditioner
Cucumbers	Milk	Setting Lotion

| Produce | Dairy | Hair Products |

HOW DIVISION-CLASSIFICATION FITS YOUR PURPOSE AND AUDIENCE

The reorganized hospital and supermarket show the way division and classification work in everyday life. But division and classification also come into play during the writing process. Because division involves breaking a subject into parts, it can be a helpful strategy during prewriting, especially if you're analyzing a broad, complex subject: the structure of a film; the motivation of a character in a novel; the problem your community has with vandalism; the controversy surrounding school prayer. An editorial examining a recent hostage crisis, for example, might divide the crisis into three areas: how the hostages were treated by (1) their captors, (2) the governments negotiating their release, and (3) the media. The purpose of the editorial might be to show readers that the governments' treatment of the hostages was particularly exploitative.

Classification can be useful for imposing order on the hodgepodge of ideas generated during prewriting. You examine that material to see which of your rough ideas are alike and which are dissimilar, so that you can cluster related items in the same category. Classification would, then, be a helpful strategy in analyzing topics like these: techniques for impressing teachers; comic styles of talkshow hosts; views on abortion; reasons for the current rise in volunteerism. You might, for instance, use classification in a paper showing that Americans are undermining their health through their obsessive pursuit of various diets. Perhaps you begin by brainstorming all the diets that have gained popularity in recent years (Weight Watchers', Slim-Fast, Jenny Craig, whatever). Then you categorize the diets according to type: high-fiber, low-protein, high-carbohydrate, and so on. Once the diets are grouped, you can discuss the problems within each category, demonstrating to readers that none of the diets is safe or effective.

Division-classification can be crucial when responding to college assignments like the following:

> Based on your observations, what kinds of appeals do television advertisers use when selling automobiles? In your view, are any of these appeals morally irresponsible?

> Analyze the components that go into being an effective parent. Indicate those you consider most vital for raising confident, well-adjusted children.

> Describe the hierarchy of the typical high school clique, identifying the various parts of the hierarchy. Use your analysis to support or refute the view that adolescence is a period of rigid conformity.

> Many social commentators have observed that discourtesy is on the rise. Indicate whether you think this is a valid observation by characterizing the types of everyday encounters you have with people.

These assignments suggest division-classification through the use of such words as *kinds, components, parts,* and *types.* Generally, though, you won't receive such clear signals to use division-classification. Instead, the broad purpose of the essay—and the point you want to make—will lead you to the analytical thinking characteristic of division-classification.

Sometimes division-classification will be the dominant technique for structuring an essay; other times it will be used as a supplemental pattern in an essay organized primarily according to another pattern of development. Let's look at some examples. Say you want to write a paper *explaining a process* (surviving divorce; creating a hit record; shepherding a bill through Congress; using the Heimlich maneuver on people who are choking).

You could *divide* the process into parts or stages, showing, for instance, that the Heimlich maneuver is an easily mastered skill that readers should acquire. Or perhaps you plan to write a light-spirited essay analyzing the *effect* that increased awareness of sexual stereotypes has had on college students' social lives. In such a case, you might use *classification*. To show readers that shifting gender roles make young men and women comically self-conscious, you could categorize the places where students scout each other out: in class, at the library, at parties, in dorms. You could then show how students—not wishing to be macho or coyly feminine—approach each other with laughable tentativeness in these four environments.

Now imagine that you're writing an *argumentation-persuasion* essay urging that the federal government prohibit the use of growth-inducing antibiotics in livestock feed. The paper could begin by *dividing* the antibiotics cycle into stages: the effects of antibiotics on livestock; the short-term effects on humans who consume the animals; the possible long-term effects of consuming antibiotic-tainted meat. To increase readers' understanding of the problem, you might also discuss the antibiotics controversy in terms of an even larger issue: the dangerous ways food is treated before being consumed. In this case, you would consider the various procedures (use of additives, preservatives, artificial colors, and so on), *classifying* these treatments into several types—from least harmful (some additives or artificial colors, perhaps) to most harmful (you might slot the antibiotics here). Such an essay would be developed using both division *and* classification: first, the division of the antibiotics cycle and then the classification of the various food treatments. Frequently, this interdependence will be reversed, and classification will precede rather than follow division.

SUGGESTIONS FOR USING DIVISION-CLASSIFICATION IN AN ESSAY

The following suggestions will be helpful whether you use division-classification as a dominant or a supportive pattern of development.

1. Select a principle of division-classification consistent with your purpose. Most subjects can be divided or classified according to a *number of different principles*. For example, when writing about an ideal vacation, you could divide your subject according to any of these principles: location, cost, recreation available. Similarly, when analyzing students at your college, you could base your classification on a variety of principles: students' majors, their racial or ethnic background, whether they belong to a fraternity or sorority. In all cases, though, the principle of division-classification you select must meet one stringent requirement: It must help you meet your overall purpose and reinforce your central point.

Sometimes a principle of division-classification seems so attractive that you latch on to it without examining whether it's consistent with your purpose. Suppose you want to write a paper asserting that several episodes of a new television comedy are destined to become classics. Here's how you might go wrong.

You begin by doing some brainstorming about the episodes. Then, as you start to organize the prewriting material, you hit on a possible principle of classification: grouping the characters in the show according to the frequency with which they appear (main characters appearing in every show, supporting characters appearing in most shows, and guest characters appearing once or twice). You name the characters and explain which characters fit where. But is this principle of classification significant? Has it anything to do with why the shows will become classics? No, it hasn't. Such an essay would be little more than a meaningless exercise in classifying things just to classify them.

In contrast, a significant principle of classification might involve categorizing a number of shows according to the easily recognized human types portrayed: the Pompous Know-It-All, the Boss Who's Out of Control, the Lovable Grouch, the Surprisingly Savvy Innocent. You might illustrate the way certain episodes offer delightful twists on these stock figures, making such shows models of comic plotting and humor.

When you write an essay that uses division-classification as its primary method of development, a *single principle* of division-classification provides the foundation for each major section of the paper. Imagine you're writing an essay showing that the success of contemporary music groups has less to do with musical talent than with the groups' ability to market themselves to a distinct segment of the listening audience. To develop your point, you might categorize several performers according to the age ranges they appeal to (preteens, adolescents, people in their late twenties) and then analyze the marketing strategies the musicians use to gain their fans' support. The essay's logic would be undermined if you switched, in the middle of your analysis, to another principle of classification—say, the influence of earlier groups on today's music scene.

Don't, however, take this caution to mean that essays can never use more than one principle of division-classification as they unfold. They can—as long as the *shift from one principle to another* occurs in *different parts* of the paper. Imagine you want to write about widespread disillusionment with student government leaders at your college. You could develop this point by breaking down the dissatisfaction into the following: disappointment with the students' qualifications for office; disenchantment with their campaign tactics; frustration with their performance once elected. That section of the essay completed, you might move to a second principle of division—how students can get involved in campus government. Perhaps you break the proposed involvement into the following possibilities: serving on nominating committees; helping to run candidates' campaigns; attending open sessions of the student government.

2. Apply the principle of division-classification logically. In an essay using division-classification, you need to demonstrate to readers that your analysis is the result of careful thought. First of all, your division-classification should be as *complete* as possible. Your analysis should include—within reason—all the parts into which you can divide your subject, or all the types into which you can categorize your subjects. Let's say you're writing an essay showing that where college students live is an important factor in determining how satisfied they are with college life. Keeping your purpose in mind, you classify students according to where they live: with parents, in dorms, in fraternity and sorority houses. But what about all the students who live in rented apartments, houses, or rooms off campus? If these places of residence are ignored, your classification won't be complete; you will lose credibility with your readers because they'll probably realize that you have overlooked several important considerations.

Your division-classification should also be *consistent:* The parts into which you break your subject or the groups into which you place your subjects should be as mutually exclusive as possible. The parts or categories should not be mixed, nor should they overlap. Assume you're writing an essay describing the animals at the zoo in a nearby city. You decide to describe the zoo's mammals, reptiles, birds, and endangered species. But such a classification is inconsistent. You begin by categorizing the animals according to scientific class (mammals, birds, reptiles), then switch to another principle when you classify some animals according to whether they are endangered. Because you drift over to a different principle of classification, your categories are no longer mutually exclusive: Endangered species could overlap with any of the other categories. In which section of the paper, for instance, would you describe an exotic parrot that is obviously a bird but is also nearly extinct? And how would you categorize the zoo's rare mountain gorilla? This impressive creature is a mammal, but it is also an endangered species. Such overlapping categories undercut the logic that gives an essay its integrity.

A helpful tip: A solid outline is invaluable when you use division-classification. The outline encourages you to do the rigorous thinking needed to arrive at divisions and classifications that are logical, complete, and consistent.

3. Prepare an effective thesis. If your essay uses division-classification as its dominant method of development, it might be helpful to prepare a thesis that does more than signal the paper's subject and suggest your attitude toward that general subject. You might also want the thesis to state the principle of division-classification at the heart of the essay. Furthermore, you might want the thesis to reveal which part or category you regard as most important.

Consider the two thesis statements that follow:

As the observant beachcomber moves from the tidal area to the upper beach to the sandy dunes, rich variations in marine life become apparent.

Although most people focus on the dangers associated with the disposal of toxic waste in the land and ocean, the incineration of toxic matter may pose an even more serious threat to human life.

The first thesis statement makes clear that the writer will organize the paper by classifying forms of marine life according to location. Because the purpose of the essay is to inform as objectively as possible, the thesis doesn't suggest the writer's opinion about which category is most significant.

The second thesis signals that the essay will evolve by dividing the issue of toxic waste according to methods of disposal. Moreover, because the paper takes a stance on a controversial subject, the thesis is worded to reveal which aspect of the topic the writer considers most important. Such a clear statement of the writer's position is an effective strategy in an essay of this kind.

You may have noted that each thesis statement also signals the paper's plan of development. The first essay, for example, will use specific facts, examples, and details to describe the kinds of marine life found in the tidal area, upper beach, and dunes. However, thesis statements in papers developed primarily through division-classification don't have to be so structured. If a paper is well written, your principle of division-classification, your opinion about which part or category is most important, and the essay's plan of development will become apparent as the essay unfolds.

4. Organize the paper logically.   Whether your paper is developed wholly or in part by division-classification, it should have a logical structure. As much as possible, you should try to discuss *comparable points* in each section of the paper. In the essay on seashore life, for example, you might describe life in the tidal area by discussing the mollusks, crustaceans, birds, and amphibians that live or feed there. You would then follow through, as much as you could, with this arrangement in the paper's other sections (upper beach and dune). Forgetting to describe the birdlife thriving in the dunes, especially when you had discussed birdlife in the tidal and upper-beach areas, would compromise the paper's structure. Of course, perfect parallelism is not always possible—there are no mollusks in the dunes, for instance. You should also use *signal devices* to connect various parts of the paper: "*Another* characteristic of marine life battered by the tides"; "A *final* important trait of both tidal and upper-beach crustaceans"; "*Unlike* the creatures of the tidal area and the upper beach." Such signals clarify the connections among the essay's ideas.

5. State any conclusions or recommendations in the paper's final section.   The analytic thinking that occurs during division-classification often leads to surprising insights. Such insights may be introduced early on, or they may be reserved for the end, where they are stated as conclusions or recommendations. A paper might categorize different kinds of coaches—from inspiring to incompetent— and make the point that athletes learn a great deal about human relations simply by having to get along with their coaches, regardless of the coaches' skills. Such a paper might conclude that participation in a team sport teaches more about human nature than several courses in psychology. Or the essay might end with a proposal: Rookies and seasoned team members should be paired so that novice players can get advice on dealing with coaching eccentricities.

STUDENT ESSAY

The following student essay was written by Gail Oremland in response to this assignment:

> In "Propaganda Techniques in Today's Advertising," Ann McClintock describes the flaws in many of the persuasive strategies used by advertisers. Choose another group of people whose job is also to communicate—for example, parents, bosses, teachers. Then, in an essay of your own, divide the group into types according to the flaws they make when communicating.

While reading Gail's paper, try to determine how effectively it applies the principles of division-classification. The annotations on Gail's paper and the commentary following it will help you look at the essay more closely.

The Truth About College Teachers

by Gail Oremland

Introduction	A recent TV news story told about a group of college professors from a nearby university who were hired by a local school system to help upgrade the teaching in the community's public schools. The professors were to visit classrooms, analyze teachers' skills, and then conduct workshops to help the teachers become more effective at their jobs. But after the first round of workshops, the superintendent of schools decided to cancel the whole project. He fired the learned professors and sent them back to their ivory tower. Why did the project fall apart? There was a simple reason. The college professors, who were supposedly going to show the public school teachers how to be more effective, were themselves poor teachers. Many college students could have predicted such a disastrous outcome. They know, firsthand, that college

1

Thesis ──────── teachers are strange. They know that professors often exhibit bizarre behaviors, relating to students in ways that make it difficult for students to stay awake, or--if awake--to learn.

2   One type of professor assumes, legitimately enough, that her function is to pass on to students the vast store of knowledge she has acquired. But

Topic sentence ────── because the "Knowledgeable One" regards herself

The first of three paragraphs on the first category of teacher

as an expert and her students as the ignorant masses, she adopts an elitist approach that sabotages learning. The Knowledgeable One enters a lecture hall with a self-important air, walks to the podium, places her yellowed-with-age notes on the stand,

The first paragraph in a three-part chronological sequence: What happens *before* class

and begins her lecture at the exact second the class is officially scheduled to begin. There can be a blizzard or hurricane raging outside the lecture hall; students can be running through freezing sleet and howling winds to get to class on time. Will the Knowledgeable One wait for them to arrive before beginning her lecture? Probably not. The Knowledgeable One's time is precious. She's there, set to begin, and that's what matters.

Topic sentence ──────► Once the monologue begins, the Knowledge-   3

The second paragraph on the first category of teacher

able One drones on and on. The Knowledgeable One is a fact person. She may be the history prof who knows the death toll of every Civil War battle, the biology prof who can diagram all the common biological molecules, the accounting prof who enumerates every clause of the federal tax form.

The second paragraph in the chronological sequence: What happens *during* class

Oblivious to students' glazed eyes and stifled yawns, the Knowledgeable One delivers her monologue, dispensing one dry fact after another. The only advantage to being on the receiving end of this boring monologue is that students do not have to worry about being called on to question a point or provide an opinion; the Knowledgeable One is not willing to relinquish one minute of her time by giving students a voice. Assume for one improbable moment that a student actually manages to stay awake during the monologue and is brave enough to ask a question. In such a case, the Knowledgeable One will address the questioning student as "Mr." or "Miss." This formality does not, as some students mistakenly suppose, indicate respect for the student as a fledgling member of the academic community. Not at all. This impersonality represents the Knowledgeable One's desire to keep as wide a distance as possible between her and her students.

Topic sentence ─────────► The Knowledgeable One's monologue always 4 comes to a close at the precise second the class is scheduled to end. No sooner has she delivered her last forgettable word than the Knowledgeable One packs up her notes and shoots out the door, heading back to the privacy of her office, where she can pursue her specialized academic interests--free of any possible interruption from students. The Knowledgeable One's hasty departure from the lecture hall makes it clear she has no desire to talk with students. In her eyes, she has met her obligations; she has taken time away from her research to transmit to students what she knows. Any closer contact might mean she would risk contagion from students, that great unwashed mass. Such a danger is to be avoided at all costs.

The third paragraph on the first category of teacher

The final paragraph in the chronological sequence: What happens *after* class

Unlike the Knowledgeable One, the "Leader of 5 Intellectual Discussion" seems to respect students. Emphasizing class discussion, the Leader encourages students to confront ideas ("What is Twain's view of morality?" "Was our intervention in Vietnam justified?" "Should big business be given tax breaks?") and discover their own truths. Then, about three weeks into the semester, it becomes clear that the Leader wants students to discover <u>his</u> version of the truth. Behind the Leader's democratic guise lurks a dictator. When a student voices an opinion that the Leader accepts, the student is rewarded by hearty nods of approval and "Good point, good point." But if a student is rash enough to advance a conflicting viewpoint, the Leader responds with killing politeness: "Well, yes, that's an interesting perspective. But don't you think that . . . ?" Grade-conscious students soon learn not to chime in with their viewpoint. They know that when the Leader, with seeming honesty, says, "I'd be interested in hearing what you think. Let's open this up for discussion," they had better figure out what the Leader wants to hear before advancing their own

Topic sentence ─────────

Paragraph on the second category of teacher

theories. "Me-tooism" rather than independent thinking, they discover, guarantees good grades in the Leader's class.

Topic sentence ⟶ 6

Paragraph on the third category of teacher

Then there is the professor who comes across as the students' "Buddy." This kind of professor does not see himself as an imparter of knowledge or a leader of discussion but as a pal, just one in a community of equals. The Buddy may start his course this way. "All of us know that this college stuff-- grades, degrees, exams, required reading--is a game. So let's not play it, okay?" Dressed in jeans, sweatshirt, and scuffed sneakers, the Buddy projects a relaxed, casual attitude. He arranges the class seats in a circle (he would never take a position in front of the room) and insists that students call him by his first name. He uses no syllabus and gives few tests, believing that such constraints keep students from directing their own learning. A free spirit, the Buddy often teaches courses like "The Psychology of Interpersonal Relations" or "The Social Dynamics of the Family." If students choose to use class time to discuss the course material, that's fine. If they want to discuss something else, that's fine, too. It's the self-expression, the honest dialogue, that counts. In fact, the Buddy seems especially fond of digressions from academic subjects. By talking about his political views, his marital problems, his tendency to drink one too many beers, the Buddy lets students see that he is a regular guy--just like them. At first, students look forward to classes with the Buddy. They enjoy the informality, the chitchat, the lack of pressure. But after a while, they wonder why they are paying for a course where they learn nothing. They might as well stay home and watch the soaps.

Conclusion

Echoes opening anecdote

Obviously, some college professors are excellent. They are learned, hardworking, and imaginative; they enjoy their work and like being with students. On the whole, though, college professors are a strange lot. Despite their advanced degrees and their own exposure to many different kinds of teachers, they do not seem to understand how to relate to students. Rather than being hired as consultants to help others upgrade their teaching 7

skills, college professors should themselves hire
consultants to tell them what they are doing wrong
and how they can improve. Who should these consultants be? That's easy: the people who know
them best--their students.

COMMENTARY

Introduction and thesis.   After years of being graded by teachers,
Gail took special pleasure in writing an essay that gave her a chance
to evaluate her teachers—in this case, her college professors. Even the
essay's title, "The Truth About College Teachers," implies that Gail
is going to have fun knocking profs down from their ivory towers. To
introduce her subject, she uses a timely news story. This brief anecdote leads directly to the essay's *thesis:* "Professors often exhibit
bizarre behaviors, relating to students in ways that make it difficult for
students to stay awake, or—if awake—to learn." Note that Gail's thesis isn't highly structured; it doesn't, for example, name the specific
categories to be discussed. Still, her thesis suggests that the essay is
going to *categorize* a range of teaching behaviors, using as a *principle
of classification* the strange ways that college profs relate to students.

Purpose.   As with all good papers developed through division-
classification, Gail's essay doesn't use classification as an end in itself.
Gail uses classification because it helps her achieve a broader *purpose*.
She wants to *convince* readers—without moralizing or abandoning
her humorous tone—that such teaching styles inhibit learning. In
other words, there's a serious underside to her essay. This additional layer of meaning is characteristic of satiric writing.

Categories and topic sentences.   The essay's body, consisting of
five paragraphs, presents the three categories that make up Gail's
analysis. According to Gail, college teachers can be categorized as
the Knowledgeable One (paragraphs 2–4), the Leader of
Intellectual Discussion (5), or the Buddy (6). Obviously, there are
other ways professors might be classified. But given Gail's purpose,
audience, tone, and point of view, her categories are appropriate;
they are reasonably *complete, consistent,* and *mutually exclusive*.
Note, too, that Gail uses *topic sentences* near the beginning of each
category to help readers see which professorial type she's discussing.

Overall organization and paragraph structure.   Gail is able to shift smoothly and easily from one category to the next. How does she achieve such graceful transitions? Take a moment to reread the sentences that introduce her second and third categories (paragraphs 5 and 6). Look at the way each sentence's beginning (in italics here) links back to the preceding category or categories: "*Unlike the Knowledgeable One,* the 'Leader of Intellectual Discussion' seems to respect students"; and "[the Buddy] . . . *does not see himself as an imparter of knowledge or a leader of discussion* but as a pal. . . ."

Gail is equally careful about providing an easy-to-follow structure within each section. She uses a *chronological sequence* to organize her three-paragraph discussion of the Knowledgeable One. The first paragraph deals with the beginning of the Knowledgeable One's lecture; the second, with the lecture itself; the third, with the end of the lecture. And the paragraphs' *topic sentences* clearly indicate this passage of time. Similarly, *transitions* are used in the paragraphs on the Leader of Intellectual Discussion and the Buddy to ensure a logical progression of points: "*Then,* about three weeks into the semester, it becomes clear that the Leader wants students to discover *his* version of the truth" (5) and "*At first,* students look forward to classes with the Buddy. . . . But *after a while,* they wonder why they are paying for a course where they learn nothing" (6).

Tone.   The essay's unity can also be traced to Gail's skill in sustaining her satiric tone. Throughout the essay, Gail selects details that fit her gently mocking attitude. She depicts the Knowledgeable One lecturing from "yellowed-with-age notes . . . , oblivious to students' glazed eyes and stifled yawns," unwilling to wait for students who "run . . . through freezing sleet and howling winds to get to class on time." Then she presents another tongue-in-cheek description, this one focusing on the way the Leader of Intellectual Discussion conducts class: "Good point, good point. . . . Well, yes, that's an interesting perspective. But don't you think that . . . ?" Finally, with similar killing accuracy, Gail portrays the Buddy, democratically garbed in "jeans, sweatshirt, and scuffed sneakers."

Other patterns of development.   Gail's satiric depiction of her three professorial types employs a number of techniques associated with *narrative* and *descriptive writing*: vigorous images, highly connotative language, and dialogue. *Definition, exemplification, causal* *analysis,* and *comparison-contrast* also come into play. Gail defines the characteristics of each type of professor; she provides numerous examples to support her categories; she explains the effects of the different teaching styles on students; and, in her description of the Leader of Intellectual Discussion, she contrasts the appearance of democracy with the dictatorial reality.

Unequal development of categories.   Although Gail's essay is unified, organized, and well-developed, you may have felt that the first category outweighs the other two. There is, of course, no need to balance the categories exactly. But Gail's extended treatment of the first category sets up an expectation that the others will be treated as fully. One way to remedy this problem would be to delete some material from the discussion of the Knowledgeable One. Gail might, for instance, omit the last five sentences in the third paragraph (about the professor's habit of addressing students as "Mr." or "Miss"). Such a change could be made without taking the bite out of her portrayal. Even better, Gail could simply switch the order of her sections, putting the portrait of the Knowledgeable One at the essay's end. Here, the extended discussion wouldn't seem out of proportion. Instead, the sections would appear in *emphatic order,* with the most detailed category saved for last.

Revising the first draft.   It's apparent that an essay as engaging as Gail's must have undergone a good deal of revising. That was in fact the case. Gail made many changes in the body of the essay, but it's particularly interesting to review what happened to the introduction as she revised the paper. Reprinted here is Gail's original introduction.

Original Version of the Introduction

Despite their high IQs, advanced degrees, and published papers, some college professors just don't know how to teach. Found in almost any department, in tenured and untenured positions, they prompt student apathy. They fail to convey ideas effectively and to challenge or inspire students. Students thus finish their courses having learned very little. Contrary to popular opinion, these professors' ineptitude is not simply a matter of delivering boring lectures or not caring about students. Many of them care a great deal. Their failure actually stems from their unrealistic perceptions of what a teacher should be. Specifically, they adopt teaching styles or roles that alienate students and undermine learning. Three of the most common ones are "The Knowledgeable One," "The Leader of Intellectual Discussion," and "The Buddy."

When Gail showed the first draft of the essay to her composition instructor, he laughed—and occasionally squirmed—as he read what she had prepared. He was enthusiastic about the paper but felt that there was a problem with the introduction's tone; it was too serious when compared to the playful, lightly satiric mood of the rest of the essay. When Gail reread the paragraph, she agreed, but she was uncertain about the best way to remedy the problem. After revising other sections of the essay, she decided to let the paper sit for a while before going back to rewrite the introduction.

In the meantime, Gail switched on the TV. The timing couldn't have been better; she tuned into a news story about several supposedly learned professors who had been fired from a consulting job because they had turned out to know so little about teaching. This was exactly the kind of item Gail needed to start her essay. Now she was able to prepare a completely new introduction, making it consistent in spirit with the rest of the paper.

With this stronger introduction and the rest of the essay well in hand, Gail was ready to write a conclusion. Now, as she worked on the concluding paragraph, she deliberately shaped it to recall the story about the fired consultants. By echoing the opening anecdote in her conclusion, Gail was able to end the paper with another poke at professors—a perfect way to close her clever and insightful essay.

ACTIVITIES: DIVISION-CLASSIFICATION

Prewriting Activities

1. Imagine you're writing two essays: One is a humorous paper outlining a *process* for impressing college instructors; the other is a serious essay examining the *causes* of the recent rise in volunteerism. What about the topics might you divide and/or classify?

2. Use group brainstorming to identify three principles of division for *one* of the topics in Set A below. Focusing on one of the principles, decide what your thesis might be if you were writing an essay. That done, use group brainstorming to identify three principles of classification that might provide the structure for *one* of the topics in Set

B. Focusing on one of the principles, decide what your thesis might be if you were writing an essay.

Set A
- Rock music
- A shopping mall
- A good horror movie

Set B
- Why people get addicted to computers
- How fast-food restaurants affect family life
- Why long-term relationships break up

Revising Activities

3. Following is a scratch outline for an essay developed through division-classification. On what principle of division-classification is the essay based? What problem do you see in the way the principle is applied? How could the problem be remedied?

   Thesis: The same experience often teaches opposite things to different people.

   - What working as a fast-food cook teaches: Some learn responsibility; others learn to take a "quick and dirty" approach.
   - What a negative experience teaches optimists: Some learn from their mistakes; others continue to maintain a positive outlook.
   - What a difficult course teaches: Some learn to study hard; others learn to avoid demanding courses.
   - What the breakup of a close relationship teaches: Some learn how to negotiate differences; others learn to avoid intimacy.

4. Following is a paragraph from the first draft of an essay urging that day care centers adopt play programs tailored to children's developmental needs. What principle of division-classification focuses the paragraph? Is the principle applied consistently and logically? Are parts/categories developed sufficiently? Revise the paragraph, eliminating any problems you discover and adding specific details where needed.

   Within a few years, preschool children move from self-absorbed to interactive play. Babies and toddlers engage in solitary play. Although they sometimes prefer being near other children, they focus primarily on their own actions. This is very different from the highly interactive play of the elementary school years. Sometime in children's second year, solitary play is replaced by parallel play, during which children engage in similar activities near one another. However, they interact only occasionally. By age three, most children show at least some cooperative play, a form that involves interaction and cooperative role-taking. Such role-taking can be found in the "pretend" games that children play to explore adult relationships (games of "Mommy and Daddy") and anatomy (games of "Doctor"). Additional signs of youngsters' growing awareness of peers can be seen at about age four. At this age, many children begin showing a special devotion to one other child and may want to play only with that child. During this time, children also begin to take special delight in physical activities such as running and jumping, often going off by themselves to expend their abundant physical energy.

William Lutz

With a dash of humor, William Lutz (1941–), Professor of English at Rutgers University and former editor of the *Quarterly Review of Doublespeak,* writes about a subject he takes very seriously: doublespeak—the use of language to evade, deceive, and mislead. An expert on language, Lutz has appeared on many national television programs, among them the *Today Show, Larry King Live,* and the *MacNeil-Lehrer News Hour.* Lutz, who has both a doctorate in English and a Doctor of Law degree, has written over two dozen articles and is the author or coauthor of fourteen books, including the best-selling *Doublespeak: From Revenue Enhancement to Terminal Living* (1989) as well as its sequels, *The New Doublespeak: Why No One Knows What Anyone's Saying Anymore* (1996) and *Doublespeak Defined: Cut Through the Bull* ✶✶✶✶ *and Get to the Point* (1999). The following piece is from *Doublespeak.*

Pre-Reading Journal Entry

At one time or another, everyone twists language in order to avoid telling the full truth. In your journal, list several instances which demonstrate that indirect, partially true language ("doublespeak") is sometimes desirable, even necessary. In each case, why was this evasive language used?

Doublespeak

There are no potholes in the streets of Tucson, Arizona, just 1 "pavement deficiencies." The Reagan Administration didn't propose any new taxes, just "revenue enhancement" through new "user's fees." Those aren't bums on the street, just "non-goal oriented members of society." There are no more poor people, just "fiscal underachievers." There was no robbery of an automatic teller machine, just an "unauthorized withdrawal." The patient didn't die because of medical malpractice, it was just a "diagnostic misadventure of a high magnitude." The U.S. Army doesn't kill the enemy anymore, it just "services the target." And the doublespeak goes on.

Doublespeak is language that pretends to communicate but 2 really doesn't. It is language that makes the bad seem good, the negative appear positive, the unpleasant appear attractive or at least tolerable. Doublespeak is language that avoids or shifts responsibility, language that is at variance with its real or purported meaning. It is language that conceals or prevents thought; rather than extending thought, doublespeak limits it. . . .

How to Spot Doublespeak

How can you spot doublespeak? Most of the time you will rec-   3
ognize doublespeak when you see or hear it. But, if you have any doubts, you can identify doublespeak just by answering these questions: Who is saying what to whom, under what conditions and circumstances, with what intent, and with what results? Answering these questions will usually help you identify as doublespeak language that appears to be legitimate or that at first glance doesn't even appear to be doublespeak.

First Kind of Doublespeak

There are at least four kinds of doublespeak. The first is the   4
euphemism, an inoffensive or positive word or phrase used to avoid a harsh, unpleasant, or distasteful reality. But a euphemism can also be a tactful word or phrase which avoids directly mentioning a painful reality, or it can be an expression used out of concern for the feelings of someone else, or to avoid directly discussing a topic subject to a social or cultural taboo.

When you use a euphemism because of your sensitivity for   5
someone's feelings or out of concern for a recognized social or cultural taboo, it is not doublespeak. For example, you express your condolences that someone has "passed away" because you do not want to say to a grieving person, "I'm sorry your father is dead." When you use the euphemism "passed away," no one is misled. Moreover, the euphemism functions here not just to protect the feelings of another person, but to communicate also your concern for that person's feelings during a period of mourning. When you excuse yourself to go to the "restroom," or you mention that someone is "sleeping with" or "involved with" someone else, you do not mislead anyone about your meaning, but you do respect the social taboos about discussing bodily functions and sex in direct terms. You also indicate your sensitivity to the feelings of your audience, which is usually considered a mark of courtesy and good manners.

However, when a euphemism is used to mislead or deceive, it   6
becomes doublespeak. For example, in 1984 the U.S. State Department announced that it would no longer use the word

"killing" in its annual report on the status of human rights in countries around the world. Instead, it would use the phrase "unlawful or arbitrary deprivation of life," which the department claimed was more accurate. Its real purpose for using this phrase was simply to avoid discussing the embarrassing situation of government-sanctioned killings in countries that are supported by the United States and have been certified by the United States as respecting the human rights of their citizens. This use of a euphemism constitutes doublespeak, since it is designed to mislead, to cover up the unpleasant. Its real intent is at variance with its apparent intent. It is language designed to alter our perception of reality.

The Pentagon, too, avoids discussing unpleasant realities when   7
it refers to bombs and artillery shells that fall on civilian targets as "incontinent ordnance." And in 1977 the Pentagon tried to slip funding for the neutron bomb unnoticed into an appropriations bill by calling it a "radiation enhancement device."

Second Kind of Doublespeak

A second kind of doublespeak is jargon, the specialized lan-   8
guage of a trade, profession, or similar group, such as that used by doctors, lawyers, engineers, educators, or car mechanics. Jargon can serve an important and useful function. Within a group, jargon functions as a kind of verbal shorthand that allows members of the group to communicate with each other clearly, efficiently, and quickly. Indeed, it is a mark of membership in the group to be able to use and understand the group's jargon.

But jargon, like the euphemism, can also be doublespeak. It can   9
be—and often is—pretentious, obscure, and esoteric terminology used to give an air of profundity, authority, and prestige to speakers and their subject matter. Jargon as doublespeak often makes the simple appear complex, the ordinary profound, the obvious insightful. In this sense it is used not to express but impress. With such doublespeak, the act of smelling something becomes "organoleptic analysis," glass becomes "fused silicate," a crack in a metal support beam becomes a "discontinuity," conservative economic policies become "distributionally conservative notions."

Lawyers, for example, speak of an "involuntary conversion" of   10
property when discussing the loss or destruction of property through theft, accident, or condemnation. If your house burns down or if your car is stolen, you have suffered an involuntary

conversion of your property. When used by lawyers in a legal situation, such jargon is a legitimate use of language, since lawyers can be expected to understand the term.

However, when a member of a specialized group uses its jargon   11
to communicate with a person outside the group, and uses it knowing that the nonmember does not understand such language, then there is doublespeak. For example, on May 9, 1978, a National Airlines 727 airplane crashed while attempting to land at the Pensacola, Florida airport. Three of the fifty-two passengers aboard the airplane were killed. As a result of the crash, National made an after-tax insurance benefit of $1.7 million, or an extra 18¢ a share dividend for its stockholders. Now National Airlines had two problems: It did not want to talk about one of its airplanes crashing, and it had to account for the $1.7 million when it issued its annual report to its stockholders. National solved the problem by inserting a footnote in its annual report which explained that the $1.7 million income was due to "the involuntary conversion of a 727." National thus acknowledged the crash of its airplane and the subsequent profit it made from the crash, without once mentioning the accident or the deaths. However, because airline officials knew that most stockholders in the company, and indeed most of the general public, were not familiar with legal jargon, the use of such jargon constituted doublespeak.

Third Kind of Doublespeak

A third kind of doublespeak is gobbledygook or bureaucratese.   12
Basically, such doublespeak is simply a matter of piling on words, of overwhelming the audience with words, the bigger the words and the longer the sentences the better. Alan Greenspan, then chair of President Nixon's Council of Economic Advisors, was quoted in *The Philadelphia Inquirer* in 1974 as having testified before a Senate committee that "It is a tricky problem to find the particular calibration in timing that would be appropriate to stem the acceleration in risk premiums created by falling incomes without prematurely aborting the decline in the inflation-generated risk premiums."

Nor has Mr. Greenspan's language changed since then.   13
Speaking to the meeting of the Economic Club of New York in 1988, Mr. Greenspan, now Federal Reserve chair, said, "I guess I should warn you, if I turn out to be particularly clear, you've probably misunderstood what I've said." Mr. Greenspan's doublespeak doesn't seem to have held back his career.

Sometimes gobbledygook may sound impressive, but when the   14
quote is later examined in print it doesn't even make sense. During
the 1988 presidential campaign, vice-presidential candidate Senator
Dan Quayle explained the need for a strategic-defense initiative by
saying, "Why wouldn't an enhanced deterrent, a more stable peace,
a better prospect to denying the ones who enter conflict in the first
place to have a reduction of offensive systems and an introduction
to defense capability? I believe this is the route the country will
eventually go."

The investigation into the Challenger disaster in 1986 revealed   15
the doublespeak of gobbledygook and bureaucratese used by too
many involved in the shuttle program. When Jesse Moore, NASA's
associate administrator, was asked if the performance of the shuttle
program had improved with each launch or if it had remained the
same, he answered, "I think our performance in terms of the liftoff
performance and in terms of the orbital performance, we knew more
about the envelope we were operating under, and we have been
pretty accurately staying in that. And so I would say the performance has not by design drastically improved. I think we have been
able to characterize the performance more as a function of our
launch experience as opposed to it improving as a function of time."
While this language may appear to be jargon, a close look will reveal
that it is really just gobbledygook laced with jargon. But you really
have to wonder if Mr. Moore had any idea what he was saying.

Fourth Kind of Doublespeak

The fourth kind of doublespeak is inflated language that is   16
designed to make the ordinary seem extraordinary; to make everyday things seem impressive; to give an air of importance to people,
situations, or things that would not normally be considered important; to make the simple seem complex. Often this kind of doublespeak isn't hard to spot, and it is usually pretty funny. While car
mechanics may be called "automotive internists," elevator operators
members of the "vertical transportation corps," used cars "pre-
owned" or "experienced cars," and black-and-white television sets
described as having "non-multicolor capability," you really aren't
misled all that much by such language.

However, you may have trouble figuring out that, when   17
Chrysler "initiates a career alternative enhancement program," it is

really laying off five thousand workers; or that "negative patient care outcome" means the patient died; or that "rapid oxidation" means a fire in a nuclear power plant.

The doublespeak of inflated language can have serious conse- 18
quences. In Pentagon doublespeak, "pre-emptive counterattack" means that American forces attacked first; "engaged the enemy on all sides" means American troops were ambushed; "backloading of augmentation personnel" means a retreat by American troops. In the doublespeak of the military, the 1983 invasion of Grenada was conducted not by the U.S. Army, Navy, Air Force, and Marines, but by the "Caribbean Peace Keeping Forces." But then, according to the Pentagon, it wasn't an invasion, it was a "predawn vertical insertion.". . .

The Dangers of Doublespeak

These . . . examples of doublespeak should make it clear that 19
doublespeak is not the product of carelessness or sloppy thinking. Indeed, most doublespeak is the product of clear thinking and is carefully designed and constructed to appear to communicate when in fact it doesn't. It is language designed not to lead but mislead. It is language designed to distort reality and corrupt thought. . . . When a fire in a nuclear reactor building is called "rapid oxidation," an explosion in a nuclear power plant is called an "energetic disassembly," the illegal overthrow of a legitimate government is termed "destabilizing a government," and lies are seen as "inoperative statements," we are hearing doublespeak that attempts to avoid responsibility and make the bad seem good, the negative appear positive, something unpleasant appear attractive; and which seems to communicate but doesn't. It is language designed to alter our perception of reality and corrupt our thinking. Such language does not provide us with the tools we need to develop, advance, and preserve our culture and our civilization. Such language breeds suspicion, cynicism, distrust, and, ultimately, hostility.

Questions for Close Reading

1. What is the selection's thesis? Locate the sentence(s) in which Lutz states his main idea. If he doesn't state the thesis explicitly, express it in your own words.

2. According to Lutz, four questions help people "spot" doublespeak. What are the questions? How do they help people distinguish between legitimate language and doublespeak?

3. Lutz's headings indicate simply "First Kind of Doublespeak," "Second Kind of Doublespeak," and so on. What terms does Lutz use to identify the four kinds of doublespeak? Cite one example of each kind.

4. What, according to Lutz, are the dangers of doublespeak?

5. Refer to your dictionary as needed to define the following words used in the selection: *variance* (paragraph 6), *esoteric* (9), *profundity* (9), *dividend* (11), and *initiative* (14).

Questions About the Writer's Craft

1. **The pattern.** Does Lutz make his four categories of doublespeak mutually exclusive, or does he let them overlap? Cite specific examples to support your answer. Why do you think Lutz took the approach he did?

2. **Other patterns.** What other patterns, besides division-classification, does Lutz use in this selection? Cite examples of at least two other patterns. Explain how each pattern reinforces Lutz's thesis.

3. Lutz quotes Alan Greenspan twice: first in paragraph 12 and again in paragraph 13. What is surprising about Greenspan's second comment (paragraph 13)? Why might Lutz have included this second quotation?

4. How would you characterize Lutz's tone in the essay? What key words indicate his attitude toward the material he discusses? Why do you suppose he chose this particular tone?

Writing Assignments Using Division-Classification as a Pattern of Development

1. According to Lutz, doublespeak "is language designed to alter our perception of reality." Using two of Lutz's categories (or any others you devise), analyze an advertisement or commercial that you think deliberately uses doublespeak to mislead consumers. Before writing your paper, read Ann McClintock's "Propaganda Techniques in Today's Advertising" (page 232). Feel free to include any of McClintock's interpretations in your paper.

2. Select *one* area of life that you know well. Possibilities include life in a college dormitory, the parent-child relationship, the dating scene, and sibling conflicts. Focus on a specific type of speech (for example, gossip, reprimands, flirtation, or criticism) that occurs in this area. Then identify the component parts of that type of speech. You might, for example, analyze dormitory gossip about individual students, couples, and professors. Reach some conclusions about the kinds of speech you discuss. Do you consider them funny, pathetic, or troubling? Your tone should be consistent with the conclusions you reach.

Writing Assignments Using Other Patterns of Development

∞ **3.** Find a spoken or written example of doublespeak that disturbs you. Possibilities include a political advertisement, television commercial, newspaper article, or legal document. Write a letter of complaint to the appropriate person or office, using convincing examples to point out what is misleading about the communication. Caroline Rego's "The Fine Art of Complaining" (page 285) offers guidelines for writing effective letters of complaint.

∞ **4.** In his essay, Lutz examines the relationship between language and perception. Identify two closely related terms, and contrast the different perceptions of reality represented by each term. For example, you might contrast "African-American" and "Negro," "Ms." and "Miss," "gay" and "homosexual," "dolls" and "action figures," or "pro-life" and "anti-abortion." Interviewing family, friends, and classmates will help you identify ideas to explore in the essay. For a discussion of the connection between language and perception, read Ann McClintock's "Propaganda Techniques in Today's Advertising" (page 232).

Writing Assignments Using a Journal Entry as a Starting Point

5. Select from your pre-reading journal entry two or three compelling instances of *beneficial* doublespeak. Use these examples in an essay arguing that doublespeak isn't always harmful. For each example cited, contrast the positive effects of doublespeak with the potentially negative consequences of *not* using it. Brainstorming with others will help you generate convincing examples.

Ann McClintock

Ann McClintock (1946–) was educated at Temple University in Philadelphia and later earned an advanced degree from the University of Pennsylvania. Formerly Director of Occupational Therapy at Ancora State Hospital in New Jersey, she has also worked as a freelance editor and writer. A frequent speaker before community groups, McClintock is especially interested in the effects of advertising on American life. The following selection, revised for this text, is part of a work in progress on the way propaganda techniques are used to sell products and political candidates.

Pre-Reading Journal Entry

How susceptible are you to ads and commercials? Do you consider yourself an easy target, or are you a "hard sell"? Have you purchased any products simply because you were won over by effective advertising strategies? What products have you not purchased because you deliberately didn't let yourself be swayed by advertisers' tactics? In your journal, reflect on these questions.

Propaganda Techniques in Today's Advertising

Americans, adults and children alike, are being seduced. They are being brainwashed. And few of us protest. Why? Because the seducers and the brainwashers are the advertisers we willingly invite into our homes. We are victims, content—even eager—to be victimized. We read advertisers' propaganda messages in newspapers and magazines; we watch their alluring images on television. We absorb their messages and images into our subconscious. We all do it—even those of us who claim to see through advertisers' tricks and therefore feel immune to advertising's charm. Advertisers lean heavily on propaganda to sell products, whether the "products" are a brand of toothpaste, a candidate for office, or a particular political viewpoint. 1

Propaganda is a systematic effort to influence people's opinions, to win them over to a certain view or side. Propaganda is not 2 necessarily concerned with what is true or false, good or bad. Propagandists simply want people to believe the messages being sent. Often, propagandists will use outright lies or more subtle deceptions to sway people's opinions. In a propaganda war, any tactic is considered fair.

When we hear the word "propaganda," we usually think of a   3 foreign menace: anti-American radio programs broadcast by a totalitarian regime or brainwashing tactics practiced on hostages. Although propaganda may seem relevant only in the political arena, the concept can be applied fruitfully to the way products and ideas are sold in advertising. Indeed, the vast majority of us are targets in advertisers' propaganda war. Every day, we are bombarded with slogans, print ads, commercials, packaging claims, billboards, trademarks, logos, and designer brands—all forms of propaganda. One study reports that each of us, during an average day, is exposed to over *five hundred* advertising claims of various types. This saturation may even increase in the future since current trends include ads on movie screens, shopping carts, videocassettes, even public television.

What kind of propaganda techniques do advertisers use? There   4 are seven basic types:

1. *Name Calling* Name calling is a propaganda tactic in   5 which negatively charged names are hurled against the opposing side or competitor. By using such names, propagandists try to arouse feelings of mistrust, fear, and hate in their audiences. For example, a political advertisement may label an opposing candidate a "loser," "fence-sitter," or "warmonger." Depending on the advertiser's target market, labels such as "a friend of big business" or "a dues-paying member of the party in power" can be the epithets that damage an opponent. Ads for products may also use name calling. An American manufacturer may refer, for instance, to a "foreign car" in its commercial—not an "imported" one. The label of foreignness will have unpleasant connotations in many people's minds. A childhood rhyme claims that "names can never hurt me," but name calling is an effective way to damage the opposition, whether it is another car maker or a congressional candidate.

2. *Glittering Generalities* Using glittering generalities is the   6 opposite of name calling. In this case, advertisers surround their products with attractive—and slippery—words and phrases. They

use vague terms that are difficult to define and that may have different meanings to different people: *freedom, democratic, all-American, progressive, Christian,* and *justice.* Many such words have strong, affirmative overtones. This kind of language stirs positive feelings in people, feelings that may spill over to the product or idea being pitched. As with name calling, the emotional response may overwhelm logic. Target audiences accept the product without thinking very much about what the glittering generalities mean—or whether they even apply to the product. After all, how can anyone oppose "truth, justice, and the American way"?

The ads for politicians and political causes often use glittering   7
generalities because such "buzz words" can influence votes. Election slogans include high-sounding but basically empty phrases like the following:

> "He cares about people." (That's nice, but is he a better candidate than his opponent?)
> "Vote for progress." (Progress by *whose* standards?)
> "They'll make this country great again." (What does "great" mean? Does "great" mean the same thing to others as it does to me?)
> "Vote for the future." (What kind of future?)
> "If you love America, vote for Phyllis Smith." (If I don't vote for Smith, does that mean I don't love America?)

Ads for consumer goods are also sprinkled with glittering gen-   8
eralities. Product names, for instance, are supposed to evoke good feelings: *Luvs* diapers, *New Freedom* feminine hygiene products, *Joy* liquid detergent, *Loving Care* hair color, *Almost Home* cookies, *Yankee Doodle* pastries. Product slogans lean heavily on vague but comforting phrases: Kinney is "The Great American Shoe Store," General Electric "brings good things to life," and Dow Chemical "lets you do great things." Chevrolet, we are told, is the "heartbeat of America," and Chrysler boasts cars that are "built by Americans for Americans."

3. *Transfer* In transfer, advertisers try to improve the image of   9
a product by associating it with a symbol most people respect, like the American flag or Uncle Sam. The advertisers hope that the prestige attached to the symbol will carry over to the product. Many

companies use transfer devices to identify their products: Lincoln Insurance shows a profile of the president; Continental Insurance portrays a Revolutionary War minuteman; Amtrak's logo is red, white, and blue; Liberty Mutual's corporate symbol is the Statue of Liberty; Allstate's name is cradled by a pair of protective, fatherly hands.

Corporations also use the transfer technique when they sponsor   10 prestigious shows on radio and television. These shows function as symbols of dignity and class. Kraft Corporation, for instance, sponsored a "Leonard Bernstein Conducts Beethoven" concert, while Gulf Oil is the sponsor of *National Geographic* specials and Mobil supports public television's *Masterpiece Theater.* In this way, corporations can reach an educated, influential audience and, perhaps, improve their public image by associating themselves with quality programming.

Political ads, of course, practically wrap themselves in the flag.   11 Ads for a political candidate often show either the Washington Monument, a Fourth of July parade, the Stars and Stripes, a bald eagle soaring over the mountains, or a white-steepled church on the village green. The national anthem or "America the Beautiful" may play softly in the background. Such appeals to Americans' love of country can surround the candidate with an aura of patriotism and integrity.

4. *Testimonial* The testimonial is one of advertisers' most-   12 loved and most-used propaganda techniques. Similar to the transfer device, the testimonial capitalizes on the admiration people have for a celebrity to make the product shine more brightly—even though the celebrity is not an expert on the product being sold.

Print and television ads offer a nonstop parade of testimonials: 13 here's William Shatner for Priceline.com; here's basketball star Michael Jordan eating Wheaties; a slew of well-known people (including rap star LL Cool J and the rock group Aerosmith) advertise clothing from the Gap; and Jerry Seinfeld assures us he never goes anywhere without his American Express card. Testimonials can sell movies, too; newspaper ads for films often feature favorable comments by well-known reviewers. And, in recent years, testimonials have played an important role in pitching books; the backs of paperbacks frequently list complimentary blurbs by celebrities.

Political candidates, as well as their ad agencies, know the value   14 of testimonials. Barbra Streisand lent her star appeal to the presidential campaign of Bill Clinton, while Arnold Schwarzenegger endorsed George Bush. Even controversial social issues are debated by celebrities. The nuclear-freeze debate, for instance, starred Paul Newman for the pro side and Charlton Heston for the con.

As illogical as testimonials sometimes are (Pepsi's Michael 15 Jackson, for instance, is a health-food adherent who does not drink soft drinks), they are effective propaganda. We like the *person* so much that we like the *product* too.

5. *Plain Folks* The plain folks approach says, in effect, "Buy 16 me or vote for me. I'm just like you." Regular folks will surely like Bob Evans's Down on the Farm Country Sausage or good old-fashioned Countrytime Lemonade. Some ads emphasize the idea that "we're all in the same boat." We see people making long-distance calls for just the reasons we do—to put the baby on the phone to Grandma or to tell Mom we love her. And how do these folksy, warmhearted (usually saccharine) scenes affect us? They're supposed to make us feel that AT&T—the multinational corporate giant—has the same values we do. Similarly, we are introduced to the little people at Ford, the ordinary folks who work on the assembly line, not to bigwigs in their executive offices. What's the purpose of such an approach? To encourage us to buy a car built by these honest, hardworking "everyday Joes" who care about quality as much as we do.

Political advertisements make almost as much use of the "plain 17 folks" appeal as they do of transfer devices. Candidates wear hard hats, farmers' caps, and assembly-line coveralls. They jog around the block and carry their own luggage through the airport. The idea is to convince voters that the candidates are average people, not the elite—not wealthy lawyers or executives but common citizens.

6. *Card Stacking* When people say that "the cards were 18 stacked against me," they mean that they were never given a fair chance. Applied to propaganda, card stacking means that one side may suppress or distort evidence, tell half-truths, oversimplify the facts, or set up a "straw man"— a false target—to divert attention from the issue at hand. Card stacking is a difficult form of propaganda both to detect and to combat. When a candidate claims that an opponent has "changed his mind five times on this important issue," we tend to accept the claim without investigating whether the candidate had good reasons for changing his mind. Many

people are simply swayed by the distorted claim that the candidate is "waffling" on the issue.

Advertisers often stack the cards in favor of the products they 19 are pushing. They may, for instance, use what are called "weasel words." These are small words that usually slip right past us, but that make the difference between reality and illusion. The weasel words are underlined in the following claims:

> "Helps control dandruff symptoms." (The audience usually interprets this as *stops* dandruff.)
>
> "Most dentists surveyed recommend sugarless gum for their patients who chew gum." (We hear the "most dentists" and "for their patients," but we don't think about how many were surveyed or whether the dentists first recommended that the patients not chew gum at all.)
>
> "Sticker price $1,000 lower than most comparable cars." (How many is "most"? What car does the advertiser consider "comparable"?)

Advertisers also use a card stacking trick when they make an 20 unfinished claim. For example, they will say that their product has "twice as much pain reliever." We are left with a favorable impression. We don't usually ask, "Twice as much pain reliever as what?" Or advertisers may make extremely vague claims that sound alluring but have no substance: Toyota's "Oh, what a feeling!"; Vantage cigarettes' "The taste of success"; "The spirit of Marlboro"; Coke's "the real thing." Another way to stack the cards in favor of a certain product is to use scientific-sounding claims that are not supported by sound research. When Ford claimed that its LTD model was "400% quieter," many people assumed that the LTD must be quieter than all other cars. When taken to court, however, Ford admitted that the phrase referred to the difference between the noise level inside and outside the LTD. Other scientific-sounding claims use mysterious ingredients that are never explained as selling points: "Retsyn," "special whitening agents," "the ingredient doctors recommend."

7. *Bandwagon* In the bandwagon technique, advertisers 21 pressure, "Everyone's doing it. Why don't you?" This kind of propaganda often succeeds because many people have a deep desire

not to be different. Political ads tell us to vote for the "winning candidate." Advertisers know we tend to feel comfortable doing what others do; we want to be on the winning team. Or ads show a series of people proclaiming, "I'm voting for the Senator. I don't know why anyone wouldn't." Again, the audience feels under pressure to conform.

In the marketplace, the bandwagon approach lures buyers. Ads   22
tell us that "nobody doesn't like Sara Lee" (the message is that you must be weird if you don't). They tell us that "most people prefer Brand X two to one over other leading brands" (to be like the majority, we should buy Brand X). If we don't drink Pepsi, we're left out of "the Pepsi generation." To take part in "America's favorite health kick," the National Dairy Council asks us, "Got Milk?" And Honda motorcycle ads, praising the virtues of being a follower, tell us, "Follow the leader. He's on a Honda."

Why do these propaganda techniques work? Why do so many of   23
us buy the products, viewpoints, and candidates urged on us by propaganda messages? They work because they appeal to our emotions, not to our minds. Often, in fact, they capitalize on our prejudices and biases. For example, if we are convinced that environmentalists are radicals who want to destroy America's record of industrial growth and progress, then we will applaud the candidate who refers to them as "treehuggers." Clear thinking requires hard work: analyzing a claim, researching the facts, examining both sides of an issue, using logic to see the flaws in an argument. Many of us would rather let the propagandists do our thinking for us.

Because propaganda is so effective, it is important to detect it   24
and understand how it is used. We may conclude, after close examination, that some propaganda sends a truthful, worthwhile message. Some advertising, for instance, urges us not to drive drunk, to become volunteers, to contribute to charity. Even so, we must be aware that propaganda is being used. Otherwise, we have consented to handing over to others our independence of thought and action.

Questions for Close Reading

1. What is the selection's thesis? Locate the sentence(s) in which McClintock states her main idea. If she doesn't state the thesis explicitly, express it in your own words.

2. What is *propaganda*? What mistaken associations do people often have with this term?
3. What are "weasel words"? How do they trick listeners?
4. Why does McClintock believe we should be better informed about propaganda techniques?
5. Refer to your dictionary as needed to define the following words used in the selection: *seduced* (paragraph 1), *warmonger* (5), and *elite* (17).

Questions About the Writer's Craft

1. **The pattern and other patterns.**   Before explaining the categories into which propaganda techniques can be grouped, McClintock provides a definition of propaganda. Is the definition purely informative, or does it have a larger objective? If you think the latter, what is the definition's broader purpose?
2. In her introduction, McClintock uses loaded words such as *seduced* and *brainwashed*. What effect do these words have on the reader?
3. Locate places in the essay where McClintock uses questions. Which are rhetorical and which are genuine queries?
4. What kind of conclusion does McClintock provide for the essay?

Writing Assignments Using Division-Classification as a Pattern of Development

∞ 1. McClintock cautions us to be sensitive to propaganda in advertising. Young children, however, aren't capable of this kind of awareness. With pen or pencil in hand, watch some commercials aimed at children, such as those for toys, cereals, and fast food. Then analyze the use of propaganda techniques in these commercials. Using division-classification, write an essay describing the main propaganda techniques you observed. Support your analysis with examples drawn from the commercials. Remember to provide a thesis that indicates your opinion of the advertising techniques. For additional insight into this issue, read Ellen Goodman's "Family Counterculture" (page 6).
2. Like advertising techniques, television shows can be classified. Avoiding the obvious system of classifying according to game shows, detective shows, and situation comedies, come up with your own original division-classification principle. Possibilities include how family life is depicted, the way work is presented, how male-female relationships are portrayed. Using one such principle, write an essay in which you categorize popular TV shows into three types. Refer to specific shows to support your classification system. Your attitude toward the shows being discussed should be made clear.

Writing Assignments Using Other Patterns of Development

3. McClintock says that card stacking "distort[s] evidence, tell[s] half-truths, oversimpli[fies] the facts" (paragraph 18). Focusing on an editorial, a political campaign, a print ad, or a television commercial, analyze the extent to which card stacking is used as a persuasive strategy. Reading William Lutz's "Doublespeak" (page 224) will deepen your understanding of the extent to which the truth can be distorted.

4. To increase further your sensitivity to the moral dimensions of propaganda, write a proposal outlining an ad campaign for a real or imaginary product or elected official. The introduction to your proposal should identify who or what is to be promoted, and the thesis or plan of development should indicate the specific propaganda techniques you suggest. In the paper's supporting paragraphs, explain how these techniques would be used to promote your product or candidate.

Writing Assignments Using a Journal Entry as a Starting Point

5. Write an essay showing that, on the whole, you are fairly susceptible to *or* are fairly immune to advertising ploys. Drawing upon your pre-reading journal entry, illustrate your position with lively details of advertising campaigns that won you over—or that failed to sway you. Draw upon some of McClintock's terminology when describing advertisers' techniques. Your essay may have a serious or a playful tone.

Deborah Tannen

The recipient of grants from the National Endowment for the Humanities, the Rockefeller Foundation, and the National Science Foundation, Deborah Tannen (1945–) is a linguistics professor at Georgetown University and has been a Distinguished McGraw Lecturer at Princeton University. She has shared her scholarly research with the general public through appearances on the *Today* show and CNN, through pieces in the *New York Times* and the *Washington Post*, and in popular books, including *That's Not What I Meant: How Conversational Style Makes or Breaks Relationships* (1987), her best-selling *You Just Don't Understand: Women and Men in Conversation* (1990), *Talking From 9 to 5* (1994), *Gender and Discourse* (1994), *The Argument Culture: Moving from Debate to Dialogue* (1998), and *I Only Say That Because I Love You* (2001). The following selection, adapted from *You Just Don't Understand,* appeared in the *New York Times* in June 1990.

Pre-Reading Journal Entry

It's been said that men and women communicate in different ways. Do you agree? Why or why not? Take a few moments to respond to this question in your journal, drawing upon your experiences and observations.

But What Do You Mean?

Conversation is a ritual. We say things that seem obviously the   1
thing to say, without thinking of the literal meaning of our words,
any more than we expect the question "How are you?" to call forth
a detailed account of aches and pains.

Unfortunately, women and men often have different ideas   2
about what's appropriate, different ways of speaking. Many of the
conversational rituals common among women are designed to take
the other person's feelings into account, while many of the conversational rituals common among men are designed to maintain the
one-up position, or at least avoid appearing one-down. As a result,
when men and women interact—especially at work—it's often

women who are at the disadvantage. Because women are not trying to avoid the one-down position, that is unfortunately where they may end up.

Here, the biggest areas of miscommunication.   3

1. Apologies

Women are often told they apologize too much. The reason   4
they're told to stop doing it is that, to many men, apologizing seems synonymous with putting oneself down. But there are many times when "I'm sorry" isn't self-deprecating, or even an apology; it's an automatic way of keeping both speakers on an equal footing. For example, a well-known columnist once interviewed me and gave me her phone number in case I needed to call her back. I misplaced the number and had to go through the newspaper's main switchboard. When our conversation was winding down and we'd both made ending-type remarks, I added, "Oh, I almost forgot—I lost your direct number, can I get it again?" "Oh, I'm sorry," she came back instantly, even though she had done nothing wrong and *I* was the one who'd lost the number. But I understood she wasn't really apologizing; she was just automatically reassuring me she had no intention of denying me her number.

Even when "I'm sorry" *is* an apology, women often assume it   5
will be the first step in a two-step ritual: I say "I'm sorry" and take half the blame, then you take the other half. At work, it might go something like this:

A: When you typed this letter, you missed this phrase I inserted.
B: Oh, I'm sorry. I'll fix it.
A: Well, I wrote it so small it was easy to miss.

When both parties share blame, it's a mutual face-saving device.   6
But if one person, usually the woman, utters frequent apologies and the other doesn't, she ends up looking as if she's taking the blame for mishaps that aren't her fault. When she's only partially to blame, she looks entirely in the wrong.

I recently sat in on a meeting at an insurance company where   7
the sole woman, Helen, said "I'm sorry" or "I apologize" repeatedly. At one point she said, "I'm thinking out loud. I apologize." Yet the meeting was intended to be an informal brainstorming session, and *everyone* was thinking out loud.

The reason Helen's apologies stood out was that she was the 8 only person in the room making so many. And the reason I was concerned was that Helen felt the annual bonus she had received was unfair. When I interviewed the colleagues, they said that Helen was one of the best and most productive workers—yet she got one of the smallest bonuses. Although the problem might have been outright sexism, I suspect her speech style, which differs from that of her male colleagues, masks her competence.

Unfortunately, not apologizing can have its price too. Since so 9 many women use ritual apologies, those who don't may be seen as hard-edged. What's important is to be aware of how often you say you're sorry (and why), and to monitor your speech based on the reaction you get.

2. Criticism

A woman who cowrote a report with a male colleague was 10 hurt when she read a rough draft to him and he leapt into a critical response—"Oh, that's too dry! You have to make it snappier!" She herself would have been more likely to say, "That's a really good start. Of course, you'll want to make it a little snappier when you revise."

Whether criticism is given straight or softened is often a mat- 11 ter of convention. In general, women use more softeners. I noticed this difference when talking to an editor about an essay I'd written. While going over changes she wanted to make, she said, "There's one more thing. I know you may not agree with me. The reason I noticed the problem is that your other points are so lucid and elegant." She went on hedging for several more sentences until I put her out of her misery: "Do you want to cut that part?" I asked—and of course she did. But I appreciated her tentativeness. In contrast, another editor (a man) I once called summarily rejected my idea for an article by barking, "Call me when you have something new to say."

Those who are used to ways of talking that soften the impact of 12 criticism may find it hard to deal with the right-between-the-eyes style. It has its own logic, however, and neither style is intrinsically better. People who prefer criticism given straight are operating on an assumption that feelings aren't involved: "Here's the dope. I know you're good; you can take it."

3. Thank-Yous

A woman manager I know starts meetings by thanking everyone   13
for coming, even though it's clearly their job to do so. Her "thank-
you" is simply a ritual.

A novelist received a fax from an assistant in her publisher's   14
office; it contained suggested catalog copy for her book. She immediately faxed him her suggested changes and said, "Thanks for running this by me," even though her contract gave her the right to
approve all copy. When she thanked the assistant, she fully expected him to reciprocate: "Thanks for giving me such a quick
response." Instead, he said, "You're welcome." Suddenly, rather
than an equal exchange of pleasantries, she found herself positioned
as the recipient of a favor. This made her feel like responding,
"Thanks for nothing!"

Many women use "thanks" as an automatic conversation starter   15
and closer; there's nothing literally to say thank you for. Like many
rituals typical of women's conversation, it depends on the goodwill
of the other to restore the balance. When the other speaker doesn't
reciprocate, a woman may feel like someone on a seesaw whose partner abandoned his end. Instead of balancing in the air, she has
plopped to the ground, wondering how she got there.

4. Fighting

Many men expect the discussion of ideas to be a ritual fight—   16
explored through verbal opposition. They state their ideas in the
strongest possible terms, thinking that if there are weaknesses someone will point them out, and by trying to argue against those objections, they will see how well their ideas hold up.

Those who expect their own ideas to be challenged will respond   17
to another's ideas by trying to poke holes and find weak links—as a
way of *helping*. The logic is that when you are challenged you will
rise to the occasion: Adrenaline makes your mind sharper; you get
ideas and insights you would not have thought of without the spur
of battle.

But many women take this approach as a personal attack. Worse,   18
they find it impossible to do their best work in such a contentious
environment. If you're not used to ritual fighting, you begin to hear
criticism of your ideas as soon as they are formed. Rather than making you think more clearly, it makes you doubt what you know.

When you state your ideas, you hedge in order to fend off potential attacks. Ironically, this is more likely to *invite* attack because it makes you look weak.

Although you may never enjoy verbal sparring, some women 19 find it helpful to learn how to do it. An engineer who was the only woman among four men in a small company found that as soon as she learned to argue she was accepted and taken seriously. A doctor attending a hospital staff meeting made a similar discovery. She was becoming more and more angry with a male colleague who'd loudly disagreed with a point she'd made. Her better judgment told her to hold her tongue, to avoid making an enemy of this powerful senior colleague. But finally she couldn't hold it in any longer, and she rose to her feet and delivered an impassioned attack on his position. She sat down in a panic, certain she had permanently damaged her relationship with him. To her amazement, he came up to her afterward and said, "That was a great rebuttal. I'm really impressed. Let's go out for a beer after work and hash out our approaches to this problem."

5. Praise

A manager I'll call Lester had been on his new job six months 20 when he heard that the women reporting to him were deeply dissatisfied. When he talked to them about it, their feelings erupted; two said they were on the verge of quitting because he didn't appreciate their work, and they didn't want to wait to be fired. Lester was dumbfounded: He believed they were doing a fine job. Surely, he thought, he had said nothing to give them the impression he didn't like their work. And indeed he hadn't. That was the problem. He had said *nothing*—and the women assumed he was following the adage "If you can't say something nice, don't say anything." He thought he was showing confidence in them by leaving them alone.

Men and women have different habits in regard to giving praise. 21 For example, Deirdre and her colleague William both gave presentations at a conference. Afterward, Deirdre told William, "That was a great talk!" He thanked her. Then she asked, "What did you think of mine?" and he gave her a lengthy and detailed critique. She found it uncomfortable to listen to his comments. But she assured herself that he meant well, and that his honesty was a signal that she, too, should be honest when he asked for a critique of his performance. As a matter of fact, she had noticed quite a few ways in which he could have improved his presentation. But she never got a chance to tell him because he never asked—and she felt put down. The worst part was that it seemed she had only herself to blame, since she *had* asked what he thought of her talk.

But had she really asked for his critique? The truth is, when she   22
asked for his opinion, she was expecting a compliment, which she felt was more or less required following anyone's talk. When he responded with criticism, she figured, "Oh, he's playing 'Let's critique each other'"—not a game she'd initiated, but one which she was willing to play. Had she realized he was going to criticize her and not ask her to reciprocate, she would never have asked in the first place.

It would be easy to assume that Deirdre was insecure, whether she   23
was fishing for a compliment or soliciting a critique. But she was simply talking automatically, performing one of the many conversational rituals that allow us to get through the day. William may have sincerely misunderstood Deirdre's intention—or may have been unable to pass up a chance to one-up her when given the opportunity.

6. Complaints

"Troubles talk" can be a way to establish rapport with a col-   24
league. You complain about a problem (which shows that you are just folks) and the other person responds with a similar problem (which puts you on equal footing). But while such commiserating is common among women, men are likely to hear it as a request to *solve* the problem.

One woman told me she would frequently initiate what she   25
thought would be pleasant complaint-airing sessions at work. She'd talk about situations that bothered her just to talk about them, maybe to understand them better. But her male office mate would quickly tell her how she could improve the situation. This left her feeling condescended to and frustrated. She was delighted to see this very impasse in a section in my book *You Just Don't Understand,* and showed it to him. "Oh," he said, "I see the problem. How can we solve it?" Then they both laughed, because it had happened again: He short-circuited the detailed discussion she'd hoped for and cut to the chase of finding a solution.

Sometimes the consequences of complaining are more serious: 26
A man might take a woman's lighthearted griping literally, and she

can get a reputation as a chronic malcontent. Furthermore, she may be seen as not up to solving the problems that arise on the job.

7. Jokes

I heard a man call in to a talk show and say, "I've worked for two women and neither one had a sense of humor. You know, when you work with men, there's a lot of joking and teasing." The show's host and guest (both women) took his comment at face value and assumed the women this man worked for were humorless. The guest said, "Isn't it sad that women don't feel comfortable enough with authority to see the humor?" The host said, "Maybe when more women are in authority roles, they'll be more comfortable with power." But although the women this man worked for *may* have taken themselves too seriously, it's just as likely that they each had a terrific sense of humor, but maybe the humor wasn't the type he was used to. They may have been like the woman who wrote to me: "When I'm with men, my wit or cleverness seems inappropriate (or lost!) so I don't bother. When I'm with my women friends, however, there's no hold on puns or cracks and my humor is fully appreciated."

The types of humor women and men tend to prefer differ. Research has shown that the most common form of humor among men is razzing, teasing, and mock-hostile attacks, while among women it's self-mocking. Women often mistake men's teasing as genuinely hostile. Men often mistake women's mock self-deprecation as truly putting themselves down.

Women have told me they were taken more seriously when they learned to joke the way the guys did. For example, a teacher who went to a national conference with seven other teachers (mostly women) and a group of administrators (mostly men) was annoyed that the administrators always found reasons to leave boring seminars, while the teachers felt they had to stay and take notes. One evening, when the group met at a bar in the hotel, the principal asked her how one such seminar had turned out. She reported, " As soon as you left, it got much better." He laughed out loud at her response. The playful insult appealed to the men—but there was a trade-off. The women seemed to back off from her after this. (Perhaps they were put off by her using joking to align herself with the bosses.)

There is no "right" way to talk. When problems arise, the cul-   30
prit may be style differences—and *all* styles will at times fail with
others who don't share or understand them, just as English won't
do you much good if you try to speak to someone who knows only
French. If you want to get your message across, it's not a question
of being "right"; it's a question of using language that's shared—or
at least understood.

Questions for Close Reading

1. What is the selection's thesis? Locate the sentence(s) in which Tannen
   states her main idea. If she doesn't state the thesis explicitly, express it in
   your own words.
2. Describe the differences in the way men and women perceive women's
   use of apologies. According to Tannen, how does this difference in perception create a problem?
3. What is the difference between "straight" and "softened" criticism
   (paragraph 11)? Does Tannen like one style more than the other? Why
   or why not?
4. What is a "ritual fight" (paragraph 16)? How, according to Tannen, do
   men and women differ in their responses to ritual fighting?
5. Refer to your dictionary as needed to define the following words used in
   the selection: *synonymous* (paragraph 4), *self-deprecating* (4), *reciprocate*
   (14), *contentious* (18), *dumbfounded* (20), *soliciting* (23), *commiserating*
   (24), and *malcontent* (26).

Questions About the Writer's Craft

1. **The pattern.**   Are Tannen's seven categories of male-female miscommunication mutually exclusive, or do they overlap? Cite specific examples to support your view. Why do you think she divided them as she did?
2. **Other patterns.**   Besides identifying the differences in men's and
   women's conversation rituals, Tannen often analyzes the causes and
   effects of these differences. Trace the causal chain in Tannen's discussion
   of apologies (paragraphs 7–9). How does this causal chain help Tannen
   reinforce her thesis?
3. Social scientists like Tannen often write impersonally, relying on statistics
   and a third-person point of view. Why do you suppose Tannen writes
   from the first-person point of view? What advantage does this point of
   view offer?
4. How would you characterize Tannen's tone in this selection? How does
   Tannen's attitude toward her subject and readers reinforce the essay's
   purpose?

Writing Assignments Using Division-Classification as a Method of Development

∞ 1. Tannen's essay shows how typical male-female conversational patterns may put women at a disadvantage. Focus on two other closely related groups whose relationship is imbalanced because the communication behaviors of one are at odds with the group's best self-interest. You might examine the relationship between parents and children, teachers and students, or employers and employees. Like Tannen, categorize the areas in which the imbalance is apparent, and be sure to explain the consequences as well as the origins of the counterproductive communication behavior. For more on miscommunication between people, you might read Dave Barry's "The Ugly Truth About Beauty" (page 323), a humorous take on gendered behaviors.

∞ 2. Given gender differences in communication styles, it's not surprising that men and women sometimes get embroiled in serious disagreements. Think about arguments between the sexes that you have participated in or observed. Write an essay categorizing the different kinds of arguments. You might, for instance, identify quarrels over money, communication, socializing, and so on. In your essay, reach some conclusions about whether these arguments are due to *gender* differences—or due to non-gender-based *personality* conflicts. To test the validity of your conclusions, confer with friends and family for their opinions about the disputes you're examining. For insights into gender-based miscommunication, read one or more of the following: Barbara Ehrenreich's "What I've Learned From Men" (page 196), Camille Paglia's "Rape: A Bigger Danger Than Feminists Know" (page 451), and Susan Jacoby's "Common Decency" (page 458).

Writing Assignments Using Other Patterns of Development

∞ 3. Tannen discusses differences in men's and women's communication rituals. Extending her work, examine another area where you perceive significant gender differences. Possibilities include the way men and women eat, socialize, shop for clothes, furnish their rooms, or watch television. Write an essay comparing and contrasting the sexes' attitudes and behaviors in this area. Brainstorm with others to gather anecdotes that convincingly exemplify the behaviors you describe. Your essay may be serious, lighthearted, or both. Before writing, read Barbara Ehrenreich's "What I've Learned From Men" (page 196) for an additional perspective on gender issues. You may also want to read relevant portions of Tannen's *You Just Don't Understand* or *Talking From 9 to 5*.

4. In this selection, Tannen shows that verbal behavior can be misunderstood. Write an essay showing that nonverbal behaviors can also be misinterpreted. Before you write, research nonverbal communication in the library and/or on the Internet. Armed with background information, spend time observing people's nonverbal communication in a variety of campus settings. When you write, do more than provide instances of misunderstanding; be sure to offer explanations of why such communication breakdowns occur.

Writing Assignments Using a Journal Entry as a Starting Point

5. Write an essay in which you agree *or* disagree with the claim that women and men have different styles of communication. To defend your contention, select and develop the most persuasive examples from your pre-reading journal entry. Brainstorming with friends, family, and classmates will help you generate additional supporting examples. Remember, too, to acknowledge the opposing argument, dismantling as much of it as you can. You might also consult two other essays that speculate about the nature of specific human behaviors: Stephen King's "Why We Crave Horror Movies" (page 349) and James Gleick's "Life As Type A" (page 387).

Additional Writing Topics

DIVISION-CLASSIFICATION

General Assignments

Choose one of the following subjects and write an essay developed wholly or in part through division-classification. Start by determining the purpose of the essay. Do you want to inform, compare and contrast, or persuade? Apply a single, significant principle of division or classification to your subject. Don't switch the principle midway through your analysis. Also, be sure that the types or categories you create are as complete and mutually exclusive as possible.

Division

1. A shopping mall
2. A video and/or stereo system
3. A fruit, such as a pineapple, an orange, or a banana
4. A tax dollar
5. A particular kind of team
6. A word-processing system
7. A human hand
8. A meal
9. A meeting
10. A favorite poem, story, or play
11. A favorite restaurant
12. A school library
13. A basement
14. A playground, gym, or other recreational area
15. A church service
16. A wedding or funeral
17. An eventful week in your life
18. A college campus
19. A television show or movie
20. A homecoming or other special weekend

Classification

1. People in a waiting room
2. Holidays
3. Closets
4. Roommates
5. Salad bars
6. Divorces

7. Beds
8. Students in a class
9. Shoes
10. Summer movies
11. Teachers
12. Neighbors
13. College courses
14. Bosses
15. TV watchers
16. Mothers or fathers
17. Commercials
18. Vacations
19. Trash
20. Relatives

Assignments With a Specific Purpose and Audience

1. You are a dorm counselor. During orientation week, you'll be talking to students on your floor about the different kinds of problems they may have with roommates. Write out your talk, describing each kind of problem and explaining how to cope.
2. As a driving instructor, you decide to prepare a lecture on the types of drivers that your students are likely to encounter on the road. In your lecture, categorize drivers according to a specific principle and show the behaviors of each type.
3. You have been asked to write a pamphlet for "new recruits"—new workers on your job, new students in your college class, new members of your sports team, or the like. In the pamphlet, identify at least three general qualities needed for the recruits' success.
4. A seasoned camp counselor, you've been asked to prepare, for new counselors, an informational sheet on children's emotional needs. Categorizing those needs into types, explain what counselors can do to nurture youngsters emotionally.
5. As your college newspaper's TV critic, you plan to write a review of the fall shows, most of which—in your opinion—lack originality. To show how stereotypical the programs are, select one type (for example, situation comedies or crime dramas). Then use a specific division-classification principle to illustrate that the same stale formulas are trotted out from show to show.
6. Asked to write an editorial for the campus paper, you decide to do a half-serious piece on taking "mental health" days off from classes. Structure your essay around three kinds of occasions when "playing hooky" is essential for maintaining sanity.

7

PROCESS ANALYSIS

WHAT IS PROCESS ANALYSIS?

Perhaps you've noticed the dogged determination of small children when they learn how to do something new. Whether trying to tie their shoelaces or tell time, little children struggle along, creating knotted tangles, confusing the hour with the minute hand. But they don't give up. Mastering such basic skills makes them feel less dependent on the adults of the world—all of whom seem to know how to do everything. Actually, none of us is born knowing how to do very much. We spend a good deal of our lives learning—everything from speaking our first word to balancing our first bank statement. Indeed, the milestones in our lives are often linked to the processes we have mastered: how to cross the street alone; how to drive a car; how to make a speech without being paralyzed by fear.

Process analysis, a technique that explains the steps or sequence involved in doing something, satisfies our need to learn as well as our curiosity about how the world works. All the self-help books flooding the market today (*Managing Stress, How to Make a Million in Real Estate, Ten Days to a Perfect Body*) are examples of process analysis. The instructions on the federal tax form and the recipes in a cookbook are also process analyses. Several television classics, now seen in reruns, also capitalize on our desire to learn how things happen: *The Wild Kingdom* shows how animals survive in faraway lands, and *Mission: Impossible* has great fun detailing elaborate plans for preventing the triumph of evil. Process analysis can be more than merely interesting or entertaining, though; it can be of critical importance. Consider a waiter hurriedly skimming the "Choking Aid" instructions posted on a restaurant wall or an air-traffic controller following emergency procedures in an effort to prevent a midair collision. In these last examples, the consequences could be fatal if the process analyses were slipshod, inaccurate, or confusing.

Undoubtedly, all of us have experienced less dramatic effects of poorly written process analyses. Perhaps you've tried to assemble a bicycle and spent hours sorting through a stack of parts, only to end up with one or two extra pieces never mentioned in the instructions. Or maybe you were baffled when putting up a set of wall shelves because the instructions used unfamiliar terms such as *mitered cleat, wing nut,* and *dowel pin.* No wonder many people stay clear of anything that actually admits "assembly required."

HOW PROCESS ANALYSIS FITS YOUR PURPOSE AND AUDIENCE

You will use process analysis in two types of writing situations: (1) when you want to give step-by-step instructions to readers showing how they can do something, or (2) when you want readers to understand how something happens even though they won't actually follow the steps outlined. The first kind of process analysis is *directional;* the second is *informational.*

When you look at the cooking instructions on a package of frozen vegetables or follow guidelines for completing a job application, you're reading directional process analysis. A serious essay explaining how to select a college and a humorous essay telling readers how to get on the good side of a professor are also examples of directional process analysis. Using a variety of tones, informational process analyses can range over equally diverse subjects; they can describe mechanical, scientific, historical, sociological, artistic, or psychological processes: for example, how the core of a nuclear reactor melts down; how television became so important in political campaigns; how abstract painters use color; how to survive a blind date.

Process analysis, both directional and informational, is often appropriate in *problem-solving situations.* In such cases, you say,

"Here's the problem and here's what should be done to solve the problem." Indeed, college assignments frequently take the form of problem-solving process analyses. Consider these examples:

> Community officials have been accused of mismanaging recent unrest over the public housing ordinance. Describe the steps the officials took, indicating why you think their strategy was unwise. Then explain how you think the situation should have been handled.

> Over the years, there have been many reports citing the abuse of small children in day care centers. What can parents do to guard against the mistreatment of their children?

> Because many colleges and universities have changed the eligibility requirements for financial aid, fewer students can depend on loans or scholarships. How can students cope with the increasing costs of obtaining a higher education?

Note that the first assignment asks students to explain what's wrong with the current approach before they present their own step-by-step solution. Problem-solving process analyses are often organized in this way. You may also have noted that none of the assignments explicitly requires an essay response using process analysis. However, the wording of the assignments—"*Describe* the steps," "*How* can students *cope*," "*What* can parents *do*"—suggests that process analysis would be an appropriate strategy for developing the responses.

Assignments don't always signal the use of process analysis so clearly. But during the prewriting stage, as you generate material to support your thesis, you'll often realize that you can best achieve your purpose by developing the essay—or part of it—using process analysis.

Sometimes process analysis will be the primary strategy for organizing an essay; other times it will be used to help make a point in an essay organized according to another pattern of development. Let's take a look at process analysis as a supporting strategy.

Assume that you're writing a *causal analysis* examining the impact of television commercials on people's buying behavior. To help readers see that commercials create a need where none existed before, you might describe the various stages in an advertising campaign to pitch a new, completely frivolous product. In an essay *defining* a good boss, you could convey the point that effective managers must be skilled at settling disputes by explaining the steps your boss took to resolve a heated disagreement between two employees. If you write an *argumentation-persuasion* paper urging the funding of programs to ease the plight of the homeless, you would have to dramatize for readers the tragedy of these people's lives. To achieve your purpose, you could devote part of the paper to an explanation of how the typical street person goes about the desperate jobs of finding a place to sleep and getting food to eat.

SUGGESTIONS FOR USING PROCESS ANALYSIS IN AN ESSAY

The suggestions that follow will be helpful whether you use process analysis as a dominant or a supportive pattern of development.

1. Identify the desired outcome of the process analysis. Many papers developed primarily through process analysis have a clear-cut purpose—simply to *inform* readers as objectively as possible about a process: "Here's a way of making french fries at home that will surpass the best served in your favorite fast-food restaurant." But a process analysis essay may also have a *persuasive* edge, with the writer advocating a point of view about the process, perhaps even urging a course of action: "If you don't want your arguments to deteriorate into ugly battles, you should follow a series of foolproof steps for having disagreements that leave friendships intact." Before starting to write, you need to decide if the essay is to be purely factual or if it will include this kind of persuasive dimension.

2. Formulate a thesis that clarifies your attitude toward the process. Like the thesis in any other paper, the thesis in a process analysis should do more than announce your subject. ("Here's how the college's work-study program operates.") It should also state or imply your attitude toward the process: "Enrolling in the college's work-study program has become unnecessarily complicated. The procedure could be simplified if the college adopted the helpful guidelines prepared by the Student Senate."

3. Keep your audience in mind. Only when you gauge how much your readers already know (or don't know) about the process can you determine how much explanation you'll have to provide. Suppose you've been asked to write an article informing students of the best way to use the university computer center. The article will be published in a newsletter for computer science majors. You would seriously misjudge your audience—and probably put them to sleep—if you explained in detail how to transfer material from disk to disk or how to delete information from a file. However, an article on the same topic prepared for a general audience—your composition class, for instance—would probably require such detailed instructions.

To determine how much explanation is needed, put yourself in your readers' shoes. Don't assume readers will know something just because you do. Ask questions such as these about your audience: "Will my readers need some background about the process before I describe it in depth?" "Are there technical terms I should define?" "If my essay is directional, should I specify near the beginning the ingredients, materials, and equipment needed to perform the process?" (For more help in analyzing your audience, see the checklist on page 20.)

4. Use prewriting to identify the steps in the process. To explain a sequence to your readers, you need to think through the process thoroughly, identifying its major parts and subparts, locating possible missteps or trouble spots. With your purpose, thesis, and audience in mind, use the appropriate prewriting techniques (brainstorming and mapping should be especially helpful) to break down the process into its component parts. In prewriting, it's a good idea to start by generating more material than you expect to use. Then the raw material can be shaped and pruned to fit your purpose and the needs of your audience. The amount of work done during the prewriting stage will have a direct bearing on the clarity of your presentation.

5. Identify the directional and informational aspects of the process analysis. Directional and informational process analyses are not always distinct. In fact, they may be complementary. Your prewriting may reveal that you'll need to provide background information about a process before outlining its steps. For example, in a paper describing a step-by-step approach for losing weight, you might first need to explain how the body burns calories. Or, in a paper on gardening, you could provide some theory about the way organic fertilizers work before detailing a plan for growing vegetables. Although both approaches may be appropriate in a paper, one generally predominates.

The kind of process analysis chosen has implications for the way you will relate to your reader. When the process analysis is *directional,* the reader is addressed in the *second person:* "You should first rinse the residue from the radiator by . . . ," or "Wrap the injured person in a blanket and then. . . ." (In the second example, the pronoun *you* is implied.)

If the process analysis has an *informational* purpose, you won't address the reader directly but will choose from a number of other options. For example, you might use the *first-person* point of view. In a humorous essay explaining how not to prepare for finals, you could cite your own disastrous study habits: "Filled with good intentions, I sit on my bed, pick up a pencil, open my notebook, and promptly fall asleep." The *third-person singular or plural* can also be used in informational process essays: "The door-to-door salesperson walks up the front walk, heart pounding, more than a bit nervous, but also challenged by the prospect of striking a deal," or "The new recruits next underwent a series of important balance tests in what was called the 'horror chamber.'" Whether you use the first, second, or third person, avoid shifting point of view midstream.

You might have noticed that in the third-person examples, the present tense ("walks up") is used in one sentence, the past tense ("underwent") in the other. The past tense is appropriate for events already completed, whereas the present tense is used for habitual or ongoing actions. ("A dominant male goose usually flies at the head of the V-wedge during migration.") The present tense is also effective when you want to lend a sense of dramatic immediacy to a process, even if the steps were performed in the past. ("The surgeon gently separates the facial skin and muscle from the underlying bony skull.") As with point of view, be on guard against changing tenses in the middle of your explanation.

6. Explain the process, one step at a time. Prewriting helped you identify key stages and sort out the directional and informational aspects of the process. Now you're ready to organize your raw material into an easy-to-follow sequence. At times your purpose will be to explain a process with a *fairly fixed chronological sequence:* how to make pizza, how to pot a plant, how to change a tire. In such cases, you should include all necessary steps, in the correct chronological order. However, if a strict chronological ordering of steps means that a particularly important part of the sequence gets buried in the middle, the sequence probably should be juggled so that the crucial step receives the attention it deserves.

Other times your goal will be to describe a process having *no commonly accepted sequence.* For example, in an essay explaining how to discipline a child or how to pull yourself out of a blue mood, you will have to come up with your own definition of the key steps and then arrange those steps in some logical order. You may also use process analyses to *reject* or *reformulate* a traditional sequence. In this case, you would propose a more logical series of steps: "Our system for electing congressional representatives is inefficient and undemocratic; it should be reformed in the following ways."

Whether the essay describes a generally agreed-on process or one that is not commonly accepted, you must provide all the details needed to explain the process. Your readers should be able to understand, even visualize, the process. There should be no fuzzy patches or confusing cuts from one step to another. Don't, however, go into obsessive detail about minor stages or steps. If you dwell for several hundred words on how to butter the pan, your readers will never stay with you long enough to learn how to make the omelet.

It's not unusual, especially in less defined sequences, for some steps in a process to occur simultaneously and overlap. When this happens, you should present the steps in the most logical order, being sure to tell your readers that several steps are not perfectly distinct and may merge. For example, in an essay explaining how a species becomes extinct, you would have to indicate that overpopulation of hardy strains and destruction of endangered breeds are often simultaneous events. You would also need to clarify that the depletion of food sources both precedes and follows the demise of a species.

7. Provide readers with the help they need to follow the sequence. As you move through the steps of a process analysis, don't forget to *warn readers about difficulties* they might encounter. For example, when writing a paper on the artistry involved in butterflying a shrimp, you might say something like this:

Next, make a shallow cut with your sharpened knife along the convex curve of the shrimp's intestinal tract. The tract, usually a faint black line along the outside curve of the shrimp, is faintly visible beneath the translucent flesh. But some shrimp have a thick orange, blue, or gray line instead of a thin black one. In all cases, be careful not to slice too deeply, or you will end up with two shrimp halves instead of one butterflied shrimp.

You have told readers what to look for, citing the exceptions, and have warned them against making too deep a cut. Anticipating spots where communication might break down is a key part of writing an effective process analysis.

Transitional words and phrases are also critical in helping readers understand the order of the steps being described. Time signals such as *first, next, now, while, after, before,* and *finally* provide readers with a clear sense of the sequence. Entire sentences can also be used to link parts of the process, reminding your audience of what has already been discussed and indicating what will now be explained: "Once the panel of experts finishes its evaluation of the exam questions, randomly selected items are field-tested in schools throughout the country."

8. Maintain an appropriate tone. When writing a process analysis essay, be sure your tone is consistent with your purpose, your attitude toward your subject, and the effect you want to have on the reader. When explaining how fraternities and sororities recruit new members, do you want to use an objective, nonjudgmental tone? To decide, take into account readers' attitudes toward your subject. Does your audience have a financial or emotional investment in the process being described? Does your own interest in the process coincide or conflict with that of your audience? Awareness of your readers' stance can be crucial. Consider another example: Assume you're writing a letter to the director of the student health center proposing a new system to replace the currently chaotic one. You'd do well to be tactful in your criticisms. Offend your reader, and your cause is lost. If, however, the letter is slated for the college newspaper and directed primarily to other students, you could adopt a more pointed, even sarcastic tone. Readers, you would assume, will probably share your view and favor change.

Once you settle on the essay's tone, maintain it throughout. If you're writing a light piece on the way computers are taking over our lives, you wouldn't include a grim step-by-step analysis of the way confidential computerized medical records may become public.

9. Open and close the process analysis effectively. A paper developed primarily through process analysis should have a strong beginning. The introduction should state the process to be described and imply whether the essay has an informational or directional intent.

If you suspect readers are indifferent to your subject, use the introduction to motivate them, telling them how important the subject is:

> Do you enjoy the salad bars found in many restaurants? If you do, you probably have noticed that the vegetables are always crisp and fresh--no matter how many hours they have been exposed to the air. What are the restaurants doing to make the vegetables look so inviting? There's a simple answer. Many restaurants dip and spray the vegetables with potent chemicals to make them appetizing.

If you think your audience may be intimidated by your subject (perhaps because it's complex or relatively obscure), the introduction is the perfect spot to reassure them that the process being described is not beyond their grasp:

> Studies show that many people willingly accept a defective product just so they won't have to deal with the uncomfortable process of making a complaint. But once a few easy-to-learn basics are mastered, anyone can register a complaint that gets results.

Most process analysis essays don't end as soon as the last step in the sequence is explained. Instead, they usually include some brief final comments that round out the piece and bring it to a satisfying close. This final section of the essay may summarize the main steps in the process—not by repeating the steps verbatim but by rephrasing and condensing them in several concise sentences. The conclusion can also be an effective spot to underscore the significance of the process, recalling what may have been said in the introduction about the subject's importance. Or the essay can end by echoing the note of reassurance that may have been included at the start.

STUDENT ESSAY

The following student essay was written by Robert Barry in response to this assignment:

> In "Your New Computer," Bill Bryson suggests that technology can sometimes waste time rather than save it. Identify another example of a technology that has turned out to be unexpectedly time-consuming. Drawing upon your own and other people's experiences, write a light-spirited essay that shows, step-by-step, how this technology ends up consuming more time than it should.

While reading Robert's paper, try to determine how effectively it applies the principles of process analysis. The annotations on Robert's paper and the commentary following it will help you look at the essay more closely.

Becoming a Videoholic
by Robert Barry

Introduction   In the last several years, videocassette   1
recorders (VCRs) have become popular additions in many American homes. A recent newspaper article notes that one in three households has a VCR, with sales continuing to climb every day. VCRs seem to be the most popular technological breakthrough since television itself. No consumer warning labels are attached to these rapidly multiplying VCRs, but they should be. VCRs can be dangerous. Barely

Start of two-sentence thesis   aware of what is happening, a person can turn into a compulsive videotaper. The descent from innocent hobby to full-blown addiction takes place in several stages.

Topic sentence ⟶   In the first innocent stage, the unsuspecting   2
person buys a VCR for occasional use. I was at this

First stage in process (VCR addiction)   stage when I asked my parents if they would buy me a VCR as a combined birthday and high school graduation gift. With the VCR, I could tape reruns of Star Trek and Miami Vice, shows I would otherwise miss on nights I was at work. The VCR was perfect. I hooked it up to the old TV in my bedroom, recorded the intergalactic adventures of Captain Kirk and the high-voltage escapades of Sonny Crockett, then watched the tapes the next day. Occasionally, I taped a movie which my friends and I watched over the weekend. I had just one cassette, but that was all I needed since I watched every show I recorded and simply taped over the preceding show when I recorded another. In these early days, my VCR was the equivalent of light social drinking.

Beginning of analogy to alcoholism

Topic sentence →

Second stage in process

In the second phase on the road to videoholism, an individual uses the VCR more frequently and begins to stockpile tapes rather than watch them. My troubles began in July when my family went to the shore for a week's vacation. I programmed the VCR to tape all five episodes of Star Trek while I was at the beach perfecting my tan. Since I used the VCR's long-play mode, I could get all five Star Treks on one cassette. But that ended up creating a problem. Even I, an avid Trekkie, didn't want to watch five shows in one sitting. I viewed two shows, but the three unwatched shows tied up my tape, making it impossible to record other shows. How did I resolve this dilemma? Very easily. I went out and bought several more cassettes. Once I had these additional tapes, I was free to record as many Star Treks as I wanted, plus I could tape reruns of classics like The Honeymooners and Mission: Impossible. Very quickly, I accumulated six Star Treks, four Honeymooners, and three Mission: Impossibles. Then a friend--who shall go nameless--told me that only eighty-two episodes of Star Trek were ever made. Excited by the thought that I could acquire as impressive a collection of tapes as a Hollywood executive, I continued recording Star Trek, even taping shows while I watched them. Clearly, my once innocent hobby was getting out of control. I was now using the VCR on a regular basis--the equivalent of several stiff drinks a day.

Continuation of analogy

Topic sentence →

Third stage in process

In the third stage of videoholism, the amount of taping increases significantly, leading to an even more irrational stockpiling of cassettes. The catalyst that propelled me into this third stage was my parents' decision to get cable TV. Selfless guy that I am, I volunteered to move my VCR and hook it up to the

3

4

Continuation of
analogy

TV in the living room, where the cable outlet was located. Now I could tape all the most recent movies and cable specials. With that delightful possibility in mind, I went out and bought two six-packs of blank tapes. Then, in addition to my regulars, I began to record a couple of other shows every day. I taped <u>Rocky III</u>, <u>Magnum Force</u>, a James Bond movie, an HBO comedy special with Eddie Murphy, and an MTV concert featuring Mick Jagger. Where did I get time to watch all these tapes? I didn't. Taping at this point was more satisfying than watching. Reason and common sense were abandoned. Getting things on tape had become an obsession, and I was taping all the time.

Topic sentence

Fourth stage in
process

Continuation of
analogy

In the fourth stage, videoholism creeps into other parts of the addict's life, influencing behavior in strange ways. Secrecy becomes commonplace. One day, my mother came into my room and saw my bookcase filled with tapes--rather than with the paperbacks that used to be there. "Robert," she exclaimed, "isn't this getting a bit out of hand?" I assured her it was just a hobby, but I started hiding my tapes, putting them in a suitcase stored in my closet. I also taped at night, slipping downstairs to turn on the VCR after my parents had gone to bed and getting down first thing in the morning to turn off the VCR and remove the cassette before my parents noticed. Also, denial is not unusual during this stage of VCR addiction. At the dinner table, when my younger sister commented, "Robert tapes all the time," I laughingly told everyone--including myself--that the taping was no big deal. I was getting bored with it and was going to stop any day, I assured my family. Obsessive behavior also characterizes the fourth stage of videoholism. Each week, I pulled out the TV magazine from the Sunday paper and went through it carefully, circling in red all the shows I wanted to tape. Another sign of addiction was my compulsive organization of all the tapes I had stockpiled. Working more diligently than I ever had for any term paper, I typed up labels and attached them to each cassette. I also created an elaborate list that showed my tapes broken down

5

into categories such as Westerns, horror movies, and comedies.

Topic sentence ———→ In the final stage of an addiction, the individual   6
either succumbs completely to the addiction or is

Continuation of
analogy

Final stage in
process

able to break away from the habit. I broke my addiction, and I broke it cold turkey. This total withdrawal occurred when I went off to college. There was no point in taking my VCR to school because TVs were not allowed in the freshman dorms. Even though there were many things to occupy my time during the school week, cold sweats overcame me whenever I thought about everything on TV I was not taping. I even considered calling home and asking members of my family to tape things for me, but I knew they would think I was crazy. At the beginning of the semester, I also had to resist the overwhelming desire to travel the three hours home every weekend so I could get my fix. But after a while, the urgent need to tape subsided. Now, months later, as I write this, I feel detached and sober.

Conclusion

Final references
to analogy

I have no illusions, though. I know that once a   7
videoholic, always a videoholic. Soon I will return home for the holidays, which, as everyone knows, can be a time for excess eating--and taping. But I will cope with the pressure. I will take each day one at a time. I will ask my little sister to hide my blank tapes. And if I feel myself succumbing to the temptations of taping, I will pick up the telephone and dial the videoholics' hotline: 1-800-VCR-TAPE. I will win the battle.

COMMENTARY

Purpose, thesis, and tone.   Robert's essay is an example of *informational process analysis;* his purpose is to describe—rather than teach—the process of becoming a "videoholic." The title, with its coined term *videoholic,* tips us off that the essay is going to be entertaining. And the introductory paragraph clearly establishes the essay's playful, mock-serious tone. The tone established, Robert briefly defines the term *videoholic* as a "compulsive videotaper" and then moves to the essay's *thesis:* "Barely aware of what is happening, a person can turn into a compulsive videotaper. The descent from innocent hobby to full-blown addiction takes place in several stages."

Throughout the essay, Robert sustains the introduction's humor by mocking his own motivations and poking fun at his quirks: "Selfless guy that I am, I volunteered to move my VCR" (paragraph 4), and "Working more diligently than I ever had for any term paper, I typed up labels" (5). Robert probably uses a bit of *dramatic license* when reporting some of his obsessive behavior, and we, as readers, understand that he's exaggerating for comic effect. Most likely he didn't break out in a cold sweat at the thought of the TV shows he was unable to tape, and he probably didn't hide his tapes in a suitcase. Nevertheless, this tinkering with the truth is legitimate because it allows Robert to create material that fits the essay's lightly satiric tone.

Organization and topic sentences.   To meet the requirements of the assignment, Robert needed to provide a *step-by-step* explanation of a process. And because he invented the term *videoholism,* Robert also needed to invent the stages in the progression of his addiction. During his prewriting, Robert discovered five stages in his videoholism: Presented *chronologically,* these stages provide the organizing focus for his paper. Specifically, each supporting paragraph is devoted to one stage, with the *topic sentence* for each paragraph indicating the stage's distinctive characteristics.

Transitions.   Although Robert's essay is playful, it is nonetheless a process analysis and so must have an easy-to-follow structure. Keeping this in mind, Robert wisely includes *transitions* to signal what happened at each stage of his videoholism: "*Once* I had these additional tapes, I was free to record" (paragraph 3); "*Then,* in addition to my regulars, I began to record" (4); "*One day,* my mother came into my room" (5); and "*But after a while,* the urgent need to tape subsided" (6). In addition to such transitions, Robert also uses crisp questions to move from idea to idea within a paragraph: "How did I resolve this dilemma? Very easily. I . . . bought several more cassettes" (3), and "Where did I get time to watch all these tapes? I didn't" (4).

Other patterns of development.   Even though Robert's essay is a process analysis, it contains elements of other patterns of development.

For example, his paper is unified by an *analogy*—a sustained *comparison* between Robert's video addiction and the obviously more serious addiction to alcohol. Handled incorrectly, the analogy could have been offensive, but Robert makes the comparison work to his advantage. The analogy is stated specifically in several spots: "In these early days, my VCR was the equivalent of light social drinking" (paragraph 2); "I was now using the VCR on a regular basis—the equivalent of several stiff drinks a day" (3). Another place where Robert touches wittily on the analogy occurs in the middle of the fourth paragraph: "I went out and bought two six-packs of blank tapes." To illustrate his progression toward video-holism, Robert depicts the *effects* of his addiction. Finally, he generates numerous lively details or *examples* to illustrate the different stages in his addiction.

Two unnecessary sentences.   Perhaps you noticed that Robert runs into a minor problem at the end of the fourth paragraph. Starting with the sentence "Reason and common sense were abandoned," he begins to ramble and repeat himself. The paragraph's last two sentences fail to add anything substantial. Take a moment to read paragraph 4 aloud, omitting the last two sentences. Note how much sharper the new conclusion is: "Where did I get time to watch all these tapes? I didn't. Taping at this point was more satisfying than watching." This new ending says all that needs to be said.

Revising the first draft.   When it was time to revise, Robert—in spite of his apprehension—showed his paper to his roommate and asked him to read it out loud. Robert knew this strategy would provide a more objective point of view on his work. His roommate, at first an unwilling recruit, nonetheless laughed as he read the essay aloud. That was just the response Robert wanted. But when his roommate got to the conclusion, Robert heard that the closing paragraph was flat and anticlimactic. Here is Robert's original conclusion.

Original Version of the Conclusion

I have no illusions, though, that I am over my videoholism. Soon I will be returning home for the holidays, which can be a time for excess taping. All I can do is ask my little sister to hide my blank tapes. After that, I will hope for the best.

Robert and his roommate brainstormed ways to make the conclusion livelier and more in spirit with the rest of the essay. They decided that the best approach would be to continue the playful, mock-serious tone that characterized earlier parts of the essay. Robert thus made three major changes in the conclusion. First, he tightened the first sentence of the paragraph ("I have no illusions, though, that I am over my videoholism"), making it crisper and more dramatic: "I have no illusions, though." Second, he added a few sentences to sustain the light, self-deprecating tone he had used earlier: "I know that once a videoholic, always a videoholic"; "But I will cope with the pressure"; "I will win the battle." Third, and perhaps most important, he returned to the alcoholism analogy: "I will take each day one at a time. . . . And if I feel myself succumbing to the temptations of taping, I will pick up the telephone and dial the videoholics' hotline. . . ."

These weren't the only changes Robert made while reworking his paper, but they give you some sense of how sensitive he was to the effect he wanted to achieve. Certainly, the recasting of the conclusion was critical to the overall success of this amusing essay.

ACTIVITIES: PROCESS ANALYSIS

Prewriting Activities

1. Imagine you're writing two essays: One *defines* the term "comparison shopping"; the other *contrasts* two different teaching styles. Jot down ways you might use process analysis in each essay.

2. Select *one* of the essay topics that follow and determine what your purpose, tone, and point of view would be for each audience indicated in parentheses. Then use brainstorming, questioning, mapping, or another prewriting technique to identify the points you'd cover for each audience. Finally, organize the raw material, noting the differences in emphasis and sequence for each group of readers.

   a. How to buy a car (*young people who have just gotten a driver's license; established professionals*)

   b. How children acquire their values (*first-time parents; elementary school teachers*)

   c. How to manage money (*grade-school children; college students*)

   d. How loans or scholarships are awarded to incoming students
       on your campus (*high school graduates applying for financial
       aid; high school guidance counselors*)
   e. How arguments can strengthen relationships (*preteen children;
       young adults*)
   f. How to relax (*college students; parents with young children*)

Revising Activities

3. Below is the brainstorming for a brief essay that describes the steps
    involved in making a telephone sales call. The paper has the follow-
    ing thesis: "Establishing rapport with customers is the most chal-
    lenging and the most important part of phone sales." Revise the
    brainstormed material by deleting anything that undermines the
    paper's unity and organizing the steps in a logical sequence.

    - Keep customers on the phone as long as possible to learn what
      they need
    - The more you know about customers' needs the better
    - The tone of the opening comments is very important
    - Gently introduce the product
    - Use a friendly tone in opening comments
    - End on a friendly tone, too
    - Don't introduce the product right away
    - Growing rudeness in society. Some people hang up right away.
      Very upsetting.
    - Try in a friendly way to keep the person on the phone
    - Many people are so lonely they don't mind staying on the phone
      so they can talk to someone--anyone
    - How sad that there's so much loneliness in the world
    - Describe the product's advantages--price, convenience, install-
      ment plan
    - If person is not interested, try in a friendly way to find out why
    - Don't tell people that their reasons for not being interested are
      silly
    - Don't push people if they're not interested
    - Encourage credit card payment--the product will arrive earlier
    - Explain payment--check, money order, or credit card payment

4. Reprinted here is a paragraph from the first draft of a humorous
    essay advising shy college students how to get through a typical day.
    Written as a process analysis, the paragraph outlines techniques for

surviving class. Revise the paragraph, deleting digressions that disrupt the paragraph's unity, eliminating unnecessary repetition, and sequencing the steps in the proper order. Also correct inappropriate shifts in person and add transitions where needed. Feel free to add any telling details.

Simply attending class can be stressful for shy people. Several strategies, though, can lessen the trauma. Shy students should time their arrival to coincide with that of most other class members--about two minutes before the class is scheduled to begin. If you arrive too early, you may be seen sitting alone, or, even worse, may actually be forced to talk with another early arrival. If you arrive late, all eyes will be upon you. Before heading to class, the shy student should dress in the least conspicuous manner possible--say, in the blue jeans, sweatshirt, and sneakers that 99.9 percent of your classmates wear. That way you won't stand out from everyone else. Take a seat near the back of the room. Don't, however, sit at the very back since professors often take sadistic pleasure in calling on students back there, assuming they chose those seats because they didn't want to be called on. A friend of mine who is far from shy uses just the opposite ploy. In an attempt to get in good with her professors, she sits in the front row and, incredibly enough, volunteers to participate. However, since shy people don't want to call attention to themselves, they should stifle any urge to sneeze or cough. You run the risk of having people look at you or offer you a tissue or cough drop. And of course, never, ever volunteer to answer. Such a display of intelligence is sure to focus all eyes on you. In other words, make yourself as inconspicuous as possible. How, you might wonder, can you be inconspicuous if you're blessed (or cursed) with great looks? Well, . . . have you ever considered earning your degree through the mail?

Bill Bryson

Bill Bryson (1951–) has kept audiences on both sides of the Atlantic chuckling by exposing, in rollicking, down-to-earth fashion, the humor inherent in the world around him. A native of Iowa who resided in England for almost twenty years, Bryson earned fame as a columnist and best-selling author in England before returning to live with his wife and four children in Hanover, New Hampshire. Bryson's cross-cultural sensibility and talent for unearthing the absurd are apparent in his books on language, including *The Mother Tongue* (1990), and in his travel writing, including *In a Sunburned Country* (2000) and *A Walk in the Woods,* his best-selling 1998 account of a hike along the Appalachian trail. The following selection first appeared in *I'm a Stranger Here Myself: Notes on Returning to America After 20 Years Away* (1999).

Pre-Reading Journal Entry

Like most people, you've probably found that today's sophisticated technologies often complicate life, rather than making it easier. Take a moment to list in your journal some of the technologies that have added stress to your life. Under each technology, jot down some specifics about the problems you've experienced.

Your New Computer

Congratulations. You have purchased an Edsel[1]/2000 Multimedia 615X Personal Computer with Digital Doo-Dah Enhancer. It will give years of faithful service, if you ever get it up and running. Also included with your PC is a bonus pack of preinstalled software—Lawn Mowing Planner, Mr. Arty-Farty, Blank Screen Saver, and Antarctica Route Finder—which will provide hours of pointless diversion while using up most of your computer's spare memory.   1

So turn the page and let's get started!   2

---

[1]Short-lived automobile (produced for only three model years, from 1958–1960), built by Ford Motors and named after Henry Ford's son. Its demise owed to the general perception that it was poorly designed and engineered—essentially, a "lemon" (editors' note).

Getting Ready

Congratulations. You have successfully turned the page and are   3
ready to proceed.

Important meaningless note: The Edsel/2000 is configured to   4
use 80386, 214J10, or higher processors running at 2472 Herz on
variable speed spin cycle. Check your electrical installations and
insurance policies before proceeding. Do not machine wash.

To prevent internal heat buildup, select a cool, dry environment   5
for your computer. The bottom shelf of the refrigerator is ideal.

Unpack the box and examine its contents. (Warning: Do not   6
open box if contents are missing or faulty, as this will invalidate your
warranty. Return all missing contents in their original packaging
with a note explaining where they have gone and a replacement will
be sent within twelve working months.)

The contents of the box should include some of the following: 7
monitor with mysterious De Gauss[2] button; keyboard; computer
unit; miscellaneous wires and cables not necessarily designed for this
model; 2,000-page Owner's Manual; Short Guide to the Owner's
Manual; Quick Guide to the Short Guide to the Owner's Manual;
Laminated Super-Kwik Set-Up Guide for People Who Are
Exceptionally Impatient or Stupid; 1,167 pages of warranties,
vouchers, notices in Spanish, and other loose pieces of paper; 292
cubic feet of Styrofoam packing material.

Something They Didn't Tell You at the Store

Because of the additional power needs of the preinstalled bonus   8
software, you will need to acquire an Edsel/2000 auxiliary software
upgrade pack, a 900-volt memory capacitator for the auxiliary software pack, a 50-megaherz oscillator unit for the memory capacitator, 2,500 mega-gigabytes of additional memory for the oscillator,
and an electrical substation.

Setting Up

Congratulations. You are ready to set up. If you have not yet   9
acquired a degree in electrical engineering, now is the time to do so.

---

[2]Refers to neutralizing a magnetic field (something a computer owner would not
want to happen to a hard drive) (editors' note).

Connect the monitor cable (A) to the portside outlet unit (D);   10
attach power offload unit suborbiter (Xii) to the coaxial AC/DC
servo channel (G); plug three-pin mouse cable into keyboard housing unit (make extra hole if necessary); connect modem (B2) to
offside parallel audio/video lineout jack. Alternatively, plug the
cables into the most likely looking holes, switch on, and see what
happens.

Additional important meaningless note: The wires in the   11
ampule modulator unit are marked as follows according to international convention: blue = neutral or live; yellow = live or blue; blue
and live = neutral and green; black = instant death. (Except where
prohibited by law.)

Switch the computer on. Your hard drive will automatically   12
download. (Allow three to five days.) When downloading is complete, your screen will say: "Yeah, what?"

Now it is time to install your software. Insert Disc A (marked   13
"Disk D" or "Disk G") into Drive Slot B or J, and type "Hello!
Anybody home?" At the DOS command prompt, enter your
License Verification Number. Your License Verification Number can
be found by entering your Certified User Number, which can be
found by entering your License Verification Number. If you are
unable to find your License Verification or Certified User numbers,
call the Software Support Line for assistance. (Please have your
License Verification and Certified User numbers handy as the support staff cannot otherwise assist you.)

If you have not yet committed suicide, then insert Installation   14
Diskette 1 in drive slot 2 (or vice versa) and follow the instructions
on your screen. (Note: Owing to a software modification, some
instructions will appear in Turkish.) At each prompt, reconfigure the
specified file path, double-click on the button launch icon, select a
single equation default file from the macro selection register, insert
the VGA graphics card in the rear aerofoil, and type "C:\>" followed
by the birthdates of all the people you have ever known.

Your screen will now say: "Invalid file path. Whoa! Abort or   15
continue?" Warning: Selecting "Continue" may result in irreversible
file compression and a default overload in the hard drive. Selecting
"Abort," on the other hand, will require you to start the installation
process all over again. Your choice.

When the smoke has cleared, insert disc A2 (marked "Disc A1")   16
and repeat as directed with each of the 187 other discs.

When installation is complete, return to file path, and type your 17
name, address, and credit card numbers and press "SEND." This will
automatically register you for our free software prize, "Blank
Screensaver IV: Nighttime in Deep Space," and allow us to pass
your name to lots and lots of computer magazines, online services,
and other commercial enterprises, who will be getting in touch
shortly.

Congratulations. You are now ready to use your computer. 18
Here are some simple exercises to get you off to a flying start.

Writing a Letter

Type "Dear ————" and follow it with a name of someone you 19
know. Write a few lines about yourself, and then write, "Sincerely
yours" followed by your own name. Congratulations.

Saving a File

To save your letter, select File Menu. Choose Retrieve from 20
Sub-Directory A, enter a backup file number, and place an insertion
point beside the macro dialogue button. Select secondary text box
from the merge menu, and double-click on the supplementary
cleared document window. Assign the tile cascade to a merge file
and insert in a text equation box. Alternatively, write the letter out
in longhand and put it in a drawer.

Advice on Using the Spreadsheet Facility

Don't.   21

Troubleshooting Section

You will have many, many problems with your computer. Here 22
are some common problems and their solutions.

Problem: My computer won't turn on.   23
Solution: Check to make sure the computer is plugged in; check 24
to make sure the power button is in the ON position; check the
cables for damage; dig up underground cables in your yard and
check for damage; drive out into country and check electricity
pylons for signs of fallen wires; call hotline.

Problem: My keyboard doesn't seem to have any keys.   25
Solution: Turn the keyboard the right way up.   26

> *Problem: My mouse won't drink its water or go on the spinning* 27
> *wheel.*

Solution: Try a high-protein diet or call your pet shop support 28
line.

> *Problem: I keep getting a message saying: "Non-System General* 29
> *Protection Fault."*

Solution: This is probably because you are trying to use the 30
computer. Switch the computer to OFF mode and any annoying messages will disappear.

> *Problem: My computer is a piece of useless junk.* 31

Correct—and congratulations. You are now ready to upgrade to 32
an Edsel/3000 Turbo model, or go back to pen and paper.

Questions for Close Reading

1. What is the selection's thesis? Locate the sentence(s) in which Bryson states his main idea. If he doesn't state the thesis explicitly, express it in your own words.
2. Paragraphs 6 and 13 target a similar flaw in computer manuals. What unfortunate tendency do the paragraphs ridicule?
3. Using humor to make a serious point, in paragraph 8 Bryson levels a not-so-funny charge against computer manufacturers. What accusation does he make? What support for this accusation does he provide?
4. Which Edsel model does Bryson cite at the beginning of the essay? Which does he refer to at the end? In what way do these two references reinforce Bryson's thesis?
5. Refer to your dictionary as needed to define the following words used in the selection: *diversion* (paragraph 1), *configured* (4), *invalidate* (6), *miscellaneous* (7), *auxiliary* (8), *convention* (11), and *pylons* (24).

Questions About the Writer's Craft

1. **The pattern.**   Is Bryson's process analysis *directional* or *informational* (see pages 257–258)? How do you know? What *purpose* (see page 256) do you think Bryson had in mind when writing the piece? Explain.
2. Although Bryson voices serious complaints about computers, their manufacturers, and computer manuals, he uses wry humor to do so. Why do you think Bryson uses humor rather than angry accusation to voice his grievances?
3. Bryson's essay is a *parody;* it mimics and ridicules the instructional manuals that come with computers. How does Bryson's use of subheads contribute to the effectiveness of his parody?

4. Bryson repeats the word "Congratulations" several times in the essay. Identify each place the word appears. What effect do you think Bryson hoped this word would have each time he used it?

Writing Assignments Using Process Analysis as a Pattern of Development

1. With lightly barbed humor, Bryson shows how needlessly frustrating it can be to set up a computer. Write a humorous essay of your own explaining to the uninitiated how to do something that is supposedly easy but in practice is unnecessarily complicated. You might explain how to correct an erroneous credit card charge, how to apply for a scholarship or loan, how to program a VCR, and so on. Like Bryson, devise several tongue-in-cheek headings that convey your attitude about the absurd complexities of the process.

2. In his essay, Bryson ironically suggests actions that in reality should *not* be done in order to get a computer functioning—for example, typing "the birthdates of all the people you have ever known" (paragraph 14). Taking a similarly ironic stance, write your own how-*not*-to guide to doing something. You could, for example, explain how *not* to get a raise, how *not* to pass a college course, how *not* to pass a driver's test. Adopt whatever tone you wish, though a lighthearted one seems particularly appropriate for this essay.

Writing Assignments Using Other Patterns of Development

3. Write an essay exploring the impact that a relatively recent technological development has had on your life. You might focus on ATMs, answering machines, cell phones, beepers, or satellite television. To illustrate how this technology has affected you personally, contrast your life *before* and *after* the introduction of the innovation. Your essay may have a serious or a lighthearted tone. Before you begin writing, consider reading Jonathan Coleman's "Is Technology Making Us Intimate Strangers?" (page 359) and James Gleick's "Life As Type A" (page 387), two essays exploring technology's impact on daily life.

4. Bryson uses humor to express his frustration with computers. But some people don't regard computers with amusement; they are upset about threats posed by computer technology. Brainstorm with others to identify some of the concerns people have about computers. They may, for example, be disturbed about unauthorized access to computerized personal information or about children's exposure to Internet pornography. Review your brainstormed material and select *one* area of concern that seems especially compelling. Also consider doing some library and/or Internet research to gain further insight into the issue. Then write an essay in which you provide dramatic examples to illustrate the validity of people's concerns. End by briefly describing steps that could be taken to minimize these problems.

Writing Assignments Using a Journal Entry as a Starting Point

5. Write an essay showing how technologies that are supposed to make life easier actually create stress. Review your pre-reading journal entry, selecting one or two technologies to write about. Draw upon the material in your journal as well as discussions with other people about their frustrating encounters with today's technologies. Your essay may have a serious or a lighthearted tone.

Nikki Giovanni

Poet and essayist Nikki Giovanni (1943–) attended Fisk University, where she became passionately interested in the link between literature and politics. In 1967, she became involved in the Black Arts movement, an informal coalition of African-American intellectuals who wrote impassioned poetry to raise awareness of Black rights and to promote the struggle for racial equality. In the wake of the assassination of Malcolm X and the rise of the Black Panthers, Giovanni's poetry became yet more political. Giovanni is now a professor at Virginia Tech, where she teaches English. Her poetry collections include *My House* (1972), *Those Who Ride the Night Winds* (1983), *The Sun Is So Quiet* (1996), and *Love Poems* (1997); her nonfiction publications include *Gemini: An Extended Autobiographical Statement on My First Twenty-Five Years Being a Black Poet* (1971), *Sacred Cows . . . and Other Edibles* (1988), and *Racism 101* (1994). The following selection is from *Racism 101*.

Pre-Reading Journal Entry

Were you exposed to racial and/or ethnic diversity while you were growing up? Looking back, do you think that this exposure—or lack of exposure—worked to your advantage or disadvantage? Use your journal to respond to these questions.

Campus Racism 101

There is a bumper sticker that reads: TOO BAD IGNORANCE ISN'T 1
PAINFUL. I like that. But ignorance is. We just seldom attribute the pain to it or recognize it when we see it. Like the postcard on my corkboard. It shows a young man in a very hip jacket smoking a cigarette. In the background is a high school with the American flag waving. The caption says: "Too cool for school. Yet too stupid for the real world." Out of the mouth of the young man is a bubble enclosing the words "Maybe I'll start a band." There could be a postcard showing a jock in a uniform saying, "I don't need school. I'm going to the NFL or NBA." Or one showing a young man or

woman studying and a group of young people saying, "So you want to be white." Or something equally demeaning. We need to quit it.

I am a professor of English at Virginia Tech. I've been here for 2 four years, though for only two years with academic rank. I am tenured, which means I have a teaching position for life, a rarity on a predominantly white campus. Whether from malice or ignorance, people who think I should be at a predominantly Black institution will ask, "Why are you at Tech?" Because it's here. And so are Black students. But even if Black students weren't here, it's painfully obvious that this nation and this world cannot allow white students to go through higher education without interacting with Blacks in authoritative positions. It is equally clear that predominantly Black colleges cannot accommodate the numbers of Black students who want and need an education.

Is it difficult to attend a predominantly white college? 3 Compared with what? Being passed over for promotion because you lack credentials? Being turned down for jobs because you are not college-educated? Joining the armed forces or going to jail because you cannot find an alternative to the streets? Let's have a little perspective here. Where can you go and what can you do that frees you from interacting with the white American mentality? You're going to interact; the only question is, will you be in some control of yourself and your actions, or will you be controlled by others? I'm going to recommend self-control.

What's the difference between prison and college? They both 4 prescribe your behavior for a given period of time. They both allow you to read books and develop your writing. They both give you time alone to think and time with your peers to talk about issues. But four years of prison doesn't give you a passport to greater opportunities. Most likely that time only gives you greater knowledge of how to get back in. Four years of college gives you an opportunity not only to lift yourself but to serve your people effectively. What's the difference when you are called nigger in college from when you are called nigger in prison? In college you can, though I admit with effort, follow procedures to have those students who called you nigger kicked out or suspended. You can bring issues to public attention without risking your life. But mostly, college is and always has been the future. We, neither less nor more than other people, need knowledge. There are discomforts attached to attending predominantly white colleges, though no more so than living in a racist world. Here are some rules to follow that may help:

Go to class. No matter how you feel. No matter how you think   5
the professor feels about you. It's important to have a consistent
presence in the classroom. If nothing else, the professor will know
you care enough and are serious enough to be there.

Meet your professors. Extend your hand (give a firm handshake)   6
and tell them your name. Ask them what you need to do to make
an A. You may never make an A, but you have put them on notice
that you are serious about getting good grades.

Do assignments on time. Typed or computer-generated. You have   7
the syllabus. Follow it, and turn those papers in. If for some reason
you can't complete an assignment on time, let your professor know
before it is due and work out a new due date—then meet it.

Go back to see your professor. Tell him or her your name again. If   8
an assignment received less than an A, ask why, and find out what
you need to do to improve the next assignment.

Yes, your professor is busy. So are you. So are your parents who   9
are working to pay or help with your tuition. Ask early what you
need to do if you feel you are starting to get into academic trouble.
Do not wait until you are failing.

Understand that there will be professors who do not like you; there   10
may even be professors who are racist or sexist or both. You must
discriminate among your professors to see who will give you the
help you need. You may not simply say, "They are all against me."
They aren't. They mostly don't care. Since you are the one who
wants to be educated, find the people who want to help.

Don't defeat yourself. Cultivate your friends. Know your ene-   11
mies. You cannot undo hundreds of years of prejudicial thinking.
Think for yourself and speak up. Raise your hand in class. Say what
you believe no matter how awkward you may think it sounds. You
will improve in your articulation and confidence.

Participate in some campus activity. Join the newspaper staff.   12
Run for office. Join a dorm council. Do something that involves you
on campus. You are going to be there for four years, so let your presence be known, if not felt.

You will inevitably run into some white classmates who are   13
troubling because they often say stupid things, ask stupid questions—and expect an answer. Here are some comebacks to some of
the most common inquiries and comments:

Q: What's it like to grow up in a ghetto?   14
A: I don't know.

Q: (from the teacher): Can you give us the Black perspective on   15
Toni Morrison,[1] Huck Finn,[2] slavery, Martin Luther King, Jr., and
others?
A: I can give you *my* perspective. (Do not take the burden of 22 million people on your shoulders. Remind everyone that you are an individual, and don't speak for the race or any other individual within it.)

Q: Why do all the Black people sit together in the dining hall?   16
A: Why do all the white students sit together?

Q: Why should there be an African-American studies course?   17
A: Because white Americans have not adequately studied the contributions of Africans and African-Americans. Both Black and white
students need to know our total common history.

Q: Why are there so many scholarships for "minority" students?   18
A: Because they wouldn't give my great-grandparents their forty
acres and the mule.[3]

Q: How can whites understand Black history, culture, literature, and   19
so forth?
A: The same way we understand white history, culture, literature,
and so forth. That is why we're in school: to learn.

Q: Should whites take African-American studies courses?   20
A: Of course. We take white-studies courses, though the universities
don't call them that.

Comment: When I see groups of Black people on campus, it's real-   21
ly intimidating.
Comeback: I understand what you mean. I'm frightened when I see
white students congregating.

---

[1]A Nobel prize-winning African-American author (editors' note).
[2]Reference to a novel by Mark Twain in which one of the main characters is a slave
(editors' note).
[3]After the Civil War, the Freedman's Bureau of the U.S. government promised
each newly freed male slave forty acres of land and a mule as part of a plan to promote economic independence; very few, if any, ex-slaves received this assistance
(editors' note).

Comment: It's not fair. It's easier for you guys to get into college   22
than for other people.
Comeback: If it's so easy, why aren't there more of us?

Comment: It's not our fault that America is the way it is.   23
Comeback: It's not our fault, either, but both of us have a responsibility to make changes.

It's really very simple. Educational progress is a national con-   24
cern; education is a private one. Your job is not to educate white
people; it is to obtain an education. If you take the racial world on
your shoulders, you will not get the job done. Deal with yourself as
an individual worthy of respect, and make everyone else deal with
you the same way. College is a little like playing grown-up. Practice
what you want to be. You have been telling your parents you are
grown. Now is your chance to act like it.

Questions for Close Reading

1. What is the selection's thesis? Locate the sentence(s) in which Giovanni
   states her main idea. If she doesn't state the thesis explicitly, express it in
   your own words.
2. How does Giovanni respond to those who question why she is teaching
   at a predominantly White college? What reasons does she give for accepting a position there?
3. What, according to Giovanni, are the most difficult challenges facing
   minority students at primarily White institutions?
4. What does Giovanni mean when she warns readers, "Do not take the
   burden of 22 million people on your shoulders" (paragraph 15)?
5. Refer to your dictionary as needed to define the following words used in
   the selection: *tenured* (paragraph 2), *predominantly* (2), *malice* (2), *authoritative* (2), *articulation* (11), *inevitably* (13), and *congregating* (21).

Questions About the Writer's Craft

1. **The pattern.** Giovanni describes two separate processes: the steps that
   Black students need to take to succeed in college and the strategies they
   can use to respond to classmates' "stupid questions" (paragraph 13). To
   what extent does Giovanni have an informative or persuasive purpose
   when explaining each process?
2. **Other patterns.** Giovanni opens her essay with brief descriptions of a
   bumper sticker and a postcard. Why do you think she chose to begin
   with these two descriptions?
3. Why do you suppose Giovanni mentions her position at Virginia Tech?
   What purpose does the reference serve?

4. Starting in paragraph 3, Giovanni addresses the reader as "you" and makes several comments using the first-person plural pronouns "we" and "us." To whom is Giovanni addressing her recommendations? How do you know?

Writing Assignments Using Process Analysis as a Pattern of Development

1. Select *one* of the suggestions that Giovanni offers in paragraphs 5–12, and expand it in an essay of your own. Explain as specifically as you can the steps that beginning college students should take to accomplish the recommendation. Illustrate the steps with concrete examples from your own and other students' experience.

2. Giovanni's suggestions highlight some of the steps that minority college students should take to get a good education. In an essay of your own, explain, step-by-step, what another group of people should do to achieve a clear-cut goal. You might explain how shy people can succeed at parties, how high school students can get good summer jobs, how friends can disagree without jeopardizing their relationship. Your tone may be serious or humorous, as long as it is consistent with your overall purpose.

Writing Assignments Using Other Patterns of Development

3. Giovanni urges her readers not to "defeat" themselves, not to sell themselves short. At one time or another, all of us have sold not only ourselves short but someone else as well. Write an essay about a time you underestimated someone's character, ability, or actions. Begin by explaining how you initially judged the person; then narrate the event(s) that altered your assessment of that person.

4. Giovanni briefly touches on, and has strong opinions about, several controversial issues: Black studies programs (17, 20), minority scholarships (18), and affirmative action in college admissions policies (22). Select *one* of these issues and write an essay defending or disputing Giovanni's position. Remember to acknowledge opposing viewpoints, refuting as many of them as you can. Where appropriate, mention points made by essayists Roger Wilkins ("Racism Has Its Privileges," page 464) and Shelby Steele ("Affirmative Action: The Price of Preference," page 475), two writers having sharply divergent views on racial issues.

Writing Assignments Using a Journal Entry as a Starting Point

5. Write an essay arguing that it is *or* is not important to expose children to racial and ethnic diversity. The material you generated in your pre-reading journal entry will help you develop your position. You'll probably find it helpful to brainstorm with others about their experiences with multiculturalism and draw on this material for specific supporting examples. Part of your essay should acknowledge the views of those who don't adopt the stance you take. Before writing, consider reading Yuh Ji-Yeon's "Let's Tell the Story of All America's Cultures" (page 445), a compelling argument advocating multicultural education.

Caroline Rego

Caroline Rego was born in 1950 in Edmond, Oklahoma. A graduate of the University of Oklahoma, she began her journalistic career as a police reporter for a daily newspaper in Montana. Later, while filling in for a vacationing colleague in the features section of another newspaper, she found her true calling: writing consumer-affairs articles that teach readers how to protect themselves against shoddy service, dangerous products, and inefficiency. A sought-after public speaker, Rego talks frequently to students and community groups on strategies for becoming an informed consumer. The following selection is part of a work in progress on consumer empowerment.

Pre-Reading Journal Entry

When you're disappointed with someone or something, how do you typically react—passively, assertively, or in some other way? In your journal, list a few disappointments you've experienced. How did you respond on each occasion? In retrospect, are you happy with your responses? Why or why not?

The Fine Art of Complaining

You waited forty-five minutes for your dinner, and when it came 1
it was cold—and not what you ordered in the first place. You washed your supposedly machine-washable, preshrunk T-shirt (the one the catalogue claimed was "indestructible"), and now it's the size of a napkin. Your new car broke down a month after you bought it, and the dealer says the warranty doesn't apply.

Life's annoyances descend on all of us—some pattering down 2
like gentle raindrops, others striking with the bruising force of hailstones. We dodge the ones we can, but inevitably, plenty of them make contact. And when they do, we react fairly predictably. Many of us—most of us, probably—grumble to ourselves and take it. We scowl at our unappetizing food but choke it down. We stash the shrunken T-shirt in a drawer, vowing never again to order from a catalogue. We glare fiercely at our checkbooks as we pay for repairs that should have been free.

A few of us go to the other extreme. Taking our cue from the 3
crazed newscaster in the 1976 movie *Network,* we go through life
mad as hell and unwilling to take it anymore. In offices, we shout
at hapless receptionists when we're kept waiting for appointments.
In restaurants, we make scenes that have fellow patrons craning
their necks to get a look at us. In stores, we argue with salespeople for not waiting on us. We may notice after a while that our
friends seem reluctant to venture into public with us, but hey—
we're just standing up for our rights. Being a patsy doesn't get you
anywhere in life.

It's true—milquetoasts live unsatisfying lives. However, people 4
who go through the day in an eye-popping, vein-throbbing state of
apoplectic rage don't win any prizes either. What persons at both
ends of the scale need—what could empower the silent sufferer and
civilize the Neanderthal—is a course in the gentle art of *effective*
complaining.

Effective complaining is not apologetic and half-hearted. It's 5
not making one awkward attempt at protest—"Uh, excuse me, I
don't think I ordered the squid and onions"—and then slinking
away in defeat. But neither is it roaring away indiscriminately,
attempting to get satisfaction through the sheer volume of our
complaint.

Effective complainers are people who act businesslike and 6
important. Acting important doesn't mean puffing up your chest
and saying, "Do you know who I am?"—an approach that would
tempt anyone to take you down a peg or two. It doesn't mean
shouting and threatening—techniques that will only antagonize the
person whose help you need. It *does* mean making it clear that you
know your request is reasonable and that you are confident it will be
taken care of. People are generally treated the way they expect to be
treated. If you act like someone making a fair request, chances are
that request will be granted. Don't beg, don't explain. Just state
your name, the problem, and what you expect to have done. Remain
polite. But be firm. "My car has been in your garage for three days,
and a mechanic hasn't even looked at it yet," you might say. "I want
to know when it is going to be worked on." Period. Now it is up to
them to give you a satisfactory response. Don't say, "Sorry to bother you about this, but . . ." or "I, uh, was sort of expecting. . . ."
You're only asking people to remedy a problem, after all; that is not
grounds for apology.

If your problem requires an immediate response, try to make   7
your complaint in person; a real, live, in-the-flesh individual has to
be dealt with in some way. Complaining over the telephone, by contrast, is much less effective. When you speak to a disembodied voice,
when the person at the other end of the line doesn't have to face
you, you're more likely to get a runaround.

Most importantly, complain to the right person. One of the   8
greatest frustrations in complaining is talking to a clerk or recep-
tionist who cannot solve your problem and whose only purpose
seems to be to drive you crazy. Getting mad doesn't help; the person you're mad at probably had nothing to do with your actual
problem. And you'll have to repeat everything you've said to the
clerk once you're passed along to the appropriate person. So make
sure from the start that you're talking to someone who can help—a
manager or supervisor.

If your problem doesn't require an immediate response, com-   9
plaining by letter is probably the most effective way to get what you
want. A letter of complaint should be brief, businesslike, and to the
point. If you have a new vacuum cleaner that doesn't work, don't
spend a paragraph describing how your Uncle Joe tried to fix the
problem and couldn't. As when complaining in person, be sure you
address someone in a position of real authority. Here's an example
of an effective letter of complaint.

Ms. Anne Lublin   10
Manager
Mitchell Appliances
80 Front Street
Newton, MA 02159

Dear Ms. Lublin: 11

First section: Explain the problem. Include facts to back up your story.   12

On August 6, I purchased a new Perma-Kool freezer from your store (a   13
copy of my sales receipt is enclosed). In the two weeks I have owned
the freezer, I have had to call your repair department three times in an
attempt to get it running properly. The freezer ran normally when it was
installed, but since then it has repeatedly turned off, causing the food
inside to spoil. My calls to your repair department have not been
responded to promptly. After I called the first time, on August 10, I waited two days for the repair person to show up. It took three days to get

a repair person here after my second call, on August 15. The freezer stopped yet again on August 20. I called to discuss this recent problem, but no one has responded to my call.

Second section: Tell how you trust the company and are confident that   14
your reader will fix the problem. This is to "soften up" the reader a bit.

I am surprised to receive such unprofessional service and poor quality   15
from Mitchell Appliances since I have been one of your satisfied customers for fifteen years. In the past, I have purchased a television, air conditioner, and washing machine from your company. I know that you value good relations with your customers, and I'm sure you want to see me pleased with my most recent purchase.

Third section: Explain exactly what you want to be done—repair,   16
replacement, refund, etc.

Although your repair department initially thought that the freezer need-   17
ed only some minor adjustments, the fact that no one has been able to permanently fix the problem convinces me that the freezer has some serious defect. I am understandably unwilling to spend any more time having repairs made. Therefore, I expect you to exchange the freezer for an identical model by the end of this week (August 30). Please call me to arrange for the removal of the defective freezer and the delivery of the new one.

Sincerely,   18

Janice Becker

P.S. (Readers always notice a P.S.) State again when you expect the   19
problem to be taken care of, and what you will do if it isn't.

P.S. I am confident that we can resolve this problem by August 30. If the   20
defective freezer is not replaced by then, however, I will report this incident to the Better Business Bureau.

Notice that the P.S. says what you'll do if your problem isn't solved.   21
In other words, you make a threat—a polite threat. Your threat must be reasonable and believable. A threat to burn down the store if your purchase price isn't refunded is neither reasonable nor believable—or if it *were* believed, you could end up in jail. A threat to

report the store to a consumer-protection agency, such as the Better   22
Business Bureau, however, is credible.

Don't be too quick to make one of the most common—and
commonly empty—threats: "I'll sue!" A full-blown lawsuit is more
trouble, and more expensive, than most problems are worth. On the
other hand, most areas have a small-claims court where suits involving modest amounts of money are heard. These courts don't use
complex legal language or procedures, and you don't need a lawyer
to use them. A store or company will often settle with you—if your   23
claim is fair—rather than go to small-claims court.

Whether you complain over the phone, in person, or by letter,
be persistent. One complaint may not get results. In that case, keep
on complaining, and make sure you keep complaining to the same
person. Chances are he or she will get worn out and take care of the   24
situation, if only to be rid of you.

Someday, perhaps, the world will be free of the petty annoyances that plague us all from time to time. Until then, however,
toasters will break down, stores will refuse to honor rainchecks, and
bills will include items that were never purchased. You can depend
upon it—there will be grounds for complaint. You might as well
learn to be good at it.

Questions for Close Reading

1. What is the selection's thesis? Locate the sentence(s) in which Rego
   states her main idea. If she doesn't state the thesis explicitly, express it in
   your own words.
2. In Rego's opinion, what types of actions and statements are *not* helpful
   when making a complaint?
3. What should be included in a letter of complaint? What should be omitted?
4. What does Rego suggest doing if a complaint is ignored?
5. Refer to your dictionary as needed to define the following words used in
   the selection: *hapless* (paragraph 3), *venture* (3), *patsy* (3), *milquetoasts*
   (4), *apoplectic* (4), *Neanderthal* (4), *indiscriminately* (5), *disembodied*
   (7), and *credible* (21).

Questions About the Writer's Craft

1. **The pattern.** Is Rego's process analysis primarily directional or primarily informational? Explain. To what extent does Rego try to persuade
   readers to follow her process?

2. **Other patterns.** Where does Rego include narrative elements in her essay? What do these brief narratives add to the piece?

3. **Other patterns.** Numerous oppositions occur throughout the essay. How do these contrasts enliven the essay and help Rego persuade readers to adopt her suggestions?

4. Reread the essay, noting where Rego shifts point of view. Where does she use the second-person (*you*), the first-person-plural (*we*), and the third-person-plural (*they*) points of view? How does her use of multiple points of view add to the essay's effectiveness?

Writing Assignments Using Process Analysis as a Pattern of Development

1. Write an essay explaining to college students how to register—with someone in a position of authority—an effective complaint about a campus problem. You could show, for example, how to complain to a professor about a course's grading policy, to the bookstore manager about the markup on textbooks, to security about the poorly maintained college parking lots. Feel free to adapt some of Rego's recommendations, but be sure to invent several strategies of your own. In either case, provide—as Rego does—lively examples to illustrate the step-by-step procedure for registering an effective complaint with a specific authority figure on campus.

2. Rego argues that "people who go through the day in an eye-popping, vein-throbbing state of apoplectic rage don't win any prizes." But sometimes, getting mad can be appropriate—even productive. Write an essay explaining the best process for expressing anger effectively. Explain how to vent emotion safely, communicate the complaint in a nonthreatening way, encourage more honest interaction, and prompt change for the better. Illustrate the process by drawing upon your own experiences and observations. Consider reading James Gleick's "Life As Type A" (page 387), which addresses the origins of high-intensity behavior, and Barbara Ehrenreich's "What I've Learned From Men" (page 196), which provides some insight into the dynamics of anger and resentment.

Writing Assignments Using Other Patterns of Development

3. Think about a service or product that failed to live up to your expectations. Perhaps you were disgruntled about your mechanic's car repair, a store's return policy, or a hotel's accommodations. Using Rego's suggestions, write a letter of complaint in which you describe the problem, convey confidence in the reader's ability to resolve the problem, and state your request for specific action. Remember that a firm but cordial

tone will persuade your reader that you have legitimate grounds for seeking the resolution you propose.

4. Rego shows that events often don't turn out as we had hoped. In an essay, contrast how you thought a specific situation would be with the way it actually turned out. Was the unexpected outcome better or worse than what you had expected? Did you have trouble adjusting, or did you adapt with surprising ease? Provide vivid specifics about the unforeseen turn of events and your reaction to it.

Writing Assignments Using a Journal Entry as a Starting Point

5. Write an essay contrasting the way you reacted to a specific disappointment with the way you wish you had reacted. Reread your pre-reading journal entry, and select *one* incident that illustrates this discrepancy most dramatically. Use vigorous narrative details to make the contrast vivid and real. In your conclusion, indicate what you've learned in hindsight. Before writing, consider reading two other essays that document personal reactions to life's minor—and major—calamities: Langston Hughes's "Salvation" (page 148) and Beth Johnson's "Bombs Bursting in Air" (page 189).

Additional Writing Topics

PROCESS ANALYSIS

General Assignments

Develop one of the following topics through process analysis. Explain the process one step at a time, organizing the steps chronologically. If there's no agreed-on sequence, design your own series of steps. Use transitions to ease the audience through the steps in the process. You may use any tone you wish, from serious to light.

Directional: How to Do Something

1. How to improve a course you have taken
2. How to drive defensively
3. How to get away with _____
4. How to succeed at a job interview
5. How to relax
6. How to show appreciation to others
7. How to get through school despite personal problems
8. How to be a responsible pet owner
9. How to conduct a garage or yard sale
10. How to look fashionable on a limited budget
11. How to protect a home from burglars
12. How to meet more people
13. How to improve the place where you work
14. How to gain or lose weight
15. How to get over a disappointment

Informational: How Something Happens

1. How a student becomes burned out
2. How a library's card catalog or computerized catalog organizes books
3. How a dead thing decays (or how some other natural process works)
4. How the college registration process works
5. How *Homo sapiens* chooses a mate
6. How a VCR (or some other machine) works
7. How a bad habit develops
8. How people fall into debt

Assignments With a Specific Purpose and Audience

1. As an author of books for elementary school children, you want to show children how to do something—take care of a pet, get along with siblings, keep a room clean. Explain the process in terms a child would understand yet not find condescending.

2. As a driver's education instructor in a high school, you decide to pre-pare a handout dealing with one of the following: making a three-point turn, parallel parking, handling a skid, or executing any other driving maneuver. Explain the process one step at a time. Remember, your audience consists of teens who are just learning how to drive.

3. Write an article for *Consumer Reports* on how to shop for a certain product. Give specific steps explaining how to save money, buy a qual-ity product, and the like.

4. Write a process analysis showing how to save a life by CPR, rescue breathing, the Heimlich maneuver, or some other method. Your audi-ence will be average, everyday people who are taking a first-aid class.

5. Your closest friend plans to move into his or her own apartment but doesn't know the first thing about how to choose one. Explain the process of selecting an apartment—where to look, what to investigate, what questions to ask before signing a lease.

6. You write an "advice to the lovelorn" column for the campus newspa-per. A correspondent asks for advice on how to break up with a steady boyfriend (or girlfriend) without hurting the person. Give the writer guidance on how to end a meaningful relationship with a minimal amount of pain.

8

COMPARISON-CONTRAST

WHAT IS COMPARISON-CONTRAST?

We frequently try to make sense of the world by finding similarities and differences in our experiences. Seeing how things are alike (comparing) and seeing how they are different (contrasting) helps us impose meaning on experiences that otherwise might remain fragmented and disconnected. Barely aware of the fact that we're comparing and contrasting, we may think to ourselves, "I woke up in a great mood this morning, but now I feel uneasy and anxious. I wonder why I feel so different." This inner questioning, which often occurs in a flash, is just one example of the way we use comparison and contrast to understand ourselves and our world.

Comparing and contrasting also helps us make choices. We compare and contrast everything—from two brands of soap we might buy to two colleges we might attend. We listen to a favorite radio station, watch a preferred nightly news show, select a particular dessert from a menu— all because we have done some degree of comparing and contrasting. We often weigh these alternatives in an unstudied, casual manner, as when we flip from one radio station to another. But when we have to make important decisions, we tend to think rigorously about how things are alike or different: Should I live in a dorm or rent an apartment? Should I accept the higher-paying job or the lower-paying one that offers more challenges? Such a deliberate approach to comparison-contrast may also provide us with needed insight into complex contemporary issues: Is television's coverage of political campaigns more or less objective than it used to be? What are the merits of the various positions on abortion?

HOW COMPARISON-CONTRAST FITS YOUR PURPOSE AND AUDIENCE

When is it appropriate in writing to use the comparison-contrast method of development? Comparison-contrast works well if you want to demonstrate any of the following: (1) that one thing is better than another (the first example below); (2) that things which seem different are actually alike (the second example below); (3) that things which seem alike are actually different (the third example below).

> Compare and contrast the way male and female relationships are depicted in *Cosmopolitan*, *Ms.*, *Playboy*, and *Esquire*. Which publication has the most limited view of men and women? Which has the broadest perspective?

> Football, basketball, and baseball differ in the ways they appeal to fans. Describe the unique drawing power of each sport, but also reach some conclusions about the appeals the three sports have in common.

> Studies show that both college students and their parents feel that post-secondary education should equip young people to succeed in the marketplace. Yet the same studies report that the two groups have a very different understanding of what it means to succeed. What differences do you think the studies identify?

Other assignments will, in less obvious ways, lend themselves to comparison-contrast. For instance, although words like *compare, contrast, differ,* and *have in common* don't appear in the following assignments, essay responses to the assignments could be organized around the comparison-contrast format:

The emergence of the two-career family is one of the major phenomena of our culture. Discuss the advantages and disadvantages of having both parents work, showing how you feel about such two-career households.

Some people believe that the 1950s, often called the golden age of television, produced several never-to-be-equaled comedy classics. Do you agree that such shows as *I Love Lucy* and *The Honeymooners* are superior to the situation comedies aired on television today?

There has been considerable criticism recently of the news coverage by the city's two leading newspapers, the *Herald* and the *Beacon*. Indicate whether you think the criticism is valid by discussing the similarities and differences in the two papers' news coverage.

Note: The last assignment shows that a comparison-contrast essay may cover similarities *and* differences, not just one or the other.

As you have seen, comparison-contrast can be the key strategy for achieving an essay's purpose. But comparison-contrast can also be a supplemental method used to help make a point in an essay organized chiefly around another pattern of development. A serious, informative essay intended for laypeople might *define* clinical depression by contrasting that state of mind with ordinary run-of-the-mill blues. Writing humorously about the exhausting *effects* of trying to get in shape, you might dramatize your plight for readers by contrasting the leisurely way you used to spend your day with your current rigidly compulsive exercise regimen. Or, in an urgent *argumentation-persuasion* essay on the need for stricter controls over drug abuse in the workplace, you might provide readers with background by comparing several companies' approaches to the problem.

SUGGESTIONS FOR USING COMPARISON-CONTRAST IN AN ESSAY

The following suggestions will be helpful whether you use comparison-contrast as a dominant or a supportive pattern of development.

1. Be sure your subjects are at least somewhat alike. Unless you plan to develop an *analogy* (see below), the subjects you choose to compare or contrast should share some obvious characteristics or qualities. It makes sense to compare different parts of the country, two comedians, or several college teachers. But a reasonable paper wouldn't result from, let's say, a comparison of a television game show with a soap opera. Your subjects must belong to the same general group so that your comparison-contrast stays within good logical bounds and doesn't veer off into pointlessness.

2. Stay focused on your purpose. When writing, remember that comparison-contrast isn't an end in itself. That is, your objective isn't to turn an essay into a mechanical list of "how A differs from B" or "how A is like B." Like the other patterns of development discussed in this book, comparison-contrast is a strategy for making a point or meeting a larger purpose.

Consider the assignment on page 297 about the two newspapers. Your purpose here might be simply to *inform,* to present information as objectively as possible: "This is what the *Herald*'s news coverage is like. This is what the *Beacon*'s news coverage is like."

More frequently, though, you'll use comparison-contrast to *evaluate* your subjects' pros and cons, your goal being to reach a conclusion or make a judgment: "Both the *Herald* and the *Beacon* spend too much time reporting local news," or "The *Herald*'s analysis of the recent hostage crisis was more insightful than the *Beacon*'s." Comparison-contrast can also be used to *persuade* readers to take action: "People interested in thorough coverage of international events should read the *Herald* rather than the *Beacon*." Persuasive essays may also propose a change, contrasting what now exists with a more ideal situation: "For the *Beacon* to compete with the *Herald*, it must assign more reporters to international stories."

Yet another purpose you might have in writing a comparison-contrast essay is to *clear up misconceptions* by revealing previously hidden similarities or differences. For example, perhaps your town's two newspapers are thought to be sharply different. However, a comparison-contrast analysis might reveal that—although one paper specializes in sensationalized stories while the other adopts a more muted approach—both resort to biased, emotionally charged analyses of local politics. Or the essay might illustrate that the tabloid's treatment of the local arts scene is surprisingly more comprehensive than that of its competitor.

Comparing and contrasting also make it possible to *draw an analogy* between two seemingly unrelated subjects. An analogy is an imaginative comparison that delves beneath the surface differences of subjects in order to expose their significant and often unsuspected similarities or differences. Your purpose may be to show that singles bars and zoos share a number of striking similarities. Or you may want to illustrate that wolves and humans raise their young in much the same way, but that wolves go about the process in a more civilized manner. The analogical approach can make a complex subject easier to understand—as when the national deficit is compared to a household budget gone awry. Analogies are often dramatic and instructive, challenging you and your audience to consider subjects in a new light. But analogies don't speak for themselves. You must make clear to the reader how the analogy demonstrates your purpose.

3. Formulate a strong thesis. An essay developed primarily through comparison-contrast should be focused by a solid thesis. Besides revealing your attitude, the thesis will often do the following:

- Name the subjects being compared and contrasted.
- Indicate whether the essay focuses on the subjects' similarities, differences, or both.
- State the essay's main point of comparison or contrast.

Not all comparison-contrast essays need thesis statements as structured as those that follow. Even so, these examples can serve as models of clarity. Note that the first thesis statement signals similarities, the second differences, and the last both similarities and differences:

Middle-aged parents are often in a good position to empathize with adolescent children because the emotional upheavals experienced by the two age groups are much the same.

The priorities of most retired people are more conducive to health and happiness than the priorities of most young professionals.

College students in their thirties and forties face many of the same pressures as younger students, but they are better equipped to withstand these pressures.

4. Select the points to be discussed.   Once you have identified the essay's subjects, purpose, and thesis, you need to decide which aspects of the subjects to compare or contrast. College professors, for instance, could be compared and contrasted on the basis of their testing methods, ability to motivate students, confidence in front of a classroom, personalities, level of enthusiasm, and so forth.

Brainstorming, freewriting, and mapping are valuable for gathering possible points to cover. Whichever prewriting technique you use, try to produce more raw material than you'll need, so that you have the luxury of narrowing the material down to the most significant points.

When selecting points to cover, be sure to consider your audience. Ask yourself: "Will my readers be familiar with this item? Will I need it to get my message across? Will my audience find this item interesting or convincing?" What your readers know, what they don't know, and what you can predict about their reactions should influence your choices. And, of course, you need to select points that support your thesis. If your essay explains the differences between healthy, sensible diets and dangerous crash diets, it wouldn't be appropriate to talk about aerobic exercise. Similarly, imagine you want to write an essay making the point that, despite their differences, hard rock of the 1960s and punk rock of the 1970s both reflected young people's disillusionment with society. It wouldn't make much sense to contrast the long, uncombed hairstyle of the 1960s with the short, spikey cuts of the 1970s. But contrasting song lyrics (protest versus nihilistic messages) would help support your thesis and lead to interesting insights.

5. Organize the points to be discussed.   After deciding which points to include, you should use a systematic, logical plan for presenting those ideas. If the points aren't organized, your essay will be little more than a confusing jumble of ideas. There are two common ways to organize an essay developed wholly or in part by comparison-contrast: the one-side-at-a-time method and the point-by-point method. Although both strategies may be used in a paper, one method usually predominates.

In the *one-side-at-a-time method* of organization, you discuss everything relevant about one subject before moving to another subject. For example, responding to the earlier assignment that asked you to analyze the news coverage in two local papers, you might first talk about the *Herald*'s coverage of international, national, and local news; then you would discuss the *Beacon*'s coverage of the same categories. Note that the areas discussed should be the same for both newspapers. It wouldn't be logical to review the *Herald*'s coverage of international, national, and local news and then to detail the *Beacon*'s magazine supplements, modern living section, and comics page. Moreover, the areas compared and contrasted should be presented in the same order.

This is how you would organize the essay using the one-side-at-a-time method:

Everything about A	*Herald*'s news coverage:
	• International
	• National
	• Local
Everything about B	*Beacon*'s news coverage:
	• International
	• National
	• Local

In the *point-by-point method* of organization, you alternate from one aspect of the first subject to the same aspect of your other subject(s). For example, to use this method when comparing or contrasting the *Herald* and the *Beacon,* you would first discuss the *Herald*'s international coverage, then the *Beacon*'s international coverage; next the *Herald*'s national coverage, then the *Beacon*'s; and finally, the *Herald*'s local coverage, then the *Beacon*'s.

Using the point-by-point method, this is how the essay would be organized:

First aspect of A and B	*Herald:* International coverage
	Beacon: International coverage
Second aspect of A and B	*Herald:* National coverage
	Beacon: National coverage
Third aspect of A and B	*Herald:* Local coverage
	Beacon: Local coverage

Deciding which of these two methods of organization to use is largely a personal choice, though there are several factors to consider.

The one-side-at-a-time method tends to convey a more unified feeling because it highlights broad similarities and differences. It is, therefore, an effective approach for subjects that are fairly uncomplicated. This strategy also works well when essays are brief; the reader won't find it difficult to remember what has been said about subject A when reading about subject B.

Because the point-by-point method permits more extensive coverage of similarities and differences, it is often a wise choice when subjects are complex. This pattern is also useful for lengthy essays since readers would probably find it difficult to remember, let's say, ten pages of information about subject A while reading the next ten pages about subject B. The point-by-point approach, however, may cause readers to lose sight of the broader picture, so remember to keep them focused on your central point.

6. Supply the reader with clear transitions.   Although a well-organized comparison-contrast format is important, it doesn't guarantee that readers will be able to follow your line of thought easily. *Transitions*—especially those signaling similarities or differences—are needed to show readers where they have been and where they are going. Such cues are essential in all writing, but they're especially crucial in a paper using comparison-contrast. By indicating clearly when subjects are being compared or contrasted, the transitions help weave the discussion into a coherent whole.

The transitions (in boldface) in the following examples could be used to *signal similarities* in an essay discussing the news coverage in the *Herald* and the *Beacon:*

- The *Beacon* **also** allots only a small portion of the front page to global news.
- **In the same way**, the *Herald* tries to include at least three local stories on the first page.
- **Likewise**, the *Beacon* emphasizes the importance of up-to-date reporting of town meetings.
- The *Herald* is **similarly** committed to extensive coverage of high school and college sports.

The transitions (in boldface) in these examples could be used to *signal differences:*

- **By way of contrast**, the *Herald*'s editorial page deals with national matters on the average of three times a week.
- **On the other hand**, the *Beacon* does not share the *Herald*'s enthusiasm for interviews with national figures.
- The *Beacon*, **however**, does not encourage its reporters to tackle national stories the way the *Herald* does.
- **But** the *Herald*'s coverage of the Washington scene is much more comprehensive than its competitor's.

STUDENT ESSAY

The following student essay was written by Carol Siskin in response to this assignment:

> In "The Ugly Truth About Beauty," Dave Barry contrasts stereotypical male and female approaches to personal beauty, ultimately praising—for unexpected reasons—one perspective over the other. In an essay of your own, contrast two personality types, lifestyles, or stages of life, showing that the one most people consider inferior is actually superior.

While reading Carol's paper, try to determine how well it applies the principles of comparison-contrast. The annotations on Carol's paper and the commentary following it will help you look at the essay more closely.

The Virtues of Growing Older
by Carol Siskin

The first of a two-paragraph introduction	→ Our society worships youth. Advertisements convince us to buy Grecian Formula and Oil of Olay so we can hide the gray in our hair and smooth the lines on our face. Television shows feature attractive young stars with firm bodies, perfect complexions, and thick manes of hair. Middle-aged folks work out in gyms and jog down the street, trying to delay the effects of age.
The second introductory paragraph	→ Wouldn't any person over thirty gladly sign with the devil just to be young again? Isn't aging an

1

2

Thesis →

First half of topic sentence for point 1: Appearance

Start of what it's like being young

Second half of topic sentence for point 1

Start of what it's like being older

First half of topic sentence for point 2: Life choices

Start of what it's like being older

Second half of topic sentence for point 2

Start of what it's like being younger

experience to be dreaded? Perhaps it is un-American to say so, but I believe the answer is "No." Being young is often pleasant, but being older has distinct advantages.

When young, you are apt to be obsessed with   3 your appearance. When my brother Dave and I were teens, we worked feverishly to perfect the bodies we had. Dave lifted weights, took megadoses of vitamins, and drank a half-dozen milk shakes a day in order to turn his wiry adolescent frame into some muscular ideal. And as a teenager, I dieted constantly. No matter what I weighed, though, I was never satisfied with the way I looked. My legs were too heavy, my shoulders too broad, my waist too big. When Dave and I were young, we begged and pleaded for the "right" clothes. If our parents didn't get them for us, we felt our world would fall apart. How could we go to school wearing loose-fitting blazers when everyone else would be wearing smartly tailored leather jackets? We would be considered freaks. I often wonder how my parents, and parents in general, manage to tolerate their children during the adolescent years. Now, however, Dave and I are beyond such adolescent agonies. My rounded figure seems fine, and I don't deny myself a slice of pecan pie if I feel in the mood. Dave still works out, but he has actually become fond of his tall lanky frame. The two of us enjoy wearing fashionable clothes, but we are no longer slaves to style. And women, I'm embarrassed to admit, even more than men, have always seemed to be at the mercy of fashion. Now my clothes--and my brother's--are attractive yet easy to wear. We no longer feel anxious about what others will think. As long as we feel good about how we look, we are happy.

Being older is preferable to being younger in   4 another way. Obviously, I still have important choices to make about my life, but I have already made many of the critical decisions that confront those just starting out. I chose the man I wanted to marry. I decided to have children. I elected to return to college to complete my education. But when you are young, major decisions await you at every turn. "What college should I attend? What career should I pursue? Should I get married? Should I have children?" These are just a few of the issues facing young people. It's no wonder that, despite their

Topic sentence for point 3: Self-concept carefree facade, they are often confused, uncertain, and troubled by all the unknowns in their future.

But the greatest benefit of being forty is know- 5

Start of what it's like being younger ing who I am. The most unsettling aspect of youth is the uncertainty you feel about your values, goals, and dreams. Being young means wondering what is worth working for. Being young means feeling happy with yourself one day and wishing you were never born the next. It means trying on new selves by taking up with different crowds. It means resenting your parents and their way of life one minute and then feeling you will never be as good or as accomplished as they are. By way of contrast, forty

Start of what it's like being older is sanity. I have a surer self-concept now. I don't laugh at jokes I don't think are funny. I can make a speech in front of a town meeting or complain in a store because I am no longer terrified that people will laugh at me; I am no longer anxious that everyone must like me. I no longer blame my parents for my every personality quirk or keep a running score of everything they did wrong raising me. Life has taught me that I, not they, am responsible for who I am. We are all human beings--neither saints nor devils.

Conclusion Most Americans blindly accept the idea that 6 newer is automatically better. But a human life contradicts this premise. There is a great deal of happiness to be found as we grow older. My own parents, now in their sixties, recently told me that they are happier now than they have ever been. They would not want to be my age. Did this surprise me? At first, yes. Then it gladdened me. Their contentment holds out great promise for me as I move into the next--perhaps even better--phase of my life.

COMMENTARY

Purpose and thesis.   In her essay, Carol disproves the widespread belief that being young is preferable to being old. The *comparison-contrast* pattern allows her to analyze the drawbacks of one and the merits of the other, thus providing the essay with an *evaluative purpose*. Using the title to indicate her point of view, Carol places the *thesis* at the end of her two-paragraph introduction: "Being young is often pleasant, but being older has distinct advantages." Note that the thesis accomplishes several things. It names the two subjects to be discussed and clarifies Carol's point of view about her subjects. The thesis also implies that the essay will focus on the contrasts between these two periods of life.

Points of support and overall organization.   To support her assertion that older is better, Carol supplies examples from her own life and organizes the examples around three main points: attitudes about appearance, decisions about life choices, and questions of self-concept. Using the *point-by-point method* to organize the overall essay, she explores each of these key ideas in a separate paragraph. Each paragraph is further focused by one or two sentences that serve as a topic sentence.

Sequence of points, organizational cues, and paragraph development.   Let's look more closely at the way Carol presents her three central points in the essay. She obviously considers appearance the least important of a person's worries, life choices more important, and self-concept the most critical. So she uses *emphatic order* to sequence the supporting paragraphs, with the phrase "But the greatest benefit" signaling the special significance of the last issue. Carol is also careful to use *transitions* to help readers follow her line of thinking: "*Now, however,* Dave and I are beyond such adolescent agonies" (paragraph 3); "*But* when you are young, major decisions await you at every turn" (4); and "*By way of contrast,* forty is sanity" (5).

Although Carol has worked hard to write a well-organized paper—and has on the whole been successful—she doesn't feel compelled to make the paper fit a rigid format. As you've seen, the essay as a whole uses the point-by-point method, but each supporting paragraph uses the *one-side-at-a-time* method—that is, everything about one age group is discussed before there is a shift to the other age group. Notice too that the third and fifth paragraphs start with young people and then move to adults, whereas the fourth paragraph reverses the sequence by starting with older people.

Other patterns of development.   Carol uses the comparison-contrast format to organize her ideas, but other patterns of development also come into play. To illustrate her points, she makes extensive use of *exemplification,* and her discussion also contains elements typical of *causal analysis.* Throughout the essay, for instance, she traces the effect of being a certain age on her brother, herself, and her parents.

A problem with unity.   As you read the third paragraph, you might have noted that Carol's essay runs into a problem. Two sentences in the paragraph disrupt the *unity* of Carol's discussion: "I often wonder how my parents, and parents in general, manage to tolerate their children during the adolescent years," and "women, I'm embarrassed to admit . . . have always seemed to be at the mercy of fashion." These sentences should be deleted because they don't develop the idea that adolescents are overly concerned with appearance.

Conclusion.   Carol's final paragraph brings the essay to a pleasing and interesting close. The conclusion recalls the point made in the introduction: Americans overvalue youth. Carol also uses the conclusion to broaden the scope of her discussion. Rather than continuing to focus on herself, she briefly mentions her parents and the pleasure they take in life. By bringing her parents into the essay, Carol is able to make a gently philosophical observation about the promise that awaits her as she grows older. The implication is that a similarly positive future awaits us, too.

Revising the first draft.   To help guide her revision, Carol asked her husband to read her first draft aloud. As he did, Carol took notes on what she sensed were the paper's strengths and weaknesses. She then jotted down her observations, as well as her husband's, on the draft. Keeping these comments in mind, Carol made a number of changes in her paper. You'll get a good sense of how she proceeded if you compare the original introduction reprinted here with the final version in the full essay.

Original Version of the Introduction

America is a land filled with people who worship youth. We admire dynamic young achievers; our middle-aged citizens work out in gyms; all of us wear tight tops and colorful sneakers--clothes that look fine on the young but ridiculous on aging bodies. Television shows revolve around perfect-looking young stars, while commercials entice us with products that will keep us young.

Wouldn't every older person want to be young again? Isn't aging to be avoided? It may be slightly unpatriotic to say so, but I believe the answer is "No." Being young may be pleasant at times, but I would rather be my forty-year-old self. I no longer have to agonize about my physical appearance, I have already made many of my crucial life decisions, and I am much less confused about who I am.

After hearing her original two-paragraph introduction read aloud, Carol was dissatisfied with what she had written. Although she wasn't quite sure how to proceed, she knew that the paragraphs were flat and that they failed to open the essay on a strong note. She decided to start by whittling down the opening sentence, making it crisper and more powerful: "Our society worships youth." That done, she eliminated two bland statements ("We admire dynamic young achievers" and "all of us wear tight tops and colorful sneakers") and made several vague references more concrete and interesting. For example, "Commercials entice us with products that will keep us young" became "Grecian Formula and Oil of Olay . . . hide the gray in our hair and smooth the lines on our face"; "perfect-looking young stars" became "attractive young stars with firm bodies, perfect complexions, and thick manes of hair." With the addition of these specifics, the first paragraph became more vigorous and interesting.

Carol next made some subtle changes in the two questions that opened the second paragraph of the original introduction. She replaced "Wouldn't every older person want to be young again?" and "Isn't aging to be avoided?" with two more emphatic questions: "Wouldn't any person over thirty gladly sign with the devil just to be young again?" and "Isn't aging an experience to be dreaded?" Carol also made some changes at the end of the original second paragraph. Because the paper is relatively short and the subject matter easy to understand, she decided to omit her somewhat awkward *plan of development* ("I no longer have to agonize about my physical appearance, I have already made many of my crucial life decisions, and I am much less confused about who I am"). This deletion made it possible to end the introduction with a clear statement of the essay's thesis.

Once these revisions were made, Carol was confident that her essay got off to a stronger start. Feeling reassured, she moved ahead and made changes in other sections of her paper. Such work enabled her to prepare a solid piece of writing that offers food for thought.

ACTIVITIES: COMPARISON-CONTRAST

Prewriting Activities

1. Imagine you're writing two essays: One explores the *effects* of holding a job while in college; the other explains a *process* for budgeting money wisely. Jot down ways you might use comparison-contrast in each essay.

2. Using your journal or freewriting, jot down the advantages and disadvantages of two ways of doing something (for example, watching movies in the theater versus watching them on a VCR at home; following trends versus ignoring them; dating one person versus playing the field; and so on). Reread your prewriting and determine what your thesis, purpose, audience, tone, and point of view might be if you were to write an essay. Make a scratch list of the main ideas you would cover. Would a point-by-point or a one-side-at-a-time method of organization work more effectively?

Revising Activities

3. Of the statements that follow, which would *not* make effective thesis statements for comparison-contrast essays? Identify the problem(s) in the faulty statements and revise them accordingly.

   a. Although their classroom duties often overlap, teacher aides are not as equipped as teachers to handle disciplinary problems.
   b. This college provides more assistance to its students than most schools.
   c. During the state's last congressional election, both candidates relied heavily on television to communicate their messages.
   d. There are many differences between American and foreign cars.

4. The following paragraph is from the draft of an essay detailing the qualities of a skillful manager. How effective is this comparison-contrast paragraph? What revisions would help focus the paragraph on the point made in the topic sentence? Where should details be added or deleted? Rewrite the paragraph, providing necessary transitions and details.

   A manager encourages creativity and treats employees courteously, while a boss discourages staff resourcefulness and views it as a threat. At the hardware store where I work, I got my boss's approval to develop a system for organizing excess stock in the storeroom. I shelved items in roughly the same order as they were displayed in the store. The system was helpful to all the salespeople, not just to me, since everyone was stymied by the boss's helter-skelter system. What he did was store overstocked items according to each wholesaler, even though most of us weren't there long enough to know which items came from which wholesaler. His supposed system created chaos. When he saw what I had done, he was furious and insisted that we continue to follow the old slapdash system. I had assumed he would welcome my ideas the way my manager did last summer when I worked in a drugstore. But he didn't and I had to scrap my work and go back to his eccentric system. He certainly could learn something about employee relations from the drugstore manager.

Rachel Carson

Once accused of being a fearmonger, biologist Rachel Carson (1907–64) is now recognized as one of the country's first environmentalists. She was the author of three popular books about the marine world: *The Sea Around Us* (1951), *Under the Sea Wind* (1952), and *The Edge of the Sea* (1955). But it was the publication of *Silent Spring* (1962), Carson's alarming study of the use of pesticides and herbicides, that brought her special attention and established her reputation as a passionate advocate for a clean environment. The following selection is taken from *Silent Spring*.

Pre-Reading Journal Entry

Take a few minutes to record in your journal your impressions of a place that has special meaning for you—but that is being threatened in one way or another. Jot down sensory details about the place, focusing on those specifics that capture its unique qualities.

A Fable for Tomorrow

There was once a town in the heart of America where all life 1 seemed to live in harmony with its surroundings. The town lay in the midst of a checkerboard of prosperous farms, with fields of grain and hillsides of orchards where, in spring, white clouds of bloom drifted above the green fields. In autumn, oak and maple and birch set up a blaze of color that flamed and flickered across a backdrop of pines. Then foxes barked in the hills and deer silently crossed the fields, half hidden in the mists of the fall mornings.

Along the roads, laurel, viburnum and alder, great ferns and 2 wildflowers delighted the traveler's eye through much of the year. Even in winter the roadsides were places of beauty, where countless birds came to feed on the berries and on the seed heads of the dried weeds rising above the snow. The countryside was, in fact, famous for the abundance and variety of its bird life, and when the flood of migrants was pouring through in spring and fall people traveled from great distances to observe them. Others came to fish the streams, which flowed clear and cold out of the hills and contained shady pools where trout lay. So it had been from the days many years ago when the first settlers raised their houses, sank their wells, and built their barns.

Then a strange blight crept over the area and everything began   3
to change. Some evil spell had settled on the community: mysterious maladies swept the flocks of chickens; the cattle and sheep sickened and died. Everywhere was a shadow of death. The farmers spoke of much illness among their families. In the town the doctors had become more and more puzzled by new kinds of sickness appearing among their patients. There had been several sudden and unexplained deaths, not only among adults but even among children, who would be stricken suddenly while at play and die within a few hours.

There was a strange stillness. The birds, for example—where   4
had they gone? Many people spoke of them, puzzled and disturbed. The feeding stations in the backyards were deserted. The few birds seen anywhere were moribund; they trembled violently and could not fly. It was a spring without voices. On the mornings that had once throbbed with the dawn chorus of robins, catbirds, doves, jays, wrens, and scores of other bird voices there was now no sound; only silence lay over the fields and woods and marsh.

On the farms the hens brooded, but no chicks hatched. The   5
farmers complained that they were unable to raise any pigs—the litters were small and the young survived only a few days. The apple trees were coming into bloom but no bees droned among the blossoms, so there was no pollination and there would be no fruit.

The roadsides, once so attractive, were now lined with browned   6
and withered vegetation as though swept by fire. These, too, were silent, deserted by all living things. Even the streams were now lifeless. Anglers no longer visited them, for all the fish had died.

In the gutters under the eaves and between the shingles of the   7
roofs, a white granular powder still showed a few patches; some weeks before it had fallen like snow upon the roofs and the lawns, the fields and streams.

No witchcraft, no enemy action had silenced the rebirth of new   8
life in this stricken world. The people had done it themselves.

This town does not actually exist, but it might easily have a thou-   9
sand counterparts in America or elsewhere in the world. I know of no community that has experienced all the misfortunes I describe. Yet every one of these disasters has actually happened somewhere, and

many real communities have already suffered a substantial number of them. A grim specter has crept upon us almost unnoticed, and this imagined tragedy may easily become a stark reality we all shall know.

Questions for Close Reading

1. What is the selection's thesis? Locate the sentence(s) in which Carson states her main idea. If she doesn't state the thesis explicitly, express it in your own words.
2. What are some of the delights of Carson's beautiful, healthy countryside?
3. When Carson writes of "a strange blight," an "evil spell" (paragraph 3), whose point of view is she adopting?
4. What are the effects of the blight?
5. Refer to your dictionary as needed to define the following words used in the selection: *viburnum* (paragraph 2), *alder* (2), *moribund* (4), and *specter* (9).

Questions About the Writer's Craft

1. **The pattern.**   To develop her essay, Carson uses the one-side-at-a-time method of comparison-contrast. What does this method enable her to do that the point-by-point approach would not?
2. **Other patterns.**   Throughout the essay, Carson appeals to the reader's senses of sight and hearing. Which paragraphs are developed primarily through visual or auditory description? How do the sensory images in these paragraphs reinforce Carson's thesis?
3. Carson's diction (word choice) and sentence rhythm often resemble those of the Bible. For example, we read, "So it had been from the days many years ago" (paragraph 2), "a strange blight crept over the area" (3), and "Everywhere was a shadow of death" (3). Why do you suppose Carson chose to echo the Bible in this way?
4. How does Carson's approach to her subject change in the last paragraph? What is the effect of this change?

Writing Assignments Using Comparison-Contrast as a Pattern of Development

1. Carson imagines a fictional town that has changed for the worse. Consider a place you know well that has changed for the *better*. You might focus on a renovated school, a rehabilitated neighborhood, a newly preserved park. Write an essay contrasting the place before and after the change. At the end of your essay, describe briefly the effects of the change.

∞ **2.** In her essay, Carson provides descriptive details unique to particular seasons. For example, she writes that "in autumn, oak and maple and birch set up a blaze of color that flamed and flickered across a backdrop of pines" (paragraph 1). Choosing a place you know well, contrast its sights, sounds, and smells during one season with those you've noticed during another time of year. Use rich sensory details to convey the differences between the two seasons. Consider first reading Joan Didion's "The Santa Ana" (page 500), which recounts, in vivid detail, a specific natural phenomenon and its impact on regional inhabitants.

Writing Assignments Using Other Patterns of Development

3. Carson cites "white granular powder" (paragraph 7) as the cause of the blight. Write an essay about a time you noticed a visible environmental problem—say, smog blurring a city skyline, soot coating a window, or medical syringes discarded on the beach. Use vivid narrative details to capture the effect of the experience on you.

∞ **4.** Carson graphically shows the effects of herbicides and pesticides on the environment. Focus on some other less global environmental problem: graffiti on a public building; vandalized trees and shrubs; beer cans thrown in a neighborhood park, for example. Discuss the effects of this situation on the physical environment and on people's attitudes and actions. Conclude with suggestions about possible ways to remedy the problem. Gordon Parks's "Flavio's Home" (page 96) will help you appreciate the interaction between the environment and human behavior.

Writing Assignments Using a Journal Entry as a Starting Point

5. Write an essay describing an endangered place that is very important to you. Describe the potential threat either at the beginning or at the end of the essay, and paint such a vivid picture of the place in the rest of the essay that readers understand why the potential threat is so unfortunate. Select from your pre-reading journal entry only those details that convey the special qualities of the place, adding more texture and specifics where needed.

Richard Rodriguez

In his autobiographical work *Hunger of Memory* (1981), from which the following selection is taken, Richard Rodriguez describes his experiences growing up in America as a first-generation Mexican-American. Born in 1944 in San Francisco, Rodriguez spoke only Spanish for the first six years of his life. After winning a scholarship to a private high school, Rodriguez attended Stanford, Columbia, and the University of California at Berkeley, where he earned a doctorate in English literature. Rodriguez now writes for a variety of publications (the *Wall Street Journal* and *Time,* to name just two), serves as an editor at Pacific News Service in San Francisco, and regularly appears on PBS's *NewsHour.* In 1997, he won the Peabody Award for achievement in broadcasting. His books include *Mexico's Children* (1991) and *Movements* (1996). The critically acclaimed *Days of Obligation: An Argument With My Mexican Father* (1992) is Rodriguez's second autobiographical book.

Pre-Reading Journal Entry

Young people often find themselves being lectured by adults claiming that kids nowadays want it easy and aren't willing to do unglamorous "real work." Do you agree with these claims? Why or why not? Drawing upon your experiences and observations, respond to these questions in your journal.

Workers

It was at Stanford, one day near the end of my senior year, that a friend told me about a summer construction job he knew was available. I was quickly alert. Desire uncoiled within me. My friend said that he knew I had been looking for summer employment. He knew I needed some money. Almost apologetically he explained: It was something I probably wouldn't be interested in, but a friend of his, a contractor, needed someone for the summer to do menial jobs. There would be lots of shoveling and raking and sweeping. Nothing too hard. But nothing more interesting either. Still, the pay would be good. Did I want it? Or did I know someone who did?

1

I did. Yes, I said, surprised to hear myself say it.

2

In the weeks following, friends cautioned that I had no idea   3
how hard physical labor really is. ("You only *think* you know what it
is like to shovel for eight hours straight.") Their objections seemed
to me challenges. They resolved the issue. I became happy with my
plan. I decided, however, not to tell my parents. I wouldn't tell my
mother because I could guess her worried reaction. I would tell my
father only after the summer was over, when I could announce that,
after all, I did know what "real work" is like.

The day I met the contractor (a Princeton graduate, it turned   4
out), he asked me whether I had done any physical labor before. "In
high school, during the summer," I lied. And although he seemed to
regard me with skepticism, he decided to give me a try. Several days
later, expectant, I arrived at my first construction site. I would take
off my shirt to the sun. And at last grasp desired sensation. No longer
afraid. At last become like a *bracero*. "We need those tree stumps out
of here by tomorrow," the contractor said. I started to work.

I labored with excitement that first morning—and all the days   5
after. The work was harder than I could have expected. But it was
never as tedious as my friends had warned me it would be. There was
too much physical pleasure in the labor. Especially early in the day, I
would be most alert to the sensations of movement and straining.
Beginning around seven each morning (when the air was still damp
but the scent of weeds and dry earth anticipated the heat of the sun),
I would feel my body resist the first thrusts of the shovel. My arms,
tightened by sleep, would gradually loosen; after only several minutes,
sweat would gather in beads on my forehead and then—a short while
later—I would feel my chest silky with sweat in the breeze. I would
return to my work. A nervous spark of pain would fly up my arm and
settle to burn like an ember in the thick of my shoulder. An hour, two
passed. Three. My whole body would assume regular movements; my
shoveling would be described by identical, even movements. Even
later in the day, my enthusiasm for primitive sensation would survive
the heat and the dust and the insects pricking my back. I would strain
wildly for sensation as the day came to a close. At three-thirty, quitting time, I would stand upright and slowly let my head fall back, luxuriating in the feeling of tightness relieved.

Some of the men working nearby would watch me and laugh.   6
Two or three of the older men took the trouble to teach me the
right way to use a pick, the correct way to shovel. "You're doing it
wrong, too fucking hard," one man scolded. Then proceeded to

show me—what persons who work with their bodies all their lives quickly learn—the most economical way to use one's body in labor.

"Don't make your back do so much work," he instructed. I 7
stood impatiently listening, half listening, vaguely watching, then noticed his work-thickened fingers clutching the shovel. I was annoyed. I wanted to tell him that I enjoyed shoveling the wrong way. And I didn't want to learn the right way. I wasn't afraid of back pain. I liked the way my body felt sore at the end of the day.

I was about to, but, as it turned out, I didn't say a thing. Rather 8
it was at that moment I realized that I was fooling myself if I expected a few weeks of labor to gain me admission to the world of the laborer. I would not learn in three months what my father had meant by "real work." I was not bound to this job; I could imagine its rapid conclusion. For me the sensations were to be feared. Fatigue took a different toll on their bodies—and minds.

It was, I know, a simple insight. But it was with this realization 9
that I took my first step that summer toward realizing something even more important about the "worker." In the company of carpenters, electricians, plumbers, and painters at lunch, I would often sit quietly, observant. I was not shy in such company. I felt easy, pleased by the knowledge that I was casually accepted, my presence taken for granted by men (exotics) who worked with their hands. Some days the younger men would talk and talk about sex, and they would howl at women who drove by in cars. Other days the talk at lunchtime was subdued; men gathered in separate groups. It depended on who was around. There were rough, good-natured workers. Others were quiet. The more I remember that summer, the more I realize that there was no single *type* of worker. I am embarrassed to say I had not expected such diversity. I certainly had not expected to meet, for example, a plumber who was an abstract painter in his off hours and admired the work of Mark Rothko. Nor did I expect to meet so many workers with college diplomas. (They were the ones who were not surprised that I intended to enter graduate school in the fall.) I suppose what I really want to say here is painfully obvious, but I must say it nevertheless: The men of that summer were middle-class Americans. They certainly didn't constitute an oppressed society. Carefully completing their work sheets; talking about the fortunes of local football teams; planning Las Vegas vacations; comparing the gas mileage of various makes of campers—they were not *los pobres* my mother had spoken about.

On two occasions, the contractor hired a group of Mexican   10
aliens. They were employed to cut down some trees and haul off
debris. In all, there were six men of varying age. The youngest in his
late twenties; the oldest (his father?) perhaps sixty years old. They
came and they left in a single old truck. Anonymous men. They were
never introduced to the other men at the site. Immediately upon
their arrival, they would follow the contractor's directions, start
working—rarely resting—seemingly driven by a fatalistic sense that
work which had to be done was best done as quickly as possible.

I watched them sometimes. Perhaps they watched me. The only   11
time I saw them pay me much notice was one day at lunchtime when
I was laughing with the other men. The Mexicans sat apart when
they ate, just as they worked by themselves. Quiet. I rarely heard
them say much to each other. All I could hear were their voices calling out sharply to one another, giving directions. Otherwise, when
they stood briefly resting, they talked among themselves in voices
too hard to overhear.

The contractor knew enough Spanish, and the Mexicans—or at   12
least the oldest of them, their spokesman—seemed to know enough
English to communicate. But because I was around, the contractor
decided one day to make me his translator. (He assumed I could
speak Spanish.) I did what I was told. Shyly I went over to tell the
Mexicans that the *patrón* wanted them to do something else before
they left for the day. As I started to speak, I was afraid with my old
fear that I would be unable to pronounce the Spanish words. But it
was a simple instruction I had to convey. I could say it in phrases.

The dark sweating faces turned toward me as I spoke. They   13
stopped their work to hear me. Each nodded in response. I stood
there. I wanted to say something more. But what could I say in
Spanish, even if I could have pronounced the words right? Perhaps
I just wanted to engage them in small talk, to be assured of their
confidence, our familiarity. I thought for a moment to ask them
where in Mexico they were from. Something like that. And maybe I
wanted to tell them (a lie, if need be) that my parents were from the
same part of Mexico.

I stood there.   14

Their faces watched me. The eyes of the man directly in front of   15
me moved slowly over my shoulder, and I turned to follow his
glance toward *el patrón* some distance away. For a moment I felt
swept up by that glance into the Mexicans' company. But then I

heard one of them returning to work. And then the others went back to work. I left them without saying anything more.

When they had finished, the contractor went over to pay them 16 in cash. (He later told me that he paid them collectively—"for the job," though he wouldn't tell me their wages. He said something quickly about the good rate of exchange "in their own country.") I can still hear the loudly confident voice he used with the Mexicans. It was the sound of the *gringo* I had heard as a very young boy. And I can still hear the quiet, indistinct sounds of the Mexican, the oldest, who replied. At hearing that voice I was sad for the Mexicans. Depressed by their vulnerability. Angry at myself. The adventure of the summer seemed suddenly ludicrous. I would not shorten the distance I felt from *los pobres* with a few weeks of physical labor. I would not become like them. They were different from me.

After that summer, a great deal—and not very much really— 17 changed in my life. The curse of physical shame was broken by the sun; I was no longer ashamed of my body. No longer would I deny myself the pleasing sensations of my maleness. During those years when middle-class black Americans began to assert with pride, "Black is beautiful," I was able to regard my complexion without shame. I am today darker than I ever was as a boy. I have taken up the middle-class sport of long-distance running. Nearly every day now I run ten or fifteen miles, barely clothed, my skin exposed to the California winter rain and wind or the summer sun of late afternoon. The torso, the soccer player's calves and thighs, the arms of the twenty-year-old I never was, I possess now in my thirties. I study the youthful parody shape in the mirror: the stomach lipped tight by muscle; the shoulders rounded by chin-ups; the arms veined strong. This man. A man. I meet him. He laughs to see me, what I have become.

The dandy. I wear double-breasted Italian suits and custom- 18 made English shoes. I resemble no one so much as my father—the man pictured in those honeymoon photos. At that point in life when he abandoned the dandy's posture, I assume it. At the point when my parents would not consider going on vacation, I register at the Hotel Carlyle in New York and the Plaza Athenée in Paris. I am as taken by the symbols of leisure and wealth as they were. For my parents, however, those symbols became taunts, reminders of all they could not achieve in one lifetime. For me those same symbols are reassuring reminders of public success. I tempt vulgarity to be reassured. I am filled with the gaudy delight, the monstrous grace of the nouveau riche.

In recent years I have had occasion to lecture in ghetto high   19
schools. There I see students of remarkable style and physical grace. (One can see more dandies in such schools than one ever will find in middle-class high schools.) There is not the look of casual assurance I saw students at Stanford display. Ghetto girls mimic high-fashion models. Their dresses are of bold, forceful color; their figures elegant, long; the stance theatrical. Boys wear shirts that grip at their overdeveloped muscular bodies. (Against a powerless future, they engage images of strength.) Bad nutrition does not yet tell. Great disappointment, fatal to youth, awaits them still. For the moment, movements in school hallways are dancelike, a procession of postures in a sexual masque. Watching them, I feel a kind of envy. I wonder how different my adolescence would have been had I been free. . . . But no, it is my parents I see—their optimism during those years when they were entertained by Italian grand opera.

The registration clerk in London wonders if I have just been to   20
Switzerland. And the man who carries my luggage in New York guesses the Caribbean. My complexion becomes a mark of my leisure. Yet no one would regard my complexion the same way if I entered such hotels through the service entrance. That is only to say that my complexion assumes its significance from the context of my life. My skin, in itself, means nothing. I stress the point because I know there are people who would label me "disadvantaged" because of my color. They make the same mistake I made as a boy, when I thought a disadvantaged life was circumscribed by particular occupations. That summer I worked in the sun may have made me physically indistinguishable from the Mexicans working nearby. (My skin was actually darker because, unlike them, I worked without wearing a shirt. By late August my hands were probably as tough as theirs.) But I was not one of *los pobres*. What made me different from them was an attitude of *mind*, my imagination of myself.

I do not blame my mother for warning me away from the sun   21
when I was young. In a world where her brother had become an old man in his twenties because he was dark, my complexion was something to worry about. "Don't run in the sun," she warns me today. I run. In the end, my father was right—though perhaps he did not know how right or why—to say that I would never know what real work is. I will never know what he felt at his last factory job. If tomorrow I worked at some kind of factory, it would go differently

for me. My long education would favor me. I could act as a public person—able to defend my interests, to unionize, to petition, to speak up—to challenge and demand. (I will never know what real work is.) I will never know what the Mexicans knew, gathering their shovels and ladders and saws.

Their silence stays with me now. The wages those Mexicans received for their labor were only a measure of their disadvantaged condition. Their silence is more telling. They lack a public identity. They remain profoundly alien. Persons apart. People lacking a union obviously, people without grounds. They depend upon the relative good will or fairness of their employers each day. For such people, lacking a better alternative, it is not such an unreasonable risk. 22

Their silence stays with me. I have taken these many words to describe its impact. Only: the quiet. Something uncanny about it. Its compliance. Vulnerability. Pathos. As I heard their truck rumbling away, I shuddered, my face mirrored with sweat. I had finally come face to face with *los pobres*. 23

Questions for Close Reading

1. What is the selection's thesis? Locate the sentence(s) in which Rodriguez states his main idea. If he doesn't state the thesis explicitly, express it in your own words.
2. What does Rodriguez find appealing about the construction job when his friend first offers it to him?
3. Once on the job, how long does it take Rodriguez to realize he will never be a "laborer"? Why does he feel this way?
4. According to Rodriguez, what makes him different from *los pobres?* Is poverty the only thing that makes them distinctive?
5. Refer to your dictionary as needed to define the following words used in the selection: *menial* (paragraph 1), *skepticism* (4), *luxuriating* (5), *diversity* (9), *ludicrous* (16), *nouveau riche* (18), and *pathos* (23).

Questions About the Writer's Craft

1. **The pattern.** One way Rodriguez develops his essay is by comparing and contrasting himself to the two groups of workers. Which group is he more like? What specifics does Rodriguez provide to show his similarity to this group and his dissimilarity to the other?
2. **Other patterns.** Rodriguez uses narration to develop his comparison-contrast of the two groups of workers. How many narrative segments appear in the essay? Why do you think Rodriguez puts the story about the Mexican workers last?

3. **Other patterns.** Rodriguez uses especially vivid language to describe the sun, his sweat, and the sensation of digging. Locate some examples of these descriptions. Which ones particularly stand out? Why?

4. Why does Rodriguez include some Spanish words in his essay? How is the use of these words related to the essay's overall theme?

Writing Assignments Using Comparison-Contrast as a Pattern of Development

1. Write an essay comparing and/or contrasting a part-time or summer job you've had with your (or someone else's) full-time or "real" job. Use examples, description, anecdotes, and illustrations to clarify the points of comparison or contrast.

2. Write an essay in which you compare and/or contrast the job you hope to have after graduation with a job you now have or have had in the past. Your analysis should reach conclusions about your interests, skills, and values.

Writing Assignments Using Other Patterns of Development

3. In an essay, define what you mean by the term *real work*. Support your definition by citing experiences you have had and/or have heard about. Before formulating your definition, discuss this subject with friends and family.

4. Former talk-show host Phil Donahue once did a show on people who had "terrible jobs." The guests included a garbage man, a toll collector, a car repossessor, an IRS auditor, and a diaper-service truck driver. Write an essay explaining what would be terrible work for you. It might be one or more of the jobs held by Donahue's guests or some other type of job. Provide abundant reasons why you would never want to do such work, and reach some conclusions about your priorities.

Writing Assignments Using a Journal Entry as a Starting Point

5. Write an essay comparing and/or contrasting the work habits of earlier generations with those of the current generation. Consider kinds of work, working conditions, benefits, hours on the job, and so on. In addition to drawing upon ideas from your pre-reading journal entry, interview an equal number of people of both generations to get their opinions. Where appropriate, include their views in your essay. Begin or end the essay with a statement indicating which generation's work habits you respect more. For additional insight into generational differences, read E. B. White's "Once More to the Lake" (page 115).

Dave Barry

Pulitzer-Prize winning humorist Dave Barry (1947–) began his writing career covering—as he puts it—"incredibly dull municipal meetings" for the *Daily Local News* of West Chester, Pennsylvania. Next came an eight-year stint trying to teach businesspeople not to write sentences like "Enclosed please find the enclosed enclosures." In 1983, Barry joined the staff of the *Miami Herald,* where his rib-tickling commentary on the absurdities of everyday life quickly brought him a legion of devoted fans. Barry's column is now syndicated in more than 150 newspapers. A popular guest on television and radio, Barry has written many books, including *Dave Barry's Complete Guide to Guys* (1995), *Dave Barry in Cyberspace* (1996), and *Big Trouble* (1999). The essay below first appeared in the *Miami Herald* in 1998.

Pre-Reading Journal Entry

To what extent would you say our images of personal attractiveness are influenced by TV commercials and magazine advertisements? Think of commercials and ads you've seen recently. What physical traits are typically identified as attractive in women? In men? List as many as you can. What assumptions does each trait suggest? Use your journal to respond to these questions.

The Ugly Truth About Beauty

If you're a man, at some point a woman will ask you how she looks.   1

"How do I look?" she'll ask.   2

You must be careful how you answer this question. The best   3 technique is to form an honest yet sensitive opinion, then collapse on the floor with some kind of fatal seizure. Trust me, this is the easiest way out. Because you will never come up with the right answer.

The problem is that women generally do not think of their   4 looks in the same way that men do. Most men form an opinion of how they look in the seventh grade, and they stick to it for the rest of their lives. Some men form the opinion that they are irresistible stud muffins, and they do not change this opinion even when their faces sag and their noses bloat to the size of eggplants and their eyebrows grow together to form what appears to be a giant forehead-dwelling tropical caterpillar.

Most men, I believe, think of themselves as average-looking.   5
Men will think this even if their faces cause heart failure in cattle at a range of 300 yards. Being average does not bother them; average is fine, for men. This is why men never ask anybody how they look. Their primary form of beauty care is to shave themselves, which is essentially the same form of beauty care that they give to their lawns. If, at the end of his four-minute daily beauty regimen, a man has managed to wipe most of the shaving cream out of his hair and is not bleeding too badly, he feels that he has done all he can, so he stops thinking about his appearance and devotes his mind to more critical issues, such as the Super Bowl.

Women do not look at themselves this way. If I had to express,   6
in three words, what I believe most women think about their appearance, those words would be: "not good enough." No matter how attractive a woman may appear to be to others, when she looks at herself in the mirror, she thinks: woof. She thinks that at any moment a municipal animal-control officer is going to throw a net over her and haul her off to the shelter.

Why do women have such low self-esteem? There are many   7
complex psychological and societal reasons, by which I mean Barbie. Girls grow up playing with a doll proportioned such that, if it were human, it would be seven feet tall and weigh 81 pounds, of which 53 pounds would be bosoms. This is a difficult appearance standard to live up to, especially when you contrast it with the standard set for little boys by their dolls . . . excuse me, by their action figures. Most of the action figures that my son played with when he was little were hideous-looking. For example, he was very fond of an action figure (part of the He-Man series) called "Buzz-Off," who was part human, part flying insect. Buzz-Off was not a looker. But he was extremely self-confident. You could not imagine Buzz-Off saying to the other action figures: "Do you think these wings make my hips look big?"

But women grow up thinking they need to look like Barbie,   8
which for most women is impossible, although there is a multibillion-dollar beauty industry devoted to convincing women that they must try. I once saw an Oprah show wherein supermodel Cindy Crawford

dispensed makeup tips to the studio audience. Cindy had all these middle-aged women applying beauty products to their faces; she stressed how important it was to apply them in a certain way, using the tips of their fingers. All the women dutifully did this, even though it was obvious to any sane observer that, no matter how carefully they applied these products, they would never look remotely like Cindy Crawford, who is some kind of genetic mutation.

I'm not saying that men are superior. I'm just saying that you're   9 not going to get a group of middle-aged men to sit in a room and apply cosmetics to themselves under the instruction of Brad Pitt, in hopes of looking more like him. Men would realize that this task was pointless and demeaning. They would find some way to bolster their self-esteem that did not require looking like Brad Pitt. They would say to Brad: "Oh YEAH? Well what do you know about LAWN CARE, pretty boy?"

Of course many women will argue that the reason they become   10 obsessed with trying to look like Cindy Crawford is that men, being as shallow as a drop of spit, WANT women to look that way. To which I have two responses:

1. Hey, just because WE'RE idiots, that does not mean YOU have   11 to be; and

2. Men don't even notice 97 percent of the beauty efforts you   12 make anyway. Take fingernails. The average woman spends 5,000 hours per year worrying about her fingernails; I have never once, in more than 40 years of listening to men talk about women, heard a man say, "She has a nice set of fingernails!" Many men would not notice if a woman had upward of four hands.

Anyway, to get back to my original point: If you're a man, and a   13 woman asks you how she looks, you're in big trouble. Obviously, you can't say she looks bad. But you also can't say that she looks great, because she'll think you're lying, because she has spent countless hours, with the help of the multibillion-dollar beauty industry, obsessing about the differences between herself and Cindy Crawford. Also, she suspects that you're not qualified to judge anybody's appearance. This is because you have shaving cream in your hair.

Questions for Close Reading

1. What is the selection's thesis? Locate the sentence(s) in which Barry states his main idea. If he doesn't state the thesis explicitly, express it in your own words.

2. Barry tells us that most men consider themselves to be "average-looking" (paragraph 5). Why, according to Barry, do men feel this way?

3. When Barry writes that most women think of themselves as "not good enough" (6), what does he mean? What, according to Barry, causes women to develop low opinions of themselves?

4. Barry implies that women could have a more rational response to the "difficult appearance standard" that pervades society (7). What would that response be?

5. Refer to your dictionary as needed to define the following words used in the selection: *regimen* (paragraph 5), *municipal* (6), *societal* (7), *dispensed* (8), *genetic* (8), *mutation* (8), *demeaning* (9), and *bolster* (9).

Questions About the Writer's Craft

1. **The pattern.** Which comparison-contrast method of organization (point-by-point or one-side-at-a-time) does Barry use to develop his essay? Why might he have chosen this pattern?

2. Barry uses exaggeration, a strategy typically associated with humorous writing. Locate instances of exaggeration in the selection. Why do you think he uses this strategy?

3. **Other patterns.** Barry demonstrates a series of cause-effect chains in his essay. Locate some of the cause-effect series. How do they help Barry reinforce his thesis?

4. Barry's title involves an *oxymoron*—a contradiction in terms. What does this title imply about Barry's attitude toward his subject?

Writing Assignments Using Comparison-Contrast as a Pattern of Development

1. Examine the pitches made in magazines and on TV for the male and female versions of *one* kind of grooming product. Possibilities include deodorant, hair dye, soap, and so on. Then write an essay contrasting the persuasive appeals that the product makes to men with those it make to women. (Don't forget to examine the assumptions behind the appeals.) To gain insight into advertising techniques, you'll find it helpful to read Ann McClintock's "Propaganda Techniques in Today's Advertising" (page 232). For useful perspectives on gender issues, consider reading Barbara Ehrenreich's "What I've Learned From Men" (page 196) and Deborah Tannen's "But What Do You Mean?" (page 241).

2. Barry contrasts women's preoccupation with looking good to men's lack of concern about their appearance. Now consider the flip side—something men care about deeply that women virtually ignore. Write an essay contrasting men's stereotypical fascination with *one* area to women's indifference. You might, for example, examine male and female attitudes

toward sports, cars, tools, even lawn care. Following Barry's example, adopt a playful tone in your essay, illustrating the absurdity of the obsession you discuss.

Writing Assignments Using Other Patterns of Development

3. Barry implies that most men, unaffected by the "multibillion-dollar beauty industry," are content to "think of themselves as average looking." Do you agree? Conduct your own research into whether or not Barry's assertions about men are true. Begin by interviewing several male friends, family members, and classmates to see how these men feel about their physical appearance. In addition, in the library or online, research magazines such as *People, Gentlemen's Quarterly,* or *Men's Health* for articles describing how everyday men as well as male celebrities view their looks. Then write an essay refuting or defending the view that being average-looking doesn't bother most men. Start by acknowledging the opposing view; then support your assertion with convincing evidence drawn from your research.

4. Barry blames Barbie dolls for setting up "a difficult appearance standard" for girls to emulate. Many would argue that the toys that *boys* play with also teach negative, ultimately damaging values. Write an essay exploring the values that are conveyed to boys through their toys. Brainstorm with others, especially males, about the toys of their youth or the toys that boys have today. Identify two to three key negative values to write about, illustrating each with several examples of toys.

Writing Assignments Using a Journal Entry as a Starting Point

5. Review your pre-reading journal entry. Focusing on the characteristics of male *or* female attractiveness conveyed by the mass media, identify two to three assumptions suggested by these standards. Illustrate each assumption with examples from TV commercials and/or magazine advertisements. Be sure to make clear how you feel about these assumptions.

Additional Writing Topics

COMPARISON-CONTRAST

General Assignments

Using comparison-contrast, write an essay on one of the following topics. Your thesis should indicate whether the two subjects are being compared, contrasted, or both. Organize the paper by arranging the details in a one-side-at-a-time or point-by-point pattern. Remember to use organizational cues to help the audience follow your analysis.

1. Two-career family versus one-career family
2. Two approaches for dealing with problems
3. Children's pastimes today and yesterday
4. Two rooms where you spend a good deal of time
5. Neighborhood stores versus shopping malls
6. Two characters in a novel or other literary work
7. Living at home versus living in an apartment or dorm
8. Two attitudes toward money
9. A sports team then and now
10. Watching a movie on television versus viewing it in a theater
11. Two attitudes about a controversial subject
12. Two approaches to parenting
13. Walking or biking versus driving a car
14. Marriage versus living together
15. The atmosphere in two classes
16. Two approaches to studying
17. The place where you live and the place where you would like to live
18. Two comedians
19. The coverage of an event on television versus the coverage in a newspaper
20. Significant trend versus passing fad
21. Two horror or adventure movies
22. Typewriter versus word processor
23. Two candidates for an office
24. Your attitude before and after getting to know someone
25. Two friends with different lifestyles

Assignments With a Specific Purpose and Audience

1. You would like to change your campus living arrangements. Perhaps you want to move from a dormitory to an off-campus apartment or

from home to a dorm. Before you do, though, you'll have to convince your parents (who are paying most of your college costs) that the move will be beneficial. Write out what you would say to your parents. Contrast your current situation with your proposed one, explaining why the new arrangement would be better.

2. As store manager, you decide to write a memo to all sales personnel explaining how to keep customers happy. Compare and/or contrast the needs and shopping habits of several different consumer groups (by age, spending ability, or sex), and show how to make each comfortable in your store.

3. As a member of the College Orientation Committee, you volunteer to write a guide entitled "Passing Exams" for first-year college students. You decide to contrast the right and wrong ways to prepare for and take exams. Although your purpose is basically serious, leaven the section with some humor on how *not* to approach exams.

4. You work as a volunteer for a mental health hot line. Many people call simply because they feel "stressed out." Prepare a brochure for these people, recommending a Type B approach to stressful situations. Focus the brochure on the contrast between Type A and Type B personalities: the former is nervous, hard-driving, competitive; the latter is relaxed and noncompetitive. Give specific examples of how each type tends to act in stressful situations.

5. As president of your student senate, you're concerned about the way your school is dealing with a particular situation (for example, advisement, parking, financial assistance). Write a letter to your college president contrasting the way your school handles the situation with another school's approach. In your conclusion, point out the advantages of adopting the other college's strategy.

6. Your old high school has invited you back to make a speech before an audience of seniors. The topic will be "how to choose the college that is right for you." Write your speech in the form of a comparison-contrast analysis. Focus on the choices available (two-year versus four-year schools, large versus small, local versus faraway, and so on), showing the advantages and/or disadvantages of each.

9

CAUSE-EFFECT

WHAT IS CAUSE-EFFECT?

Superstition has it that curiosity killed the cat. Maybe so. Yet our science, technology, storytelling, and fascination with the past and future all spring from our determination to know "Why" and "What if." Seeking explanations, young children barrage adults with endless questions: "Why do trees grow tall?" "What would happen if the sun didn't shine?" But children aren't the only ones who wonder in this way. All of us think in terms of cause and effect, sometimes consciously, sometimes unconsciously: "Why did they give me such an odd look?" we wonder, or "How would I do at another college?" we speculate. This exploration of reasons and results is also at the heart of most professions: "What led to our involvement in Vietnam?" historians question; "What will happen if we administer this experimental drug?" scientists ask.

Cause-effect writing, often called *causal analysis,* is rooted in this elemental need to make connections. Because the drive to understand reasons and results is so fundamental, causal analysis is a common kind of writing. An article analyzing the unexpected outcome of an election, a report linking poor nutrition to low academic achievement, an editorial analyzing the impact of a proposed tax cut—all are examples of cause-effect writing.

Done well, cause-effect pieces can uncover the subtle and often surprising connections between events or phenomena. By rooting out causes and projecting effects, causal analysis enables us to make sense of our experiences, revealing a universe that is somewhat less arbitrary and chaotic.

HOW CAUSE-EFFECT FITS YOUR PURPOSE AND AUDIENCE

Many assignments and exam questions in college involve writing essays that analyze causes, effects, or both. Sometimes, as in the following examples, you'll be asked to write an essay developed primarily through the cause-effect pattern:

> Although divorces have leveled off in the last few years, the number of marriages ending in divorce is still greater than it was a generation ago. What do you think are the causes of this phenomenon?

> Political commentators were surprised that so few people voted in the last election. Discuss the probable causes of this weak voter turnout.

> Americans never seem to tire of gossip about the rich and famous. What effect has this fascination with celebrities had on U.S. culture?

> The federal government is expected to pass legislation that will significantly reduce the funding of student loans. Analyze the possible effects of such a cutback.

Other assignments and exam questions may not explicitly ask you to address causes and effects, but they may use words that suggest causal analysis would be appropriate. Consider these examples, paying special attention to the words in boldface:

> In contrast to the socially involved youth of the 1960s, many young people today tend to remove themselves from political issues. What do you think are the **sources** of the political apathy found among 18- to 25-year-olds? *(cause)*

A number of experts forecast that drug abuse will be the most significant factor affecting U.S. productivity in the coming decade. Evaluate the validity of this observation by discussing the **impact** of drugs in the workplace. *(effect)*

According to school officials, a predictable percentage of entering students drop out of college at some point during their first year. What **motivates** students to drop out? What **happens** to them once they leave? *(cause and effect)*

In addition to serving as the primary strategy for achieving an essay's purpose, causal analysis can also be a supplemental method used to help make a point in an essay developed chiefly through another pattern of development. Assume, for example, that you want to write an essay *defining* the term *the homeless*. To help readers see that unfavorable circumstances can result in nearly anyone becoming homeless, you might discuss some of the unavoidable, everyday factors causing people to live on streets and in subway stations. Similarly, in a *persuasive* proposal urging your college administration to institute an honors program, you would probably spend some time analyzing the positive effect of such a program on students and faculty.

SUGGESTIONS FOR USING CAUSE-EFFECT IN AN ESSAY

The following suggestions will be helpful whether you use causal analysis as a dominant or a supportive pattern of development.

1. Stay focused on the purpose of your analysis.   When writing a causal analysis, don't lose sight of your overall purpose. Consider, for example, an essay on the causes of widespread child abuse. If you're concerned primarily with explaining the problem of child abuse to your readers, you might take a purely *informative* approach:

Although parental stress is the immediate cause of child abuse, the more compelling reason for such behavior lies in the way parents were themselves mistreated in their own families.

Or you might want to *persuade* the audience about some point or idea concerning child abuse:

> The tragic consequences of child abuse provide strong support for more aggressive handling of such cases by social workers and judges.

Then again, you could choose a *speculative* approach, your main purpose being to suggest possibilities:

> Psychologists disagree about the potential effect on youngsters of all the media attention to child abuse. Will children exposed to this media coverage grow up assertive, self-confident, and able to protect themselves? Or will they become fearful and distrustful?

These examples illustrate that an essay's causal analysis may have more than one purpose. For instance, although the last example points to a paper with a primarily speculative purpose, the essay would probably start by informing readers of experts' conflicting views. The paper would also have a persuasive slant if it ended by urging readers to complain to the media about their sensationalized treatment of the child-abuse issue.

2. Adapt content and tone to your purpose and readers.   Your purpose and audience determine what supporting material and what tone will be most effective in a cause-effect essay. Assume you want to direct your essay on child abuse to general readers who know little about the subject. To *inform* readers, you might use facts, statistics, and expert opinion to provide an objective discussion of the causes of child abuse. Your analysis might show the following: (1) adults who were themselves mistreated as children tend to abuse their own offspring; (2) marital stress contributes to the mistreatment of children; and (3) certain personality disorders increase the likelihood of child abuse. Sensitive to what your readers would and wouldn't understand, you would stay away from a technical or formal tone. Rather than writing "Pathological preabuse symptomatology predicts adult transference of high aggressivity," you would say "Psychologists can often predict, on the basis of family histories, who will abuse children."

Now imagine that your purpose is to *convince* future social workers that the failure of social service agencies to act authoritatively in child-abuse cases often has tragic consequences. Hoping to encourage more responsible behavior in the prospective social workers, you would adopt a more emotional tone in the essay, perhaps citing wrenching case histories that dramatize what happens when child abuse isn't taken seriously.

3. Think rigorously about causes and effects.   To write a meaningful causal analysis, you should do some careful thinking about the often complex relationship between causes and effects. Children tend to oversimplify causes and effects ("Mommy and Daddy are getting divorced because I was bad the other day"), and adults' arguments can be characterized by hasty, often slipshod thinking ("All these immigrants willing to work cheaply have made us lose our jobs"). But imprecise thinking has no place in essay writing. You should be willing to dig for causes, to think creatively about effects. You should examine your subject in depth, looking beyond the obvious and superficial.

Brainstorming, freewriting, and mapping will help you explore causes and effects thoroughly. No matter which prewriting technique you use, generate as many explanations as possible by asking yourself questions like these:

> *Causes:* What happened? What are the possible reasons? Which are most likely? Who was involved? Why?
>
> *Effects:* What happened? Who was involved? What were the observable results? What are some possible future consequences? Which consequences are negative? Which are positive?

If you remain open and look beyond the obvious, you'll discover that a cause may have many effects. Imagine that you're writing a paper on the effects of cigarette smoking. Prewriting would probably generate a number of consequences that could be discussed, some less obvious but perhaps more interesting than others: increased risk of lung cancer and heart disease, harm traced to secondhand smoke, legal battles regarding the rights of smokers and nonsmokers, lower birth weights in babies of mothers who smoke, and developmental problems experienced by such underweight infants.

In the same way, prewriting will help you see that an effect may have multiple causes. An essay analyzing the reasons for world hunger could discuss many causes, again some less evident but perhaps more thought-provoking than others: climatic changes, inefficient use of land, cultural predispositions for large families, and poor management of international relief funds.

Your analysis may also uncover a *causal chain* in which one cause (or effect) brings about another, which, in turn, brings about another, and so on. Here's an example of a causal chain: Prohibition went into effect; bootleggers and organized crime stepped in to supply public demand for alcoholic beverages; ordinary citizens began breaking the law by buying illegal alcohol and patronizing speakeasies; disrespect for legal authority became widespread and acceptable. As you can see, a causal chain often leads to interesting points. In this case, the subject of Prohibition leads not just to the obvious (illegal consumption of alcohol) but also to the more complex issue of society's decreasing respect for legal authority.

Don't grapple with so complex a chain, however, that you become hopelessly entangled. If your subject involves multiple causes and effects, limit what you'll discuss. Identify which causes and effects are *primary* and which are *secondary.* How extensively you cover secondary factors will depend on your purpose and audience. In an essay intended to inform a general audience about the harmful effects of pesticides, you would most likely focus on everyday dangers—polluted drinking water, residues in food, and the like. You probably wouldn't include a discussion of more long-range consequences (evolution of resistant insects, disruption of the soil's acid-alkaline balance).

Similarly, decide whether to focus on *immediate,* more obvious causes and effects, or on less obvious, more *remote* ones. Or perhaps you need to focus on both. In an essay about a faculty strike at your college, should you attribute the strike simply to the faculty's failure to receive a salary increase? Or should you also examine other factors: the union's failure to accept a salary package that satisfied most professors; the administration's inability to coordinate its negotiating efforts? It may be more difficult to explore more remote causes and effects, but it can also lead to more original and revealing essays. Thoughtful analyses take these less obvious considerations into account.

When developing a causal analysis, be careful to avoid the *post hoc fallacy.* Named after the Latin phrase *post hoc, ergo propter hoc,* meaning "after this, therefore because of this," this kind of faulty thinking occurs when you assume that simply because one event *followed* another, the first event *caused* the second. For example, if the Republicans win a majority of seats in Congress and, several months later, the economy collapses, can you conclude that the Republicans caused the collapse? A quick assumption of "Yes" fails the test of logic, for the timing of events could be coincidental and not indicative of any cause-effect relationship. The collapse may have been triggered by uncontrolled inflation that began well before the congressional elections. (For more information on the *post hoc* fallacy, see page 424.)

Also, be careful not to mistake *correlation* for *causation*. Two events correlate when they occur at about the same time. Such co-occurrence, however, doesn't guarantee a cause-effect relationship. For instance, while the number of ice-cream cones eaten and the instances of heat prostration both increase during the summer months, this doesn't mean that eating ice cream causes heat prostration! A third factor—in this case, summer heat—is the actual cause. When writing causal analyses, then, use with caution words that imply a causal link (such as *therefore* and *because*). Words that express simply time of occurrence (like *following* and *previously*) are safer and more objective.

Finally, keep in mind that a rigorous causal analysis involves more than loose generalizations about causes and effects. Creating plausible connections may require library research, interviewing, or both. Often you'll need to provide facts, statistics, details, personal observations, or other corroborative material if readers are going to accept the reasoning behind your analysis.

4. Write a thesis that focuses the paper on causes, effects, or both. The thesis in an essay developed through causal analysis often indicates whether the essay will deal mostly with causes, effects, or both. Here, for example, are three thesis statements for causal analyses dealing with the public school system. You'll see that each thesis signals that essay's particular emphasis:

Our school system has been weakened by an overemphasis on trendy electives. *(causes)*

An ineffectual school system has led to crippling teachers' strikes and widespread disrespect for the teaching profession. *(effects)*

Bureaucratic inefficiency has created a school system unresponsive to children's emotional, physical, and intellectual
needs. *(causes and effects)*

Note that the thesis statement—in addition to signaling whether
the paper will discuss causes or effects or both—may also point to
the essay's plan of development. Consider the last thesis statement; it makes clear that the paper will discuss children's emotional needs first, their physical needs second, and their intellectual needs last.

The thesis statement in a causal analysis doesn't have to specify
whether the essay will discuss causes, effects, or both. Nor does the
thesis have to be worded in such a way that the essay's plan of development is apparent. But when first writing cause-effect essays, you
may find that a highly focused thesis will keep your analysis on track.

5. Choose an organizational pattern. There are two basic ways to
organize the points in a cause-effect essay: You may use a chronological or an emphatic sequence. If you select a *chronological order,*
you discuss causes and effects in the order in which they occur or
will occur. Suppose you're writing an essay on the causes for the
popularity of imported cars. These causes might be discussed in
chronological sequence: American plant workers became frustrated
and dissatisfied on the job; some workers got careless while others
deliberately sabotaged the production of sound cars; a growing
number of defective cars hit the market; consumers grew dissatisfied
with American cars and switched to imports.

Chronology might also be used to organize a discussion about
effects. Imagine you want to write an essay about the need to guard
against disrupting delicate balances in the country's wildlife. You
might start the essay by discussing what happened when the starling,
a non-native bird, was introduced into the American environment.
Because the starling had few natural predators, the starling population soared out of control; the starlings took over food sources and
habitats of native species; the bluebird, a native species, declined and
is now threatened with extinction.

Although a chronological pattern can be an effective way to
organize material, a strict time sequence can present a problem if
your primary cause or effect ends up buried in the middle of the
sequence. In such a case, you might use *emphatic order,* reserving

the most significant cause or effect for the end. For example, time order could be used to present the reasons behind a candidate's unexpected victory: Less than a month after the candidate's earlier defeat, a full-scale fund-raising campaign for the next election was started; the candidate spoke to many crucial power groups early in the campaign; the candidate did exceptionally well in the pre-election debates; good weather and large voter turnout on election day favored the candidate. However, if you believe that the candidate's appearance before influential groups was the key factor in the victory, it would be more effective to emphasize that point by saving it for the end. This is what is meant by emphatic order—saving the most important point for last.

Emphatic order is an especially effective way to sequence cause-effect points when readers hold what, in your opinion, are mistaken or narrow views about a subject. To encourage readers to look more closely at the issues, you present what you consider the erroneous or obvious views first, show why they are unsound or limited, then present what you feel to be the actual causes and effects. Such a sequence nudges the audience into giving further thought to the causes and effects you have discovered. Here are informal outlines for two causal analyses using this approach.

Subject: The causes of the riot at the rock concert

1. Some commentators blame the excessively hot weather.
2. Others cite drug use among the concertgoers.
3. Still others blame the liquor sold at the concessions.
4. But the real cause of the disaster was poor planning by the concert promoters.

Subject: The effects of campus crime

1. Immediate problems
   a. Students feel insecure and fearful.
   b. Many nighttime campus activities have been curtailed.
2. More significant long-term problems
   a. Unfavorable publicity about campus crime will affect future student enrollments.
   b. Hiring faculty will become more difficult.

When using emphatic order in a causal analysis, you might want to word the thesis in such a way that it signals which point your essay will stress. Look at the following thesis statements:

Although many immigrants arrive in this country without marketable skills, their most pressing problem is learning how to make their way in a society whose language they don't know.

The space program has led to dramatic advances in computer technology and medical science. Even more important, though, the program has helped change many people's attitudes toward the planet we live on.

These thesis statements reflect an awareness of the complex nature of cause-effect relationships. While not dismissing secondary issues, the statements establish which points the writer considers most noteworthy. The second thesis, for instance, indicates that the paper will touch on the technological and medical advances made possible by the space program but will emphasize the way the program has changed people's attitudes toward the earth.

Whether you use a chronological or emphatic pattern to organize your essay, you'll need to provide clear *signals* to identify when you're discussing causes and when you're discussing effects. Expressions such as "Another reason" and "A final outcome" help readers follow your line of thought.

6. Use language that hints at the complexity of cause-effect relationships. Because it's difficult—if not impossible—to identify causes and effects with certainty, you should avoid such absolutes as "It must be obvious" and "There is no doubt." Instead, try phrases like "Most likely" or "It's probable that." Using such language is not indecisive; rather, it reflects your understanding of the often tangled nature of causes and effects. Be careful, though, of going to the other extreme and being reluctant to take a stand on the issues. If you've thought carefully about causes and effects, you have a right to state your analysis with conviction. Don't undercut the hard work you've done by writing as if your ideas were unworthy of your reader's attention.

STUDENT ESSAY

The following student essay was written by Carl Novack in response to this assignment:

In "Is Technology Making Us Intimate Strangers?" Jonathan Coleman examines the way cell phones, e-mail, and other technologies affect the way we relate to each other. Think of another aspect of everyday life that has changed recently, and discuss those factors that you believe are responsible for the change.

   While reading Carl's paper, try to determine how well it applies the principles of causal analysis. The annotations on Carl's paper and the commentary following it will help you look at the essay more closely.

Americans and Food
by Carl Novack

Introduction

An offbeat but timely cartoon recently appeared in the local newspaper. The single panel showed a gravel-pit operation with piles of raw earth and large cranes. Next to one of the cranes stood the owner of the gravel pit--a grizzled, tough-looking character, hammer in hand, pointing proudly to the new sign he had just tacked up. The sign read, "Fred's Fill Dirt and Croissants." The cartoon illustrates an interesting phenomenon: the changing food habits of Americans. Our meals used to consist of something like home-cooked pot roast, mashed potatoes laced with butter and salt, a thick slice of apple pie topped with a healthy scoop of vanilla ice cream--plain, heavy meals, cooked from scratch, and eaten leisurely at home. But America

Thesis

has changed, and as it has, so have what we Americans eat and how we eat it.

We used to have simple, unsophisticated tastes and looked with suspicion at anything more exotic than hamburger. Admittedly, we did adopt some foods from the various immigrant groups who flocked to our shores. We learned to eat Chinese food, pizza, and bagels. But in the last few years, the

Topic sentence: Background paragraph

international character of our diet has grown tremendously. We can walk into any mall in Middle America and buy pita bread, quiche, and tacos. Such foods are often changed on their journey from exotic imports to ordinary "American" meals (no Pakistani, for example, eats frozen-on-a-stick boysenberry-flavored yogurt), but the imports are still a long way from hamburger on a bun.

1

2

Topic sentence: ——→ Why have we become more worldly in our   3
Three causes   tastes? For one thing, television blankets the coun-
answer the   try with information about new food products and
question   trends. Viewers in rural Montana know that the lat-
    est craving in Washington, D.C., is Cajun cooking or
First cause ——   that something called tofu is now available in the
    local supermarket. Another reason for the growing
Second cause ——   international flavor of our food is that many young
    Americans have traveled abroad and gotten hooked
    on new tastes and flavors. Backpacking students
    and young professionals vacationing in Europe
    come home with cravings for authentic French
    bread or German beer. Finally, continuing waves of
Third cause ——   immigrants settle in the cities where many of us
    live, causing significant changes in what we eat.
    Vietnamese, Haitians, and Thais, for instance, bring
    their native foods and cooking styles with them and
    eventually open small markets or restaurants. In
    time, the new food will become Americanized
    enough to take its place in our national diet.

Topic sentence: ——→ Our growing concern with health has also   4
Another cause   affected the way we eat. For the last few years, the
    media have warned us about the dangers of our tra-
    ditional diet, high in salt and fat, low in fiber. The
    media also began to educate us about the dangers
    of processed foods pumped full of chemical addi-
    tives. As a result, consumers began to demand
Start of a causal ——   healthier foods, and manufacturers started to
chain   change some of their products. Many foods, such as
    lunch meat, canned vegetables, and soups, were
    made available in low-fat, low-sodium versions.
    Whole-grain cereals and higher-fiber breads also
    began to appear on the grocery shelves. Moreover,
    the food industry started to produce all-natural
    products--everything from potato chips to ice
    cream--without additives and preservatives. Not
    surprisingly, the restaurant industry responded to
    this switch to healthier foods, luring customers with
    salad bars, broiled fish, and steamed vegetables.

Topic sentence: ——→ Our food habits are being affected, too, by the   5
Another cause   rapid increase in the number of women working out-
    side the home. Sociologists and other experts believe
    that two important factors triggered this phenome-
    non: the women's movement and a changing

economic climate. Women were assured that it was acceptable, even rewarding, to work outside the home; many women also discovered that they had to work just to keep up with the cost of living. As the traditional role of homemaker changed, so did the way families ate. With Mom working, there wasn't time for her to prepare the traditional three square meals a day. Instead, families began looking for alternatives to provide quick meals. What was the result?

Start of a causal chain

For one thing, there was a boom in fast-food restaurants. The suburban or downtown strip that once contained a lone McDonald's now features Wendy's, Roy Rogers, Taco Bell, Burger King, and Pizza Hut. Families also began to depend on frozen foods as another time-saving alternative. Once again, though, demand changed the kind of frozen food available. Frozen foods no longer consist of foil trays divided into greasy fried chicken, watery corn niblets, and lumpy mashed potatoes. Supermarkets now stock a range of supposedly gourmet frozen dinners--from fettucini in cream sauce to braised beef en brochette.

Conclusion

It may not be possible to pick up a ton of fill dirt 6 and a half-dozen croissants at the same place, but America's food habits are definitely changing. If it is true that "you are what you eat," then America's identity is evolving along with its diet.

COMMENTARY

Title and introduction.   Asked to prepare a paper analyzing the reasons behind a change in our lives, Carl decided to write about a shift he had noticed in Americans' eating habits. The title of the essay, "Americans and Food," identifies Carl's subject but could be livelier and more interesting.

Despite his rather uninspired title, Carl starts his *causal analysis* in an engaging way—with the vivid description of a cartoon. He then connects the cartoon to his subject with the following sentence: "The cartoon illustrates an interesting phenomenon: the changing food habits of Americans." To back up his belief that there has been a revolution in our eating habits, Carl uses the first paragraph to summarize the kind of meal that people used to eat. He then moves into his *thesis:* "But America has changed, and as it has, so have what Americans eat and how we eat it." The thesis implies that Carl's paper will focus on both causes and effects.

Purpose.   Carl's *purpose* was to write an *informative* causal analysis. But before he could present the causes of the change in eating habits, he needed to show that such a change had, in fact, taken place. He therefore uses the second paragraph to document one aspect of this change—the internationalization of our eating habits.

Topic sentences.   At the beginning of the third paragraph, Carl uses a question—"Why have we become more worldly in our tastes?"—to signal that his discussion of causes is about to begin. This question also serves as the paragraph's *topic sentence,* indicating that the paragraph will focus on reasons for the increasingly international flavor of our food. The next two paragraphs, also focused by topic sentences, identify two other major reasons for the change in eating habits: "Our growing concern with health has also affected the way we eat" (paragraph 4), and "Our food habits are being affected, too, by the rapid increase in the number of women working outside the home" (5).

Other patterns of development.   Carl draws on two patterns— comparison-contrast and exemplification—to develop his causal analysis. At the heart of the essay is a basic *contrast* between the way we used to eat and the way we eat now. And throughout his essay, Carl provides convincing *examples* to demonstrate the validity of his points. Consider for a moment the third paragraph. Here Carl asserts that one reason for our new eating habits is our growing exposure to international foods. He then presents concrete evidence to show that we have indeed become more familiar with international cuisine: Television exposes rural Montana to Cajun cooking; students traveling abroad take a liking to French bread; urban dwellers enjoy the exotic fare served by numerous immigrant groups. The fourth and fifth paragraphs use similarly specific evidence (for example, "low-fat, low-sodium versions" of "lunch meat, canned vegetables, and soups") to illustrate the soundness of key ideas.

Causal chains.   Let's look more closely at the evidence in the essay. Not satisfied with obvious explanations, Carl thought through his ideas carefully and even brainstormed with friends to arrive at as comprehensive an analysis as possible. Not surprisingly, much of the evidence Carl uncovered took the form of *causal chains*. In the fourth paragraph, Carl writes, "The media also began to educate us about the dangers of processed foods pumped full of chemical additives. As a result, consumers began to demand healthier foods, and manufacturers started to change some of their products." And the next paragraph shows how the changing role of American women caused families to search for alternative ways of eating. This shift, in turn, caused the restaurant and food industries to respond with a wide range of food alternatives.

Making the paper easy to follow.   Although Carl's analysis digs beneath the surface and reveals complex cause-effect relationships, he wisely limits his pursuit of causal chains to *primary causes and effects*. He doesn't let the complexities distract him from his main purpose: to show why and how the American diet is changing. Carl is also careful to provide his essay with abundant *connecting devices,* making it easy for readers to see the links between points. Consider the use of *transitions* (signaled by italics) in the following sentences: "*Another* reason for the growing international flavor of our food is that many young Americans have traveled abroad" (paragraph 3); "*As a result,* consumers began to demand healthier foods" (4); and "*As* the traditional role of homemaker changed, so did the way families ate" (5).

A problem with the essay's close.   When reading the essay, you probably noticed that Carl's conclusion is a bit weak. Although his reference to the cartoon works well, the rest of the paragraph limps to a tired close. Ending an otherwise vigorous essay with such a slight conclusion undercuts the effectiveness of the whole paper. Carl spent so much energy developing the body of his essay that he ran out of the stamina needed to conclude the piece more forcefully. Careful budgeting of his time would have allowed him to prepare a stronger concluding paragraph.

Revising the first draft.   When Carl was ready to revise, he showed the first draft of his essay to several classmates. Listening carefully to what they said, he jotted down their most helpful comments and eventually transferred them, numbered in order of importance, to his draft. Comparing Carl's original version of his fourth paragraph (shown here) with his final version in the essay will show you how he went about revising.

Original Version of the Fourth Paragraph

A growing concern with health has also affected the way we eat, especially because the media have sent us warnings the last few years about the dangers of salt, sugar, food additives, high-fat and low-fiber diets. We have started to worry that our traditional meals may have been shortening our lives. As a result, consumers demanded healthier foods and manufacturers started taking some of the salt and sugar out of canned foods. "All-natural" became an effective selling point, leading to many preservative-free products. Restaurants, too, adapted their menus, luring customers with light meals. Because we now know about the link between overweight and a variety of health problems, including heart attacks, we are counting calories. In turn, food companies made fortunes on diet beer and diet cola. Sometimes, though, we seem a bit confused about the health issue; we drink soda that is sugar-free but loaded with chemical sweeteners. Still, we believe we are lengthening our lives through changing our diets.

On the advice of his classmates, Carl decided to omit all references to the way our concern with weight has affected our eating habits. It's true, of course, that calorie-counting has changed how we eat. But as soon as Carl started to discuss this point, he got involved in a causal chain that undercut the paragraph's unity. He ended up describing the paradoxical situation in which we find ourselves. In an attempt to eat healthy, we stay away from sugar and use instead artificial sweeteners that probably aren't very good for us. This is an interesting issue, but it detracts from the point Carl wants to make: that our concern with health has affected our eating habits in a *positive* way.

Carl's editing team also pointed out that the fourth paragraph's first sentence contained too much material to be an effective topic sentence. Carl corrected the problem by breaking the overlong sentence into two short ones: "Our growing concern with health has also affected the way we eat. For the last few years, the media have warned us about the dangers of our traditional diet, high in salt and fat, low in fiber." The first of these sentences serves as a crisp topic sentence that focuses the rest of the paragraph.

Finally, Carl agreed with his classmates that the fourth paragraph lacked convincing specifics. When revising, he changed "manufacturers started taking some of the salt and sugar out of canned foods" to the more specific "Many foods, such as lunch meats, canned vegetables, and soups, were made available in low-fat, low-sodium versions." Similarly, generalizations about "light meals" and "all-natural products" gained life through the addition of concrete examples: restaurants lured "customers with salad bars, broiled fish, and steamed vegetables," and the food industry produced "everything from potato chips to ice cream—without additives and preservatives."

Carl did an equally good job revising other sections of his paper. With the exception of the weak spots already discussed, he made the changes needed to craft a well-reasoned essay, one that demonstrates his ability to analyze a complex phenomenon.

ACTIVITIES: CAUSE-EFFECT

Prewriting Activities

1. Imagine you're writing two essays: One *argues* the need for high school courses in personal finance (how to budget money, balance a checkbook, and the like); the other explains a *process* for showing appreciation. Jot down ways you might use cause-effect in each essay.

2. Use mapping, collaborative brainstorming, or another prewriting technique to generate possible causes and/or effects for *one* of the topics below. Be sure to keep in mind the audience indicated in parentheses. Next, devise a thesis and decide whether your purpose would be informative, persuasive, speculative, or some combination of these. Finally, organize your raw material into a brief outline, with related causes and effects grouped in the same section.

   a. Pressure on students to do well (*high school students*)
   b. Children's access to pornography on the Internet (*parents*)
   c. Being physically fit (*those who are out of shape*)
   d. Spiraling costs of a college education (*college officials*)

Revising Activities

3. Explain how the following statements demonstrate *post hoc* thinking and confuse correlation and cause-effect.

   a. Our city now has many immigrants from Latin American countries. The crime rate in our city has increased. Latin American immigrants are the cause of the crime wave.

    b. The divorce rate has skyrocketed. More women are working outside the home than ever before. Working outside the home destroys marriages.

    c. A high percentage of people in Dixville have developed cancer. The landfill, used by XYZ Industries, has been located in Dixville for twenty years. The XYZ landfill has caused cancer in Dixville residents.

4. The following paragraph is from the first draft of an essay arguing that technological advances can diminish the quality of life. How solid is the paragraph's causal analysis? Which causes and/or effects should be eliminated? Where is the analysis simplistic? Where does the writer make absolute claims even though cause-effect relationships are no more than a possibility? Keeping these questions in mind, revise the paragraph.

    How did the banking industry respond to inflation? It simply introduced a new technology--the automated teller machine (ATM). By making money more available to the average person, the ATM gives people the cash to buy inflated goods--whether or not they can afford them. Not surprisingly, automated teller machines have had a number of negative consequences for the average individual. Since people know they can get cash at any time, they use their lunch hours for something other than going to the bank. How do they spend this new-found time? They go shopping, and machine-vended money means more impulse buying, even more than with a credit card. Also, because people don't need their checkbooks to withdraw money, they can't keep track of their accounts and therefore develop a casual attitude toward financial matters. It's no wonder children don't appreciate the value of money. Another problem is that people who would never dream of robbing a bank try to trick the machine into dispensing money "for free." There's no doubt that this kind of fraud contributes to the immoral climate in the country.

Stephen King

Probably the best-known living horror writer, Stephen King (1947–) is the author of more than thirty books. Before earning fame through his vastly popular books, including *Carrie* (1974), *The Shining* (1977), *Cujo* (1981), and *Tommyknockers* (1987), King worked as a high school English teacher and an industrial laundry worker. Much of King's prolific output has been adapted for the screen; movies based on King's work include *Misery* (1990), *Stand By Me* (1986), and *The Green Mile* (1999). In *On Writing: A Memoir of the Craft* (2000), King offers insight into the writing process and examines the role that writing has played in King's own life—especially following a near-fatal accident in 1999. Most recently, he coauthored *Black House* (2001). King lives with his family in Bangor, Maine. The following essay first appeared in *Playboy* in 1982.

Pre-Reading Journal Entry

Several forms of entertainment, besides horror movies, are highly popular despite what many consider a low level of quality. In your journal, list as many "lowbrow" forms of entertainment as you can. Possibilities include professional wrestling, aggressive video games, Internet chat rooms, and so on. Review your list, and respond to the following question in your journal: What is it about each form of entertainment that attracts such popularity— and inspires such criticism?

Why We Crave Horror Movies

I think that we're all mentally ill: those of us outside the asylums only hide it a little better—and maybe not all that much better, after all. We've all known people who talk to themselves, people who sometimes squinch their faces into horrible grimaces when they believe no one is watching, people who have some hysterical fear— of snakes, the dark, the tight place, the long drop . . . and, of course, those final worms and grubs that are waiting so patiently underground. 1

When we pay our four or five bucks and seat ourselves at tenth-row center in a theater showing a horror movie, we are daring the nightmare. 2

Why? Some of the reasons are simple and obvious. To show that 3
we can, that we are not afraid, that we can ride this roller coaster.
Which is not to say that a really good horror movie may not surprise
a scream out of us at some point, the way we may scream when the
roller coaster twists through a complete 360 or plows through a lake
at the bottom of the drop. And horror movies, like roller coasters,
have always been the special province of the young; by the time one
turns 40 or 50, one's appetite for double twists or 360-degree loops
may be considerably depleted.

We also go to re-establish our feelings of essential normality; the 4
horror movie is innately conservative, even reactionary. Freda
Jackson as the horrible melting woman in *Die, Monster, Die!* confirms for us that no matter how far we may be removed from the
beauty of a Robert Redford or a Diana Ross, we are still light-years
from true ugliness.

And we go to have fun. 5

Ah, but this is where the ground starts to slope away, isn't it? 6
Because this is a very peculiar sort of fun indeed. The fun comes
from seeing others menaced—sometimes killed. One critic has suggested that if pro football has become the voyeur's version of combat, then the horror film has become the modern version of the
public lynching.

It is true that the mythic, "fairytale" horror film intends to take 7
away the shades of gray. . . . It urges us to put away our more civilized and adult penchant for analysis and to become children again,
seeing things in pure blacks and whites. It may be that horror
movies provide psychic relief on this level because this invitation to
lapse into simplicity, irrationality and even outright madness is
extended so rarely. We are told we may allow our emotions a free
rein . . . or no rein at all.

If we are all insane, then sanity becomes a matter of degree. If 8
your insanity leads you to carve up women like Jack the Ripper or the
Cleveland Torso Murderer, we clap you away in the funny farm (but
neither of those two amateur-night surgeons was ever caught, heh-
heh-heh); if, on the other hand your insanity leads you only to talk to
yourself when you're under stress or to pick your nose on the morning bus, then you are left alone to go about your business . . . though
it is doubtful that you will ever be invited to the best parties.

The potential lyncher is in almost all of us (excluding saints, past 9
and present; but then, most saints have been crazy in their own

ways), and every now and then, he has to be let loose to scream and roll around in the grass. Our emotions and our fears form their own body, and we recognize that it demands its own exercise to maintain proper muscle tone. Certain of these emotional muscles are accept-ed—even exalted—in civilized society; they are, of course, the emo-tions that tend to maintain the status quo of civilization itself. Love, friendship, loyalty, kindness—these are all the emotions that we applaud, emotions that have been immortalized in the couplets of Hallmark cards. . . .

When we exhibit these emotions, society showers us with posi-   10
tive reinforcement; we learn this even before we get out of diapers. When, as children, we hug our rotten little puke of a sister and give her a kiss, all the aunts and uncles smile and twit and cry, "Isn't he the sweetest little thing?" Such coveted treats as chocolate-covered graham crackers often follow. But if we deliberately slam the rotten little puke of a sister's fingers in the door, sanctions follow—angry remonstrance from parents, aunts and uncles; instead of a chocolate-covered graham cracker, a spanking.

But anticivilization emotions don't go away, and they demand   11
periodic exercise. We have such "sick" jokes as, "What's the difference between a truckload of bowling balls and a truckload of dead babies?" (You can't unload a truckload of bowling balls with a pitchfork . . . a joke, by the way, that I heard originally from a ten-year-old.) Such a joke may surprise a laugh or a grin out of us even as we recoil, a pos-sibility that confirms the thesis: If we share a brotherhood of man, then we also share an insanity of man. None of which is intended as a defense of either the sick joke or insanity but merely as an explanation of why the best horror films, like the best fairy tales, manage to be reactionary, anarchistic, and revolutionary all at the same time.

The mythic horror movie, like the sick joke, has a dirty job to   12
do. It deliberately appeals to all that is worst in us. It is morbidity unchained, our most base instincts let free, our nastiest fantasies realized . . . and it all happens, fittingly enough, in the dark. For those reasons, good liberals often shy away from horror films. For myself, I like to see the most aggressive of them—*Dawn of the Dead,* for instance—as lifting a trap door in the civilized forebrain and throwing a basket of raw meat to the hungry alligators swimming around in that subterranean river beneath.

Why bother? Because it keeps them from getting out, man. It   13
keeps them down there and me up here. It was Lennon and

McCartney who said that all you need is love, and I would agree with that.

As long as you keep the gators fed.   14

Questions for Close Reading

1. What is the selection's thesis? Locate the sentence(s) in which King states his main idea. If he doesn't state the thesis explicitly, express it in your own words.
2. In what ways do King's references to "Jack the Ripper" and the "Cleveland Torso Murderer" (paragraph 8) support his thesis?
3. What does King mean in paragraph 4 when he says that horror movies are "innately conservative, even reactionary"? What does he mean in paragraph 11 when he calls them "anarchistic, and revolutionary"?
4. In paragraphs 12 and 14, King refers to "alligators" and "gators." What does the alligator represent? What does King mean when he says that all the world needs is love—"[a]s long as you keep the gators fed"?
5. Refer to your dictionary as needed to define the following words used in the selection: *hysterical* (paragraph 1), *reactionary* (4), *voyeur's* (6), *lynching* (6), *penchant* (7), *immortalized* (9), *anarchistic* (11), and *morbidity* (12).

Questions About the Writer's Craft

1. **The pattern.** Does King's causal analysis have an essentially informative, speculative, or persuasive (see pages 333–34) purpose? What makes you think so? How might King's profession as a horror writer have influenced his purpose?
2. **Other patterns.** King compares and contrasts horror movies to roller coasters (3), public lynchings (6), and sick jokes (11–12). How do these comparisons and contrasts reinforce King's thesis about horror movies?
3. **Other patterns.** Throughout the essay, King uses several examples involving children. Identify these instances. How do these examples help King develop his thesis?
4. What is unusual about paragraphs 2, 5, and 14? Why do you think King might have designed these paragraphs in this way?

Writing Assignments Using Cause-Effect as a Pattern of Development

1. King argues that horror movies have "a dirty job to do": they feed the hungry monsters in our psyche. Write an essay in which you put King's thesis to the test. Briefly describe the first horror movie you ever saw;

then explain its effect on you. Like King, speculate about the nature of your response—your feelings and fantasies—while watching the movie.

2. Many movie critics claim that horror movies nowadays are more violent and bloody than they used to be. Write an essay about *one* other medium of popular culture that you think has changed for the worse. You might consider action movies, televised coverage of sports, men's or women's magazines, radio talk shows, TV sitcoms, and so on. Briefly describe key differences between the medium's past and present forms. Analyze the reasons for the change, and, at the end of the essay, examine the effects of the change.

Writing Assignments Using Other Patterns of Development

3. King advocates the horror movie precisely because "It deliberately appeals to all that is worst in us." Write an essay in which you rebut King. Argue instead that horror movies should be avoided precisely *because* they satisfy monstrous feelings in us. To refute King, provide strong examples drawn from your own and other people's experience. Consider supplementing your informal research with material gathered in the library and/or on the Internet.

4. Write an essay in which you illustrate, contrary to King, that humans are by nature essentially benevolent and kind. Brainstorm with others to generate vivid examples in support of your thesis. Consider referring in your paper to points made by Lewis Thomas in "The Lie Detector" (page 354).

Writing Assignments Using a Journal Entry as a Starting Point

5. King believes that horror movies involve "a very peculiar sort of fun." Review your pre-reading journal entry, and select *one* other form of popular entertainment that you think provides its own strange kind of enjoyment. Like King, write an essay in which you analyze the causes of people's enjoyment of this type of entertainment. Brainstorm with others to identify convincing examples. You may, like King, endorse the phenomenon you examine—or you may condemn it.

Lewis Thomas

Lewis Thomas (1913–94) earned a reputation as an outstanding scientist and physician. A graduate of Princeton University and Harvard Medical School, Thomas held both the deanship of Yale University's medical school and the presidency of Sloan-Kettering Memorial Cancer Center. But more remarkable than Thomas's professional accomplishments was his gift for communicating the wonder of medicine and biology to the average reader. His essays, many of which first appeared in the *New England Journal of Medicine,* are less about medicine than they are about what he called the "mystery of being." Thomas published many books: a memoir, *The Youngest Science* (1983); and five essay collections, *Lives of a Cell* (1974), which won a National Book Award; *The Medusa and the Snail* (1979); *Late Night Thoughts on Listening to Mahler's Ninth Symphony* (1984); *Etcetera, Etcetera* (1990); and *The Fragile Species* (1992). The following selection is from *Late Night Thoughts.*

Pre-Reading Journal Entry

It's been argued that many technological developments of the last century reflect the worst in human nature. Consider the flip side of this claim. What three inventions of the last hundred years do you find reflect *positively* on human nature? List them in your journal, jotting down what about each invention inspires optimism about human beings.

The Lie Detector

Every once in a while the reasons for discouragement about the human prospect pile up so high that it becomes difficult to see the way ahead, and it is then a great blessing to have one conspicuous and irrefutable good thing to think about ourselves, something solid enough to step onto and look beyond the pile. 1

Language is often useful for this, and music. A particular painting, if you have the right receptors, can lift the spirits and hold them high enough to see a whole future for the race. The sound of laughter in the distance in the dark can be a marvelous encouragement. But these are chancy stimuli, ready to work only if you happen to be ready to receive them, which takes a bit of luck. 2

I have been reading magazine stories about the technology of   3
lie detection lately, and it occurs to me that this may be the thing
I've been looking for, an encouragement propped up by genuine,
hard scientific data. It is promising enough that I've decided to take
as given what the articles say, uncritically, and to look no further. For
a while, anyway.

Lying Is a Strain

As I understand it, a human being cannot tell a lie, even a small   4
one, without setting off a kind of smoke alarm somewhere deep in
a dark lobule of the brain, resulting in the sudden discharge of nerve
impulses, or the sudden outpouring of neurohormones of some
sort, or both. The outcome, recorded by the lie-detector gadgetry,
is a highly reproducible cascade of changes in the electrical conduc-
tivity of the skin, the heart rate, and the manner of breathing, similar to the responses to various kinds of stress.

Lying, then, is stressful, even when we do it for protection, or   5
relief, or escape, or profit, or just for the pure pleasure of lying and
getting away with it. It is a strain, distressing enough to cause the
emission of signals to and from the central nervous system warning
that something has gone wrong. It is, in a pure physiological sense,
an unnatural act.

Now I regard this as a piece of extraordinarily good news,   6
meaning, unless I have it all balled up, that we are a moral species
by compulsion, at least in the limited sense that we are biologically
designed to be truthful to each other. Lying doesn't hurt, mind you,
and perhaps you could tell lies all day and night for years on end
without being damaged, but maybe not—maybe the lie detector
informs us that repeated, inveterate untruthfulness will gradually
undermine the peripheral vascular system, the sweat glands, the
adrenals, and who knows what else. Perhaps we should be looking
into the possibility of lying as an etiologic agent for some of the
common human ailments still beyond explaining, recurrent head
colds, for instance, or that most human of all unaccountable disorders, a sudden pain in the lower mid-back.

Truth: Genetically Required?

It makes a sort of shrewd biological sense, and might therefore   7
represent a biological trait built into our genes, a feature of humanity

as characteristic for us as feathers for birds or scales for fish, enabling us to live, at our best, the kinds of lives we are designed to live. This is, I suppose, the "sociobiological" view to take, with the obvious alternative being that we are brought up this way as children in response to the rules of our culture. But if the latter is the case, you would expect to encounter, every once in a while, societies in which the rule does not hold, and I have never heard of a culture in which lying was done by everyone as a matter of course, all life through, nor can I imagine such a group functioning successfully. Biologically speaking, there is good reason for us to restrain ourselves from lying outright to each other whenever possible. We are indeed a social species, more interdependent than the celebrated social insects; we can no more live a solitary life than can a bee; we are obliged, as a species, to rely on each other. Trust is a fundamental requirement for our kind of existence, and without it all our linkages would begin to snap loose.

The restraint is a mild one, so gentle as to be almost impercep-   8
tible. But it is there; we know about it from what we call guilt, and now we have a neat machine to record it as well.

It seems a trivial thing to have this information, but perhaps it   9
tells us to look again, and look deeper. If we had better instruments, designed for profounder probes, we might see needles flipping, lines on charts recording quantitative degrees of meanness of spirit, or a lack of love. I do not wish for such instruments, I hope they will never be constructed; they would somehow belittle the issues involved. It is enough, quite enough, to know that we cannot even tell a plain untruth, betray a trust, without scaring some part of our own brains. I'd rather guess at the rest.

Questions for Close Reading

1. What is the selection's thesis? Locate the sentence(s) in which Thomas states his main idea. If he doesn't state the thesis explicitly, express it in your own words.
2. For what reasons does Thomas call lying an "unnatural act"? How does he feel about its being "unnatural"?
3. Thomas writes that receptivity to language, music, art, and laughter "takes a bit of luck" (paragraph 2). What do you think he means by this statement?
4. To his "sociobiological" view of truth telling, Thomas contrasts another viewpoint. What is this other interpretation? Does he give this other interpretation equal support? Why or why not?

5. Refer to your dictionary as needed to define the following words used in the selection: *irrefutable* (paragraph 1), *receptors* (2), *stimuli* (2), *lobule* (4), *neurohormones* (4), *inveterate* (6), and *etiologic* (6).

Questions About the Writer's Craft

1. **The pattern.** At the heart of Thomas's essay is a causal chain consisting of a series of interwoven causes and effects. What is this causal chain?
2. Thomas mixes technical terms from neuroscience with a rather informal style, involving contractions, the first-person ("I") point of view, colloquial expressions ("unless I have it all balled up"), and sentence fragments. Why might he have chosen to blend two such contrasting styles?
3. When presenting his viewpoint, Thomas uses a number of qualifiers: "it occurs to me" (paragraph 3), "as I understand it" (4), "unless I have it all balled up" (6), and "I suppose" (7). What is the effect of these qualifiers? Do they contribute to or detract from his credibility?
4. Thomas's next-to-last paragraph is shorter than any other in the essay. What function does this brief paragraph serve?

Writing Assignments Using Cause-Effect as a Pattern of Development

∞ 1. Reasons for lying, Thomas writes, include profit, protection, pleasure, and kindness. Write an essay tracing the reasons for a lie that you or someone else (a parent, friend, or public figure) once told. Also analyze the effect of the lie. Langston Hughes's "Salvation" (page 148) and William Lutz's "Doublespeak" (page 224) may provide some insight into the psychology of lying. End the paper with some conclusions about when lying is and is not acceptable.

∞ 2. Thomas welcomes the use of the lie detector but has qualms about the development of similar technologies. Focus on one technological breakthrough (word processors, cell phones, DVDs, handheld computers) and discuss its negative and positive effects. Although your analysis may be serious or playful, it should have a basically persuasive intent. You might read Jonathan Coleman's "Is Technology Making Us Intimate Strangers?" (page 359) for an additional perspective on the human impact of technology.

Writing Assignments Using Other Patterns of Development

3. Thomas claims, "Trust is a fundamental requirement for our . . . existence." In an essay, define the word *trust*. Consider dramatic examples, brief anecdotes, or a comparison of two people when developing the definition. Your essay should illustrate Thomas's point that without trust "all our linkages would . . . snap loose."

∞ 4. According to Thomas, "We are a moral species by compulsion." Write an essay in which you argue for or against this contention. Remembering to consider the opposing opinion, develop your argument by citing several examples of human behavior. Before writing the paper, you might want to read Stephen King's "Why We Crave Horror Movies" (page 349), an essay that presents a point of view very different from Thomas's.

Writing Assignments Using a Journal Entry as a Starting Point

5. Write an essay showing that the very existence of a specific invention provides evidence of higher-level human attributes. From your pre-reading journal entry, select the *one* invention that you think offers the most compelling proof. Brainstorming with others will help you identify reasons and examples worth developing.

Jonathan Coleman

Jonathan Coleman (1951–), a frequent contributor to *Time* and the *New York Times,* was born in Allentown, Pennsylvania, and graduated from the University of Virginia. He was an editor with Alfred A. Knopf and Simon & Schuster before moving to CBS News in the early 1980s. While at CBS, Coleman began investigating the story that led to his first book, *At a Mother's Request* (1985). A best-seller, the book provided the basis for a popular CBS miniseries. Coleman is also the author of *Exit the Rainmaker* (1989) and *Long Way to Go: Black and White in America* (1997). A lecturer on the subject of race at universities across the country, Coleman has been interviewed on most major television and radio shows. He makes his home in Charlottesville, Virginia. The following selection first appeared in *Newsweek* in 2000.

Pre-Reading Journal Entry

You've probably observed that people today have such full schedules, they often do several things at once. What examples of "multi-tasking" have you seen in yourself and in others? What do you think about this tendency to multi-task? Do you consider it productive? Do you think it overcomplicates life? Use your journal to respond to these questions.

Is Technology Making Us Intimate Strangers?

Every day when I walk out of my house I feel surrounded. 1
Surrounded by mere civilians so loaded down with the latest equipment that any military commander would be envious. Cell phones, beepers, headsets, watches that both tell time and give good e-mail—smart, sleek, technological fashion statements that enable you to be reached any time, anywhere; devices that allow you to keep up and keep track and that keep you tethered to the daily grind. America is on the move, utterly self-absorbed, multi-tasking, busy, busy, busy.

So what's the matter with me, daring to go about the streets 2
without any of these things, a dinosaur sorely out of step with the

times? Why can't I just capitulate, go along with The Program? After all, it might make me more efficient and productive, perhaps even give me a sense of power and importance.

Frankly, I worry about the freedom we give up, the time to   3
think and reflect, the time to consider where we've been in order to see where we are—or want to be—going. For many people these are painful things they don't necessarily want to dwell on. Self-reflection is far different—and far more difficult—than self-absorption, but the pain that self-absorption can inflict on others is acute.

Last summer, on as lovely an evening as one can hope for in   4
central Virginia, I was at my daughter's lacrosse practice. Standing next to me was a father more intent on the cell-phone conversation he was having (which did not sound terribly pressing) than on watching his daughter play. Time and again, she would look toward him, craving his attention, but he never saw her. Nor, for that matter, did another girl's mother see her child, focused as she was on her laptop, merrily tapping away.

Before you get antsy (or feel too guilty), stop reading this and   5
zero in on the next dot-com start-up vying for your attention, some confessions are in order. I've had e-mail only for a little more than a year, and I worry that I'm starting to become obsessed with it. In the intoxicating game of popularity that we all play, e-mail has presented another way for others to reach out to us. If someone hasn't left us a phone message or a fax, there is always the chance that an e-mail awaits. I can't even finish this essay without checking—three times already—to see if another one came through. I have also checked my stocks and a favorite Web site—all because they are there and are so tantalizingly *available*. I am not proud of my lack of discipline, but there you have it. Nor am I proud of the fact that when I read to my 6-year-old daughter at night, I sometimes reach for the phone when it rings, only to have her admonish me— "Daddy, don't!"—a sharp rebuke for being so quick to interrupt our sacred time together.

Speaking of which, do you remember when you and your   6
friends would go to the beach to swim and sun and take leave of your lives for an afternoon or longer? These days, I go to the beach and see teenagers come out of the water and instantly get on their cell phones. They can't imagine a life without a cell phone, and they can't image coming to the beach without it. In their view of the world, I am just a guy from the old days. A guy who needs to chill.

Nonetheless, I still say: why not step back and view all this   7
progress from a different angle? Instead of trying to figure out ways
to do a hundred things at once, why not slow things down? After
all, the greatest gift you can offer another person is your ability to
listen, to let that person feel that you are intent on what he or she is
saying, that you have all the time in the world. (The individuals I
know who can do that are few, but they stand out conspicuously in
my mind.) Through interviewing people I write about, I have come
to learn how much people yearn to be understood, how much they
want and need to be able to explain themselves.

Technology, for the most part, creates the illusion of intimacy.   8
As marvelous as it can be, it also foils us. It keeps us from the best
of ourselves and enables us to avoid others. It makes us into intimate
strangers.

To me, the most splendid thing about a place like New York   9
City, where I lived for a long time, is that you can walk the streets
day after day, year after year, and always see something new, something that will astonish or touch you. It may be a detail on a building, or the way the light hits the magnificent public library at a particular time, or even the moment when your doorman has an extra
spring in his step. But if you're not open to these things, if you're
too busy walking down the street glued to your phone and cut off
from all that is around you, you're going to miss something. It may
seem intangible and, therefore, unimportant, but those somethings
have a way of adding up.

Questions for Close Reading

1. What is the selection's thesis? Locate the sentence(s) in which Coleman
   states his main idea. If he doesn't state the thesis explicitly, express it in
   your own words.
2. Early in his essay, Coleman lists some of the technological devices we rely
   upon nowadays. Name some of these devices. What, according to
   Coleman, are their advantages and disadvantages?
3. What, in Coleman's opinion, is the difference between "self-reflection"
   and "self-absorption" (paragraphs 1 and 3)? What does he suggest are
   the effects of each?
4. Where in the essay does Coleman admit that he, too, has trouble resist-
   ing the seductive quality of modern technology? Who, besides Coleman,
   is affected by his inability to resist? Explain.
5. Refer to your dictionary as needed to define the following words
   used in the selection: *tethered* (paragraph 1), *capitulate* (2), *vying* (5),

intoxicating (5), *tantalizing* (5), *rebuke* (5), *conspicuously* (7), *yearn* (7), *illusion* (8), *foils* (8), and *intangible* (9).

Questions About the Writer's Craft

1. **The pattern.** What seems to be Coleman's purpose in pointing out the effects of technology on our day-to-day lives? Is his purpose mainly informative, speculative, or persuasive? How do you know?
2. Coleman organizes his essay around a causal chain showing technology's effect on our relationships with ourselves and with those around us. Trace the development of this causal chain.
3. At various points in his essay, Coleman poses a single question or a number of related questions. Identify these instances of question-asking. In each case, why do you think Coleman adopted this questioning strategy?
4. **Other patterns.** Reread the first and final paragraphs of Coleman's essay. What are the similarities between the two? What are the differences? Why do you suppose Coleman decided to open and close his essay this way?

Writing Assignments Using Cause-Effect as a Pattern of Development

1. Coleman expresses frustration with parents who are too engrossed in technological devices to notice their children. Increasingly, however, it's children and teenagers who are becoming addicted to such devices. Brainstorm with others about the devices that commonly lure young people. What is the appeal—and the downside—of each device? Review your brainstorming notes, and pick *one* device to focus on. Then write an essay explaining to parents the negative consequences of youngsters' overuse of the technology. Consider ending the essay with brief suggestions for scaling back kids' reliance on the device. You'll probably find it helpful to supplement your ideas with information gathered in the library and/or on the Internet.
2. In all likelihood, you know someone who hasn't been seduced by recent technological devices. Perhaps the person resists having voice mail, owning a cell phone, or using the Internet. Write an essay exploring possible reasons why this individual hasn't been lured by one or more technological advancements. Examine too the effect on others of the person's decision, as Coleman puts it, not to "go along with The Program." Your essay may be lighthearted or serious. In either case, indicate, explicitly or implicitly, how you feel about the person's reluctance to embrace technology. For insight into why many people avoid computer technology, read Bill Bryson's spirited essay "Your New Computer" (page 271).

Writing Assignments Using Other Patterns of Development

3. Coleman believes that technology "enables us to avoid others." Focusing on one or two specific technologies, write an essay in which you argue against this view. Show instead that technology can enhance interpersonal relations. Acknowledge Coleman's viewpoint near the beginning of the essay. Like Coleman, support your position with vigorous images, heartfelt commentary, and lively examples.

4. Coleman observes that teenagers today, unlike those in the past, can't even go to the beach without their cell phones. Identify several activities that you participated in as a child and teenager but that you think young people experience differently nowadays because of technology's dominant role in the culture. Possibilities include dating, doing homework, shopping, celebrating holidays with family. Write an essay illustrating how technology has changed young people's experience of these activities. To illustrate the change, contrast your childhood *or* adolescent experience of these activities with the experience of children *or* teenagers today. Be sure to convey whether you think the change has or has not been for the better.

Writing Assignments Using a Journal Entry as a Starting Point

∞ **5.** Write an essay illustrating the advantages and disadvantages of "multi-tasking"—doing more than one thing at a time. To develop your discussion, draw upon the examples in your pre-reading journal entry and upon the experiences and observations of others. Your essay should indicate whether, on the whole, you think multi-tasking is a positive or negative phenomenon. Before writing, you might read James Gleick's "Life As Type A" (page 387), an essay that speculates about the consequences of today's high-intensity lifestyles.

Additional Writing Topics

CAUSE-EFFECT

General Assignments

Write an essay that analyzes the causes and/or effects of one of the following topics. Determine your purpose before beginning to write: Will the essay be informative, persuasive, or speculative? As you prewrite, think rigorously about causes and effects; try to identify causal chains. Provide solid evidence for the thesis and use either chronological or emphatic order to organize your supporting points.

1. Sleep deprivation
2. Having the parents you have
3. Lack of communication in a relationship
4. Overexercising or not exercising
5. A particular TV or rock star's popularity
6. Skill or ineptitude in sports
7. A major life decision
8. Stiffer legal penalties for drunken driving
9. Changing attitudes toward protecting the environment
10. A particular national crisis
11. The mass movement of women into the workforce
12. Choosing to attend this college
13. "Back to basics" movement in schools
14. Headaches
15. An act of violence
16. A natural event: leaves turning, birds migrating, animals hibernating, an eclipse occurring
17. Pesticide use
18. Use of computers in the classroom
19. Banning disposable cans and bottles
20. A bad habit
21. A fear of _____
22. Legalizing drugs
23. Abolishing the F grade
24. Joining a particular organization
25. Owning a pet

Assignments With a Specific Purpose and Audience

1. A debate about the prominence of athletics at colleges and universities is going to be broadcast on the local cable station. For this debate, prepare

a speech pointing out either the harmful or the beneficial effects of "big-time" college athletic programs.

2. Why do students "flunk out" of college? Write an article for the campus newspaper outlining the main causes of failure. Your goal is to steer students away from dangerous habits and situations that lead to poor grades or dropping out.

3. Write a letter to the editor of your favorite newspaper, analyzing the causes of the country's current "trash crisis." Be sure to mention the nationwide love affair with disposable items and the general disregard of the idea of thrift.

4. Employed by your college's work-study office, you've been asked to write a brief pamphlet: "Things to Keep in Mind If You Plan to Work While Attending College." The pamphlet will be given to your fellow students, and it will focus on the effects—both negative and positive—of combining a part-time job with college studies.

5. Why do you think teenage suicide is on the rise? Write a fact sheet for parents of teenagers and for high school guidance counselors, describing the factors that could make a young person desperate enough to attempt suicide. At the end, suggest what parents and counselors can do to help confused, unhappy young people.

6. Some communities have conducted campaigns encouraging residents to give up television for a fixed period of time. You feel your community should participate in such an experiment. Write a letter to your mayor encouraging a public relations effort in favor of "Turn Off the TV Month." Cite specifically the positive effects such a program would have on parents, children, and the community in general.

10

DEFINITION

WHAT IS DEFINITION?

In Lewis Carroll's wise and whimsical tale *Through the Looking Glass,* Humpty Dumpty proclaims, "When *I* use a word . . . , it means just what I choose it to mean—neither more nor less." If the world were filled with characters like Humpty Dumpty, all of them bending words to their own purposes and accepting no challenges to their personal definitions, communication would be an exercise in frustration. You would say a word, and it would mean one thing to you but perhaps something completely different to a close friend. Without a common understanding, the two of you would talk at cross-purposes, missing each other's meanings as you blundered through a conversation.

For language to communicate, words must have accepted *definitions*. Dictionaries, the sourcebooks for accepted definitions, are compilations of current word meanings, enabling speakers of a language to understand one another. But as you might suspect, things are not as simple as they first appear. We all know that a word like *discipline* has a standard dictionary definition. We also know, though, that parents argue over what constitutes "discipline" and that controversies about the meaning of "discipline" rage within school systems year after year. Moreover, many of the wrenching moral debates of our time also boil down to questions of definition. Much of the controversy over abortion, for instance, centers on what is meant by "life" and when it "begins."

Words can, in short, be slippery. Each of us has unique experiences, attitudes, and values that influence the way we use words and the way we interpret the words of others. Lewis Carroll may have been exaggerating, but Humpty Dumpty's attitude exists—in a very real way—in all of us.

In addition to the idiosyncratic interpretations that may attach to words, some words may shift in meaning over time. The word *pedagogue*, for instance, originally meant "a teacher or leader of children." However, with time, *pedagogue* has come to mean "a dogmatic, pedantic teacher." And, of course, we invent other words (*modem, byte*) as the need arises.

Writing a definition, then, is no simple task. Primarily, the writer tries to answer basic questions: "What does _____ mean?" and "What is the special or true nature of _____?" The word to be defined may be an object, a concept, a type of person, a place, or a phenomenon. Potential subjects might be the "user-friendly" computer, animal rights, a model teacher, cabin fever. As you will see, there are various strategies for expanding definitions far beyond the single-word synonyms or brief phrases that dictionaries provide.

HOW DEFINITION FITS YOUR PURPOSE AND AUDIENCE

Many times, short-answer exam questions call for definitions. Consider the following examples:

Define the term *mob psychology.*

What is the difference between a metaphor and a simile?

How would you explain what a religious cult is?

In such cases, a good response might involve a definition of several sentences or several paragraphs.

Other times, definition may be used in an essay organized mainly around another pattern of development. In this situation, all that's needed is a brief formal definition or a short definition given in your own words. For instance, a *process analysis* showing readers how computers have revolutionized the typical business office might start with a textbook definition of the term *artificial intelligence*. In an *argumentation-persuasion* paper urging students to support recent efforts to abolish fraternities and sororities, you could refer to the definitions of *blackballing* and *hazing* found in the university handbook. Or your personal definition of *hero* could be the starting point for a *causal analysis* that explains to readers why there are few real heroes in today's world.

But the most complex use of definition, and the one we are primarily concerned with in this chapter, involves exploring a subject through an *extended definition*. Extended definition allows you to apply a personal interpretation to a word, to make a case for a revisionist view of a commonly accepted meaning, to analyze words representing complex or controversial issues. "Pornography," "gun control," "secular humanism," and "right-to-life" would be excellent subjects for extended definition—each is multifaceted, often misunderstood, and fraught with emotional meaning. "Junk food," "anger," "leadership," "anxiety" could make interesting subjects, especially if the extended definition helped readers develop a new understanding of the word. You might, for example, define "anxiety" not as a negative state to be avoided but as a positive force that propels us to take action.

An extended definition could perhaps run several paragraphs or a few pages. Keep in mind, however, that an extended definition may require a chapter or even an entire book to develop. If this seems unlikely, remember that theologians, philosophers, and pop psychologists have devoted entire texts to such concepts as "evil" and "love."

SUGGESTIONS FOR USING DEFINITION IN AN ESSAY

The following suggestions will be helpful whether you use definition as a dominant or a supportive pattern of development.

1. Stay focused on the essay's purpose, audience, and tone. Since your purpose for writing an extended definition shapes the entire paper, you need to keep that objective in mind when developing your definition. Suppose you decide to write an essay defining *jazz*. The essay could be purely *informative* and discuss the origins of jazz, its characteristic tonal patterns, and some of the great jazz musicians of the past. Or the essay could move beyond pure information and take on a *persuasive* edge. It might, for example, argue that jazz is the only contemporary form of music worth considering seriously.

Just as your purpose in writing will vary, so will your tone. A strictly informative definition will generally assume a detached, objective tone ("Apathy is an emotional state characterized by listlessness and indifference"). By way of contrast, a definition essay with a persuasive slant might be urgent in tone ("To combat student apathy, we must design programs that engage students in campus life"), or it might take a satiric approach ("An apathetic stance is a wise choice for any thinking student").

As you write, keep thinking about your audience as well. Not only do your readers determine what terms need to be defined (and in how much detail), but they also keep you focused on the essay's purpose and tone. For instance, you probably wouldn't write a serious, informative piece for the college newspaper about the "mystery meat" served in the campus cafeteria. Instead, you would adopt a light tone as you defined the culinary horror and might even make a persuasive pitch about improving the food prepared on campus.

2. Formulate an effective definition.   A definition essay sometimes begins with a brief *formal definition*—the dictionary's, a textbook's, or the writer's—and then expands that initial definition with supporting details. Formal definitions are traditionally worded as three-part statements that consist of the following: the *term*, the *class* to which the term belongs, and the *characteristics* that distinguish the term from other members of its class.

Term	Class	Characteristics
The peregrine falcon,	an endangered bird,	is the world's fastest flyer.
A bodice-ripper	is a paperback book,	that deals with highly charged romance in exotic places and faraway times.
Back to basics	is a trend in education	that emphasizes skill mastery through rote learning.

A definition that meets these guidelines will clarify what your subject *is* and what it *is not*. These guidelines also establish the boundaries of your definition, removing unlike items from consideration in your (and your reader's) mind. For example, defining "back to basics" as a trend that emphasizes rote learning signals a certain boundary; it lets readers know that other educational trends, such as those that emphasize children's social or emotional development, will not be part of the essay's definition.

If you decide to include a formal definition, avoid tired openers like "the dictionary says" or "according to Webster." Such weak starts are just plain boring and often herald an unimaginative essay. You should also keep in mind that a strict dictionary definition may actually confuse readers. Suppose you're writing a paper on the way all of us absorb ideas and values from the media. Likening this automatic response to the process of osmosis, you decide to open the paper with a dictionary definition. If you write, "Osmosis is the tendency of a solvent to disperse through a semipermeable membrane into a more concentrated medium," readers are apt to be baffled, even hostile. Remember: The purpose of a definition is to clarify meaning, not obscure it.

You should also stay clear of ungrammatical "is when" definitions: "Blind ambition is when you want to get ahead, no matter how much other people are hurt." Instead, write "Blind ambition is wanting to get ahead, no matter how much other people are hurt." A final pitfall to avoid in writing formal definitions is *circularity,* saying the same thing twice and therefore defining nothing: "A campus tribunal is a tribunal composed of various members of the university community." Circular definitions like this often repeat the term being defined (*tribunal*) or use words having the same meaning (*campus; university community*). In this case, we learn nothing about what a campus tribunal is; the writer says only that "X is X."

3. Develop the extended definition. You can choose from a variety of patterns when formulating an extended definition. Description, narration, process analysis, and comparison-contrast can be used— alone or in combination. Imagine that you're planning to write an extended definition of "robotics." You might develop the term by providing *examples* of the ways robots are currently being used in scientific research; by *comparing* and *contrasting* human and robot capabilities; or by *classifying* robots, starting with the most basic and moving to the most advanced or futuristic models.

Which patterns of development to use will often become apparent during the prewriting stage. Here is a list of prewriting questions as well as the pattern of development implied by each question.

Question	Pattern of Development
How does X look, taste, smell, feel, and sound?	Description
What does X do? When? Where?	Narration
What are some typical instances of X?	Exemplification
What are X's component parts? What different forms can X take?	Division-classification
How does X work?	Process analysis
What is X like or unlike?	Comparison-contrast
What leads to X? What are X's consequences?	Cause-effect

Those questions yielding the most material often suggest the effective pattern(s) for developing an extended definition.

4. Organize the material that develops the definition.   If you use a single pattern to develop the extended definition, apply the principles of organization suited to that pattern, as described in the appropriate chapter of this book. Assume that you're defining "fad" by means of *process analysis.* You might organize your paragraphs according to the steps in the process: a fad's slow start as something avant-garde or eccentric; its wildfire acceptance by the general public; the fad's demise as it becomes familiar or tiresome. If you want to define "character" by means of a single *narration,* you would probably organize paragraphs chronologically.

In a definition essay using several methods of development, you should devote separate paragraphs to each pattern. A definition of "relaxation," for instance, might start with a paragraph that *narrates* a particularly relaxing day; then it might move to a paragraph that describes several *examples* of people who find it difficult to unwind; finally, it might end with a paragraph that explains a *process* for relaxing the mind and body.

5. Write an effective introduction.   It can be helpful to provide—near the beginning of a definition essay—a brief formal definition of the term you're going to develop in the rest of the paper.

Beyond this basic element, the introduction may include a number of other features. You might explain the *origin* of the term being defined: "Acid rock is a term first coined in the 1960s to describe music that was written or listened to under the influence of the drug LSD." Similarly, you could explain the *etymology*, or linguistic origin, of the key word that focuses the paper. "The term *vigilantism* is derived from the Latin word meaning 'to watch and be awake.'"

You may also use the introduction to clarify what the subject is *not*. Such *definition by negation* can be an effective strategy at the beginning of a paper, especially if readers don't share your view of the subject. In such a case, you might write something like this: "The gorilla, far from being the vicious killer of jungle movies and popular imagination, is a sedentary, gentle creature living in a closely knit family group." Such a statement provides the special focus of your essay and signals some of the misconceptions or fallacies soon to be discussed.

In addition, you may include in the introduction a *stipulative definition,* one that puts special restrictions on a term: "Strictly defined, a mall refers to a one- or two-story enclosed building containing a variety of retail shops and at least two large anchor stores. Highway-strip shopping centers or downtown centers cannot be considered true malls." When a term has multiple meanings, or when its meaning has become fuzzy through misuse, a stipulative definition sets the record straight right at the start, so that readers know exactly what is, and is not, being defined.

Finally, the introduction may end with a *plan of development* that indicates how the definition essay will unfold. A student who returned to school after having raised a family decided to write a paper defining the *midlife crisis* that led to her enrollment in college. After providing a brief formal definition of "midlife crisis," the student rounded off her introduction with this sentence: "Such a midlife crisis starts with vague misgivings, turns into depression, and ends with a significant change in lifestyle."

STUDENT ESSAY

The following student essay was written by Laura Chen in response to this assignment:

> In "Entropy," K. C. Cole takes a scientific term from physics and gives it a broader definition and a wider

application. Choose another specialized term and define it in such a way that you reveal something significant about contemporary life.

While reading Laura's paper, try to determine how well it applies the principles of definition. The annotations on Laura's paper and the commentary following it will help you look at the essay more closely.

Physics in Everyday Life
by Laura Chen

Introduction

A boulder sits on a mountainside for a thousand years. The boulder will remain there forever unless an outside force intervenes. Suppose a force does affect the boulder--an earthquake, for instance. Once the boulder begins to thunder down the mountain, it will remain in motion and head in one direction only--downhill--until another force interrupts its progress. If the boulder tumbles into a gorge, it will finally come to rest as gravity anchors it to the earth once more. In both cases, the boulder is exhibiting the physical principle of inertia: the tendency of matter to remain at rest or, if moving, to keep moving in one direction unless affected by an outside force. Inertia, an important factor in the world of physics, also plays a crucial role in the human world. Inertia affects our individual lives as well as the direction taken by society as a whole.

Formal definition

Thesis

Plan of development

Topic sentence

Inertia often influences our value systems and personal growth. Inertia is at work, for example, when people cling to certain behaviors and views. Like the boulder firmly fixed to the mountain, most people are set in their ways. Without thinking, they vote Republican or Democratic because they have always voted that way. They regard with suspicion a couple having no children, simply because everyone else in the neighborhood has a large family. It is only when an outside force--a jolt of some sort-- occurs that people change their views. A white American couple may think little about racial discrimination, for instance, until they adopt an Asian child and must comfort her when classmates tease

Start of a series of causes and effects

1

2

her because she looks different. Parents may consider promiscuous any unmarried teenage girl who has a baby until their seventeen-year-old honor student confesses that she is pregnant. Personal jolts like these force people to think, perhaps for the first time, about issues that now affect them directly.

Topic sentence ⟶ To illustrate how inertia governs our lives, it is 3 helpful to compare the world of television with real

Start of a series of contrasts ⟶ life. On TV, inertia does not exist. Television shows and commercials show people making all kinds of drastic changes. They switch brands of coffee or try a new hair color with no hesitation. In one car commercial, an ambitious young accountant abandons her career with a flourish and is seen driving off into the sunset as she heads for a small cabin by the sea to write poetry. In a soap opera, a character may progress from homemaker to hooker to nun in a single year. But in real life, inertia rules. People tend to stay where they are, to keep their jobs, to be loyal to products. A second major difference between television and real life is that, on television, everyone takes prompt and dramatic action to solve problems. The construction worker with a thudding headache is pain-free at the end of the sixty-second commercial; the police catch the murderer within an hour; the family learns to cope with their son's life-threatening drug addiction by the time the made-for-TV movie ends at eleven. But in the real world, inertia persists, so that few problems are solved neatly or quickly. Illnesses drag on, few crimes are solved, and family conflicts last for years.

Topic sentence ⟶ Inertia is, most importantly, a force at work in 4 the life of our nation. Again, inertia is two-sided. It keeps us from moving and, once we move, it keeps us pointed in one direction. We find ourselves mired in a certain path, accepting the inferior, even the

Start of a series of examples ⟶ dangerous. We settle for toys that break, winter coats with no warmth, and rivers clogged with pollution. Inertia also compels our nation to keep moving in one direction--despite the uncomfortable suspicion that it is the wrong direction. We are not sure if manipulating genes is a good idea, yet we continue to fund scientific projects in genetic engineering. More than fifty years ago, we were shaken when we saw the devastation caused by an atomic bomb. But we went on to develop weapons hundreds of times more destructive. Although warned that excessive television viewing may be harmful, we continue to watch hours of television each day.

Conclusion   We have learned to defy gravity, one of the   5 basic laws of physics; we fly high above the earth, even float in outer space. But most of us have not learned to defy inertia. Those special individuals who are able to act when everyone else seems paralyzed are rare. But the fact that such people do exist means that inertia is not all-powerful. If we use our reasoning ability and our creativity, we can conquer inertia, just as we have conquered gravity.

COMMENTARY

Introduction.   As the title of her essay suggests, Laura has taken a scientific term (*inertia*) from a specialized field and drawn on the term to help explain some everyday phenomena. Using the *simple-to-complex* approach to structure the introduction, she opens with a vivid *descriptive* example of inertia. This description is then followed by a *formal definition* of inertia: "the tendency of matter to remain at rest or, if moving, to keep moving in one direction unless affected by an outside force." Laura wisely begins the paper with the easy-to-understand description rather than with the more-difficult-to-grasp scientific definition. Had the order been reversed, the essay would not have gotten off to nearly as effective a start. She then ends her introductory paragraph with a *thesis*, "Inertia, an important factor in the world of physics, also plays a crucial role in the human world," and with a *plan of development*, "Inertia affects our individual lives as well as the direction taken by society as a whole."

Organization.   To support her definition of inertia and her belief that it can rule our lives, Laura generates a number of compelling examples. She organizes these examples by grouping them into three major points, each point signaled by a *topic sentence* that opens each of the essay's three supporting paragraphs (2–4).

A definite organizational strategy determines the sequence of Laura's three central points. The essay moves from the way inertia affects the individual to the way it affects the nation. The phrase "most importantly" at the beginning of the fourth paragraph shows that Laura has arranged her points emphatically, believing that inertia's impact on society is most critical.

A weak example.   When reading the fourth paragraph, you might have noticed that Laura's examples aren't sequenced as effectively as they could be. To show that we, as a nation, tend to keep moving in the same direction, Laura discusses our ongoing uneasiness about genetic engineering, nuclear arms, and excessive television viewing. The point about nuclear weapons is most significant, yet it gets lost because it's sandwiched in the middle. The paragraph would be stronger if it ended with the point about nuclear arms. Moreover, the example about excessive television viewing doesn't belong in this paragraph since, at best, it has limited bearing on the issue being discussed.

Other patterns of development.   In addition to using numerous *examples* to illustrate her points, Laura draws on several other patterns of development to show that inertia can be a powerful force. In the second and fourth paragraphs, she uses *causal analysis* to explain how inertia can paralyze people and nations. The second paragraph indicates that only "an outside force—a jolt of some sort—" can motivate inert people to change. To support this view, Laura provides two examples of parents who experience such jolts. Similarly, in the fourth paragraph, she contends that inertia causes the persistence of specific national problems: shoddy consumer goods and environmental pollution.

Another pattern, *comparison-contrast,* is used in the third paragraph to highlight the differences between television and real life: on television, people zoom into action, but in everyday life, people tend to stay put and muddle through. The essay also contains a distinct element of *argumentation-persuasion,* since Laura clearly wants readers to accept her definition of inertia and her view that it often governs human behavior.

Conclusion.   Laura's *conclusion* rounds off the essay nicely and brings it to a satisfying close. Laura refers to another law of physics, one with which we are all familiar—gravity. By creating an *analogy* between gravity and inertia, she suggests that our ability to defy gravity should encourage us to defy inertia. The analogy enlarges the scope of the essay; it allows Laura to reach out to her readers by challenging them to action. Such a challenge is, of course, appropriate in a definition essay having a persuasive bent.

Revising the first draft.   When it was time to rework her essay, Laura began by reading her paper aloud. She noted in the margin of her draft the problems she detected, numbering them in order of importance. After reviewing her notes, she started to revise in earnest, paying special attention to her third paragraph. The first draft of that paragraph is reprinted here:

Original Version of the Third Paragraph

The ordinary actions of daily life are, in part, determined by inertia. To understand this, it is helpful to compare the world of television with real life, for, in the TV-land of ads and entertainment, inertia does not exist. For example, on television, people are often shown making all kinds of drastic changes. They switch brands of coffee or try a new hair color with no hesitation. In one car commercial, a young accountant leaves her career and sets off for a cabin by the sea to write poetry. In a soap opera, a character may progress from homemaker to hooker to nun in a single year. In contrast, inertia rules in real life. People tend to stay where they are, to keep their jobs, to be loyal to products (wives get annoyed if a husband brings home the wrong brand or color of bathroom tissue from the market). Middle-aged people wear the hairstyles or makeup that suited them in high school. A second major difference between television and real life is that, on TV, everyone takes prompt and dramatic action to solve problems. A woman finds the solution to dull clothes at the end of a commercial; the police catch the murderer within an hour; the family learns to cope with a son's disturbing lifestyle by the time the movie is over. In contrast, the law of real-life inertia means that few problems are solved neatly or quickly. Things, once started, tend to stay as they are. Few crimes are actually solved. Medical problems are not easily diagnosed. Messy wars in foreign countries seem endless. National problems are identified, but Congress does not pass legislation to solve them.

After rereading what she had written, Laura realized that her third paragraph rambled. To give it more focus, she removed the last two sentences ("Messy wars in foreign countries seem endless" and "National problems are identified, but Congress does not pass legislation. . . .") because they referred to national affairs but were

located in a section focusing on the individual. Then, she eliminated two flat, unconvincing examples: wives who get annoyed when
their husbands bring home the wrong brand of bathroom tissue and
middle-aged people whose hairstyles and makeup are outdated.
Condensing the two disjointed sentences that originally opened the
paragraph also helped tighten this section of the essay. Note how
much crisper the revised sentences are: "To illustrate how inertia
rules our lives, it is helpful to compare the world of television with
real life. On TV, inertia does not exist."

Laura also worked to make the details and the language in the
paragraph more specific and vigorous. The vague sentence "A
woman finds the solution to dull clothes at the end of the commercial" is replaced by the more dramatic "The construction worker
with a thudding headache is pain-free at the end of the sixty-second
commercial." Similarly, Laura changed a "son's disturbing lifestyle"
to a "son's life-threatening drug addiction"; "by the time the movie
is over" became "by the time the made-for-TV movie ends at
eleven"; and "a young accountant leaves her career and sets off for
a cabin by the sea to write poetry" was changed to "an ambitious
young accountant abandons her career with a flourish and is seen
driving off into the sunset as she heads for a small cabin by the sea
to write poetry."

After making these changes, Laura decided to round off the
paragraph with a powerful summary statement highlighting how
real life differs from television: "Illnesses drag on, few crimes are
solved, and family conflicts last for years."

These third-paragraph revisions are similar to those that Laura
made elsewhere in her first draft. Her astute changes enabled her to
turn an already effective paper into an especially thoughtful analysis
of human behavior.

ACTIVITIES: DEFINITION

Prewriting Activities

1. Imagine you're writing two essays: one explains the *process* for registering a complaint that gets results; the other *contrasts* the styles
   of two stand-up comics. Jot down ways you might use definition in
   each essay.

2. Select a term whose meaning varies from person to person or one for which you have a personal definition. Some possibilities include:

success	femininity	a liberal
patriotism	affirmative action	a housewife
individuality	pornography	intelligence

Brainstorm with others to identify variations in the term's meaning. Then examine your prewriting material. What thesis comes to mind? If you were writing an essay, would your purpose be informative, persuasive, or both? Finally, prepare a scratch list of the points you might cover.

Revising Activities

3. Explain why each of the following is an effective or ineffective definition. Rewrite those you consider ineffective.

   a. *Passive aggression* is when people show their aggression passively.
   b. A *terrorist* tries to terrorize people.
   c. *Being assertive* means knowing how to express your wishes and goals in a positive, noncombative way.
   d. *Pop music* refers to music that is popular.
   e. *Loyalty* is when someone stays by another person during difficult times.

4. The following introductory paragraph is from the first draft of an essay contrasting walking and running as techniques for reducing tension. Although intended to be a definition paragraph, it actually doesn't tell us anything we don't already know. It also relies on the old-hat "*Webster's* says." Rewrite the paragraph so it is more imaginative. You might use a series of anecdotes or one extended example to define *tension* and introduce the essay's thesis more gracefully.

> According to Webster's, tension is "mental or nervous strain, often accompanied by muscular tightness or tautness." Everyone feels tense at one time or another. It may occur when there's a deadline to meet. Or it could be caused by the stress of trying to fulfill academic, athletic, or social goals. Sometimes it comes from criticism by family, bosses, or teachers. Such tension puts wear and tear on our bodies and on our emotional well-being. Although some people run to relieve tension, research has found that walking is a more effective tension reducer.

K. C. Cole

K. C. Cole's writings about science, especially physics, have made a great deal of specialized knowledge available to the general public. A graduate of Barnard College, Cole has contributed numerous articles to such publications as the *New York Times,* the *Washington Post,* and *Long Island Newsday,* and writes a regular column for *Discover* magazine. Her work with the Exploratorium, a San Francisco science museum, led her to write several books on the exhibits there. In 1985, Cole published a collection of essays, *Sympathetic Vibrations: Reflections on Physics as a Way of Life.* Other books include *What Only a Mother Can Tell You About Having a Baby* (1986), *The Universe and the Teacup* (1998), *First You Build a Cloud* (1999), and *The Hole in the Universe* (2000). She is currently a science writer and editor at the *L.A. Times.* The following selection was first published as a "Hers" column in the *New York Times* in 1982.

Pre-Reading Journal Entry

Do you consider yourself an orderly or a disorderly person? What about those around you? What are the benefits and the drawbacks of being orderly? Of being disorderly? Use your journal to reflect on these questions.

Entropy

It was about two months ago when I realized that entropy was getting the better of me. On the same day my car broke down (again), my refrigerator conked out and I learned that I needed root-canal work in my right rear tooth. The windows in the bedroom were still leaking every time it rained and my son's baby sitter was still failing to show up every time I really needed her. My hair was turning gray and my typewriter was wearing out. The house needed paint and I needed glasses. My son's sneakers were developing holes and I was developing a deep sense of futility. 1

After all, what was the point of spending half of Saturday at the Laundromat if the clothes were dirty all over again the following Friday? 2

Disorder, alas, is the natural order of things in the universe. 3
There is even a precise measure of the amount of disorder, called
entropy. Unlike almost every other physical property (motion, gravity, energy), entropy does not work both ways. It can only increase.
Once it's created it can never be destroyed. The road to disorder is
a one-way street.

Because of its unnerving irreversibility, entropy has been called 4
the arrow of time. We all understand this instinctively. Children's
rooms, left on their own, tend to get messy, not neat. Wood rots,
metal rusts, people wrinkle and flowers wither. Even mountains wear
down; even the nuclei of atoms decay. In the city we see entropy in
the rundown subways and worn-out sidewalks and torn-down buildings, in the increasing disorder of our lives. We know, without asking, what is old. If we were suddenly to see the paint jump back on
an old building, we would know that something was wrong. If we
saw an egg unscramble itself and jump back into its shell, we would
laugh in the same way we laugh at a movie run backward.

Entropy is no laughing matter, however, because with every 5
increase in entropy energy is wasted and opportunity is lost. Water
flowing down a mountainside can be made to do some useful work
on its way. But once all the water is at the same level it can work no
more. That is entropy. When my refrigerator was working, it kept all
the cold air ordered in one part of the kitchen and warmer air in
another. Once it broke down the warm and cold mixed into a luke-
warm mess that allowed my butter to melt, my milk to rot and my
frozen vegetables to decay.

Of course the energy is not really lost, but it has diffused and 6
dissipated into a chaotic caldron of randomness that can do us no
possible good. Entropy is chaos. It is loss of purpose.

People are often upset by the entropy they seem to see in the 7
haphazardness of their own lives. Buffeted about like so many molecules in my tepid kitchen, they feel that they have lost their sense
of direction, that they are wasting youth and opportunity at every
turn. It is easy to see entropy in marriages, when the partners are too
preoccupied to patch small things up, almost guaranteeing that they
will fall apart. There is much entropy in the state of our country, in
the relationships between nations—lost opportunities to stop the
avalanche of disorders that seems ready to swallow us all.

Entropy is not inevitable everywhere, however. Crystals and 8
snowflakes and galaxies are islands of incredibly ordered beauty in

the midst of random events. If it was not for exceptions to entropy, the sky would be black and we would be able to see where the stars spend their days; it is only because air molecules in the atmosphere cluster in ordered groups that the sky is blue.

The most profound exception to entropy is the creation of life. 9
A seed soaks up some soil and some carbon and some sunshine and some water and arranges it into a rose. A seed in the womb takes some oxygen and pizza and milk and transforms it into a baby.

The catch is that it takes a lot of energy to produce a baby. It 10
also takes energy to make a tree. The road to disorder is all downhill but the road to creation takes work. Though combating entropy is possible, it also has its price. That's why it seems so hard to get ourselves together, so easy to let ourselves fall apart.

Worse, creating order in one corner of the universe always creates more disorder somewhere else. We create ordered energy from 11
oil and coal at the price of the entropy of smog.

I recently took up playing the flute again after an absence of several months. As the uneven vibrations screeched through the house, 12
my son covered his ears and said, "Mom, what's wrong with your flute?" Nothing was wrong with my flute, of course. It was my ability to play it that had atrophied, or entropied, as the case may be. The only way to stop that process was to practice every day, and sure enough my tone improved, though only at the price of constant work. Like anything else, abilities deteriorate when we stop applying our energies to them.

That's why entropy is depressing. It seems as if just breaking 13
even is an uphill fight. There's a good reason that this should be so. The mechanics of entropy are a matter of chance. Take any ice-cold air molecule milling around my kitchen. The chances that it will wander in the direction of my refrigerator at any point are exactly 50-50. The chances that it will wander away from my refrigerator are also 50-50. But take billions of warm and cold molecules mixed together, and the chances that all the cold ones will wander toward the refrigerator and all the warm ones will wander away from it are virtually nil.

Entropy wins not because order is impossible but because there 14
are always so many more paths toward disorder than toward order. There are so many more different ways to do a sloppy job than a good one, so many more ways to make a mess than to clean it up. The obstacles and accidents in our lives almost guarantee that constant collisions

will bounce us on to random paths, get us off the track. Disorder is the path of least resistance, the easy but not the inevitable road.

Like so many others, I am distressed by the entropy I see   15
around me today. I am afraid of the randomness of international events, of the lack of common purpose in the world; I am terrified that it will lead into the ultimate entropy of nuclear war. I am upset that I could not in the city where I live send my child to a public school; that people are unemployed and inflation is out of control; that tensions between sexes and races seem to be increasing again; that relationships everywhere seem to be falling apart.

Social institutions—like atoms and stars—decay if energy is not   16
added to keep them ordered. Friendships and families and economies all fall apart unless we constantly make an effort to keep them working and well oiled. And far too few people, it seems to me, are willing to contribute consistently to those efforts.

Of course, the more complex things are, the harder it is. If there   17
were only a dozen or so air molecules in my kitchen, it would be likely—if I waited a year or so—that at some point the six coldest ones would congregate inside the freezer. But the more factors in the equation—the more players in the game—the less likely it is that their paths will coincide in an orderly way. The more pieces in the puzzle, the harder it is to put back together once order is disturbed. "Irreversibility," said a physicist, "is the price we pay for complexity."

Questions for Close Reading

1. What is the selection's thesis? Locate the sentence(s) in which Cole states her main idea. If she doesn't state the thesis explicitly, express it in your own words.
2. How does entropy differ from the other properties of the physical world? Is the image "the arrow of time" helpful in establishing this difference?
3. Why is the creation of life an exception to entropy? What is the relationship between entropy and energy?
4. Why does Cole say that entropy "is no laughing matter"? What is so depressing about the entropy she describes?
5. Refer to your dictionary as needed to define the following words used in the selection: *futility* (paragraph 1), *dissipated* (6), *buffeted* (7), *tepid* (7), and *atrophied* (12).

Questions About the Writer's Craft

1. **The pattern.**   What is Cole's underlying purpose in defining the scientific term *entropy?* What gives the essay its persuasive edge?

2. What tone does Cole adopt to make reading about a scientific concept more interesting? Identify places in the essay where her tone is especially prominent.

3. Cole uses such words as *futility, loss,* and *depressing*. How do these words affect you? Why do you suppose she chose such terms? Find similar words in the essay.

4. **Other patterns.**   Many of Cole's sentences follow a two-part pattern involving a contrast: "The road to disorder is all downhill but the road to creation takes work" (paragraph 10). Find other examples of this pattern in the essay. Why do you think Cole uses it so often?

Writing Assignments Using Definition as a Pattern of Development

1. Write an essay in which you define *order* or *disorder* by applying the term to a system that you know well—for example, your school, dorm, family, or workplace. Develop your definition through any combination of writing patterns: by supplying examples, by showing contrasts, by analyzing the process underlying the system.

2. Choose, as Cole does, a technical term that you think will be unfamiliar to most readers. In a humorous or serious paper, define the term as it is used technically; then show how the term can shed light on some aspect of your life. For example, the concept in astronomy of a *supernova* could be used to explain your sudden emergence as a new star on the athletic field, in your schoolwork, or on the social scene. Here are a few suggested terms:

symbiosis	volatility	resonance
velocity	erosion	catalyst
neutralization	equilibrium	malleability

Writing Assignments Using Other Patterns of Development

∞ 3. Can one person make much difference in the amount of entropy—disorder and chaos—in the world? Share your view in an essay. Use examples of people who have tried to overcome the tendency of things to "fall apart." Make clear whether you think these people succeeded or failed in their attempts. To inform your perspective before writing, consider reading James Gleick's "Life As Type A" (page 387), an evaluation of the factors that influence people's compulsion for order.

∞ 4. Cole claims that we humans are "buffeted about like so many molecules." Write an essay arguing that people either do or do not control their own fates. Support your point with a series of specific examples. For different perspectives on the issue, you might want to read "Sister Flowers" (page 106) by Maya Angelou, "So Tsi-Fai" (page 153) by

Sophronia Liu, and "Campus Racism 101" (page 278) by Nikki Giovanni.

Writing Assignments Using a Journal Entry as a Starting Point

5. Write an essay arguing that disorder can be liberating *or* that it can be stifling. Review your pre-reading journal entry, and select strong, compelling examples that support your position. Aim to refute as many opposing arguments as possible. Your essay may have a serious or a humorous tone.

James Gleick

After graduating from Harvard College in 1976, James Gleick helped found *Metropolis,* an alternative newspaper in Minneapolis. He then spent ten years as a reporter and editor with the *New York Times,* where he wrote a column about the impact of science and technology on modern life. His earlier books, *Chaos: Making a New Science* (1987) and *Genius: The Life and Science of Richard Feynman* (1992), were both finalists for the National Book Award and Pulitzer Prize. Formerly McGraw Distinguished Lecturer at Princeton University, Gleick lives with his wife, writer Cynthia Crossen, in New York. The following piece is taken from Gleick's most recent book, *Faster: The Acceleration of Just About Everything* (1999).

Pre-Reading Journal Entry

Like many people, you may feel harried and under pressure at least some of the time. Use your journal to reflect on the sources of stress in your everyday life. List several examples. For each, consider the factors leading to this frenzied feeling.

Life As Type A

Everyone knows about Type A. This magnificently bland 1 coinage, put forward by a pair of California cardiologists in 1959, struck a collective nerve and entered the language. It is a token of our confusion: are we victims or perpetrators of the crime of haste? Are we living at high speed with athleticism and vigor, or are we stricken by hurry sickness?

The cardiologists, Meyer Friedman and Ray Rosenman, listed a 2 set of personality traits which, they claimed, tend to go hand in hand with one another and also with heart disease. They described these traits rather unappealingly, as characteristics about and around the theme of impatience. Excessive competitiveness. Aggressiveness. "A harrying sense of time urgency." The Type A idea emerged in technical papers and then formed the basis of a popular book and made its way into dictionaries. The canonical Type A, as these doctors portrayed him, was "Paul":

A very disproportionate amount of his emotional energy is consumed in struggling against the normal constraints of time. "How can I move faster, and do more and more things in less and less time?" is the question that never ceases to torment him.

Paul hurries his thinking, his speech and his movements. He also strives to hurry the thinking, speech, and movements of those about him; they must communicate rapidly and relevantly if they wish to avoid creating impatience in him. Planes must arrive and depart precisely on time for Paul, cars ahead of him on the highway must maintain a speed he approves of, and there must never be a queue of persons standing between him and a bank clerk, a restaurant table, or the interior of a theater. In fact, he is infuriated whenever people talk slowly or circuitously, when planes are late, cars dawdle on the highway, and queues form.

Let's think . . . Do we know anyone like "Paul"?

This was the first clear declaration of *hurry sickness*—another 3 coinage of Friedman's. It inspired new businesses: mind-body workshops; videotapes demonstrating deep breathing; anxiety-management retreats; seminars on and even institutes of stress medicine. "I drove all the way in the right-hand lane," a Pacific Gas and Electric Company executive said proudly one morning in 1987 to a group of self-confessed hurriers, led by Friedman himself, by then seventy-six years old. In the battle against Type A jitters, patients tried anything and everything—the slow lane, yoga, meditation, visualization: "Direct your attention to your feet on the floor. . . . Be aware of the air going in your nostrils cool and going out warm. . . . Visualize a place you like to be. . . . Experience it and see the objects there, the forms and shadows. Take another deep breath and experience the sounds, the surf, the wind, leaves, a babbling brook." Some hospital television systems now feature a "relaxation channel," with hour after hour of surf, wind, leaves, and babbling brooks.

We believe in Type A—a triumph for a notion with no particu- 4 lar scientific validity. The Friedman-Rosenman claim has turned out to be both obvious and false. Clearly some heart ailments do result from, or at least go along with, stress (itself an ill-defined term), both chronic and acute. Behavior surely affects physiology, at least once in a while. Sudden dashes for the train, laptop computer in one hand and takeout coffee in the other, can accelerate heartbeats and raise blood pressure. That haste makes coronaries was already a kind of folk wisdom—that is, standard medical knowledge untainted by research. "Hurry has a clearly debilitating effect upon the tissues and may in time injure the heart," admonished Dr. Cecil Webb-Johnson in *Nerve Troubles,* an English monograph of the early 1900s. "The great men of the centuries past were never in a hurry," he added sanctimoniously, "and that is why the world will never forget them in a hurry." It might be natural—even appealing—to expect certain less-great people to receive their cardiovascular comeuppance. But in reality, three decades of attention from cardiologists and psychologists have failed to produce any carefully specified and measurable set of character traits that predict heart disease—or to demonstrate that people who change their Type A behavior will actually lower their risk of heart disease.

Indeed, the study that started it all—Friedman and Rosenman's 5 "Association of Specific Overt Behavior Pattern with Blood and Cardiovascular Findings"—appears to have been a wildly flawed piece of research. It used a small sample—eighty-three people (all men) in what was then called "Group A." The selection process was neither random nor blind. White-collar male employees of large businesses were rounded up by acquaintances of Friedman and Rosenman on a subjective basis—they fit the type. The doctors further sorted the subjects by interviewing them personally and observing their appearance and behavior. Did a man gesture rapidly, clench his teeth, or exhibit a "general air of impatience"? If so, he was chosen. It seems never to have occurred to these experienced cardiologists that they might have been consciously or unconsciously selecting people whose physique indicated excess weight or other markers for incipient heart disease. The doctors' own data show that the final Group A drank more, smoked more, and weighed more than Group B. But the authors dismissed these factors, asserting, astonishingly, that there was no association between heart disease and cigarette smoking.

In the years since, researchers have never settled on a reliable 6 method for identifying Type A people, though not for want of trying. Humans are not reliable witnesses to their own impatience. Researchers have employed questionnaires like the Jenkins Activity Survey, and they have used catalogues of grimaces and frowns—Ekman and Friesen's Facial Action Coding System, for example, or the Cook-Medley Hostility Inventory. In the end, nothing conclusive emerges.

Some studies have found Type A people to have *lower* blood pressure. The sedentary and obese have cardiac difficulties of their own.

The notion of Type A has expanded, shifted, and flexed to suit   7 the varying needs of different researchers. V.A. Price adds *hypervigilance* to the list of traits. Some doctors lose patience with the inconclusive results and shift their focus to anger and hostility—mere subsets of the original Type A grab-bag. Cynthia Perry finds that Type A people have fewer daydreams. How does she know? She asks them to monitor lines flashing across a computer screen for forty painfully boring minutes and finds that, when interrupted by a beep (1000 hertz at 53 decibels), they are less likely to press a black button to confess that irrelevant thoughts had strayed into their minds. Studies have labeled as Type A not only children (those with a tendency to interrupt and to play competitively at games) but even babies (those who cry more). Meanwhile, researchers interested in pets link the Type A personality to petlessness; a National Institutes of Health panel reports: "The description of a 'coronary-prone behavior pattern,' or Type A behavior, and its link to the probability of developing overt disease provided hope that, with careful training, individuals could exercise additional control over somatic illness by altering their lifestyle. . . . Relaxation, meditation, and stress management have become recognized therapies. . . . It therefore seems reasonable that pets, who provide faithful companionship to many people, also might promote greater psychosocial stability for their owners, and thus a measure of protection from heart disease." This is sweet, but it is not science.

Typically a Type A study will begin with researchers who assume   8 that there are some correlations to be found, look for a wide variety of associations, fail to find some and succeed in finding others. For example, a few dozen preschool children are sorted according to their game-playing styles and tested for blood pressure. No correlation is found. Later, however, when performing a certain "memory game," the supposed Type A children rank somewhat higher in, specifically, systolic pressure. Interesting? The authors of various published papers evidently think so, but they are wrong, because if their technique is to keep looking until they find some correlation, somewhere, they are bound to succeed. Such results are meaningless.

The categorizations are too variable and the prophecies too self-   9 fulfilling. It is never quite clear which traits *define* Type A and which are fellow travelers. The "free-floating, but well-rationalized form of hostility"? The "deep-seated insecurity"? "Their restlessness, their tense facial muscles, their tics, or their strident-staccato manner of speaking"? If you are hard-driving yet friendly, chafing yet self-assured—if you race for the airport gate and then settle *happily* into your seat—are you Type A or not? If you are driven to walk briskly, briskly, all the time, isn't that good for your heart?

Most forget that there is also supposed to be a Type B, defined   10
not by the personality traits its members possess but by the traits they lack. Type B people are the shadowy opposites of Type A people. They are those who are not so very Type A. They do *not* wear out their fingers punching that elevator button. They do *not* allow a slow car in the fast lane to drive their hearts to fatal distraction; in fact, they are at the wheel of that slow car. Type B played no real part in that mass societal gasp of recognition in the 1970's. Type B-ness was just a foil. Doctors Friedman and Rosenman actually claimed to have had trouble finding eighty men in all San Francisco who were not under any time pressure. They finally came up with a few, they wrote solemnly, "in the municipal clerks' and the embalmers' unions."

Even more bizarrely, that first Friedman-Rosenman study also   11
included a Group C, comprising forty-six unemployed blind men. Not much haste in Group C. "The primary reason men of Group C exhibited little ambition, drive, or desire to compete," the doctors wrote, "was the presence of total blindness for ten or more years and the lack of occupational deadlines because none was gainfully employed." No wonder they omitted Type C from the subsequent publicity.

If the Type A phenomenon made for poor medical research, it   12
stands nonetheless as a triumph of social criticism. Some of us yield more willingly to impatience than others, but on the whole Type A is who we are—not just the coronary-prone among us, but all of us, as a society and as an age. No wonder the concept has proven too rich a cultural totem to be dismissed.

Questions for Close Reading

1. What is the selection's thesis? Locate the sentence(s) in which Gleick states his main idea. If he doesn't state the thesis explicitly, express it in your own words.
2. What is Gleick's opinion of the study Friedman and Rosenman conducted? List at least two elements of the study that Gleick uses to support his assessment.

3. In paragraph 7, Gleick observes that the concept of Type A has changed since Friedman and Rosenman's study first chronicled it. How has it changed? What accounts for this change?
4. According to Gleick, how do Friedman and Rosenman define the Type B personality? Why does Gleick find fault with their definition of this personality type?
5. Refer to your dictionary as needed to define the following words used in the selection: *coinage* (paragraph 1), *harrying* (2), *canonical* (2), *circuitously* (2), *sanctimoniously* (4), *overt* (5), *incipient* (5), *sedentary* (6), *hypervigilance* (7), *correlations* (8), *strident* (9), *staccato* (9), *foil* (10), and *totem* (12).

Questions About the Writer's Craft

1. **The pattern.** In their work, Friedman and Rosenman use a description of Paul to define "canonical Type A" behavior (paragraph 2). Why do you suppose that Gleick, who criticizes Friedman and Rosenman's research, quotes their portrait of Paul at such length?
2. **The pattern.** Gleick uses a sequence of three fragments when discussing (in paragraph 2) how Type A has been defined. Identify these fragments. What effect do you think Gleick wanted the fragments to have?
3. Locate places where Gleick uses the first-person pronouns "we," "us," and "our." What do you think Gleick's purpose is in using these pronouns?
4. In paragraph 1, Gleick sarcastically refers to the phrase *Type A* as "magnificently bland." Find other places in the essay where he uses sarcasm. Why might he have chosen to employ such language?

Writing Assignments Using Definition as a Pattern of Development

1. Write an essay offering a fuller definition of the Type B personality than Gleick's essay provides. Rather than defining Type B through negation, as Friedman and Rosenman do, marshal convincing evidence that illustrates the validity of the Type B phenomenon. Brainstorming with friends, family, and classmates will help you generate strong examples of this personality type. At some point in the essay, you might offer a brief personality sketch of the "canonical" Type B as well as discuss the factors that shape the Type B personality as you define it.
2. Gleick notes that, like *Type A, stress* is an ill-defined term. Brainstorm with others to identify as many examples of different kinds of stress as you can. Review the brainstormed material, and select a specific type of stress to focus on. Then write an essay providing a *clear* definition of that particular stress. Possibilities include "dating stress," "workplace stress," "online stress," "fitness stress." Near the end of the essay, you might

provide concise hints for managing the stress you define. Your essay may have a humorous or a serious tone—whichever seems appropriate to your subject.

Writing Assignments Using Other Patterns of Development

3. Write an essay contrasting situations in which being Type A would be beneficial with situations in which it would be counterproductive. Under what circumstances would Type A characteristics be desirable? Under what circumstances would they be undesirable? Drawing upon your own experiences and observations, reach some conclusions about the advantages and/or limitations of the Type A personality.

4. Gleick observes that "hurry sickness" is a trait induced by society at large. Identify a trait of yours that you think is also a reflection of the society in which you live. You might discuss your tendency to be aggressive or nonassertive, materialistic or idealistic, studious or fun-loving. Write an essay illustrating this character trait at work in your everyday behavior. Explain whether you think this trait works to your advantage or disadvantage.

Writing Assignments Using a Journal Entry as a Starting Point

5. Gleick claims that the Type A phenomenon is pervasive in our society. Write an essay of your own illustrating the extent to which your life reflects this phenomenon. Draw upon the most dramatic examples in your pre-reading journal entry. At the end of the essay, describe steps that you or anyone with similar pressures could take to slow down the frenetic pace of everyday life. Gathering information in the library and/or on the Internet might be helpful when you develop the final section of your paper.

William Raspberry

Journalist William Raspberry was born in Okolona, Mississippi. From his mother, an English teacher and poet, Raspberry learned to care "about the rhythm and grace of words." His father, a shop teacher, taught him "that neither end tables nor arguments are worthwhile unless they stand solidly on all four legs." Raspberry graduated from Indiana Central College and later joined the staff of the Indianapolis *Recorder* as a reporter and editor. Following a two-year stint in the army, he was hired by the *Washington Post,* where his nationally syndicated column has originated since 1971. His coverage of the Watts race riots in 1965 won him the Capital Press Club Journalist of the Year award, and he later went on to win the Pulitzer Prize for commentary in 1994. *Looking Backward at Us,* a collection of Raspberry's columns, was published in 1991. The following selection appeared in Raspberry's *Washington Post* column in 1982.

Pre-Reading Journal Entry

Which do you think plays a more important role in determining what a person accomplishes: innate talent or belief in oneself? Take a few minutes to respond to this question in your journal, jotting down examples drawn from your experiences and observations.

The Handicap of Definition

I know all about bad schools, mean politicians, economic deprivation and racism. Still, it occurs to me that one of the heaviest burdens black Americans—and black children in particular—have to bear is the handicap of definition: the question of what it means to be black. 1

Let me explain quickly what I mean. If a basketball fan says that the Boston Celtics' Larry Bird plays "black," the fan intends it—and Bird probably accepts it—as a compliment. Tell pop singer Tom Jones he moves "black" and he might grin in appreciation. Say to Teena Marie or the Average White Band that they sound "black" and they'll thank you. 2

But name one pursuit, aside from athletics, entertainment or sexual performance, in which a white practitioner will feel 3 complimented to be told he does it "black." Tell a white broadcaster he talks "black" and he'll sign up for diction lessons. Tell a white reporter he writes "black" and he'll take a writing course. Tell a white lawyer he reasons "black" and he might sue you for slander.

What we have here is a tragically limited definition of blackness, and it isn't only white people who buy it.   4

Think of all the ways black children can put one another down   5
with charges of "whiteness." For many of these children, hard study and hard work are "white." Trying to please a teacher might be criticized as acting "white." Speaking correct English is "white." Scrimping today in the interest of tomorrow's goals is "white." Educational toys and games are "white."

An incredible array of habits and attitudes that are conducive to   6
success in business, in academia, in the nonentertainment professions are likely to be thought of as somehow "white." Even economic success, unless it involves such "black" undertakings as numbers banking, is defined as "white."

And the results are devastating. I wouldn't deny that blacks   7
often are better entertainers and athletes. My point is the harm that comes from too narrow a definition of what is black.

One reason black youngsters tend to do better at basketball, for   8
instance, is that they assume they can learn to do it well, and so they practice constantly to prove themselves right.

Wouldn't it be wonderful if we could infect black children with   9
the notion that excellence in math is "black" rather than white, or possibly Chinese? Wouldn't it be of enormous value if we could create the myth that morality, strong families, determination, courage and love of learning are traits brought by slaves from Mother Africa and therefore quintessentially black?

There is no doubt in my mind that most black youngsters could   10
develop their mathematical reasoning, their elocution and their attitudes, the way they develop their jump shots and their dance steps: by the combination of sustained, enthusiastic practice and the unquestioned belief that they can do it.

In one sense, what I am talking about is the importance of   11
developing positive ethnic traditions. Maybe Jews have an innate talent for communication; maybe the Chinese are born with a gift for mathematical reasoning; maybe blacks are naturally blessed with athletic grace. I doubt it. What is at work, I suspect, is assumption, inculcated early in their lives, that this is a thing our people do well.

Unfortunately, many of the things about which blacks make this   12
assumption are things that do not contribute to their career success—except for that handful of the truly gifted who can make it as
entertainers and athletes. And many of the things we concede to
whites are the things that are essential to economic security.

So it is with a number of assumptions black youngsters make   13
about what it is to be a "man": physical aggressiveness, sexual
prowess, the refusal to submit to authority. The prisons are full of
people who, by this perverted definition, are unmistakably men.

But the real problem is not so much that the things defined as   14
"black" are negative. The problem is that the definition is much too
narrow.

Somehow, we have to make our children understand that they   15
are intelligent, competent people, capable of doing whatever they
put their minds to and making it in the American mainstream, not
just in a black subculture.

What we seem to be doing, instead, is raising up yet another   16
generation of young blacks who will be failures—by definition.

Questions for Close Reading

1. What is the selection's thesis? Locate the sentence(s) in which Raspberry states his main idea. If he doesn't state the thesis explicitly, express it in your own words.
2. In paragraph 14, Raspberry emphasizes that the word *black* presents a problem not because it's negative but because it has become "much too narrow." According to Raspberry, what limitations have become associated with the term *black*? What negative consequences does he see resulting from these limitations?
3. In paragraph 11, Raspberry talks about "positive ethnic traditions." What does he mean by this term? What examples does he provide?
4. In Raspberry's opinion, what needs to be done to ensure the future success of African-American children?
5. Refer to your dictionary as needed to define the following words used in the selection: *diction* (paragraph 3), *scrimping* (5), *array* (6), *quintessentially* (9), *elocution* (10), *inculcated* (11), and *concede* (12).

Questions About the Writer's Craft

1. **The pattern.** Raspberry is primarily concerned with showing how limited the definition of *black* has come to be in our society. In the course of the essay, though, he also defines three other terms. Locate these terms and their definitions. How do the definitions and the effects of the

definitions help Raspberry make his point about the narrowness of the term *black*?

2. **Other patterns.** In his opening paragraph, Raspberry uses the argumentation technique of refutation. What does he refute? What does he achieve by using this strategy at the very beginning of the essay?

3. A Black journalist, Raspberry writes a nationally syndicated column that originates in the *Washington Post,* a major newspaper serving the nation's capital and the nation as a whole. Consider these facts when examining Raspberry's use of the pronouns *I, we,* and *our* in the essay. What do these pronouns seem to imply about Raspberry's intended audience? What is the effect of these pronouns?

4. Raspberry has chosen a relatively abstract topic to write about—the meaning of the term *black.* What techniques does he use to draw in readers and keep them engaged? Consider his overall tone, choice of examples, and use of balanced sentence structure.

Writing Assignments Using Definition as a Pattern of Development

1. Raspberry points out how restrictive the definitions of *black* and *white* can be. Do you think that the definitions of *male* and *female* can be equally restrictive? Focusing on the term *male* or *female,* write an essay showing how the term was defined as you were growing up. Considering the messages conveyed by your family, the educational system, and society at large, indicate whether you came to perceive the term as limiting or liberating. Before planning your paper, you may want to read one or more of the following essays, all of which deal with the way gender roles influence behavior: Barbara Ehrenreich's "What I've Learned From Men" (page 196), Deborah Tannen's "But What Do You Mean?" (page 241), and Dave Barry's "The Ugly Truth About Beauty" (page 323).

2. In paragraph 15, Raspberry seems to define *success* as "making it in the American mainstream," but not everyone would agree that this is what constitutes success. Write an essay in which you offer your personal definition of *success.* One way to proceed might be to contrast what you consider success with what you consider failure. Or you might narrate the success story of a person you respect highly. No matter how you proceed, be sure to provide telling specifics that support your definition.

Writing Assignments Using Other Patterns of Development

3. Like most people, you've probably had a "defining" term applied to you at one time or another. Perhaps you've been called "shy" or "stubborn" or "the class clown" or "the athlete in the family." Focusing on one such label that's been applied to you, write an essay showing the effect of this

term on your life. Be sure to explain why you got the label and how you felt about it. The following essay will give you an additional perspective on the ways that labels and names affect people's lives and self-image: Shelby Steele's "Affirmative Action: The Price of Preference" (page 475).

4. In his conclusion, Raspberry makes a plea for providing the younger generation with a more positive, more expansive definition of *black*. Consider the beliefs and principles that today's older generation seems to impart to the younger generation. Write an essay showing which aspects of this value system seem helpful and valid and which do not. Also explain what additional values and convictions the older generation should be passing on. How should parents, teachers, and others convey these precepts? For a discussion of some obstacles to children's moral instruction, read Ellen Goodman's "Family Counterculture" (page 6).

Writing Assignments Using a Journal Entry as a Starting Point

5. Developing the material in your pre-reading journal entry, write an essay arguing that an individual's innate talent *or* self-confidence is the critical factor in determining achievement. Consider brainstorming with others to generate examples in support of your contention. At some point in the essay, you should acknowledge the opposing viewpoint, dismantling as much of it as you can.

Additional Writing Topics

DEFINITION

General Assignments

Use definition to develop any of the following topics. Once you fix on a limited subject, decide if the essay has an informative or a persuasive purpose. The paper might begin with the etymology of the term, a stipulative definition, or a definition by negation. You may want to use a number of writing patterns—such as description, comparison, narration, process analysis—to develop the definition. Remember, too, that the paper doesn't have to be scholarly and serious. There is no reason it can't be a lighthearted discussion of the meaning of a term.

1. Fads
2. A family fight
3. Helplessness
4. An epiphany
5. A workaholic
6. A Pollyanna
7. A con artist
8. A stingy person
9. A team player
10. A Yiddish term like *mensch, klutz, chutzpah,* or *dreck,* or a term from some other ethnic group
11. Adolescence
12. Fast food
13. A perfect day
14. Hypocrisy
15. Inner peace
16. Obsession
17. Generosity
18. Exploitation
19. Depression
20. A double bind

Assignments With a Specific Purpose and Audience

1. *Newsweek* magazine runs a popular column called "My Turn," consisting of readers' opinions on subjects of general interest. Write a piece for this column defining *today's college students.* Use the piece to dispel some negative stereotypes (for example, that college students are apathetic, ill-informed, self-centered, and materialistic).

2. You're an attorney arguing a case of sexual harassment—a charge your client has leveled against her boss, a business executive. To win the case, you must present to the jury a clear definition of exactly what *sexual harassment* is and isn't. Write such a definition for your opening remarks in court.

3. You have been asked to write part of a pamphlet for students who come to the college health clinic. For this pamphlet, define *one* of the following conditions and its symptoms: *depression, stress, burnout, test anxiety, addiction* (to alcohol, drugs, or TV), *workaholism*. Part of the pamphlet should describe ways to cope with the condition described.

4. A new position has opened in your company. Write a job description to be sent to employment agencies that will screen candidates. Your description should define the job's purpose, state the duties involved, and outline essential qualifications.

5. Part of your job as peer counselor in your college's counseling center involves helping people communicate more effectively. To assist students, write a definition of some term that you think represents an essential component of a strong interpersonal relationship. You might, for example, define *respect, sharing, equality,* or *trust.* Part of the definition should employ definition by negation, a discussion of what the term is *not.*

6. Having waited on tables for several years at a resort hotel, you've been asked by the hotel manager to give some pointers to this year's new dining hall staff. Prepare a talk in which you define *courtesy,* the quality you consider most essential to the job. Use specific examples to illustrate your definition.

11

ARGUMENTATION-PERSUASION

WHAT IS ARGUMENTATION-PERSUASION?

"You can't possibly believe what you're saying."
"Look, I know what I'm talking about, and that's that."

Does this heated exchange sound familiar? Probably. When we hear the word *argument,* most of us think of a verbal battle propelled by stubbornness and irrational thought, with one person pitted against the other.

Argumentation in writing, though, is a different matter. Using clear thinking and logic, the writer tries to convince readers of the soundness of a particular opinion on a controversial issue. If, while trying to convince, the writer uses emotional language and dramatic appeals to readers' concerns, beliefs, and values, then the piece is called *persuasion.* Besides encouraging acceptance of an opinion, persuasion often urges readers (or another group) to commit themselves to a course of action. Assume you're writing an essay protesting the federal government's policy of offering aid to those suffering from hunger in other countries while many Americans go hungry. If your purpose is to document, coolly and objectively, the presence of hunger in the United States, you would prepare an argumentation essay. Such an essay would be filled with statistics, report findings, and expert opinion to demonstrate how widespread hunger is nationwide. If, however, your purpose is to shake up readers, even motivate them to write letters to their congressional representatives and push for a change in policy, you would write a persuasive essay. In this case, your essay might contain emotional accounts of undernourished children, ill-fed pregnant women, and nearly starving elderly people.

Because people respond rationally *and* emotionally to situations, argumentation and persuasion are usually *combined*. Suppose you decide to write an article for the campus newspaper advocating a pre-Labor Day start for the school year. Your audience includes the college administration, students, and faculty. The article might begin by *arguing* that several schools starting the academic year earlier were able to close for the month of January and thus reduce heating and other maintenance expenses. Such an argument, supported by documented facts and figures, would help convince the administration. Realizing that you also have to gain student and faculty support for your idea, you might argue further that the proposed change would mean that students and faculty could leave for winter break with the semester behind them—papers written, exams taken, grades calculated and recorded. To make this part of your argument especially compelling, you could adopt a *persuasive* strategy by using emotional appeals and positively charged language: "Think how pleasant it would be to sleep late, spend time with family and friends, toast the New Year—without having to worry about work awaiting you back on campus."

When argumentation and persuasion blend in this way, emotion *supports* rather than *replaces* logic and sound reasoning. Although some writers resort to emotional appeals to the exclusion of rational thought, when you prepare argumentation-persuasion essays, you should advance your position through a balanced appeal to reason and emotion.

HOW ARGUMENTATION-PERSUASION FITS YOUR PURPOSE AND AUDIENCE

You probably realize that argumentation, persuasion, or a combination of the two is everywhere: an editorial urging the overhaul of an ill-managed literacy program; a commercial for a new shampoo; a scientific report advocating increased funding for AIDS research. Your own writing involves argumentation-persuasion as well. When you prepare a *causal analysis, descriptive piece, narrative,* or *definition essay,* you advance a specific point of view: MTV has a negative influence on teens' view of sex; Cape Cod in winter is imbued with a special kind of magic; a disillusioning experience can teach people much about themselves; *character* can be defined as the willingness to take unpopular positions on difficult issues. Indeed, an essay organized around any of the patterns of development described in this book may have a persuasive intent. You might, for example, encourage readers to try out a *process* you've explained, or to see one of the two movies you've *compared.*

Argumentation-persuasion, however, involves more than presenting a point of view and providing evidence. Unlike other forms of writing, it assumes controversy and addresses opposing viewpoints. Consider the following assignments, all of which require the writer to take a position on a controversial issue:

> In parts of the country, communities established for older citizens or childless couples have refused to rent to families with children. How do you feel about this situation? What do you think are the rights of the parties involved?

> Citing the fact that the highest percentage of automobile accidents involve young men, insurance companies consistently charge their highest rates to young males. Is this policy fair? Why or why not?

> Some colleges and universities have instituted a "no pass, no play" policy for athletes. Explain why this practice is or is not appropriate.

It's impossible to predict with absolute certainty what will make readers accept the view you advance or take the action you propose. But the ancient Greeks, who formulated our basic concepts of logic, isolated three factors crucial to the effectiveness of argumentation-persuasion: *logos, pathos,* and *ethos.*

Your main concern in an argumentation-persuasion essay should be with the *logos,* or soundness, of your argument: the facts, statistics, examples, and authoritative statements you gather to support your viewpoint. This supporting evidence must be unified, specific, adequate, accurate, and representative (see pages 38–43). Imagine, for instance, you want to convince people that a popular charity misappropriates the money it receives from the public. Your readers, inclined to believe in the good works of the charity, will probably dismiss your argument unless you can substantiate your claim with valid, well-documented evidence that enhances the *logos* of your position.

Sensitivity to *pathos,* or the emotional power of language, is another key consideration for writers of argumentation-persuasion essays. *Pathos* appeals to readers' needs, values, and attitudes, encouraging them to commit themselves to a viewpoint or course of action. The *pathos* of a piece derives partly from the writer's language. *Connotative* language—words with strong emotional overtones—can move readers to accept a point of view and may even spur them to act.

Advertising and propaganda generally rely on *pathos* to the exclusion of logic, using emotion to influence and manipulate. Consider the following pitches for a man's cologne and a woman's perfume. The language—and the attitudes to which it appeals—is different in each case:

> Brawn: Experience the power. Bold. Yet subtle. Clean. Masculine. The scent for the man who's in charge.

> Black Lace is for you—the woman who dresses for success but who dares to be provocative, slightly naughty. Black Lace. Perfect with pearls by day and with diamonds by night.

The appeal to men plays on the impact that words like *Brawn, bold, power,* and *in charge* may have for some males. Similarly, the charged words *Black Lace, provocative, naughty,* and *diamonds* are intended to appeal to businesswomen who—in the advertiser's mind, at least—may be looking for ways to reconcile sensuality and professionalism. (For more on slanted language, read Ann McClintock's "Propaganda Techniques in Today's Advertising," page 232.)

Like an advertising copywriter, you must select language that reinforces your message. In a paper supporting an expanded immigration policy, you might use evocative phrases like "land of liberty," "a nation of immigrants," and "America's open-door policy." However, if you were arguing for strict immigration quotas, you might use language like "save jobs for unemployed Americans," "flood of unskilled labor," and "illegal aliens." Remember, though: Such language should support, not supplant, clear thinking.

Finally, whenever you write an argumentation-persuasion essay, you should establish your *ethos,* or credibility and integrity. You cannot expect readers to accept or act on your viewpoint unless you convince them that you know what you're talking about and that you're worth listening to. Be sure, then, to tell readers about any experiences you've had that make you knowledgeable about the issue being discussed. You will also come across as knowledgeable and trustworthy if you present a logical, reasoned argument that takes opposing views into account. And make sure that your appeals to emotion aren't excessive. Overwrought emotionalism undercuts credibility. Remember, too, that *ethos* isn't constant. A writer may have credibility on one subject but not on another: An army general might be a reliable source for information on military preparedness but not for information on federal funding of day care.

Writing an effective argumentation-persuasion essay involves an interplay of *logos, pathos,* and *ethos.* The exact balance among these factors is determined by your audience and purpose (that is, whether you want the audience simply to agree with your view or whether you also want them to take action). More than any other kind of writing, argumentation-persuasion requires that you *analyze your readers* and tailor your approach to them. You need to determine how much they know about the issue, how they feel about you and your position, what their values and attitudes are, what motivates them.

In general, most readers will fall into one of three broad categories: supportive, wavering, or hostile. Each type of audience requires a different blend of *logos, pathos,* and *ethos* in an argumentation-persuasion essay.

1. A supportive audience. If your audience agrees with your position and trusts your credibility, you don't need a highly reasoned argument dense with facts, examples, and statistics. Although you may want to solidify support by providing additional information (*logos*), you can rely primarily on *pathos*—a strong emotional appeal—to reinforce readers' commitment to your shared viewpoint. Assume that you belong to a local fishing club and have volunteered to write an article encouraging members to support threatened fishing rights in state parks. You might begin by stating that fishing strengthens the fish population by thinning out over-crowded streams. Since your audience would certainly be familiar with this idea, you wouldn't need to devote much discussion to it. Instead, you would attempt to move them emotionally. You might evoke the camaraderie in the sport, the pleasure of a perfect cast, the beauty of the outdoors, and perhaps conclude with "If you want these enjoyments to continue, please make a generous contribution to our fund."

2. A wavering audience.   At times, readers may be open to what you have to say but may not be committed fully to your viewpoint. Or perhaps they're not as informed about the subject as they should be. In either case, you don't want to risk alienating them with a heavy-handed emotional appeal. Concentrate instead on *ethos* and *logos,* bolstering your image as a reliable source and providing the evidence needed to advance your position. If you want to convince an audience of high school seniors to take a year off to work between high school and college, you might establish your credibil-ity by recounting the year you spent working and by showing the positive effects it had on your life (*ethos*). In addition, you could cite studies indicating that delayed entry into college is related to high-er grade point averages. A year's savings, you would explain, allows students to study when they might otherwise need to hold down a job to earn money for tuition (*logos*).

3. A hostile audience.   An apathetic, skeptical, or hostile audi-ence is obviously most difficult to convince. With such an audience, you should avoid emotional appeals because they might seem irra-tional, sentimental, or even comical. Instead, weigh the essay heavi-ly in favor of logical reasoning and hard-to-dispute facts (*logos*). Assume your college administration is working to ban liquor from the student pub. You plan to submit to the campus newspaper an open letter supporting this generally unpopular effort. To sway other students, you cite the positive experiences of schools that have gone dry. Many colleges, you explain, have found their tavern rev-enues actually increase because all students—not just those of drink-ing age—can now support the pub. With the greater revenues, some schools have upgraded the food served in the pubs and have hired disc jockeys or musical groups to provide entertainment. Many schools have also seen a sharp reduction in alcohol-related vandalism. Readers may not be won over to your side, but your sound, logical argument may encourage them to be more tolerant of your viewpoint. Indeed, such increased receptivity may be all you can reasonably expect from a hostile audience. (For more help in analyzing your audience, see pages 19–20.)

SUGGESTIONS FOR USING ARGUMENTATION-PERSUASION IN AN ESSAY

1. At the beginning of the paper, identify the controversy surrounding the issue and state your position in the thesis. Your introduction should clarify the controversy about the issue. In addition, it should provide as much background information as your readers are likely to need.

The thesis of an argumentation-persuasion paper is often called the *assertion* or *proposition*. Occasionally, the proposition appears at the paper's end, but it is usually stated at the beginning. If you state the thesis right away, your audience knows where you stand and is better able to evaluate the evidence presented.

Remember: Argumentation-persuasion assumes conflicting viewpoints. Be sure your proposition focuses on a controversial issue and indicates your view. Avoid a proposition that is merely factual; what is demonstrably true allows little room for debate. To see the difference between a factual statement and an effective thesis, examine the two statements that follow:

> *Fact:* In the past decade, the nation's small farmers have suffered financial hardships.

> *Thesis:* Inefficient management, rather than competition from agricultural conglomerates, is responsible for the financial plight of the nation's small farmers.

The first statement is certainly true. It would be difficult to find anyone who believes that these are easy times for small farmers. Because the statement invites little opposition, it can't serve as the focus of an argumentation-persuasion essay. The second statement, though, takes a controversial stance on a complex issue. Such a proposition is a valid starting point for a paper intended to argue and persuade. However, don't assume that such advice means that you should take a highly opinionated position in your thesis. A dogmatic, overstated proposition ("Campus security is staffed by overpaid, badge-flashing incompetents") is bound to alienate some readers.

Remember also to keep the proposition narrow and specific, so you can focus your thoughts in a purposeful way. Consider the following statements:

> *Broad thesis:* The welfare system has been abused over the years.

> *Narrow thesis:* Welfare payments should be denied to unmarried teenage girls who have more than one child out of wedlock.

If you tried to write a paper based on the first statement, you would face an unmanageable task—showing all the ways that welfare has been abused. Your readers would also be confused about what to expect in the paper: Will it discuss unscrupulous bureaucrats, fraudulent bookkeeping, dishonest recipients? In contrast, the revised thesis is limited and specific. It signals that the paper will propose severe restrictions on welfare payments. Such a proposal will surely have opponents and is thus appropriate for argumentation-persuasion.

The thesis in an argumentation-persuasion essay can simply state your opinion about an issue, or it can go a step further and call for some action:

> *Opinion:* The lack of affordable day care centers discriminates against lower-income families.

> *Call for action:* The federal government should support the creation of more day care centers in low-income neighborhoods.

In either case, your stand on the issue must be clear to your readers.

2. Provide readers with strong support for the thesis. Finding evidence that relates to the readers' needs, values, and experience is a crucial part of writing an effective argumentation-persuasion essay. Readers will be responsive to evidence that is *unified, adequate,* *specific, accurate,* and *representative* (see pages 38–43). It might consist of personal experiences or observations. Or it could be gathered from outside sources—statistics; facts; examples; or expert authority taken from books, articles, reports, interviews, and documentaries. A paper arguing that elderly Americans are better off than they used to be might incorporate the following kinds of evidence:

- *Personal observation or experience:* A description of the writer's grandparents who are living comfortably on Social Security and pensions.
- *Statistics from a report:* A statement that the per capita after-tax income of older Americans is $335 greater than the national average.
- *Fact from a newspaper article:* The point that the majority of elderly Americans do not live in nursing homes or on the streets; rather, they have their own houses or apartments.
- *Examples from interviews:* Accounts of several elderly couples living comfortably in well-managed retirement villages in Florida.
- *Expert opinion cited in a documentary:* A statement by Dr. Marie Sanchez, a specialist in geriatrics: "An over-sixty-five American today is likely to be healthier, and have a longer life expectancy, than a fifty-year-old living only a decade ago."

As you seek outside evidence, you may—perhaps to your dismay—come across information that undercuts your argument. Resist the temptation to ignore such material; instead, use the evidence to arrive at a more balanced, perhaps somewhat qualified viewpoint. Conversely, don't blindly accept points made by sources agreeing with you. Retain a healthy skepticism, analyzing the material as rigorously as if it were advanced by the opposing side.

Also, keep in mind that outside sources aren't infallible. They may have biases that cause them to skew evidence. So be sure to evaluate your sources. If you're writing an essay supporting a woman's right to abortion, the National Abortion Rights Action League (NARAL) can supply abundant statistics, case studies, and reports. But realize that NARAL most likely won't give you the complete picture; it will probably present evidence that supports its "pro-choice" position only. To counteract such bias, you should review what those with differing opinions have to say. You should, for example, examine material published by such "pro-life" organizations as the National Right-to-Life Committee—keeping in mind, of course, that this material is also bound to present support for its viewpoint only. Remember, too, that there are more than two sides to a complex issue. To get as broad a perspective as possible, you should also track down sources that have no axe to grind—that is, sources that make a deliberate effort to examine all sides of the issue. For example, published proceedings from a debate on abortion or an in-depth article that aims to synthesize various views on abortion would broaden your understanding of this controversial subject.

Whatever sources you use, be sure to *document* (give credit to) that material. Otherwise, readers may dismiss your evidence as nothing more than your subjective opinion, or they may conclude that you have *plagiarized*—tried to pass off someone else's ideas as your own. (Documentation isn't necessary when material is commonly known or is a matter of historical or scientific record.) In brief informal papers, documentation may consist of simple citations like "Psychologist Aaron Beck believes depression is the result of distorted thoughts" or "*Time* (Dec. 4, 2000) reports a decline in the enrollment of male students in colleges across the country." In longer, more formal papers, documentation is more detailed (see the Appendix, "A Concise Guide to Finding and Documenting Sources"). One additional point: Because documentation lends a note of objectivity to writing, it may not be appropriate in a paper that cites sources to use the first-person point of view ("I, like many college students, agree with the government report that . . ."). To be on the safe side, check with your instructor to see if you should use the third-person point of view ("Many college students agree with the government report that . . .") instead.

3. Seek to create goodwill.   To avoid alienating readers with views different from your own, stay away from condescending expressions like "Anyone can see that . . ." or "It's obvious that . . ." Also, guard against personalizing the debate and being confrontational: "*My opponents* find the law ineffective" sounds adversarial, whereas "*Those opposed* to the law find it ineffective" or "*Opponents* of the law find it ineffective" is more evenhanded. The last two statements also focus—as they should—on the issue, not on the people involved in the debate.

Goodwill can also be established by finding a *common ground*— some points on which all sides can agree, despite their differences.

Assume a township council has voted to raise property taxes. The additional revenues will be used to preserve, as parkland, a wooded area that would otherwise be sold to developers. Before introducing its tax-hike proposal, the council would do well to remind homeowners of everyone's shared goals: maintaining the town's beauty and preventing the community's overdevelopment. This reminder of the common values shared by the town council and homeowners will probably make residents more receptive to the tax hike. (For more on establishing common ground, see pages 412–14.)

4. Organize the supporting evidence.   The support for an argumentation-persuasion paper can be organized in a variety of ways. Any of the patterns of development described in this book (description, narration, definition, causal analysis, and so on) may be used— singly or in combination—to develop the essay's proposition. Imagine you're writing a paper arguing that car racing should be banned from television. Your essay might contain a *description* of a horrifying accident that was televised in graphic detail; you might devote part of the paper to a *causal analysis* showing that the broadcast of such races encourages teens to drive carelessly; you could include a *process analysis* to explain how young drivers "soup up" their cars in a dangerous attempt to imitate the racers seen on television. If your essay includes several patterns, you may need a separate paragraph for each.

When presenting evidence, arrange it so you create the strongest possible effect. In general, you should end with your most compelling point, leaving readers with dramatic evidence that underscores your proposition's validity.

5. Use Rogerian strategy to acknowledge differing viewpoints.   If your essay has a clear thesis and strong logical support, you've taken important steps toward winning readers over. However, because argumentation-persuasion focuses on controversial issues, you should also consider contrary points of view. A good argument seeks out and acknowledges conflicting viewpoints. Such a strategy strengthens your argument in several ways. It helps you anticipate objections, alerts you to flaws in your own position, and makes you more aware of the other sides' weaknesses. Further, by acknowledging dissenting views, you come across as reasonable and thorough—qualities that may disarm readers and leave them more receptive to your argument. You may not convince them to surrender their views, but you can enlarge their perspectives and encourage them to think about your position.

Psychologist Carl Rogers took the idea of acknowledging contrary viewpoints a step further. He believed that argumentation's goal should be to *reduce conflict,* rather than to produce a "winner" and a "loser." But he recognized that people identify so strongly with their opinions that they experience any challenge to those opinions as highly threatening. Such a challenge feels like an attack on their very identity. And what's the characteristic response to such a perceived attack? People become defensive; they dig in their heels and become more adamant than ever about their position. Indeed, when confronted with solid information that calls their opinion into question, they devalue that evidence rather than allow themselves to be persuaded. The old maxim about the power of first impressions demonstrates this point. Experiments show that after people form a first impression of another person, they are unlikely to let future conflicting information affect that impression. If, for example, they initially perceive someone to be unpleasant and disagreeable, they tend to reject subsequent evidence that casts the person in a more favorable light.

Taking into account this tendency to cling tenaciously to opinions in the face of a challenge, Rogerian strategy rejects the adversarial approach that often characterizes argumentation. It adopts, instead, a respectful, conciliatory posture—one that demonstrates a real understanding of opposing views, one that emphasizes shared interests and values. Such an approach makes it easier to negotiate differences and arrive at—ideally—a synthesis: a new position that both parties find at least as acceptable as their original positions.

How can you apply Rogerian strategy in your writing? Simply follow these steps:

- Begin by making a conscientious effort to *understand* the viewpoints of those with whom you disagree. As you listen to or read about their opinions, try to put yourself in their shoes; focus on *what they believe* and *why they believe* it, rather than on how you will challenge their beliefs.
- Open your essay with an unbiased, even-handed *restatement of opposing points of view.* Such an objective summary shows that you're fair and open-minded—and not so blinded by the righteousness of your own position that you can't consider any other. Typically, people respond to such a respectful

approach by lowering their defenses. Because they appreciate your ability to understand what they have to say, they become more open to your point of view.

- When appropriate, *acknowledge the validity* of some of the arguments raised by those with differing views. What should you do if they make a well-founded point? You'll enhance your credibility if you concede that point while continuing to maintain that, overall, your position is stronger.
- Point out areas of *common ground* (see pages 410–11) by focusing on interests, values, and beliefs that you and those with opposing views share. When you say to them, "Look at the beliefs we share. Look at our common concerns," you communicate that you're not as unlike them as they first believed.
- Finally, *present evidence* for your position. Since those not agreeing with you have been "softened up" by your non-combative stance and disarmed by the realization that you and they share some values and beliefs, they're more ready to consider your point of view.

Let's consider, more specifically, how you might draw upon essentially Rogerian strategy when writing an argumentation-persuasion essay. In the following paragraphs, we discuss three basic strategies. As you read about each strategy, keep in mind this key point: The earlier you acknowledge alternate viewpoints, the more effective your argument will be. Establishing—right at the outset—your awareness of opposing positions shows you to be fair-minded and helps reduce resistance to what you have to say.

First, you may acknowledge the opposing viewpoint in a two-part proposition consisting of a subordinate clause followed by a main clause. The *first part of the proposition* (the subordinate clause) *acknowledges opposing opinions;* the *second part* (the main clause) *states your opinion* and implies that your view stands on more solid ground. (When using this kind of proposition, you may, but don't have to, discuss opposing opinions.) The following thesis illustrates this strategy (the opposing viewpoint is underlined once; the writer's position is underlined twice):

Although some instructors think that standardized finals restrict academic freedom, such exams are preferable to those prepared by individual professors.

Second, *in the introduction,* you may provide—separate from the proposition—a *one- or two-sentence summary of the opposing viewpoint.* Suppose you're writing an essay advocating a ten-day waiting period before an individual can purchase a handgun. Before presenting your proposition at the end of the introductory paragraph, you might include sentences like these: "Opponents of the waiting period argue that the ten-day delay is worthless without a nationwide computer network that can perform background checks. Those opposed also point out that only a percentage of states with a waiting period have seen a reduction in gun-related crime."

Third, you can take *one or two body paragraphs* near the beginning of the essay to *present in greater detail arguments raised by opposing viewpoints.* After that, you *grant* (when appropriate) the validity of some of those points ("It may be true that . . . ," "Granted, . . ."). Then you go on to *present evidence* for your position ("Even so . . . ," "Nevertheless . . ."). Imagine you're preparing an editorial for your student newspaper arguing that fraternities and sororities on your campus should be banned. Realizing that many students don't agree with you, you "research" the opposing viewpoint by seeking out supporters of Greek organizations and listening respectfully to the points they raise. When it comes time to write the editorial, you decide not to begin with arguments for your position; instead, you start by summarizing the points made by those supporting fraternities and sororities. You might, for example, mention their argument that Greek organizations build college spirit, contribute to worthy community causes, and provide valuable contacts for entry into the business world. Following this summary of the opposing viewpoint, you might concede that the point about the Greeks' contributions to community causes is especially valid; you could then reinforce this conciliatory stance by stressing some common ground you share—perhaps you acknowledge that you share your detractors' belief that enjoyable social activities with like-minded people are an important part of campus life. Having done all that, you would be in a good position to present arguments why you nevertheless think fraternities and sororities should be banned. Because you prepared readers to listen to your opinion, they would tend to be more receptive to your argument.

6. Refute differing viewpoints.   There will be times, though, that acknowledging opposing viewpoints and presenting your own case won't be enough. Particularly when an issue is complex and when readers strongly disagree with your position, you may have to refute all or part of the *dissenting views*. *Refutation* means pointing out the problems with opposing viewpoints, thereby highlighting your own position's superiority. You may focus on the opposing sides' inaccurate or inadequate evidence, or you may point to their faulty logic. (Some common types of illogical thinking are discussed on pages 417, 419–20, and 423–26.)

Let's consider how you could refute a competing position in an essay you're writing that supports sex education in public schools. Adapting the Rogerian approach to suit your purposes, you might start by acknowledging the opposing viewpoint's key argument: "Sex education should be the prerogative of parents." After granting the validity of this view in an ideal world, you might show that many parents don't provide such education. You could present statistics on the number of parents who avoid discussing sex with their children because the subject makes them uncomfortable; you could cite studies revealing that children in single-parent homes are apt to receive even less parental guidance about sex; and you could give examples of young people whose parents provided sketchy, even misleading information.

There are various ways to develop a paper's refutation section. The best method to use depends on the paper's length and the complexity of the issue. Two possible sequences are outlined here:

First Strategy	**Second Strategy**
• State your proposition.	• State your proposition.
• Cite opposing viewpoints and the evidence for those views.	• Cite opposing viewpoints and the evidence for those views.
• Refute opposing viewpoints by presenting counterarguments.	• Refute opposing viewpoints by presenting counterarguments.
	• Present additional evidence for your proposition.

In the first strategy, you simply refute all or part of the opposing positions' arguments. The second strategy takes the first one a step further by presenting *additional evidence* to support your proposition. In such a case, the additional evidence *must be different* from the points made in the refutation. The additional evidence may appear at the essay's end (as in the preceding outline), or it may be given near the beginning (after the proposition); it may also be divided between the beginning and end.

No matter which strategy you select, you may refute opposing views *one side at a time* or *one point at a time.* When using the one-side-at-a-time approach, you cite all the points raised by the opposing side and then present your counterargument to each point. When using the one-point-at-a-time strategy, you mention the first point made by the opposing side, refute that point, then move on to the second point and refute that, and so on. (For more on comparing and contrasting the sides of an issue, see pages 298–303.)

Throughout the essay, be sure to provide clear signals so that readers can distinguish your arguments from the other side's: "Despite the claims of those opposed to the plan, many think that . . ." and "Those not in agreement think that. . . ."

7. Use induction or deduction to think logically about your argument.   The line of reasoning used to develop an argument is the surest indicator of how rigorously you have thought through your position. There are two basic ways to think about a subject: *inductively* and *deductively.* Though the following discussion treats induction and deduction as separate processes, the two often overlap and complement each other.

Inductive reasoning involves examination of specific cases, facts, or examples. Based on these specifics, you then draw a conclusion or make a generalization. This is the kind of thinking scientists use when they examine evidence (the results of experiments, for example) and then draw a *conclusion:* "Smoking increases the risk of cancer." All of us use inductive reasoning in everyday life. We might think the following: "My head is aching" (evidence); "My nose is stuffy" (evidence); "I'm coming down with a cold" (conclusion). Based on the conclusion, we might go a step further and take some action: "I'll take an aspirin."

With inductive reasoning, the conclusion reached can serve as the proposition for an argumentation essay. (Of course, the essay will most likely include elements of persuasion since strict argumentation—with no appeal to emotions—is uncommon.) If the paper advances a course of action, the proposition often mentions the action, signaling an essay with a distinctly persuasive purpose.

Let's suppose that you're writing a paper about a crime wave in the small town where you live. You might use inductive thinking to structure the essay's argument:

Several people were mugged last month while shopping in the center of town. (*evidence*)

Several homes and apartments were burglarized in the past few weeks. (*evidence*)

Several cars were stolen from people's driveways over the weekend. (*evidence*)

The police force hasn't adequately protected town residents. (*conclusion, or proposition, for an argumentation essay with probable elements of persuasion*)

The police force should take steps to upgrade its protection of town residents. (*conclusion, or proposition, for an argumentation essay with a clearly persuasive intent*)

This inductive sequence highlights a possible structure for the essay. After providing a clear statement of your proposition, you might detail recent muggings, burglaries, and car thefts. Then you could move to the opposing viewpoint: a description of the steps the police say they have taken to protect town residents. At that point, you would refute the police's claim, citing additional evidence that shows the measures taken have not been sufficient. Finally, if you wanted your essay to have a decidedly persuasive purpose, you could end by recommending specific action the police should take to improve its protection of the community.

As in all essays, your evidence should be *specific, unified, adequate,* and *representative* (see pages 38–43). These last two characteristics are critical when you think inductively; they guarantee that your conclusion would be equally valid even if other evidence were presented. Insufficient or atypical evidence often leads to *hasty generalizations* that mar the essay's logic. For example, you might think the following: "Some elderly people are very wealthy and do not need Social Security checks" (evidence), and "Some Social Security recipients illegally collect several checks" (evidence). If you then conclude, "Social Security is a waste of taxpayers' money," your conclusion is invalid and hasty because it's based on only a few atypical examples. Millions of Social Security recipients aren't wealthy and don't abuse the system. If you've failed to consider the full range of evidence, any action you propose ("The Social Security system should be disbanded") will probably be considered suspect by thoughtful readers. It's possible, of course, that Social Security should be disbanded, but the evidence leading to such a conclusion must be sufficient and representative.

When reasoning inductively, you should also be careful that the evidence you collect is both *recent* and *accurate*. No valid conclusion can result from dated or erroneous evidence. To ensure that your evidence is sound, you also need to evaluate the reliability of your sources. When a person who is legally drunk claims to have seen a flying saucer, the evidence is shaky, to say the least. But if two respected scientists, both with 20/20 vision, saw the saucer, their evidence is worth considering.

Finally, it's important to realize that there's always an element of uncertainty in inductive reasoning. The conclusion can never be more than an *inference*, involving what logicians call an *inductive leap*. There could be other explanations for the evidence cited and thus other positions to take and actions to advocate. For example, given a small town's crime wave, you might conclude not that the police force has been remiss but that residents are careless about protecting themselves and their property. In turn, you might call for a different kind of action—perhaps that the police conduct public workshops in self-defense and home security. In an inductive argument, your task is to weigh the evidence, consider alternative explanations, then choose the conclusion and course of action that seem most valid.

Unlike inductive reasoning, which starts with a specific case and moves toward a generalization or conclusion, *deductive reasoning* begins with a generalization that is then applied to a specific case. This movement from general to specific involves a three-step form of reasoning called a *syllogism*. The first part of a syllogism is called the *major premise,* a general statement about an entire group. The second part is the *minor premise,* a statement about an individual within that group. The syllogism ends with a *conclusion* about that individual.

Just as you use inductive thinking in everyday life, you use deductive thinking—often without being aware of it—to sort out your experiences. When trying to decide which car to buy, you might think as follows:

> *Major premise:* In an accident, large cars are safer than small cars.
>
> *Minor premise:* The Turbo Titan is a large car.
>
> *Conclusion:* In an accident, the Turbo Titan will be safer than a small car.

Based on your conclusion, you might decide to take a specific action, buying the Turbo Titan rather than the small car you had first considered.

To create a valid syllogism and thus arrive at a sound conclusion, you need to avoid two major pitfalls of deductive reasoning. First, be sure not to start with a *hasty generalization* (see page 417) as your *major premise*. Second, don't accept as truth a *faulty conclusion*. Let's look at each problem.

Sweeping major premise.   Perhaps you're concerned about a trash-to-steam incinerator scheduled to open near your home. Your thinking about the situation might follow these lines:

Major premise:	Trash-to-steam incinerators have had serious problems and pose significant threats to the well-being of people living near the plants.
Minor premise:	The proposed incinerator in my neighborhood will be a trash-to-steam plant.
Conclusion:	The proposed trash-to-steam incinerator in my neighborhood will have serious problems and pose significant threats to the well-being of people living near the plant.

Having arrived at this conclusion, you might decide to join organized protests against the opening of the incinerator. But your thinking is somewhat illogical. Your *major premise* is a *sweeping* one because it indiscriminately groups all trash-to-steam plants into a single category. It's unlikely that you're familiar with the operations of all trash-to-steam incinerators in this country and abroad; it's probably not true that *all* such plants have had serious difficulties that endangered the public. For your argument to reach a valid conclusion, the major premise must be based on repeated observations or verifiable facts. You would have a better argument, and thus reach a more valid conclusion, if you restricted or qualified the major premise, applying it to some, not all, of the group:

Major premise:	A number of trash-to-steam incinerators have had serious problems and posed significant threats to the well-being of people living near the plants.
Minor premise:	The proposed incinerator in my neighborhood will be a trash-to-steam plant.
Conclusion:	It's possible that the proposed trash-to-steam incinerator in my neighborhood will run into serious problems and pose significant threats to the well-being of people living near the plant.

This new conclusion, the result of more careful reasoning, would probably encourage you to learn more about trash-to-steam incinerators in general and about the proposed plant in particular. If further research still left you feeling uncomfortable about the plant, you would probably decide to join the protest. On the other hand, your research might convince you that the plant has incorporated into its design a number of safeguards that have been successful at other plants. This added information could reassure you that your original fears were unfounded. In either case, the revised deductive process would lead to a more informed conclusion and course of action.

Faulty conclusion.   Your syllogism—and thus your reasoning—would also be invalid if your *conclusion reverses the "if . . . then" relationship implied in the major premise.* Assume you plan to write a letter to the college newspaper urging the resignation of the student government president. Perhaps you pursue a line of reasoning that goes like this:

Major premise:	Students who plagiarize papers must appear before the Faculty Committee on Academic Policies and Procedures.
Minor premise:	Yesterday, Jennifer Kramer, president of the student government, appeared before the Faculty Committee on Academic Policies and Procedures.
Conclusion:	Jennifer must have plagiarized a paper.
Action:	Jennifer should resign her position as president of the student government.

Such a chain of reasoning is illogical and unfair. Here's why. *If* students plagiarize their papers and are caught, *then* they must appear before the committee. However, the converse isn't necessarily true—that *if* students appear before the committee, *then* they must have plagiarized. In other words, not *all* students appearing before the committee have been called up on plagiarism charges. For example, Jennifer could have been speaking on behalf of another student; she could have been protesting some action taken by the committee; she could have been seeking the committee's help on an article she plans to write about academic honesty. The conclusion doesn't allow for these other possible explanations.

Now that you're aware of potential problems associated with deductive reasoning, let's look at the way you can use a syllogism to structure an argumentation-persuasion essay. Suppose you decide to write a paper advocating support for a projected space mission. You know that controversy surrounds the space program, especially since seven astronauts died in a 1986 launch. Confident that the tragedy has led to more rigorous controls, you want to argue that the benefits of an upcoming mission outweigh its risks. A deductive pattern could be used to develop your argument. In fact, outlining your thinking as a syllogism might help you formulate a proposition, organize your evidence, deal with opposing viewpoints, and—if appropriate—propose a course of action:

Major premise:	Space programs in the past have led to important developments in technology, especially in medical science.
Minor premise:	The Cosmos Mission is the newest space program.
Proposition (essay might be persuasive):	The Cosmos Mission will most likely lead to important developments in technology, especially in medical science.
Proposition (essay clearly is persuasive):	Congress should continue its funding of the Cosmos Mission.

Having outlined the deductive pattern of your thinking, you might begin by stating your proposition and then discuss some new procedures developed to protect the astronauts and the rocket system's structural integrity. With that background established, you could detail the opposing claim that little of value has been produced by the space program so far. You could then move to your refutation, citing significant medical advances derived from former space missions. Finally, the paper might conclude on a persuasive note, with a plea to Congress to continue funding the latest space mission.

8. Use Toulmin logic to establish a strong connection between your evidence and your thesis.   Whether you use an essentially inductive or deductive approach, your argument depends on strong evidence. In *The Uses of Argument,* Stephen Toulmin describes a useful approach for strengthening the connection between evidence and thesis. Toulmin divides a typical argument into three parts:

- **Claim**—The thesis, proposition, or conclusion.
- **Data**—The evidence (facts, statistics, examples, observations, expert opinion) used to convince readers of the claim's validity.
- **Warrant**—The underlying assumption that justifies moving from evidence to claim.

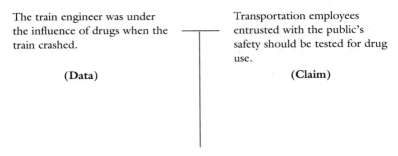

The train engineer was under the influence of drugs when the train crashed.

(Data)

Transportation employees entrusted with the public's safety should be tested for drug use.

(Claim)

Transportation employees entrusted with the public's safety should not be allowed on the job if they use drugs.

(Warrant)

As Toulmin explains in his book, readers are more apt to consider your argument valid if they know what your warrant is. Sometimes your warrant will be so obvious that you won't need to state it explicitly; an *implicit warrant* will be sufficient. Assume you want to argue that the use of live animals to test product toxicity should be outlawed. To support your claim, you cite the following evidence: first, current animal tests are painful and usually result in the animal's death; second, human cell cultures frequently offer more reliable information on how harmful a product may be to human tissue; and third, computer simulations often can more accurately rate a substance's toxicity. Your warrant, although not explicit, is nonetheless clear: "It is wrong to continue product testing on animals when more humane and valid test methods are available."

Other times, you'll do best to make your warrant *explicit*. Suppose you plan to argue that students should be involved in deciding which faculty members are granted tenure. To develop your claim, you present some evidence. You begin by noting that, currently, only faculty members and administrators review candidates for tenure. Next, you call attention to the controversy surrounding two professors, widely known by students to be poor teachers, who were nonetheless granted tenure. Finally, you cite a decision, made several years ago, to discontinue using student evaluations as part of the tenure process; you emphasize that since that time complaints about teachers' incompetence have risen dramatically. Some readers, though, still might wonder how you got from your evidence to your claim. In this case, your argument could be made stronger by stating your warrant explicitly: "Since students are as knowledgeable as the faculty and administrators about which professors are competent, they should be involved in the tenure process."

The more widely accepted your warrant, Toulmin explains, the more likely it is that readers will accept your argument. If there's no consensus about the warrant, you'll probably need to *back it up*. For the preceding example, you might mention several reports that found students evaluate faculty fairly (most students don't, for example, use the ratings to get back at professors against whom they have a personal grudge); further, students' ratings correlate strongly with those given by administrators and other faculty.

Toulmin describes another way to increase receptivity to an argument: *qualify the claim*—that is, explain under what circumstances it might be invalid or restricted. For instance, you might grant that most students know little about their instructors' research activities, scholarly publications, or participation in professional committees. You could, then, qualify your claim this way: "Because students don't have a comprehensive view of their instructors' professional activities, they should be involved in the tenure process but play a less prominent role than faculty and administrators."

As you can see, Toulmin's approach provides strategies for strengthening an argument. So, when prewriting or revising, take a few minutes to ask yourself the following questions:

- What data (*evidence*) should I provide to support my claim (*thesis*)?
- Is my warrant clear? Should I state it explicitly? What backup can I provide to justify my warrant?
- Would qualifying my claim make my argument more convincing?

Your responses to these questions will help you structure a convincing and logical argument.

9. Recognize logical fallacies.   When writing an argumentation-persuasion essay, you need to recognize *logical fallacies* both in your

own argument and in points raised by opposing sides. Work to eliminate such gaps in logic from your own writing and, when they
appear in opposing arguments, try to expose them in your refutation. Logicians have identified many logical fallacies—including the
sweeping or hasty generalization and the faulty conclusion discussed
on pages 417 and 420. Other logical fallacies are described in Ann
McClintock's "Propaganda Techniques in Today's Advertising"
(page 232) and in the paragraphs that follow.

The *post hoc fallacy* (short for a Latin phrase meaning "after this,
therefore because of this") occurs when you conclude that a cause-
effect relationship exists simply because one event preceded another. Let's say you note the growing number of immigrants settling in
a nearby city, observe the city's economic decline, and conclude that
the immigrants' arrival caused the decline. Such a chain of thinking
is faulty because it assumes a cause-effect relationship based purely
on co-occurrence. Perhaps the immigrants' arrival was a factor in the
economic slump, but there could also be other reasons: the lack of
financial incentives to attract business to the city, restrictions on the
size of the city's manufacturing facilities, citywide labor disputes that
make companies leery of settling in the area. Your argument should
also consider these possibilities. (For more on the *post hoc* fallacy, see
pages 336–37.)

The *non sequitur fallacy* (Latin for "it does not follow") is an
even more blatant muddying of cause-effect relationships. In this
case, a conclusion is drawn that has no logical connection to the evidence cited: "Millions of Americans own cars, so there is no need to
fund public transportation." The faulty conclusion disregards the
millions of Americans who don't own cars; it also ignores pollution
and road congestion, both of which could be reduced if people had
access to safe, reliable public transportation.

An *ad hominem argument* (from the Latin meaning "to the
man") occurs when someone attacks a person rather than a point of
view. Suppose your college plans to sponsor a physicians' symposium on the abortion controversy. You decide to write a letter to the
school paper opposing the symposium. Taking swipes at two of the
invited doctors who disapprove of abortion, you mention that one
was recently involved in a messy divorce and that the other is
alleged to have a drinking problem. By hurling personal invective,
you avoid discussing the issue. Mudslinging is a poor substitute for
reasoned argument.

Appeals to questionable or faulty authority also weaken an argument. Most of us have developed a healthy suspicion of phrases like *sources close to, an unidentified spokesperson states, experts claim,* and *studies show.* If these people and reports are so reliable, they should be clearly identified.

Begging the question involves failure to establish proof for a debatable point. The writer expects readers to accept as given a premise that's actually controversial. For instance, you would have trouble convincing readers that prayer should be banned from public schools if you based your argument on the premise that school prayer violates the U.S. Constitution. If the Constitution does, either explicitly or implicitly, prohibit prayer in public education, your essay must demonstrate that fact. You can't build a strong argument if you pretend there's no controversy surrounding your premise.

A *false analogy* wrongly implies that because two things share *some* characteristics, they are therefore *alike in all respects.* You might, for example, compare nicotine and marijuana. Both, you could mention, involve health risks and have addictive properties. If, however, you go on to conclude, "Driving while smoking a cigarette isn't illegal, so driving while smoking marijuana shouldn't be illegal either," you're employing a false analogy. You've overlooked a major difference between nicotine and marijuana: Marijuana impairs perception and coordination—important aspects of driving—while there's no evidence that nicotine does the same.

The *either-or fallacy* occurs when you assume that a particular viewpoint or course of action can have only one of two diametrically opposed outcomes—either totally this or totally that. Say you argue as follows: "Unless colleges continue to offer scholarships based solely on financial need, no one who is underprivileged will be able to attend college." Such a statement ignores the fact that bright, underprivileged students could receive scholarships based on their potential or their demonstrated academic excellence.

Finally, a *red herring argument* is an intentional digression from the issue—a ploy to deflect attention from the matter being discussed. Imagine that you're arguing that condoms shouldn't be dispensed to high school students. You would introduce a red herring if you began to rail against parents who fail to provide their children with any information about sex. Most people would agree that parents *should* provide such information. However, the issue being discussed is not parents' irresponsibility but the pros and cons of schools' distributing condoms to students.

STUDENT ESSAY

The following student essay was written by Mark Simmons in response to this assignment:

> Mary Sherry's "In Praise of the 'F' Word" invites controversy by attacking the popular notion that failing students is a harmful practice. Select another controversial issue, one that you feel strongly about. Conduct library research to gather evidence in support of your position, and brainstorm with others to identify some points that might be raised by those who oppose your view. Then, using logic and formal, documented evidence, convince readers that your viewpoint is valid.

Your instructor may not ask you to include research in your essay. But, if you're asked—as Mark was—to research your paper and to provide *formal documentation,* you'll want to pay special attention to the way Mark credits his sources. (In *your* paper, the Works Cited list should be double-spaced—along with the rest of the paper—and placed at the end on a separate page.) You'll also find it helpful to refer to the Appendix, "A Concise Guide to Finding and Documenting Sources" (page 505). If your instructor wants you to research your paper but will accept *informal documentation,* the material on page 410 should come in handy.

Whether or not you include research in your paper, the annotations on Mark's essay and the comments following it will help you determine how well it applies the principles of argumentation-persuasion.

Compulsory National Service
by Mark Simmons

Beginning of two-paragraph introduction	Our high school history class spent several weeks studying the events of the 1960s. The most interesting thing about that decade was the spirit of service and social commitment among young people. In the '60s, young people thought about issues

1

beyond themselves; they joined the Peace Corps, worked in poverty-stricken Appalachian communities, and participated in freedom marches against segregation. Most young people today, despite their concern with careers and getting ahead, would also like an opportunity to make a worthwhile contribution to society.

Common knowledge: No need to document

Convinced that many young adults are indeed   2 eager for such an opportunity, President Clinton's administration implemented in 1994 a pilot program of voluntary national service. The following year, the program was formalized, placed under the management of the Corporation for National Service (CNS), and given the name AmeriCorps. In the years 1994–2000, approximately 175,000 AmeriCorps volunteers provided varied assistance in communities across the country ("President Releases"). The pro-

Parenthetic citation of unpaged anonymous material obtained through the Internet

Start of two-sentence thesis

gram holds out so much promise that it seems only natural to go one step further and make young people's participation in this or some kind of national service mandatory. By instituting a program of compulsory national service, the country could tap youth's idealistic desire to make a difference. Such a system would yield significant benefits.

Definition paragraph

What exactly is meant by compulsory national   3 service? Traditionally, it has tended to mean that everyone between the ages of seventeen and twenty-five would serve the country for two years. These young people could choose between two major options: military service or a public-service corps. They could serve their time at any point within an eight-year span. The unemployed or the uncertain could join immediately after high school; college-bound students could complete their education before joining the national service. Years ago, Senator Sam Nunn and Representative Dave McCurdy gave a new twist to the definition of com-

Beginning of summary of a source's ideas

pulsory national service. They proposed a plan that would require all high school graduates applying for federal aid for college tuition to serve either in the military or in a Citizens Corps. Anyone in the Citizens Corps would be required to work full-time at public-service duties for one or two years. During that time, participants would receive a weekly stipend, and, at the end, be given a voucher worth $10,000 for each year of civilian service. The voucher could then be applied toward college credit, employment training, or a down payment on a house (Sudo 9).

Parenthetic citation—page number *and* author are given since the author is not cited earlier in the sentence

The traditional plan for compulsory national service and the one proposed by Nunn and McCurdy are just two of many variations that have been discussed over the years. While this country debates the concept, some nations such as France have gone ahead and accepted it enthusiastically. The idea could be workable in this country too. Unfortunately, opponents are doing all they can to prevent the idea from taking hold. They contend, first of all, that the program would cost too much. A great deal of money, they argue, would be spent administering the program, paying young people's wages, and providing housing for participants. Another argument against compulsory national service is that it would demoralize young people; supposedly, the plan would prevent the young from moving ahead with their careers and would make them feel as though they were engaged in work that offered no personal satisfaction. A third argument is that compulsory service would lay the groundwork for a dictatorship. The picture is painted of an army of young people, controlled by the government, much like the Hitler Youth of the Second World War.

4

Topic sentence

Beginning of summary of three points made by the opposing viewpoint

Despite opponents' claims that compulsory national service would involve exorbitant costs, the program would not have to be that expensive to run. AmeriCorps has already provided an excellent model for achieving substantial benefits at reasonable cost. For example, a study conducted by universities in Iowa and Michigan showed that each dollar spent on AmeriCorps programs yielded $2.60 in reduced welfare costs, increased earnings, and other benefits (Garland 120). Also, the sums required for wages and housing could be reduced considerably through payments made by the towns, cities, and states using the corps' services. And the economic benefits of the program could be significant. AmeriCorps's official website gives an idea of the current scope of the program's activities.

5

Topic sentence: Refutation of first point

Information comes from two sources. Sources, separated by a semicolon, are given in the order they appear in the Works Cited list. First source is ———→ unpaged electronic text. No page given for second source because it runs only one page.

Topic sentence: Refutation of second point ———

Attribution giving author's full name and area of expertise ———

Full-sentence quotation is preceded by a comma and begins with a ——— capital letter

Where secondary source was quoted

Quotation is blended into the sentence (no comma and the ——— quotation begins with a lowercased word)

Quotation with ——— ellipsis

Just the page ——— number is provided because the author's name is cited in the preceding attribution

Volunteers provide crucial services including building affordable homes for families, reducing crime in neighborhoods, responding to natural disasters, and tutoring children ("AmeriCorps"). A compulsory national corps could also clean up litter, provide day care services, staff libraries, immunize children, and care for the country's growing elderly population (Clinton; Eng). All these projects would help solve many of the problems that plague our nation, and they would probably cost less than if they were handled by often inefficient government bureaucracies. It's important to note, then, that AmeriCorps isn't administered by a complex, multi-tiered federal agency; rather it is run by the streamlined nonprofit CNS, whose efficiency and cost-control measures have been recognized by many major corporations (Garland 120).

Also, rather than undermining the spirit of young people, as opponents contend, the program would probably boost their morale. Many young people feel enormous pressure and uncertainty; they are not sure whether they want to find a job or further their education. Compulsory national service could give these young people much-needed breathing space. As Edward Lewis, president of St. Mary's College, says, "Many students are not ready for college at seventeen or eighteen. This kind of program responds to that need" (qtd. in Fowler 3). Robert Coles, psychiatrist and social activist, argues that a public-service stint enriches participants' lives in yet another way. Coles points out that young people often have little sense of the job market. When they get involved in community service, though, they frequently "discover an area of interest . . . that launches them on a career" (93). Equally important, compulsory national service can provide an emotional boost for the young; all of them would experience the pride that comes from working hard, reaching goals, acquiring skills, and handling responsibilities (Waldman and Wofford). A positive mind-set would also result from the sense of community that would be created by serving in the national service. All young people--rich or poor, educated or not, regardless of sex and social class--would come together and perceive not their

6

Parenthetic
citation for
electronic source
having two
authors. No page
given since elec-
tronic text is
unpaged.

differences but their common interests and similarities (Waldman and Wofford). As President Clinton
proclaimed at the Year 2000 swearing-in of Ameri-
Corps's recruits in Philadelphia, AmeriCorps gives
volunteers a chance "to tear down barriers of distrust and misunderstanding and old-fashioned
ignorance, and build a genuine American community" (Clinton).

Topic sentence:
Refutation of
third point

Finally, in contrast to what opponents claim,   7
compulsory national service would not signal the
start of a dictatorship. Although the service would
be required, young people would have complete
freedom to choose any two years between the ages
of seventeen and twenty-five. They would also have
complete freedom to choose the branch of the military or public-service corps that suits them best.
And the corps would not need to be outfitted in military uniforms or to live in barrack-like camps. It
could be set up like a regular job, with young people
living at home as much as possible, following a
nine-to-five schedule, enjoying all the personal freedoms that would ordinarily be theirs. Also, a dictatorship would no more likely emerge from compulsory national service than it has from our present
military system. We would still have a series of
checks and balances to prohibit the taking of power
by one group or individual. We should also keep in
mind that our system is different from that of fascist
regimes; our long tradition of personal liberty makes
improbable the seizing of absolute power by one
person or faction. A related but even more important point to remember is that freedom does not
mean people are guaranteed the right to pursue
only their individual needs. That is mistaking selfishness for freedom. And, as everyone knows, selfishness leads only to misery. The national service
would not take away freedom. On the contrary, serving in the corps would help young people grasp this
larger concept of freedom, a concept that is badly
needed to counteract the deadly "look out for number one" attitude that is spreading like a poison
across the nation.

Beginning of
two-paragraph
conclusion

Perhaps there will never be a time like the   8
1960s when so many young people were concerned
with remaking the world. Still, a good many of

Attribution leading to a long quotation. Attribution is followed by a colon since the lead-in is a full sentence. If the lead-in isn't a full sentence, use a comma after the attribution.

today's young people want meaningful work. They want to feel that what they do makes a difference. A program of compulsory national service would harness this idealism and help young people realize the best in themselves. Such a program would also help resolve some of the country's most critical social problems.

When President Bush was in office, political commentator Donald Eberly expressed his belief in the power of national service. Urging the inauguration of such a program, Eberly wrote the following:

9

Long quotation is indented ten spaces. Don't leave any extra space within, above, or below the quotation.

> The promise of national service can be manifested in many ways: in cleaner air and fewer forest fires, in well-cared-for infants and old folks; in a better-educated citizenry and better-satisfied work force; perhaps in a more peaceful world. National service has a lot of promise. It's a promise well worth keeping. (651)

For an indented quotation, the period is placed *before* the parenthetic citation.

In *your* paper, the Works Cited list would be double-spaced like the rest of the paper, with no extra space after the heading or between entries. Also, in *your* paper, the Works Cited would start on a *separate* page.

Several years later, President Clinton took office, gave his support to the concept, and AmeriCorps was born. Although there was pressure to reduce AmeriCorps's funding, such efforts were motivated by a political agenda intent on undercutting the accomplishments of the Clinton administration (Molyneux 39). Indeed, even among conservative Republicans today, there is growing support for AmeriCorps; in September 2000, forty-nine of fifty U.S. governors sponsored a bipartisan letter urging Congress to extend national service ("49 Governors"). An efficient and successful program of voluntary service, AmeriCorps has paved the way. Now seems to be the perfect time to expand the concept and make compulsory national service a reality.

Anonymous material obtained on the Internet. Names of website and of sponsoring organization appear. Electronic text is five paragraphs long. Web address always required.

Works Cited

"AmeriCorps: Who We Are." AmeriCorps. The Corporation for National Service. May 2000: 5 pars. 26 Jan. 2001 <http://www.americorps.org/ whoweare.html>.

Authored ———▶ Clinton, William. "Remarks by the President to
material on the   AmeriCorps." AmeriCorps. The Corporation
Internet. Dates   for National Service. 11 Oct. 2000: 28 pars. 7
the material was   Jan. 2001 <http://www.americorps.org/news/
published and   pr/potus_remarks101100.html>.
accessed both
provided.   ┌▶ Coles, Robert. The Call of Service. Boston: Houghton
Book by one ─┘   Mifflin, 1993.
author   ┌──▶ Eberly, Donald. "What the President Should Do About
Published ─┘   National Service." Vital Speeches of the Day 15
speech   Aug. 1989: 561–63.

Newspaper ———▶ Eng, Lily. "Congressional Pressure Puts AmeriCorps
article whose text   Under the Gun." Philadelphia Inquirer 18 Apr.
is only one page   1996, late ed.: B1.

Internet ——————▶ "49 Governors Urge Congress to Extend National
article with   Service." National Service Newsletter. Office
unnumbered   of the Governor of the State of Montana. 20
paragraphs or   Sept. 2000. 26 Jan. 2001 <http://
pages   www.nationalservice.org/news/pr/
                       92000.html>.

                    Fowler, Margaret. "New Interest in National Youth
                       Corps." New York Times 16 May 1989, natl.
                       ed.: A25.

Article from ———▶ Garland, Susan B. "A Social Program CEOs Want to
weekly magazine   Save." Business Week 19 June 1996: 120–21.

                    Molyneux, Guy. "When Success Fails." Rolling Stone
                       4 May 1995: 38–39.

                    "President Releases Study on Success of
                       AmeriCorps Tutoring." AmeriCorps. The
                       Corporation for National Service. 11 Oct. 2000:
                       6 pars. 7 Jan. 2001 <http://
                       www.americorps.org/news/pr/101100.html>.

                    Sudo, Phil. "Mandatory National Service?" Scholastic
                       Update 23 Feb. 1990: 9.

Article (by ———▶ Waldman, Steven, and Harris Wofford. "AmeriCorps
two authors)   the Beautiful? Habitat for Conservative Values."
from scholarly   Policy Review Sept.–Oct. 1997: 49 pars.
journal on CD-   CD-ROM. EBSCOhost.
ROM

COMMENTARY

Blend of argumentation and persuasion.   In his essay, Mark tackles a controversial issue. He takes the position that compulsory national service would benefit both the country as a whole and its young people in particular. Mark's essay is a good example of the way argumentation and persuasion often mix: Although the paper presents Mark's position in a logical, well-reasoned manner (argumentation), it also appeals to readers' personal values and suggests a course of action (persuasion).

Audience analysis.   When planning the essay, Mark realized that his audience—his composition class—would consist largely of two kinds of readers. Some, not sure of their views, would be inclined to agree with him if he presented his case well. Others would probably be reluctant to accept his view. Because of this mixed audience, Mark knew he couldn't depend on *pathos* (an appeal to emotion) to convince readers. Rather, his argument had to rely mainly on *logos* (reason) and *ethos* (credibility). So Mark organized his essay around a series of logical arguments—many of them backed by expert opinion—and he evoked his own authority by drawing on his knowledge of history and his "inside" knowledge of young people.

Introduction and thesis.   Mark introduces his subject by discussing an earlier decade when large numbers of young people worked for social change. Mark's references to the Peace Corps, community work, and freedom marches reinforce his image as a knowledgeable source and establish a context for his position. These historical references, combined with the comments about AmeriCorps, the program of voluntary national service, lead into the two-sentence thesis at the end of the two-paragraph introduction: "By instituting a program of compulsory national service, the country could tap youth's idealistic desire to make a difference. Such a system would yield significant benefits."

The second paragraph in the introduction also illustrates Mark's first use of outside sources. Because the assignment called for research in support of an argument, Mark went to the library and identified sources that helped him defend his position. If Mark's instructor had required extensive investigation of an issue, Mark would have been obligated both to dig more deeply into his subject and to use more scholarly and specialized sources. But given the instructor's requirements, Mark proceeded just as he should have: He searched out expert opinion that supported his viewpoint; he presented that evidence clearly; he documented his sources carefully.

Background paragraph and use of outside sources.   The third paragraph provides a working *definition* of compulsory national service by presenting two common interpretations of the concept. Such background information guarantees that Mark's readers will share his understanding of the essay's central concept.

Acknowledging the opposing viewpoint.   Having explained the meaning of compulsory national service, Mark is now in a good position to launch his argument. Even though he wasn't required to research the opposing viewpoint, Mark wisely decided to get together with some friends to brainstorm some issues that might be raised by the dissenting view. He acknowledges this position in the *topic sentence* of the essay's fourth paragraph: "Unfortunately, opponents are doing all they can to prevent the idea from taking hold." Next he summarizes the main points the dissenting opinion might advance: compulsory national service would be expensive, demoralizing to young people, and dangerously authoritarian. Mark uses the rest of the essay to counter these criticisms.

Refutation.   The next three paragraphs (5–7) *refute* the opposing stance and present Mark's evidence for his position. Mark structures the essay so that readers can follow his *counterargument* with ease. Each paragraph argues against one opposing point and begins with a *topic sentence* that serves as Mark's response to the dissenting view. Note the way the italicized portion of each topic sentence recalls a dissenting point cited earlier: "Despite opponents' claims that *compulsory national service would involve exorbitant costs,* the program would not have to be that expensive to run" (paragraph 5); "Also, rather than *undermining the spirit of young people,* as opponents contend, the program would probably boost their morale" (6); "Finally, in contrast to what opponents claim, *compulsory national service would not signal the start of a dictatorship*" (7). Mark also guides the reader through the various points in the refutation by using *transitions* within paragraphs: "*And* the economic benefits . . . could be significant" (5); "*Equally important,* compulsory national service could provide an emotional boost . . ." (6); "*Also,* a dictatorship would no more likely emerge . . ." (7).

Throughout the three-paragraph refutation, Mark uses outside sources to lend power to his argument. If the assignment had called for in-depth research, he would have cited facts, statistics, and case studies to develop this section of his essay. Given the nature of the assignment, though, Mark's reliance on expert opinion is perfectly acceptable.

Mark successfully incorporates material from these outside sources into his refutation. He doesn't, for example, string one quotation numbingly after another; instead he usually develops his refutation by *summarizing* expert opinion and saves *direct quotations* for points that deserve emphasis. Moreover, whenever Mark quotes or summarizes a source, he provides clear signals to indicate that the material is indeed borrowed. (If you'd like some suggestions for citing outside sources in an essay of your own, see pages 422 and 520–25.)

Some problems with the refutation.   Overall, Mark's three-paragraph refutation is strong, but it would have been even more effective if the paragraphs had been resequenced. As it now stands, the last paragraph in the refutation (7) seems anticlimactic. Unlike the preceding two paragraphs, which are developed through fairly extensive reference to outside sources, paragraph 7 depends entirely on Mark's personal feelings and interpretations for its support. Of course, Mark was under no obligation to provide research in all sections of the paper. Even so, the refutation would have been more persuasive if Mark had placed the final paragraph in the refutation in a less emphatic position. He could, for example, have put it first or second in the sequence, saving for last either of the other two more convincing paragraphs.

You may also have felt that there's another problem with the third paragraph in the refutation. Here, Mark seems to lose control of his counterargument. Beginning with "And, as everyone knows . . . ," Mark falls into the *logical fallacy* called *begging the question*. He shouldn't assume that everyone agrees that a selfish life inevitably brings misery. He also indulges in charged emotionalism when he refers—somewhat melodramatically—to the "deadly 'look out for number one' attitude that is spreading like a poison across the nation."

Inductive reasoning.   In part, Mark arrived at his position *inductively*, through a series of *inferences* or *inductive leaps*. He started with some personal *observations* about the nation and its young people. Then, to support those observations, he added his friends' insights as well as information gathered through research. Combined, all this material led him to the general *conclusion* that compulsory national service would be both workable and beneficial.

Other patterns of development.   To develop his argument, Mark draws on several patterns of development. The third paragraph relies on *definition* to clarify what is meant by compulsory national service. The first paragraph of both the introduction and conclusion *compares* and *contrasts* young people of the 1960s with those of today. And, to support his position, Mark uses a kind of *causal analysis;* he both speculates on the likely consequences of compulsory national service and cites expert opinion to illustrate the validity of some of those speculations.

Conclusion.   Despite some problems in the final section of his refutation, Mark comes up with an effective two-paragraph conclusion for his essay. In the first closing paragraph, he echoes the point made in the introduction about the 1960s and restates his thesis. That done, he moves to the second paragraph of his conclusion. There, he quotes a dramatic statement from a knowledgeable source, cites efforts to undermine AmeriCorps, and ends by pointing out that AmeriCorps has earned the respect of some unlikely supporters. All that Mark does in this final paragraph lends credibility to the crisp assertion and suggested course of action at the very end of his essay.

Revising the first draft.   Given the complex nature of his argument, Mark found that he had to revise his essay several times. One way to illustrate some of the changes he made is to compare his final introduction with the original draft reprinted here:

Original Version of the Introduction

   "There's no free lunch." "You can't get something for nothing." "You have to earn your way." In America, these sayings are not really true. In America, we gladly take but give back little. In America, we receive economic opportunity, legal protection, the right to vote, and, most of all, a personal freedom unequaled throughout the world. How do we repay our country for such gifts? In most cases, we don't. This unfair relationship must be changed. The best way to make a start is to institute a system of national compulsory service for young people. This system would be of real benefit to the country and its citizens.

When Mark met with a classmate for a feedback session, he found that his partner had a number of helpful suggestions for revising various sections of the essay. But Mark's partner focused most of her comments on the essay's introduction because she felt it needed special attention. Following his classmate's suggestion, Mark deleted the original introduction's references to Americans in general. He made this change because he wanted readers to know—from the very start of the essay—that the paper would focus not on all Americans but on American youth. To reinforce this emphasis, he also added the point about the social commitment characteristic of young people in the 1960s. This reference to an earlier period gave the discussion an important historical perspective and lent a note of authority to Mark's argument. The decision to mention the '60s also helped Mark realize that his introduction should point out more recent developments—specifically, the promising start-up of AmeriCorps. Mark was pleased to see that adding this new material not only gave the introduction a sharper focus, but it also provided a smoother lead-in to his thesis.

These are just a few of the many changes Mark made while reworking his essay. Because he budgeted his time carefully, he was able to revise thoroughly. With the exception of some weak spots in the refutation, Mark's essay is well-reasoned and convincing.

ACTIVITIES: ARGUMENTATION-PERSUASION

Prewriting Activities

1. Imagine you're writing two essays: One *defines* hypocrisy; the other *contrasts* license and freedom. Identify an audience for each essay (college students, professors, teenagers, parents, employers, employees, or some other group). Then jot down how each essay might argue the merits of certain ways of behaving.

2. Following are several thesis statements for argumentation-persuasion essays. For each thesis, determine whether the three audiences indicated in parentheses are apt to be supportive, wavering, or hostile. Then select *one* thesis and use group brainstorming to identify,

for each audience, specific points you would make to persuade each group.

a. Students should not graduate from college until they have passed a comprehensive exam in their majors (*college students, their parents, college officials*).

b. Abandoned homes owned by the city should be sold to low-income residents for a nominal fee (*city officials, low-income residents, general citizens*).

c. The town should pass a law prohibiting residents who live near the reservoir from using pesticides on their lawns (*environmentalists, homeowners, members of the town council*).

d. Faculty advisors to college newspapers should have the authority to prohibit the publication of articles that reflect negatively on the school (*alumni, college officials, student journalists*).

Revising Activities

3. Each set of statements that follows contains at least one of the logical fallacies described earlier in the chapter and in Ann McClintock's essay "Propaganda Techniques in Today's Advertising" (page 232). Identify the fallacy or fallacies in each set and explain why the statements are invalid.

a. Grades are irrelevant to learning. Students are in college to get an education, not good grades. The university should eliminate grading altogether.

b. The best policy is to put juvenile offenders in jail so that they can get a taste of reality. Otherwise, they will repeat their crimes again and again.

c. So-called sex education programs do nothing to decrease the rate of teenage pregnancy. Further expenditures on these programs should be curtailed.

d. If we allow abortion, people will think it's acceptable to kill the homeless or pull the plug on sick people—two groups that are also weak and frail.

e. The curfews that some towns impose on teenagers are as repressive as the curfews in totalitarian countries.

4. Following is the introduction from the first draft of an essay advocating the elimination of mandatory dress codes in public schools. Revise the paragraph, being sure to consider these questions: How effectively does the writer deal with the opposing viewpoint? Does the paragraph encourage those who might disagree with the writer

to read on? Why or why not? Do you see any logical fallacies in the writer's thinking? Where? Does the writer introduce anything that veers away from the point being discussed? Where? Before revising, you may find it helpful to do some brainstorming—individually or in a group—to find ways to strengthen the paragraph.

After reworking the paragraph, take a few minutes to consider how the rest of the essay might unfold. What persuasive strategies could be used? How could Rogerian argument win over readers? What points could be made? What action could be urged in the effort to build a convincing argument?

In three nearby towns recently, high school administrators joined forces to take an outrageously strong stand against students' constitutional rights. Acting like fascists, they issued an edict in the form of a preposterous dress code that prohibits students from wearing expensive jewelry, designer jeans, leather jackets--anything that the administrators, in their supposed wisdom, consider ostentatious. Perhaps the next thing they'll want to do is forbid students to play rock music at school dances. What prompted the administrators' dictatorial prohibition against certain kinds of clothing? Somehow or other, they got it into their heads that having no restrictions on the way students dress creates an unhealthy environment, where students vie with each other for the flashiest attire. Students and parents alike should protest this and any other dress code. If such codes go into effect, we might as well throw out the Constitution.

Mary Sherry

Following her graduation from Dominican University in 1962 with a degree in English, Mary Sherry (1940–) wrote freelance articles and advertising copy while raising her family. Over the years, a love of writing and an interest in education have been integral to all that Sherry does professionally. Founder and owner of a small research and publishing firm in Minnesota, she has taught creative and remedial writing to adults for more than sixteen years. The following selection first appeared as a 1991 "My Turn" column in *Newsweek*.

Pre-Reading Journal Entry

Imagine you had a son or daughter who didn't take school seriously. How would you go about motivating the child to value academic success? Would your strategies differ depending on the age and gender of the child? If so, how and why? What other factors might influence your approach? Use your journal to respond to these questions.

In Praise of the "F" Word

Tens of thousands of 18-year-olds will graduate this year and be 1 handed meaningless diplomas. These diplomas won't look any different from those awarded their luckier classmates. Their validity will be questioned only when their employers discover that these graduates are semiliterate.

Eventually a fortunate few will find their way into educational 2 repair shops—adult-literacy programs, such as the one where I teach basic grammar and writing. There, high-school graduates and high-school dropouts pursuing graduate-equivalency certificates will learn the skills they should have learned in school. They will also discover they have been cheated by our educational system.

As I teach, I learn a lot about our schools. Early in each session 3 I ask my students to write about an unpleasant experience they had in school. No writers' block here! "I wish someone would have had made me stop doing drugs and made me study." "I liked to party and no one seemed to care." "I was a good kid and didn't cause any trouble, so they just passed me along even though I didn't read well and couldn't write." And so on.

I am your basic do-gooder, and prior to teaching this class I 4 blamed the poor academic skills our kids have today on drugs, divorce and other impediments to concentration necessary for doing well in school. But, as I rediscover each time I walk into the classroom, before a teacher can expect students to concentrate, he has to get their attention, no matter what distractions may be at hand. There are many ways to do this, and they have much to do with teaching style. However, if style alone won't do it, there is another way to show who holds the winning hand in the classroom. That is to reveal the trump card[1] of failure.

I will never forget a teacher who played that card to get the 5 attention of one of my children. Our youngest, a world-class charmer, did little to develop his intellectual talents but always got by. Until Mrs. Stifter.

Our son was a high-school senior when he had her for English. 6 "He sits in the back of the room talking to his friends," she told me. "Why don't you move him to the front row?" I urged, believing the embarrassment would get him to settle down. Mrs. Stifter looked at me steely-eyed over her glasses. "I don't move seniors," she said. "I flunk them." I was flustered. Our son's academic life flashed before my eyes. No teacher had ever threatened him with that before. I regained my composure and managed to say that I thought she was right. By the time I got home I was feeling pretty good about this. It was a radical approach for these times, but, well, why not? "She's going to flunk you," I told my son. I did not discuss it any further. Suddenly English became a priority in his life. He finished out the semester with an A.

I know one example doesn't make a case, but at night I see a 7 parade of students who are angry and resentful for having been passed along until they could no longer even pretend to keep up. Of average intelligence or better, they eventually quit school, concluding they were too dumb to finish. "I should have been held back" is a comment I hear frequently. Even sadder are those students who are high-school graduates who say to me after a few weeks of class, "I don't know how I ever got a high-school diploma."

Passing students who have not mastered the work cheats them 8 and the employers who expect graduates to have basic skills. We

[1]In cards, an advantage held in reserve until it's needed (editors' note).

excuse this dishonest behavior by saying kids can't learn if they come from terrible environments. No one seems to stop to think that—no matter what environments they come from—most kids don't put school first on their list unless they perceive something is at stake. They'd rather be sailing.

Many students I see at night could give expert testimony on unemployment, chemical dependency, abusive relationships. In spite of these difficulties, they have decided to make education a priority. They are motivated by the desire for a better job or the need to hang on to the one they've got. They have a healthy fear of failure.   9

People of all ages can rise above their problems, but they need to have a reason to do so. Young people generally don't have the maturity to value education in the same way my adult students value it. But fear of failure, whether economic or academic, can motivate both.   10

Flunking as a regular policy has just as much merit today as it did two generations ago. We must review the threat of flunking and see it as it really is—a positive teaching tool. It is an expression of confidence by both teachers and parents that the students have the ability to learn the material presented to them. However, making it work again would take a dedicated, caring conspiracy between teachers and parents. It would mean facing the tough reality that passing kids who haven't learned the material—while it might save them grief for the short term—dooms them to long-term illiteracy. It would mean that teachers would have to follow through on their threats, and parents would have to stand behind them, knowing their children's best interests are indeed at stake. This means no more doing Scott's assignments for him because he might fail. No more passing Jodi because she's such a nice kid.   11

This is a policy that worked in the past and can work today. A wise teacher, with the support of his parents, gave our son the opportunity to succeed—or fail. It's time we return this choice to all students.   12

Questions for Close Reading

1. What is the selection's thesis? Locate the sentence(s) in which Sherry states her main idea. If she doesn't state the thesis explicitly, express it in your own words.
2. Sherry opens her essay with these words: "Tens of thousands of 18-year-olds will graduate this year and be handed meaningless diplomas." Why does Sherry consider these diplomas meaningless?

3. According to Sherry, what justification do many teachers give for "passing students who have not mastered the work" (paragraph 8)? Why does Sherry think that it is wrong to pass such students?
4. What does Sherry think teachers should do to motivate students to focus on school despite the many "distractions . . . at hand" (4)?
5. Refer to your dictionary as needed to define the following words used in the selection: *validity* (paragraph 1), *semiliterate* (1), *equivalency* (2), *impediments* (4), *composure* (6), *radical* (6), *priority* (6), *resentful* (7), *testimony* (9), *motivate* (10), *merit* (11), *conspiracy* (11), and *illiteracy* (11).

Questions About the Writer's Craft

1. **The pattern.** To write an effective argumentation-persuasion essay, writers need to establish their credibility. How does Sherry convince readers that she is qualified to write about her subject? What does this attempt to establish credibility say about Sherry's perception of her audience's point of view?
2. Sherry's title is deliberately misleading. What does her title lead you to believe the essay will be about? Why do you think Sherry chose this title?
3. Why do you suppose Sherry quotes her students rather than summarizing what they had to say? What effect do you think Sherry hopes the quotations will have on readers?
4. **Other patterns.** What example does Sherry provide to show that the threat of failure can work? How does this example reinforce her case?

Writing Assignments Using Argumentation-Persuasion as a Pattern of Development

1. Like Sherry, write an essay arguing your position on a controversial school-related issue. Possibilities include but need not be limited to the following: College students should *or* should not have to fulfill a physical education requirement; high school students should *or* should not have to demonstrate computer proficiency before graduating; elementary school students should *or* should not be grouped according to ability; a course in parenting should *or* should not be a required part of the high school curriculum. Once you select a topic, brainstorm with others to gather insight into varying points of view. When you write, restrict your argument to one level of education, and refute as many opposing arguments as you can. The following essays will help you identify educational issues worth writing about: Sophronia Liu's "So Tsi-Fai" (page 153), Charles Sykes's "The 'Values' Wasteland" (page 178), Nikki Giovanni's "Campus Racism 101" (page 278), and William Raspberry's "The Handicap of Definition" (page 394).
2. Sherry acknowledges that she used to blame students' poor academic skills on "drugs, divorce and other impediments." To what extent

should teachers take these and similar "impediments" into account when grading students? Are there certain situations that call for leniency, or should out-of-school forces affecting students not be considered? To gain perspective on this issue, interview several friends, classmates, and instructors. Then write an essay in which you argue your position. Provide specific examples to support your argument, being sure to acknowledge and—when possible—to refute opposing viewpoints.

Writing Assignments Using Other Patterns of Development

3. You probably feel, as Sherry does, that Mrs. Stifter is a strong, committed professional. Write an essay illustrating the qualities you think a teacher needs to have to be effective. Ask friends, classmates, family members, and instructors for their opinions; however, in your paper, focus on only those attributes you believe are most critical. To highlight the importance of these qualities, begin with a dramatic example of an ineffective teacher—someone who lacks the attributes you consider most important. To gain insight into some of the factors that make teachers effective or ineffective, read Sophronia Liu's "So Tsi-Fai" (page 153).

4. Where else, besides in the classroom, do you see people acting irresponsibly, expending little effort, and taking the easy way out? You might consider the workplace, a school-related club or activity, family life, or interpersonal relationships. Select *one* area and write an essay illustrating the effects of this behavior on everyone concerned. For a broader perspective on the issue of personal responsibility, read Charles Sykes's "The 'Values' Wasteland" (page 178) and William Raspberry's "The Handicap of Definition" (page 394).

Writing Assignments Using a Journal Entry as a Starting Point

5. Write the text for a brochure presenting parents with a step-by-step guide for dealing with academically unmotivated students. Focus your discussion on a specific level of schooling. From your pre-reading journal entry, select those strategies you consider most realistic and productive. When presenting your ideas, take into account children's likely resistance to the strategies described, and instruct parents how to deal with this resistance. Interviewing others (especially parents) and doing some research in the library and/or on the Internet will broaden your understanding of the issues involved.

Yuh Ji-Yeon

At the age of five, Yuh Ji-Yeon (1965–) immigrated from Seoul, Korea, to the United States, settling in Chicago with her parents. After graduating from Stanford University, she worked as a reporter for the *Omaha World-Herald* and *New York Newsday.* Currently, she is writing her doctoral dissertation at the University of Pennsylvania. The dissertation examines the parallels between the experiences of Korean women immigrating to the United States as wives of U.S. soldiers and the larger context of U.S.-Korean relations. Nearly all of Yuh's writing reflects the concerns of people struggling for liberation in the face of oppression. The following selection first appeared in the *Philadelphia Inquirer* in 1991.

Pre-Reading Journal Entry

Which events in American history do you consider shameful? List these events in your journal. For each, jot down what your teachers taught you about the event when you were a child. Does what you were taught as a child differ from what you know now? In what way? If you did later on learn harsher truths about these events, how did you feel? Do you believe that you should have been told the truth from the beginning? Why or why not?

Let's Tell the Story of All America's Cultures

I grew up hearing, seeing and almost believing that America was 1 white—albeit with a little black tinge here and there—and that white was best.

The white people were everywhere in my 1970s Chicago child- 2 hood: Founding Fathers, Lewis and Clark, Lincoln, Daniel Boone, Carnegie, presidents, explorers and industrialists galore. The only black people were slaves. The only Indians were scalpers.

I never heard one word about how Benjamin Franklin was so 3 impressed by the Iroquois federation of nations that he adapted that model into our system of state and federal government. Or that the Indian tribes were systematically betrayed and massacred by a greedy young nation that stole their land and called it the United States.

I never heard one word about how Asian immigrants were   4
among the first to turn California's desert into fields of plenty. Or
about Chinese immigrant Ah Bing, who bred the cherry now on sale
in groceries across the nation. Or that plantation owners in Hawaii
imported labor from China, Japan, Korea and the Philippines to
work the sugar cane fields. I never learned that Asian immigrants
were the only immigrants denied U.S. citizenship, even though they
served honorably in World War I. All the immigrants in my textbook
were white.

I never learned about Frederick Douglass, the runaway slave   5
who became a leading abolitionist and statesman, or about black
scholar W.E.B. Du Bois. I never learned that black people rose up in
arms against slavery. Nat Turner wasn't one of the heroes in my
childhood history class.

I never learned that the American Southwest and California were   6
already settled by Mexicans when they were annexed after the
Mexican-American War. I never learned that Mexico once had a problem keeping land-hungry white men on the U.S. side of the border.

So when other children called me a slant-eyed chink and told   7
me to go back where I came from, I was ready to believe that I was-
n't really an American because I wasn't white.

America's bittersweet legacy of struggling and failing and get-   8
ting another step closer to democratic ideals of liberty and equality
and justice for all wasn't for the likes of me, an immigrant child from
Korea. The history books said so.

Well, the history books were wrong.   9

Educators around the country are finally realizing what I real-   10
ized as a teenager in the library, looking up the history I wasn't getting in school. America is a multicultural nation, composed of many
people with varying histories and varying traditions who have little
in common except their humanity, a belief in democracy and a desire
for freedom.

America changed them, but they changed America too.   11

A committee of scholars and teachers gathered by the New York   12
State Department of Education recognizes this in their recent
report, "One Nation, Many Peoples: A Declaration of Cultural
Interdependence."

They recommend that public schools provide a "multicultural   13
education, anchored to the shared principles of a liberal democracy."

What that means, according to the report, is recognizing that   14
America was shaped and continues to be shaped by people of diverse

backgrounds. It calls for students to be taught that history is an ongoing process of discovery and interpretation of the past, and that there is more than one way of viewing the world.

Thus, the westward migration of white Americans is not just a   15 heroic settling of an untamed wild, but also the conquest of indigenous peoples. Immigrants were not just white, but Asian as well. Blacks were not merely passive slaves freed by northern whites, but active fighters for their own liberation.

In particular, according to the report, the curriculum should   16 help children "to assess critically the reasons for the inconsistencies between the ideals of the U.S. and social realities. It should provide information and intellectual tools that can permit them to contribute to bringing reality closer to the ideals."

In other words, show children the good with the bad, and give   17 them the skills to help improve their country. What could be more patriotic?

Several dissenting members of the New York committee publicly worry that America will splinter into ethnic fragments if this   18 multicultural curriculum is adopted. They argue that the committee's report puts the focus on ethnicity at the expense of national unity.

But downplaying ethnicity will not bolster national unity. The   19 history of America is the story of how and why people from all over the world came to the United States, and how in struggling to make a better life for themselves, they changed each other, they changed the country, and they all came to call themselves Americans.

E pluribus unum. Out of many, one.   20

This is why I, with my Korean background, and my childhood   21 tormentors, with their lost-in-the-mist-of-time European backgrounds, are all Americans.

It is the unique beauty of this country. It is high time we let all   22 our children gaze upon it.

Questions for Close Reading

1. What is the selection's thesis? Locate the sentence(s) in which Yuh states her main idea. If she doesn't state the thesis explicitly, express it in your own words.
2. Yuh makes the rather shocking claim that "the history books were wrong" (paragraph 9). Why does she make this statement? What evidence does she offer to support it?
3. According to Yuh, what changes are needed in U.S. history courses?

4. Why does Yuh feel it is critical that U.S. students receive more than the traditional whites-only version of our nation's history? Who will be served by making history books more multicultural?

5. Refer to your dictionary as needed to define the following words used in the selection: *albeit* (paragraph 1), *tinge* (1), *galore* (2), *multicultural* (10, 13, 18), *interdependence* (12), *indigenous* (15), *dissenting* (18), *ethnicity* (18), and *bolster* (19).

Questions About the Writer's Craft

1. The pattern. Where in her argument does Yuh present the opposing viewpoint? Why do you suppose she waits so long to deal with the dissenting opinion? What effect does this delay have on her argument's effectiveness?

2. Other patterns. Why might Yuh have decided to use so many examples in paragraphs 2 through 6? How do these examples contribute to the persuasiveness of her position? Why might she have placed these examples before her thesis statement?

3. Yuh mixes the subjective and the objective in her argument. Where does she use specifics from her own life? How do these personal details help persuade readers to accept her viewpoint?

4. Yuh often uses parallelism and repetition of phrases, particularly in paragraphs 1 through 6 and paragraph 15. What effect do you think she intended these two stylistic devices to have on her readers?

Writing Assignments Using Argumentation-Persuasion as a Pattern of Development

1. Using the resources of the library and/or Internet, read several articles about the ongoing debate over multiculturalism's role in contemporary education. You should find coverage of the 1991 New York State Department of Education Study (cited by Yuh in paragraph 12) and historian Arthur Schlesinger's *Time* essay "The Cult of Ethnicity: Good and Bad" (July 8, 1991) especially helpful. Review your research, and decide whether or not you support the idea of a multicultural curriculum. Then write an essay in which you argue your position, refuting as many of the opposing views as possible. Draw upon your own experiences as well as your research when developing your point of view.

2. Yuh cites a problem she encountered in her education. What problems or insufficiencies have you found in your own education? Perhaps you perceive an overemphasis on athletics, a reliance on rote memorization, a tendency to discourage female students from pursuing an interest in math and science. Select a single problem at one level of education, and brainstorm with others to gather material about the problem. Then write an essay directed at those who think all is well in our educational system. Be sure your argument illustrates the inaccuracy of these individuals' overly positive view. Before writing your paper, you may want to read Charles Sykes's "The 'Values' Wasteland" (page 178), which offers a critique of U.S. education.

Writing Assignments Using Other Patterns of Development

3. Because the mainstream culture they lived in didn't recognize the presence of minorities, the author's classmates considered Yuh an outsider, almost a nonbeing. To what extent, in your opinion, does television contribute to the dehumanization of minorities? For several days, watch a variety of television shows, noting how a particular ethnic or minority group (such as African-Americans, Hispanic-Americans, or the elderly) is portrayed. Then write an essay showing that the depiction of this group on television is either accurate *or* distorted. Support your main idea with plentiful references to specific television shows, including newscasts, situation comedies, talk shows, and so forth.

4. In her essay, Yuh refers to a report issued by the New York State Department of Education. The report argues that curriculum should encourage students to examine "the reasons for the inconsistencies between the ideals of the U.S. and social realities." Like most people, you probably detected such disparities when you were growing up. Perhaps as a ten-year-old, you heard an admired neighbor brag about padding an expense account. As an eighth-grader, you may have visited your state legislature, where you saw chaos and rudeness instead of order and respect. As a high school student, you might have learned that an esteemed coach took kickbacks from college recruiters. Focus on one such clash between the ethical ideal and the everyday reality, and write about the incident's effect on you. Provide dramatic details to show how you reacted, what you did to explain the discrepancy to yourself, and whether you asked adults to help you understand the situation. At the end, reach some conclusions about the way children can be helped to deal with such collisions between ideals and reality. Before writing your paper, you may want to read Langston Hughes's "Salvation" (page 148), a powerful essay that explores a child's disillusionment with adult realities.

Writing Assignments Using a Journal Entry as a Starting Point

5. Write an essay in which you argue for *or* against schools' revealing harsh historical realities to children. Review your pre-reading journal entry, and select *one* historical event to focus on. Provide plentiful reasons to support your position, whenever possible pointing out weaknesses in opposing viewpoints. To deepen your understanding of the issue, consider reading Beth Johnson's "Bombs Bursting in Air" (page 189), an essay exploring parents' quandary between protecting their children and educating them about life's painful realities.

Camille Paglia

Before 1990, Camille Paglia, Professor of Humanities at Philadelphia's University of the Arts, was known primarily for her electrifying performance in the classroom. Then came the publication of Paglia's *Sexual Personae: Art and Decadence From Nefertiti to Emily Dickinson,* a sweeping book that moves with dizzying speed from the days of cave art to the nineteenth century. *Sexual Personae* makes the case that man creates art as a defensive response to woman's terrifying cosmic power—specifically, her sexual and procreative force. Suddenly Paglia became an international celebrity and had many opportunities to express her controversial views. She has been both revered and reviled for making statements like these: "Male aggression and lust are the energizing factors in culture" and "If I ever got into a dating situation where I was overpowered and raped, I would say, 'Oh well, I misread the signals.'" Born in 1947, Paglia earned her doctorate from Yale University, where her doctoral thesis was an early version of *Sexual Personae. Sex, Art, and American Culture: Essays* (1992), *Vamps and Tramps: New Essays* (1994), and *Alfred Hitchcock's "The Birds"* (1998) are Paglia's latest works. She is also a regular columnist for *Salon* online magazine. The following selection, written in Paglia's characteristically provocative style, first appeared in *New York Newsday* in 1991.

Pre-Reading Journal Entry

How would you define "date rape"? Use your journal to formulate a preliminary definition. Working as quickly as you can, jot down your preliminary thoughts about what it is and what it isn't.

Rape: A Bigger Danger Than Feminists Know

Rape is an outrage that cannot be tolerated in civilized society. 1 Yet feminism, which has waged a crusade for rape to be taken more seriously, has put young women in danger by hiding the truth about sex from them.

In dramatizing the pervasiveness of rape, feminists have told 2 young women that before they have sex with a man, they must give consent as explicit as a legal contract's. In this way, young women have been convinced that they have been the victims of rape. On elite campuses in the Northeast and on the West Coast, they have held consciousness-raising sessions, petitioned administrations, demanded inquests. At Brown University, outraged, panicky "victims" have scrawled the names of alleged attackers on the walls of women's rest rooms. What marital rape was to the '70s, "date rape" is to the '90s.

The incidence and seriousness of rape do not require this kind of exaggeration. Real acquaintance rape is nothing new. It has been a horrible problem for women for all of recorded history. Once, father and brothers protected women from rape. Once, the penalty for rape was death. I come from a fierce Italian tradition where, not so long ago in the motherland, a rapist would end up knifed, castrated, and hung out to dry.   3

But the old clans and small rural communities have broken down. In our cities, on our campuses far from home, young women are vulnerable and defenseless. Feminism has not prepared them for this. Feminism keeps saying the sexes are the same. It keeps telling women they can do anything, go anywhere, say anything, wear anything. No, they can't. Women will always be in sexual danger.   4

One of my male students recently slept overnight with a friend in a passageway of the Great Pyramid in Egypt. He described the moon and sand, the ancient silence and eerie echoes. I am a woman. I will never experience that. I am not stupid enough to believe I could ever be safe there. There is a world of solitary adventure I will never have. Women have always known these somber truths. But feminism, with its pie-in-the-sky fantasies about the perfect world, keeps young women from seeing life as it is.   5

We must remedy social injustice whenever we can. But there are some things we cannot change. There are sexual differences that are based in biology. Academic feminism is lost in a fog of social constructionism. It believes we are totally the product of our environment. This idea was invented by Rousseau.[1] He was wrong. Emboldened by dumb French language theory, academic feminists repeat the same hollow slogans over and over to each other. Their view of sex is naive and prudish. Leaving sex to the feminists is like letting your dog vacation at the taxidermist's.   6

[1]A French political writer and philosopher (1712–78) (editors' note).

The sexes are at war. Men must struggle for identity against the   7
overwhelming power of their mothers. Women have menstruation
to tell them they are women. Men must do or risk something to be
men. Men become masculine only when other men say they are.
Having sex with a woman is one way a boy becomes a man.

College men are at their hormonal peak. They have just left   8
their mothers and are questing for their male identity. In groups,
they are dangerous. A woman going to a fraternity party is walking
into Testosterone Flats, full of prickly cacti and blazing guns. If she
goes, she should be armed with resolute alertness. She should arrive
with girlfriends and leave with them. A girl who lets herself get dead
drunk at a fraternity party is a fool. A girl who goes upstairs alone
with a brother at a fraternity party is an idiot. Feminists call this
"blaming the victim." I call it common sense.

For a decade, feminists have drilled their disciples to say, "Rape   9
is a crime of violence but not of sex." This sugar-coated Shirley
Temple nonsense has exposed young women to disaster. Misled by
feminism, they do not expect rape from the nice boys from good
homes who sit next to them in class.

Aggression and eroticism, in fact, are deeply intertwined. Hunt,   10
pursuit and capture are biologically programmed into male sexuali-
ty. Generation after generation, men must be educated, refined, and
ethically persuaded away from their tendency toward anarchy and
brutishness. Society is not the enemy, as feminism ignorantly claims.
Society is woman's protection against rape. Feminism, with its
solemn Carry Nation[2] repressiveness, does not see what is for men
the eroticism or fun element in rape, especially the wild, infectious
delirium of gang rape. Women who do not understand rape cannot
defend themselves against it.

The date-rape controversy shows feminism hitting the wall of its   11
own broken promises. The women of my '60s generation were the
first respectable girls in history to swear like sailors, get drunk, stay
out all night—in short, to act like men. We sought total sexual freedom and equality. But as time passed, we woke up to cold reality.
The old double standard protected women. When anything goes,
it's women who lose.

Today's young women don't know what they want. They see that   12
feminism has not brought sexual happiness. The theatrics of public

[2]A nineteenth-century reformer who advocated the abolition of alcohol (editors'
note).

rage over date rape are their way of restoring the old sexual rules that were shattered by my generation. Yet nothing about the sexes has really changed. The comic film *Where the Boys Are* (1960), the ultimate expression of '50s man-chasing, still speaks directly to our time. It shows smart, lively women skillfully anticipating and fending off the dozens of strategies with which horny men try to get them into bed. The agonizing date-rape subplot and climax are brilliantly done. The victim, Yvette Mimieux, makes mistake after mistake, obvious to the other girls. She allows herself to be lured away from her girlfriends and into isolation with boys whose character and intentions she misreads. *Where the Boys Are* tells the truth. It shows courtship as a dangerous game in which the signals are not verbal but subliminal.

Neither militant feminism, which is obsessed with politically cor- 13
rect language, nor academic feminism, which believes that knowledge and experience are "constituted by" language, can understand preverbal or nonverbal communication. Feminism, focusing on sexual politics, cannot see that sex exists in and through the body. Sexual desire and arousal cannot be fully translated into verbal terms. This is why men and women misunderstand each other.

Trying to remake the future, feminism cut itself off from sexual 14
history. It discarded and suppressed the sexual myths of literature, art and religion. Those myths show us the turbulence, the mysteries and passions of sex. In mythology we see men's sexual anxiety, their fear of woman's dominance. Much sexual violence is rooted in men's sense of psychological weakness toward women. It takes many men to deal with one woman. Woman's voracity is a persistent motif. Clara Bow,[3] it was rumored, took on the USC[4] football team on weekends. Marilyn Monroe, singing "Diamonds Are a Girl's Best Friend," rules a conga line of men in tuxes. Half-clad Cher, in the video for "If I Could Turn Back Time," deranges a battleship of screaming sailors and straddles a pink-lit cannon. Feminism, coveting social power, is blind to woman's cosmic sexual power.

To understand rape, you must study the past. There never was 15
and never will be sexual harmony. Every woman must be prudent and cautious about where she goes and with whom. When she makes a mistake, she must accept the consequences and, through self-criticism, resolve never to make that mistake again. Running to

[3]A movie star from the Roaring Twenties era (editors' note).
[4]University of Southern California (editors' note).

mommy and daddy on the campus grievance committee is unworthy of strong women. Posting lists of guilty men in the toilet is cowardly, infantile stuff.

The Italian philosophy of life espouses high-energy confrontation. A male student makes a vulgar remark about your breasts? Don't slink off to whimper with the campus shrinking violets. Deal with it. On the spot. Say, "Shut up, you jerk! And crawl back to the barnyard where you belong!" In general, women who project this take-charge attitude toward life get harassed less often. I see too many dopey, immature, self-pitying women walking around like melting sticks of butter. It's the Yvette Mimieux syndrome: make me happy. And listen to me weep when I'm not. 16

The date-rape debate is already smothering in propaganda churned out by the expensive Northeastern colleges and universities, with their overconcentration of boring, uptight academic feminists and spoiled, affluent students. Beware of the deep manipulativeness of rich students who were neglected by their parents. They love to turn the campus into hysterical psychodramas of sexual transgression, followed by assertions of parental authority and concern. And don't look for sexual enlightenment from academe, which spews out mountains of books but never looks at life directly. 17

As a fan of football and rock music, I see in the simple, swaggering masculinity of the jock and in the noisy posturing of the heavy-metal guitarist certain fundamental, unchanging truths about sex. Masculinity is aggressive, unstable, combustible. It is also the most creative cultural force in history. Women must reorient themselves toward the elemental powers of sex, which can strengthen or destroy. 18

The only solution to date rape is female self-awareness and self-control. A woman's number-one line of defense against rape is herself. When a real rape occurs, she should report it to the police. Complaining to college committees because the courts "take too long" is ridiculous. College administrations are not a branch of the judiciary. They are not equipped or trained for legal inquiry. Colleges must alert incoming students to the problems and dangers of adulthood. Then colleges must stand back and get out of the sex game. 19

Questions for Close Reading

1. What is the selection's thesis? Locate the sentence(s) in which Paglia states her main idea. If she doesn't state the thesis explicitly, express it in your own words.

2. In Paglia's opinion, why are women more "vulnerable and defenseless" now than in the past?
3. According to Paglia, what "truth about sex" has feminism hidden from young women?
4. What does Paglia believe is "the only solution to date rape"?
5. Refer to your dictionary as needed to define the following words used in the selection: *inquests* (paragraph 2), *testosterone* (8), *constituted* (13), *grievance* (15), and *judiciary* (19).

Questions About the Writer's Craft

1. **The pattern.** Examine the way Paglia develops her argument in paragraphs 6 and 8. Which of her assertions in these paragraphs can be assumed to be true without further proof? Why do you think Paglia includes these essentially incontestable statements? Conversely, which of her assertions in paragraphs 6 and 8 require further proof before their truth can be demonstrated? Does Paglia provide such support? Explain.
2. **Other patterns.** How does Paglia use the comparison-contrast pattern to develop her argument?
3. Paglia's style is frequently characterized by short sentences strung together with few transitions. Locate some examples of this style. Why might Paglia have chosen this style? What is its effect?
4. Where does Paglia use emotional, highly connotative language? Where does she employ strongly worded absolute statements? Do you think that this use of pathos makes Paglia's argument more or less convincing? Explain.

Writing Assignments Using Argumentation-Persuasion as a Pattern of Development

∞ 1. Read Susan Jacoby's "Common Decency" (page 458), an essay that takes exception to Paglia's view of date rape. Decide which writer presents her case more convincingly. Then write an essay arguing that the *other writer* has trouble making a strong case for her position. Consider the merits and flaws (including any logical fallacies) in the argument, plus such issues as the writer's credibility, strategies for dealing with the opposing view, and use of emotional appeals. Throughout, support your opinion with specific examples drawn from the selection. Keep in mind that you're critiquing the effectiveness of the writer's argument. It's not appropriate, then, simply to explain why you agree or disagree with the writer's position or merely to summarize what the writer says.

∞ 2. Paglia criticizes those who claim that the environment, or social climate, is primarily responsible for shaping gender differences. She believes that such differences "are based in biology." Write an essay arguing your own position about the role that environment and biology play in determining sex-role attitudes and behavior. Remembering to acknowledge opposing views, defend your own viewpoint with plentiful examples based on your experiences and observations. You may also need to conduct some library research to gather support for your position. The following essays will provide insights that you may want to draw upon in your paper: Barbara Ehrenreich's "What I've Learned From Men" (page 196), Deborah Tannen's "But What Do You Mean?" (page 241), and Dave Barry's "The Ugly Truth About Beauty" (page 323).

Writing Assignments Using Other Patterns of Development

3. Paglia writes in paragraph 7 that "men become masculine only when other men say they are. Having sex with a woman is one way a boy becomes a man." Write an essay constructing your own definition of masculinity. Comment on the extent to which you feel being sexually active is an important criterion, but also include other hallmarks of masculinity.

4. Date rape seems to be on the rise. Brainstorm with others to identify what may be leading to its growing occurrence. Focusing on several related factors, write an essay showing how these factors contribute to the problem. Possible factors include the following: the way males and females are depicted in the media (advertisements, movies, television, rock videos); young people's use of alcohol; the emergence of coed college dorms. At the end of the essay, offer some recommendations about what can be done to create a safer climate for dating. You should consider supporting your speculations with information about date rape gathered in the library and/or on the Internet.

Writing Assignments Using a Journal Entry as a Starting Point

5. Drawing upon the material in your pre-reading journal entry, write an essay in which you present a carefully considered definition of the term *date rape*. Explain clearly what constitutes date rape and what doesn't. To deepen your understanding of this thorny issue, consider brainstorming with others as well as conducting research in the library and/or on the Internet. One issue to consider: Do males and females define the term differently? If so, how do they define it, and why might their definitions differ?

Susan Jacoby

In her first job as a newspaper reporter, Susan Jacoby (1945–) carefully avoided doing "women's stories," believing that such features weren't worthy of a serious journalist. However, Jacoby's opinion changed with the times, especially as women's issues began to gain increasing attention. Indeed, many of her essays—including those in the *New York Times* and *McCall's*—have dealt with women's concerns. Several of Jacoby's essays have been collected in *The Possible She* (1979) and *Money, Manners, and Morals* (1993). In 1994, she coauthored the biography *Soul to Soul: A Black Russian American Family 1865–1992*. Jacoby's most recent books include *Body* and *Geotrivia Sports*, both published in 1996, and *Half-Jew: A Daughter's Search for Her Family's Buried Past* (2000). The following selection, published in the *New York Times* in April 1991, was written in response to the book *Sexual Personae* by Camille Paglia (see page 451).

Pre-Reading Journal Entry

The phrase "boys will be boys" is often cited to explain certain types of male behavior. What kinds of actions typically fall into this category? List a few of these in your journal. Which behaviors are positive? Why? Which are negative? Why?

Common Decency

She was deeply in love with a man who was treating her badly. 1
To assuage her wounded ego (and to prove to herself that she could get along nicely without him), she invited another man, an old boyfriend, to a dinner *à deux* in her apartment. They were on their way to the bedroom when, having realized that she wanted only the man who wasn't there, she changed her mind. Her ex-boyfriend was understandably angry. He left her apartment with a not-so-politely phrased request that she leave him out of any future plans.

And that is the end of the story—except for the fact that he was 2
eventually kind enough to accept her apology for what was surely a classic case of "mixed signals."

I often recall this incident, in which I was the embarrassed 3
female participant, as the controversy over "date rape"—intensified

by the assault that William Kennedy Smith[1] has been accused of—
heats up across the nation. What seems clear to me is that those who
place acquaintance rape in a different category from "stranger
rape"—those who excuse friendly social rapists on grounds that they
are too dumb to understand when "no" means no—are being even
more insulting to men than to women.

These apologists for date rape—and some of them are women— 4
are really saying that the average man cannot be trusted to exercise
any impulse control. Men are nasty and men are brutes—and a
woman must be constantly on her guard to avoid giving a man any
excuse to give way to his baser instincts.

If this view were accurate, few women would manage to get 5
through life without being raped, and few men would fail to commit rape. For the reality is that all of us, men as well as women, send
and receive innumerable mixed signals in the course of our sexual
lives—and that is as true in marital beds at age fifty as in the back
seats of cars at age fifteen.

Most men somehow manage to decode these signals without 6
using superior physical strength to force themselves on their partners. And most women manage to handle conflicting male signals
without, say, picking up carving knives to demonstrate their dis-
pleasure at sexual rejection. This is called civilization.

Civilized is exactly what my old boyfriend was being when he 7
didn't use my muddleheaded emotional distress as an excuse to rape
me. But I don't owe him excessive gratitude for his decent behavior—any more than he would have owed me special thanks for not
stabbing him through the heart if our situations had been reversed.
Most date rapes do not happen because a man honestly mistakes a
woman's "no" for a "yes" or a "maybe." They occur because a
minority of men—an ugly minority, to be sure—can't stand to take
"no" for an answer.

This minority behavior—and a culture that excuses it on 8
grounds that boys will be boys—is the target of the movement
against date rape that has surfaced on many campuses during the
past year.

---

[1]William Kennedy Smith, the nephew of John, Robert, and Edward Kennedy, was
accused of raping a woman in 1991. Kennedy was acquitted, but the trial, broadcast on television, created a national furor and generated heated debate on the issue
of date rape (editors' note).

It's not surprising that date rape is an issue of particular impor-   9
tance to college-age women. The campus concentration of large
numbers of young people, in an unsupervised environment that
encourages drinking and partying, tends to promote sexual aggression and discourage inhibition. Drunken young men who rape a
woman at a party can always claim they didn't know what they were
doing—and a great many people will blame the victim for having
been there in the first place.

That is the line adopted by antifeminists like Camille Paglia,[2]   10
author of the controversial *Sexual Personae: Art and Decadence From
Nefertiti to Emily Dickinson*. Paglia, whose views strongly resemble
those expounded twenty years ago by Norman Mailer[3] in *The
Prisoner of Sex*, argues that feminists have deluded women by telling
them they can go anywhere and do anything without fear of rape.
Feminism, in this view, is both naïve and antisexual because it ignores
the power of women to incite uncontrollable male passions.

Just to make sure there is no doubt about a woman's place,   11
Paglia also links the male sexual aggression that leads to rape with
the creative energy of art. "There is no female Mozart," she has
declared, "because there is no female Jack the Ripper." According
to this "logic," one might expect to discover the next generation of
composers in fraternity houses and dorms that have been singled out
as sites of brutal gang rapes.

This type of unsubtle analysis makes no distinction between sex   12
as an expression of the will to power and sex as a source of pleasure.
When domination is seen as an inevitable component of sex, the act
of rape is defined not by a man's actions but by a woman's signals.

It is true, of course, that some women (especially the young)   13
initially resist sex not out of real conviction but as part of the elaborate persuasion and seduction rituals accompanying what was once
called courtship. And it is true that many men (again, especially the
young) take pride in the ability to coax a woman a step further than
she intended to go.

But these mating rituals do not justify or even explain date rape.   14
Even the most callow youth is capable of understanding the difference between resistance and genuine fear; between a halfhearted "no,
we shouldn't" and tears or screams; between a woman who is physically free to leave a room and one who is being physically restrained.

[2]For information on Camille Paglia, see page 451 (editors' note).
[3]An American essayist and novelist (editors' note).

The immorality and absurdity of using mixed signals as an   15
excuse for rape is cast in high relief when the assault involves one
woman and a group of men. In cases of gang rape in a social setting
(usually during or after a party), the defendants and their lawyers
frequently claim that group sex took place but no force was
involved. These upright young men, so the defense invariably contends, were confused because the girl had voluntarily gone to a party
with them. Why, she may have even displayed sexual interest in *one*
of them. How could they have been expected to understand that she
didn't wish to have sex with the whole group?

The very existence of the term "date rape" attests to a slow   16
change in women's consciousness that began with the feminist movement of the late 1960s. Implicit in this consciousness is the conviction that a woman has the right to say no at any point in the process
leading to sexual intercourse—and that a man who fails to respect her
wishes should incur serious legal and social consequences.

The other, equally important half of the equation is respect for   17
men. If mixed signals are the real cause of sexual assault, it behooves
every woman to regard every man as a potential rapist.

In such a benighted universe, it would be impossible for a woman   18
(and, let us not forget, for a man) to engage in the tentative emotional and physical exploration that eventually produces a mature
erotic life. She would have to make up her mind right from the start
in order to prevent a rampaging male from misreading her intentions.

Fortunately for everyone, neither the character of men nor the   19
general quality of relations between the sexes is that crude. By cen-
suring the minority of men who use ordinary socializing as an excuse
for rape, feminists insist on sex as a source of pure pleasure rather
than as a means of social control. Real men want an eager sexual
partner—not a woman who is quaking with fear or even one who is
ambivalent. Real men don't rape.

Questions for Close Reading

1. What is the selection's thesis? Locate the sentence(s) in which Jacoby
   states her main idea. If she doesn't state the thesis explicitly, express it in
   your own words.
2. Why does Jacoby feel that she doesn't owe her old boyfriend a great deal
   of gratitude, even though she sent mixed signals about what type of relationship she wanted?
3. What does Jacoby mean in paragraph 6 by her comment, "This is called
   civilization"? How does this comment support her thesis?

4. Why does Jacoby think that it's insulting to men to accept Paglia's notion that men are ruled by uncontrollable passions?

5. Refer to your dictionary as needed to define the following words used in the selection: *apologists* (paragraph 4), *deluded* (10), *unsubtle* (12), *implicit* (16), *benighted* (18), *erotic* (18), *rampaging* (18), and *ambivalent* (19).

Questions About the Writer's Craft

1. The pattern. One way to refute an idea is to carry it to its logical extreme, thus revealing its inherent falsity or absurdity. This technique is called *reduction ad absurdum*. Examine paragraphs 4–5 and 15 and explain how Jacoby uses this technique to refute Paglia's position on date rape.

2. Other patterns. Locate places in the essay where Jacoby compares and contrasts male and female behavior or the behavior of rapists and non-rapists. How does her use of comparison-contrast help her build her argument?

3. What introduction technique (see pages 60–62) does Jacoby use to begin the essay? How does this type of introduction help her achieve her persuasive goal?

4. How would you characterize Jacoby's tone? Identify specific sentences and words that convey this tone. What effect might Jacoby have hoped this tone would have on readers?

Writing Assignments Using Argumentation-Persuasion as a Pattern of Development

1. Jacoby feels that Camille Paglia and others "excuse . . . rapists." If you haven't already done so, read "Rape: A Bigger Danger Than Feminists Know" (page 451) to see what Paglia says about who bears primary responsibility for preventing rape. Then decide to what degree you feel men who commit date rape should be held accountable for their actions. Argue your position in an essay, making reference to both Jacoby's and Paglia's ideas to support your case. Also include reasons and evidence of your own.

2. Determine what your campus is doing about date rape. Does it have a formal policy defining date rape, a hearing process, ongoing workshops, discussions during orientation for incoming students? Write a paper explaining how your college deals with date rape. Then argue either that more attention should be devoted to this issue or that your college has adopted fair and comprehensive measures to deal with the problem. If you feel the college should do more, indicate what additional steps should be taken.

Writing Assignments Using Other Patterns of Development

3. Jacoby acknowledges that males and females often send "mixed signals" and cause each other confusion. Select one time that you found "mixed signals" with a person of the opposite sex to be a problem. For example, you might have conflicted because of different ways of expressing anger or because of dissimilar styles in asking for support. Describe what happened and explain why you think such mixed signals occurred. Before writing the paper, you may want to read "But What Do You Mean?" (page 241) to see what Deborah Tannen has to say about some basic differences between men and women.

4. Interview some people, both males and females, to determine their definition of date rape. In an essay, discuss any differences between the two sexes' perspectives. That done, present your own definition of date rape, explaining what it is and what it isn't.

Writing Assignments Using a Journal Entry as a Starting Point

5. Some people believe that "boys-will-be-boys" behavior is potentially dangerous and therefore not acceptable. Others argue that it is perfectly innocent and therefore permissible. What do you think? Drawing upon your pre-reading journal entry, write an essay taking a position on this issue. Provide persuasive examples to support your viewpoint, refuting as much of the opposing argument as you can. Discussing the topic with others and doing some research in the library and/or on the Internet will broaden your understanding of this complex issue.

Roger Wilkins

Pulitzer Prize-winning journalist Roger Wilkins (1932–) is the author of many works, including *A Man's Life: An Autobiography* (1982), *Quiet Riots: Race and Poverty in the U.S.* (1988), and *Jefferson's Pillow* (2001). A member of the editorial board at *The Nation*, Wilkins is professor of history at George Mason University in Virginia. Senior advisor to Jesse Jackson during Jackson's presidential campaigns, Wilkins also served as national coordinator of the visit that South African president Nelson Mandela made to the United States in 1988. The following essay was first published in *The Nation* in 1995.

Pre-Reading Journal Entry

Do you think schools should engage in discussions of racism, a sensitive and painful topic? Why do you feel as you do? Would such discussions be appropriate at some levels of schooling but not at others? Take some time to explore these questions in your journal.

Racism Has Its Privileges

The storm that has been gathering over affirmative action for the past few years has burst. Two conservative California professors are leading a drive to place an initiative on the state ballot in 1996 that will ask Californians to vote affirmative action up or down.[1] Since the state is beloved in political circles for its electoral votes, advance talk of the initiative has put the issue high on the national agenda. Three Republican presidential contenders—Bob Dole, Phil Gramm and Lamar Alexander—have already begun taking shots at various equal opportunity programs. Congressional review of the Clinton Administration's enforcement of these programs has begun. The President has started his own review, promising adherence to principles of nondiscrimination and full opportunity while asserting the need to prune those programs that are unfair or malfunctioning.

1

---

[1]Approved by 54 percent of the voters in California, Proposition 209 took effect in August 1997, ending affirmative action efforts in the state (editors' note).

It is almost an article of political faith that one of the major influ-   2
ences in last November's election was the backlash against affirmative
action among "angry white men," who are convinced it has stacked the
deck against them. Their attitudes are shaped and their anger heightened by unquestioned and virtually uncheckable anecdotes about victimized whites flooding the culture. For example, *Washington Post*
columnist Richard Cohen recently began what purported to be a serious analysis and attack on affirmative action by recounting that he had
once missed out on a job someplace because they "needed a woman."

Well, I have an anecdote too, and it, together with Cohen's,   3
offers some important insights about the debate that has flared
recently around the issues of race, gender and justice. Some years
ago, after watching me teach as a visiting professor for two semesters,
members of the history department at George Mason University
invited me to compete for a full professorship and endowed chair.
Mason, like other institutions in Virginia's higher education system,
was under a court order to desegregate. I went through the appropriate application and review process and, in due course, was appoint-
ed. A few years later, not long after I had been honored as one of the
university's distinguished professors, I was shown an article by a
white historian asserting that he had been a candidate for that chair
but that at the last moment the job had been whisked away and
handed to an unqualified black. I checked the story and discovered
that this fellow had, in fact, applied but had not even passed the first
threshold. But his "reverse discrimination" story is out there pollut-
ing the atmosphere in which this debate is taking place.

Affirmative action, as I understand it, was not designed to pun-   4
ish anyone; it was, rather—as a result of a clear-eyed look at how
America actually works—an attempt to enlarge opportunity for
everybody. As amply documented in the 1968 Kerner Commission
report on racial disorders, when left to their own devices, American
institutions in such areas as college admissions, hiring decisions and
loan approvals had been making choices that discriminated against
blacks. That discrimination, which flowed from doing what came
naturally, hurt more than blacks: it hurt the entire nation, as the
riots of the late 1960s demonstrated. Though the Kerner report
focused on blacks, similar findings could have been made about
other minorities and women.

Affirmative action required institutions to develop plans enabling   5
them to go beyond business as usual and search for qualified people

in places where they did not ordinarily conduct their searches or their business. Affirmative action programs generally require some proof that there has been a good-faith effort to follow the plan and numerical guidelines against which to judge the sincerity and the success of the effort. The idea of affirmative action is *not* to force people into positions for which they are unqualified but to encourage institutions to develop realistic criteria for the enterprise at hand and then to find a reasonably diverse mix of people qualified to be engaged in it. Without the requirements calling for plans, good-faith efforts and the setting of broad numerical goals, many institutions would do what they had always done: assert that they had looked but "couldn't find anyone qualified," and then go out and hire the white man they wanted to hire in the first place.

Affirmative action has done wonderful things for the United   6
States by enlarging opportunity and developing and utilizing a far broader array of the skills available in the American population than in the past. It has not outlived its usefulness. It was never designed to be a program to eliminate poverty. It has not always been used wisely, and some of its permutations do have to be reconsidered, refined or, in some cases, abandoned. It is not a quota program, and those cases where rigid numbers are used (except under a court or administrative order after a specific finding of discrimination) are a bastardization of an otherwise highly beneficial set of public policies.

President Clinton is right to review what is being done under pres-   7
ent laws and to express a willingness to eliminate activities that either don't work or are unfair. Any program that has been in place for thirty years should be reviewed. Getting rid of what doesn't work is both good government and good politics. Gross abuses of affirmative action provide ammunition for its opponents and undercut the moral authority of the entire effort. But the President should retain—and strengthen where required—those programs necessary to enlarge social justice.

What makes the affirmative action issue so difficult is that it   8
engages blacks and whites exactly at those points where they differ the most. There are some areas, such as rooting for the local football team, where their experiences and views are virtually identical. There are others—sometimes including work and school—where their experiences and views both overlap and diverge. And finally, there are areas such as affirmative action and inextricably related notions about the presence of racism in society where the divergences draw out almost all the points of difference between the races.

This Land Is My Land

Blacks and whites experience America very differently. Though 9
we often inhabit the same space, we operate in very disparate psychic spheres.

Whites have an easy sense of ownership of the country; they feel 10
they are entitled to receive all that is best in it. Many of them believe
that their country—though it may have some faults—is superior to
all others and that, as Americans, they are superior as well. Many of
them think of this as a white country and some of them even experience it that way. They think of it as a land of opportunity—a good
place with a lot of good people in it. Some suspect (others *know*)
that the presence of blacks messes everything up. . . .

For most blacks, America is either a land of denied opportunity 11
or one in which the opportunities are still grudgingly extended and
extremely limited. For some—that one-third who are mired in poverty, many of them isolated in dangerous ghettos—America is a land of
desperadoes and desperation. In places where whites see a lot of idealism, blacks see, at best, idealism mixed heavily with hypocrisy.
Blacks accept America's greatness but are unable to ignore ugly warts
that many whites seem to need not to see. I am reminded here of
James Baldwin's searing observation from *The Fire Next Time:*

> The American Negro has the great advantage of having
> never believed that collection of myths to which white
> Americans cling: that their ancestors were all freedom-lov-
> ing heroes, that they were born in the greatest country the
> world has ever seen, or that Americans are invincible in bat-
> tle and wise in peace, that Americans have always dealt hon-
> orably with Mexicans and Indians and all other neighbors
> or inferiors, that American men are the world's most direct
> and virile, that American women are pure.

It goes without saying, then, that blacks and whites remember 12
America differently. The past is hugely important since we argue a
lot about who we are on the basis of who we think we have been,
and we derive much of our sense of the future from how we think
we've done in the past. In a nation in which few people know much
history these are perilous arguments, because in such a vacuum,
people tend to weave historical fables tailored to their political or
psychic needs.

Blacks are still recovering the story of their role in America, 13 which so many white historians simply ignored or told in a way that made black people ashamed. But in a culture that batters us, learning the real history is vital in helping blacks feel fully human. It also helps us understand just how deeply American we are, how richly we have given, how much has been taken from us and how much has yet to be restored. Supporters of affirmative action believe that broad and deep damage has been done to American culture by racism and sexism over the whole course of American history and that they are still powerful forces today. We believe that minorities and women are still disadvantaged in our highly competitive society and that affirmative action is absolutely necessary to level the playing field. . . .

The Politics of Denial

The successful public relations assault on affirmative action 14 flows on a river of racism that is as broad, powerful and American as the Mississippi. And, like the Mississippi, racism can be violent and deadly and is a permanent feature of American life. But while nobody who is sane denies the reality of the Mississippi, millions of Americans who are deemed sane—some of whom are powerful and some even thought wise—deny, wholly or in part, that racism exists.

It is critical to understand the workings of denial in this debate 15 because it is used to obliterate the facts that created the need for the remedy in the first place. One of the best examples of denial was provided recently by the nation's most famous former history professor, House Speaker Newt Gingrich. According to *The Washington Post*, "Gingrich dismissed the argument that the beneficiaries of affirmative action, commonly African Americans, have been subjected to discrimination over a period of centuries. 'That is true of virtually every American,' Gingrich said, noting that the Irish were discriminated against by the English, for example."

That is breathtaking stuff coming from somebody who should 16 know that blacks have been on this North American continent for 375 years and that for 245 the country permitted slavery. Gingrich should also know that for the next hundred years we had legalized subordination of blacks, under a suffocating blanket of condescension and frequently enforced by nightriding terrorists. We've had only thirty years of something else.

That something else is a nation trying to lift its ideals out of a 17 thick, often impenetrable slough of racism. Racism is a hard word for what over the centuries became second nature in America—preferences across the board for white men and, following in their wake, white women. Many of these men seem to feel that it is un-American to ask them to share anything with blacks—particularly their work, their neighborhoods or "their" women. To protect these things— apparently essential to their identity—they engage in all forms of denial. For a historian to assert that "virtually every American" shares the history I have just outlined comes very close to lying.

Denial of racism is much like the denials that accompany addictions to alcohol, drugs or gambling. It is probably not stretching the analogy too much to suggest that many racist whites are so addicted to their unwarranted privileges and so threatened by the prospect of losing them that all kinds of defenses become acceptable. . . . 18

"Those People" Don't Deserve Help

Before the 1950s, whites who were busy denying that the nation was unfair to blacks would simply assert that we didn't deserve equal treatment because we were *inferior.* These days it is not permissible in most public circles to say that blacks are inferior, but it is perfectly acceptable to target the *behavior* of blacks, specifically poor blacks. . . . 19

While I don't hold the view that all blacks who behave badly are blameless victims of a brutal system, I do believe that many poor blacks have, indeed, been brutalized by our culture, and I know of *no* blacks, rich or poor, who haven't been hurt in some measure by the racism in this country. The current mood (and, in some cases like the Speaker's, the cultivated ignorance) completely ignores the fact that some blacks never escaped the straight line of oppression that ran from slavery through the semislavery of sharecropping to the late mid-century migration from Southern farms into isolated pockets of urban poverty. Their families have always been excluded, poor and without skills, and so they were utterly defenseless when the enormous American economic dislocations that began in the mid-1970s slammed into their communities, followed closely by deadly waves of crack cocaine. One would think that the double-digit unemployment suffered consistently over the past two decades by blacks who were *looking for work* would be a permanent feature of the discussions about race, responsibility, welfare and rights. 20

But people's attention is kept trained on the behavior of some poor blacks by politicians and television news shows, reinforcing the stereotypes of blacks as dangerous, as threats, as unqualified. 21

Frightened whites direct their rage at pushy blacks rather than at the corporations that export manufacturing operations to low-wage countries, or at the Federal Reserve, which imposes interest rate hikes that slow down the economy.

Who Benefits? We All Do

There is one final denial that blankets all the rest. It is that only   22
society's "victims"—blacks, other minorities and women (who should, for God's sake, renounce their victimological outlooks)— have been injured by white male supremacy. Viewed in this light, affirmative action remedies are a kind of zero-sum game in which only the "victims" benefit. But racist and sexist whites who are not able to accept the full humanity of other people are themselves badly damaged—morally stunted—people. The principal product of a racist and sexist society is damaged people and institutions—victims and victimizers alike. Journalism and education, two enterprises with which I am familiar, provide two good examples.

Journalistic institutions often view the nation through a lens   23
that bends reality to support white privileges. A recent issue of *U.S. News & World Report* introduced a package of articles on these issues with a question on its cover: "Does affirmative action mean NO WHITE MEN NEED APPLY?" The words "No white men need apply" were printed in red against a white background and were at least four times larger than the other words in the question. Inside, the lead story was illustrated by a painting that carries out the cover theme, with a wan white man separated from the opportunity ladders eagerly being scaled by women and dark men. And the story yielded up the following sentence: "Affirmative action poses a conflict between two cherished American principles: the belief that all Americans deserve equal opportunities and the idea that hard work and merit, not race or religion or gender or birthright, should determine who prospers and who does not."

Whoever wrote that sentence was in the thrall of one of the   24
myths that Baldwin was talking about. The sentence suggests—as many people do when talking about affirmative action—that America is a meritocratic society. But what kind of meritocracy excludes women and blacks and other minorities from all meaningful competition? And even in the competition among white men, money, family and connections often count for much more than merit, test results (for whatever they're worth) and hard work.

The *U.S. News* story perpetuates and strengthens the view that 25
many of my white students absorb from their parents: that white
men now have few chances in this society. The fact is that white men
still control virtually everything in America except the wealth held
by widows. According to the Urban Institute, 53 percent of black
men aged 25–34 are either unemployed or earn too little to lift a
family of four from poverty.

Educational institutions that don't teach accurately about why 26
America looks the way it does and why the distribution of winners
and losers is as it is also injure our society. Here is another anecdote.

A warm, brilliant young white male student of mine came in just 27
before he was to graduate and said that my course in race, law and culture, which he had just finished, had been the most valuable and the
most disturbing he had ever taken. I asked how it had been disturbing.

"I learned that my two heroes are racists," he said. 28

"Who are your heroes and how are they racists?" I asked. 29

"My mom and dad," he said. "After thinking about what I was 30
learning, I understand that they had spent all my life making me into
the same kind of racists they were."

Affirmative action had brought me together with him when he 31
was 22. Affirmative action puts people together in ways that make
that kind of revelation possible. Nobody is a loser when that happens. The country gains.

And that, in the end, is the case for affirmative action. The argu- 32
ments supporting it should be made on the basis of its broad contributions to the entire American community. It is insufficient to vilify white males and to skewer them as the whiners that journalism of
the kind practiced by *U.S. News* invites us to do. These are people
who, from the beginning of the Republic, have been taught that
skin color is destiny and that whiteness is to be revered. Listen to
Jefferson, writing in the year the Constitution was drafted:

> The first difference that strikes us is that of colour. . . . And
> is the difference of no importance? Is it not the foundation
> of a greater or less share of beauty in the two races? Are not
> the fine mixtures of red and white . . . in the one, preferable
> to that eternal monotony, which reigns in the counte-
> nances, that immoveable veil of black which covers all the
> emotions of the other race? Add to these, flowing hair, a
> more elegant symmetry of form, their own judgment in

favor of the whites, declared by their preference for them, as uniformly as is the preference of the Oran-ootan for the black women over those of his own species. The circumstance of superior beauty, is thought worthy attention in the propagation of our horses, dogs, and other domestic animals; why not in that of man?

In a society so conceived and so dedicated, it is understandable that white males would take their preferences as a matter of natural right and consider any alteration of that a primal offense. But a nation that operates in that way abandons its soul and its economic strength, and will remain mired in ugliness and moral squalor because so many people are excluded from the possibility of decent lives and from forming any sense of community with the rest of society. . . .

It may be that we will need affirmative action until most white   33
males are really ready for a color-blind society—that is, when they are ready to assume "the rank of a mere citizen." As a nation we took a hard look at that special favoritism thirty years ago. Though the centuries of cultural preference enjoyed by white males still overwhelmingly skew power and wealth their way, we have in fact achieved a more meritocratic society as a result of affirmative action than we have ever previously enjoyed in this country.

If we want to continue making things better in this society, we'd   34
better figure out ways to protect and defend affirmative action against the confused, the frightened, the manipulators and, yes, the liars in politics, journalism, education and wherever else they may be found. In the name of longstanding American prejudice and myths and in the service of their own narrow interests, power-lusts or blindness, they are truly victimizing the rest of us, perverting the ideals they claim to stand for and destroying the nation they pretend to serve.

Questions for Close Reading

1. What is the selection's thesis? Locate the sentences in which Wilkins states his main idea. If he doesn't state the thesis explicitly, express it in your own words.
2. How does Wilkins define *affirmative action?* What must an affirmative-action program include in order to be successful?
3. According to Wilkins, what "myths" do White people believe? How have these myths prevented White people from seeing the need for affirmative action?
4. How, in Wilkins's opinion, does affirmative action benefit *all* Americans?

5. Refer to your dictionary as needed to define the following words used in the selection: *initiative* (paragraph 1), *adherence* (1), *purported* (2), *permutations* (6), *bastardization* (6), *inextricably* (8), *disparate* (9), *invincible* (11), *obliterate* (15), *meritocratic* (24), *perpetuates* (25), *vilify* (32), and *skew* (33).

Questions About the Writer's Craft

1. **The pattern.** Where in his argument does Wilkins acknowledge conflicting viewpoints? What is his attitude toward these opposing views? How does this attitude help Wilkins reinforce his thesis?

2. **Other patterns.** Why do you suppose Wilkins places the anecdote about his being hired at George Mason University (paragraph 3) near the beginning of his essay? How does this anecdote add to the effectiveness of his argument?

3. **Other patterns.** Locate places in the essay where Wilkins uses comparison-contrast. How do these comparisons and contrasts help Wilkins develop his central argument?

4. Sometimes Wilkins uses provocative language, as when he refers to the beliefs of those opposed to affirmative action as "myths." What other emotionally loaded words does he use? What assumptions about his audience might have motivated Wilkins to employ this charged language?

Writing Assignments Using Argumentation-Persuasion as a Pattern of Development

∞ 1. Wilkins argues that "affirmative action is absolutely necessary to level the playing field" for minorities in this country. Do you agree? Focusing on a specific minority group, write an essay in which you support or challenge Wilkins's argument. To ensure that your position is more than a reflexive opinion, conduct some library research on the group in question, and read Shelby Steele's "Affirmative Action: The Price of Preference" (page 475), an essay that is in sharp opposition to Wilkins's. No matter which side you take, assume that some readers are opposed to your point of view. Acknowledge and try to dismantle as many of their objections as possible. Refer, whenever it's relevant, to Steele's argument in your paper.

∞ 2. Wilkins suggests that it is appropriate for schools to celebrate the admirable and heroic aspects of our history. But, he believes, schools must also be willing to acknowledge the "ugly warts" in that history. Do you agree? Write an essay arguing that schools should *or* should not teach students about the non-heroic aspects of our national story. Your essay should acknowledge and refute as many opposing arguments as possible. To broaden your understanding of the issue, interview classmates, family members, friends, and instructors. Also read "Let's Tell the Story of All America's Cultures" (page 445) by Yuh Ji-Yeon.

Writing Assignments Using Other Patterns of Development

∞ 3. Wilkins believes that people who consider themselves victims should "renounce their victimological outlooks." Select a group that you believe perceives itself as being victimized. Possibilities include a specific racial, ethnic, or religious group; the disabled; the overweight; those in abusive relationships. Write an essay explaining the steps these individuals could take to overthrow their victimhood. End the paper by discussing the effects of abandoning a victimological perspective. What would be gained? What might be lost? Before writing, read one or more of the following essays to sharpen your understanding of the concept of victimhood: Maya Angelou's "Sister Flowers" (page 106), William Raspberry's "The Handicap of Definition" (page 394), and Camille Paglia's "Rape: A Bigger Danger Than Feminists Know" (page 451).

4. One student told Wilkins that the course Wilkins taught was "the most valuable . . . he had ever taken." Write an essay showing how a course or school experience made you, like Wilkins's student, realize something important about yourself, society, or life in general. Develop your essay by contrasting what you were like before with what you were like after the educational experience.

Writing Assignments Using a Journal Entry as a Starting Point

∞ 5. Write an essay arguing that schools should *or* should not encourage students to discuss the issue of racism. Review your pre-reading journal entry, and select a specific level of schooling to focus on before taking a position. Supplement the material in your journal by gathering the opinions, experiences, and observations of friends, family, and classmates. No matter which position you take, remember to cite opposing arguments, refuting as many of them as you can. Before writing, consider reading "Let's Tell the Story of All America's Cultures" (page 445), in which Yuh Ji-Yeon forcefully argues the need for honest discussion of race and ethnicity in the classroom.

Shelby Steele

Currently a professor of English at San Jose State University, Shelby Steele (1946–) was born in Chicago and earned his doctoral degree at the University of Utah. The recipient of a National Magazine Award in 1989, Steele has published widely. His writing on racial issues has appeared in publications including *Harper's,* the *New York Times,* the *Washington Post,* and *American Scholar.* One of his pieces on race was selected for *The Best American Essays 1989,* and a number of his most compelling essays were published in *The Content of Our Character: A New Vision of Race in America* (1990). Most recently, he wrote *A Dream Deferred: The Second Betrayal of Black Freedom in America* (1998). The following essay, which originally appeared in the *New York Times Magazine* (1990), is reprinted from *The Content of Our Character.*

Pre-Reading Journal Entry

What do you think would happen if college affirmative-action admission policies were ruled illegal and were subsequently outlawed? What positive effects might there be? What negative effects? Take some time to respond to these questions in your journal.

Affirmative Action: The Price of Preference

In a few short years, when my two children will be applying to college, the affirmative-action policies by which most universities offer black students some form of preferential treatment will present me with a dilemma. I am a middle-class black, a college professor, far from wealthy, but also well removed from the kind of deprivation that would qualify my children for the label "disadvantaged." Both of them have endured racial insensitivity from whites. They have been called names, have suffered slights and have experienced first hand the peculiar malevolence that racism brings out of people. Yet they have never experienced racial discrimination, have never been stopped by their race on any path they have chosen to follow. Still,

1

their society now tells them that if they will only designate them-selves as black on their college applications, they will probably do better in the college lottery than if they conceal this fact. I think there is something of a Faustian[1] bargain in this.

Of course many blacks and a considerable number of whites   2 would say that I was sanctimoniously making affirmative action into a test of character. They would say that this small preference is the meagerest recompense for centuries of unrelieved oppression. And to these arguments other very obvious facts must be added. In America, many marginally competent or flatly incompetent whites are hired every day—some because their white skin suits the con-scious or unconscious racial preference of their employers. The white children of alumni are often grandfathered[2] into elite univer-sities in what can only be seen as a residual benefit of historic white privilege. Worse, white incompetence is always an individual matter, but for blacks it is often confirmation of ugly stereotypes. Given that unfairness cuts both ways, doesn't it only balance the scales of his-tory, doesn't this repay, in a small way, the systematic denial under which my children's grandfather lived out his days?

In theory, affirmative action certainly has all the moral symmetry   3 that fairness requires. It is reformist and corrective, even repentant and redemptive. And I would never sneer at these good intentions. Born in the late 1940s in Chicago, I started my education (a chari-table term, in this case) in a segregated school, and suffered all the indignities that come to blacks in a segregated society. My father, born in the South, made it only to the third grade before the white man's fields took permanent priority over his formal education. And though he educated himself into an advanced reader with an almost professorial authority, he could only drive a truck for a living, and never earned more than $90 a week in his entire life. So yes, it is cru-cial to my sense of citizenship, to my ability to identify with the spir-it and the interests of America, to know that this country, however imperfectly, recognizes its past sins and wishes to correct them.

Yet good intentions can blind us to the effects they generate   4 when implemented. In our society affirmative action is, among other things, a testament to white good will and to black power, and in the

---

[1]A reference to the legend of Faust, a scholar who sold his soul to the devil in return for unlimited power. Faust later regretted the bargain (editors' note).
[2]Permitted to enter on the basis of longtime association with an institution without having to satisfy existing entrance requirements (editors' note).

midst of these heavy investments its effects can be hard to see. But after 20 years of implementation I think that affirmative action has shown itself to be more bad than good and that blacks—whom I will focus on in this essay—now stand to lose more from it than they gain.

In talking with affirmative-action administrators and with blacks and whites in general, I found that supporters of affirmative action focus on its good intentions and detractors emphasize its negative effects. It was virtually impossible to find people outside either camp. The closest I came was a white male manager at a large computer company who said, "I think it amounts to reverse discrimination, but I'll put up with a little of that for a little more diversity." But this only makes him a half-hearted supporter of affirmative action. I think many people who don't really like affirmative action support it to one degree or another anyway. 5

I believe they do this because of what happened to white and black Americans in the crucible of the 1960s,[3] when whites were confronted with their racial guilt and blacks tasted their first real power. In that stormy time white absolution and black power coalesced into virtual mandates for society. Affirmative action became a meeting ground for those mandates in the law. At first, this meant insuring equal opportunity. The 1964 civil-rights bill was passed on the understanding that equal opportunity would not mean racial preference. But in the late 60's and early 70's, affirmative action underwent a remarkable escalation of its mission from simple anti-discrimination enforcement to social engineering by means of quotas, goals, timetables, set-asides and other forms of preferential treatment. 6

Legally, this was achieved through a series of executive orders and Equal Employment Opportunity Commission guidelines that allowed racial imbalances in the workplace to stand as proof of racial discrimination. Once it could be assumed that discrimination explained racial imbalances, it became easy to justify group remedies to presumed discrimination rather than the normal case-by-case redress. 7

Even though blacks had made great advances during the 60's without quotas, the white mandate to achieve a new racial innocence and the black mandate to gain power, which came to a head in the 8

---

[3]A decade characterized by both nonviolent and violent civil rights protests that forced mainstream America finally to acknowledge the injustices endured by Black Americans (editors' note).

very late 60's, could no longer be satisfied by anything less than racial preferences. I don't think these mandates, in themselves, were wrong, because whites clearly needed to do better by blacks and blacks needed more real power in society. But as they came together in affirmative action, their effect was to distort our understanding of racial discrimination. By making black the color of preference, these mandates have reburdened society with the very marriage of color and preference (in reverse) that we set out to eradicate. . . .

I think one of the most troubling effects of racial preferences for   9 blacks is a kind of demoralization. Under affirmative action, the quality that earns us preferential treatment is an implied inferiority. However this inferiority is explained—and it is easily enough explained by the myriad deprivations that grew out of our oppression—it is still inferiority. There are explanations and then there is the fact. And the fact must be borne by the individual as a condition apart from the explanation, apart even from the fact that others like himself also bear this condition. In integrated situations in which blacks must compete with whites who may be better prepared, these explanations may quickly wear thin and expose the individual to racial as well as personal self-doubt. (Of course whites also feel doubt, but only personally, not racially.)

What this means in practical terms is that when blacks deliver   10 themselves into integrated situations they encounter a nasty little reflex in whites, a mindless, atavistic reflex that responds to the color black with negative stereotypes, such as intellectual ineptness. I think this reflex embarrasses most whites today and thus it is usually quickly repressed. On an equally atavistic level, the black will be aware of the reflex his color triggers and will feel a stab of horror at seeing himself reflected in this way. He, too, will do a quick repression, but a lifetime of such stabbings is what constitutes his inner realm of racial doubt. Even when the black sees no implication of inferiority in racial preferences, he knows that whites do, so that— consciously or unconsciously—the result is virtually the same. The effect of preferential treatment—the lowering of normal standards to increase black representation—puts blacks at war with an expanded realm of debilitating doubt, so that the doubt itself becomes an unrecognized preoccupation that undermines their ability to perform, especially in integrated situations.

I believe another liability of affirmative action comes from the   11 fact that it indirectly encourages blacks to exploit their own past victimization. Like implied inferiority, victimization is what justifies preference, so that to receive the benefits of preferential treatment one must, to some extent, become invested in the view of one's self as a victim. In this way, affirmative action nurtures a victim-focused identity in blacks and sends us the message that there is more power in our past suffering than in our present achievements.

When power itself grows out of suffering, blacks are encouraged 12 to expand the boundaries of what qualifies as racial oppression, a situation that can lead us to paint our victimization in vivid colors even as we receive the benefits of preference. The same corporations and institutions that give us preference are also seen as our oppressors. At Stanford University, minority-group students—who receive at least the same financial aid as whites with the same need—recently took over the president's office demanding, among other things, more financial aid.

But I think one of the worst prices that blacks pay for preference 13 has to do with an illusion. I saw this illusion at work recently in the mother of a middle-class black student who was going off to his first semester of college: "They owe us this, so don't think for a minute that you don't belong there." This is the logic by which many blacks, and some whites, justify affirmative action—it is something "owed," a form of reparation. But this logic overlooks a much harder and less digestible reality, that it is impossible to repay blacks living today for the historic suffering of the race. If all blacks were given a million dollars tomorrow it would not amount to a dime on the dollar for three centuries of oppression, nor would it dissolve the residues of that oppression that we still carry today. The concept of historic reparation grows out of man's need to impose on the world a degree of justice that simply does not exist. Suffering can be endured and overcome, it cannot be repaid. To think otherwise is to prolong the suffering. . . .

But if not preferences, what? The impulse to discriminate is 14 subtle and cannot be ferreted out unless its many guises are made clear to people. I think we need social policies that are committed to two goals: the educational and economic development of disadvantaged people regardless of race and the eradication from our society—through close monitoring and severe sanctions—of racial, ethnic or gender discrimination. Preferences will not get us to either of these goals, because they tend to benefit those who are not disadvantaged—middle-class white women and middle-class blacks—and attack one form of discrimination with another. Preferences are inexpensive and carry the glamour of good intentions—change the numbers and the good deed is done. To be against them is to be unkind. But I think the unkindest cut is to bestow on children like my own an undeserved advantage while neglecting the development of those disadvantaged children in the poorer sections of my city who will most likely never be in a position to benefit from a preference. Give my children fairness; give disadvantaged children a better shot at development—better elementary and secondary schools, job training, safer neighborhoods, better financial assistance for college and so on. A smaller percentage of black high school graduates go to college today than 15 years ago; more black males are in prison, jail or in some other way under the control of the criminal-justice system than in college. This despite racial preferences.

The mandates of black power and white absolution out of which   15
preferences emerged were not wrong in themselves. What was wrong was that both races focused more on the goals of those mandates than on the means to the goals. Blacks can have no real power without taking responsibility for their own educational and economic development. Whites can have no racial innocence without earning it by eradicating discrimination and helping the disadvantaged to develop. Because we ignored the means, the goals have not been reached and the real work remains to be done.

Questions for Close Reading

1. What is the selection's thesis? Locate the sentence(s) in which Steele states his main idea. If he doesn't state the thesis explicitly, express it in your own words.
2. Why doesn't Steele want his children to designate themselves as Black on their college applications? Why does he call such labeling "a Faustian bargain"?
3. Why does Steele believe that affirmative action "demoralizes" Blacks?
4. What does Steele suggest as an alternative to affirmative action in hiring and in education?
5. Refer to your dictionary as needed to define the following words used in the selection: *malevolence* (paragraph 1), *sanctimoniously* (2), *meagerest* (2), *recompense* (2), *residual* (2), *symmetry* (3), *diversity* (5), *absolution* (6), *mandates* (6), *eradicate* (8), *demoralization* (9), *myriad* (9), *ineptness* (10), *debilitating* (10), *reparation* (13), and *residues* (13).

Questions About the Writer's Craft

1. **The pattern.** Which of the two possible strategies for organizing a refutation (see pages 415–16) does Steele use in his essay? Do you consider the points he makes in the refutation sufficiently persuasive? Explain.
2. **Other patterns.** Why do you suppose Steele begins with the example of his own children? How does this example prepare readers for his argument?
3. Steele often uses "I think" or "I believe" when making his points. (One example is at the end of the first paragraph.) Find additional instances elsewhere in the essay. Why do you think he uses these expressions so frequently?
4. In paragraph 9, which two key words does Steele repeat? Why might he have used this repetition?

Writing Assignments Using Argumentation-Persuasion as a Pattern of Development

∞ 1. To support his argument that affirmative action has negative effects, Steele makes a number of key points, including the following:

   - Preferential treatment implies an inherent inferiority and thus leads to corrosive self-doubt.
   - Preferential treatment fosters a feeling of victimhood that strips people of the ability to take strong action on their own behalf.
   - Preferential treatment creates a dangerous illusion of entitlement that ultimately works to the detriment of those who feel they are owed something.

   Focusing on a specific minority group, write an essay defending or challenging *one* of these points (or any other that Steele makes). Remember to acknowledge and, when possible, to refute opposing opinions. Before formulating your position, read William Raspberry's "The Handicap of Definition" (page 394) and Roger Wilkins's "Racism Has Its Privileges" (page 464). Raspberry provides additional evidence for Steele's viewpoint, while Wilkins presents a sharply divergent point of view. Where appropriate, refer to Raspberry and/or Wilkins in your paper.

∞ 2. Choose another social program or common practice with which you are familiar, and write an essay arguing—as Steele does—that it has had an effect very different from that which was intended. Like Steele, include specific examples of the program's ill effects, making sure to acknowledge the views of those who support the program. For additional insight into the way practices can have unintended negative consequences, read

Jonathan Coleman's "Is Technology Making Us Intimate Strangers?" (page 359) before writing your paper.

Writing Assignments Using Other Patterns of Development

3. Imagine what your life might be like if you were a member of another race, religion, or ethnic group. Or consider what life might be like if you were the opposite sex. Then write an essay in which you provide examples showing how your life would or would *not* change if you did indeed have another identity. Reach some conclusions about whether life would be easier or more difficult with this other identity.

4. Steele states that "Blacks can have no real power without taking responsibility for their own . . . development." The same could be said for all people. Write an essay telling about a time that you took charge of your life at a difficult point. Perhaps you rallied your strength to end a painful relationship or insisted on furthering your education even though others believed additional schooling was unnecessary. Provide vivid narrative details to show how hard you worked to take responsibility for your life. End by explaining how this concerted effort on your own behalf affected you and those who are important to you. Maya Angelou's "Sister Flowers" (page 106) and William Raspberry's "The Handicap of Definition" (page 394) should spark ideas worth exploring.

Writing Assignments Using a Journal Entry as a Starting Point

5. Write an essay exploring the positive and negative consequences that might ensue if colleges nationwide were required to dismantle their affirmative-action admission programs. To develop your discussion, draw upon the material in your pre-reading journal entry as well as the opinions of friends, classmates, and family members. Consider supplementing your informal research with material gathered in the library and/or on the Internet. At the end of your essay, indicate whether you think disbanding affirmative-action admission policies would be a good idea or a bad one.

Additional Writing Topics

ARGUMENTATION-PERSUASION

General Assignments

Using argumentation-persuasion, develop one of the topics below in an essay. After choosing a topic, think about your purpose and audience. Remember that the paper's thesis should state the issue under discussion as well as your position on the issue. As you work on developing evidence, you might want to do some outside research. Keep in mind that effective argumentation-persuasion usually means that some time should be spent acknowledging and perhaps refuting opposing points of view. Be careful not to sabotage your argument by basing your case on a logical fallacy.

1. Mercy killing
2. Hiring quotas
3. Giving birth-control devices to teenagers
4. Prayer in the schools
5. Living off campus
6. The drinking age
7. Spouses sharing housework equally
8. Smoking in public places
9. Big-time sports in college
10. Music videos
11. Working mothers with young children
12. Acid rain
13. Drugs on campus
14. Political campaigns
15. Requiring college students to pass a comprehensive exam in their majors before graduating
16. Fifty-five-mile-per-hour speed limit
17. Putting elderly parents in nursing homes
18. An optional pass-fail system for courses
19. The homeless
20. Nonconformity in a neighborhood: allowing a lawn to go wild, keeping many pets, painting a house an odd color, or some other atypical behavior

Assignments With a Specific Purpose and Audience

1. A college has rejected your or your child's application on the basis of low SAT scores. Write to the college admissions director, arguing that SAT scores are not a fair indicator of your or your child's abilities and potential.

2. As a staff writer for the college opinion magazine, you've been asked to nominate the "Outstanding Man or Woman on Campus," to be featured on the magazine's cover. Write a letter to your supervising editor in support of your nominee.

3. You and your parents don't agree on some aspect of your romantic life (you want to live with your partner and they don't approve; you want to get married and they want you to wait; they simply don't like your partner). Write your parents a letter explaining why your preference is reasonable. Try hard to win them over to your side, and remember not to be antagonistic.

4. As a high school teacher, you support some additional restriction on students. The restriction might be "no radios in school," "no T-shirts," "no food in class," "no smoking on school grounds." Write an article for the school newspaper, justifying this new rule to the student body.

5. Someone you know is convinced that the music you listen to is trashy or boring. Write a letter to the person arguing that your music has value. Support your contention with specific references to lyrics, musical structure, and performers' talent.

6. Assume you're a member of a racial, ethnic, religious, or social minority. You might, for example, be a Native American, an elderly person, a female executive. On a recent television show or in a TV commercial, you saw something that depicts your group in an offensive way. Write a letter (to the network or the advertiser) expressing your feelings and explaining why you feel the material should be taken off the air.

12

COMBINING THE PATTERNS

Throughout this book, you've studied the patterns of development—narration, process analysis, definition, and so on—in depth. You've seen how the patterns are used as strategies for generating, developing, and organizing ideas for essays. You've also learned that, in practice, most types of writing combine two or more patterns. The two sections that follow provide additional information about these important points. The rest of the chapter then gives you an opportunity to look more closely at the way several writers use the patterns of development in their work.

THE PATTERNS IN ACTION: DURING THE WRITING PROCESS

The patterns of development come into play throughout the composing process. In the prewriting stage, awareness of the patterns encourages you to think about your subject in fresh, new ways. Assume, for example, that you've been asked to write an essay about the way children are disciplined in school. However, you draw a blank as soon as you try to limit this general subject. To break the logjam, you could apply one or more patterns of development to your subject. *Comparison-contrast* might prompt you to write an essay investigating the differences between your parents' and your own feelings about school discipline. *Division-classification* might lead you to another paper—one that categorizes the kinds of discipline used in school. And *cause-effect* might point to still another essay—one that explores the way students react to being suspended.

Further along in the writing process—after you've identified your limited subject and your thesis—the patterns of development can help you generate your paper's evidence. Imagine that your thesis is "Teachers shouldn't discipline students publicly just to make an example of them." You're not sure, though, how to develop this thesis. Calling upon the patterns might spark some promising possibilities. *Narration* might encourage you to recount the disastrous time you were singled out and punished for the misdeeds of an entire class. Using *definition,* you might explain what is meant by an *autocratic* disciplinary style. *Argumentation-persuasion* might prompt you to advocate a new plan for disciplining students fairly and effectively.

The patterns of development also help you organize your ideas by pointing the way to an appropriate framework for a paper. Suppose you plan to write an essay for the campus newspaper about the disturbingly high incidence of shoplifting among college students; your purpose is to persuade young people not to get involved in this tempting, supposedly victimless crime. You believe that many readers will be deterred from shoplifting if you tell them about the harrowing *process* set in motion once a shoplifter is detected. With this step-by-step explanation in mind, you can now map out the essay's content: what happens when a shoplifter is detained by a salesperson, questioned by store security personnel, led to a police car, booked at the police station, and tried in a courtroom.

THE PATTERNS IN ACTION: IN AN ESSAY

Although this book devotes a separate chapter to each of the nine patterns of development, all chapters emphasize the same important point: Most writing consists of several patterns, with the dominant pattern providing the piece's organizational framework. To reinforce this point, each chapter contains a section, "How [the Pattern] Fits Your Purpose and Audience," that shows how a writer's purpose often leads to a blending of patterns. You might also have noticed that one of the "Questions About the Writer's Craft" following each professional selection asks you to analyze the piece's combination of patterns. Further, the "Writing Assignments Using Other Patterns of Development" encourage you to discover for yourself which mix of patterns would work best in a given piece of writing. In short, all through *The Longman Reader: Brief Edition* we emphasize that the patterns of development are far from being mechanical formulas. On the contrary: They are practical strategies that open up options in every stage of the composing process.

In this section of the book, you'll have a chance to focus on the way writers combine patterns in their essays. The following three selections are by three writers whose styles and subjects differ sharply. (Before reading the selections, you'll probably find it helpful to glance back at pages 27–28 so you can review the broad purpose of each pattern of development.) As you read each selection, ask yourself these questions:

1. What is the writer's *purpose* and *thesis?*
2. What *pattern of development dominates* the essay? How does this pattern help the writer support the essay's thesis and fulfill the essay's purpose?
3. What *other patterns appear* in the essay? How do these secondary patterns help the writer support the essay's thesis and fulfill the essay's purpose?

Your responses to these three questions will reward you with a richer understanding of the way writers work and with a deeper appreciation of three skilled prose stylists. To give you an even clearer sense of how writers mix patterns, we have annotated Virginia Woolf's "The Death of the Moth" (page 488), using the preceding three questions as a guide. By making your own annotations on Woolf's essay and then comparing them to ours, you can measure your ability to analyze Woolf's use of the patterns. You can further evaluate your analysis of the piece by answering the three questions on your own and then comparing your responses to ours on pages 492–94.

Virginia Woolf

Virginia Woolf is considered one of the most innovative writers of the twentieth century. Born in 1882 in London, Woolf was educated at home by her father, a well-known biographer, critic, and scholar. Along with her sister, Woolf became a key member of the Bloomsbury Group, a circle of writers and artists committed to the highest standards in art and literature. Woolf married a fellow Bloomsbury member, author and publisher Leonard Woolf. Together, they established Hogarth Press, which went on to publish Woolf's groundbreaking writings, including the novels *Mrs. Dalloway* (1923) and *To the Lighthouse* (1927), as well as the collection of essays *A Room of One's Own* (1920). Woolf's experimentation with point of view and her use of stream of consciousness earned her a place as a pivotal figure in English literature. Although Woolf's work met with critical acclaim and her collaboration with her husband was productive, Woolf was troubled all her life by severe depression. She committed suicide in 1941. "The Death of the Moth" appeared in the volume *The Death of the Moth and Other Essays* (1948).

The Death of the Moth

Description of
the moth

Definition (by
negation): How
this moth differs
from the usual
kind

Moths that fly by day are not properly to be 1
called moths; they do not excite that pleasant
sense of dark autumn nights and ivy-blossom
which the commonest yellow-underwing asleep
in the shadow of the curtain never fails to rouse
in us. They are hybrid creatures, neither gay like
butterflies nor sombre like their own species.
Nevertheless the present specimen, with his narrow hay-coloured wings, fringed with a tassel of
the same colour, seemed to be content with life.
It was a pleasant morning, mid-September, mild,
benignant, yet with a keener breath than that of
the summer months. The plough was already
scoring the field opposite the window, and where
the share had been, the earth was pressed flat and

Part of implied purpose/thesis: Nature's energy

gleamed with moisture. Such vigour came rolling in from the fields and the down beyond that it was difficult to keep the eyes strictly turned upon the book. The rooks too were keeping one of

Description of nature's energy here *contrasts* with *description* of nature in ¶5 (part of purpose/thesis)

their annual festivities; soaring round the tree tops until it looked as if a vast net with thousands of black knots in it had been cast up into the air; which, after a few moments, sank slowly down upon the trees until every twig seemed to have a knot at the end of it. Then, suddenly, the net would be thrown into the air again in a wider circle this time, with the utmost clamour and vociferation, as though to be thrown into the air and

Comparison between nature's energy and the moth's strong life force (part of purpose/thesis)

settle slowly down upon the tree tops were a tremendously exciting experience.

The same energy which inspired the rooks, the ploughmen, the horses, and even, it seemed, the lean bare-backed downs, sent the moth fluttering from side to side of his square of the win-

Start of *narrative* (main pattern) about the moth's plight

dow-pane. One could not help watching him. One was, indeed, conscious of a queer feeling of pity for him. The possibilities of pleasure seemed that morning so enormous and so various that to

Start of *narrative* about Woolf's reaction to the moth's plight

have only a moth's part in life, and a day moth's at that, appeared a hard fate, and his zest in enjoying his meagre opportunities to the full, pathetic. He flew vigorously to one corner of his compart-

Description of moth's strong life force—despite its small size (these two contrasting qualities are part of purpose/thesis)

ment, and, after waiting there a second, flew across to the other. What remained for him but to fly to a third corner and then to a fourth? That was all he could do, in spite of the size of the downs, the width of the sky, the far-off smoke of houses, and the romantic voice, now and then, of a steamer out at sea. What he could do he did. Watching him, it seemed as if a fibre, very thin but pure, of the enormous energy of the world had been thrust into his frail and diminutive

Part of purpose/thesis: The moth represents life

body. As often as he crossed the pane, I could fancy that a thread of vital light became visible. He was little or nothing but life.

2

Narrative about Woolf's reaction continues

Restatement of part of purpose/ thesis: The moth's two contrasting qualities

Restatement of part of purpose/ thesis: The moth represents life

Narrative about the moth's plight continues; tension builds

Narrative about Woolf's reaction continues

Yet, because he was so small, and so simple a 3 form of the energy that was rolling in at the open window and driving its way through so many narrow and intricate corridors in my own brain and in those of other human beings, there was something marvellous as well as pathetic about him. It was as if someone had taken a tiny bead of pure life and decking it as lightly as possible with down and feathers, had set it dancing and zigzagging to show us the true nature of life. Thus displayed one could not get over the strangeness of it. One is apt to forget all about life, seeing it humped and bossed and garnished and cumbered so that it has to move with the greatest circumspection and dignity. Again, the thought of all that life might have been had he been born in any other shape caused one to view his simple activities with a kind of pity.

After a time, tired by his dancing apparently, 4 he settled on the window ledge in the sun, and, the queer spectacle being at an end, I forgot about him. Then, looking up, my eye was caught by him. He was trying to resume his dancing, but seemed either so stiff or so awkward that he could only flutter to the bottom of the windowpane; and when he tried to fly across it he failed. Being intent on other matters I watched these futile attempts for a time without thinking, unconsciously waiting for him to resume his flight, as one waits for a machine, that has stopped momentarily, to start again without considering the reason of its failure. After perhaps a seventh attempt he slipped from the wooden ledge and fell, fluttering his wings, on to his back on the window sill. The helplessness of his attitude roused me. It flashed upon me that he was in difficulties; he could no longer raise himself; his legs struggled vainly. But, as I stretched out a pencil, meaning to help him to right himself, it came over me that the failure and awkwardness

Hint of the resolution of the *narrative* about the moth

Narrative about Woolf's reaction continues

Description of nature's indifference here contrasts with description of nature in ¶1 (part of purpose/thesis)

Restatement of part of purpose/thesis: The strength of the moth's life force—despite small size

Part of purpose/thesis: Death's inevitability

Narrative about moth continues

Narrative about Woolf's reaction continues

Restatement of part of purpose/thesis: The strength of the moth's life force—despite its size

Resolution of the narrative about the moth

were the approach of death. I laid the pencil down again.

The legs agitated themselves once more. I 5 looked as if for the enemy against which he struggled. I looked out of doors. What had happened there? Presumably it was midday, and work in the fields had stopped. Stillness and quiet had replaced the previous animation. The birds had taken themselves off to feed in the brooks. The horses stood still. Yet the power was there all the same, massed outside, indifferent, impersonal, not attending to anything in particular. Somehow it was opposed to the little hay-coloured moth. It was useless to try to do anything. One could only watch the extraordinary efforts made by those tiny legs against an oncoming doom which could, had it chosen, have submerged an entire city, not merely a city, but masses of human beings; nothing, I knew, had any chance against death. Nevertheless after a pause of exhaustion the legs fluttered again. It was superb, this last protest, and so frantic that he succeeded at last in righting himself. One's sympathies, of course, were all on the side of life. Also, when there was nobody to care or to know, this gigantic effort on the part of an insignificant little moth, against a power of such magnitude, to retain what no one else valued or desired to keep, moved one strangely. Again, somehow, one saw life, a pure bead. I lifted the pencil again, useless though I knew it to be. But even as I did so, the unmistakable tokens of death showed themselves. The body relaxed, and instantly grew stiff. The struggle was over. The insignificant little creature now knew death. As I looked at the dead moth, this minute wayside triumph of so great a force over so mean an antagonist filled me with wonder. Just as life had been strange a few minutes before, so death was now as strange. The moth having righted himself now lay most decently and uncomplainingly

Restatement of
part of purpose/
thesis: Death's
inevitability

composed. O yes, he seemed to say, death is
stronger than I am.

The following answers to the questions on page 487 will help
you analyze Virginia Woolf's use of the patterns of development in
the essay "The Death of the Moth."

1. *What is the writer's purpose and thesis?*

Woolf's *purpose* is to show that the tiny moth's courageous but ultimately futile battle to cling to life embodies the struggle at the very heart
of all existence. Woolf achieves her purpose by relating the story of the
moth's efforts to resist death. Her *thesis* might be expressed this way:
Although living creatures may make "extraordinary efforts" (paragraph
5) to hold onto life, these attempts aren't strong enough to defy death.
Nothing, Woolf writes, has "any chance against death" (5).

Woolf's purpose and thesis first become apparent at the end of paragraph 2. There she shows that the moth, with his "frail and diminutive
body," represents "nothing but life." Although "small . . . and . . . simple" (3), the moth is suffused with the same extraordinary energy that is
evident in the natural world beyond Woolf's window. This energy, combined with the moth's tiny size, makes the creature both "marvellous"
and "pathetic" (3)—two qualities that are particularly apparent during
the moth's final struggles. During those moments, the moth makes a
final "superb" (5) protest against death, but ultimately the "insignificant" (5) creature—like all forms of life—must cease his valiant struggle
and die.

2. *What pattern of development dominates the essay? How does this pattern
help the writer support the essay's thesis and fulfill the essay's purpose?*

Although the essay's first paragraph is largely descriptive, it becomes
clear by paragraph 2 that the description is in service of a larger narrative
about the moth's struggles. It's this narrative that dominates the essay.

At the beginning, the moth is imbued with vitality, as he flies "vigorously" (paragraph 2) and with "zest" (2) from one side of the window
to the other. But narrative tension begins to build in paragraph 4. There
Woolf writes that the moth tries once again to cross the windowpane,
fails repeatedly, and slips "on to his back," seemingly defeated. However,
even then, the moth doesn't abandon his hold on life, for—as Woolf
relates in paragraph 5—he tries, despite exhaustion, to right himself.

Against all odds, he finally succeeds, but his frantic struggle to hold onto life takes its toll, and the tiny creature soon dies. This detailed story of the moth's futile battle against death is presented as an emblem of the fate of all life. Through this narrative, Woolf achieves her purpose and thesis: to convey the power of nature and the inability of living creatures—despite heroic efforts—to defy this power.

Paralleling the tale of the moth's struggle is another *narrative*: the story of Woolf's changing understanding of the event that unfolds before her. When the moth is "dancing" (3), energetic, and vital, Woolf "could not help watching him" (2) and feels a kind of wonderment at this "tiny bead of pure life" (3). Then in paragraph 4, Woolf writes that she forgets about the moth for a while until she happens to look up and see his "futile attempts" to "resume . . . dancing." For a few moments, she watches the moth's "stiff" and "awkward" efforts to fly, expecting him to demonstrate the same vitality as before. Suddenly, she understands that the moth is "in difficulties" and can no longer lift himself up. She tries to help but abandons her efforts when she realizes that the moth's labored efforts signify the "approach of death." Paragraph 5 presents the final stage of Woolf's interior narrative. She looks outside her window for an explanation of the moth's plight. But now she finds that the forces of nature—earlier so exuberant and vibrant—are, if anything, "opposed to the little hay-coloured moth." With that, her attention is once again drawn to the moth and the fluttering of his legs. Although drained, the tiny creature makes one last effort to resist death—and, improbably enough, picks himself up one more time. Struck by the sheer power of the moth's life force, Woolf is prompted, as before, to help the creature, even though she recognizes the futility. But then the "unmistakable tokens of death" appear, and the moth gives up his struggle, succumbing—as all forms of life must—to the forces of nature. With the moth lying "uncomplainingly composed," Woolf comes to accept the fact that death is stronger than life.

3. *What other patterns appear in the essay? How do these secondary patterns help the writer support the essay's thesis and fulfill the essay's purpose?*

Although the essay is predominantly a narrative, it also contains other patterns. The *descriptive* passage at the beginning of the essay includes a brief *definition by negation* in which Woolf explains how the creature she is observing differs from the usual, more colorful night moth. The rest of paragraph 1 draws upon description to evoke the sense of early autumn and nature's extraordinary energy. This description of the natural world's vibrancy and abundance, exemplified by the rooks and plowed earth, *contrasts* with Woolf's later characterization of the natural world in paragraph 5. There she writes, "Stillness and quiet . . . replaced the previous animation," and she senses not that nature fosters vitality, but that it is "indifferent, impersonal, not attending to anything in particular."

Shifting her focus in paragraph 2 from the natural world to the moth, Woolf exercises her *descriptive* powers to convey the moth's extraordinary zest as he flies across the windowpane. In this paragraph, Woolf also draws upon *comparison-contrast* to show that despite *differences* in their sizes, the tiny moth and the vast natural world embody the *same* primal energy. Woolf's consideration of this elemental similarity leads her to the basic *contrast* at the heart of the essay: While the moth's tiny size makes him "pathetic," his formidable life spirit makes him "marvellous." He may be small and lightweight, but he is abuzz with vitality. When contrasted to the enormous power of nature, the moth—like all forms of life—may be puny, but his impulse to defy such power inspires awe and reverence.

Martin Luther King, Jr.

More than thirty years after his assassination, Martin Luther King, Jr. (1929–68), is still recognized as the towering figure in the struggle for civil rights in the United States. Born in Atlanta, Georgia, King earned doctorates from Boston University and Chicago Theological Seminary and served as pastor of a Baptist congregation in Montgomery, Alabama. Advocating a philosophy of nonviolent resistance to racial injustice, he led bus boycotts, marches, and sit-ins that brought about passage of the 1964 Civil Rights Act and the Voting Rights Act of 1965. Dr. King was awarded the Nobel Peace Prize in 1964. The following selection by King is taken from *Where Do We Go From Here: Community or Chaos?* (1967).

Where Do We Go From Here: Community or Chaos?

A final problem that mankind must solve in order to survive in the world house that we have inherited is finding an alternative to war and human destruction. Recent events have vividly reminded us that nations are not reducing but rather increasing their arsenals of weapons of mass destruction. The best brains in the highly developed nations of the world are devoted to military technology. The proliferation of nuclear weapons has not been halted, in spite of the limited-test-ban treaty. 1

In this day of man's highest technical achievement, in this day of dazzling discovery, of novel opportunities, loftier dignities and fuller freedoms for all, there is no excuse for the kind of blind craving for power and resources that provoked the wars of previous generations. There is no need to fight for food and land. Science has provided us with adequate means of survival and transportation, which make it possible to enjoy the fullness of this great earth. The question now is, do we have the morality and courage required to live together as brothers and not be afraid? 2

One of the most persistent ambiguities we face is that everybody talks about peace as a goal, but among the wielders of power peace is practically nobody's business. Many men cry "Peace! Peace!" but they refuse to do the things that make for peace. 3

The large power blocs talk passionately of pursuing peace while   4
expanding defense budgets that already bulge, enlarging already
awesome armies and devising ever more devastating weapons. Call
the roll of those who sing the glad tidings of peace and one's ears
will be surprised by the responding sounds. The heads of all the
nations issue clarion calls for peace, yet they come to the peace table
accompanied by bands of brigands each bearing unsheathed swords.

The stages of history are replete with the chants and choruses of   5
the conquerors of old who came killing in pursuit of peace.
Alexander, Genghis Khan, Julius Caesar, Charlemagne and
Napoleon were akin in seeking a peaceful world order, a world fash-
ioned after their selfish conceptions of an ideal existence. Each
sought a world at peace which would personify his egotistic dreams.
Even within the life span of most of us, another megalomaniac
strode across the world stage. He sent his blitzkrieg-bent legions
blazing across Europe, bringing havoc and holocaust in his wake.
There is grave irony in the fact that Hitler could come forth, following nakedly aggressive expansionist theories, and do it all in the
name of peace.

So when in this day I see the leaders of nations again talking   6
peace while preparing for war, I take fearful pause. When I see our
country today intervening in what is basically a civil war, mutilating
hundreds of thousands of Vietnamese children with napalm, burning villages and rice fields at random, painting the valleys of that
small Asian country red with human blood, leaving broken bodies
in countless ditches and sending home half-men, mutilated mentally and physically; when I see the unwillingness of our government to
create the atmosphere for a negotiated settlement of this awful conflict by halting bombings in the North and agreeing unequivocally
to talk with the Vietcong—and all this in the name of pursuing the
goal of peace—I tremble for our world.[1] I do so not only from dire
recall of the nightmares wreaked in the wars of yesterday, but also
from dreadful realization of today's possible nuclear destructiveness
and tomorrow's even more calamitous prospects.

Before it is too late, we must narrow the gaping chasm between   7
our proclamations of peace and our lowly deeds which precipitate
and perpetuate war. We are called upon to look up from the

[1]Only after more than 58,000 Americans had been killed did the United States
withdraw from Vietnam. The war then continued until the North Vietnamese,
aided by the Vietcong, took over all of Vietnam (editors' note).

quagmire of military programs and defense commitments and read the warnings on history's signposts.

One day we must come to see that peace is not merely a distant 8
goal that we seek but a means by which we arrive at that goal. We must pursue peaceful ends through peaceful means. How much longer must we play at deadly war games before we heed the plaintive pleas of the unnumbered dead and maimed of past wars?

President John F. Kennedy said on one occasion, "Mankind 9
must put an end to war or war will put an end to mankind." Wisdom born of experience should tell us that war is obsolete. There may have been a time when war served as a negative good by preventing the spread and growth of an evil force, but the destructive power of modern weapons eliminates even the possibility that war may serve any good at all. If we assume that life is worth living and that man has a right to survive, then we must find an alternative to war. In a day when vehicles hurtle through outer space and guided ballistic missiles carve highways of death through the stratosphere, no nation can claim victory in war. A so-called limited war will leave little more than a calamitous legacy of human suffering, political turmoil and spiritual disillusionment. A world war will leave only smoldering ashes as mute testimony of a human race whose folly led inexorably to ultimate death. If modern man continues to flirt unhesitatingly with war, he will transform his earthly habitat into an inferno such as even the mind of Dante[2] could not imagine.

Therefore I suggest that the philosophy and strategy of non- 10
violence become immediately a subject for study and for serious experimentation in every field of human conflict, by no means excluding the relations between nations. It is, after all, nation-states which make war, which have produced the weapons that threaten the survival of mankind and which are both genocidal and suicidal in character.

We have ancient habits to deal with, vast structures of power, 11
indescribably complicated problems to solve. But unless we abdicate our humanity altogether and succumb to fear and impotence in the presence of the weapons we have ourselves created, it is as possible and as urgent to put an end to war and violence between nations as it is to put an end to poverty and racial injustice.

---

[2]In *The Divine Comedy* (1321), Italian poet Dante depicts the burning torments of hell endured by a lost soul before it can attain salvation (editors' note).

The United Nations is a gesture in the direction of nonviolence   12
on a world scale. There, at least, states that oppose one another have
sought to do so with words instead of with weapons. But true nonviolence is more than the absence of violence. It is the persistent and
determined application of peaceable power to offenses against the
community—in this case the world community. As the United Nations
moves ahead with the giant tasks confronting it, I would hope that it
would earnestly examine the uses of nonviolent direct action.

I do not minimize the complexity of the problems that need to   13
be faced in achieving disarmament and peace. But I am convinced
that we shall not have the will, the courage and the insight to deal
with such matters unless in this field we are prepared to undergo a
mental and spiritual re-evaluation, a change of focus which will
enable us to see that the things that seem most real and powerful are
indeed now unreal and have come under sentence of death. We need
to make a supreme effort to generate the readiness, indeed the
eagerness, to enter into the new world which is now possible, "the
city which hath foundation, whose Building and Maker is God."

It is not enough to say, "We must not wage war." It is necessary   14
to love peace and sacrifice for it. We must concentrate not merely on
the eradication of war but on the affirmation of peace. A fascinating
story about Ulysses and the Sirens[3] is preserved for us in Greek literature. The Sirens had the ability to sing so sweetly that sailors could
not resist steering toward their island. Many ships were lured upon
the rocks, and men forgot home, duty and honor as they flung themselves into the sea to be embraced by arms that drew them down to
death. Ulysses, determined not to succumb to the Sirens, first decided to tie himself tightly to the mast of his boat and his crew stuffed
their ears with wax. But finally he and his crew learned a better way
to save themselves: They took on board the beautiful singer Orpheus,
whose melodies were sweeter than the music of the Sirens. When
Orpheus sang, who would bother to listen to the Sirens?

So we must see that peace represents a sweeter music, a cos-   15
mic melody that is far superior to the discords of war. Somehow
we must transform the dynamics of the world power struggle from
the nuclear arms race, which no one can win, to a creative contest
to harness man's genius for the purpose of making peace and

---

[3]Ulysses and the Sirens, as well as Orpheus (mentioned later in the paragraph), are
all figures in Greek mythology (editors' note).

prosperity a reality for all the nations of the world. In short, we must shift the arms race into a "peace race." If we have the will and determination to mount such a peace offensive, we will unlock hitherto tightly sealed doors of hope and bring new light into the dark chambers of pessimism.

Joan Didion

Known for her taut prose style and sharp social commentary, Joan Didion (1934–) graduated from the University of California at Berkeley. Her essays have appeared in the *Saturday Evening Post*, the *American Scholar*, and the *National Review*, as well as in three collections: *Slouching Towards Bethlehem* (1969), *The White Album* (1979), and *After Henry* (1992). *Salvador* (1983) is a book-length essay about a 1982 visit to Central America. The coauthor of several screenplays (including *A Star Is Born* in 1976 and *Up Close and Personal* in 1996), Didion has also written novels, including *Run River* (1963), *A Book of Common Prayer* (1977), *Democracy* (1984), and *The Last Thing He Wanted* (1996). The following selection is from *Slouching Towards Bethlehem*.

The Santa Ana

There is something uneasy in the Los Angeles air this afternoon,   1
some unnatural stillness, some tension. What it means is that tonight
a Santa Ana will begin to blow, a hot wind from the northeast whin-
ing down through the Cajon and San Gorgonio Passes, blowing up
sandstorms out along Route 66, drying the hills and the nerves to
the flash point. For a few days now we will see smoke back in the
canyons, and hear sirens in the night. I have neither heard nor read
that a Santa Ana is due, but I know it, and almost everyone I have
seen today knows it too. We know it because we feel it. The baby
frets. The maid sulks. I rekindle a waning argument with the telephone company, then cut my losses and lie down, given over to
whatever is in the air. To live with the Santa Ana is to accept, consciously or unconsciously, a deeply mechanistic view of human
behavior.

I recall being told, when I first moved to Los Angeles and was   2
living on an isolated beach, that the Indians would throw themselves
into the sea when the bad wind blew. I could see why. The Pacific
turned ominously glossy during a Santa Ana period, and one woke
in the night troubled not only by the peacocks screaming in the

olive trees but by the eerie absence of surf. The heat was surreal. The sky had a yellow cast, the kind of light sometimes called "earthquake weather." My only neighbor would not come out of her house for days, and there were no lights at night, and her husband roamed the place with a machete. One day he would tell me that he had heard a trespasser, the next a rattlesnake.

"On nights like that," Raymond Chandler[1] once wrote about   3 the Santa Ana, "every booze party ends in a fight. Meek little wives feel the edge of the carving knife and study their husbands' necks. Anything can happen." That was the kind of wind it was. I did not know then that there was any basis for the effect it had on all of us, but it turns out to be another of those cases in which science bears out folk wisdom. The Santa Ana, which is named for one of the canyons it rushes through, is a *foehn* wind, like the *foehn* of Austria and Switzerland and the *hamsin* of Israel. There are a number of persistent malevolent winds, perhaps the best known of which are the mistral of France and the Mediterranean sirocco, but a *foehn* wind has distinct characteristics: it occurs on the leeward slope of a mountain range and, although the air begins as a cold mass, it is warmed as it comes down the mountain and appears finally as a hot dry wind. Whenever and wherever a *foehn* blows, doctors hear about headaches and nausea and allergies, about "nervousness," about "depression." In Los Angeles some teachers do not attempt to conduct formal classes during a Santa Ana, because the children become unmanageable. In Switzerland the suicide rate goes up during the *foehn,* and in the courts of some Swiss cantons the wind is considered a mitigating circumstance for crime. Surgeons are said to watch the wind, because blood does not clot normally during a *foehn.* A few years ago an Israeli physicist discovered that not only during such winds, but for the ten or twelve hours which precede them, the air carries an unusually high ratio of positive to negative ions. No one seems to know exactly why that should be; some talk about friction and others suggest solar disturbances. In any case the positive ions are there, and what an excess of positive ions does, in the simplest terms, is make people unhappy. One cannot get much more mechanistic than that.

---

[1]Chandler (1888–1959) was an American novelist, best known for his detective novels featuring the character of Philip Marlowe (editors' note).

Easterners commonly complain that there is no "weather" at all   4
in Southern California, that the days and the seasons slip by relent-
lessly, numbingly bland. That is quite misleading. In fact the climate
is characterized by infrequent but violent extremes: two periods of
torrential subtropical rains which continue for weeks and wash out
the hills and send subdivisions sliding toward the sea; about twenty
scattered days a year of the Santa Ana, which, with its incendiary
dryness, invariably means fire. At the first prediction of a Santa Ana,
the Forest Service flies men and equipment from northern
California into the southern forests, and the Los Angeles Fire
Department cancels its ordinary non-firefighting routines. The
Santa Ana caused Malibu to burn the way it did in 1956, and Bel
Air in 1961, and Santa Barbara in 1964. In the winter of 1966–67
eleven men were killed fighting a Santa Ana fire that spread through
the San Gabriel Mountains.

Just to watch the front-page news out of Los Angeles during a   5
Santa Ana is to get very close to what it is about the place. The
longest single Santa Ana period in recent years was in 1957, and it
lasted not the usual three or four days but fourteen days, from
November 21 until December 4. On the first day 25,000 acres of
the San Gabriel Mountains were burning, with gusts reaching 100
miles an hour. In town, the wind reached Force 12, or hurricane
force, on the Beaufort Scale; oil derricks were toppled and people
ordered off the downtown streets to avoid injury from flying
objects. On November 22 the fire in the San Gabriels was out of
control. On November 24 six people were killed in automobile
accidents, and by the end of the week the Los Angeles *Times* was
keeping a box score of traffic deaths. On November 26 a prominent
Pasadena attorney, depressed about money, shot and killed his wife,
their two sons, and himself. On November 27 a South Gate
divorcée, twenty-two, was murdered and thrown from a moving car.
On November 30 the San Gabriel fire was still out of control, and
the wind in town was blowing eighty miles an hour. On the first day
of December four people died violently, and on the third the wind
began to break.

It is hard for people who have not lived in Los Angeles to real-   6
ize how radically the Santa Ana figures in the local imagination. The
city burning is Los Angeles's deepest image of itself: Nathanael West
perceived that, in *The Day of the Locust;* and at the time of the 1965
Watts riots what struck the imagination most indelibly were the

fires.[2] For days one could drive the Harbor Freeway and see the city on fire, just as we had always known it would be in the end. Los Angeles weather is the weather of catastrophe, of apocalypse, and, just as the reliably long and bitter winters of New England determine the way life is lived there, so the violence and the unpredictability of the Santa Ana affect the entire quality of life in Los Angeles, accentuate its impermanence, its unreliability. The wind shows us how close to the edge we are.

[2]Set in Hollywood, West's 1939 novel, *The Day of the Locust,* ends with a description of Los Angeles engulfed in flames. In 1965, the Watts section of Los Angeles experienced widespread riots, leaving much of the area devastated by fire (editors' note).

Appendix
A CONCISE GUIDE TO FINDING AND DOCUMENTING SOURCES

Many assignments in *The Longman Reader: Brief Edition* suggest that you might want to do some research in the library and/or on the Internet. Such research enlarges your perspective and enables you to move beyond off-the-top-of-your-head opinions to those that are firmly supported. This appendix will be useful if you do decide to draw upon outside sources when preparing a paper. The appendix explains how to: (1) use the library to find books, reference works, and periodicals on a subject; (2) research a topic using the Internet; and (3) document print and electronic sources.

USING THE LIBRARY TO FIND BOOKS ON YOUR SUBJECT

To locate books on a specific topic, go to your college's *library catalog*, which lists all the books in the library. Although most college libraries have a *computerized catalog* of their book holdings, some use a *card catalog,* a list of alphabetically arranged cards in a series of drawers. Library technology is changing rapidly. With each passing year, a greater number of college (and local) libraries can be accessed online. That means that you can check—at any time of the day or night—a library's book holdings from your home or dorm computer.

Searching the Library Catalog by Author, Title, or Subject

Whether you use your own computer to visit a library's holdings online or use the library's computerized (or card) catalog, you need to familiarize yourself with the three ways to look up a book: by author, title, or subject. To locate a specific book, you can do either an *author* or a *title search.* To search by author, look up the book under the author's last name; to search by title, use the first word in the title, or the second word if the first is *A, An,* or *The.* To identify books on a specific topic, do a *subject search.* Following are some strategies for searching a computerized catalog by subject. (If your library's holdings aren't computerized, it's easy to adapt the suggestions to card-catalog research.) To do a subject search, type in a word or phrase that summarizes your topic. You may have to try several key terms to discover under which term(s) the computer lists sources on your topic. Assume you're conducting research to identify classroom strategies that undermine student success. You might start by typing the word "Education." But that word would probably yield so many possibilities that you wouldn't know where to start. You might narrow your search by keying in "Teaching techniques," "Classroom practices," or "Academic failure." For help in identifying appropriate key terms, speak with your college librarian. He or she will probably have you consult the *Library of Congress Subject Headings* or a bound or on-screen thesaurus of headings used in your library's database.

When you search for a book by subject, the screen usually indicates narrower subheadings under that topic. When you click on one of those subheads, a list of books on that subject will appear. To get complete bibliographic information about a specific book, follow the computer's instructions. The book's publisher, publication date, call number (see page 508), and so on will then appear on the screen. Most computerized catalogs also indicate the status of a book—whether it is available, on reserve, out on loan, overdue, lost, or available through an interlibrary loan system. (If all copies of the book are checked out, fill out a form to be notified when the book is returned.) Here is one college's computerized catalog display for a book on education in the inner city:

Other subject headings to look under to find additional relevant books. The underlining indicates that these are links to related subjects in the computerized catalog.

AUTHOR:	Rathbone, Cristina.
TITLE:	**On the Outside Looking In: A Year at an Inner-City High School**
PUBLICATION INFO:	**New York: Atlantic Monthly Press, 1998.**
PAGING AND SIZE:	**387p.; 24 cm.**
SUBJECTS:	<u>**Education, Urban, Case Studies—United States.**</u> <u>**Economically Disadvantaged Youth, Education (Secondary)—United States.**</u> <u>**New York City High Schools.**</u>

1. CALL NUMBER: LC5131.R38 1998—STACKS—Checked Out

2. CALL NUMBER: LC5131.R38 1998—STACKS—Available

Indicates the book's call number, location, and availability in the library. In this case, the library owns two copies, one checked out, the other available.

Once the computer identifies books on your subject, you can copy down the authors, titles, and call numbers of promising books; or, in many libraries, you can direct the computer to print out a list. Mastering your library's computerized catalog enables you to identify in minutes sources that once might have taken you several hours to track down.

Locating Books in the Stacks

Most college libraries contain several floors of bookshelves (called *stacks*). There you'll find fiction, nonfiction, periodicals, microfilm and microfiche files, reserved books, government documents, reference works (see below), and special collections. To locate a book in the stacks, use its *call number* (a number used to classify a book and indicate its location in the library). The call number appears both in the catalog entry and on the spine of the book. There are two systems of call numbers in use in the United States—the *Dewey Decimal* and the *Library of Congress*. Once you have a book's call number, consult a map or list (usually posted near the front desk) to see where in the library you'll find the book. For example, to track down Cristina Rathbone's *On the Outside Looking In*, you'd need to find where the library shelves books with the call number *LC5131.R38*. If your library has closed stacks, make out a call slip, and a member of the staff will get the book for you.

USING THE LIBRARY TO FIND REFERENCE WORKS ON YOUR SUBJECT

Though they present highly condensed information, *reference works* can be helpful, especially in the early stages of your research. Some reference volumes cover a wide range of subjects (*Encyclopedia Britannica* and the *World Almanac and Book of Facts*), while others are more specialized (*Mathematics Dictionary* and *Dance Encyclopedia*). Many reference volumes are available on CD-ROM or can be accessed online. Those that aren't are most likely arranged on library shelves alphabetically by subject ("Art," "Economics," "History"), making it easy to browse for useful reference volumes. Keep in mind that reference materials can't be checked out; you must consult them while in the library. Here are representative reference books found in most college libraries. Check with the librarian to see if any you're interested in are available electronically.

Biography: *International Who's Who, Who's Who in America*

Business/Economics: *Dictionary of Banking and Finance, Encyclopedia of Economics*

Ethnic/Feminist Studies: *Encyclopedia of Feminism, Harvard Encyclopedia of American Ethnic Groups*

Fine Arts: *New Grove Dictionary of American Music, The Oxford Companion to Art*

Literature: *Benét's Reader's Encyclopedia, The Oxford Companion to American Literature*

History/Political Science: *Editorials on File, Facts on File, A Political Handbook of the World*

Philosophy/Religion: *The Encyclopedia of American Religions, An Encyclopedia of Philosophy*

Science/Technology/Mathematics: *McGraw-Hill Encyclopedia of Science and Technology, A Dictionary of Mathematics*

Psychology/Education: *Encyclopedia of Education, Encyclopedia of Psychology*

Social Sciences: *International Encyclopedia of the Social Sciences, Encyclopedia of Crime and Justice*

USING THE LIBRARY TO FIND ARTICLES ON YOUR SUBJECT

Periodicals are publications issued at intervals throughout the year. Generally, periodicals contain material that is more recent than that found in books or reference works. There are three broad types of periodicals: general, scholarly, and serious. Written for the average reader, *general periodicals* (daily newspapers and magazines such as *Time* and *Newsweek*) contain articles that provide background information rather than comprehensive coverage of a subject. Intended for readers with specialized knowledge, *scholarly publications* (such as the *Journal of Experimental Child Psychology* and the *Journal of Renaissance Drama*) provide in-depth analyses written by authorities in the field. Designed for well-educated lay people rather than those having specialized knowledge, *serious publications* (for example, *Scientific American* and *Smithsonian*) develop subjects with less depth than scholarly publications.

Using Periodical Indexes, Abstracts, and Bibliographies

Periodical indexes are cumulative directories that list articles published in specific journals, newspapers, and magazines. (Major newspapers, such as the *New York Times,* publish their own directories.) Most periodical indexes list articles under subject headings. Beneath the headings, individual articles are organized alphabetically by authors' last names.

When you were in high school, you may have used the *Readers' Guide to Periodical Literature,* which lists highly accessible, general-interest articles published by popular newsstand magazines like *U.S. News & World Report* and *Sports Illustrated.* The college equivalents of the *Readers' Guide* are the *Humanities Index* and the *Social Sciences Index.* To locate articles appropriate for college-level research, you'll need to consult these indexes as well as those listing articles from more academic, professional, and specialized publications.

Some specialized indexes provide brief descriptions of the articles they list. These indexes are usually called *abstracts.* Examples are *Abstracts of Folklore Studies* and *Psychological Abstracts.* Abstracts usually contain fewer listings than other types of indexes and are restricted to a limited field. In contrast to indexes that list only articles, *bibliographies* like the *Modern Language Association International Bibliography* list books as well as articles.

You shouldn't end your search for appropriate material until you've consulted the most pertinent indexes and bibliographies. For a paper on the psychology of child abuse, you might start with the *New York Times Index* and then move to more specialized volumes, such as *Psychological Abstracts, Child Development Abstracts,* and *Mental Health Book Review Index.* To ensure that you don't miss current developments in your subject area, start with the most recent years and work your way back.

Most college libraries offer computerized databases of the major periodical indexes, abstracts, and bibliographies. The databases, which group directories alphabetically by subject, can be accessed through the library's computer terminals—and often through a campus-wide computer network, making it possible for you to conduct part of your research from your own room. In some libraries, periodical databases are maintained in the same system as the computerized catalog for books. In other libraries, the databases are available at a separate bank of terminals. These terminals are usually hooked up to a CD-ROM player containing compact discs that contain periodical indexes. (If your school library isn't computerized, you'll probably find the periodical indexes located in the periodicals section, arranged alphabetically by title. Simply scan the shelves to find the index you want.)

Listed here is a small sample of the indexes, abstracts, and bibliographies found in most college libraries. Check with the librarian to see which can be accessed electronically.

> **General:** *Academic Search FullTEXT, Dialog, EBSCOhost, Humanities Index, InfoTrac Academic Index, InfoTrac Magazine Index, InfoTrac National Newspaper Index, Magazine Index Plus, National Newspaper Index, Readers' Guide to Periodical Literature, Social Sciences Index*
>
> **Education:** *Education Abstracts, Education Index, ERIC (Educational Resources Information Center)*
>
> **History, Political Science, Government:** *Government Publications Index, Historical Abstracts, Monthly Index to United States Government Publications, Political Science Bibliographies, Public Affairs Information Service, Vertical File Index*
>
> **Philosophy/Religion:** *Philosopher's Index, Religion Index*
>
> **Psychology/Sociology:** *Psychological Abstracts, Sociological Abstracts*
>
> **Sciences:** *Applied Science and Technology Index, Biological Abstracts, Botanical Bibliographies, Chemical Abstracts, Engineering Index Annual, Environment Index, International Computer Bibliography*
>
> **Women's and Ethnic Studies:** *Bibliography on Women, Ethnic Newswatch, Hispanic American Periodicals Index, Index to Periodical Articles by and About Blacks*

Whether a periodicals directory is in computerized or print form, you identify titles of relevant articles by looking under keywords that describe your subject. If you don't find your subject listed in a printed index, or if a computerized database yields no titles when you type in keywords, try alternate terms for your topic. Suppose you're researching the subject of business ethics. In addition to using "Business ethics" as keywords, you might try "Bribery" or "Fraud" to find relevant articles. Computerized and print indexes also show cross-references. By looking under "Business ethics," you might see suggested search terms such as "Advertising ethics," "Banking, ethical aspects," and "Commercial crime." In many libraries, the computer terminals at which you view database listings are hooked up to printers, enabling you to print out the listings rather than record them from the screen. Some online and CD-ROM databases offer access to the full text of selected articles or books. These texts may be read on screen and, if the computer terminal connects to a printer, printed out.

Here's an entry from the computerized database EBSCOhost. The entry gives all the information you need to track down the article in the library.

EBSCOhost

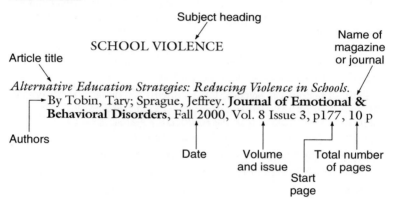

SCHOOL VIOLENCE

Subject heading

Article title

Name of magazine or journal

Alternative Education Strategies: Reducing Violence in Schools.
By Tobin, Tary; Sprague, Jeffrey. **Journal of Emotional & Behavioral Disorders**, Fall 2000, Vol. 8 Issue 3, p177, 10 p

Authors

Date

Volume and issue

Start page

Total number of pages

Locating a Specific Issue of a Periodical

If you don't have the option of printing out the text of relevant online articles, you'll need to obtain the original text. To do so, you have to determine whether the library owns the specific periodicals and issues you want. If your library catalogs its periodicals online, search for a periodical by typing in its name. Does that particular name appear on screen? If it does, your library owns issues of that publication. With a few additional keystrokes, you can obtain more detailed information—such as which issues of the periodical the library holds and their location in the library.

If your library doesn't catalog its periodicals online, look for a card catalog of holdings. The library probably has a separate periodicals card catalog in the periodicals section. Look up the periodicals by name. A periodical card will usually tell you the issues owned by the library and their location.

Recent issues of magazines, newspapers, and journals are kept in the library's periodicals section, where they are arranged alphabetically by title. Less current issues can be found in bound volumes in the periodicals section, in the stacks, or on microfilm. Usually, periodicals must be read in the library. Back issues of major newspapers are generally stored on microfilm filed in cabinets in a separate location.

USING THE INTERNET TO RESEARCH YOUR SUBJECT

Computer technology isn't, of course, limited to college libraries. It's everywhere. Nothing demonstrates the staggering impact of the computer revolution more powerfully than the growth of the Internet. This global network of interlinked computer systems puts a massive storehouse of information within the reach of anyone with access to a personal computer and a modem. Such a wealth of material presents obvious research benefits to you as a student. However, when faced with the task of using the Internet, you may feel overwhelmed and unsure of how to proceed. The following pages will introduce you to the Internet, show you how to access its resources, and offer pointers on evaluating the material you find there.

The Internet is the catch-all term for the global network that links individual computers throughout the world. The *World Wide Web* refers to a global information system existing *within* the Internet. The Web consists of uncounted millions of *websites*. Some websites feature text only; others also contain graphics; still others include audio and video components. Although there's great variation in the content and design of websites, all contain a *home page* that provides the site's title, descriptive material about the site, and a menu consisting of *links* to the information that can be accessed at the site. A link is a stepping stone to other pages on the site or to a related website. You can jump from the first location to the next just by clicking on the link. (For more on links, see page 516.)

Accessing the Web

Access to the Web is provided through a software program called a *web browser*. Netscape, Internet Explorer, and Mosaic are several widely used browsers. If you attend one of the many colleges or universities providing Web access to students, you'll probably use one of these browsers. At these schools, you can do your research online by accessing the library's catalog of holdings, its databases, and other resources. If your school doesn't offer Web access and you have a computer and modem at home, you can subscribe to a commercial online service, such as America Online, Earthlink, Prodigy, or CompuServe, all of which have their own browsers.

The Advantages and Limitations of the Web

The World Wide Web offers a collection of data that surpasses anything else the world has seen. With the click of a mouse, you can read electronic versions of the *Washington Post* or the *London Times;* you can check the temperature in Cairo or get up-to-the-minute stock quotes; you can read reviews of a best-selling novel or learn about alternative treatments for arthritis. Because the Web (unlike a library) *doesn't have a centralized organizational structure,* you're automatically—and somewhat haphazardly—exposed to this staggering array of material.

Keep in mind, too, that anyone—from Nobel Prize winners to members of extreme fringe groups—can post material on the Web at any time. Not surprisingly, then, the quality of information found on the Web ranges from authoritative to speculative to fraudulent. Unlike sources in the library, which may be dated or even no longer accurate, online material is generally up-to-date because it can be posted on the Web as soon as it's created. Yet the instantaneous nature of Web postings can create problems. Library materials certainly aren't infallible, but most have gone through a process of editorial review before being published. This is often *not* the case with material on the Web. Given this basic limitation, it's a good idea not to rely solely on the Web when you research a topic. Consider using the Web as a supplement to, rather than a substitute for, library research. (For more about evaluating the currency and validity of material on the Web, see pages 518–19.)

Using Online Time Productively

Whether you access the Web through a university service or a commercial provider, the following suggestions will help you use online time productively. First, just as you do when conducting library research (see pages 505–13), be sure to record accurate and sufficient information about your online source so you can provide full documentation when it comes time to write your paper. Specifically, be sure to record the material's title and date, as well as the date of your retrieval. You also need to copy the source's full *URL* (*uniform resource locator*), or Internet *address*. Here, for example is the address for the *Boston Globe* newspaper: *www.boston.com/globe*. Having the address makes it possible for you—and the reader of your research paper—to return to this page in the future. Type the address *exactly* as it appears on the website's home page. Don't capitalize something that originally was in lowercase letters, and don't leave extra space between elements in the address. Typing even slight changes in the address usually makes it impossible to access the site. Second, when you find a helpful website that you may want to visit again, use your browser's *Bookmark* or *Favorite Places* option. After you "bookmark" a site, its address is saved in your personal file, so you can click on its name and instantly return to the site, without having to remember (or type) its address.

Using the Internet to Find Books on Your Topic

Assume that you've used your library's computerized catalog to track down several books on your subject. Now you'd like to go online to see if there are additional books you might find helpful. In such a case, you could access the site of one or both of the following national booksellers: Barnes and Noble (at *www.bn.com*) and Amazon (at *www.amazon.com*). At either site, you would use the "Browse Subjects" box on the bookseller's home page to identify relevant books. Let's say you want to investigate how the experience of childhood poverty affected the politics of certain American presidents. Using the "Browse Subjects" box, you note that one of the subject listings is "Biography." Clicking on "Biography," you see that one of the subcategories is "Presidents." Click on "Presidents," and a list of books on American presidents appears. By clicking on specific titles from the list, you obtain information about each book, including reviewer and reader comments. With this information, you can usually determine which books are appropriate for your purpose. At that point, you check the availability of those books in the library or, if you wish, purchase them online.

Online booksellers can also help you narrow your topic. Perhaps you want to research the topic of illiteracy. As soon as you type the word "illiteracy" in the "Key Words" box on the bookseller's home page, you receive a long list of books on the subject. Simply looking at the range of titles can help you narrow your research. You might, for example, decide to focus on illiteracy in the workplace, teenagers' declining reading scores, or programs that teach marginally literate parents how to read to their children.

Using the Internet to Find Articles and Other Materials on Your Topic

What do you do if you want to go online to track down articles, speeches, legislation, TV transcripts, and so on about your subject? How, given the array of online material, can you identify pertinent sources? Search directories and search engines will help.

Search Directories.   A *search directory*, a service that lists websites organized by categories, will point you in the right direction. If you're not sure how to narrow your topic, seeing the search directory's categories may help you by identifying directions you wouldn't have thought of on your own. New search directories crop up regularly, but one of the most popular and user-friendly is Yahoo! On page 517 is an approximation of what you'll see when you go to Yahoo's home page. (Bear in mind that websites change constantly. What appears on your computer screen will not be identical to what's presented here.)

As you see, Yahoo! divides websites into fourteen categories: Arts & Humanities, Business & Economy, and so on. Each category is presented as a *link* (see page 513). Typically, a link shows up as an underlined word or phrase that's a different color from the type elsewhere on the page. When you click on a link, you're automatically transported to a related site. There you're presented with a more focused list of websites to choose from. As you move from link to link, you go from the general topic to more specific aspects of the topic. For example, say you're researching the legal rights of the disabled. You notice that there's a section titled "Law" under the category "Government." Click on "Law" and you're presented with a screen that lists several dozen law-related links, from "arbitration and mediation" to "trade." (There's even a link for "lawyer jokes.") When you see the link "disabilities," you know you're on the right track. As soon as you click on "disabilities," links to related sites appear on screen. From those, you select the sites you think will be most useful in your research.

Search Engines.   Search directories are wonderful tools when you begin exploring your topic. But when you're refining your investigation, you'll want to use another kind of resource—the *search engine*. Search engines comb through the vast amount of information on the Web for sites that match your research needs. You activate a search engine by typing in key words or phrases that tell the engine what to

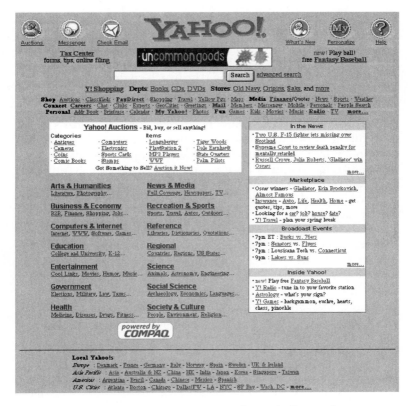

look for. Increasingly, search engines and search directories are combined, making it possible to access both from the site's home page. Here's a list of some popular search directories and search engines and their addresses.

About at *www.about.com*

AltaVista at *www.altavista.com*

Excite! at *www.excite.com*

Google at *www.google.com*

GoTo at *www.goto.com*

Lycos at *www.lycos.com*

Northern Light at *www.northernlight.com*

Refdesk at *www.refdesk.com*

Yahoo! at *www.yahoo.com*

Tips for Using Search Engines.   When you reach the home page of a search engine, it's a good idea to click on the "help" or "tips" button. When you do, you'll receive specific guidelines for using that particular search engine efficiently. As you proceed, don't forget to "bookmark" (see page 515) the search engines you use so you can return to them easily at a later date.

Return to the example of a Yahoo! home page (page 517). Note that at the top, there's an empty box beside "Search." That's where you type in keyword(s) describing your research topic. After you click on "Search" (or whatever your search engine calls its "search" command), the engine scans the Web for your keyword(s). It then provides you with a list of "hits," or links, to websites where your keyword is found. Most search engines also provide a brief description of each site.

The success of your search depends on how carefully you follow your search engine's guidelines and on how specific and descriptive your search terms are. For example, say you're doing research on animal-rights activism. Depending upon your search engine, if you simply enter the words "animal rights activism" in the search box, the engine may provide a list of *every* document that contains the word "animal" or "rights" or "activism"—hundreds of thousands of hits. To limit the number of hits you get, follow with great care your search engine's specific guidelines. For example, you might be told to enclose the keywords in quotation marks ("animal rights activism") or to place plus signs between the words (animal + rights + activism) to find documents in which all three words appear.

Evaluating Internet Materials

You need to take special care to evaluate the worth of material you find on the Web. Electronic documents often seem to appear out of nowhere and can disappear without a trace. And anyone—from scholar to con artist—can create a Web page. How, then, do you know if an Internet source is credible? Here are some questions to ask when you work with online material:

- Who is the author of the material? Does the author offer his or her credentials in a résumé or biographical note? Do these credentials qualify the author to provide reliable information on the topic? Does the author provide an e-mail address so you can request more information? The less you know about an author, the more suspicious you should be about using the data.

- Can you verify the accuracy of the information presented? Does the author refer to studies or to other authors you can investigate? If the author doesn't cite other works or other points of view, that may suggest the document is opinionated and one-sided. In such a case, it's important to track down material addressing alternative points of view.

- Who's sponsoring the website? Many sites are established by organizations—businesses, agencies, lobby groups—as well as by individuals. If a sponsor pushes a single point of view, you should use the material with great caution. Once again, make an extra effort to locate material addressing other sides of the issue.

- Is the cited information up-to-date? Being on the Internet doesn't guarantee that information is current. To assess the timeliness of Internet materials, check at the top or bottom of the document for copyright date, publication date, and/or revision date. Having those dates will help you determine whether the material is recent enough for your purposes.

DOCUMENTING SOURCES

In Chapter 11, you learned the importance of *documentation*—giving credit to the print and electronic sources whose words and ideas you borrow in an essay (see page 410). That earlier discussion showed you how to document sources in informal papers. The following pages will show you how to use the documentation system of the Modern Language Association (MLA)[1] when citing sources in more formal papers.

The discussion here covers key features of the MLA system. For more detailed coverage, you may want to consult a recent composition handbook or the latest edition of the *MLA Handbook for*

---

[1]MLA documentation is appropriate in papers written for humanities courses, such as your composition class. If you're writing a paper for a course in the social sciences (for example, psychology, economics, or sociology), your professor will probably expect you to use the citation format developed by the American Psychological Association (APA). For information about APA documentation, consult a composition handbook or the most recent edition of the *Publication Manual of the American Psychological Association.*

Writers of Research Papers. For a sample paper that uses MLA documentation, turn to the student essay on pages 426–32.

WHAT TO DOCUMENT

You may inadvertently fall into the trap of *plagiarizing*—passing off someone else's ideas as your own—if you're not sure when you need to acknowledge outside sources in an essay. To avoid plagiarism, you must provide documentation in the following situations:

- When you include *word-for-word quotations* from a source.
- When you *summarize or restate in your own words* ideas or information from a source, unless that material is *commonly known* or is a *matter of historical or scientific record.*
- When you *combine a summary and a quotation.*

An important note: On the whole, you should try to state borrowed material in your own words. A string of quotations signals that you haven't sufficiently evaluated and distilled your sources. Use quotations sparingly; draw upon them only when they dramatically illustrate key points you want to make. Also, keep in mind that quotations won't, by themselves, make your case for you. You need to interpret and comment on them, showing how they support your points.

HOW TO DOCUMENT

The MLA documentation system uses the *parenthetic reference,* a brief note in parentheses inserted into the text after borrowed material. The parenthetic reference doesn't provide full bibliographic information but it presents enough so that readers can turn to the Works Cited list (see page 525) at the end of the paper for complete information. If the method of documentation you learned in high school involved footnotes or endnotes, you will be happy to know that parenthetic documentation—currently the preferred method—is much easier to use. While it is now accepted by most college professors, be sure to check with your professors to determine their documentation preferences.

Whenever you quote or summarize material from an outside source, you must do two things: (1) *identify the author* and (2) *specify the page(s)* in your source on which the material appears. The author's name may be given *either* in a lead-in sentence (often called the *attribution*) *or* in the parentheses following the borrowed material. The page number *always* appears in parentheses. The examples below illustrate the MLA documentation style and are based on the following excerpt from page 8 of Julian Stamp's book *The Homeless and History:*

> The key to any successful homeless program requires a clear understanding of just who make up the homeless in our country. Since fifty percent of shelter residents have drug and alcohol addictions, programs need to provide not only a place to sleep but also comprehensive substance-abuse treatment. Since roughly one-third of the homeless population is mentally ill, programs need to offer psychiatric care, even institutionalization, not just housing subsidies. Since the typical head of a homeless family often lacks the know-how needed to maintain a job and a home, programs need to supply employment and life skills training.
>
> When we switch our focus to larger *economic* issues, we see that homelessness cannot be resolved solely at the level of the individual. Since the 1980s, the gap between the rich and the poor has widened, buying power has stagnated, jobs have fled overseas, and funding for low-cost housing has been almost eliminated. Given these developments, homelessness begins to look like a product of history, and only by addressing shifts in the American economy can we begin to find effective solutions.

Using Parentheses Only

Counseling and support services are not enough to solve the problem of homelessness; proposed solutions must also address the complex economic issues at the heart of homelessness (Stamp 8).

If we look beyond the problems of homelessness, to "larger *economic* issues, we see that homelessness cannot be resolved solely at the level of the individual" (Stamp 8).

Given the fact that a significant percentage of the homeless suffer from mental illness, "programs need to offer psychiatric care [. . .], not just housing subsidies" (Stamp 8).

Using Parentheses and Attributions

Historian Julian Stamp argues that homelessness must be addressed in terms of economics, not simply in terms of individual counseling, addiction therapy, or job training (8).

Because half of those taking refuge in shelters have problems with drugs and alcohol, Stamp argues that "programs need to provide not only a place to sleep but also comprehensive substance-abuse treatment" (8).

As Stamp states, "The key to any successful homeless program requires a clear understanding of just who make up the homeless [. . .]" (8).

Key Points to Remember

Take a moment to look again at the preceding examples and note the following points:

- The parenthetic reference is placed *immediately after* the borrowed material, at a natural pause in the sentence or at the end of the sentence.
- The parenthetic reference is placed *before* any *internal punctuation* (a comma or semicolon) as well as *before* any *terminal punctuation* (a period or question mark).
- If you want to call attention to a specific author, use an attribution indicating the author's name.
- When the author's name is provided in the attribution, the name is *not* repeated in the parentheses.
- The first time an author is referred to in an attribution, the author's *full name* is given; afterwards, only the *last name* is provided.
- Sometimes, to inform readers of an author's area of expertise, the person may be identified by profession ("Historian Julian Stamp argues that . . ."), title, or affiliation.
- When the author's name is provided in the parentheses, only the last name is given.
- The page number comes directly after the author's name. (If the source is only one page long, only the author's name is needed.)

- There is no punctuation between the author's name and the page number.
- There is no *p.* or *page* preceding the page number.
- Words may be deleted from a quotation as long as the author's original meaning isn't changed. In such a case, three spaced periods—called an *ellipsis* (. . .)—are inserted in place of the deleted words. To make it clear that the ellipsis stands for material that you rather than your source deleted, place brackets around the ellipsis.[2] An ellipsis is not needed when material is omitted from the start of a quotation.

Three Other Important Points

Here are three additional situations you may encounter when documenting sources.

1. More than one source by the same author.   When your paper includes references to more than one work by the same author, you must specify—either in the parentheses or in the attribution—the particular work being cited. You do this by providing the *title*, as well as the author's name and the page(s). As with the author's name, the title may be given in *either* the attribution *or* the parenthetic citation. Here are some examples:

In The Language and Thought of the Child, Jean Piaget states that "discussion forms the basis for a logical point of view" (240).

Piaget considers dialogue essential to the development of logical thinking (Language and Thought 240).

The Child's Conception of the World shows that young children think that the name of something can never change (Piaget 81).

Young children assume that everything has only one name and that no others are possible (Piaget, Child's Conception 81).

[2]The 1999 edition of the *MLA Handbook for Writers of Research Papers* was the first edition calling for the use of brackets with ellipsis points. Earlier editions required only the ellipses. To be consistent with the most recent guidelines, the examples here and on pages 521–22 use brackets with the ellipses. Check with your instructors to see which guidelines they want you to follow.

Notice that when a work is named in the attribution, the full title appears; when a title is given in the parenthetic citation, though, only the first few significant words appear. (However, don't use the ellipsis to indicate that some words have been omitted from the title; the ellipsis is used only when quoting a source.)

2. Long quotations.   A quotation extending beyond four typed lines starts on a new line and is indented ten spaces from the left margin throughout. Since this so-called *block format* already indicates a quotation, quotation marks are unnecessary. Double-space the block quotation, as you do the rest of your paper. Don't leave extra space above or below the quotation. Long quotations, which should be used sparingly, require a lead-in. A lead-in that *isn't* a full sentence is followed by a comma, while a lead-in that *is* a full sentence (as in the accompanying example) is followed by a colon:

Stamp cites changing economic conditions as the key to a national homeless policy:

> Since the 1980s, the gap between the rich and the poor has widened, buying power has stagnated, jobs have fled overseas, and funding for low-cost housing has been almost eliminated. Given these developments, homelessness begins to look like a product of history, and only by addressing shifts in the American economy can we begin to find effective solutions. (8)

Notice that the page number appears in parentheses, just as in a short quotation. But in a long quotation, the parenthetic citation is placed two spaces *after* the period that ends the quotation.

3. Quoting or summarizing a source within a source.   If you quote or summarize a *secondhand source* (someone whose ideas come to you only through another source), you need to make this clear. The parenthetic documentation should indicate "as quoted in" with the abbreviation *qtd. in:*

According to Sherman, "Recycling has, in several communities, created unanticipated expenses" (qtd. in Pratt 3-4).

Sherman explains that recycling can be surprisingly costly (qtd. in Pratt 3-4).

Your Works Cited list would include the source you actually read (Pratt), rather than the source you refer to secondhand (Sherman).

LIST OF WORKS CITED

A documented paper ends with a list of Works Cited, which includes only those sources you actually acknowledge in the paper. Placed on its own page, the Works Cited list provides the reader with full bibliographic information about the sources cited in the parenthetic references (see pages 520–24). By referring to the Works Cited list that appears at the end of the student essay on pages 431–32, you will notice the following:

- The list is organized alphabetically by authors' last names. Entries without an author are alphabetized by the first major word in the title (that is, not *A, An,* or *The*).
- Entries are not numbered.
- If an entry runs longer than one line, each additional line is indented five spaces. Entries are double-spaced with no extra space between entries.

Sample Works Cited Entries

Listed here are sample Works Cited entries for the most commonly used kinds of sources. Refer to these samples when you prepare your own Works Cited list, taking special care to reproduce the punctuation and spacing exactly. If you don't spot an entry for the kind of source you need to document, consult the *MLA Handbook* for more comprehensive examples.

CITING BOOKS

Book by One Author

List the author's last name followed by a comma and first name. Then type the title (underlined) and city of publication, followed by a colon and the shortened version of the publisher's name (for example, use "UP" for "University Press" and "Norton" for "W.W. Norton & Co."). End with the year of publication.

Young, Iris Marion. <u>Inclusion and Democracy</u>. New York: Oxford UP, 2000.

Book by Two or Three Authors

Provide all the authors' names in the order they appear on the title page of the book, but reverse only the first name.

Ward, Jeffrey C., and Ken Burns. Jazz: A History of America's Music. New York: Knopf, 2000.

Wallerstein, Judith S., Julia M. Lewis, and Sandra Blakeslee. The Unexpected Legacy of Divorce: A 25 Year Landmark Study. New York: Hyperion, 2000.

Book by Four or More Authors

For a work by four or more authors, give only the first author's name followed by a comma and "et al." (Latin for "and others").

Frye, Northrop, et al. The Harper Handbook to Literature. New York: Longman, 1997.

Two or More Works by the Same Author

If you use more than one work by the same author, list each book separately. Give the author's name in the first entry only; begin the entries for other books by that author with three hyphens followed by a period. Arrange the works alphabetically by title.

Sommers, Christina Hoff. The War Against Boys: How Misguided Feminism Is Harming Our Young Men. New York: Simon & Schuster, 2000.

---. Who Stole Feminism? How Women Have Betrayed Women. New York: Simon & Schuster, 1995.

Revised Edition

Indicate a revised edition ("Rev. ed.," "2nd ed.," "3rd ed.," "4th ed.," and so on) after the title.

Eagleton, Terry. Literary Theory: An Introduction. 2nd ed. Minneapolis: U of Minnesota P, 1996.

Kobliner, Beth. Get a Financial Life: Personal Finance in Your
    Twenties and Thirties. Rev. ed. New York: Simon & Schuster,
    2000.

Book With an Editor or Translator

Following the title, type "Ed." or "Trans.," followed by the
name of the editor or translator.

Jacobs, Harriet. Incidents in the Life of a Slave Girl, Written by
    Herself. Ed. Jean Fagan Yellin. Cambridge: Harvard UP, 2000.

Anthology or Compilation of Works by Different Authors

List anthologies according to the editor or editors' names, followed by "ed."

Gates, Henry Louis, Jr., and Nellie Y. McKay, ed. The Norton
    Anthology of African American Literature. New York: Norton,
    1997.

Section of an Anthology or Compilation

Begin this entry with the author and title of the selection (in
quotation marks), followed by the title of the anthology. The editors' names are listed after the anthology title and are preceded by
"Ed." Note that the entry ends with the page numbers on which the
selection appears.

Baldwin, James. "Everybody's Protest Novel." The Norton Anthology
    of African American Literature. Ed. Henry Louis Gates, Jr. and
    Nellie Y. McKay. New York: Norton, 1997. 1654-59.

Section or Chapter in a Book by One Author

Murphy, Tom. "Interactivity: Taking Control." Web Rules: How the
    Internet Is Changing the Way Consumers Make Choices.
    Chicago: Dearborn Trade, 2000. 77-89.

Reference Work

"Temperance Movements." Columbia Encyclopedia. 6th ed. New
    York: Columbia UP, 2000.

Book by an Institution or Corporation

United Nations Commission on Women. The World's Women, 2000:
    Trends and Statistics. New York: United Nations, 2000.

CITING PERIODICALS

Article in a Weekly or Biweekly Magazine

Provide the author's name (if the article is signed), article title
(in quotation marks), periodical name (underlined), and date of
publication, followed by a colon and page number(s) of the article.

Mannix, Margaret. "The Web's Dark Side." U.S. News & World
    Report 28 Aug. 2000: 36-45.

Article in a Monthly or Bimonthly Magazine

Stone, Robin D. "Reading, Writing, Roulette." Essence Sept. 2000:
    153-62.

Article in a Daily Newspaper

If the article is printed on multiple, nonconsecutive pages, simply list the first page (including both section and page numbers or
letters) followed by a plus sign (+). (Note: Omit the initial *The* from
newspaper names.)

Zernike, Kate. "New Tactic on College Drinking: Play It Down." New
    York Times 3 Oct. 2000: A1+.

Editorial, Letter to the Editor, or Reply to a Letter

List as you would any signed or unsigned article, but indicate
the type of piece after the article's title.

Steele, Shelby. "A New Front in the Culture War." Editorial. Wall
    Street Journal 2 Aug. 2000: A22.

Article in a Scholarly Journal

Some journals are paged continuously; the first issue of each year
starts with page one, and each subsequent issue picks up where the
previous one left off. For such journals, use numerals to indicate the
volume number after the title, and then indicate the year in parentheses. Note that neither "volume" nor "vol." is used. The article's
page(s) appear at the end, separated from the year by a colon.

"Standing Up to School Bullies." Congressional Quarterly Researcher
    9 (1999): 604-11.

For a journal that pages each issue separately, use numerals to
indicate the *volume and issue numbers;* separate the two with a period but leave no space after the period.

Staples, J. Scott. "Violence in Schools: Rage Against a Broken World."
    Annals of the American Academy of Political & Social Science
    56.1 (2000): 30-42.

CITING ELECTRONIC SOURCES

Article in an Online Periodical

For an article obtained online, supply the same information you
would for printed text: author's name, selection's title, source, and
(when available) publication date and page or paragraph numbers.
When page or paragraph numbers are provided, list them after the
date of publication (using "pp." for "pages" or "par." for "paragraphs").

Complete your listing with the date on which you accessed the
material, followed by the exact address of the website (in angle
brackets) and then a final period. (Since online material can be
revised at any time, it's critical that you provide your date of access
to identify the version you retrieved.) Note that long Web addresses should be broken up only after slashes.

Nordland, Rod. "Sanctioning Starvation?" <u>Newsweek Online</u> 3 Aug.
     2000. 6 Feb. 2001 <http//:www.msnbc.com/news/
     NW-front_Front.asp>.

Ramos, Dante. "Public Health vs. Private Medicine." <u>Salon</u> 31 July
     2000: 17 pars. 2 Mar. 2001 <http://salon.com/health/
     feature/2000/07/31/betrayaloftrust/index/html>.

Article in a Full-Text Online Periodicals Index

For full-text articles accessed through an online index (general-ly only available to libraries by subscription), begin with the same information as for online periodicals. After the publication informa-tion (issue, date, and page numbers), list the title of the index (underlined), its vendor, and the library through which you gained access to it. Complete the entry with the date you accessed the index and the index's Web address.

Casella, Ronnie. "The Benefits of Peer Mediation in the Context of
     Urban Conflict." <u>Urban Education</u> 35.3 (2000): 324-56.
     <u>EBSCOhost</u>. MasterFILE Premier. Camden County Lib.,
     Voorhees. 19 May 2001 <http://ehostvg.wl.epnet.com>.

Online Book

When it's available, include the book's original publication information between the book's title and the underlined database name. Also include (when available) the name of the site's editor, its electronic publication date, its sponsoring organization, your date of access, and the Web address.

Franklin, Benjamin. <u>The Autobiography of Benjamin Franklin</u>. London,
     1793. <u>Electronic Text Center</u>. Ed. David Seaman. 1998. U of
     Virginia Lib. 16 July 2001 <http://
     etext.lib.virginia.edu>.

Online Reference Work

"Salem Witch Trials." <u>Britannica.com</u>. Apr. 2000. Encyclopedia
     Britannica. 29 Sept. 2000 <http://britannica.com/bcom/eb/
     article/html?/query=salem%20witch%20trials>.

Professional or Personal Website

John Steinbeck's Life and Work. Sept. 1999. San Jose Center for
    Steinbeck Studies, San Jose State U. 24 Jan. 2001
    <http://www.sjsu.edu/depts/steinbec/steinbio.html>.

Mallen, Enrique. Online Picasso Project. 18 Apr. 2001 <http://
    www.tamu.edu/mocl/picasso>.

Article on CD-ROM

Supplement basic publication information with the title of the
database (underlined), publication medium (CD-ROM), CD-ROM
publisher, and CD-ROM publication date.

Krauss, Clifford. "Crime Statistics in the Big Apple." New York Times
    12 Mar. 1998, late ed.: B1. New York Times Ondisc. CD-ROM.
    UMI-ProQuest. 11 Dec. 2000.

Computer Software

Cite the following information (when available); author of the
software, title (underlined), medium (CD-ROM or diskette), version, publication city, publisher, and year of publication.

Compton's Encyclopedia 2000 Deluxe. CD-ROM. 2000 ed.
    Mindscape, 2000.

E-mail Message

Bernard, Lynn. "Regional Adult Literacy Seminar." E-mail to Ronnie
    Hotis. 30 Aug. 2001.

CITING OTHER NONPRINT SOURCES

Television or Radio Program

"Underground Culture Hits Main Street." Nightline. Narr. Robert
    Krulwich. Part 1 of 3. ABC. WPVI-TV, Philadelphia. 6 Sept.
    2000.

Movie, Recording, Videotape, DVD, Filmstrip, or Slide Program

Provide the author or composer of the piece (if appropriate); title (underlined); director, conductor, or performer; medium; distributor; and year of release.

The Matrix. Dir. Andy Wachowski and Larry Wachowski. DVD.
    Warner Bros, 1999.

Personal or Phone Interview

Langdon, Paul. Personal interview. 26 Jan. 2001.

Lecture

Akers, Sharon. "Stock Market Savvy." Investing Made Easy Seminar.
    Camden County Adult Education Program.   East Hills High
    School, New Jersey. 27 Mar. 2001.

GLOSSARY

Abstract and concrete language refers to two different qualities of words. Abstract words and phrases convey concepts, qualities, emotions, and ideas that we can think and talk about but not actually see or experience directly. Examples of abstract words are *conservatism, courage, avarice, joy,* and *hatred.* Words or phrases whose meanings are directly seen or experienced by the senses are concrete terms. Examples of phrases using concrete words are *split-level house, waddling penguin,* and *short pink waitress uniform.*

Adequate—see *Evidence.*

***Ad hominem* argument**—see *Logical fallacies.*

Analogy refers to an imaginative comparison between two subjects that seem to have little in common. Often a complex idea or topic can be made understandable by comparing it to a more familiar subject, and such an analogy can be developed over several paragraphs or even an entire essay. For example, to explain how the economic difficulties of farmers weaken an entire nation, a writer might create an analogy between failing farms and a cancer that slowly destroys a person's life.

Argumentation-persuasion tries to encourage readers to accept a writer's point of view on some controversial issue. In *argumentation,* a writer uses objective reasoning, facts, and hard evidence to demonstrate the soundness of a position. In *persuasion,* the writer uses appeals to the readers' emotions and value systems, often in the hope of encouraging them to take a specific action. Argumentation and persuasion are frequently used together in an essay. For example, a writer might argue for the construction of a highway through town by pointing out that the road would bring new business, create new jobs, and lighten traffic. The writer also might try to persuade readers to vote for a highway appropriations bill by appealing to their emotions, claiming that the highway would allow people to get home faster, thus giving them more time for family life and leisure activities. A whole essay can be organized around argumentation-persuasion, or an essay developed chiefly through another pattern may contain elements of argumentation-persuasion.

Assertion refers to the *thesis* of an *argumentation-persuasion* essay. The assertion, or *proposition,* is a point of view or opinion on a controversial issue or topic. The assertion cannot be merely a statement of a fact. Such statements as "Women still experience discrimination in the job market," "General Rabb would make an ideal mayor for our town," and "This university should devote more funds to raising the quality of the food services" are examples of assertions that could serve as theses for argumentation-persuasion essays.

Audience refers to a writer's intended readers. In planning the content and tone of an essay, you should identify your audience and consider its needs. How similar are the members of your audience to you in knowledge and point of view? What will they need to know for you to achieve your *purpose?* What *tone* will make them open to receiving your message? For example, if you were to write a description of a trip to Disney World, you would have to explain a lot more to an eighty-year-old grandmother who had never seen a theme park than to a young parent who has probably visited several. If you wrote about the high cost of clothing for an economics professor, you would choose a serious, analytic tone and supply statistical evidence for your points. If you wrote about the same topic for the college newspaper, you might use a tone tinged with humor and provide helpful hints on finding bargain clothing.

Begging the question—see *Logical fallacies.*

Brainstorming is a technique used in the *prewriting* stage. It helps you discover the limited subject you can successfully write about and also generates raw material—ideas and details—to develop that subject. In brainstorming, you allow your mind to play freely with the subject. You try to capture fleeting thoughts about it, no matter how random, minor, or tangential, and jot them down rapidly before they disappear from your mind.

Causal analysis—see *Cause-effect.*

Causal chain refers to a series of causes and effects, in which the result or effect of a cause becomes itself the cause of a further effect, and so on. For example, a person's alarm clock failing to buzz might begin a causal chain by causing the person to oversleep. Oversleeping then causes the person to miss the bus, and missing the bus causes the person to arrive late to work. Arriving late causes the person to miss an important phone call, which causes the person to lose a chance at a lucrative contract.

Cause-effect, sometimes called *causal analysis,* involves analyzing the reasons for or results of an event, action, decision, or phenomenon. Writers develop an essay through an analysis of causes whenever they attempt to answer such questions as "Why has this happened?" or "Why does this exist?" When writers explore such questions as "What happens or would happen if a certain change occurs?" or "What will happen if a condition continues?" their essays involve a discussion of effects. Some cause-effect essays concentrate on the causes of a situation, some focus on the effects, and others present both causes and effects. Causal analysis can be an essay's central pattern, or it can be used to help support a point in an essay developed primarily through another pattern.

Characteristics—see *Formal definition.*

Chronological sequence—see *Narrative sequence* and *Organization.*

Circularity is an error in *formal definition* resulting from using variations of the to-be-defined word in the definition. For example, "A scientific hypothesis is a hypothesis made by a scientist about the results of an experiment" is circular because the unknown term is used to explain itself.

Class—see *Formal definition.*

Coherence refers to the clear connection among the various parts of an essay. As a writer, you can draw upon two key strategies to make writing coherent. You can use a clear *organizational format* (for example, a chronological, spatial, emphatic, or simple-to-complex sequence). You can also provide *appropriate signaling* or *connecting devices* (transitions, bridging sentences, repeated words, synonyms, and pronouns).

Comparison-contrast means explaining the similarities and/or differences between events, objects, people, ideas, and so on. The comparison-contrast format can be used to meet a purely factual purpose ("This is how A and B are alike or different"). But usually writers use comparison-contrast to make a judgment about the relative merits of the subjects under discussion. Sometimes a writer will concentrate solely on similarities *or* differences. For instance, when writing about married versus single life, you would probably devote most of your time to discussing the differences between these lifestyles. Other times, comparison and contrast are found together. In an essay analyzing two approaches to U.S. foreign policy, you would probably discuss the similarities *and* the differences in the goals and methods characteristic of each approach. Comparison-contrast can be the dominant pattern in an essay, or it can help support a point in an essay developed chiefly through another pattern.

Conclusion refers to the one or more paragraphs that bring an essay to an end. Effective conclusions give the reader a sense of completeness and finality. Writers often use the conclusion as a place to reaffirm the *thesis* and to express a final thought about the subject. Methods of conclusion include summarizing main points, using a quotation, predicting an outcome, and recommending an action.

Conflict creates tension in the readers of a *narration*. It is produced by the opposition of characters or other forces in a story. Conflict can occur between individuals, between a person and society or nature, or within a person. Readers wonder how a conflict will be resolved and read on to find out.

Connotative and denotative language describe the ability of language to emphasize one or another aspect of a word's range of meaning. *Denotative language* stresses the dictionary meaning of words. *Connotative language* emphasizes the echoes of feeling that cluster around some words. For example, the terms *weep, bawl, break down,* and *sob* all denote the same thing: to cry. But they have different associations and call up different images. A writer employing the connotative resources of language would choose the term among these that suggested the appropriate image.

Controlling idea—see *Thesis*.

Deductive reasoning is a form of logical thinking in which general statements believed to be true are applied to specific situations or cases. The result of deduction is a conclusion or prediction about the specific situation. Deduction is often expressed in a three-step pattern called a *syllogism*. The first part of the syllogism is a general statement about a large class of items or situations, the *major premise*. The second part is the *minor premise,* a more limited statement about a specific item or case. The third part is the *conclusion*, drawn from the major premise, about that specific case or item. Deductive reasoning is very common in everyday thinking. For example, you might use deduction when car shopping:

In an accident, large cars are safer than small cars. (*major premise*)

The Turbo Titan is a large car. (*minor premise*)

In an accident, the Turbo Titan will be safer than a small car. (*conclusion*)

Definition explains the meaning of a word or concept. The brief formal definitions found in the dictionary can be useful if you need to clarify or restrict the meaning of a term used in an essay. In such cases, the definition is short and to the point. But you may also use an *extended definition* in an essay, taking several paragraphs, even the entire piece, to develop the meaning of a term. You may use extended definition to convey a personal slant on a well-known term, to refute a commonly held interpretation of a word, or to dissect a complex or controversial issue. Definition can be the chief method of development in an essay, or it can help support a point in an essay organized around another pattern.

Definition by negation is a method of defining a term by first explaining what the term is *not*, and then going on to explain what it is. For example, you might begin a critical essay about television with a definition by negation: "Television, far from being a medium that dispenses only light, insubstantial fare, actually disseminates a dangerously distorted view of family life." Definition by negation can provide a stimulating introduction to an essay.

Denotative language—see *Connotative and denotative language.*

Description involves the use of vivid word pictures to express what the five senses have experienced. The subject of a descriptive essay can be a person, a place, an object, or an event. Description can be the dominant pattern in an essay, or it can be used as a supplemental method in an essay developed chiefly through another pattern.

There are two main types of description. In an *objective description,* a writer provides details about a subject without conveying the emotions the subject arouses. For example, if you were involved in a traffic accident, your insurance agent might ask you to write an objective description of the events leading up to and during the crash. But in a *subjective description,* the writer's goal is to evoke in the reader the emotions felt during the experience. For example, in a cautionary letter to a friend who has a habit of driving dangerously, you might write a subjective description of your horrifyingly close call with death during a car accident.

Development—see *Evidence.*

Dialogue is the writer's way of directly presenting the exact words spoken by characters in a *narration.* By using dialogue, writers can convey people's individuality and also add drama and immediacy to an essay.

Directional process analysis—see *Process analysis.*

Division-classification refers to a logical method for analyzing a single subject or several related subjects. Though often used together in an essay, division and classification are separate processes. *Division* involves breaking a subject or idea into its component parts. For instance, the concept "an ideal vacation" could be divided according to its destination, accommodations, or cost. *Classification* involves organizing a number of related items into categories. For example, in an essay about the overwhelming flow of paper in our everyday lives, you might classify the typical kinds of mail most people receive: personal mail (letters, birthday cards, party invitations), business mail (bills, bank statements, charge-card receipts), and junk mail (flyers about bargain sales, solicitations to donate, contest announcements). Division-classification can be the dominant pattern in a paper, or it may be used to support a point in an essay organized chiefly around another pattern of development.

Dominant impression refers to the purpose of a descriptive essay. While some descriptive essays have a thesis, others do not; instead, they convey a dominant impression or main point. For example, one person writing a descriptive essay about New York City might use its architectural diversity as a focal point. Another person writing a description of Manhattan might concentrate on the overpowering sense of hustle and speed about everyone and everything in the city. Both writers would select only those details that supported their dominant impressions.

Dramatic license refers to the writer's privilege, when writing a narrative, to alter facts or details to strengthen the support of the *thesis* or *narrative point*. For example, a writer is free to flesh out the description of an event whose specific details may be partially forgotten or to modify or omit details of a narrative that do not contribute to the meaning the writer wishes to convey.

Either-or fallacy—see *Logical fallacies.*

Emphatic sequence—see *Organization.*

Ethos refers to a writer's reliability or credibility. Such an image of trustworthiness is particularly important to readers of an *argumentation-persuasion* essay or piece. Writers establish their *ethos* by using reason and logic, by being moderate in their appeals to emotions, by avoiding a hostile tone, and by demonstrating overall knowledgeability of the subject. The most effective argumentation-persuasion involves an interplay of *ethos, logos,* and *pathos.*

Etymology refers to the history of a word or term. All English words have their origins in other, often ancient, languages. Giving a brief etymology of a word can help a writer establish the context for developing an *extended definition* of the word. For example, the word *criminal* is derived from a Latin word meaning "accusation" or "accused." Today, our word *criminal* goes beyond the concept of "accused" to mean "guilty."

Evidence lends substance to a writer's main ideas and thus helps the reader to accept the writer's viewpoint. Evidence should meet several criteria. First of all, it should be *unified,* in the sense that all supporting ideas and details should relate directly to the key point the writer is making. Second, evidence should be *adequate;* there should be enough evidence to convince the reader to agree with the thesis. Third, evidence should be *specific;* that is, vivid and detailed rather than vague and general. Fourth, evidence must be *accurate* and not overstate or understate information. Fifth, evidence should be *representative,* relying on the typical rather than the atypical to make a point. The bulk of an essay is devoted to supplying evidence. Supporting the thesis with solid evidence is the third stage in the writing process.

Exemplification, at the heart of all effective writing, involves using concrete specifics to support generalizations. In exemplification, writers provide examples or instances that support or clarify broader statements. You might support the thesis statement "I have a close-knit family" by using such examples as the following: "We have a regular Sunday dinner at my grandmother's house with at least ten family members present"; "My sisters and brothers visit my parents every week"; "I spend so much time on the phone talking with my sisters that sometimes I have trouble finding time for my new college friends." Exemplification may be an essay's central pattern, or it may supplement an essay developed mainly around another pattern.

Extended definition—see *Definition.*

Fallacies—see *Logical fallacies.*

False analogy—see *Logical fallacies.*

Figures of speech are imaginative comparisons between two things usually thought of as dissimilar. Some major figures of speech are *simile, metaphor,* and *personification. Similes* are comparisons that use the signal words *like* or *as:* "Superman was as powerful as a locomotive." *Metaphors,* which do not use signal words, directly equate unlike things: "The boss is a tiger when it comes to landing a contract." "The high-powered pistons of the boxer's arms pummeled his opponent." *Personification* attributes human characteristics to inanimate things or nonhuman beings: "The angry clouds unleashed their fury on the town"; "The turtle shyly poked his head out of his shell."

First draft refers to the writer's first try at producing a basic, unpolished version of the whole essay. It is often referred to as the "rough" draft, and nothing about it is final or unchangeable. The process of writing the first draft often brings up new ideas or details. Writers sometimes break off writing the draft to *brainstorm* or *freewrite* as new ideas occur to them and then return to the draft with new inspiration. You shouldn't worry about spelling, grammar, or style in the first-draft stage; instead, you should keep focused on casting your ideas into sentence and paragraph form. Writing the first draft is the fifth stage in the writing process.

Flashback—see *Narrative sequence.*

Flashforward—see *Narrative sequence.*

Formal definition involves stating a definition in a three-part pattern of about one sentence in length. In presenting a formal definition, a writer puts the *term* in a *class* and then lists the *characteristics* that separate the term from other members of its class. For example, a formal definition of a word processor might be, "A word processor (term) is an electronic machine (class) that is used to write, edit, store, and produce typewritten documents (characteristics)." Writers often use a formal definition to prepare a reader for an extended definition that follows.

Freewriting is most often used during the *prewriting* stage to help writers generate ideas about a limited topic. To use this method, write nonstop for five or ten minutes about everything your topic brings to mind. Disregard grammar, spelling, and organization as you keep your pen and mind moving. Freewriting is similar to *brainstorming*, except that the result is a rambling, detail-filled paragraph rather than a list. Freewriting can also be used to generate ideas during later stages of the writing process.

Gender-biased language gives the impression that one sex is more important, powerful, or valuable than the other. When writing, you should work to replace such sexist language with *gender-neutral* or *nonsexist* terms that convey no sexual prejudice. First of all, try to avoid *sexist vocabulary* that demeans or excludes one of the sexes: *stud, jock, chick, fox,* and so on. Also, just as adult males should be called *men,* adult females should be referred to as *women,* not *girls.* And men shouldn't be empowered with professional and honorary titles (*President* Clinton) while professional women—such as congressional representatives—are assigned only personal titles (*Mrs.* Shroeder). Here are some examples of the way you can avoid words that exclude women: Change "chairman" to *chairperson,* "layman" to *layperson,* "congressman" to *congressional representative,* "workmen" to *workers,* the "average guy" to the *average person.* Second, be aware of the fact that indefinite singular nouns—those representing a general group of people consisting of both genders—can lead to *sexist pronoun use:* for example, "On *his* first day of school, a young child often experiences separation anxiety." This sentence excludes female children from consideration, although the situation being described applies equally to them. Third, recognize that indefinite pronouns like *anyone, each,* and *everybody* may also pave the way to sexist pronoun use. Although such pronouns often refer to a number of individuals, they're considered singular. So, wanting to be grammatically correct, you may write a sentence like the following: "Everybody wants *his* favorite candidate to win." The sentence, however, is sexist because *everybody* is certainly not restricted to men. One way to avoid this type of sexist construction is to use both male and female pronouns: "Everybody wants *his* or *her* favorite candidate to win." Another approach is to use *s/he* in place of *he*. A third possibility is to use the gender-neutral pronouns *they, their,* or *themselves:* "Everybody wants *their* favorite candidate to win." Be warned, though. Some people object to using these plural pronouns with singular indefinite pronouns, even though the practice is common in everyday speech. Two alternative strategies enable you to eliminate the need for *any* gender-marked singular pronouns. First, you can change singular general nouns or indefinite pronouns to their plural equivalents and then use nonsexist plural pronouns. For example, you may change "A *workaholic* feels anxious when *he* isn't busy" to "*Workaholics* feel anxious when *they're* not busy" and "*Everyone* in the room expressed *his* opinion freely" to "*Those* in the room expressed *their* opinions freely." Second, you can recast the sentence to omit the singular pronoun: For instance, you may change "A *manager* usually spends part of each day settling squabbles among *his* staff" to "A manager usually spends part of each day settling *staff squabbles*" and "No *one* wants *his* taxes raised" to "No one wants *to pay more taxes.*"

Hasty generalization—see *Logical fallacies.*

Inductive reasoning is a form of logical thinking in which specific cases and facts are examined to draw a wider-ranging conclusion. The result of inductive reasoning is a generalization that is applied to situations or cases similar to the ones examined. Induction is typical of scientific investigation and of everyday thinking. For example, on the basis of specific experiences, you may have concluded that when you feel chilly in a room where everyone else is comfortable, you are likely to develop a cold and fever in the next day or two. In an *argumentation-persuasion* essay, the conclusion reached by induction would be your *assertion* or *thesis.*

Inference is the term for a conclusion based on *inductive reasoning.* Because the reasoning behind specific cases may not be simple, there is usually an element of uncertainty in an inductive conclusion. Choosing the correct explanation for specific cases is a matter of carefully weighing and selecting alternative conclusions.

Informational process analysis—see *Process analysis.*

Introduction refers to the first paragraph or several paragraphs of an essay. The introduction serves three purposes. It informs readers of the general subject of the essay, it catches their attention, and it presents the controlling idea or thesis. The methods of introducing an essay include the use of an anecdote, a quotation or surprising statistic or fact, and questions. Or you may narrow your discussion down from a broad subject to a more limited one.

Irony occurs when a writer or speaker implies (rather than states directly) a discrepancy or incongruity of some kind. *Verbal irony,* which is often tongue-in-cheek, involves a discrepancy between the literal words and what's actually meant ("I know you must be unhappy about receiving the highest grade in the course"). If the ironic comment is designed to be hurtful or insulting, it qualifies as *sarcasm* ("Congratulations! You failed the final exam"). In *situational irony,* the circumstances are themselves incongruous. For example, although their constitutional rights were violated when the federal government detained them in internment camps, Japanese-Americans nevertheless played American football, sang American songs, and saluted the American flag during their imprisonment.

Journal writing is a form of prewriting in which writers make daily entries in a private journal, much as they would in a diary. Whether they focus on one topic or wander freely, journal writers jot down striking incidents, images, and ideas encountered in the course of a day. Such journal material can produce ideas for future essays.

Logical fallacies are easily committed mistakes in reasoning that writers must avoid, especially when writing *argumentation-persuasion* essays. There are many kinds of logical fallacies. Here are several:

Ad hominem argument occurs when someone attacks another person's point of view by criticizing that person, not the issue. Often called "mudslinging," *ad hominem* arguments try to invalidate a person's ideas by revealing unrelated, past or present, personal or ethical flaws. For example, to claim that a person cannot govern the country well because it can be proven he or she has little sense of humor is to use an *ad hominem* argument.

Begging the question is a fallacy in which the writer assumes the truth of something that needs to be proven. Imagine a writer argues the following: "A law should be passed requiring dangerous pets like German shepherds and Doberman pinschers to be restrained by fences, leashes, and muzzles." Such an argument begs the question since it assumes readers will automatically accept the view that such dogs are indeed dangerous.

Either-or fallacies occur when it's argued that a complex situation can be resolved in only one of two possible ways. Here's an example: "If the administration doesn't grant striking professors more money, the college will never be able to attract outstanding teachers in years ahead." Such an argument oversimplifies matters. Excellent teachers might be attracted to a college for a variety of reasons, not just because of good salaries: the school's location, research facilities, reputation for scholarship, hardworking students, and so on.

False analogy erroneously suggests that because two things are alike in some regards, they are similar in all ways. In the process, significant differences between the two are disregarded. If you argue that a woman prosecuting a rapist is subjected to a second rape in court, you're guilty of a false analogy. As embarrassing, painful, and hurtful as the court proceedings may be, the woman is not physically assaulted, as she was when she was raped. Also, as difficult as her decision to seek justice might be, she's in court by choice and not against her will.

Hasty generalizations are unsound *inductive inferences* based on too few instances of a behavior, situation, or process. For example, it would be a hasty generalization to conclude that you're allergic to a food such as curry because you once ate it and became ill. There are several other possible explanations for your illness, and only repetitions of this experience or a lab test could prove conclusively that you're allergic to this spice.

Non sequiturs are faulty conclusions about cause and effect. Here's an example: "Throughout this country's history, most physicians have been male. Women apparently have little interest in becoming doctors." The faulty conclusion accords one factor—the possible vocational preferences of women—the status of sole cause. The conclusion fails to consider pressures on women to devote themselves to homemaking and to avoid an occupation sexually stereotyped as "masculine."

Post hoc thinking results when it's presumed that one event caused another just because it occurred first. For instance, if your car broke down the day after you lent it to your brother, you would be committing the *post hoc* fallacy if you blamed him, unless you knew he did something to your car's engine.

Questionable authority, revealed by such phrases as "studies show" and "experts claim," undercuts a writer's credibility. Readers become suspicious of such vague and unsubstantial appeals to authority. Writers should demonstrate the reliability of their sources by citing them specifically.

Red herring arguments are deliberate attempts to focus attention on a peripheral matter rather than examine the merits of the issue under discussion. Imagine that a local environmental group advocates stricter controls for employees at a nearby chemical plant. The group points out that plant employees are repeatedly exposed to high levels of toxic chemicals. If you respond, "Many of the employees are illegal aliens and shouldn't be allowed to take jobs from native-born townspeople," you're throwing in a red herring. By bringing in immigration policies, you sidetrack attention from the matter at hand: the toxic level to which plant employees—illegal aliens or not—are exposed.

Logos is a major factor in creating an effective argument. It refers to the soundness of *argumentation,* as created by the use of facts, statistics, information, and commentary by authoritative sources. The most effective arguments involve an interplay among *logos, pathos,* and *ethos.*

Major premise—see *Deductive reasoning.*

Minor premise—see *Deductive reasoning*.

MLA documentation is the system developed by the Modern Language Association for citing sources in a paper. When you quote or summarize source material, you must do two things within your paper's text: (1) identify the author and (2) specify the pages on which the material appears. You may provide the author's name in a lead-in sentence or within parentheses following the borrowed material; the page number always appears in parentheses, inserted in the text after the borrowed material. The material in the parentheses is called a *parenthetic reference*. A paper using MLA documentation ends with a *Works Cited* list, which includes only those sources actually acknowledged in the paper. Entries are organized alphabetically by authors' last names. Entries without an author are alphabetized by the first major word in the title.

Narration means recounting an event or a series of related events to make a point. Narration can be an essay's principal pattern of development, or it can be used to supplement a paper organized primarily around another pattern. For instance, to persuade readers to avoid drug use, a writer might use the narrative pattern by recounting the story of an abuser's addiction and recovery.

Narrative point refers to the meaning the writer intends to convey to a reader by telling a certain story. This narrative point might be a specific message, or it might be a feeling about the situation, people, or place of the story. This underlying meaning is achieved by presenting details that support it and eliminating any that are nonessential. For example, in an essay about friendship, a writer's point might be that friendships change when one of the friends acquires a significant partner of the opposite sex. The writer would focus on the details of how her close female friend had less time for her, changed their usual times of getting together, and confided in her less. The writer would omit judgments of the friend's choice of boyfriend and her friend's declining grades because these details, while real for the writer, would distract the reader from the essay's narrative point.

Narrative sequence refers to the order in which a writer recounts events. When you follow the order of the events as they happened, you're using *chronological sequence*. This sequence, in which you begin at the beginning and end with the last event, is the most basic and commonly used narrative sequence. If you interrupt this flow to present an event that happened before the beginning of the narrative sequence, you're employing a *flashback*. If you skip ahead to an event later than the one that comes next in your narrative, you're using the *flashforward* technique.

Non sequiturs—see *Logical fallacies*.

Objective description—see *Description*.

One-side-at-a-time method refers to one of the two techniques for organizing a *comparison-contrast* essay. In using this method, a writer discusses all the points about one of the compared and contrasted subjects before going on to the other. For example, in an essay titled "Single or Married?" a writer might first discuss single life in terms of amount of independence, freedom of career choice, and companionship. Then the writer would, within reason, discuss married life in terms of these same three subtopics. The issues the writer discusses in each half of the essay would be identical and presented in the same order. See also *Point-by-point method.*

Organization refers to the process of arranging evidence to support a thesis in the most effective way. When organizing, a writer decides what ideas come first, next, and last. In *chronological* sequence, details are arranged according to occurrence in time. In *spatial* sequence, details appear in the order in which they occur in space. In *emphatic* order, ideas are sequenced according to importance, with the most significant, outstanding, or convincing evidence being reserved for last. In *simple-to-complex* order, easy-to-grasp material is presented before more-difficult-to-comprehend information. Organizing is the fourth stage of the writing process.

Outlining involves making a formal plan before writing a *first draft.* Writing an outline helps you determine whether your supporting evidence is logical and adequate. As you write, you can use the outline to keep yourself on track. Many writers use the indentation system of Roman numerals, letters, and Arabic numbers to outline; sometimes writers use a less formal system.

Paradox refers to a statement that seems impossible, contrary to common sense, or self-contradictory, yet that can—after consideration—be seen to be plausible or true. For example, Oscar Wilde produced a paradox when he wrote "When the gods wish to punish us, they answer our prayers." The statement doesn't contradict itself because often, Wilde believes, that which we wish for turns out to be the very thing that will bring us the most pain.

Parenthetic reference—see *MLA documentation.*

Pathos refers to the emotional power of an *argumentation-persuasion* essay. By appealing to the needs, values, and attitudes of readers and by using *connotative language,* writers can increase the chances that readers will come to agree with the ideas in an essay. Although *pathos* is an important element of persuasion, such emotional appeals should reinforce rather than replace reason. The most effective argumentation-persuasion involves an interplay among *pathos, logos,* and *ethos.*

Peer review is the critical reading of another person's writing with the intention of suggesting changes. To be effective, peer review calls for readers who are objective, skilled, and tactful enough to provide useful feedback. Begin by giving your readers a clear sense of what you expect from the review. To promote specific responses, ask the reviewers targeted (preferably written) questions. Following the review, rank the problems and solutions that the reviewers identified. Then enter your own notes for revising in the margins of your draft so that you'll know exactly what changes need to be made in your draft as you rework it.

Plan of development refers to a technique whereby the writer supplies the reader with a brief map of the main points to be covered in an essay. If used, the plan of development occurs as part of the *thesis* or in a sentence following the thesis. In it, the main ideas are mentioned in the order in which they'll appear in the supporting paragraphs. Longer essays and term papers usually need a plan of development to maintain unity, but shorter papers may do without one.

Point-by-point method refers to one of the two techniques for organizing a *comparison-contrast* essay. A writer using this method moves from one aspect of one subject to the same aspect of another subject before going on to the second aspect of each subject. For example, in an essay titled "Single or Married?" a writer might first discuss the amount of independence a person has when single and when married. Then, the writer might go on to discuss how much freedom of career choice a person has when single and when married. Finally, the writer might discuss, in turn, the amount of companionship available in each of the two lifestyles. See also *One-side-at-a-time method*.

Point of view refers to the perspective a writer chooses when writing about a subject. If you narrate events as you experience them, you're using the *first-person* point of view. You might say, for example, "*I* noticed jam on the child's collar and holes in her shirt." If you relate the events from a distance—as if you observed them but did not experience them personally—you're using the *third-person* point of view; for instance, "Jam splotched the child's collar, and her shirt had several holes in it." The point of view should be consistent throughout an essay.

Post hoc **thinking**—see *Logical fallacies*.

Prewriting is the first stage of the writing process. During prewriting, you jot down rough ideas about your subject without yet moving to writing a draft of your essay. Your goals at this stage are to (1) understand the boundaries of the assignment, (2) discover the limited subject you could write about, (3) generate raw material about the limited subject, and (4) organize the raw material into a very rough *scratch outline*. If you keep in mind that prewriting is "unofficial," it can be a low-pressure, even enjoyable activity.

Process analysis refers to writing that explains the steps involved in doing something or the sequence of stages in an event or behavior. There are two types of process analysis. In *directional process analysis*, readers are shown how to do something step-by-step. Cookbook recipes, tax form instructions, and how-to books are some typical uses of directional process analysis. In *informational process analysis,* the writer explains how something is done or occurs, without expecting the reader to attempt the process. "A Senator's Road to Political Power," "How a Bee Makes Honey," and "How a Convict Gets Paroled" would be titles of essays developed through informational process analysis. Process analysis can be the dominant mode in an essay, as in these examples, or it may help make a point in an essay developed chiefly through another pattern. For example, in a cause-effect essay that explores the impact of the two-career family, process analysis might be used to explain how parents arrange for day care.

Proofreading involves rereading a final draft carefully to catch any errors in spelling, grammar, punctuation, or typing that have slipped by. While such errors are minor, a significant number of them can seriously weaken the effectiveness of an essay. Proofreading is the last stage in the writing process.

Proposition—see *Assertion.*

Purpose is the reason a writer has for preparing a particular essay. Usually, writers frame their purposes in terms of the effect they wish to have on their *audience.* They may wish to explore the personal meaning of a subject or experience, explain an idea or process, provide information, influence opinion, or entertain. Many essays combine purposes, with one purpose predominating and providing the essay's focus.

Red herring argument—see *Logical fallacies.*

Refutation is an important strategy in *argumentation-persuasion.* In refutation, writers acknowledge that there are opposing views on the subject under discussion and then go on to do one of two things. Sometimes they may admit that the opposing views are somewhat valid but assert that their own position has more merit and devote their essay to demonstrating that merit. For example, a writer might assert, "Business majors often find interesting and lucrative jobs. However, in the long run, liberal arts graduates have many more advantages in the job market because the breadth of their background helps them think better, learn faster, and communicate more effectively." This writer would concentrate on proving the advantages that liberal arts graduates have. At other times, writers may choose to argue actively against an opposing position by dismantling that view point by point. Such refutation of opposing views can strengthen the writer's own arguments.

Repeated words, synonyms, and pronouns—see *Signaling devices.*

Revision means, literally, "reseeing" a *first draft* with a fresh eye, as if the writer had not actually prepared the draft. When revising, you move from more global issues (like clarifying meaning and organization) to more specific matters (like fine-tuning sentences and word choice). While revising, you make whatever changes are necessary to increase the essay's effectiveness. You might strengthen your thesis, resequence paragraph order, or add more transitions. Such changes often make the difference between mediocre and superior writing. Revision, itself a multi-stage process, is the last stage of the writing process.

Satire is a humorous form of social criticism usually aimed at society's institutions or human behavior. Often irreverent as well as witty, satire is serious in purpose: to point out evil, injustice, and absurdity and bring about change through an increase in awareness. Satire ranges widely in tone: it may be gentle or biting; it may sarcastically describe a real situation or use fictional characters and events to spoof reality. Satire often makes use of *irony*.

Scratch outline refers to your first informal plan for an essay, devised at the end of the *prewriting* stage. In making a scratch outline, you select ideas and details from your raw material for inclusion in your essay and discard the rest. You also arrange these ideas in an order that makes sense and that will help you achieve your *purpose*. A scratch outline is tentative and flexible, and can be reshaped as needed.

Sensory description vividly evokes the sights, smells, tastes, sounds, and physical feelings of a scene or event. For example, if a writer carefully chooses words and images, readers can see the vibrant reds and oranges of falling leaves, taste the sourness of an underripe grapefruit, hear the growling of motorcycles as a gang sweeps through a town, smell the spicy aroma of a grandmother's homemade tomato soup, and feel the pulsing pain of a jaw after Novocain wears off. Sensory description is particularly important in writing *description* or *narration*.

Sentence variety adds interest to the style of an essay or paragraph. In creating sentence variety, writers mix different kinds of sentences and sentence patterns. For example, you might vary the way your sentences open or intersperse short sentences with long ones, simple sentences with complex ones. Repetitive sentence patterns tend to make readers lose interest.

Signaling devices indicate the relationships among ideas in an essay. They help the reader follow the train of thought from sentence to sentence and from paragraph to paragraph. There are three types of connectives. *Transitions* are words that clarify flow of meaning. They can signal an additional or contrasting point, an enumeration of ideas, the use of an example, or other movement of ideas. *Linking sentences* summarize a point just made and then introduce a follow-up point. *Repeated words, synonyms,* and *pronouns* create a sense of flow by keeping important concepts in the mind of the reader.

Spatial sequence—see *Organization*.

Specific—see *Evidence.*

Stipulative definition is a way of restricting a term for the purposes of discussion. Many words have multiple meanings that can get in the way of clarity when a writer is creating an *extended definition.* For example, you might stipulate the following definition of *foreign car:* "While many American automobiles use parts or even whole engines made by foreign car manufacturers, for the purposes of discussion, 'foreign car' refers only to those automobiles designed and manufactured wholly by a company based in another country. By this definition, a European vehicle made in Pennsylvania is *not* a foreign car."

Subjective description—see *Description.*

Support—see *Evidence.*

Syllogism—see *Deductive reasoning.*

Term—see *Formal definition.*

Thesis is the central idea in any essay, usually expressed in a one- or two-sentence *thesis statement.* Writers accomplish two things by providing a thesis statement in an essay: They indicate the essay's limited subject and express an attitude about that subject. Also called the *controlling idea,* the thesis statement consists of a particular slant, angle, or point of view about the limited subject. Stating the thesis is the second stage of the writing process.

Tone conveys your attitude toward yourself, your purpose, your topic, and your readers. As in speaking, tone in writing may be serious, playful, sarcastic, and so on. Generally, readers detect tone more by how you say something (that is, through your sentence structure and word choice) than by what you say.

Topic sentence is the term for the sentence(s) that convey the main idea of a paragraph. Such sentences are often, but not always, found at the start of a paragraph. They provide a statement of the subject to be discussed and an indication of the writer's attitude toward that subject. Writers usually concern themselves with topic sentences during the writing of the first draft, the fifth stage of the writing process.

Transitions—see *Signaling devices.*

Unified—see *Evidence.*

Works Cited—see *MLA documentation.*

ACKNOWLEDGMENTS

INDEX

Abstract language, 86–88, 533
Accurate support in an essay, 43, 167
Additional writing assignments
   argumentation-persuasion,
     483–84
   cause-effect, 347–48
   comparison-contrast, 328–29
   definition, 379–80
   description, 124–25
   division-classification, 251–52
   exemplification, 203–04
   narration, 159–60
   process analysis, 292–93
Adequate support in an essay, 42–43,
   166–67, 533
Ad hominem argument, 424, 533
"Affirmative Action: The Price of
     Preference" (Steele), 475–82
Analogy, 533
   in comparison-contrast essay, 298
   in definition essay, 377–78
   in process analysis essay, 263–65,
    267
Angelou, Maya, 106
   "Sister Flowers," 106–14

Argumentation-persuasion, 38,
   401–84, 533–34
   activities in, 437–39
   audience in, 402–05, 433
   common ground, 410–11,
    411–14
   deductive reasoning, 416–17,
    417–20, 536
   defined, 401–02, 533–34
   documentation in, 410, 426–32
   factors in
    ethos, 403–05, 433, 538
    logos, 403–05, 433, 543
    pathos, 403–05, 433, 545
   goodwill in, 410–11
   inductive reasoning, 416–17,
    435–36, 541
    inductive leap, 418, 435–36
    inference, 418, 435–36, 541
   logical fallacies
    ad hominem argument, 424,
     533
    begging the question, 425,
     435, 534
    either-or fallacy, 425, 538

Argumentation-persuasion,
  logical fallacies *(continued)*
    false analogy, 425, 539
    faulty conclusion, 420
    hasty or sweeping generaliza-
      tions, 167, 417, 419, 541
    non sequitur thinking, 424,
      544
    post hoc thinking, 424, 546
    questionable or faulty
      authority, 425, 543
    red herring argument, 425–26,
      547
  organization in, 411, 412–14
  in other rhetorical patterns, 218,
    377, 401–03
  prewriting for, 437–38
  purpose, 402–07, 483–84
  refutation of opposition, 414–16,
    434–35
  Rogerian strategy, 411–14
  student essay and commentary,
    426–37
  suggestions for using, 407–26
  syllogism in, 418–20, 549
  thesis in, 407–08, 433–34, 534
  tone in, 401–07, 433
  Toulmin logic, 421–23
  ways of thinking
    deductive reasoning, 416–17,
      417–20, 536
    inductive reasoning, 416–17,
      541
    use of syllogism, 418–20, 549
  when to use, 401–07
Assertion, 407–08, 433–34, 534
Attitude expressed in a thesis, 32–33
Audience, 534
  awareness of, in outlining, 49–52
  awareness of, in writing, 19–20,
    51–52, 64, 77
  in argumentation-persuasion,
    402–05, 433
  in cause-effect, 332–35, 364–65
  in comparison-contrast, 296–97,
    300, 302–03, 328–29
  in definition, 368–69, 399–400
  in description, 82–84, 84–86

  in division-classification, 207–08
  in exemplification, 162–65
  in narration, 128
  in process analysis, 254–56,
    292–93
Authority, faulty or questionable,
  425, 543

Barry, Dave, 323
  "The Ugly Truth About Beauty,"
    323–27
Begging the question, 425, 435, 534
"Bombs Bursting in Air" (Johnson),
  189–95
Brainstorming, 24–26, 534
  in argumentation-persuasion,
    437–38
  in cause-effect, 335
  in comparison-contrast, 300
  in description, 84–86
  in division-classification, 210–11
  in exemplification, 165
  in narration, 130
  in process analysis, 257, 268
Bridging sentences, 59, 548
Bryson, Bill, 271
  "Your New Computer," 271–77
"But What Do You Mean?"
  (Tannen), 241–50

"Campus Racism 101" (Giovanni),
  278–84
Carson, Rachel, 311
  "A Fable for Tomorrow," 311–14
Causal analysis. *See* Cause-effect
Causal chain, 336, 535. *See also*
  Cause-effect
Cause-effect, 38, 331–65, 535
  activities in, 347–48
  audience in, 332–33, 334–35,
    364–65
  causal chain, 336, 535
  correlation, 337
  defined, 331–32, 535
  kinds of order
    chronological, 338
    emphatic, 338–40
  organization in, 338–40

Cause-effect *(continued)*
    in other rhetorical patterns, 163,
        333, 411
    post hoc thinking, 336–37, 546
    prewriting for, 335–36
    purpose in, 332–35, 344, 364–65
    student essay and commentary,
        340–47
    suggestions for using, 333–40
    thesis in, 337–38, 344
    tone in, 334–35
    when to use, 332–33
"Chase, The" (Dillard), 142–47
Checklist for outlining, 49–50
Checklist for revision, 72–74
Chronological method of
        organization, 46–47, 78, 86,
        545
    in cause-effect, 338
    in description, 86
    in narration, 131, 138
    in process analysis, 258–59
Circularity, 371, 535
Classification. *See* Division-
        classification
Coherence, 39–40, 57–58, 535
Cole, K. C., 381
    "Entropy," 381–86
Coleman, Jonathan, 359
    "Is Technology Making Us
        Intimate Strangers?" 359–63
Commentary for student essays
    argumentation-persuasion,
        433–37
    cause-effect, 343–47
    comparison-contrast, 305–08
    definition, 376–79
    description, 90–94
    division-classification, 218–21
    exemplification, 172–76
    narration, 137–39
    process analysis, 265–68
"Common Decency" (Jacoby),
        458–63
Common ground, 410–11, 411–14
Comparison-contrast, 38, 56,
        295–329, 535–36
    activities in, 309–10
    analogy in, 298, 533

    audience in, 296–97, 300, 328–29
    defined, 295–96, 535–36
    methods of
        one-side-at-a-time, 300–02,
            306, 545
        point-by-point, 300–02, 306,
            546
    in other rhetorical patterns, 163,
        172, 297, 377
    prewriting for, 300
    purpose in, 296–97, 328–29
    student essay and commentary,
        303–08
    suggestions for using, 297–303
    thesis in, 299, 305–06, 328–29
    when to use, 296–97
Conclusion to an essay, 536
    methods of, 62–64
        in argumentation-persuasion,
            436
        in cause-effect, 345–46
        in comparison-contrast, 307
        in definition, 377–78
        in description, 92
        in narration, 137
        in process analysis, 261,
            267–68
    purpose of, 62–63
Concrete language, 86–88, 91,
        138–39, 219–20, 533
Conflict, 129, 536
Connotative language, 21, 86–88,
        404, 536
Controlling idea, 31–35, 84–85,
        129–31, 137–38, 165–67,
        172, 212–13, 218, 265–66,
        299, 328–29, 337–38,
        343–44, 376, 407–08,
        433–34, 536

"Death of the Moth, The" (Woolf),
        488–94
Deductive reasoning, 416–17,
        417–20, 536
Definition, 38, 367–400, 537
    activities in, 379–80
    audience in, 368–69, 399–400

Definition *(continued)*
  circularity in, 371, 535
  defined, 367–68, 537
  extended, 369, 371–72, 537
  formal, 370–71, 540
  by negation, 373, 537
  in other rhetorical patterns, 46,
    91, 368–69, 434
  prewriting for, 372
  purpose in, 368–69, 376,
    399–400
  stipulative, 373, 549
  student essay and commentary,
    373–79
  suggestions for using, 369–73
  thesis in, 368–69
  tone in, 369–70
  when to use, 368–69
Definition by negation, 373, 537
Denotative language, 21, 83–84, 537
Description, 38, 81–126, 537
  activities in, 94–95
  audience in, 82–83, 124–25
  defined, 81, 537
  dominant impression in, 84–86,
    90–91, 538
  language in, 83–84, 86–87, 91–92
    connotative, 83–84, 86–87,
      536
    denotative, 83–84, 536
  organization in, 86, 92
  in other rhetorical patterns, 46,
    82–83, 137–38, 219–20,
    377, 411
  prewriting for, 84–86
  purpose in, 82–84, 90–91
  sensory impressions, 83–88, 91,
    132–34, 548
  student essay and commentary,
    88–94
  suggestions for using, 84–88
  thesis in, 82–84, 90–91, 538
  tone in, 82–84
  types of
    objective, 82–84, 544
    subjective, 82–84, 537
  when to use, 83–84
Dialogue, 537
  in narrative writing, 133, 138–39

Didion, Joan, 500
  "Santa Ana, The," 500–03
Dillard, Annie, 142
  "The Chase," 142–47
Directional process analysis, 254–55,
    257–58, 537
Division-classification, 38, 205–52,
    537–38
  activities in, 221–23
  audience in, 207–09, 252
  defined, 205–07, 537–38
  organization in, 213
  in other rhetorical patterns,
    208–09
  prewriting for, 207–08, 210
  principle of, 209–12, 218
  purpose in, 207–09, 218, 252
  student essay and commentary,
    214–21
  suggestions for using, 209–14
  thesis in, 212–13, 218
  tone in, 219
  when to use, 207–09
Documentation. *See also* MLA docu-
    mentation
  formal, 43, 410, 426–32, 519–32
  informal, 43, 410, 431
Dominant impression, 84–86, 90–91,
    538
"Doublespeak" (Lutz), 224–31
Dramatic license, 131, 266, 538

Ehrenreich, Barbara, 196
  "What I've Learned From Men,"
    196–202
Either-or fallacy, 425, 538
Ellipsis, 523
Emphatic method of organization,
    47, 77–78, 538
  in cause-effect, 338–40
  in comparison-contrast, 306
  in definition, 376–77
  in description, 86, 92
  in division-classification, 220
  in exemplification, 169
  in narration, 131–32
"Entropy" (Cole), 381–86
Essays
  reading, 1–12

Essays *(continued)*
  by students
    argumentation-persuasion,
      426–32
    cause-effect, 340–43
    comparison-contrast, 303–05
    definition, 373–76
    description, 88–94
    division-classification, 214–21
    documented, 431–32
    exemplification, 170–76
    first draft, 64–66
    model, 74–79
    narration, 135–40
    process analysis, 262–65
    traditional format of, 64–65
    writing, 13–79
Ethos, 403–05, 433, 538
Etymology in definitions, 373, 538
Evidence, 36–43, 538–39
  characteristics of
    accurate, 43, 167, 408–10
    adequate, 42–43, 84–86,
      129–31, 257, 300, 334–35,
      371–72, 408–10
    documented, 43, 334–35, 410,
      431–32, 519–32
    relevant, 39–40, 77–78,
      129–31, 165–67, 300
    representative, 43, 129–31,
      165–67, 300, 371–72,
      408–10
    specific, 40–41, 84–86, 86–88,
      129–31, 165, 408–10
    unified, 39–40, 84–86, 408–10
  types of, 37
  variety in, 165–67
Exemplification, 38, 161–204, 539
  activities in, 176–77
  audience in, 162–65, 204
  defined, 161–62, 539
  extended example, 167
  organization of, 168–69
  in other rhetorical patterns,
    162–65, 219–20, 265–66,
    305–06, 344, 377
  prewriting for, 165
  purpose in, 162–65, 204

student essay and commentary,
  170–76
suggestions for using, 165–69
thesis in, 165–67, 172
tone in, 162–65, 174
value of using examples, 162–65
when to use, 162–65
Extended definition, 369, 371–72,
  539

"Fable for Tomorrow, A" (Carson),
  311–14
False analogy, 425, 539
"Family Counterculture"
  (Goodman), 6–12
Figures of speech, 86–88, 91–92,
  539
  metaphors, 87–88
  personification, 87–88
  similes, 87
"Fine Art of Complaining, The"
  (Rego), 285–91
First draft, 53–67, 539
Flashback, 131–32, 539
Flashforward, 131–32, 540
"Flavio's Home" (Parks), 96–105
Formal definition, 370–71, 539
Freewriting, 25–26, 300, 540

Gender-biased language, 73, 540–41
Generalizations, hasty, 167, 417,
  419, 541
General subject of any essay, 21–23,
  31–33
Giovanni, Nikki, 278
  "Campus Racism 101," 278–84
Gleick, James, 387
  "Life As Type A," 387–93
Goodman, Ellen, 6
  "Family Counterculture," 6–12
Goodwill, in argumentation, 410–11,
  411–14
Group brainstorming, 26

"Handicap of Definition, The"
  (Raspberry), 394–98
Hasty generalization, 167, 417, 419,
  541
Hughes, Langston, 148
  "Salvation," 148–52

Inductive leap, 418, 435–36
Inductive reasoning, 416–17,
    435–36, 727
Inference, 418, 435–36, 541
Informational process analysis,
    254–55, 257–58, 265–66,
    541
"In Praise of the 'F' Word" (Sherry),
    440–44
Internet, 513–19
    advantages and limitations of, 514
    evaluating materials on, 518–19
    World Wide Web, 513–19
        address, 514, 516–17
        bookmark option, 515
        browser, 513–14
        link, 513, 516–18
        search directory for, 516
        search engine for, 516–18
        site, 513, 515, 516, 518, 519
Introduction to an essay, 60–62
    methods of, 60–62
    purpose of, 60
    used in
        argumentation-persuasion,
            407–08, 433–34
        cause-effect, 343–44
        comparison-contrast, 307–08
        definition, 372–73, 376
        description, 88–89, 90–91
        division-classification, 218,
            220–21
        narration, 137–38
        process analysis, 261
Irony, 541–42
"Is Technology Making Us Intimate
    Strangers?" (Coleman),
    359–63

Jacoby, Susan, 458
    "Common Decency," 458–63
Johnson, Beth, 189
    "Bombs Bursting in Air," 189–95
Journals, 15–18, 542
Journal writing, sample, 15

King, Martin Luther, Jr., 495
    "Where Do We Go From Here:
        Community or Chaos?"
        495–99
King, Stephen, 349
    "Why We Crave Horror Movies,"
        349–53

"Let's Tell the Story of All America's
    Cultures" (Yuh), 445–50
Library research, 505–13
    author search, 506–07
    bibliographies and indexes,
        509–12
    call numbers, 507–08
    card catalog, 505–07
    computerized catalog, 506–07
    computerized periodicals index,
        508–09, 510–12
    Dewey Decimal System, 508
    Library of Congress, 508
    periodicals, 509–13
    reference section, 508–09
    subject search, 506–07
    title search, 506–07
"Lie Detector, The" (Thomas),
    354–58
"Life As Type A" (Gleick), 387–93
Limited subject of an essay, 21–30,
    31–33
Linking sentences. See Bridging
    sentences
Liu, Sophronia, 153
    "So Tsi-Fai," 153–58
Logical fallacies, 423–26, 542–43
Logic in argument, 416–26
Logos, 403–05, 433, 543
Lutz, William, 224
    "Doublespeak," 224–31

Mapping, 26–27, 335
McClintock, Ann, 232
    "Propaganda Techniques in
        Today's Advertising,"
        232–40
Metaphors, 87–88, 539

MLA documentation, 426–32,
    519–32, 544

Narration, 38, 127–52, 544
    activities in, 140–41
    audience in, 128, 159–60
    conflict in, 129, 137, 536
    defined, 127–28, 544
    details in, 129–31
    dialogue in, 133–34, 138–39
    dramatic license in, 131, 538
    narrative sequence in, 131–32, 544
        flashback, 131–32, 544
        flashforward, 131–32, 544
    in other rhetorical patterns, 128,
        219–20, 371–72
    point in, 129, 137–38, 544
    point of view, 134–35, 137, 546
        first-person, 134, 137, 546
        third-person, 135, 546
    prewriting for, 130
    purpose in, 128, 159–60
    sensory description in, 132–34,
        548
    student essay and commentary,
        135–39
    suggestions for using, 129–35
    thesis in, 129, 137–38, 544
    tone in, 129
    when to use, 127–28
Narrative point, 129, 137–38, 544
Narrative sequence, 131–32, 544
Non sequitur thinking, 424, 544

Objective description, 82–84, 91, 544
"Once More to the Lake" (White),
    115–23
One-side-at-a-time method, 300–02,
    306, 545
Organization in an essay, 45–52,
    55–57, 77–78
    conclusion, 62–64, 78–79,
        267–68, 536
    connecting devices, 57–60, 77–78
    introduction, 60–62, 541
    methods of
        chronological, 46–47, 545

    emphatic, 47, 545
    simple-to-complex, 48, 545
    spatial, 47, 545
    by outlining, 48–50, 545
    plan of development, 62, 77, 546
    rhetorical patterns of
        development, 27–28, 37–38
    thesis, 31–35, 549
    topic sentences, 55–56, 64–65,
        549
    traditional format, 64–65
Outlining, 48–50, 545
    checklist for, 49–50
    scratch, 29–30, 548

Paglia, Camille, 451
    "Rape: A Bigger Danger Than
        Feminists Know," 451–57
Parenthetic reference. *See* MLA
    documentation
Parks, Gordon, 96
    "Flavio's Home," 96–105
Pathos, 403–05, 433, 545
Patterns of development, rhetorical
    combining, 82, 128, 162–65,
        207–09, 254–56, 296–97,
        333–34, 368–69, 402–03,
        485–87
    as strategies, 27–28, 37–38,
        45–46, 56–57, 485–87
Peer review, 69–73, 545–46
Personification, 87–88
Persuasion. *See* Argumentation-
    persuasion
Plagiarizing, 410, 520
Plan of development, 62, 77, 546
    in definition, 372–73, 376
    in exemplification, 172
Point-by-point method, 300–02,
    306, 546
Point of view in narration, 134–35,
    137, 546
Post hoc thinking, 424, 546
Premises
    faulty, 418–21
    major, 418–21, 543
    minor, 418–21, 544

Prewriting, 14–30, 546
  in cause-effect, 335–36
  in comparison-contrast, 300
  in definition, 372
  in description, 84–86
  in division-classification, 207–08,
    210
  in exemplification, 165
  in narration, 130
  in process analysis, 257
Process
  reading, 1–12
  writing, 13–79
Process analysis, 38, 253–93, 546–47
  activities in, 268–70
  audience in, 254–56, 257, 292–93
  defined, 253–54, 546–47
  kinds of
    directional, 254–55, 257–58,
      537
    informational, 254–55,
      257–58, 265–66, 541
  organization in, 258–59, 266
  in other rhetorical patterns,
    402–03
  prewriting for, 257
  purpose in, 254–56, 265–66,
    292–93
  signal devices in, 259–60, 266
  student essay and commentary,
    262–68
  suggestions for using, 256–61
  thesis in, 256, 265–66
  tone in, 260–61, 265–66
  when to use, 254–56
Proofreading, 73–74, 547
"Propaganda Techniques in Today's
    Advertising" (McClintock),
    232–40
Proposition. See Assertion
Purpose, 547
  awareness of, in outlining, 49–52
  awareness of, in writing, 19, 54,
    64, 72–73, 77
  in argumentation-persuasion,
    401–07, 483–84
  in cause-effect, 332–35, 344,
    364–65

  in comparison-contrast, 296–97,
    328–29
  in definition, 368–69, 376,
    399–400
  in description, 82–84, 90–91
  in division-classification, 207–08,
    218, 252
  in exemplification, 162–65, 204
  in narration, 128, 159–60
  in process analysis, 254–56,
    265–66, 292–93

Questioning
  to limit a subject, 21–23
  when evaluating an essay, 4–5,
    486–87
  when revising, 72–73
Quoting sources, 43, 520–25

"Racism Has Its Privileges"
    (Wilkins), 464–74
"Rape: A Bigger Danger Than
    Feminists Know" (Paglia),
    451–57
Raspberry, William, 394
  "The Handicap of Definition,"
    394–98
Readers' Guide to Periodical
    Literature, 510
Reading process, 1–5
  model selection, 6–12
  questions for evaluating essays,
    4–5, 486–87
  steps in effective reading, 1–5
Red herring argument, 425–26, 547
Refutation of the opposition,
    414–16, 434–35, 547
Rego, Caroline, 285
  "The Fine Art of Complaining,"
    285–91
Repeated words, synonyms, and pro-
    nouns, 59–60, 78, 547
Representative support in an essay,
    43, 129–31, 165–67, 300,
    371–72, 408–10
Revision, 14, 68–74, 547–48
  checklist for, 72–75

Revision *(continued)*
  in student essays, 78–79, 93–94,
    139–40, 174–76, 220–21,
    267–68, 307–08, 329,
    378–79, 436–37
Rhetorical patterns of development,
    27–28, 38, 45–46, 56–57,
    485–87
Rodriguez, Richard, 315
  "Workers," 315–22
Rogerian strategy, 411–14

"Salvation" (Hughes), 148–52
"Santa Ana, The" (Didion), 500–03
Satire, 174, 218, 219, 548
Scratch outline, 29–30, 548
Sensory description, 83–88, 91,
    132–34, 548
Sentence variety, 73, 86–88, 134,
    378–79, 548
"Sexism and Language" (Nilsen),
    225–33
Sherry, Mary, 440
  "In Praise of the 'F' Word,"
    440–44
Signaling devices, 58–60, 78, 548
  bridging sentences, 59
  repeated words, synonyms, and
    pronouns, 59–60
  transitions, 58, 549
  used in
    argumentation-persuasion, 435
    cause-effect, 345
    comparison-contrast, 302–03,
      306
    description, 92
    division-classification, 213, 219
    exemplification, 173
    narration, 132, 138
    process analysis, 259–60, 266
Simile, 87, 539
"Sister Flowers" (Angelou), 106–14
"So Tsi-Fai" (Liu), 153–58
Spatial method of organization, 47,
    545
  in description, 86, 92
  in exemplification, 168–69

Specific support in an essay, 40–41,
    84–86, 86–88, 129–31, 165,
    408–10
Steele, Shelby, 475
  "Affirmative Action: The Price of
    Preference," 475–82
Stipulative definition, 373, 549
Student essays. *See* Essays
Subjective description, 82–84, 549
Supporting paragraphs in an essay,
    55–60, 64–65
Sykes, Charles, 178
  "The 'Values' Wasteland, 178–88

Tannen, Deborah, 241
  "But What Do You Mean?"
    241–50
Thesis, 3–5, 14, 31–35, 549
  in argumentation-persuasion,
    407–08, 433–34, 533–34
  in cause-effect, 337–38, 344
  in comparison-contrast, 299,
    305–06, 535–36
  in definition, 368–69
  in description, 82–84, 90–91, 538
  in division-classification, 212–13,
    218
  in exemplification, 165–67, 172
  in narration, 129, 137–38, 544
  in process analysis, 256, 265–66
Thomas, Lewis, 354
  "The Lie Detector," 354–58
Title, in essays, 3, 55, 64
Tone, 549
  awareness of, in outlining, 49
  awareness of, in writing, 20–21,
    64–65, 72, 77
  in argumentation-persuasion,
    401–07, 433
  in cause-effect, 334–35
  in definition, 369–70
  in description, 82–84
  in exemplification, 162–65, 174
  in narration, 129
  in process analysis, 260–61,
    265–66

Topic sentences, 55–56, 549
    in argumentation-persuasion,
        434–35
    in cause-effect, 344
    in comparison-contrast, 306
    in definition, 376
    in division-classification, 218–19
    in exemplification, 173
    in narration, 132, 138
    in process analysis, 266
Toulmin logic, 421–23
Transitions, 549
    in argumentation-persuasion,
        434–35
    in cause-effect, 345
    in comparison-contrast, 302–03
    in description, 92
    in division-classification, 213, 219
    in exemplification, 173
    in narration, 132, 138
    in process analysis, 259–60, 266

"Ugly Truth About Beauty, The"
    (Barry), 323–27
Unified support in an essay, 39–40,
    84–88, 408–10, 549

"'Values' Wasteland, The" (Sykes),
    178–88

"What I've Learned From Men"
    (Ehrenreich), 196–202
"Where Do We Go From Here:
    Community or Chaos?"
    (King), 495–99
White, E. B., 115
    "Once More to the Lake,"
        115–23

"Why We Crave Horror Movies"
    (King), 349–53
Wilkins, Roger, 464
    "Racism Has Its Privileges,"
        464–74
Woolf, Virginia, 488
    "The Death of the Moth,"
        488–94
"Workers" (Rodriguez), 315–22
Works cited list. See MLA
    documentation
Writing process, 13–79
    activities in
        identify the thesis, 35–36
        organize the evidence, 53–54
        prewrite, 30–31
        revise, 79–80
        support the thesis, 44–45
        write the first draft, 68
    audience, 19–20, 51–52, 64–65,
        77, 534
    purpose, 19, 49–50, 64, 77
    stages in
        identify the thesis, 31–35
        organize the evidence, 45–52
        prewrite, 14–30
        revise, 68–79
        support the thesis, 38–43
        write the first draft, 53–67
    student essay and commentary,
        66–67, 74–79
    tone, 20–21, 49–50, 64, 72, 77,
        549

"Your New Computer" (Bryson),
    271–77
Yuh, Ji-Yeon, 445
    "Let's Tell the Story of All
        America's Cultures," 445–50

To the Student
From the Authors

By now, you realize that almost all writing goes through a series of revisions. The same was true for this book. *The Longman Reader,* Sixth Edition, *Brief Edition,* has been reworked a number of times, with each revision taking into account students' and instructors' reactions to drafts of material.

Before we prepare the seventh edition of *The Longman Reader: Brief Edition,* we'd like to know how you, the student, feel about the book. We hope you'll spend a few minutes completing this brief questionnaire. You can be sure that your responses will help shape subsequent editions. Please send your completed survey to the College English Editor, Longman Publishers, 1185 Avenue of the Americas, New York, NY 10036.

Thanks for your time.

College _____ City and state _____

Course title _____ Instructor _____

	I really liked it.	It was okay.	I didn't like it.	I didn't read it.
DESCRIPTION				
Parks, *Flavio's Home*	___	___	___	___
Angelou, *Sister Flowers*	___	___	___	___
White, *Once More to the Lake*	___	___	___	___
NARRATION				
Dillard, *The Chase*	___	___	___	___
Hughes, *Salvation*	___	___	___	___
Liu, *So Tsi-Fai*	___	___	___	___
EXEMPLIFICATION				
Sykes, *The "Values" Wasteland*	___	___	___	___
Johnson, *Bombs Bursting in Air*	___	___	___	___
Ehrenreich, *What I've Learned From Men*	___	___	___	___

DIVISION-CLASSIFICATION

	I really liked it.	It was okay.	I didn't like it.	I didn't read it.
Lutz, *Doublespeak*	____	____	____	____
McClintock, *Propaganda Techniques in Today's Advertising*	____	____	____	____
Tannen, *But What Do You Mean?*	____	____	____	____

PROCESS ANALYSIS

Bryson, *Your New Computer*	____	____	____	____
Giovanni, *Campus Racism 101*	____	____	____	____
Rego, *The Fine Art of Complaining*	____	____	____	____

COMPARISON-CONTRAST

Carson, *A Fable for Tomorrow*	____	____	____	____
Rodriguez, *Workers*	____	____	____	____
Barry, *The Ugly Truth About Beauty*	____	____	____	____

CAUSE-EFFECT

King, *Why We Crave Horror Movies*	____	____	____	____
Thomas, *The Lie Detector*	____	____	____	____
Coleman, *Is Technology Making Us Intimate Strangers?*	____	____	____	____

DEFINITION

Cole, *Entropy*	____	____	____	____
Gleick, *Life As Type A*	____	____	____	____
Raspberry, *The Handicap of Definition*	____	____	____	____

ARGUMENTATION-PERSUASION

Sherry, *In Praise of the "F" Word*	____	____	____	____
Yuh, *Let's Tell the Story of All America's Cultures*	____	____	____	____
Paglia, *Rape: A Bigger Danger Than Feminists Know*	____	____	____	____
Jacoby, *Common Decency*	____	____	____	____
Wilkins, *Racism Has Its Privileges*	____	____	____	____
Steele, *Affirmative Action: The Price of Preference*	____	____	____	____

COMBINING THE PATTERNS

	I really liked it.	It was okay.	I didn't like it.	I didn't read it.
Woolf, *The Death of the Moth*	_____	_____	_____	_____
King, *Where Do We Go From Here: Community or Chaos?*	_____	_____	_____	_____
Didion, *The Santa Ana*	_____	_____	_____	_____

Any general comments or suggestions?

Name ——————————————————— Date ————————————

Address ————————————————————————————————

THANKS AGAIN!